- Should you use automation?
- Should you use single- or double-blind procedures?
- Do you use tasks with experimental realism?
- Should you hide measurement tasks using unobtrusive te̶c̶
- Do you provide a placebo for control group?
- Should you disguise conditions with deception or a field experiment?

Considering ethical issues

- Are there physical risks to participants?
- Are there psychological risks to participants?
- Can you eliminate or minimize risks?
- Can you justify risks in terms of the scientific value of results?
- Will you obtain informed consent?
- Will you provide debriefing and care for participants after the study?
- Will you submit the planned procedure to the IRB for review?

Considering participant variables

- Do the characteristics of participants limit generalizability?
- Is the sample size *(N)* sufficient to represent the population?
- Does the volunteer bias or subject sophistication influence the results?
- Are extraneous participant variables strongly correlated with the independent or dependent variable?
- Will fluctuating participant variables within conditions reduce reliability and the relationship's strength?
- Will fluctuating participant variables between conditions reduce internal validity and the relationship's strength?

Considering a between-subjects design

- Will random assignment control important participant variables?
- Will balancing control important participant variables?
- Will matching control important participant variables?
- Will pretesting create major problems?
- Will limiting the population restrict generalizability?
- Will controls add error variance that weakens the relationship?

Considering a within-subjects design

- Must many participant variables be controlled?
- Are subject history, maturation, and mortality a problem?
- Do stimuli and other aspects fit a repeated-measures design?
- Will nonsymmetrical carry-over effects occur?
- Is randomization or partial or complete counterbalancing of order of conditions needed?

Research Methods in Psychology

Second Edition

Gary W. Heiman
Buffalo State College

Houghton Mifflin Company   *Boston*   *New York*

To Karen, for the "good stuff inside"

Editor-in-Chief: Kathi Prancan
Senior Associate Editor: Jane Knetzger
Editorial Assistant: Lou Gum
Project Editor: Anne Holm
Manufacturing Manager: Florence Cadran
Marketing Manager: Pamela J. Laskey

Cover design: Harold Burch Design NYC
Cover illustration: Harold Burch

Printed in the U.S.A.

Library of Congress Catalog Card Number: 98-72040

ISBN: 0-395-90335-1

123456789-DC-02 01 00 99 98

Contents

Preface   *xvii*

Part I   Introduction to Psychological Research   *1*

1   Introduction to the Scientific Method   *2*
2   An Overview of Designing and Interpreting Research   *32*
3   Creating a Reliable and Valid Experiment   *75*
4   Risk, Deception, and the Ethics of Research   *108*
5   Controlling Participant Variables Using Between-Subjects and Within-Subjects Designs   *135*

Part II   The Statistical Analysis of Experiments   *169*

6   Applying Descriptive and Inferential Statistics to Simple Experiments   *170*
7   Designing and Analyzing Multifactor Experiments   *202*

Part III   Beyond the Typical Laboratory Experiment   *243*

8   Correlational Research and Questionnaire Construction   *244*
9   Field Experiments and Single-Subject Designs   *285*
10   Quasi-Experiments and Descriptive Designs   *311*

Part IV   Putting It All Together   *347*

11   Examples of Designing and Evaluating Research   *348*

Appendixes   *383*

Appendix A   Reporting Research Using APA Format   *383*
Appendix B   Sample APA-Style Research Report   *417*
Appendix C   Statistical Procedures   *429*
Appendix D   Statistical Tables   *477*
Glossary   *495*
References   *507*
Name Index   *513*
Subject Index   *515*

Contents

Preface   *xvii*

Part I: Introduction to Psychological Research   *1*

Chapter 1:   Introduction to the Scientific Method   *2*

Getting Started   **2**

The Scientific Method   **3**

    The Assumptions of Science   4

The Attitudes of Scientists   **6**

    The Criteria for Scientific Evidence   8

The Goals of Psychological Research   **10**

    Meeting the Goals of Science   12
    Applied and Basic Research   13
    The Role of a Single Study   13

Scientific Hypotheses   **14**

    Creating Hypotheses   14
    The Criteria for Scientific Hypotheses   15
    Sources of Hypotheses   17
    Testing Hypotheses through Research   19
    Experimental Methods   20
    Descriptive Methods   21

The Flaws in Scientific Research   **21**

    The Flaws in the Evidence   22
    The Flaws in Testing Hypotheses   23
    Using Replication to Build Confidence in Psychological
    Findings   26

Putting It All Together   **27**

    CHAPTER SUMMARY   28
    KEY TERMS   29
    REVIEW QUESTIONS   29
    DISCUSSION QUESTIONS   30

Chapter 2: *An Overview of Designing and Interpreting Research* 32

Getting Started 32

Beginning the Design: Asking the Question 33

Considering the Context of the Behavior 34
Identifying the Population and the Sample 35
Identifying the Hypothetical Constructs 36
Identifying Component Variables of a Construct 37
Creating Operational Definitions 38

Testing a Hypothesis by Discovering a Relationship 40

Interpreting a Relationship 42
The Flow of a Study 43

Critically Evaluating a Study 44

Understanding Reliability 47

Understanding Validity 48

Drawing Valid Inferences about Measurements 48
Drawing Internally Valid Inferences about the Relationship 49
Drawing Externally Valid Inferences about the Relationship 51

Minimizing Threats to Validity and Reliability 53

Controlling Extraneous Variables 54
Deciding on the Controls to Use 56

Descriptive Research Methods 56

Issues of Validity and Reliability in Descriptive Studies 57
Problems in Inferring the Causes of a Behavior 58

Experimental Research Methods 59

The Independent Variable 59
Conditions of the Independent Variable 60
The Dependent Variable 61
True versus Quasi-Experiments 62
Issues of Validity and Reliability in Experiments 63
Laboratory versus Field Experiments 66

Selecting a Design 67

Putting It All Together 69

CHAPTER SUMMARY 69
KEY TERMS 71
REVIEW QUESTIONS 71
DISCUSSION QUESTIONS 73

Chapter 3:　Creating a Reliable and Valid Experiment　　*75*

Getting Started　75

Selecting the Independent Variable　76

Approaches to Manipulating an Independent Variable　76
Selecting a Valid and Reliable Manipulation　78

Selecting the Conditions of the Independent Variable　79

Control Groups　80
Creating a Powerful Design through a Strong Manipulation　81
Manipulation Checks　85

Selecting the Dependent Variable　86

Approaches to Measuring the Dependent Variable　86
Selecting a Valid and Reliable Dependent Variable　87

Designing the Dependent Variable　89

Creating a Powerful Design through a Sensitive Measure　90
Avoiding a Restricted Range of Scores　91
Observing Reliable Behaviors　92
The Problem of Order Effects　94
Counterbalancing Order Effects　95
Judging a Behavior and Inter-rater Reliability　96

Controlling Extraneous Variables　98

Instructions to Participants　99
Using Automation　100
Testing Participants in Groups　100
Pilot Studies　101
Eliminating Participants from the Data　101

Putting It All Together　102

CHAPTER SUMMARY　104
KEY TERMS　105
REVIEW QUESTIONS　105
DISCUSSION QUESTIONS　107

Chapter 4:　Risk, Deception, and the Ethics of Research　　*108*

Getting Started　108

Demand Characteristics　109

General Controls for Demand Characteristics　111
Using Unobtrusive Measures and Deception　113

Concealing the Experiment   115

Research Ethics   117

The Cooperativeness of Participants   117
The APA Principles of Ethical Conduct   118
The Ethics of Unobtrusive Measures and Field Research   121
Role Playing and Simulations   124

Research Involving Animals   124

Controls Used with Animal Research   125
The Ethics of Animal Research   126

Scientific Fraud   127

Putting It All Together   128

CHAPTER SUMMARY   131
KEY TERMS   132
REVIEW QUESTIONS   132
DISCUSSION QUESTIONS   134

Chapter 5:   *Controlling Participant Variables Using Between-Subjects and Within-Subjects Designs*   *135*

Getting Started   135

How Participant Variables Influence External Validity   136

Defining the Population   136
Limitations on the Representativeness of a Sample   137
Sample Size and Representativeness   138
Limitations on the Representativeness of Volunteers   139

How Fluctuating Variables Influence a Relationship through Error Variance   140

The Connection between a Powerful Relationship and Reliability and Validity   142

Controlling Participant Variables in a Between-Subjects Design   144

Random Assignment   144
Balancing Participant Variables   146
Matched-Groups Designs   148
Limiting the Population   150
Selecting the Approach for Dealing with Participant Variables   151

Controlling Participant Variables in a Within-Subjects Design   152

    Pros and Cons of Repeated Measures   154

Methods for Controlling Order Effects   156

    Complete Counterbalancing of Conditions   157
    Partial Counterbalancing of Conditions   159
    Randomizing the Order of Conditions   160

Choosing a Design   161

Putting It All Together   164

CHAPTER SUMMARY   164
KEY TERMS   166
REVIEW QUESTIONS   166
DISCUSSION QUESTIONS   167

Part II: The Statistical Analysis of Experiments   *169*

Chapter 6:   *Applying Descriptive and Inferential Statistics to Simple Experiments*   *170*

Getting Started   170

Selecting the Statistical Procedures   171

    Impact of a Particular Scale of Measurement   172
    Understanding the Characteristics of a Relationship   173

Applying Descriptive Statistics to Experiments   178

    Describing Central Tendency   178
    Graphing the Results of an Experiment   180
    Describing Variability   182
    Interpreting the Overall Relationship   183

Applying Inferential Statistical Procedures   184

    The Logic of Inferential Statistics   185
    Selecting an Inferential Procedure   186

Interpreting Significant Results   189

    Comparing the Conditions in ANOVA   190
    Estimating the Population Mean   190
    Restrictions on Interpreting Significant Results   191

Interpreting Nonsignificant Results   192

Statistical Power and Research Design   193

Putting It All Together   195

CHAPTER SUMMARY   195
KEY TERMS   197
REVIEW QUESTIONS   198
DISCUSSION QUESTIONS   201

Chapter 7:   *Designing and Analyzing Multifactor Experiments*   202

Getting Started   202

The Reason for Multifactor Studies   203

The Two-Way Between-Subjects ANOVA   203

Main Effects   206
Interaction Effects   208
Interpreting the Two-Way Experiment   215

Using Counterbalanced Variables to Produce Two-Way Designs   216

The Two-Way Within-Subjects ANOVA   218

The Two-Way Mixed ANOVA   220

The Three-Way Design   223

Main Effects   224
Two-Way Interactions   225
The Three-Way Interaction   226

The Two-Way Chi Square   227

Describing Effect Size   229

Understanding the Proportion of Variance Accounted For   230
Computing the Proportion of Variance Accounted For   233

A Word about Multivariate Statistics and Meta-Analysis   234

Putting It All Together   235

CHAPTER SUMMARY   235
KEY TERMS   237
REVIEW QUESTIONS   237
DISCUSSION QUESTIONS   240

Part III: *Beyond the Typical Laboratory Experiment* *243*

Chapter 8: *Correlational Research and Questionnaire Construction* *244*

Getting Started   **244**

The Difference between True Experiments and Correlational Studies   **245**

Interpreting Correlational Designs   247
Reasons for Using the Correlational Approach   248

Analyzing Data with Correlational Statistics   **249**

Linear Regression   253
Errors in Prediction and the Variance Accounted For   254
Maximizing the Power of the Correlation Coefficient   257

Additional Uses of Correlation   **259**

Ascertaining Reliability   259
Ascertaining Validity   260

Conducting Research Using Interviews and Questionnaires   **263**

Using Closed-Ended versus Open-Ended Questions   263
Using Interviews versus Questionnaires   265
Constructing Questions   266
Dealing with Order Effects   270
Creating Catch Trials   272
Conducting Pilot Studies   273
Administering the Questionnaire or Interview   273

A Word about Advanced Correlational Procedures   **276**

Multiple Correlation and Regression   276
Discriminant Analysis   276
Partial Correlation   276
Factor Analysis   277

Putting It All Together   **278**

CHAPTER SUMMARY   278
KEY TERMS   280
REVIEW QUESTIONS   281
DISCUSSION QUESTIONS   283

Chapter 9: Field Experiments and Single-Subject Designs   *285*

Getting Started   285

Field Experiments   286

Sampling Techniques   287
Field Experiments with the General Public   290
Field Experiments with Selected Groups   293
Ethics and Field Experiments   296

Small *N* Research and the Single-Subject Design   296

The Argument for Small *N* Designs   297
The Logic of Baseline Designs   298
Reversal Designs   299
Multiple-Baseline Designs   300
Design Concerns with Baseline Research   303
Other Approaches to Single-Subject Designs   304
Choosing between Single-Subject and Group Designs   305

Putting It All Together   306

CHAPTER SUMMARY   307
KEY TERMS   308
REVIEW QUESTIONS   308
DISCUSSION QUESTIONS   309

Chapter 10: Quasi-Experiments and Descriptive Designs   *311*

Getting Started   311

Understanding Quasi-Experiments   312

Quasi-Independent Variables Involving Participant Variables   314

Creating the Conditions Using a Participant Variable   314
The Problem of Regression Toward the Mean   316
Interpreting the Quasi-Experiment   317

Quasi-Independent Variables Involving Environmental Events: The Time-Series Design   318

One-Group Pretest-Posttest Designs   319
Nonequivalent Control Group Designs   320
Interrupted Time-Series Designs   322
Multiple Time-Series Designs   324

The Quasi-Independent Variable of the Passage of Time   325

    Longitudinal Designs   325
    Cross-Sectional Designs   327
    Cohort Designs   328

Descriptive Research   329

    Field Surveys   331
    Observational Studies   335
    The Pros and Cons of Observational Designs   336
    Additional Sources of Data in Descriptive Approaches   337
    Ethical Issues in Descriptive Research   338

A Word about Program Evaluation   339

Putting It All Together   340

CHAPTER SUMMARY   341
KEY TERMS   342
REVIEW QUESTIONS   343
DISCUSSION QUESTIONS   344

Part IV   Putting It All Together   *347*

Chapter 11:   Examples of Designing and Evaluating Research   *348*

Topic 1:   Attribution of Arousal   350

Topic 2:   Time Perception   356

Topic 3:   Fear of Success in Females   363

Topic 4:   Creativity   367

Additional Research Topics   374

    Belief in Astrology   374
    Serial-Position Effects   375
    Attractiveness and Height   377
    The Influence of Color   379
    Self-Consciousness and "Choking under Pressure"   380

Putting It All Together   381

Appendixes   *383*

Appendix A: *Reporting Research Using APA Format*   *383*

Getting Started   383

An Example Study   384

The Research Literature   385

What Constitutes the Research Literature?   386
Searching the Literature   386
Completing the Droodle Study   388

Organization of a Research Article   391

The Assumptions of the Author and Reader   393
Some Rules of Style   394

The Components of an APA-Style Research Article   395

The Title   396
The Abstract   398
The Introduction   398
The Method   401
The Results   405
The Discussion   409
The Reference Page   412

Putting It All Together   413

CHAPTER SUMMARY   413
KEY TERMS   414
REVIEW QUESTIONS   415
DISCUSSION QUESTIONS   416

Appendix B: *Sample APA-Style Research Report*   *417*

Appendix C: *Statistical Procedures*   *429*

C.1   **Measures of Central Tendency**   430

C.2   **Measures of Variability**   431

C.3   **The Two-Sample *t*-Test**   432

C.4   **The One-Way Analysis of Variance**   435

C.5   **The Two-Way Between-Subjects Analysis of Variance**   440

C.6   The Two-Way Within-Subjects Analysis of
        Variance   445

C.7   The Two-Way Mixed-Design Analysis of Variance   452

C.8   Tukey HSD Post Hoc Comparisons   457

C.9   Measures of Effect Size in *t*-Tests and ANOVA   460

C.10   Confidence Intervals   461

C.11   Pearson Correlation Coefficient, Linear Regression, and
        Standard Error of the Estimate   463

C.12   Spearman Correlation Coefficient   465

C.13   Chi Square Procedures   466

C.14   Mann-Whitney *U* and Wilcoxon *T* Tests   469

C.15   Kruskal-Wallis *H* and Friedman χ^2 Tests   471

Appendix D: *Statistical Tables*   *477*

Glossary   495
References   507
Name Index   513
Subject Index   515

Preface

I wrote the first edition of this book because, after teaching introductory research methods for more years than I care to admit, I could not find a methods book whose style and organization satisfied the demands of the course. My goal was to write a book that allowed students to (1) understand the terminology, logic, and procedures used in research; (2) integrate statistical procedures with research methods; (3) develop critical thinking skills regarding research; and (4) learn to design and conduct research and write APA-style reports. I have attempted to create a textbook that recognizes students' initial weaknesses in all of these areas but that still brings students to the level of understanding most instructors seek.

 ## Pedagogical Approach

Rather than present a laundry list of the components and characteristics of various research approaches, I have attempted to teach methods (and statistical applications) in an integrated, cohesive manner. My approach is to place students in the role of researchers, focusing on the specific decisions they make. I believe this teaches students the critical-thinking skills and understanding of concepts necessary for designing research. Within this framework, the book presents concepts, procedures, and evaluation of research in an organized manner; provides an integrated review and discussion of statistics with methods; reviews terminology and concepts frequently, especially as they are reintroduced in new settings; and fosters understanding through application to specific examples.

By rehearsing new terms and concepts as they reappear throughout the book, I have tried to anticipate and alleviate students' confusion over terminology, recognizing that an introductory methods course is in part a language course and that achieving literacy requires practice. When introducing a general technique, I also cite several examples so that students gain an appreciation of the variety and scope of the technique. I then present the material in more depth using one or two detailed example studies. Throughout, I have sought simple examples that are easy to understand, avoiding unnecessarily sophisticated studies that might obscure the illustrative purpose of the example. I have also attempted to select interesting examples that convey the elegance and challenge of research, and I have stuck to studies that relate to psychology and that students can easily replicate in class projects.

Teaching critical thinking is not easy. Often textbook discussions end abruptly, just prior to answering the question "So what?" I have tried to include the "so what" by pointing out the logical ramifications behind each issue and providing critical analysis. Several themes recur throughout the text. Reliability and validity appear repeatedly as the basis for making decisions among various design options. The interaction between statistics and design recurs in demonstrating relationships and maximizing statistical power. Basic issues such as confounding, demand characteristics, and counterbalancing are also repeatedly addressed. Revisiting these issues in their different contexts allows students to retain and integrate them. My intent is that students understand that the nature of the research question and the goals of the researcher dictate the design. The design has strengths and weaknesses, which in turn dictate the interpretation of the results.

New to the Second Edition

In response to instructor feedback, I have changed the order in which several topics occur. The essential revisions are: (1) creating a separate chapter on research ethics, (2) holding off on a review of statistics until later in the text, (3) combining the discussion of independent and dependent variables into one chapter, and (4) discussing APA-style reports at the end of the text. With these changes, the material is presented in a more linear fashion that mirrors the steps a researcher follows in conducting a study.

The entire text was revised to ensure a clear and tight explanation of each concept, and a number of additional pedagogical devices were added. *Getting Started* sections now open each chapter, providing new learning objectives as well as identifying concepts from previous chapters students should review before reading the chapter. In addition, new running *Checklists* that build across chapters have been added, covering the major issues to consider when designing and analyzing an experiment. The culminating checklist appears on the inside front cover of the text. Finally, a *Key Terms* list now appears at the end of every chapter for student review.

Organization of the Text

Overall, this text uses a "top-down" approach that stresses context and the interrelatedness of topics. Unlike many textbooks, the text focuses on laboratory experiments first and other types of designs later. Once students understand the basics of a controlled laboratory study, they can more easily understand the strengths and weaknesses of other types of designs. Further, discussing experiments early in the course leaves more of the semester for students to practice designing and reporting them in lab exercises.

To give students a background for thinking scientifically and to enable them to begin conducting lab exercises, Part I provides an overview of the conceptual, design, and ethical issues in the research process. The goal is to provide a general context for all research designs that is centered on the common task of demonstrating relationships. Chapter 1 introduces the goals of research, the basics of the scientific method, and the logic of research, using simple, everyday examples. Chapter 2 presents the conceptual issues in research, identifying the major design and interpretive concerns by examining a sample study of the kind beginning students often create. Potential flaws in descriptive and experimental studies are introduced here in terms of validity and reliability. I took great care to prevent Chapters 1 and 2 from reading like a disjointed list of definitions. Rather, I show how each concept affects our confidence in a study's conclusions. Chapter 3, a new chapter, introduces the major common techniques used to ensure reliability and validity. Essentially, this chapter answers the question: "How do you conduct a psychological study?" Chapter 4, another new chapter, discusses the ethics of research and the APA guidelines. Rather than presenting ethics as a dry set of prescriptions, however, the chapter explores the realistic dilemmas that researchers face when they encounter potentially risky procedures and variables and when they use deception and unobtrusive measures to deal with demand characteristics. Throughout Part I, students examine the ways their design decisions affect their data through the issue of designing a powerful study. The discussion is simplified, however, by presenting the individual scores in idealized examples of relationships instead of using more obtuse summary statistics.

Part II presents more advanced design issues and the statistical analysis of experiments. Chapter 5 discusses controlling participant variables and presents the pros and cons of between-subjects and within-subjects designs. A complete discussion of counterbalancing is included. Chapter 6 reviews common descriptive and inferential statistics and shows how they are used to interpret simple experiments. This chapter was written without assuming that students perfectly recall their previous statistics course, but without talking down to them either. Chapter 7 expands the discussion to multifactor designs and includes common advanced statistical procedures. These chapters emphasize understanding the practical uses of statistics in the research process without clouding the issue with statistical theories or formulas. Further, all statistical discussions go beyond the mere numbers, covering the psychological interpretation of each study in terms of behaviors and variables. (Computational formulas and critical values are presented in Appendixes C and D.)

With this background in laboratory experiments, students are ready to learn about and evaluate other types of designs presented in Part III. These chapters have been revised to provide a more straightforward presentation while integrating relevant design, ethical, and statistical issues. Chapter 8 presents correlational designs, including questionnaire development and a brief discussion of advanced correlational statistics. Chapter 9 discusses field experiments and single-subject designs. Chapter 10 presents quasi-experiments, survey techniques, and observational and descriptive methods.

The final chapter, Chapter 11, is a unique review chapter designed to help students apply and integrate issues covered throughout the entire course. It walks students through an analysis of several research studies from start to finish, focusing on the logic of design, evaluation, and interpretation. This material may serve as an end-of-course capstone chapter. Alternatively, because it includes most of the designs discussed in the text, specific examples may be used in conjunction with earlier chapters.

Appendix A, "Reporting Research Using APA Format," is a full-fledged chapter designed for use at any point in the course. It provides a comprehensive look at how to search the literature and how to read and write a research report using APA format. A complete example manuscript is featured in Appendix B, describing a simple yet engaging two-sample experiment.

Special Features

A full set of learning tools provides extensive pedagogical support in every chapter.

• Each chapter begins with a new *Getting Started* section that lists the learning objectives for the chapter and identify relevant concepts from previous chapters for students to review.

• Important points are emphasized throughout the text by *Remember* statements, which are summary reminders set off from the text.

• Key terms are highlighted in bold type, and formal definitions are accompanied by numerous mnemonics and analogies to promote retention and understanding. A new *Key Terms* list appears at the end of each chapter, and a complete glossary appears at the end of the text.

• Summary reference tables and new *Checklists* that build across chapters integrate topics and help students select from various design options.

• At the end of each chapter, a *Putting It All Together* section provides advice, cautions, and ways to integrate material from different chapters.

• Each *Chapter Summary* provides a substantive review of the material, not merely a list of the topics covered.

• *Review Questions* at the end of each chapter review definitions and concepts and present real-world application problems. More involved *Discussion Questions* (including challenging ethical questions) are also provided for use in class. Answers to Review Questions and suggestions for Discussion Questions are provided in the instructor's resource manual.

Supplements

The accompanying instructor's resource manual and test bank includes suggestions for classroom activities and discussions and multiple-choice and short-answer test items. The test questions are also available on disk in a program that allows instructors to add or edit questions and generate exams. In addition, a student manual called *Using SPSS for Windows,* by Charles Stangor of the University of Maryland, and a set of accompanying datasets are available for shrinkwrapping with the text. You can also visit the Houghton Mifflin College Psychology Website for additional teaching and learning activities that support this course.

Acknowledgments

Many people contributed to the production of this text. At Houghton Mifflin Company, I want to thank all those who saw the project through to completion, including David Lee, Jane Knetzger, Anne Holm, Jane Judge Bonassar, and Barbara Sutton.

I am also grateful to the following reviewers, who in evaluating the first edition, provided invaluable feedback:

Richard W. Bowen, Loyola University, Chicago

Stephen L. Crites, Jr., University of Texas at El Paso

Loraina L. Ghiraldi, St. Lawrence University

Rory O'Brien McElwee, Randolph-Macon Woman's College

Walena C. Morse, West Chester University

P. Michael Politano, The Citadel

Holly R. Straub, University of South Dakota

Lori R. Van Wallendael, University of North Carolina at Charlotte

Christine B. Ziegler, Kennesaw State University

—Gary W. Heiman

Part I

Introduction to Psychological Research

OK, so now you're taking a course in research methods. Because you are a student of psychology and psychology is a science, you are in some sense training to be a scientist. Regardless of whether you intend to become an active researcher, if you want to understand, use, and evaluate psychological information, you must understand the methods used in psychological research. This book will teach you those methods.

Research methods are the most enjoyable—and the easiest to learn—when you are actively involved, so this text places you in the role of a researcher. As a researcher, you will learn the goals of science and how scientists operate. You will learn how to phrase questions scientifically, how to design and conduct scientific research, and how to interpret and communicate your results. Along the way, you will also learn about the imperfections and limitations of scientific research. Ultimately, you will not only understand the research of others but also be able to conduct and correctly interpret research on your own.

This course aims to discipline your mind so that you can answer questions scientifically. Toward this end, you must deal with three major concerns. First, being a researcher involves a combination of thinking logically, being creative, and, more than anything else, applying a critical eye to all phases of your research. Second, although knowing the rules of science is important, learning to *apply* those rules in the contexts of different research problems is vital. Third, research has its own language. Psychologists use very specific terms—with very specific meanings—that you must learn. You must strive for a degree of precision that you seldom experience in your day-to-day life, so that you can accurately and concisely communicate the procedures and findings of a study. Practice using the special vocabulary of research at every opportunity.

1

Introduction to the Scientific Method

GETTING STARTED

As you read this chapter, your goals are to learn:

- The assumptions and attitudes of scientists.

- The goals of science.

- The difference between basic and applied research.

- The criteria for scientific hypotheses and for acceptable evidence for testing them.

- Why literal and conceptual replication are necessary.

*P*sychology is often defined as the scientific study of behavior, where a "behavior" may be any external physical action or any internal mental action. Accordingly, psychologists want to understand every aspect of behavior—and not just human behavior but the behavior of all organisms. Because the behaviors of organisms constitute a part of the natural world, psychologists study part of "nature," just as biologists, physicists, and other scientists do. And, as in all sciences, there is only one acceptable source for the "facts": Everything psychologists think they know in the science of psychology is obtained through research.

On the one hand, research is exciting and challenging, because nature is very secretive and not easily understood. The fun in research is in devising a way to unlock the mysteries of behavior. On the other hand, creating, conducting, and interpreting research require mental effort, because it is easy to draw *incorrect* conclusions about any behavior. To understand how such errors occur, you need first to understand the general characteristics of scientific research. Therefore, this chapter introduces you to the scientific method, and points out some of the major pitfalls that psychologists try to avoid when learning about nature.

The Scientific Method

If you are at all curious about your behavior or the behavior of others, you are already part of the way toward becoming a researcher. All sciences are based on curiosity about nature, and psychology is based on curiosity about behavior. Your curiosity is important, because it is the basis for deciding what you want to learn and how to go about learning it.

> **REMEMBER** Every decision a researcher makes depends first and foremost on the question the researcher is asking.

But being curious is not enough. The primary difference between scientists and nonscientists lies in the way scientists go about answering the questions they ask about nature: They use the "scientific method." This is a rather broad term, referring to a philosophy and set of rules that have evolved over the past several hundred years. Essentially, the **scientific method** consists of certain assumptions, attitudes, goals, and procedures for creating and answering questions about nature.

Why should psychologists—including yourself—worry about their methods? Because there are many ways to learn about behavior, and some are better than others. Most people think they know a lot about behavior: They have intuitions and personal experiences, they make logical deductions, they use common sense, and they defer to authority figures. But these sources of information are not acceptable to scientists. We do not trust intuitions or personal experience because everyone has different feelings about and experiences of the world. (Whose should we believe?) We do not trust logic because nature does not always conform to our logic. We cannot rely on common sense because it is often contradictory. (Which is true: "Absence makes the heart grow fonder" or "Out of sight, out of mind"?) And we cannot rely on what authority figures or the so-called experts say, because there is no reason to believe that they correctly understand how nature works either.

The problem with the preceding sources of knowledge is that they ultimately rely on opinions or beliefs that may be created by someone who is biased or wrong (or downright crazy). After all, merely because someone says something about the nature of a behavior does not make it true. Implicit in our goals as psychologists is that we will *accurately* understand behavior. In addition, psychology is a source of knowledge used by society in a way that can and does have a serious impact on the lives and well-being of others. For example, at one time people with a criminal history were thought to have "defective" personalities, which were "remedied" by surgical lobotomy, the removal of portions of their brains. Unfortunately for those undergoing the surgery, this approach was just plain wrong! Thus, because we seek to understand behavior, and because this knowledge can drastically influence the lives of others, psychology's ideal goal is to be perfectly accurate.

Psychology relies on the scientific method because it is the best approach for eliminating bias and opinion, for reaching a consensus about how a behavior truly operates, and for correcting errors. It does this by requiring that whenever someone makes a statement about behavior, we ask that person, "How do you *know* that?" We do not mean "believe," "feel," or "think"; we mean *know,* with certainty! In the science of psychology—just as in a court of law—it is the evidence supporting a statement that is most important. The scientific method provides the most convincing evidence, because it is based on the events as they occur in nature. That is, rather than relying on the opinions and beliefs of others, we look to nature directly; and as nature is available for all of us to see, we all have the same basis for examining it and coming to an agreement about how it works. Thus, the scientific study of psychology is specifically geared toward learning about an organism's behavior by *observing* that behavior, while minimizing the influences of bias or opinion.

The remainder of this chapter examines the components of the scientific method as they apply to the study of behavior. To start with, the following sections look at how scientists approach the task of science.

The Assumptions of Science

What first distinguishes scientists from nonscientists is the philosophy about nature that scientists adopt. At first glance, any aspect of nature, especially human behavior, seems to be overwhelmingly complex, verging on the chaotic. Scientists have the audacity to try to understand such a complicated topic because they do not consider nature to be chaotic. Instead, scientists make certain assumptions about nature that allow them to approach it as a regulated and consistent system. These assumptions are that nature is lawful, deterministic, and understandable.

By saying that nature is **lawful**, we mean that every event can be understood as a sequence of natural causes and effects. We assume that behavior is lawful, because if it wasn't (and instead is random), then we could never understand it. Thus, in the same way that the "law of gravity" governs the behavior of planets or the "laws of aerodynamics" govern the behavior of airplanes, psychologists assume that there are laws of nature that govern the behavior of living organisms. Although some natural laws do not apply to all species (for example, laws dealing with nest building among birds do not apply to humans), a specific law does apply to all members of a group. Thus, when psychologists study the mating behavior of penguins, or the development of language in people, they are studying laws of nature.

Recognize that most psychologists would think it too grandiose to claim that any single study directly examines a law of nature. As you'll see, any study will have a very narrow focus, and researchers are frequently confronted with contradictory findings and opposing explanations. Thus, a considerable amount of research is required to reach a consensus about even a small aspect of a behavior, and so a conclusive definition of any law requires an extremely slow and complicated process. We do assume, however, that eventually all of the diverse findings will be integrated so that we can truly understand each law of nature.

Viewing behavior as lawful leads to a second, related assumption: We assume that the behavior of organisms is "determined." **Determinism** means that behavior is solely influenced by natural causes and does not depend on choice or "free will." If instead we assumed that organisms freely decide their behavior, then behavior truly would be chaotic, because the only explanation for every behavior would be "because he or she wanted to." Therefore, we reject the idea that free will plays a role. After all, you cannot walk off a cliff and "will" yourself not to fall, because the law of gravity forces you to fall. Anyone else in the same situation will also fall because that is how gravity operates. Likewise, we assume that you cannot freely choose to exhibit a particular personality or behave in a particular way in a given situation. The laws of behavior force you to have certain attributes and to behave in a certain way in a certain situation. Anyone else in the same situation will be similarly influenced, because that's how the laws of behavior operate. There are, of course, individual differences, so no two individuals will behave identically. The term **individual differences**, however, is really just another way of saying that so many influences are operating on a behavior at any moment that the situation is unique for each individual. Still, we assume that there are laws of nature that govern even individual differences. Thus, in a sense, determinism views all living organisms as machinelike: When a specific situation in nature is present, organisms behave in a predictable, lawful way.

Note that determinism is not the same as *predestination*. Predestination suggests that our actions follow some universal plan that is already laid out for us. Determinism, however, means that there are identifiable, natural causes for every behavior. Thus, there is no grand scheme governing your life so that at noon on Tuesday you'll walk off a cliff. If you do walk off a cliff, however, it's because specific natural causes make you do this—causes operating in a lawful manner so that anyone else similarly exposed to them would also walk off the cliff.

The third assumption is that the laws of nature are *understandable*. Regardless of how complicated nature may appear or how confused we currently are about some aspect of nature, we assume that we will eventually understand it (or there is no point in studying it). Thus, any scientific statement must logically and rationally fit with the known facts, so that it can be understood. Part of an explanation can never be that we must accept a mystery or an unresolvable contradiction. If two statements contradict each other at present, it must be logically possible to resolve the debate eventually so that only one statement applies.

Notice that the preceding assumptions exclude certain topics from being studied scientifically. For example, miracles cannot be studied scientifically because, by definition, miracles do not obey the laws of nature. Likewise, because of determinism, we cannot study free will. (We can study people's *perceptions* of miracles or free will, because their perceptions are behaviors that fit our assumptions about nature.) Further, because nature is assumed to be understandable, any topic that requires faith cannot be studied scientifically. Faith is the acceptance of the truth of a statement without questions or needing proof. But in science it is *always* appropriate to question and to ask for proof. Thus, for example, according to the Judeo-Christian tradition, God created the universe in six days. Some people refer to the study of this idea as "creationism science." There can be no *science* of creationism, however, because creationism requires belief in God, but science does not allow for such a requirement. Likewise, although scientists are entitled to the same religions and beliefs as anyone else, these beliefs simply cannot play a part when producing and evaluating scientific evidence. After all, if science did allow statements of faith, whose faith would we use . . . yours or mine?

REMEMBER   To be studied scientifically, any behavior must be assumed to be lawful, determined, and understandable.

The Attitudes of Scientists

To help prevent their own biases and beliefs from creeping into their conclusions, scientists explicitly adopt certain attitudes toward the process of learning about nature. Therefore, as a scientist, you should be uncertain, open-minded, skeptical, cautious, and ethical.

The starting point is to recognize that the purpose of science is to learn about nature, admitting that no one already knows everything about how nature operates. There is always some degree of *uncertainty*. For psychologists, this means that no one knows precisely what a particular behavior entails, what the factors are that influence it, or what the one correct way to study it is. All other steps in scientific research stem from this simple admission.

If no one knows for certain how nature operates, then any explanation or description of it may be just as appropriate as any other. Therefore, you should be *open-minded,* leaving your biases and preconceptions behind. An explanation may offend your sensibilities or contradict your beliefs, but that is no reason to dismiss it. You must look in all directions, at all possible explanations, when trying to understand a behavior.

At the same time, you should be *skeptical:* never automatically accept the truth of any scientific description. Because no one already knows how nature works, any description of a behavior may be incorrect (no one is perfect, not even psychologists). After all, the history of science is littered with descriptions that at first appeared accurate but later turned out to misrepresent nature. (The earth is not flat!) Therefore, you must skeptically and critically evaluate the evidence produced by any study: using logic and your knowledge of psychology, always question whether the factors proposed as important might actually be irrelevant (or at least not the whole story) and whether the factors proposed as irrelevant might actually be important. To aid in this process, researchers share their research findings through professional publications, meetings, and so on. Then, eventually, psychology will identify and rectify any mistakes, to arrive at the best, most accurate information.

If we assume that critical analysis will eventually produce an error-free understanding of nature, then we must also recognize that we are currently in the process of discovering which parts of our information are incorrect. Therefore, you must be *cautious* when dealing with scientific findings. Any scientific conclusion implicitly contains the qualifying statement "given our present knowledge and abilities." Never treat the results of any single study as a "fact" in the usual sense. Instead, phrase your conclusions using words such as *possibly* or *suggests*—in essence saying, "It *appears* that the behavior *might* operate in such-and-such a way." Always consider that a research finding is merely a piece of evidence that provides some degree of confidence in a description about nature but that it may actually misrepresent nature.

Finally, there is one other attitude that scientists adopt: you must behave *ethically* when conducting research. In Chapter 4 we'll discuss the specifics of **research ethics,** but the basic principle is that neither researchers nor their research should cause harm to others.

Table 1.1 will help you to remember these attitudes by relating each one to the approach that scientists take. Whenever you conduct research or encounter that of others, be sure that these attitudes are present.

REMEMBER Scientists are uncertain, open-minded, skeptical, cautious, and ethical.

As scientists, psychologists are led by their assumptions to continually evaluate their own research and the research of others. Evaluating a study means evaluating the evidence the study provides. As with the rules of evidence in a court of law, science has rules governing what evidence is admissible and how it must be gathered.

Table 1.1 How the Attitudes of Researchers Influence Their Approach to Psychological Findings

Attitude	Approach
Uncertain	No one already knows how a behavior operates.
Open-minded	Any approach or statement may be correct.
Skeptical	Any approach or statement may contain error.
Cautious	Any conclusion is not a "fact."
Ethical	Research should not harm others.

The Criteria for Scientific Evidence

When people think of scientific research, they usually think of "experiments." Although psychologists often perform experiments, they also conduct other types of research. In fact, there is an infinite number of different ways to "design" a study. The **design** of a study is the specific manner in which the study is set up and conducted. First, the design must identify the specific people or animals to study. (Note that historically, published psychological research has referred to these individuals as **subjects.** As discussed in Appendix A, however, beginning with research published after 1994, these individuals are now called **participants.**) In addition, a design includes the specific situation or sequence of situations under which participants are studied, the way their behavior is examined, and the components of the situation and behavior that are considered.

As an example of a behavior for which we might design a study, let's discuss one simple, familiar behavior: the irritating tendency of people to "channel surf"—to grab the television's remote control and change the channel whenever a commercial appears. (If this seems too mundane a behavior to be "psychological," stay tuned . . .) In designing a study of this behavior, remember that we seek the most convincing evidence for answering the question "How do you know that?" In science, convincing evidence is empirical, objective, systematic, and controlled.

First, the evidence must be **empirical**—meaning learned by *observation*. Psychologists study everything that an individual does, feels, thinks, wants, or remembers, from the microlevel of neurological functioning to the macrolevel of complex, lifelong behaviors. Yet ultimately, all evidence is collected and all debates are resolved by attending to observable, public behaviors. Thus, to understand channel changing, we should *observe* channel changing. Because anyone else can potentially observe this behavior in the same way, everyone then shares the same basis for determining how it operates.

Second, several people can observe the same event and still have different personal impressions of it. Therefore, science requires **objectivity**. This means that, ideally, a researcher's personal biases, attitudes, or subjective impressions do not influence the observations or conclusions. Although people can't be perfectly objective, scientists strive for this by obtaining *measurements* that are as empirical, as objective, and as precise as possible. It is through empirical, objective measurement of behavior that a researcher obtains the data in a study. For example, counting the number of times a person changes channels during a specified time period results in objective, precise data. Or, in other studies, we may use equipment that times someone's responses or measures his or her physiological reactions, we may interview participants or have them perform mental or physical tests, we may observe people surreptitiously, and so on. In any of these approaches, we try to be as objective as possible, so that the data reflect precisely what participants actually do in a given situation and not our personal interpretations of what they do.

In addition, nature is very complex. Consequently the research situation must be simplified so that we are not confused by all that is going on. Therefore, evidence is gathered systematically. Being **systematic** means that observations are obtained in a methodical, step-by-step fashion. For example, say we think that boring commercials cause channel changing. After we've objectively measured "boring," we would then objectively measure the channel changing that occurs with very boring commercials, with less boring commercials, and again with interesting commercials. If we also think that the number of people in the room influences channel changing, we would observe a person's responses to the preceding commercials first when alone, then when another person is present, then when two other people are present, and so on. By being systematic, we determine the role of each factor and combination of factors as they apply to a behavior.

Finally, evidence must be obtained under controlled conditions. **Control** is another way to simplify the situation by eliminating any extraneous factors that might influence the observed behaviors and thus create confusion. For example, while observing whether more boring commercials produce more channel changing, we would try to control how boring the television program is, so that this factor would not influence channel changing. Likewise, we'd control the situation by having people only watch television so that other distractions won't influence their channel changing. In short, with control, researchers attempt to create a clearly defined situation in which to observe only the specific behavior and the relevant factors that interest them.

Table 1.2 will help you remember these criteria by relating them to the rules for designing research. The more that a study deviates from these rules, the more its results are likely to misrepresent nature, and so the less convincing they are.

REMEMBER Acceptable scientific evidence is obtained through empirical, objective, systematic, and controlled research.

Table 1.2   How the Criteria for Scientific Research Translate into the Rules for Designing Research

Criteria	Rule
Empirical	All information is based on observation.
Objective	Observations must be free from bias.
Systematic	Observations are made in a step-by-step fashion.
Controlled	Potentially confusing factors are eliminated.

As you will see, many different research designs are possible that meet the preceding criteria. Which approach to take depends first on the type of question being asked—the specific goal of the study.

The Goals of Psychological Research

Overall, the goal of psychology is to understand behavior. But what does "understand" mean? Science defines understanding an event in terms of the four simultaneous and equally important goals of being able to describe, explain, predict, and control the event.

Obviously, psychologists want to know what behavior does and does not occur in nature, so the first goal is to **describe** each behavior and the conditions under which it occurs. To describe channel changing, we would specify how frequently channels are changed, whether they are changed during all commercials, whether they are changed at all times of the day, and so on. We could also describe channel changing from various perspectives, in terms of the hand movements necessary to operate the remote, or the cognitive decision making involved, or the neurological activity occurring in the brain.

Mere description of a behavior, however, is not enough to completely understand it: We also need to know *why* the behavior occurs. Therefore, another goal is to **explain** behaviors in terms of their specific causes. Thus, we want to explain what aspect of a commercial, either present or absent, causes channel changing and why. Also, we want to identify the factors—the channel changer's personality, the type of program, the presence of other people in the room—that cause more or less channel changing and why. And again, there are various perspectives we can take, such as neurological, cognitive, motivational, or environmental causes.

Note that in explaining a behavior, it is important to avoid pseudo-explanations. A **pseudo-explanation** is circular, giving as the reason for an event another name for that event. For example, a pseudo-explanation of channel changing is that it is caused by the motivation to see what is on other channels—really just another way of saying that people change channels because they want to change channels. The key to avoiding a pseudo-explanation is to provide an *independent* verification of the supposed cause. If, for example, we could discover a gene that motivates people to change channels, then we would be confident that we were talking about two different things—a cause (the gene) and an effect (changing channels)—and not merely renaming one thing.

A third aspect of understanding a behavior is to know when it will occur or what will bring it about, so an additional goal of psychology is to **predict** behaviors. Thus, we want to be able to accurately predict when channel changing will and will not occur, the amount or degree of the behavior to expect from a particular person, or when and how the behavior will change as a person's physiological, cognitive, social, or environmental conditions change. In addition, the accuracy with which a behavior can be predicted is an indication of how well we have explained it. If we say that a behavior has a particular cause but the presence of the cause does not allow us to accurately predict the behavior, then the explanation is wrong, or at least incomplete.

Finally, if we truly understand a behavior, we should be able to create the situation in which it occurs. Therefore, the fourth goal is to **control** behavior. Thus, in studying channel changing, we want to know how to alter the situation to produce, increase, decrease, or eliminate the behavior. And note that being able to control events is another test of an explanation. If a cause of a behavior is identified, then *manipulating* that cause—turning it on and off or providing more or less of it—should produce changes in the behavior. If it does not, the explanation is again either wrong or incomplete.

Table 1.3 will help you to remember these goals by relating them to the types of activities psychologists pursue when conducting research. Any psychological study will entail one or more of these activities.

Table 1.3 How the Goals of Science Translate into the Activities of Psychologists

Goal	Activity
Describe	Learn what a behavior entails and the situations in which it occurs.
Explain	Learn the causes that determine when and why a behavior occurs.
Predict	Learn to identify the factors needed to predict when a behavior will occur.
Control	Learn to manipulate the factors needed to produce or eliminate a behavior.

REMEMBER To completely understand a behavior, researchers strive to describe it, explain its causes, and predict and control its occurrence.

Meeting the Goals of Science

You can now see how the science of psychology proceeds. As shown in Figure 1.1, it is through the combination of the required attitudes plus the requirements of research that we expect to understand behavior. That is, psychologists attempt to learn about a behavior by obtaining empirical, objective, systematic, and controlled observations that allow them to describe, explain, predict, and control the behavior. Each finding is rigorously evaluated in a cautious, skeptical, and open-minded manner, so that an accurate understanding of the laws of behavior can be developed.

You may think that this approach is massive overkill when studying a behavior as mundane as channel changing. Is it really necessary to be that fussy? Well, yes, if we want to *fully* understand the behavior. Granted, it would be easier to see why we should be so fussy if, for example, we were studying something like airplane pilots who turn off their planes' engines in midflight. There is an urgency to this behavior, so that understanding it in such great detail would not be overkill (pardon the pun). But recognize that channel changing is not so mundane. This behavior involves major psychological processes such as decision making, information processing, communication, neural-pathways control, motivation, and social processes. Thus, an in-depth study of channel changing is worthwhile because, for example, by studying the decision making involved in channel changing, we can learn about decision making processes in general. Further, another reason for a detailed study of channel changing is that research often leads to **serendipitous** findings: In the process of studying one aspect of nature, researchers may accidentally discover another aspect, unrelated to the original research. (In studying channel changing, we may stumble onto a cure for

Figure 1.1 How a scientist's attitudes plus the criteria for acceptable evidence lead to meeting the goals of science

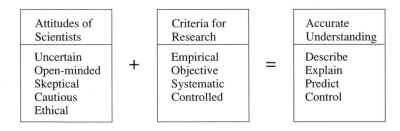

Attitudes of Scientists		Criteria for Research		Accurate Understanding
Uncertain Open-minded Skeptical Cautious Ethical	+	Empirical Objective Systematic Controlled	=	Describe Explain Predict Control

boredom.) Thus, because we never know where an investigation will lead, we take the study of every behavior very seriously and do the best, most complete job we can.

Applied and Basic Research

Studying the errors an airplane pilot makes involves a greater urgency, because this behavior represents a real-life problem. Such research is called applied research. **Applied research** is conducted for the purpose of solving an existing, real-life problem. For example, the companies that pay for television commercials might conduct applied research into channel changing during their commercials so that they can eliminate the resulting problem of wasted advertising money.

On the other hand, **basic research** is conducted simply for the knowledge it produces. Thus, we might study channel changing simply because it is interesting and adds to our understanding of behavior in general. Although people often have a hard time understanding why it's important to conduct basic research, such research is justified first and foremost because science seeks to understand *all* aspects of nature. Also, basic and applied research often overlap. For example, basic research into channel changing may provide information that advertising agencies can apply to solve their problem (and applied research designed to eliminate channel changing will add to our basic understanding of the behavior). A third justification of basic research is that past basic research may someday be valuable in a future applied setting. Say that we learn that channel changing and turning off airplane engines in midflight share some common factor (perhaps both are caused by boredom). At that point, our basic research into channel changing would be very useful for the applied problem of preventing airplane crashes. And, finally, a justification for basic research is that it often results in serendipitous applied findings. For example, some of the most common medicinal drugs have been discovered totally by accident during the course of basic research.

In sum, the terms *basic* and *applied* are general, describing a study only in terms of its obvious, stated purposes. In reality, we never know the ultimate purpose that research will serve (which is another reason for employing very rigorous methods).

REMEMBER The primary purpose of basic research is to obtain knowledge; the primary purpose of applied research is to solve an existing problem.

The Role of a Single Study

Regardless of whether we conduct applied or basic research, *completely* describing, explaining, predicting, and controlling a behavior constitute the *ultimate* goal of research. But, because of the extreme complexity of behaviors, no single study can fully meet this goal. Consider the variety of perspectives we can take when studying channel changing and the many factors that might influence it. Because we cannot study everything at once, we must simplify nature by examining one factor and taking one perspective at a time. Thus, one study will describe certain aspects of a behavior, another will examine an explanation, other studies will investigate ways to predict the behavior, and still others will focus on controlling it. Any specific study is therefore a momentary "snapshot" of one small portion of a behavior. As a result of this piecemeal approach, the discipline of psychology—and publications describing it—may appear to be disjointed and unfocused, going off in many directions at once. Yet, as these individual pieces of information gradually combine, we eventually do come to understand all aspects of a behavior.

> **REMEMBER** Any study represents a very limited and simplified view of the complexity found in nature and contributes minutely to the goals of describing, explaining, predicting, and controlling a behavior.

Every decision researchers make depends first and foremost on whether their primary goal is to describe, explain, predict, or control a behavior. Therefore, the first step in any study is to formulate the specific question you wish to answer. That question is called a hypothesis.

Scientific Hypotheses

You might ask the question, "What causes channel changing?" However, this is actually a very ambiguous question, with no hint as to the type of "snapshot" needed to answer it. Do you mean "what" in terms of the cognitive, physiological, or environmental causes? And which aspect of the cognitive, physiological, or environmental causes are you talking about? Such an ambiguous question cannot be directly answered by a study. After all, at some point you must go out and actually collect some data, so sooner or later you need to know precisely which behavior to examine and how to examine it. Therefore, you must translate any general question into a specific hypothesis that directs the research.

Creating Hypotheses

A **hypothesis** is a formally stated expectation about how a behavior operates. It is, in essence, a tentative guess about a behavior that usually relates the behavior to some other behavior or influence. Rather than asking a question beginning with "why" or "what," a hypothesis is phrased as a declarative statement or description. Then we test the hypothesis: We conduct an empirical, controlled, systematic study that provides data that help us determine if the statement is correct or not.

There are two general types of hypotheses. In keeping with the goal of explaining and controlling the causes of behavior, one type is a **causal hypothesis**: This tentatively identifies a particular cause for or influence on a behavior. For example, we might hypothesize that "channel changing is caused by the boring content of commercials." (Implicitly, we recognize that there may be many other influences on channel changing, but for now, this is the one we'd study.)

On the other hand, in keeping with the goal of describing and predicting behavior, the other type is a **descriptive hypothesis**: This tentatively describes a behavior in terms of its characteristics or the situation in which it occurs, and allows us to predict when it occurs. For example, we might hypothesize that "channel changing occurs more frequently when someone is watching television alone than when other people are present." Notice that even though the number of people present might partially cause channel changing, we have not stated this. A descriptive hypothesis does *not* attempt to identify the causes of a behavior. In fact, sometimes it states simply that certain behaviors occur and can be measured, giving a general goal and direction to our observations. For example, we might hypothesize that "channel changers have certain personality characteristics" and then set out to discover and describe them.

> **REMEMBER** A causal hypothesis postulates a particular causal influence on a behavior, and a descriptive hypothesis postulates particular characteristics of the behavior or provides a goal for observations.

It is extremely important to state explicitly whether a study is examining the causes of a behavior, because this is a critical factor in determining the design of the study. Before designing the study, however, you must be sure the hypothesis reflects the assumptions about the lawfulness and understandability of nature. If it does not, then the hypothesis is not scientific, and the evidence that supports it is not scientifically admissible. Therefore, there are specific rules for creating scientific hypotheses.

The Criteria for Scientific Hypotheses

A scientific hypothesis should be testable, falsifiable, precise, rational, and parsimonious.

A hypothesis must first be testable and falsifiable. **Testable** means that it is possible to devise a test of a hypothesis. **Falsifiable** means that the test can show that the hypothesis is incorrect. Our previous channel-changing hypotheses are testable and falsifiable because we can devise a study to test them, and we may find evidence indicating they are incorrect. It is possible, however, to create hypotheses that are not testable or falsifiable. Consider the hypothesis "When people die, they see a bright light." This is not a testable hypothesis because it's not possible to study people's experience after death—they're dead! (Studying people who are declared dead and then revived is a poor substitute, because they are not truly dead.) Because it's not testable, the hypothesis is also not falsifiable. Or, consider Sigmund Freud's hypothesis that the "id" leads people to express aggression directly as well as indirectly through superficially nonaggressive behaviors. Although this hypothesis is testable through observation, it cannot be shown to be false: If we observe aggression, it's because of the id. If we don't observe aggression, it's still because of the id, expressing its aggression through nonaggressive behavior. Given the circular logic here, this hypothesis cannot tell us anything about the id (even Freud wasn't perfect). If a hypothesis is not testable or falsifiable, it's impossible to determine its accuracy. Instead, we must take the hypothesis on faith, which is a nonscientific approach.

A hypothesis must also add to knowledge about the laws of nature in a meaningful and understandable way, so a hypothesis must be precise and rational. A **precise** hypothesis contains terms that are clearly defined. The use of ambiguous terms opens the hypothesis to interpretation and opinion, making it less clearly testable and falsifiable. A **rational** hypothesis logically fits what is already known about the laws of behavior. For example, our hypothesis about boring commercials causing channel changing fits with what we already know about behavior and, if shown to be correct, will mesh easily with existing knowledge. In contrast, consider the claim that some people exhibit extrasensory perception (ESP), the ability to send and receive mental messages. Any hypothesis about this supposed ability is not rational, because it contradicts existing knowledge about the brain and physical energy that's been developed in psychology, biology, and physics.

Finally, a hypothesis must be parsimonious. A **parsimonious** hypothesis is one that is as simple as possible. The assumption that nature is lawful implies that many diverse events can be accounted for by an economical combination of relatively few laws. If we propose new laws or mechanisms for every situation, we are merely renaming nature without explaining it. Therefore, the rule of parsimony says that we begin with relatively simple hypotheses that apply to broad categories of behaviors. Then only if the simple explanation fails to account for a behavior can we propose new, more complex ones. Thus, any hypothesis about ESP would not be parsimonious, because it would require proposing all sorts of new brain components and new energy waves, just to make it a viable hypothesis. To be parsimonious, however, there would first need to be scientific evidence for ESP that could not be explained using brain mechanisms and energy forms that are already established by previous research. Only then would it be acceptable to propose the existence of new brain components and new energy waves.

Checklist 1.1 will help you remember the criteria for acceptable hypotheses by relating them to the question you should ask about a hypothesis for each. The more that a hypothesis deviates from these criteria, the less confidence we have in any conclusions about it.

REMEMBER Scientific hypotheses must be testable, falsifiable, precise, rational, and parsimonious.

CHECKLIST 1.1 Questions to consider when determining whether a hypothesis meets the five criteria for scientific acceptability

Criteria	Question about the Hypothesis
❏ Testable	Can a test be designed for it?
❏ Falsifiable	Can it be possibly proved false?
❏ Precise	Are its terms clearly defined?
❏ Rational	Does it fit with the known information?
❏ Parsimonious	Does it involve the simplest possible approach?

Sources of Hypotheses

How do you come up with a hypothesis? One obvious source for generating a hypothesis is a researcher's own opinions, observations, or experiences. It is perfectly acceptable to base a hypothesis on such sources, as long as you then conduct an empirical, objective study to provide evidence for the hypothesis. A second source is existing research: When reading the results of a study that tested one hypothesis, you'll usually see the basis for several additional hypotheses. For example, if we find that channel changing increases when someone is alone, we would then want to determine why, identify the factors that modify this influence, and so on. A third source of a hypothesis, as we'll see, is the retesting of a hypothesis previously tested by another researcher.

Theories are another source of hypotheses. A **theory** is a logically organized set of statements that defines, explains, organizes, and interrelates knowledge about many behaviors. Theoreticians may develop a theory beginning with certain ideas and concepts for which there is little scientific evidence. The theory then provides a direction for the evidence researchers will seek. Or theoreticians may develop a theory after substantial evidence has been collected, providing a way to organize diverse findings. Either way, a theory is a framework of abstract concepts that helps to explain and describe a broad range of behaviors in a parsimonious way. For example, "Freudian theory" attempted to explain and relate a vast array of normal and abnormal behaviors using such abstract concepts as id, ego, and superego. Likewise, the most common psychological terms are actually theoretical concepts, such as learning, memory, intelligence, creativity, personality, and schizophrenia. These are not real things; you cannot place your personality on a table. Rather, they are abstract general descriptions that help you to understand specific behaviors.

Theories serve two major functions. First, they help to *organize* empirical findings. Additional research can then be tied to the theory, providing a framework for developing the "big picture" regarding a behavior. Thus, for the sake of rational and parsimonious hypotheses, especially when research begins with your personal opinions or experiences, you need to relate any behavior being researched to theoretical concepts. For example, you might tie your ideas about boring commercials to existing concepts of "information processing" and "motivation" to explain channel changing, and then design a study using these concepts. If you find evidence that supports the hypothesis, your description and explanation is then likely to mesh with existing knowledge in an understandable way.

The other, simultaneous function that theories serve is to *guide* research. To test or add to a theory, researchers derive a specific hypothesis, test it in a research study, and then apply the study's outcome to the theoretical concepts, either adding to or correcting the theory. Then, from the modified theory, researchers develop additional hypotheses, which, after testing, are used to further modify the theory. (Note: A study cannot test a theory; it can only test a hypothesis derived from a theory. Be careful when using the word *theory*.)

A final, related source of hypotheses is a model. A **model** is a generalized, hypothetical description that, by analogy, explains the process underlying particular behaviors. Consider a model airplane: It provides a solid way to discuss and understand how the components of an airplane really operate. Contrast this with the theory of aerodynamics that explains the general principles of flight. Likewise, in psychology, a theory accounts for broad, abstract components of behaviors, whereas a model provides a more concrete analogy for thinking about how these concepts actually operate. This provides a way to discuss and understand the components of a behavior. A psychological model usually involves a flow chart or diagram relating different psychological processes. For example, Figure 1.2 illustrates the Information Processing Model of human memory. Although no one believes the brain contains little boxes labeled short-term and long-term memory, they are useful for deriving specific hypotheses about how and when

Figure 1.2   The information processing model of memory

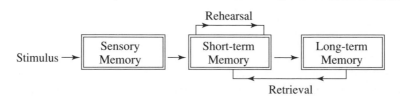

information remains in temporary or more permanent memory. We then conduct research to test these hypotheses and use the results to modify the model, in the same way that theories are modified.

Testing Hypotheses through Research

Once we've created a hypothesis, we design a specific study to test it. In doing so, we distinguish between a hypothesis and a prediction. Whereas a hypothesis is a general statement about how a behavior operates, a **prediction** is a specific statement about how we will see the behavior manifested in the research situation, describing the specific results that we expect in our study. We test the accuracy of a hypothesis using the logic that, if the hypothesis is true, we should obtain certain data: The behavior should occur in such a way that the corresponding scores will be high or low, or will change in a predictable manner. For example, let's say we hypothesize that channel changing occurs because of a theoretical cognitive mechanism in humans that is affected by the boring content in commercials. We predict that as more boring commercials occur, participant's scores will reflect more frequent, more rapid, or more motivated channel changing.

With a prediction in hand, we then actually conduct the study. Just how you do that, of course, is the topic of this book. Suffice it to say that there are many designs to use, depending on whether the primary goal of the study is to describe, explain, predict, or control a behavior. Regardless of the design, we attempt to obtain objective, systematic, and controlled measurements of the intended behaviors, so that we can clearly and confidently test the hypothesis.

It is after collecting the data that statistical procedures come into play. There are various types of statistics to use, depending on the specific design of a study. Regardless, statistics essentially make sense out of data so that it is possible to see if the scores form the predicted pattern. Thus, if we are testing whether more frequent channel changing occurs with more boring commercials, we'll use statistical procedures to determine if this pattern occurs in the data. (Notice, by the way, that the word *data* is a plural, like *people*.)

Finally, based on whether the data fit the prediction, we have evidence that either does or does not support the original hypothesis. Therefore, we will have learned something about how the behavior operates. Then we integrate these results with existing knowledge, models, or theories and start the process all over again.

The "model" in Figure 1.3 summarizes the flow that most research follows. The first step is to create a rational and parsimonious hypothesis that relates to the concepts in a theory or model so as to better describe, explain, predict, and control a behavior. The second step is to design a study that will test the hypothesis. Third, the predictions of the study must be derived: If the hypothesis is correct, then in a particular situation, participants should exhibit the behavior in a certain way. The next step is to conduct the study and measure the behavior, and,

Figure 1.3   The flow of scientific research

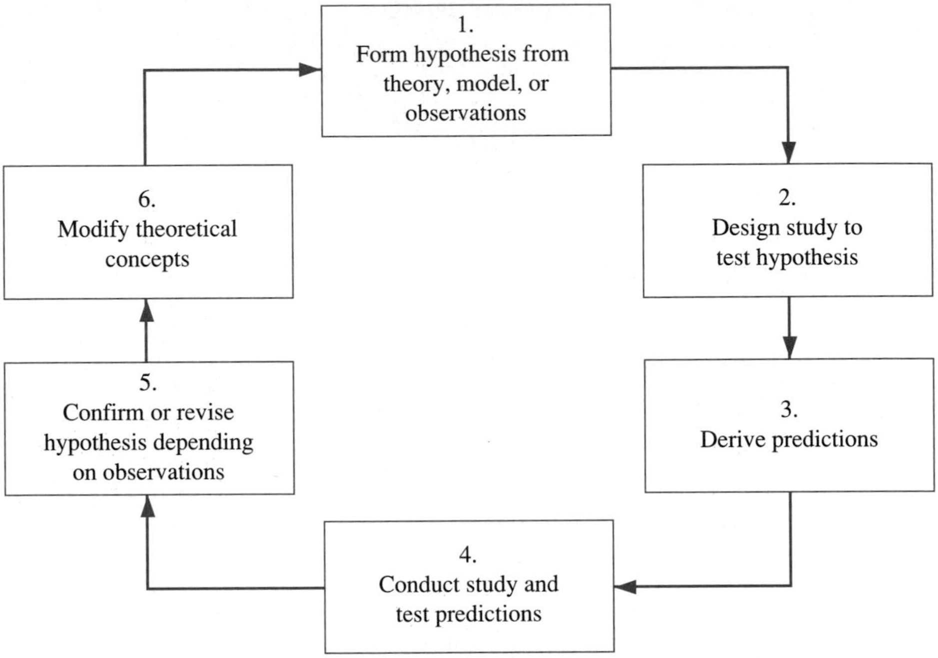

using statistical procedures, determine if the data confirm the prediction. If they do, there is support for the hypothesis. If they do not, there is not support for the hypothesis. Then, from the conclusions about the hypothesis, we work back to the theoretical concepts or model from step 1, either adding to or correcting the description. Future research then uses the modified theory or model, testing additional hypotheses that are used to further modify the description, and the cycle begins again. It is through this continual cycle that the science of psychology collates, organizes, and resolves the diverse "snapshots" of behaviors that individual studies provide, so that we can eventually understand the broader laws of nature.

Although research in general follows the preceding cycle, we use different types of designs depending on whether the primary goal of a study is to test a descriptive or causal hypothesis. As we shall see, there are many variations, but a design falls in one of two broad categories: experimental or descriptive methods.

Experimental Methods

Recall that with a causal hypothesis we propose the causes of and influences on a behavior. To test such a hypothesis, we employ **experimental methods,** in which the researcher actively manipulates a proposed influence and then measures the behavior. The logic behind experimental methods is this: If the hypothesis is correct, then if we *do* this or that to participants, we should see an influence or change in their behaviors. Thus, if we hypothesize that boring commercials *cause* more channel changing, we would systematically *manipulate* whether people view more or less boring commercials to see if we can cause greater channel changing with more boring commercials.

Usually an experiment implies a laboratory setting, but this need not be the case. Though the term *laboratory* might conjure up images of elaborate equipment and mad scientists, a laboratory is simply a location in which the researcher can conduct a study while controlling the situation, the environment, and the behavior of participants. As you'll see in later chapters, the hallmark of experimental methods is that researchers actively manipulate or change certain aspects of a situation. Then they examine whether their manipulations cause or influence the behavior being studied.

Descriptive Methods

Recall that with a descriptive hypothesis we identify the characteristics of a behavior or the situations in which it occurs, so that we can describe or predict the behavior. We test descriptive hypotheses using **descriptive** or **nonexperimental methods,** in which the researcher only measures—without manipulation—a behavior and its possible influences. The logic behind descriptive methods is this: If the hypothesis is accurate, then when we observe the behavior, we should also observe the predicted characteristics of the behavior, participants, or situation we have hypothesized. Researchers usually conduct descriptive studies in natural "field" settings, not in the laboratory. Thus, to test our hypothesis that channel changing occurs more frequently when a person is alone, we could observe (or obtain records of) people as they view television in their homes, measuring how frequently they changed channels when different numbers of people are present. We'll examine different descriptive procedures in later chapters, but in this approach, the researcher is always a rather passive observer who does not manipulate the situation or behavior under study.

> **REMEMBER** In *experimental* designs, the researcher actively manipulates the behavior or situation. In *descriptive* designs, the researcher only observes and measures the behavior or situation.

 ## The Flaws in Scientific Research

Recall that it's easy to make mistakes when studying nature because nature is complex and mysterious, and we don't already know how it works. Although the rules we've examined may seem sufficient to eliminate bias and error, they do not guarantee this. There are many opportunities for researchers to make errors. Therefore, as scientists, you must always remember that what you know—or *think* you know—depends on (1) the evidence presented and (2) how it is interpreted.

First, let's consider the evidence.

The Flaws in the Evidence

An ideal study would produce perfectly accurate measurement of the exact behavior we seek to describe, with only the relevant factors coming into play. However, *no study is ideal*. Rather, four factors can weaken confidence in the data.

First, some behaviors cannot be studied in a completely empirical, objective, systematic, and controlled manner. For example, it's impossible to directly observe "thinking." Instead, we must observe some other behavior—such as errors in logic that people make—from which to draw inferences about thinking. However, the greater the inferential leap from the observed to the unseen behavior, the less confidence we have in a conclusion. Also, there is no "yardstick" for objectively measuring some behaviors (such as aggressiveness or love). Instead, we must employ more subjective measurement procedures that may include bias and error. Finally, researchers cannot always observe a behavior in a systematic and controlled fashion. For example, in studying the attitudes of women toward childbearing, we cannot separate the fact that participants have female personalities from the fact that they have female genes. Therefore, it's impossible to be sure whether it's a woman's personality or her physiology (or both) that influences her attitudes. Because similar limitations are found in every study, we are never completely confident that we *know* what the measurements reflect about the behavior or which factors were truly operating.

Second, the decisions made when designing a study may also reduce confidence in the findings. For example, if we study channel changing as it occurs in someone's living room, we cannot control such distractions as whether the phone rings in the middle of a commercial and thus prevents channel changing. But if we study channel changing in a controlled "laboratory" setting, we create an artificial and thus biased picture of the behavior: People do not normally watch television in a laboratory! Likewise, the particular participants in a study, the way a behavior is measured, and the way factors are controlled may all result in biased evidence.

Third, often there are technical limitations that produce misleading information. For example, in the late 1800s, psychologists studied "phrenology," the idea that various personality traits are reflected by the size of bumps on the skull. Considering current techniques for studying personality and brain physiology, however, phrenology now seems silly. Always consider the inherent limitations arising from current technical abilities.

And finally, the results of one study can never tell the whole story. A single study is a "snapshot" that necessarily provides a biased perspective, considering certain factors and ignoring others (some of which we don't even know about). The problem is this: By taking one approach, a study automatically excludes others, and thus may misrepresent nature. This is illustrated by a fable about several blind men trying to describe an elephant (Shah, 1970). One, touching the animal's trunk, describes the elephant as like a snake. Another, touching the ear, says the elephant is like a fan. Another, touching the leg, describes the elephant as resembling a tree. And so on. In studying a behavior, researchers are like the blind men, trying to describe the entire elephant from one limited perspective at a time. For example, say our study supports the hypothesis that channel changing is caused by boring commercials. If we do not consider the television program during which the commercials appear, however, then a different study may indicate that channel changing is caused by boring programs. The problem is that either study alone does not give the complete picture if channel changing is actually caused by a combination of boring commercials and a boring program. Remember, being skeptical means not falling for the obvious explanation provided. Always consider whether your attention has been misdirected by the limited perspective of a study.

From the preceding, it should be clear that all research is not created equal! Individual studies can vary greatly in the extent to which they provide "good" data that accurately reflect the behavior and situation as they occur in nature. Therefore, the most important factor to consider when evaluating scientific evidence is the design of the study that produced it. As you will see in later chapters, the design and interpretation of a study are completely interrelated. So, whether you're evaluating a study performed by you or by someone else, always consider if there are flaws that suggest reasons for doubting the study's conclusions.

REMEMBER A study's design determines the "snapshot" of a behavior it produces and thus ultimately the evidence for a particular hypothesis.

Even when the evidence from a study contains a minimum of flaws, you still cannot have as much confidence in the conclusions as you might think. This is because of the intrinsic difficulty in "proving" that a hypothesis is true.

The Flaws in Testing Hypotheses

To see how difficult it is to be sure of the truth of any hypothesis, consider the deck of cards shown in Figure 1.4. The card on the top of the pile shows a "4." Say our hypothesis is "If there is an even number on one side of any card, there is a vowel on the other side."[1] The way to test this hypothesis is to turn over the card showing the "4" and see if we find a vowel. First, say we find the consonant "T." Then the hypothesis has been *disconfirmed,* so we are confident it is false. Note, however, that although we have disproved the hypothesis as stated, it may contain some element of truth. Maybe the rule does apply, but only if the even number is greater than 4.

---

[1]From the four-card problem in Wason (1968).

Figure 1.4   Testing a hypothesis

Shown here is a deck of cards used to test the hypothesis "If there is an even number on one side of any card, there is a vowel on the other side."

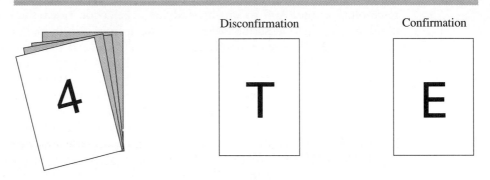

Disconfirmation   Confirmation

Instead, say we turn over the card and the vowel "E" is there. Our observation of a "4" and an "E" is consistent with, or is a *confirming* instance of, the hypothesis that even numbers are paired with vowels. But does this prove that the hypothesis is true? Absolutely not! We have not proved that our hypothesis is true because the true hypothesis may involve some other mix of vowels and numbers. The card we observe may *coincidentally* fit what is actually an incorrect hypothesis. In other words, there may be a competing or rival hypothesis that actually describes the cards. For example, our observation also fits the hypothesis "When there is any kind of number on one side, there is any kind of letter on the other side." Our observation supports both the original hypothesis and the rival hypothesis. Therefore, we do not *know* for sure which hypothesis is true, so we have not proved our hypothesis.

You might claim that if we examined more cards and they also confirm our hypothesis, we would prove it to be true. However, for as many cards as we examine, a vowel and an even number will confirm both of the above hypotheses, so we can never know which is true. Only if we can disconfirm and thus eliminate one hypothesis can we be confident that the other is true. Thus, you must fight the urge to seek only confirming evidence. *The best evidence comes from disconfirming rival hypotheses while simultaneously confirming your own hypothesis.*

Even then, confirming a hypothesis is not the same as proving it. Confirming a hypothesis is actually a failure to disconfirm it. We may fail to "disprove" it for one of two reasons: (1) It is the correct hypothesis, or (2) it is an incorrect hypothesis, but our observations coincidentally fit it. We can never "prove" that our original hypothesis is correct, because for as many cards as are drawn, we can always argue that one more card might be the one to disprove it.

Although this is a serious objection when we've examined only a few cards, it becomes less convincing as we observe more cards. After enough tries we can argue that if a disproving card was out there, we would have found it. If we continually fail to disconfirm the hypothesis, we come to believe that we have eliminated the coincidence argument and that the hypothesis is not disprovable—that it is correct. Thus, the best we can expect is that if we repeatedly find cards that confirm our hypothesis while disconfirming competing hypotheses, we become *confident* that our hypothesis is true. Eventually, with enough cards, we will come to accept the truth of the hypothesis, even though, technically, we can never "prove" it.

The same rationale applies to the channel-changing experiment. Say we find that people change channels more frequently with more boring commercials. We haven't proved that the boring content of commercials causes channel changing, because the results are merely consistent with what we would expect *if* our hypothesis were true. It may be, for example, that our boring commercials coincidentally contain less visual stimulation. Then the correct hypothesis may be that participants change channels to obtain more visual stimulation, and would do so *regardless* of how boring a commercial is. Given this possibility, we cannot be sure whether the amount of boredom or the amount of visual stimulation in a commercial actually causes channel changing. Only by performing additional experiments in which we confirm our original hypothesis and disconfirm the visual stimulation hypothesis (and any other competing hypotheses) can we confidently conclude that boring commercials cause channel changing.

Testing hypotheses in real research is even more difficult, because some data may confirm a hypothesis, while other data may disconfirm it. Therefore, we must critically evaluate the evidence and the design that produced it. For example, do you accept the hypothesis that dreams predict the future? If you do, it's probably because you've occasionally dreamt of events that later occurred. But consider the quality and quantity of this evidence. First, such a hypothesis is suspect because it's neither rational nor parsimonious. (How in the world could your dreams know what the future holds?) Second, your belief that you accurately recall dreams and that they match up with real events lacks objectivity and is thus also suspect. Third, you are relying on confirmation: Your observation is merely consistent with the hypothesis that dreams predict the future. But weigh this weak evidence against the amount of disconfirmation that is available. How many times have your dreams *failed* to come true? On balance, the preponderance of evidence heavily disconfirms the hypothesis that dreams predict the future. It makes much more sense to say that those few confirming instances are nothing more than coincidence: Some event occurred after you had coincidentally dreamt about it.

Likewise, our confidence in any scientific hypothesis is based on the quantity and quality of evidence that confirms *and* disconfirms it. Do we accept the hypothesis that "positive reinforcement" facilitates learning? Yes, there is a tremendous body of convincing evidence that confirms this hypothesis, while there is little disconfirming evidence. Do we accept the hypothesis that UFOs exist? Most scientists are not convinced because we have not seen enough confirming, scientifically acceptable evidence, and also because the observations may be explained by alternative hypotheses. (Reports in supermarket tabloids never concern themselves with these criteria.) Of course, some people may feel that there is sufficient evidence to believe in UFOs. As in all scientific debates, additional evidence must be gathered so that, eventually, we'll all be convinced one way or the other.

And remember, any statement must be precise so that it accurately reflects the current evidence. Above, I said that we are not convinced that UFOs exist; I did not say that UFOs *don't* exist. Being both open-minded and cautious means that when one hypothesis has not been confirmed sufficiently to accept with confidence, our conclusion must be that the jury is still out, not that the opposite of the hypothesis is true.

> **REMEMBER** If we *confirm* a hypothesis, we are merely more confident that it is true than we were before testing it, so the more times we confirm it, the greater our confidence in it.

Using Replication to Build Confidence in Psychological Findings

Researchers ultimately develop confidence in a hypothesis by repeatedly confirming the hypothesis while disconfirming competing hypotheses. This final component of the scientific method is called replication. **Replication** is the process of repeatedly conducting studies that test and confirm a hypothesis so that we develop confidence in its truth. The logic behind replication is that because nature is lawful, it is also consistent. Over many studies, therefore, the correct hypotheses will be consistently supported, while the erroneous, coincidental ones will not.

Researchers perform two types of replication. In a **literal replication**, the researcher tries to duplicate precisely the specific design and results of a previous study. This approach, also called *direct* or *exact* replication, is used because there are always chance factors at work—the particular participants, the unique environment of the study, and so on—that may mislead us. But chance factors that appear in one study are unlikely to appear consistently in others. Therefore, literal replication demonstrates that the original results are not likely to be due to chance factors. If different researchers can repeatedly obtain the same evidence in similar situations, we are more confident that the hypothesis is accurate.

On the other hand, in a **conceptual replication**, the researcher provides additional confirmation of a hypothesis, but does so while measuring the behavior in a different way, examining different types of participants, or using a different design. Conceptual or *indirect* replication provides for greater confidence in the general applicability of the hypothesis while testing and disconfirming competing hypotheses. Thus, for example, conceptual replications of our channel-changing study might involve observing children watching Saturday-morning cartoons and adults watching late-night shows, or include various commercials for toys, automobiles, and so on. Then, by combining the findings from these different studies, researchers can determine how the behavior generally operates and which factors influence it.

Note that there is a name for how conceptual replications build confidence in a particular explanation. **Converging operations** are two or more procedures that together eliminate competing hypotheses and bolster our conclusions about a particular behavior. By comparing studies that employ different procedures—different "operations"—we can eliminate some hypotheses and obtain different perspectives that "converge" to provide an accurate picture of a behavior. Thus, we might define boring commercials in terms of their content in one study and in terms of their visual stimulation in another. Then these different lines of research converge on what the term *boring* means in this situation, and whether it is the content, the visual stimulation, or both that causes channel changing.

Thus, scientists use replication to build confidence in their "facts" in the same way that lawyers build a legal case. Literal replication is analogous to repeatedly questioning the same witnesses to make sure they keep their stories straight. Conceptual replication is akin to finding a number of witnesses who, from different vantage points, all report the same event. With enough consistent evidence from both sources, we eventually come to believe that we have discovered a law of nature.

The need for replication often frustrates society because it thinks science should quickly provide a solution to every problem. For example, a newspaper story may report the discovery of a new drug for treating cancer, but sadly, the researcher notes that it could be many years before the drug is available to the public. This reflects the recognition that consistent, convincing evidence of the effectiveness of the drug can be obtained only through time-consuming replication. After all, we accept the "law" of gravity because it always works, in every situation, from every perspective. The same logic must be used when making any other scientific claim as well.

 ## Putting It All Together

As should be painfully obvious by now, a study never provides unquestionable "proof." First, we can never be completely confident that the data reflect the precise behavior we wish to measure, in the precise situation we wish to observe. Further, even with good, convincing data that confirm a hypothesis, the hypothesis may still be incorrect. For that matter, even when a hypothesis is disconfirmed, it may still contain some elements of truth.

Given these problems, you may be wondering why we even bother to conduct research. Well, the issues we've discussed are reasons for being skeptical about any single research finding, not for being negative about the research process. Instead of being paralyzed by such limitations, you should view dealing with them as a challenge. Simply recognize that testing a hypothesis involves translating a general statement about a behavior into a concrete measurable situation, and then translating the measurements back into conclusions about the general behavior. There is always room for error in the translation.

Do not automatically accept or dismiss any single study. On the one hand, researchers try to design the best study they can, providing the clearest evidence for answering the question at hand. Thus, even with flaws, a study usually tells us something about a behavior. On the other hand, what seems to describe a behavior correctly from one perspective may be incorrect when viewed from a different perspective. Look for that different perspective. And always keep in mind that a single study will not tell us everything about a behavior. A complete understanding can be gained only by replication, as we repeatedly obtain numerous and varied "snapshots" of the behavior.

CHAPTER SUMMARY

1. The *scientific method* includes certain assumptions, attitudes, goals, and procedures for creating and answering questions about nature.

2. The assumptions of psychology are that behaviors are *lawful, determined,* and *understandable.*

3. Scientists are *uncertain, open-minded, skeptical, cautious,* and *ethical.*

4. The *design* of a study is the specific manner in which the study is conducted. It should provide for *empirical, objective, systematic,* and *controlled* observations of a behavior. "Control" refers to the control of factors that might influence the behavior or our observations of it.

5. The goals of psychological research are to *describe, explain, predict,* and *control* behavior.

6. A *pseudo-explanation* is circular, explaining the causes of an event by merely renaming the event. Pseudo-explanations are avoided by obtaining independent verification of a supposed cause.

7. The primary purpose of *basic research* is to obtain knowledge. The primary purpose of *applied research* is to solve an existing problem.

8. A *hypothesis* is a formally stated expectation about how a behavior operates. A *causal hypothesis* postulates a particular causal influence on a behavior. A *descriptive hypothesis* postulates particular characteristics or aspects of the behavior.

9. Scientific hypotheses must be *testable, falsifiable, precise, rational,* and *parsimonious.*

10. A *theory* is a logically organized set of statements that defines, explains, organizes, and interrelates knowledge about many behaviors.

11. A *model* is a hypothetical description that, by analogy, explains the process underlying a set of common behaviors.

12. A *prediction* is a statement about the data that are expected in a specific study if the hypothesis is correct.

13. With *experimental methods* the researcher actively manipulates a proposed influence and then measures the behavior. With *descriptive methods* the researcher only measures a behavior and its possible influences.

14. When the results of a study *confirm* a hypothesis, this does not prove that the hypothesis is true, because the results may only coincidentally fit it. *Disconfirming* a hypothesis provides the greatest confidence in a conclusion about the hypothesis.

15. *Replication* is the process of repeatedly conducting studies to build confidence in a hypothesis. *Literal replication* is the precise duplication of a previous study. *Conceptual replication* repeats the test of a hypothesis but uses a different design.

16. Converging operations are two or more procedures that together eliminate rival hypotheses about a behavior.

KEY TERMS

applied research *(13)*
basic research *(13)*
causal hypothesis *(15)*
conceptual replication *(26)*
control *(9)*
converging operations *(27)*
descriptive hypothesis *(15)*
descriptive methods *(21)*
descriptive study *(10)*

design *(8)*
determinism *(5)*
empirical *(8)*
experimental methods *(20)*
falsifiable *(15)*
individual differences *(5)*
lawfulness *(5)*
literal replication *(26)*
objectivity *(9)*
parsimonious *(16)*
participants *(8)*
precise *(16)*

prediction *(19)*
pseudo-explanation *(10)*
rational *(16)*
replication *(26)*
research ethics *(7)*
scientific method *(3)*
subjects *(8)*
systematic *(9)*
testable *(15)*
theory *(17)*

REVIEW QUESTIONS

1. What three assumptions do scientists make about nature?

2. (a) What attitudes characterize scientists? (b) Why are they necessary?

3. (a) What are the four goals of research? (b) What are the four criteria for scientific evidence, and what does each term mean?

4. (a) What is the difference between a theory and a model? (b) How do theories and models simplify nature for us?

5. What are the five criteria for a scientific hypothesis, and what does each term mean?

6. What is the difference between a causal hypothesis and a descriptive hypothesis?

7. What is the difference between a hypothesis and a prediction?

8. Why must we critically evaluate the design of any study?

9. Why does disconfirmation provide greater confidence than confirmation?

10. What is replication, and why does science rely on it?

11. What is the difference between literal replication and conceptual replication?

12. On a television talk show, a panelist says that listening to rock music causes the listener to become a devil worshiper, a homicidal maniac, or a suicide victim. What questions would you ask the panelist before voting to ban this kind of music?

13. You've read some research in a developmental psychology text that contradicts what you've observed about your younger brother. Whose claim should you believe, yours or the researcher's? Why?

14. A theorist claims that men become homosexual when, as they are growing up, their mother either (1) tried to control them or (2) did not try to control them. Scientifically speaking, what is wrong with this hypothesis?

15. The government has announced a large monetary grant awarded to a scientist to study the sex life of a nearly extinct butterfly. A commentator claims that such research is a waste of money. Why do you agree or disagree?

16. A researcher explains that the reason people can remember smells is because they have a memory for smells. What is wrong with this explanation?

17. Researchers who accept the existence of extrasensory perception argue that the reason others have not found convincing evidence for it is that they do not believe such mental powers exist. What rule of science is violated by this argument?

18. An old tale states that if you dream you are falling off a cliff, you must wake up prior to dreaming that you hit the ground, or you will actually die. (a) Why couldn't you devise a test that confirms this hypothesis? (b) What is the way to test this hypothesis? (c) Even if you collect the appropriate dream information, what problems remain?

DISCUSSION QUESTIONS

1. (a) Is astrology a science? List the reasons why or why not. (b) Explain the problems involved in "proving" that statements from astrology are true.

2. Some students argue that they learn better while listening to the radio when studying. (a) What descriptive and causal hypotheses might you create about this behavior? (b) What predictions do these hypotheses lead to? (c) How

would you obtain empirical and objective observations of the behavior? (d) What factors might you manipulate or control to identify the causes of the behavior? (e) Why would the study need to be replicated?

3. Select a behavior and create both a descriptive hypothesis and a causal hypothesis about it. In general terms, how would you design a study to test each hypothesis?

4. Some people argue that the U.S. Food and Drug Administration should not require extensive replication studies before allowing the use of drugs for treating AIDS, so that the drugs can be made available sooner. Identify the two sides of the ethical dilemma here. (Hint: The drug may work, or it may not.)

2

An Overview of Designing and Interpreting Research

GETTING STARTED

To understand this chapter, recall the following:

■ We create either a descriptive or causal hypothesis about a behavior.

■ Then we conduct a study that measures the behavior of participants.

■ Depending on whether the data support our predictions, we have evidence that either confirms or disconfirms the hypothesis.

Your goals in this chapter are to learn:

■ How to translate hypothetical constructs into a variable and then an operational definition.

■ What a relationship is and how relationships fit into the logic of research.

■ What is meant by reliability and the different types of validity.

■ How extraneous variables threaten reliability and validity.

■ What a confounding is.

■ What the difference between descriptive and experimental designs is and what true experiments, quasi-experiments, and correlational designs are.

■ How experimental and descriptive designs differ in terms of reliability and validity.

As you now know, in research we translate a hypothesis about a behavior into objective measurements and then translate the measurements back into conclusions about the behavior. This chapter expands on this translation process, filling in some of the details so that you understand the overall flow of most research. We'll also discuss the major types of flaws in research, as well as how they affect the major research designs.

Beginning the Design: Asking the Question

It's pointless to design a study by simply grabbing some behavior out of the blue to examine: If you do, you end up with an answer in search of a question. Instead, research proceeds well only when you first determine the question you want to answer and then design a study to answer it. Therefore, the starting point of any study is to form a specific hypothesis about a specific behavior.

The behavior you choose to study is determined first by the topic you find interesting. Animal psychologists find animals interesting, for example, and child psychologists find children interesting. However, you should not start from scratch when then studying the behavior. An important preliminary step is to examine the *psychological literature,* the published research related to the behavior. The literature contains a large body of established evidence, terminology, hypotheses, and theories regarding virtually any behavior. Here you'll find numerous ideas for interesting studies, as well as useful research procedures that make designing your study *much* easier. (The specifics of how to "search" the literature are discussed in Appendix A.)

Your hypothesis may stem from questions raised by previous research, from theories or models, or from literal or conceptual replications of previous studies. It may also develop from your experiences or from your observations of a behavior. The key to developing a hypothesis based on your own experience, however, is in recognizing the general psychological principles that it reflects, so that the hypothesis rationally and parsimoniously fits previous research and theory. For example, let's say you observe that your friends are more successful at making dates with members of the opposite sex at the student union than you are. (Aren't they always?) You believe this is so because they are better looking than you. (Aren't they always!) There is not, however, much psychological research on making dates at your student union. But your observation is related to the broader issue of how people form first impressions. Many published studies from social psychology have shown that first impressions are influenced by physical attractiveness (e.g., Eagly, Ashmore, MaKijani & Longo, 1991). Although this finding holds for *both* genders, say that you decide to examine the descriptive hypothesis that females form more positive first impressions of males who are more physically attractive. (If this hypothesis offends you because it suggests people are shallow and insensitive, remember that scientists must be open-minded and accept nature as it is, warts and all.)

Now the goal is to design a study that will provide a clear test of the hypothesis. The first step is to take a moment and think about the behavior.

Considering the Context of the Behavior

When designing a study, it is *extremely* important that you first consider the overall context or situation in which the behavior occurs. Using your knowledge of psychology and some common sense, try to identify all of the factors that may influence the behavior and your study of it. This approach not only provides numerous ideas for the specific study, but it also allows you to foresee potential problems. As you do this, consider that there are four general components to any study: The *researcher* observes the *participants* in a specific *environment* and applies a *measurement procedure* to a specific behavior. When designing a study, it is these components that you must consider. So, what's involved when a woman forms a first impression and judges a man as attractive?

First, what might a woman consider when determining a man's physical attractiveness? She probably considers his facial attractiveness, the color and style of his hair, his height and weight, his posture, his body's shape, his style of dress, his cleanliness, and so on. She might also consider his behavior when they meet: Whether he is silent or talkative, what he says and how he says it, whether he is friendly or condescending. Does he exhibit nervous tics or irritating mannerisms? Does he make eye contact? Does he smile? Does he make physical contact, and how? (Is his handshake firm or mushy?)

The personal characteristics of a woman can also influence her perceptions. Her height and weight determine whether she judges a male as tall or short, heavy or thin. Also, is she different from him in age, style of dress, educational level, culture, or language? Is she actively seeking to meet men, or is she happily married and thus disinterested? Further, how does she form a first impression? It may involve whether she judges him to be intelligent, creative, sexy, likable, interesting, decisive, or some combination of these qualities. How long after she meets him is she beyond first impressions and getting to know him?

You should also consider the environment for the meeting. Is she interviewing him for a job or is the meeting social? Is the meeting in a crowded room or an empty one? Does it occur at a shopping mall, a party, or a funeral? Is the place noisy or quiet, dark or well-lit? Remember, too, that you must somehow observe her behavior. Doing so may make her nervous and interfere with her normal reactions. Does the gender of the researcher make her more or less self-conscious? How will you measure her impressions? Will she answer questions honestly?

As this partial list shows, a female's first impression of a male and his attractiveness may be defined in numerous ways, influenced by a host of factors, and examined from many perspectives. We cannot study all aspects of this situation at once, so our observations must be systematic and controlled. In other words, we must "whittle down" the complexity of the situation so that we can clearly examine one aspect of it. The way to accomplish this is by more precisely defining the hypothesis. We must decide precisely what we mean to study, selecting one specific aspect of "attractiveness," of "first impressions," of a "male meeting a female," and of every other component of the situation. Then we will have a simplified and, we hope, understandable "snapshot" of attractiveness and first impressions.

As you'll see, all design decisions are ultimately made simultaneously because any one decision has an impact on other decisions. A useful starting point, however, is to identify the relevant population and sample.

Identifying the Population and the Sample

By speculating that females form more positive first impressions of more attractive males, we have essentially hypothesized a component of a law of nature. A law applies to members of a specific group, which is called the **population.** We must specifically define the target population of the study. Are we talking about young children, college students, senior citizens, or all of the above? Does the hypothesis apply to all cultures, socioeconomic classes, intelligence levels, and personality types? As usual, check the literature for help in defining the appropriate population. Typically we strive for the broadest population possible, so say that we decide to study the population of sighted adult women who are citizens of this country.

By defining the population, we also define the participants we will examine. We now know that we will study the first impressions of a specific type of adult female (and we are most concerned with reading the literature dealing with such people). Of course, we cannot study all females, so we will study a sample of females. A **sample** is a relatively small subset of a population that is selected to represent or stand in for the population. When thinking about your sample, you must also consider how you will obtain and select the actual participants. The basic technique for selecting a sample is random sampling.

Simple random sampling is the selection of participants in an unbiased manner, so that all members of the population have an equal chance of being selected. Ideally, we might place the names of everyone in the population in a large hat. After mixing thoroughly, we would randomly select the individuals that constitute the sample. Or we might use books containing tables of random numbers; by closing our eyes and selecting numbers, we would select participants having the same identification numbers. Or we might program a computer to randomly select in this way.

An alternative approach is **systematic random sampling.** Here we select every nth person from a list of the population. After randomly selecting a starting point in the list, we might then select every third or every tenth name in the list. This technique is faster than simple random sampling, but be careful that everyone has an equal chance of being selected: If females are listed by age, for example, then we run the risk of filling a sample with young women before selecting any older ones further down the list.

REMEMBER   Simple random sampling is selecting participants from the population in an unbiased fashion. Systematic random sampling is selecting every *n*th person from the population in an unbiased fashion.

The reason for using random and unbiased selection is that it allows all of the diverse characteristics of individuals in the population to occur in our sample. Consequently, we hope, it is representative. In a **representative sample,** the characteristics of the participants and thus their behaviors accurately reflect the characteristics and behaviors of those in the population. Likewise, because we measure a behavior, a representative sample provides scores that are a good example of the scores we would find if we could measure the behavior of the entire population. Ultimately, the conclusions based on a representative sample will accurately apply to the population, so we will meet the goal of understanding a law of behavior as it applies to everyone.

Random sampling implies that we have a list of the population and that everyone is available to us. In actual practice, however, researchers can seldom identify or contact *all* members of the population. Instead, they must randomly select from the segment of the population that is at hand. For this reason, there are some members of the population who have *no* chance of being selected. In reality, therefore, a truly random sample is an ideal that is seldom attained. The result is that a sample may not be completely representative because we may miss some individuals having important characteristics that are found in the population.

Thus we must find a way of obtaining our "random" sample of females and determine how this selection process influences their representativeness. In later chapters we'll return to the issue of representative samples, but for now, given your initial observations at the student union, let's say that we decide to sample from the women attending your college. In fact, let's go to the most common source for participants—the current introductory psychology course. Notice that such a decision will have an impact on the study: The participants will be most representative of the population of females who attend your college or a similar one and who are taking introductory psychology, because we are excluding those who don't. Nonetheless, we now know that we are interested in those aspects of attractiveness and first impressions that apply to college females.

Identifying the Hypothetical Constructs

To investigate the relationship between attractiveness and first impressions, we must decide what we mean by these concepts. Like other concepts in psychology—learning, perception, thinking, motivation, or intelligence—*attractiveness* and *first impressions* are general terms that refer to a wide variety of reactions, judgments, and behaviors that people exhibit. They represent general ideas that we "construct" on the basis of many observations of related behaviors, so such terms are called hypothetical constructs. A **hypothetical construct** is an abstract concept used in a particular theoretical manner to relate different behaviors according to their underlying features or causes. It is used to describe, organize, summarize, and communicate our *interpretations* of behaviors. Thus, we interpret the differences among individuals' mental capabilities using the construct of "intelligence." Or, we summarize the activities of mentally storing and retrieving information using the construct of "memory." We summarize a person's reactions when first meeting someone using the construct of a "first impression." And we describe a person's reactions to someone's appearance using the construct of "attractiveness."

> **REMEMBER**   A hypothetical construct is an abstract term used to summarize and describe behaviors that share certain attributes.

The way to ensure that a hypothesis is rational and parsimonious is to incorporate accepted hypothetical concepts. That's because when we talk about understanding a behavior, we are really talking about understanding the constructs that describe and govern the behavior.

We *study* constructs, however, by observing components of the physical world that we think reflect them. But because these terms are intentionally general, they may be examined from many perspectives. Therefore, in designing a study you must define each hypothetical construct in terms of a specific measurable event that reflects the construct.

Identifying Component Variables of a Construct

The way we learn about hypothetical constructs is by measuring variables. In psychological research, a **variable** is any measurable aspect of a behavior or influence on behavior that may change. By measuring a variable we obtain scores, and the scores then constitute the data. A variable might reflect a physical action or a physiological response, or it might be a characteristic of the participants, of the situation, or of a stimulus to which participants respond. By identifying specific variables that reflect a hypothetical construct, we define the construct using more concrete and measurable terms. This allows us to "whittle away" at the complexity of behavior, while simultaneously obtaining empirical evidence that anyone else can also collect.

When selecting the variables for a study, first consider the many variables that may reflect a construct. When we considered the overall context of first impressions, we saw that a male's physical attractiveness might be reflected by such variables as the attractiveness of his face, his body, or his manner of dress. Each of these can be further reduced into component variables: Facial attractiveness, for instance, includes such variables as the size and shape of the mouth, the nose, and the eyes. Likewise, the hypothetical construct of a first impression may involve such variables as how intelligent, likable, creative, or honest a female judges a male to be.

Once you've identified the component variables of your constructs, from them you select the specific variables that you'll examine. The variables you select should be a good example of the hypothetical constructs, they should allow for objective and precise measurement as much as possible, and, as you'll see, they must be compatible with other aspects of the design.

> **REMEMBER**   We examine an aspect of a hypothetical construct by selecting a specific variable that can be measured.

Let's say we decide that to reflect a male's physical attractiveness we will measure the variable of "facial attractiveness." To measure a component of a first impression, we'll measure how much a male is initially "liked" by a female, measuring the variable of "likability." We have now translated the general hypothesis that first impressions are related to physical attractiveness into the more specific hypothesis that a male's initial likability is related to his facial attractiveness. However, this is still too general.

Creating Operational Definitions

Even after selecting a variable, you are still confronted by a variety of ways in which to measure it, so you must choose the *one* way to measure the variable. An **operational definition** defines a concept by the operations used to measure it. Operational definitions are very important because they allow researchers to communicate without ambiguity exactly what they mean when discussing any aspect of a study. For example, although you and I may disagree about what the concept of "intelligence" means, in a study I might operationally define it as a person's score on the XYZ intelligence test. Now at least there is no debate about what I had my participants do, how I've measured their intelligence, and what you'd need to do to replicate my study. Contrast this with if I simply left it as "I determined each person's intelligence."

It is thus important to first think about how you might operationally define the variables in a study. We might define a male's facial attractiveness using some definition based upon symmetry, artistic quality, or the lack of scars or blemishes. Alternatively, we could ask a panel of judges to rate each male or simply ask female participants how attractive a male is. Likewise, we might define likability as asking each female whether she agrees that a man meets some definition of lik-ability. We might record the number of times she uses the word *like* when describing him. Or we could simply ask her how much she likes him.

Give considerable thought to the particular operational definitions you select. Operational definitions are a major source of potential flaws in a study and can produce all kinds of controversy among researchers. When studying intelligence, for example, I would be in big trouble if most researchers did not accept that the XYZ test reflects anything about intelligence. As with everything else, your first line of defense is to look for definitions that have been used in successful replications of previous research. (Note that Chapter 1 showed you that replications improve confidence in a finding through *converging operations*, the process of using different procedures that together eliminate competing hypotheses. These different "operations" result from using different "operational" definitions.)

Notice that the variable you select is essentially an operational definition of your hypothetical construct: We defined the construct of "first impressions" in terms of the variable we will use to measure it—namely, "likability." Now, say we operationally define the variable of likability as a participant's response to the question "How much do you like this person?" measured on a 6-point rating scale ranging from "Dislike" (1) to "Like" (6). Say we operationally define a male's facial attractiveness as a woman's response to the question "How attractive is this person's face?," which is also measured on a scale ranging from "unattractive" (1) to "attractive" (6). Thus, participants will answer

How much do you like this person?

1   2   3   4   5   6

Dislike   Like

How attractive is this person's face?

1   2   3   4   5   6

Unattractive   Attractive

By translating hypothetical constructs into specific operational definitions of variables in this way, we attempt to meet the scientific goal of obtaining empirical, objective, systematic, and controlled observations. Likewise, designing the remainder of the study essentially involves creating the necessary operational definitions of the variables that characterize the situation in which we are examining the behavior. Thus, we must define what we mean by "an initial meeting between a male and our female participants." Let's say we define our "participants" as 12 sighted female volunteers randomly selected from an introductory psychology class. We define the "meeting" as a social, one-on-one introduction, and "initial" as lasting 2 minutes. And we define "meeting males" as bringing each female to a student lounge and introducing her to each of 10 of our male friends (call them our male models). After each meeting, the female will rate the model on his likability and attractiveness, answering our questions using pencil and paper.

REMEMBER   Each variable in a study must be operationally defined in terms of the procedure that is used to measure it.

So that you remember the terminology, Table 2.1 summarizes the steps in defining a concept in psychological research.

Table 2.1   The Steps in Defining a Research Concept

Step	Definition
1. Hypothetical construct	General theoretical term that summarizes common behaviors or processes.
2. Variable	Measurable component of a construct.
3. Operational definition	Definition of variable in terms of the method used to measure it.

You may think that the above likability design is finished. It's *not,* because we haven't completely thought it through. However, we now have the most precise translation of our hypothesis: Females who produce higher attractiveness ratings for a male will also produce higher likability scores for him.

Testing a Hypothesis by Discovering a Relationship

Notice that by operationally defining the variables, we have translated our hypothesis into a *prediction* about the scores that will be observed in the study. If the hypothesis is correct, then when a female produces the same attractiveness rating for two models, she should also produce the same likability ratings for them. If a female's attractiveness rating for one model is higher than that for another model, her likability rating should also be higher. In other words, we have predicted a "relationship" between attractiveness and likability. A **relationship** occurs when a change in one variable is accompanied by a consistent change in another variable. Because we measure the variables, a mathematical relationship occurs when certain scores on one variable are paired with certain scores on another variable, so that as the scores on one variable increase or decrease, the scores on the other variable also change in a consistent manner.

For example, let's say that some of the data we obtain in the likability study are shown in Table 2.2. For each attractiveness rating given a model in the left-hand column, the corresponding likability rating he received is in the right-hand column. Sure enough, models receiving higher attractiveness scores also tend to receive higher likability scores. Further, when attractiveness scores do *not* change (for example, the two models rated as "2"), the corresponding likability scores also tend to not change (they both received 3). Thus, a relationship reflects an *association* between the variables: In the same way that your shadow's movements are associated with your movements, low attractiveness scores are associ-

Table 2.2 Some Data from the Likability Study Showing a Relationship

Attractiveness Score	Likability Score
1	1
2	3
2	3
3	4
5	5
6	5
6	6

ated with low likability scores and high attractiveness scores are associated with high likability scores. Similarly, another name for a relationship is a *correlation,* and so in the data above, attractiveness and likability are *correlated.*

The simplest relationships fit either the pattern "the more you X, the *more* you Y" or the pattern "the more you X, the *less* you Y." More complicated relationships are formed when some scores on variable X are associated with increasing Y scores, while other X scores are associated with decreasing Y scores. (And note that a score may refer to a quantity or a quality. For example, men tend to be taller than women. If you think of male and female as "scores" on the variable of gender, then this is a relationship, because as gender scores change—going from male to female—height scores tend to decrease.)

On the other hand, when no relationship is present, there is no discernible pattern of change in Y scores as X scores change. Instead, essentially the same batch of Y scores shows up with each X. For example, say that the likability study produced data similar to that in Table 2.3. Here no particular likability scores are associated with a particular attractiveness score, and likability scores do not consistently change as attractiveness increases.

Table 2.3 Some Data from the Likability Study Showing No Relationship

Attractiveness Score	Likability Score
1	2
2	1
2	2
3	1
5	2
6	1
6	2

We'll discuss relationships more in later chapters. For now, it is important to understand why, as the next section shows, a relationship in the data provides evidence that a law of nature is at work.

Interpreting a Relationship

Most scientific research is designed to demonstrate and examine a relationship. The reason for this is that if *Y* is influenced by or otherwise *related* to *X* by a law of nature, then *different* amounts or categories of *Y* will occur when *different* amounts or categories of *X* occur. Thus, we originally hypothesized that the constructs of attractiveness and first impressions are related in nature, such that as attractiveness improves, first impressions also improve. If this is true, then, as facial attractiveness scores increase, likability scores should also increase. Thus, after we have collected the data, we first examine the relationship between the scores in the sample. With real data, however, researchers are invariably confronted with a mind-boggling array of different numbers that may have a relationship hidden in it. Therefore, we employ statistical procedures to bring order to this chaos. Using them, we answer such questions as: Is the predicted relationship present? What *Y* score tends to be paired with each *X* score? and How consistent is the association between *X* and *Y*? If we observe the predicted relationship in the sample data, we *begin* to have evidence that supports the hypothesis that the variables of likability and facial attractiveness are related in nature.

Our interpretation does not stop there, however, because we are interested in more than just the relationship observed in the sample. Using the sample data, we seek to estimate, or *infer,* that the relationship between the variables would also be found for other individuals in the population, if we could measure them. Here, too, we use statistical procedures that essentially allow us to determine whether we should or should not conclude that we would find the predicted relationship in the population. (We'll discuss the application of statistics more in Chapters 6 and 7.) If we can argue that any sample of similar females would produce a similar relationship, we can argue that all females in the population would behave in this way. "All females in the population" constitute a part of nature. Thus, by concluding that this relationship holds for all females, we are describing a law of nature: The laws of nature operate such that greater likability is associated with greater facial attractiveness.

By claiming that our observations provide evidence for the general case, we are generalizing. To **generalize** means to apply the conclusions of a study to other individuals or situations. In interpreting research we generalize in two ways. First, as above, we generalize the relationship between the variables in the sample to a relationship between the variables in the population. Second, we then generalize the relationship between the variables to the relationship between the hypothetical constructs we originally set out to study. That is, we translate the scores back into the behaviors and events they reflect and then argue that a similar relationship would be found with other variables and operational definitions. Thus, we want to conclude that as scores on *any* variable reflecting a male's physical attractiveness increase, scores on *any* variable reflecting a female's positive first impression will also increase. If we can make this claim, then we have come full circle, confirming the original hypothesis that nature lawfully operates in such a way that when more of the quality we call physical attractiveness occurs, more of the reaction we call a positive first impression also occurs.

> **REMEMBER**   The focus of research is to examine and then generalize relationships.

The Flow of a Study

The previous sections described the steps involved in a typical study as you translate from the general to the specific and then back to the general again. You can visualize these translations as the double funnels shown in Figure 2.1.

Figure 2.1   The steps in a typical research study

The flow of a study is from a general hypothesis to the specifics of the study, and then back to the general hypothesis.

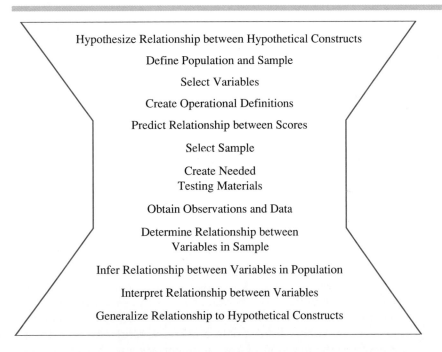

Hypothesize Relationship between Hypothetical Constructs

Define Population and Sample

Select Variables

Create Operational Definitions

Predict Relationship between Scores

Select Sample

Create Needed
Testing Materials

Obtain Observations and Data

Determine Relationship between
Variables in Sample

Infer Relationship between Variables in Population

Interpret Relationship between Variables

Generalize Relationship to Hypothetical Constructs

Begin with broad hypothetical constructs regarding a behavior. Then narrow the scope by identifying the applicable population and specify the hypothesis as a relationship between variables. Next, whittle down the situation to a very specific one by creating operational definitions for the variables and then predict the relationship between the scores that you seek. Then select a "random" sample from the population and design a method for obtaining participants' scores. If you find the relationship between the scores in the sample, begin widening the scope by inferring that the variables are related in the population. Finally, on the basis of this inference, generalize to the relationship in nature involving the broad hypothetical constructs that you began with.

Note that this flow from the general to the specific and back to the general is mirrored in the organization that psychologists use when publishing research reports in psychological journals. This organization was created by the American Psychological Association (APA), the national association of psychologists in the United States, and is known as "APA-style" or "APA-format." (This format is presented in detail in Appendix A.) A published report will basically follow the previous discussion, although the sequence may not be so obvious. The trick to reading the literature is to look for what the author is saying about each of the above steps.

Critically Evaluating a Study

So far, we've seen what is apparently a pretty straightforward process: We look for a relationship between the variables and, if found, use the relationship to draw conclusions about the underlying hypothesis. You may be wondering why, then, in Chapter 1, I made such a big deal about the potential flaws in research and the need for skeptical and critical evaluation of every research finding. Well, although *overall* a study *seems* straightforward, it is in the specifics of planning and conducting it that all sorts of misleading errors can creep in. Here's how.

Say that you conducted the likability study and obtained data similar to that in Table 2.4. I've arranged the data a different way, sorting the likability scores into two columns, based on whether a model was rated as less attractive (rated a 3 or below) or as more attractive (rated a 4 or above). Sure enough, higher likability scores were given to more attractive models. It appears we can conclude that, in general, a woman's first impressions of a man are related to his physical attractiveness.

But recall that the goal is to *know* how a behavior operates. The problem is, in any study, the only thing we know is that each participant produced a particular score—a number—at a particular time. We *don't* know what these numbers actually reflect: We don't know that participants are really—and only—reacting to the stimuli or variables we want them to, so we don't know what a score really means, and so we don't know what the relationship really shows. That's why you must always critically evaluate any study. Critically evaluating a study means answering the question "How confident are you that the scores actually reflect the hypothetical constructs, variables, and behaviors you think they reflect, and that the observed relationship actually reflects the relationship you think it reflects?"

Table 2.4 Example Data from the Likability Study

	Less Attractive Models	More Attractive Models
Likability Scores →	2	5
	1	6
	2	6
	1	5
	3	4
	3	4
	3	6

There are many aspects of the likability study that we took for granted. Consequently, there are numerous potential flaws that reduce our confidence that the scores indicate what we think they indicate, and that the relationship reflects what we think it reflects. Here are just some of the things that could go wrong.

1. "Facial attractiveness" cannot be accurately measured by our procedure.
2. Some models are wearing a more pleasant aftershave, have more muscular bodies, and dress better than others, and some talk warmly to the females while others talk only of car engines and beer blasts. Some models will be rated as more attractive, but *not* because of their faces.
3. Some participants barely speak English. Their answers to our questions are partially a test of their English.
4. Some meetings actually last only 30 seconds, while others last over 2 minutes, so we don't always measure the same kind of first impression.
5. Some participants already know the models. Their responses don't reflect an *initial* anything.
6. Some females cannot decide between a "4" and a "5" on the rating scales, and mentally flip a coin when responding. Others are extremely nearsighted (but don't wear glasses). They can barely see the model and instead guess at his attractiveness.
7. Sometimes the lounge is hot, sometimes it's noisy, and sometimes other people are wandering through it. Therefore some participants don't pay much attention to the model.
8. The researcher is a female who introduces the more attractive models in a more positive manner. Or the researcher is a male who's jealous of the attractive models and gives negative introductions for them. Either way, likability scores reflect the tone of the introduction.
9. The lounge is usually lit by sunlight, but when clouds pass by, some participants meet the models in a darkened room. Everyone looks more attractive in a dark room.

10. Two females are inadvertently given a pencil with a broken point and think that their reaction to this is what is being studied. They focus not on attractiveness or likability but on where the hidden camera might be.

Although such problems may strike you as unlikely, they can and do occur. For example, May and Hamilton (1980) found that something as mundane as the type of background music being played influenced how females rated a male's attractiveness. Therefore, because we are skeptical and open-minded, always consider whether such things might be occurring in any study. In general, there are two aspects of a study to examine.

First, always critically examine the operational definitions being used. There are many ways to define a construct or variable, and each definition will provide a very narrow perspective and type of evidence that may produce a misleading picture of the behavior. Rely on the research literature for accepted definitions that produce the most precise and objective data possible.

Second, recall that the more systematic and controlled a study is, the greater our confidence that we are not being misled by other things that are going on. The problems in the likability study occur because of the many unintended and misleading influences that might affect the participants. Therefore, always examine a study to identify potential unintended influences. These influences are called extraneous variables. An **extraneous variable** is any variable that can potentially influence our results, but is not a variable we wish to study. Such variables come from those four components of a study: the researcher, the participants, the environment, and the measurement task. Critically examining a study boils down to trying to identify the extraneous variables related to each component.

1. *Participant variables:* the personal characteristics and experiences of subjects that may influence their responses.
2. *Researcher variables:* the behaviors and characteristics of the researcher that may influence participants' reactions.
3. *Environmental variables:* the aspects of the environment that can influence scores.
4. *Measurement variables:* the aspects of the stimulus presentation and the measurement procedure that may influence scores.

Thus, extraneous variables are operating if a researcher's rudeness or the environment's temperature influences attractiveness scores, or if participants' near-sightedness or the difficulty of the measurement task alters likability scores.

Notice that extraneous variables are extremely important at all stages of a study. It was extraneous variables that we actually considered originally when we considered the context of the behavior and designed the study. If you missed any, these are then the variables that come back to haunt you, causing problems when interpreting the study.

Sometimes an extraneous variable changes *unsystematically*—that is, changing with no consistent pattern. For example, if the lounge is sometimes dark and sometimes light in a random pattern, then lounge lighting changes unsystematically. Unsystematic extraneous variables produce problems, because if an influence on a behavior is inconsistent from moment to moment, then the behavior will be inconsistent. Yet, the whole logic of research is to demonstrate a relationship: We look for a consistent behavior in one situation that then changes to a different, consistent behavior when the situation is different.

An extraneous variable may also change *systematically,* either increasing or decreasing in a way that forms a consistent pattern. For example, say that meeting and rating our 10 models is physically tiring. Then each participant's fatigue changes systematically over the course of the 10 meetings, going from not so tired on the first meeting to very tired by the tenth meeting. The problem is that systematic extraneous variables undermine our intention of simplifying the situation: Now we must also consider the role of fatigue in first impressions, because if we don't, it may confuse our interpretation of the situation and of the data.

Thus, whether designing a study or evaluating someone else's, critically evaluating a study involves considering its operational definitions and looking for potentially influential unsystematic and systematic extraneous variables. The question is always whether the data reflect what we think they do. However, we have special terminology, that allows us to communicate different aspects of this question. These aspects fall under two general concerns called reliability and validity.

Understanding Reliability

When asking what the data actually reflect, one concern is whether the measurements are reliable. **Reliability** is the degree to which a measurement is consistent and reproducible. We ask, "Regardless of what the scores actually measure, do they measure it consistently, without introducing error, so that measuring an event produces the same score whenever we measure it?" For example, we assume a woman's liking of a particular model will not change rapidly. If she indicates she likes him today, she should like him to the same degree tomorrow. If her two scores differ, then we've incorporated some measurement error: Either today's score, tomorrow's score, or both contain error. The problem is that obtaining different scores each time we measure the behavior will lead to different conclusions each time, so we don't know which conclusion is correct. Thus, unreliable data are "untrustworthy" in the sense that they reflect error and lead to inconsistent conclusions.

> **REMEMBER**   Reliability is the degree to which measurements are consistent and do not contain measurement error.

Reliability is often reduced by unsystematic extraneous variables, so any aspect of a study that is inconsistent threatens reliability. Thus, we have unreliable scores if, because of their eyesight or indecision, females guess when rating the attractiveness of the models. Or we have unreliable scores if the stopwatch is inaccurate, and so meetings sometimes last 30 seconds and sometimes 2 minutes. Instead, to obtain reliable data, we seek to keep all aspects of any research situation as consistent as possible.

Understanding Validity

The other concern is whether the data accurately reflect the constructs, variables, and relationships we think they do. Any time researchers question whether they are drawing the correct inferences from results, they are concerned with validity. **Validity** is the extent to which a procedure measures what it is intended to measure. When a procedure lacks validity, it is "untrustworthy" because it reflects the "wrong" aspects of a situation to some degree, so we cannot trust our inferences about the situation.

Researchers break the issue of validity into several subparts, depending on the particular inference being drawn.

Drawing Valid Inferences about Measurements

First, we are concerned with whether a score actually reflects what we think it does, in terms of the variable and in terms of the hypothetical construct we wish to measure. For each type of inference, we have a corresponding type of validity.

Content validity is the degree to which measurements actually reflect the *variable* of interest. In particular, we question whether a procedure actually and only measures all dimensions of the behavior we seek. (Are we tapping the appropriate and complete "contents" of the target behavior?) Thus, when females are supposedly rating attractiveness, we ask, "Are their scores actually and only measuring all intended aspects of the attractiveness of the model?"

A procedure lacks content validity, first, if it lacks reliability. For example, if participants are guessing somewhat when rating a model's attractiveness, then a score partly reflects his attractiveness and partly reflects the random error of guessing. Second, content validity is decreased if any systematic or unsystematic extraneous variable is also measured by a score. For example, we lose content validity in measuring attractiveness when participants barely speak English, because their scores partially reflect the variable of language ability. Likewise, content validity is decreased if a woman's rating partially reflects fatigue or her response to a model's behavior or style of dress. By reflecting these other variables, such scores can mislead us about the variable of facial attractiveness. In essence, we don't know what we're talking about when it comes to facial attractiveness, because we have not measured facial attractiveness alone.

On the other hand, **construct validity** is the extent to which a measurement reflects the *hypothetical construct* of interest. Here we question whether the variable we are measuring actually reflects the construct as it is conceptualized from a particular theoretical viewpoint. If a procedure lacks construct validity, then any inferences drawn about the broad, underlying psychological processes will be in error.

A classic question of construct validity occurs with intelligence tests, which measure people on such variables as vocabulary or problem-solving ability. While content validity is the question of whether we really measure these variables, construct validity is the question of whether these variables really measure "intelligence." Perhaps other variables more accurately reflect this construct. Likewise, some females might argue that they are not so shallow as to judge a male's attractiveness based on his facial appearance. They are essentially theorizing about what should constitute the construct of attractiveness and its relationship to first impressions. For them, our study lacks construct validity because it examines the "wrong" variable—facial attractiveness—and thus will lead to an incorrect interpretation of behavior.

> *REMEMBER*   Content validity refers to whether we actually and only measure an intended variable. Construct validity refers to whether a variable actually and only reflects the intended hypothetical construct.

In addition to considering the content and construct validity of any single variable, we are also concerned with the validity of conclusions about the relationship between the variables. Because we can consider the relationship either in terms of the sample data or when generalizing beyond the study, we have two types of validity—internal and external.

Drawing Internally Valid Inferences about the Relationship

Internal validity is the degree to which the mathematical relationship we observe between participants' scores actually and only reflects the *relationship* between the variables of interest. Thus, we have internal validity if the X and Y scores reflect only the relationship between the X and Y variables we think they do, so that we draw the correct inferences about what was going on *in* ("internal" to) the study. We lose internal validity, however, if the apparent relationship between the X and Y scores actually reflects other, unintended variables. Thus, internal validity is our confidence that the results actually and only reflect the relationship between the variables that we think are present. When a relationship lacks internal validity, it is "untrustworthy" in that it does not only reflect the relationship between variables that we think it does. If we are inaccurate about what occurred internal to our study, then we cannot confidently draw inferences about the relationship in nature.

Don't confuse internal validity with content or construct validity. If, for example, our questions actually measure how participants view a model's likability and attractiveness as we intended, then we have content and construct validity. But, say that the researcher inadvertently gave some models a more positive introduction, making them seem *both* more attractive and more likable. Then we have lost internal validity, because the "real" relationship we're studying is between the variable of how positive the introduction is and the combination variable of how attractive/likable a model is.

> **REMEMBER**   Internal validity is the degree to which we correctly infer what the relationship between the scores reflects about the relationship between the intended variables.

Internal validity is most important when discussing experiments and the causes of a behavior. The primary threat to internal validity is from confounding variables.

Confounding Variables   A **confounding** variable is an extraneous variable that systematically changes along with a variable of interest. Then we cannot tell which variable is actually operating in the study (we are confused or "confounded" by the extraneous variable). Say that coincidentally our more attractive models were better dressed. Then style of dress would be a confounding variable. This confounding is shown in Table 2.5. Again, the models are in two groups, rated either less attractive or more attractive. However, the less attractive models can also be described as poorly dressed, while the more attractive models can be described as well-dressed. We have the predicted relationship here, because what we are *calling* the more attractive models receive higher likability scores. The trouble is, we don't know if we've labeled the groups with the correct variable. Maybe facial attractiveness was irrelevant in this situation. Maybe we should be calling the groups "poorly dressed" and "well-dressed" because that was the relevant variable. Thus, we would say that "a confounding is present," or that "attractiveness and manner of dress are confounded."

Table 2.5   A Confounded Relationship

Intended Variable ⟶	*Less Attractive Models*	*More Attractive Models*
Confounding Variable ⟶	*Poorly Dressed*	*Well-Dressed*
Likability Scores ⟶	2	5
	1	6
	2	6
	1	5
	3	4
	3	4
	3	6

REMEMBER If an extraneous variable changes simultaneously with a variable of interest, then the variables are confounded.

Internal validity is most important when discussing experiments because their purpose is to test hypotheses about the causes or influences of a behavior. If confoundings are present, however, then our inferences about the cause of the behavior are not correct—not valid. Instead, the observed relationship actually reflects other laws of nature. The above data also confirm the rival hypothesis that "better dress produces greater likability.") Because the observed relationship confirms both hypotheses, we have little support for our original hypothesis.

As in this example, identifying a confounding *after* the study is conducted just makes interpreting the study impossible: Therefore, the goal is to identify and eliminate *potential* confounding variables when designing the study. Confounding variables arise from any source. There's a confounding if a male researcher introduces the unattractive models and a female researcher introduces the attractive ones. Or, we have confoundings if, along with changes in the models' attractiveness, there are systematic changes in the temperature or noise level of the lounge, or in how interested participants are in meeting men. Or, say in a different study we looked at the influence of different types of background music on the models' likability, comparing a song that has lyrics with another that does not. Confoundings would be present if one song is louder than the other, or if one is more familiar than the other. In each case, we will not be able to determine which variable is the one that produced differences in a model's likability.

REMEMBER Always be on the lookout for confounding variables.

Drawing Externally Valid Inferences about the Relationship

Recall that once we conclude what was going on *in* a study, we then *generalize* the conclusion beyond the study. But, are we correct in this conclusion? **External validity** is the degree to which the results accurately generalize to other individuals and other situations. Thus, external validity is the question of whether the study provides a good example of the relationship that occurs in situations "external" to our study.

External validity is threatened by any extraneous variable that makes observations unique and atypical, so that they are unrepresentative of the relationship generally found in nature. For example, our female participants are all from the same college, so the sample represents the type of women who attend that college. And by testing only college women, we have less confidence that the relationship generalizes to the population of all women, including those who don't go to college. Likewise, the way we operationally defined the variables and the specifics of the procedure may result in scores or a relationship that would not be found in other settings. If a similar relationship cannot be found with other participants in other settings, then we have a biased and misleading perspective: We will incorrectly describe the relationship between likability and facial attractiveness—as well as incorrectly describing the relationship between the constructs of first impressions and physical attractiveness.

> **REMEMBER**   External validity is the degree to which we can draw the correct inferences when generalizing beyond a study.

Several subparts to external validity arise depending on the researcher's perspective when generalizing. Two important subparts are ecological validity and temporal validity.

Ecological Validity   The term **ecological validity** refers to the extent to which research can be generalized to *common* behaviors and natural situations. If a design does not have ecological validity, we end up focusing on what participants *can* do in a study instead of what they *usually* do in everyday life. This issue is most important in highly controlled laboratory experiments. For example, for years researchers studied "paired-associate learning," in which participants learned pairs of nonsense syllables (for example, learning that BIM and YOB go together). But learning nonsense syllables is not an everyday, real-life behavior, and so such research lacks ecological validity: We cannot be confident that it accurately generalizes to and describes natural learning processes.

Researchers often lose ecological validity in their quest for internal validity, developing a rather unusual measurement task in order to control and simplify the behavior. (Paired-associate learning allows for much more controlled observations than, say, classroom learning.) However, where possible, a balance between internal and ecological validity is best. The challenge is to maintain control while having participants perform tasks that bear some resemblance to those found in the real world.

> **REMEMBER**   Ecological validity is the extent to which the situation and behaviors in a study are those found in the natural environment.

Temporal Validity   Another aspect of external validity is **temporal validity,** the extent to which results can be generalized to other time periods. Temporal validity has two applications. First, any study incorporates certain time frames, such as our measuring likability after a 2-minute meeting. Temporal validity is the extent to which the observed relationship generalizes to other time frames (such as to a 1- or 5-minute meeting). Second, any study is conducted in a particular month and particular year. Temporal validity is also the extent to which results generalize to other months, years, or eras. Recognize that research published a number of years ago often *does* have temporal validity for today, so don't automatically dismiss an "old" study as outdated. Basic behaviors such as memory or emotion are not greatly influenced by societal changes over time so findings

CHECKLIST 2.1   Questions to consider when drawing inferences from a study

Research Term	Inferences Made
❐ Reliability	Do the scores reflect error?
❐ Content Validity	Do the scores reflect the variable?
❐ Construct Validity	Do the scores reflect the hypothetical construct?
❐ Internal Validity	Does the relationship reflect the variables in the study?
❐ External Validity	Does the relationship generalize beyond the study?
❐ Ecological Validity	Do the results generalize to natural behaviors and situations?
❐ Temporal Validity	Do the results generalize to other time frames?

regarding them tend to generalize well. However, social processes, attitudes, and other behaviors that are influenced by societal changes may generalize less well.

REMEMBER   Temporal validity is the extent to which generalizations are accurate across other time periods.

The preceding issues of reliability and validity are *the* issues in designing and interpreting research, so they are summarized for you in Checklist 2.1. (You need to know these terms.)

Minimizing Threats to Validity and Reliability

All research suffers to some extent from problems of reliability and validity. The best you can do is minimize the *major* threats to reliability and validity, so that you are as confident in a conclusion as possible. The problem with the likability study was that we did not take the necessary steps to minimize these threats. After a study is completed, however, there is no way to solve such problems. The design and interpretation of a study are totally interwoven, so the appropriate time to worry about the interpretation is when you are designing the study.

Notice that although we focus on identifying threats to reliability and validity, such issues are ultimately empirical questions. That is, we rely on replication to determine whether we've made a mistake when interpreting a study. In particular, literal or direct replications—studies that duplicate a previous study—increase confidence that a particular approach is internally valid. Conceptual replications—studies that employ somewhat different procedures—increase confidence that the overall approach is externally valid.

As a consequence, researchers first rely on the psychological literature to find operational definitions of constructs and variables that are reliable and have the various types of validity. Instead, you can devise your own procedures, but then you run the risk that they will have weak validity and reliability. In such cases, you must demonstrate that a procedure is reliable and valid. (Some techniques for demonstrating this are discussed in Chapter 8). Whenever possible, however, it's best to adopt procedures that are commonly accepted in the literature.

In addition, you'll make decisions about how to test a hypothesis so that in some ways your study is unique, with its own threats to validity and reliability. The first step in dealing with such threats is to identify potentially important extraneous variables. Use your knowledge of research and psychology to examine the general context of the behavior, as we did in the likability study. Throughout, look for variables that might reduce your confidence that the scores and relationship actually reflect what you think they reflect.

Once you identify serious threats, often you will want to control them.

Controlling Extraneous Variables

It is by controlling extraneous variables that we meet the scientific goal of obtaining controlled observations. Later chapters will examine control techniques in detail, but for now the basic approach is to use a more precise operational definition of each component of a study. More precise definitions automatically limit extraneous variables. Typically, researchers control extraneous variables by eliminating them, keeping them constant, or balancing their effects.

Many problems can be solved by eliminating extraneous variables. For example, in the likability study, we could improve the reliability and content validity of the scores by eliminating distracting noises by moving to a lounge where they do not occur. We could refuse to admit intruders who might distract participants. We could ensure the models are all unknown to participants by obtaining them from a different school, and we could avoid the use of broken pencils.

If we cannot eliminate an extraneous variable, we may keep it at a constant level for all participants. For example, to improve the reliability and validity of scores, and to eliminate potential confoundings, we should keep the temperature and illumination in the lounge at constant, normal levels, and we should keep the researcher's behavior constant, precisely defining how all participants are treated. Also, we could redefine our participants, selecting females who all speak

English well and have corrected vision. Likewise, we could select models with the same body type and manner of dress, and provide them with a "script" of what to say and how to behave.

Sometimes an extraneous variable cannot be eliminated (for example, we cannot eliminate the variable of a researcher's gender). Likewise, keeping the variable constant may not be feasible, because if it is present in one particular way it may create a rather unique situation, reducing external validity for generalizing our findings (employing only a male researcher or only a female researcher might influence participants in a particular way, and this would reduce generalizability). In such cases, we may intentionally change the variable to "balance" its biasing influence. For example, we could balance the researcher's gender as shown in Table 2.6. Each *X* represents a likability score. We would have a male researcher introduce half of the less attractive and half of the more attractive models, while a female researcher would introduce the remaining models. In one sense, this design is consistent, because across all participants and all models, the potential positive or negative influence of the male researcher should balance out any potential effects of the female researcher. Then we show a more general relationship between attractiveness and likability that occurs despite the sex of the researcher present.

Likewise, if we thought the time of day participants were tested might have a biasing influence, we'd balance those tested early in the day with others tested later. Or, if we thought a particular decor in the lounge could influence first impressions, we'd balance testing some participants in each of several different lounges. Such active balancing not only adds to external validity, but it also eliminates potential confoundings so that we increase internal validity. (We'll see more about balancing variables in later chapters.)

REMEMBER To control extraneous variables, we eliminate them, keep them constant, or balance their influence.

Table 2.6   Likability Study in Which Researcher's Gender Is Balanced

	Less Attractive Models	*More Attractive Models*
Likability Scores with Male Experimenter	X X X X	X X X X
Likability Scores with Female Experimenter	X X X X	X X X X

Deciding on the Controls to Use

Ideally, of course, we seek the best possible study from all perspectives, so we always correct any flaws that we can. It is a fact of life, however, that the things that influence reliability and validity are interrelated. There are always trade-offs, so that improving one aspect of a study may have a negative impact on another aspect. (For example, the most reliable procedure may not be construct valid.) In particular, as we'll see repeatedly, those procedures that increase internal validity often decrease external validity, and vice versa.

Therefore, there is no set of rules to follow when deciding whether to control an extraneous variable. How to deal with any issue of reliability and validity depends on your particular research hypothesis and how you examine the behavior. You may simply accept a threat to reliability or a certain type of validity because the threat is not all that important to your study. In doing so, however, recognize the limitations produced by the threat and refrain from drawing inferences that are invalid because of them.

> **REMEMBER** Whether you should deal with a threat to reliability or validity depends on whether it seriously threatens the purpose of your study.

How to deal with threats to reliability and validity is determined primarily by the type of hypothesis you are testing and thus by the type of design you use.

Descriptive Research Methods

In the likability study, we hypothesized the reactions a female has when first meeting a male without proposing a cause for these reactions. Recall that we test such descriptive hypotheses using descriptive or nonexperimental methods. In a **descriptive design** we do not manipulate *the variables of interest*. Rather, descriptive research observes behaviors and relationships so that we can describe them. Thus, we did not try to alter the facial attractiveness of our male models or attempt to make them more or less likable.

As in our study, we often measure the variables using a questionnaire, but we might also directly measure physical actions, interview participants, or examine their records. We may perform an in-depth study of the behavior or history of one individual or conduct a survey of many people. Or we may surreptitiously watch people or animals in their natural habitats.

The likability study employed the most common descriptive method, called a correlational design. In a **correlational design** we measure participants' scores on at least two variables and then determine whether the scores form a relationship. We may test a hypothesis that specific variables are related, or we may set out to discover variables that are related. In doing so, we might look for a relationship between participants' scores on two tests or questionnaires (e.g., determining whether higher IQ scores occur with higher creativity test scores). We might "correlate" test scores with some measure of physical or mental performance (e.g., relating personality types to problem-solving ability). Or we might relate a participant's record to his or her performance (e.g., relating school-attendance records to measures of subsequent job success). If we find such relationships, then, as usual, we generalize from the specific variables we observe to a more general description in terms of hypothetical constructs and broad behaviors.

Correlational designs are especially useful for meeting the goal of *predicting* behaviors. Once we've established a relationship, we can use a participant's score on one variable to predict the corresponding score (and underlying behavior) on the other variable. For example, from the likability study we'll know a male's typical likability rating when he has a certain facial attractiveness score. Using this relationship, we can predict how likable other females will find a particular male, if we know how attractive they find him.

Not all descriptive designs, however, are correlational designs. Sometimes the hypothesis is that certain behaviors, situations, or participants will have certain characteristics, and we simply set out to describe them. Thus, in studying first impressions, we might surreptitiously observe people when they meet, simply to describe this behavior. Or we might distribute a survey containing questions reflecting many variables that we think constitute a first impression, so that we can describe it, develop theoretical constructs, or derive hypotheses for later study.

REMEMBER   Descriptive designs are used to demonstrate a relationship, predict behaviors, and describe a behavior or participant.

Issues of Validity and Reliability in Descriptive Studies

What characterizes descriptive designs is that the researcher does not tinker with the situation and manipulate the variables of interest. Descriptive studies are often conducted outside of the laboratory in natural, "field" settings, where few extraneous variables are controlled, and so a wide range of natural behaviors is likely. Descriptive studies therefore tend to produce high external validity: They tend to be repeatable with other participants and settings. For example, our original likability study has much in common with the way that people meet in the real world. Consequently, our results should generalize to other such meetings in the real world.

It is because of their greater external validity that descriptive methods are best for testing hypotheses about describing and predicting behaviors. Here the goal is to describe behaviors as they normally occur and to predict behaviors based on their occurrence in natural settings. Thus, we use the methods that produce observations and relationships that are typical of such behaviors in the real world.

Different designs result in trade-offs, however. The cost of high external validity in a descriptive study is reduced control. Uncontrolled fluctuating variables in a student lounge, for example, can reduce the reliability, content validity, and construct validity of the measurements. *Most important, descriptive research tends to have weak internal validity because of likely confoundings.* In the likability study, the models rated as more attractive might also, coincidentally, be better dressed, be better mannered, or be given a better introduction. Because such confounding variables are so likely, we have little confidence that the relationship between scores that we observe *actually and only* reflects the relationship between attractiveness and likability.

REMEMBER   Descriptive designs tend to have high external validity but reduced internal validity.

It is because of their weak internal validity that descriptive approaches cannot be used to make valid inferences about the causes of a behavior.

Problems in Inferring the Causes of a Behavior

When most people hear of a relationship between X and Y, they automatically conclude that it is a causal relationship, thinking that changes in X *cause* changes in Y. This conclusion is a mistake, however, because one variable can be related to another variable without causing it to change. For example, a person's weight is related to his or her height, but weight does not cause height. The key to inferring a causal relationship lies not only in demonstrating a relationship but also in the *manner* in which it is demonstrated. Two components are needed.

First, it is necessary to produce the correct temporal sequence: To say that X causes Y, we have to show that X occurs *before* Y. In evaluating any finding that claims to show causality, be sure that the supposed cause did in fact occur first. Descriptive methods *cannot* be used to infer a causal relationship, because they do not establish positively which variable occurs first. In the likability study, we cannot say that greater attractiveness causes greater likability, because we are unsure of the order in which these reactions occur. Perhaps females first perceived a model as more attractive and this then caused greater likability. Or, perhaps females first decided that they liked the model, and greater likability then caused him to be rated as more attractive.

The second requirement for demonstrating a behavior's cause is to be sure that no extraneous variable could actually be the cause: in other words, that no confoundings are present. However, we tend not to control extraneous variables in descriptive designs, and so there is a great potential for confoundings. We therefore have little confidence about the actual causes operating in descriptive studies. Even if, for example, we conducted a more controlled version of the likability study in the lounge, we would still be introducing males and females who might behave in all sorts of ways, and in an environment we cannot control. Thus it is very likely that confounding extraneous variables are changing along with likability and attractiveness. Although the data may *seem* to show that greater attractiveness causes greater likability, with so many other potential causes present, we have virtually no internal validity for making this claim.

Thus, with descriptive designs, we only describe the relationship between the variables, without inferring that one causes the other. Changes in X might cause changes in Y, but it's also possible that (1) changes in Y cause changes in X, or (2) some other, third variable causes both X and Y to change. (This latter idea is often called "the third variable problem.") Therefore, all we can say with confidence is that a relationship exists between the scores on the two variables.

REMEMBER In descriptive designs, we are unsure that changes in X cause changes in Y, because we cannot be sure that X changes first or that it is the only variable that could cause Y to change.

The way to demonstrate a relationship so that we have greater confidence about the causes of a behavior is to conduct an experiment.

Experimental Research Methods

We test a causal hypothesis using **experimental methods.** In an **experiment** the researcher changes one variable and measures the participant's resulting behavior by measuring another variable. Then we see if the manipulation changed the behavior so that the predicted relationship is observed.

Say we had originally proposed that greater attractiveness *causes* better first impressions. We would follow the same logical flow we did previously, selecting the population, considering the hypothetical constructs, and so on, except here we would attempt to demonstrate the relationship in a different way: Experiments typically imply a highly controlled situation in which we try to "make" the predicted relationship occur. Here we'd manipulate the attractiveness of the models a female meets, and then see if their likability scores change as predicted. In the lingo of experiments, we look for a relationship such that, as we change the independent variable, scores on the dependent variable change in a consistent fashion.

The Independent Variable

An **independent variable** is one that is systematically changed or manipulated by the experimenter. Implicitly, it is the variable that we think causes a change in behavior. In the preceding scenario we'd manipulate facial attractiveness because we think it influences likability, so attractiveness is our independent variable. You can remember the independent variable as the one that the experimenter manipulates *independent* of what the participant wishes: Some of our participants may meet an ugly model whether they want to or not. (An independent variable is also called a **factor.**)

We select an independent variable because it's a component of a construct or part of the physical environment that we think influences a behavior. Then we create an operational definition of the variable, stating how we'll measure and manipulate it. The goal is to create a reliable and valid procedure so that, for example, when we want certain females to see a model having a certain facial attractiveness, *all* of those females will be actually and only exposed to that level of attractiveness as intended. An independent variable may be quantitative, in which case we manipulate the *amount* of a variable that is present in a given situation. Or an independent variable may be qualitative, in which case we manipulate a *quality* or *attribute* of the situation. (If, in a different study, we compare meeting a model in a lounge vs. in a classroom, we are manipulating a quality of the meeting room.)

Although the variety of independent variables is unlimited, common approaches to manipulating them include changing a physical aspect of stimuli (e.g., changing the color or brightness of geometric shapes or the loudness or pitch of tones that people must recognize) or changing the meaning of stimuli (e.g., manipulating whether words to be remembered have similar meanings or have a positive or negative emotional connotation). Sometimes we manipulate the environment (e.g., changing the color of the walls in a room where participants study, altering the furniture arrangement in an office to alter efficiency, or varying the number of people present when someone gives a speech). Or we may change the attributes of the stimuli or task (e.g., providing different instructions, varying the rewards or punishments given, or altering the social setting in which participants are placed).

REMEMBER   The independent variable is a variable the researcher changes to produce a corresponding change in participants' behavior and thus demonstrate a relationship.

Conditions of the Independent Variable

An independent variable is the *overall* variable a researcher examines that may have many different amounts or categories we could examine. Therefore, we must select exactly which of these we'll include in the experiment. A **condition** is a specific amount or category of the independent variable that the researcher selects to create the specific situation under which the participants are observed. Thus, a model's attractiveness can be at any point on the continuum from very attractive to very unattractive, so we must select specific amounts of the variable for participants to experience. To show a relationship you must have at least two conditions, but you can have more than two if appropriate. To start, let's define a model's facial attractiveness as its rating by a panel of judges prior to the study. We'll select one model consistently rated as "low," one rated as "medium," and one rated as "high" (defining these terms as well). Eventually when participants meet the low-rated model they'll be in the "low-attractiveness condition"; when they see the medium-rated model they'll be in the "medium-attractiveness condition"; and when they meet the high-rated model they'll be in the "high-attractiveness condition." Likewise, if we compare meetings in a lounge or classroom, the independent variable is *any* type of room, and our conditions are "lounge" and "classroom." (A condition is also known as a **level** or a **treatment**.)

REMEMBER   The independent variable is the entire causal variable of interest. Conditions are the specific amounts or categories of the variable under which participants are tested.

A useful way to diagram an experiment is shown in Table 2.7. Each column represents a condition under which participants are tested. The scores in a column are those obtained by measuring participants on the dependent variable.

The Dependent Variable

The **dependent variable** reflects some aspect of participants or their response in each condition of the independent variable. You can identify the dependent variable in a study as the one measuring scores that are presumably caused by, or *depend* on, the condition of the independent variable. We've proposed that a model's likability depends on his facial attractiveness, so likability is our dependent variable. Thus, as in Table 2.7, we expect to see a relationship in which low likability ratings tend to occur in the low-attractiveness condition, medium ratings occur with medium attractiveness, and higher ratings are associated with high attractiveness. To see this as a relationship, think of the condition under which participants are tested as their "score" on the independent variable.

Table 2.7   Experiment to Study the Influence of a Model's Attractiveness on His Likability

	Conditions of the Independent Variable (Attractiveness of Model)		
	Condition 1: Low Attractiveness	Condition 2: Medium Attractiveness	Condition 3: High Attractiveness
Participants' Scores on Dependent Variable (Likability)	1	2	5
	1	3	5
	2	3	6
	1	2	6
	3	4	6
	1	4	5

For example, females in Condition 1 have a score equivalent to "low" on the variable of attractiveness. Then we look to see if, as "scores" on the independent variable change, corresponding scores on the dependent variable change in a consistent fashion. If we find the relationship, then, as usual, we generalize from the specific variables we observe to a broader description in terms of the hypothetical constructs we began with.

> **REMEMBER** In experiments, we look for a relationship such that as we change the *conditions* of the *independent variable,* participants' behavior as measured by scores on the *dependent variable* change in a consistent fashion.

As with everything, you must operationally define the dependent variable so that you measure it in a reliable and valid manner. Most of the time, the dependent variable *quantifies* a behavior, measuring the amount or degree of a behavior—how strongly it is exhibited, or its frequency of occurrence. At other times, the variable *qualifies* the behavior, distinguishing one behavior from another in terms of a quality or characteristic. For example, if we look at the causes of different personalities, personality type is the dependent variable, even though instead of measuring more or less personality, we would just identify different ones.

Essentially the dependent variable measures participants' *responses* to a particular situation. Just some of the dependent variables you'll find in the literature include those that measure physical actions, such as measures of coordination or ability; perceptual and sensory responses; or internal physiological reactions. They may also measure how well or how often a behavior is performed to reflect a participant's degree of learning, memory, or motivation. Other measures include asking participants to describe their feelings, beliefs, or attitudes that a situation elicits. Or we might examine participants' social judgments about or actions toward others.

True versus Quasi-Experiments

Although all experiments have the above components, it's important to understand that there are two major types of independent variables and, therefore, that there are two major types of experiments. On the one hand, a **true experiment** involves a **true independent variable**, in which the experimenter manipulates the variable by doing something *to* the participants. You can recognize a true independent variable because participants can be randomly assigned to any condition. **Random assignment** means that the condition of the independent variable a participant experiences is determined by random chance. Random assignment is a second step that occurs after we use random sampling to select the individuals for a study. For example, we might write the names of the three attractiveness conditions on slips of paper. Then, when a participant we've randomly selected arrives for the study, we would select a slip to randomly assign her to one of the conditions.

> ___
> **REMEMBER**   A true experiment, with a true independent variable, allows random assignment of participants to any condition.

While a true independent variable is something to which a researcher exposes participants, there are many behavior-influencing variables—for instance, age, race, background, or personality—that we cannot manipulate in this way. Such variables are called "quasi-independent variables," and studies that employ them are called **quasi-experiments.** A **quasi-independent variable** is *not* something that the experimenter does *to* participants, and so they cannot be randomly assigned to conditions. Instead, participants are assigned to a particular condition because they *already* qualify for that condition based upon some *inherent* characteristic. For example, say that in a different study we hypothesize that 18-year-old females will like a particular male more than 22-year-old females will. We cannot select a group of females and then *make* some of them 18 and make others 22. Or, say we want to determine whether males like a model more or less than females do. We can't randomly assign some *people* to be male and others to be female. Instead, we would create the conditions of 18- and 22-year-olds by randomly selecting one sample of females who are *already* 18 years old and another sample of 22-year-old females. Or, for the quasi-independent variable of gender, a random sample of males and a random sample of females would create the conditions. We also create conditions in this way when studying the influence of accidental events, such as that of experiencing a hurricane or being assigned to instructors with different teaching styles.

> ___
> **REMEMBER**   A quasi-experiment does not involve random assignment of participants to conditions.

Otherwise, quasi-experiments have the same purpose as true experiments. In conducting them we seek to demonstrate a relationship in which scores on the dependent variable change as the conditions of the quasi-independent variable change. Thus, we would look to see whether a model's likability changes as the age of participants changes. Or we would look for a change in his likability as gender changes.

Quasi-experiments are very common in psychological research and *are legitimate forms of research*. However, as you'll see in the next section, the lack of random assignment is a flaw in quasi-experiments that severely reduces their internal validity.

Issues of Validity and Reliability in Experiments

Ideally, in our likability study, if we could control all extraneous variables so that the only variable that systematically distinguished the models was their facial attractiveness, then we could confidently claim that attractiveness causes likability. Typically we associate laboratory experiments with such control, because here we solicit participants to come to our controlled environment and be tested under situations we determine. For example, here are some controls we could use. After having identified the models with low, medium, or high facial attractiveness, we could eliminate extraneous variables stemming from the model's behavior by only showing participants a *photograph* of each model. To eliminate influences from a model's clothes or physique, the photo would show only the model's face (as in May & Hamilton, 1980). To give all models the same personality characteristics, all participants would read the same paragraph describing the model. Finally, we'd conduct the study in a controlled laboratory, keep the environment constant, keep the researcher's behavior constant for each participant, and balance the researcher's gender so that half the participants in each condition are tested by a male and the other half are tested by a female. Then we would hope to see the relationship in which, as the conditions change so that a model's attractiveness increases, his likability score also increases. Now, however, by controlling many extraneous variables, we have substantial reliability and validity, so that we have a much clearer idea of what these scores and the relationship reflect.

In particular, the above controls eliminate potential confoundings, providing much greater internal validity. Internal validity in experiments is our confidence that it was our changing of the independent variable *alone* that produced the observed changes in the dependent variable. With the preceding controls we have greater internal validity for concluding that the relationship actually and only reflects the variables of facial attractiveness and likability: Because participants don't experience a model's behavior or dress, it makes no sense to argue that differences in likability were due to these variables. Because the environment and the researcher are much more consistent, it's also unlikely that these variables influenced participants' ratings. And so on.

There is a trade-off, however, between internal and external validity. The more controls we add, the more atypical and unnatural the situation becomes. For example, above we've created a rather strange situation, because women do not normally form first impressions of men from meetings with a photograph! By creating an unusual situation, we reduce external validity, because the results generalize poorly beyond the study and are not repeatable with other participants and settings. Thus, with experimental methods, we have greater internal validity for understanding a particular relationship, but at the cost of getting results that may be atypical of, and thus less generalizable to, other settings.

REMEMBER   Experiments tend to have greater internal validity but less external validity.

Although experiments generally provide greater control, not all experiments are created equal. In particular, there is a major difference between true and quasi-experiments. The random assignment of participants to conditions in true experiments is very important, because it is a way of "balancing" and thus controlling extraneous participant variables. Quasi-experiments, by not allowing for random assignment, are likely to be confounded by participant variables.

For example, say we conduct a quasi-experiment to determine whether a model's likability changes depending on a whether a female participant is 18 or 22 years old. For each condition we must select participants who are already the appropriate age. In the process, however, we may end up with two groups who also differ in terms of all sorts of other variables. For example, older women are likely to have had a greater amount of dating experience. Thus, we might produce the study diagrammed in Table 2.8. The quasi-independent variable of age is confounded by the extraneous participant variable of amount of dating experience. Further, the women in these two age groups may also differ in terms of their year in college, their maturity, their preferences in men, or—who knows—perhaps the amount of their exposure to makeup. It might be differences in any of these variables that actually cause the differences in likability ratings. We therefore cannot confidently identify which variable is actually the cause. In other words, the absence of random assignment severely reduces internal validity.

Note that the lack of random assignment also limits the internal validity of descriptive designs. Here we simply measure participants on the variables, so we cannot prevent extraneous participant variables from producing a confounding. For example, when we measured likability and attractiveness in the lounge, those women who found certain models less attractive might coincidentally have been younger, shorter, or less experienced. These variables might have then determined likability.

On the other hand, the previous likability experiment in the laboratory involved the true independent variable of the attractiveness of a model that a participant sees, because we could randomly assign participants to conditions. Then we could be confident that the above confoundings do not occur, because by luck, we should obtain various types of women in each condition, so that differences in participant variables should balance out. Thus, we'd expect each condi-

Table 2.8 Quasi-Experiment Showing a Confounding of the Independent Variable of Age with Amount of Dating Experience

Independent Variable	*18-Year-Olds*	*22-Year-Olds*
Confounding Variable	*Little Dating Experience*	*Much Dating Experience*
Likability Scores →	1	4
	2	5
	1	5
	3	6
	3	4

tion to contain some women who are experienced daters and some not, some older and some younger, some taller and some shorter, some freshmen and some seniors, some who have worn more makeup and some who have worn less, and so on. Overall, each condition should contain a balanced mix of the same types of women as the other conditions. Therefore, we have greater confidence that this true independent variable is not confounded by extraneous participant variables.

> **REMEMBER** Random assignment to conditions balances participant variables, so true independent variables provide greater internal validity than quasi-independent variables.

Thus, on the one hand, a true experiment provides the greatest confidence that we have demonstrated a causal relationship. First, by presenting the conditions of the independent variable and then measuring the dependent variable, we're confident of the temporal sequence between the supposed cause and its effect. Second, random assignment balances extraneous participant variables, reducing their potential as confoundings. And third, by controlling other extraneous variables, we hope to be able to say that the "only" variable that systematically changed was the independent variable, so that it must be the cause of changes in dependent scores.

On the other hand, being skeptical, we recognize that we've eliminated only *some* of the many extraneous variables that might be operating, and so it's always possible that we've missed an important one. (Perhaps, for example, the researcher's expectations of how the different models should be rated was communicated to participants.) Also, we cannot be positive that the measurements are otherwise valid or perfectly reliable. (Perhaps our judges did not rate a model's attractiveness as our participants will see him, so we may not actually manipulate a model's attractiveness in their eyes.) And so on.

Thus, although a well-controlled, true experiment provides substantial confidence that we have validly and reliably demonstrated a causal relationship, it will not be "proof." A quasi-experiment has the added problem of lacking random assignment, so there is the likelihood of confounding by participant variables. Consequently we have even less confidence in conclusions about causality with these designs. Thus, *at best,* the results of any single experiment allow us to *argue* to some degree that we have identified a causal relationship. Only as researchers conduct replication studies that control different extraneous variables do we become truly confident of the cause of a behavior.

Laboratory versus Field Experiments

Laboratory experiments have reduced external validity because a laboratory setting is not a slice of real life. The situation is artificial, participants know they are being tested, and a researcher is present who in some way "studies" their behavior. Also, the participants may be unrepresentative because we can study only those who will come to the laboratory.

To increase external validity, we may leave the laboratory and conduct a field experiment. A **field experiment** is a true or quasi-experiment conducted in a natural setting. Field experiments are common in social psychology, industrial psychology, and other areas when it is appropriate to study a behavior as it occurs in the real world. The setting may be a factory, a school, a shopping mall, a street corner, or any place the behavior occurs. One common approach is to disguise the fact that an experiment is being conducted and secretly study the public so that we can generalize to the typical person. The other approach is to study an existing group—such as a group of police, teachers, or medical personnel—because only they experience certain situations or exhibit certain behaviors.

A field experiment is still an experiment, so we try to randomly select and assign participants to conditions, systematically manipulate the conditions of the independent variable, control extraneous variables, and measure the dependent variable in a valid and reliable manner. Then, because the experiment is conducted in a more natural setting, we should have greater external validity when generalizing the results. On the other hand, in the field we tend to have less control of all extraneous variables. We therefore usually have the trade-off in which—you guessed it—we lose internal validity. Thus, the result is that we have increased confidence that a natural behavior operates in a particular way but less confidence that there is not some hidden extraneous variable at work.

> *REMEMBER* Field experiments tend to have greater external validity but less internal validity than laboratory experiments.

Selecting a Design

Researchers use the terms *descriptive* and *experimental* as a shorthand way of communicating the overall approach of a design. These terms distinguish the extent to which variables are controlled and, often, the degree to which observations are reliable and have certain types of validity. However, in creating a specific design, you have wide latitude in applying controls and mixing experimental and descriptive methods. In general, there are three major factors that determine the overall approach to select.

First and foremost, the method selected depends on the question being answered. Use correlational and other descriptive designs when testing descriptive hypotheses. True experiments are best for testing a causal hypothesis, because they provide the greatest control over potentially confounding variables. Sometimes you may not have a choice, however, because some behaviors simply cannot be studied using a particular method. For example, we cannot *make* people be Republican or Democrat, have a certain personality, be alcoholic, be the victim of sexual abuse, or have a criminal record. Although these variables may influence behavior, they cannot be true independent variables to which we expose participants. Thus, regardless of the nature of the hypothesis, we are sometimes forced to accept weaker evidence. We may have to study alcoholics using a quasi-experiment, in which the conditions are formed by people who already exhibit different degrees of alcoholism. We may be forced to merely describe the relationship between sexual abuse and other variables by asking questions of abuse victims using a correlational design. And we may have to examine records in order to study criminals. Based on such studies, we may propose the causes of behaviors, but without conducting true experiments, we recognize that the evidence only *suggests* possible causes.

Second, how you conduct a study using a particular method is determined by your concerns with reliability and validity. In particular, you must decide whether the primary concern is for internal or external validity. On the one hand, we can study a highly controlled situation that is easier to understand, but it may also be a rather atypical situation that does not generalize well. On the other hand, with fewer controls, we can study a situation that is more natural and realistic, so that the results generalize better, but we may also experience greater confusion about what specifically influenced the behavior *in* the study. Fortunately, the choice is not completely all-or-nothing. If we added controls to the original likability study in the lounge, we would have a more internally valid correlational design. If we went further and introduced models representing conditions of low, medium, and high attractiveness, we would have a less controlled but more externally valid field experiment.

For "basic" research in which we seek the underlying causes of behavior or test hypotheses derived from theories, we are usually concerned with internal validity and thus lean toward highly controlled laboratory experiments. These procedures help to develop our understanding of basic processes, even though they may create a unique or artificial situation that is less externally valid. Conversely, for "applied" research or when we seek to determine whether theoretical explanations are supported in the real world, we lean toward less controlled field experiments or toward descriptive designs that are less artificial and thus have greater external validity.

The third consideration is to be ethical and practical. We must not harm participants, either physically or emotionally, and we must respect their rights. (Another reason not to make people alcoholic.) In deference to such ethical requirements, we always accept reduced reliability and validity. We also must be practical and realistic, accepting that we cannot devise a perfectly reliable and valid study. For example, many studies have tested participants drawn from college Introductory Psychology courses, because they are easily accessible. Such selection is not random, however, because people are not randomly selected for college, and students are not randomly assigned to Introductory Psychology. This may reduce external validity, because such subjects primarily represent the population of Introductory Psychology students and may not represent any broader population. But unless there is a compelling reason to select a different type of participant, we are practical and use these students.

Putting It All Together

Designing a study is a problem-solving task. The problem is to produce the best and clearest evidence you can for testing a particular hypothesis. Solve the problem by designing the study in such a way that it shows the relationship between the variables, minimizes confusion produced by extraneous variables and untrustworthy measurements, and generalizes appropriately.

The key to designing a good, convincing study is to anticipate potential threats to reliability and validity and build in controls that eliminate them. Therefore, keep these pointers in mind. (1) State the hypothesis clearly, asking one question about one specific behavior. (2) Be a psychologist, using your knowledge of behavior to identify potential flaws in the design. (3) Rely on the research literature, using solutions that others have already developed. And (4) assume that "Murphy's Law" always applies: Anything that can go wrong will go wrong. Design your study accordingly.

At the same time, recognize that you cannot control every aspect of a situation. Therefore, deal with the *serious* threats to validity and reliability. You can never create the perfect study, so every decision must necessarily be "the lesser of two evils." Any study ultimately involves two major concerns. First, try to eliminate flaws that can be dealt with practically. Second, consider any remaining flaws when interpreting the results. Leave everything else for the next study.

CHAPTER SUMMARY

1. A *sample* is a relatively small subset of a *population* which consists of all members of a specific, defined group.

2. *Simple random sampling* is the unbiased selection of participants so that all members of the population have an equal chance of being selected. *Systematic random sampling* involves selecting every *n*th individual from a list of the members of the population. The goal of both techniques is to obtain a *representative sample* that accurately reflects the characteristics and behaviors of the population from which it is drawn.

3. A *hypothetical construct* is an abstract concept used in a particular theoretical manner to relate different behaviors according to their common underlying features or causes. A *variable* is any measurable aspect of a behavior or influence on behavior that may change.

4. An *operational definition* defines a construct or variable in terms of the operations used to measure it.

5. Most studies focus on demonstrating a *relationship,* a pattern in which, as the scores on one variable change, scores on another variable also change in a consistent fashion.

6. A relationship between the variables in a sample is used to infer a relationship between the variables in the population, which in turn is used to make inferences about hypothetical constructs.

7. *Extraneous variables* potentially influence a study's results, but they are not variables we wish to study. They may be participant variables, researcher variables, environmental variables, or measurement variables. We attempt to control extraneous variables by eliminating, keeping constant, or balancing their influence.

8. When determining what a measurement reflects, researchers consider (a) *reliability,* the degree to which a measurement is consistent, can be reproduced and avoids error; (b) *content validity,* the degree to which a measurement accurately and completely reflects the variable or behavior of interest; and (c) *construct validity,* the degree to which a measurement reflects the hypothetical construct of interest.

9. When determining what a relationship reflects, researchers consider (a) *internal validity,* the degree to which there are no unintended variables operating that produced the relationship; and (b) *external validity,* the degree to which the relationship generalizes to other individuals and situations.

10. *Ecological validity* is the extent to which the situation and behavior found in a study are those found in the natural environment. *Temporal validity* is the extent to which generalizations are accurate across other time periods.

11. If two (or more) potential causal variables simultaneously change, then the variables are *confounded.*

12. In *descriptive designs,* we do not manipulate or change the variables of interest. With a *correlational design,* we measure variables to determine whether a predicted relationship occurs.

13. Descriptive methods are best for testing descriptive hypotheses because they tend to have greater external validity. However, they also have less internal validity.

14. To demonstrate that changes in variable X cause variable Y to change, we must show that X occurs first and is the only changing variable.

15. In experimental designs, the researcher systematically changes the *independent variable* and, for each *condition,* measures participants' responses on the *dependent variable.*

16. Experimental methods are best for testing causal hypotheses because they tend to have greater internal validity. However, they also have less external validity.

17. In a *true experiment* with a *true independent variable,* participants are randomly assigned to conditions. This should balance out differences in participant variables across conditions.

18. In a *quasi-experiment* with a *quasi-independent* variable, participants cannot be randomly assigned to any condition but, instead, are assigned to a condition based on some inherent characteristic. Because of potential confounding by extraneous participant variables, quasi-experiments have much less internal validity than true experiments.

19. A *field experiment* is an experiment conducted in a natural setting. Field research tends to have greater external validity but reduced internal validity.

KEY TERMS

condition *(60)*
confounding *(50)*
construct validity
  (48)
content validity *(48)*
correlational design
  (56)
dependent variable
  (61)
ecological validity
  (52)
experiment *(59)*
external validity *(51)*
extraneous variable
  (46)

factor *(59)*
field experiment *(67)*
generalize *(42)*
hypothetical construct
  (36)
independent variable
  (59)
internal validity *(49)*
operational definition
  (38)
population *(35)*
quasi-experiment
  (63)
random assignment
  (62)

relationship *(40)*
reliability *(47)*
representative sample
  (36)
sample *(35)*
simple random
  sampling *(35)*
systematic random
  sampling *(35)*
temporal validity *(52)*
true experiment *(62)*
validity *(48)*
variable *(37)*

REVIEW QUESTIONS

1. (a) What's the difference between a sample and a population? (b) How are samples used in research? (c) What produces a representative sample?

2. (a) What is simple random sampling? (b) What is systematic random sampling?

3. (a) What does the term *hypothetical construct* mean? (b) How do hypothetical constructs simplify nature? (c) Why does incorporating hypothetical constructs help us to create scientifically acceptable hypotheses?

4. (a) How are constructs studied? (b) What's the difference between a variable and an operational definition? (c) Why are operational definitions important to researchers?

5. (a) How can you recognize when a relationship exists between two variables? (b) Why do researchers look for relationships between variables?

6. Explain what researchers mean when they express concern about (a) reliability, (b) content validity, (c) construct validity, (d) internal validity, and (e) external validity.

7. (a) What question about a study is raised by the term *ecological validity?* (b) What are the two ways the term *temporal validity* is applied?

8. After taking a test, you hear the following complaints. Each is actually about whether the test is reliable or valid. Identify the specific issue raised by each. (a) "The test is unfair because it does not reflect my knowledge of the material." (b) "The questions were tricky and required that I be good at solving riddles." (c) "My essay makes the same points as my friend's, but I got a lower grade." (d) "From this course, I know how well I'll do in other courses." (e) "I doubt that what caused students to perform poorly or well on the test was how much they studied."

9. (a) What is the difference between a correlational study and other descriptive methods? (b) What is the difference between an experiment and a correlational study?

10. (a) What is the difference between descriptive and experimental research methods? (b) What aspect of your study directs you to select one approach over the other?

11. (a) What are the advantages and disadvantages of descriptive research methods? (b) How do they influence a researcher's conclusions?

12. (a) What are the advantages and disadvantages of experimental research methods? (b) How do they influence a researcher's conclusions?

13. (a) What is the difference between the independent variable and the conditions of the independent variable? (b) What is a dependent variable?

14. What do we mean by the term *confounding variable?*

15. (a) What is the difference between a true independent variable and a quasi-independent variable? (b) What is the problem with using the latter to draw causal inferences?

16. You study participants' memory for a story, comparing the recall of some who read it silently with that of others who read it aloud. (a) Will you have greater external validity if you test only males, only females, or both genders? (b) Draw a diagram showing how you would balance participants' gender.

17. (a) What are field experiments? (b) What is their major strength? (c) What is their major potential weakness?

18. In each of the following, identify the independent variable, the conditions, and the dependent variable. (a) A researcher studies whether scores on a final exam are influenced when background music is played soft, is played loud, or is absent. (b) A researcher compares freshmen, sophomores, juniors, and seniors with respect to how much fun they have during the semester.

(c) A researcher investigates whether being first-born, second-born, or third-born is related to intelligence. (d) A researcher examines whether length of daily exposure to a sun lamp (15 minutes versus 60 minutes) accounts for differences in self-reported depression. (e) A researcher investigates whether being in a room with blue walls, green walls, red walls, or beige walls influences aggressive behavior in a group of adolescents.

19. In question 18, which are true experiments and which are quasi-experiments?

20. Drinking red wine daily may help prevent heart disease. To test this hypothesis, we select elderly people who have typically drunk zero, one, or two glasses of red wine daily during their lives and determine the health of their hearts. (a) What type of design is this? (b) What term do we use to refer to the amount of wine a person drinks? (c) What do we call the amounts we examine? (d) What do we call the healthiness of participants' hearts? (e) How confident can be we be in our conclusion that drinking more wine causes reduced heart disease? Why?

21. How would you conduct the preceding study using a correlational design?

22. Red wine contains an acid that causes headaches, so people who drink more red wine probably take more aspirin. Taking aspirin may prevent heart disease. (a) In questions 20 and 21, what term do we use to refer to the amount of aspirin that people take? (b) What problem of validity pertains to this situation, and how does it affect our conclusions?

23. In question 20, describe how you would control the variable of aspirin by (a) eliminating it, (b) keeping it constant, and (c) balancing it.

24. When conducting a study, a researcher wears a white "lab coat" and carries a clipboard and stopwatch. How might these details influence the internal and external validity of the study?

25. We hypothesize that a person's frequency of changing sexual partners is caused by the degree to which that person fears sexually transmitted diseases. How should we study this relationship, and what inherent research flaws must we accept?

DISCUSSION QUESTIONS

1. Consider the hypothesis that greater exposure to violence from television or movies results in more aggressive behavior. (a) For ethical reasons, what might be the best design for determining whether this relationship exists? (b) What is the trade-off involved in being ethical?

2. A nurse claims that when she wore one of those silly-looking hats, patients followed instructions better than they do now that she no longer wears it. (a) What hypothetical constructs might this situation reflect? (b) Outline an

experiment for studying this situation in a laboratory. (c) Outline a correlational design for studying it in the real world.

3. A researcher reads numerous traffic accident reports and finds that brighter-colored automobiles are involved in more traffic accidents, with red autos having the worst record. He concludes that certain colors cause more accidents. (a) What type of research method has been used in this study? (b) Are the researcher's inferences correct? Why? (c) What confounding variables might have been operating? (Hint: Who drives red cars?) (d) What steps must be taken to more convincingly support this hypothesis?

4. Create a descriptive hypothesis about a behavior and decide how you would test it. What problems do you foresee?

5. Create a causal hypothesis about a behavior and decide how you would test it. What problems do you foresee?

3

Creating a Reliable and Valid Experiment

GETTING STARTED

To understand this chapter, recall the following from Chapter 2:

- What a relationship is.
- What an independent variable is and that it is also called a factor.
- What the conditions of an independent variable are, and that they are also called levels or treatments.
- What a dependent variable is.
- What extraneous variables are and how they threaten reliability and validity.

Your goals in this chapter are to learn:

- How to select the conditions of a factor, how control groups are used, and why a strong manipulation is needed.
- How to design scoring criteria, create a sensitive dependent variable, and observe reliable behaviors.
- What order effects are and how to deal with them.
- How to maintain consistency in a study.

*T*his chapter presents the specific techniques used in designing a reliable and valid study. For now, we'll focus on *true experiments,* because they provide the greatest opportunity to control extraneous variables. Similar techniques, however, are used when conducting quasi-experiments and descriptive research.

As you know, we begin a design by creating an acceptable scientific hypothesis, identifying the relevant population, and considering the sample we'll select. In conjunction with this, there are essentially three steps to designing an experiment: operationally defining the independent variable, defining the dependent variable, and designing the remainder of the testing situation to control extraneous variables. In the following sections, we'll discuss each of these steps separately, although in real research, they must all be considered simultaneously.

Selecting the Independent Variable

Once you have developed a hypothesis about a behavior's cause, you then select and define the independent variable. There are, however, no hard and fast rules that determine the appropriate independent variable. The specifics of the treatments depend on the specific behavior, variables, and participants being studied. As you'll see repeatedly, design decisions are always made in response to the questions "What is it you wish to study?" and then "What aspects must you control?"

In the literature you'll typically find manipulations involving one of the following approaches.

Approaches to Manipulating an Independent Variable

Researchers often manipulate a factor by presenting participants with different stimuli or changing the characteristics of a stimulus. Thus, we might present stimuli that differ along some physical dimension and then measure participants' detection or recognition of the stimuli. Or we may measure participants' attitudes when children play with different types of toys or adults are exposed to words having different meanings or connotations. We can study the causes of aggression and such by showing participants films or television programs that depict different behaviors and then measuring participants' subsequent aggression or other reactions.

The independent variable may also be the context in which a stimulus is presented, while the stimulus itself is kept constant. For example, we might present various amounts of background noise, alter the temperature, change the arrangement of furniture, or vary the number of people present while measuring participants' performance of a task. We may examine how people develop attitudes by presenting a point of view using different types of arguments or speakers. We may study learning processes by presenting different rewards or punishments and measuring participants' rate of learning. Or we can examine participants' memory or thought processes using conditions of different moods that are created by exposure to different words or stories, or even through hypnosis.

A factor may instead consist of the instructions or information given to participants in each condition. We might tell different participants that they are involved in different social situations or levels of competition. We can study participants' recall for an event by varying the type and amount of information conveyed in questions about the event. We might tell participants different types of information about another person or event to see how they then react to the person. Or we may expose participants to situations that conflict with an attitude they advocate or have them fail at a task, to study how they resolve conflicts or attribute blame.

To manipulate a social setting, researchers often employ confederates. **Confederates** are people enlisted by a researcher to act as other participants or "accidental" passersby, creating a particular social situation to which the "real" participants then respond. For example, we may create various types of tasks, games, or competitions involving a participant and a confederate to study the participants' cooperativeness, aggressiveness, or competitiveness. Researchers have had confederates claim to have health problems, be lost, or need money, and then measured participants' helpfulness depending on the characteristics of the confederate or situation. Or we may increase peer pressure in a situation by varying the number of confederates present.

Some researchers manipulate internal, physiological processes. Here the conditions may involve giving participants different amounts of alcohol or other drugs, manipulating the amount of food, water, or sleep participants get or varying the levels of sensory stimulation they receive. Using animal subjects, researchers employ surgical techniques to create different conditions in which parts of the brain are removed or altered and then measure the type and degree of differences produced in such behaviors as motivation, emotion, or memory.

Often researchers manipulate a variable because they believe it changes an internal psychological state, which then influences a behavior. This internal state is called an intervening variable. An **intervening variable** is influenced by the independent variable, which in turn influences the dependent variable. It "intervenes" or comes between the independent and dependent variable. For example, let's say we hypothesize that being frustrated makes people angry, and that greater anger then leads to more aggressive behavior. Here we would manipulate the independent variable of frustration—for example, by blocking participants from obtaining a desired reward. This should change the intervening variable of anger, which should then influence participants' scores on the dependent variable of aggressiveness.

Recognize that psychologists distinguish between two general types of internal psychological states. A **state characteristic** is a temporary, changeable attribute that is influenced by situational factors. For example, you have a certain "state anxiety," the level of anxiety you experience depending on the situation you are in. (Suddenly realizing you have an exam will raise your state anxiety.)

Conversely, a **trait characteristic** is stable over time and not easily influenced by situational factors. (Think "personality traits" here.) For example, self-esteem is generally defined as a trait characteristic, because it is relatively unaffected by the situation you're in. Some attributes have both state and trait components: A person has a momentary state anxiety as well as a general trait anxiety. Other attributes, such as self-esteem, are considered to have only a trait component. State characteristics can be studied in experiments, because they will change in response to the conditions of an independent variable. Trait characteristics are not studied in this way, because, being rather permanent, they are not influenced by most manipulations.

> **REMEMBER** State characteristics are transient and can be experimentally manipulated. Trait characteristics are rather permanent and cannot be easily manipulated.

Selecting a Valid and Reliable Manipulation

When selecting an independent variable, remember that if you find a relationship, you'll then want to infer that it demonstrates an aspect of nature. In Chapter 2 we discussed several types of *validity,* the degree to which we can be confident in such inferences. Each of these is a concern when selecting the independent variable.

First, consider whether an independent variable has *construct validity:* Does it allow valid inferences about the underlying construct as we conceptualize it? For example, are we truly increasing the "social pressure" a person experiences by increasing the number of confederates in a room? Or, if we are manipulating participants' anxiety level in different conditions to then influence their performance of a task, are we erroneously trying to manipulate what is an immutable trait characteristic? If the variable lacks construct validity, then any inferences we draw about underlying psychological processes will be in error.

Likewise, we are concerned with *content validity:* Does the procedure allow accurate inferences about the variable of interest? If, for example, the objective is to expose people to films containing different amounts of violence, then we must measure and manipulate *this* aspect of the films. But if we inadvertently select different films based on their humorous content or their plots, then we are not actually and only studying the influence of a film's violent content.

Of paramount importance is to consider *internal validity:* An experiment is supposed to show that changing the independent variable causes changes in the dependent variable, so you must be sure that you can eliminate the influences of extraneous, confounding variables that might actually be a cause. Thus, we want to be sure that whether a participant helps a confederate does not depend on such extraneous variables as the confederate's looks, mannerisms, and so on. Or, if we show participants films depicting violence, we want to be sure their responses are to the film and not to the social situation created by the presence of the experimenter. Different factors and the situations they create implicitly allow you more or less control of potentially confounding variables. Be sure that the procedure you select allows you to maintain a level of internal validity sufficient for your purposes.

In addition, we also seek *external validity:* Can we confidently generalize the results to other individuals and situations? The independent variable should not create situations that are so atypical that they generalize to a limited type of participant or situation. Also, look for *ecological validity:* Do the conditions create natural, everyday situations that, along with the dependent variable, elicit natural behaviors? And consider *temporal validity,* which here is whether (1) the duration of each treatment and the time between a treatment and measuring the dependent variable generalizes to other time frames, and (2) the period during which the study is conducted generalizes to other seasons or years.

Don't forget that you also want a procedure that will be reliable. Here reliability translates into an independent variable that we can consistently manipulate: All participants in a condition should receive the same amount or category of the variable, and when we change to another level, all participants there should receive exactly the same new amount. If there is inconsistency in a manipulation, then we are not always presenting the condition we think we are, and our conclusions will be based on the wrong amounts of the independent variable. Also, if the situation is different for each participant, this may cause different responses among participants within the same condition, so that we do not consistently observe the predicted behavior in each condition.

And finally, a procedure must be *ethical:* As you'll see in the next chapter, researchers do not have the right to callously harm others in the name of science.

Questions of reliability and validity are ultimately resolved by theoretical discussion, replications, and research showing that a procedure is reliable or valid because it produces the same results as other accepted procedures. If, however, you are too inventive when defining your variables, you run the risk of threatening the reliability and validity of your study. Instead, it is best to adopt procedures that are commonly accepted in the literature.

Selecting the Conditions of the Independent Variable

Assuming you've selected a valid and reliable independent variable, the next step is to select the specific conditions to expose participants to. As an example, say that we wish to pursue the independent variable of room temperature, testing the hypothesis that people become more aggressive as room temperature increases. We'll place participants in a laboratory room under a particular temperature level, and the dependent variable will measure participants' aggressiveness toward the experimenter. Now there are two decisions about the conditions to simultaneously consider.

First, you must decide on the number of levels of the independent variable to include. You can examine virtually any number of conditions, but you need at least two to show a relationship: to show that aggressiveness increases with higher temperatures, we must show that aggression scores increase when changing from one temperature to at least one other temperature. Beyond that, the number of levels you should include depends on the specific hypothesis you're testing (and on a small statistical issue we'll discuss later.) At the same time, remember that the purpose of research is to learn about nature, and the more conditions you include, the more you learn. In fact, once you've gone to the trouble of creating a procedure, contacting participants, and so on, it's not much more work to test another condition or two.

The other decision is to select the specific amount or category of the independent variable that each condition will present. The particular levels you choose also depend first on the hypothesis. We're investigating the influence of "hot" temperatures, so we don't want conditions where it's cold. Of course, we don't want to kill anybody either, so we'll avoid extremely high temperatures. So we might compare the influence of some temperatures between, say, 70 and 90 degrees Fahrenheit.

When selecting the levels of an independent variable, there are two important issues to consider: control groups and strong manipulations.

Control Groups

Sometimes we create a condition under which we measure participants on the dependent variable after presenting zero amount of the independent variable. A **control group** is a group that receives zero amount of the independent variable or otherwise does not receive any treatment. Groups that receive a nonzero amount of the independent variable or otherwise *do* experience the treatment are called **experimental groups.** A control group shows how individuals behave without the treatment, providing a "baseline" or starting point for evaluating the influence of the variable in the experimental groups. For example, say that in a different experiment we have students study for various amounts of time and then measure their performance on a later exam. The control group would be students who spend zero time studying for the exam. Their exam scores then provide a starting point for determining, literally, whether other amounts of studying in the experimental groups are better than nothing.

A control group is not always essential to a design—whether to include one depends on the question being asked. Control groups are especially useful, however, for eliminating rival hypotheses about what causes dependent scores to change. For example, say that in a memory study, we present a loud background noise to people while they read a story, and find that they poorly remember the story. It appears that the noise interferes with memory, but only if we assume that participants would otherwise retain the story well. Perhaps the story is intrinsically difficult to recall. To eliminate this rival hypothesis, we compare the noise condition to a control condition, an otherwise identical condition but with no noise. If retention is poor in both conditions, we could conclude that this result is due to the story and that the presence of noise literally does not make a difference. But if retention is lower with noise, then we'd have support for the hypothesis that noise lowers retention.

Sometimes it's not possible to administer zero amount of an independent variable, and then the control group is tested under a "normal" or "neutral" condition. For example, for the variable of temperature, there must be *some* temperature present, so using a 70-degree condition would actually be the control condition of normal room temperature. Or, if we are presenting cheerful or sad statements to alter participants' mood, the control condition might involve emotionally neutral statements.

And sometimes the equivalent of a control condition involves comparing participants' performance to the result we would expect if they were guessing. For example, to study "psychic abilities," researchers "send" participants a telepathic message about a card drawn from a deck of playing cards. The number of cards someone correctly selects is then compared to the number we'd expect if the person was merely guessing. (As it turns out, "psychics" do not perform above a chance level [Hanssel, 1980].)

REMEMBER *Control conditions* provide a clearer indication of the influence of a manipulation and of the causes of participants' responses.

Creating a Powerful Design through a Strong Manipulation

As you know, we cannot claim to have demonstrated anything about a behavior unless we find a relationship in the sample data. However, a relationship is not an all-or-nothing thing, and so it's possible to find a very *unc*lear relationship in the sample data. For example, let's jump ahead and say that in the temperature study, we decide to measure participants' aggressiveness toward the experimenter in a way that higher scores indicate greater aggressiveness. Then say that, as we increase room temperature, participants' aggression scores barely increase in a consistent fashion, as in Table 3.1.

Table 3.1 Example of an Unconvincing Relationship between Room Temperature and Aggression Scores

	Conditions of Room Temperature		
	Low Temperature	*Medium Temperature*	*High Temperature*
Aggression Scores ⟶	5	6	6
	4	5	6
	3	5	6
	4	6	7
	$\overline{X} = 4.0$	$\overline{X} = 5.5$	$\overline{X} = 6.25$

The consistency or inconsistency in a relationship is called the *strength of a relationship*. How do we determine strength? Later we'll review statistical procedures for this, but essentially it is the extent to which the data meet the definition of a relationship (showing a pattern in which, as the conditions of the independent variable change, scores on the dependent variable change in a consistent fashion). In a very consistent or *strong relationship*, there would be one or close to one aggression score for everyone in the low-temperature condition, and then a new, different score for everyone in the medium-temperature condition, and then again another, different score for everyone in the high-temperature condition. Instead, Table 3.1 shows a relatively *weak relationship* because within each condition there is a group of different scores that overlaps with the scores in other conditions so that more or less the same batch of scores occurs in each condition; consequently there is only a slight trend toward increasing aggression with higher temperatures.

In a real study, for reliability we would test considerably more participants, producing many scores per condition. We would then use *descriptive statistics* to summarize the data and the relationship. The starting point in most experiments is to compute the average or *mean* of the scores in each condition (each column). As shown in Table 3.1, the symbol for a sample mean is $\overline{X}$, and the means here are 4, 5.5, and 6.25 for the three levels of temperature, respectively. These means also suggest a weak relationship, because quite literally, increasing temperature did not, *on average,* produce much of a difference in aggression.

With such data, we—and our statistical procedures—could easily conclude that there really is no relationship here, and that the changes in scores actually result from random fluctuations that signify nothing. We can do little if the predicted relationship does not exist in nature. However, what would really be a shame is to miss a substantial relationship that exists in nature because we obtain such a weak and unconvincing relationship in the sample data. That is, we may obtain a poor example of the relationship in nature. Through some flaw in the design, strange participants, fluctuating variables or just plain luck, we may obtain some weird scores that form little or no relationship, even though there is a very consistent, strong, and impressive relationship in nature.

On the other hand, say we obtained more convincing data like that in Table 3.2. Although there is still inconsistency among the scores within each condition (each column), it is now relatively small compared to the large differences in scores *between* the conditions. Thus, the scores within each condition do not overlap with the scores in other conditions, so that each increase in temperature produces a dramatic increase in aggression scores. Likewise, the means of the scores in each column suggest a stronger relationship, because quite literally, increasing temperature *did,* on average, produce a substantial difference in aggression. When a sample relationship looks like this, we—and our statistical procedures—are unlikely to miss it, or interpret it as a coincidence. (It may be unrealistic to expect to actually obtain data as dramatic as in the example, but they would be the goal.)

Remember that your data are always tied to your design. It is therefore important to design any study so that if a relationship exists between the vari-

Table 3.2 Example of a Convincing Relationship between Room Temperature and Aggression Scores

	Conditions of Room Temperature		
	Low Temperature	*Medium Temperature*	*High Temperature*
Aggression	5	26	46
Scores	4	21	45
	3	25	44
$\longrightarrow$	4	20	45
	$\overline{X} = 4$	$\overline{X} = 23$	$\overline{X} = 45$

ables in nature, the data are likely to clearly and convincingly show it. The term that applies to this strategy is to maximize the *power* of a design. Power is actually a statistical concept, so you'll see a precise definition in Chapter 6 when we review statistics. For now, remember that a **powerful design** is more likely to produce a clear, convincing, and strong sample relationship. If the data show a convincing relationship, then we are likely to draw the correct inference when generalizing to the relationship in nature. Designs that lack power, however, may show little or no relationship in the sample, so that we miss the relationship that exists in nature.

> **REMEMBER** A *powerful* design is likely to produce a clear and convincing sample relationship.

Thus your goal is to create a powerful design. As you'll see, you can do a number of things to maximize the power of a design. It starts with your independent variable. As you've just seen, large differences in scores *between* the conditions help to produce a convincing relationship. We assume that changing the conditions of the independent variable cause differences in the scores, so we select conditions that will produce large differences. A **strong manipulation** involves conditions that will produce large differences in scores between the conditions. It will "strongly" influence participants' behavior and produce large, obvious differences in their scores between the conditions. And, if there are large differences in the scores between conditions, then there will also be large differences between the means from the conditions. Thus, a strong manipulation produces a powerful design by producing large convincing differences between the means of the conditions. You can create strong manipulations in two ways.

First, select amounts or categories of the independent variable that are substantially different from one another. For example, using temperatures of 70, 80, and 90 degrees Fahrenheit seems to be a reasonably strong manipulation of room temperature: If higher temperatures do influence aggressiveness, adding 10 degrees in each treatment should show this. Conversely, comparing temperatures of 70, 71, and 72 degrees Fahrenheit would not be a strong manipulation: Even if temperature does influence aggression, we might not detect a change in behavior with such subtle temperature changes. Likewise, in a different study, say we are presenting happy or sad words to alter participants' mood. For a strong manipulation, the happy words should be *very* happy and the sad ones should be *very* sad.

The second aspect of a strong manipulation is to have participants experience a condition sufficiently for it to dramatically influence their behavior. For example, a strong manipulation would also have participants experience the temperature for a long enough period of time (say 20 minutes) so that we dramatically alter their aggressiveness. Being in the room for only a minute or two would hardly be expected to "strongly" influence anything. Or, if we're presenting happy or sad words to influence participants' mood, a strong manipulation would be to present *many* happy words or *many* sad ones. Or, say we are studying how different speaking styles influence the persuasiveness of a message. Rather than presenting a short message with only one example of the style, we'd present a longer message with many aspects conveying that style.

> **REMEMBER** For *power,* create a *strong manipulation* so that the conditions are likely to produce large differences in dependent scores.

One other way to ensure a strong manipulation is to prevent diffusion of treatment.

Diffusion of Treatment   A **diffusion of treatment** occurs when participants in one condition are aware of the treatment given in other conditions. People who have already participated in a condition may tell future participants about their experience, or while participating in the study, some may "figure out" what we're doing. Either way, participants are now aware of the various treatments, and so the influence of a particular condition may be reduced or eliminated. Thus, if participants are aware that we're manipulating room temperature, they may not react normally to any temperature condition they're in. And, not only will the strength of a treatment be reduced, but internal validity will be threatened as well: Instead of being influenced only by a condition, participants will be influenced by information they have about the overall nature of the study.

Our first line of defense against diffusion of treatment is to explain to people after they've participated why they should not tell other potential participants about the study. Recognize, however, that the more interesting, creative, or bizarre your treatments, the more people will want to talk about them. Therefore, another strategy is to try to complete the study in a brief period, to minimize the time during which people discuss it. Or we can test participants from different locations so that they have little contact with one another. And finally, as you'll see, we can also disguise a treatment.

Manipulation Checks

So far, we've been *planning* the conditions of an independent variable that *should* influence participants in predicted ways. We can, however, also check that the manipulation *does* have its intended effect. A **manipulation check** is a measurement, in addition to the dependent variable, that determines whether each condition of the independent variable had its intended effect. Usually this check is made after participants have been measured on the dependent variable (otherwise it might provide cues that create diffusion of treatment). Then we may ask participants to answer questions about their experience in a condition, have them complete a task that reflects its influence, or measure their physiological responses to it. So, if the goal was to test people in a hot room, we will check that they thought it really was hot. Or, if the intent was to make participants happy, we will check that they really were happy. Such procedures are especially important for checking on an intervening variable. Thus, if we thought that higher room temperature produced greater aggressiveness by way of the intervening variable of producing greater anger, we could also directly measure each participant's anger. Such checks increase our confidence that the independent variable worked as intended, which in turn increases internal validity for explaining why dependent scores changed as they did.

> **REMEMBER** When designing the independent variable, create a strong manipulation and consider including control groups and a manipulation check.

For help remembering the questions to ask when designing the independent variable, consult Checklist 3.1.

CHECKLIST 3.1 Questions to consider when designing an independent variable

- ☐ Will the variable provide content and construct validity?
- ☐ Will the operational definition prevent confounding?
- ☐ Will the conditions generalize well?
- ☐ Will the temporal aspects of the design generalize?
- ☐ Does the factor reflect common, real-life situations?
- ☐ Is a control group appropriate?
- ☐ Is the manipulation strong, without diffusion of treatment?
- ☐ Is a manipulation check needed?

Selecting the Dependent Variable

Along with designing the conditions of the independent variable, you must also develop an operational definition of the dependent variable. As with everything, which dependent variable you select and how you measure it depend on the hypothesis and behavior you're investigating, your participants, and the perspective you're taking. Most dependent variables, however, employ one of the following approaches.

Approaches to Measuring the Dependent Variable

Often the dependent variable involves direct observation and measurement of the behavior under study. For example, we measure eating behavior by measuring the quantity of food that participants eat, or in learning studies we count the frequency of the to-be-learned behavior. Or if studying helping behavior, we measure whether participants help or not.

At other times the behavior we observe is an indirect measure of an unseen, internal process. The dependent variable measures an observable response that we think is correlated with the unseen process, so we use changes in the response to make inferences about changes in the unseen process. For example, researchers take physiological measurements of respiration and heart rate to make inferences about a person's anxiety or stress level. In memory research, the number of words correctly or incorrectly recalled or recognized under various conditions is used to infer the cognitive processes of retention and forgetting. Or the number of associations between objects or words that participants provide is used as a measure of their creativity. In studying social processes, we may infer a person's response to peer pressure by measuring the amount of time they need to complete a task or the number of mistakes they make while doing it.

A common indirect measure is **reaction time,** the amount of time a participant takes to respond to a stimulus. After presenting stimuli that differ along a physical or mental dimension, we use differences in reaction time to infer underlying cognitive or emotional processes involved.

Another measurement approach is to ask people to make judgments about a stimulus, and then to observe how the judgments change as a function of the conditions. Often this approach involves a **forced-choice** procedure, in which participants must select from the possible choices we provide (e.g., a multiple-choice test). The simplest of these is a **yes-no task.** Researchers in perception, for example, might manipulate characteristics of a visual illusion and have participants indicate whether they still perceive the illusion. Note that any recognition judgment about a stimulus actually reflects two components: a basic ability to detect the stimulus and a bias toward making a particular response. (For example, are we cautious or liberal when saying yes?) Researchers use a statistical procedure called "signal detection analysis" to separate these two components. (Many introductory perception texts discuss this procedure.)

Sometimes, instead of an all-or-none choice, researchers obtain more refined judgments. For example, in studying how people perceive the passage of time, we might ask them to indicate the duration of an interval in seconds. Or we might use more symbolic responses, such as having them draw a line to indicate the perceived duration of an interval. Or we may use a **sorting task,** in which participants indicate their judgments by sorting stimuli into different groups, thus showing the categories they are using to organize them.

Of course, to determine the internal processes occurring in participants, we can explicitly ask them to describe these processes. When people provide descriptions about their feelings or thoughts, they are providing **self-reports.** Often self-reports involve completing a rating scale called a **Likert-type question.** Here a statement is presented, and participants then rate their response to it typically using a scale between "strongly agree" and "strongly disagree". (We used Likert questions in the previous chapter when measuring a female's judgment of a male's attractiveness and likability.) Similar rating scales can be used to measure such things as participants' attitudes, their perceptions of an event, or their confidence in their memory for an event. In another form of self-reports, researchers ask people to provide a running commentary of the mental steps they perform in problem solving, in making judgments, or in social settings.

Selecting a Valid and Reliable Dependent Variable

Ultimately, our conclusions from a study hinge on the scores we obtain. Remember, however, that just because we obtain a particular set of scores in a condition does not necessarily mean that the behavior occurs as proposed, and differences between the conditions do not necessarily mean that the behavior or internal process changes as we think it does. Therefore, you must critically evaluate the operational definition of the dependent variable using the same criteria we previously applied when evaluating the independent variable.

First determine whether the dependent variable provides *construct validity,* reflecting the hypothetical construct as we conceptualize it. In particular, state characteristics are transient attributes that we can change by manipulating an independent variable, so it's appropriate to study them as a dependent variable. Trait characteristics, however, are rather immune to momentary situational events, so it is usually pointless to see if manipulating an independent variable causes changes in them.

The dependent variable should also provide *content validity,* such that we actually and only measure the variable of interest. A score should not depend on a person's abilities and experiences unrelated to the behavior we are studying. We also seek *internal validity,* such that changes in scores reflect the influence of the independent variable but do not reflect changes in extraneous variables. And we seek *external validity,* such that the observed relationship generalizes to other individuals and settings. This includes considering ecological validity, whether we measure a participant's real-world behaviors so that we can generalize to real-world psychological processes. And we seek *reliability*, so that there is minimal error or inconsistency in measurement of the behavior.

Any approach to defining a dependent variable will have some weakness in terms of reliability and validity. When directly observing a behavior, for example, we may observe an unreliable example of the behavior: By watching people eat, we may cause them to eat less than usual. Self-reports can be unreliable and invalid because people may not know or care to divulge their true feelings. Asking participants to sort words into categories might reduce content validity because the sorting process could partially be a test of vocabulary, or asking people to indicate a response by drawing may partially be a test of their drawing ability. We also must be careful when making inferences about any internal construct: If participants fail to recall a stimulus, is it because they initially "stored" it poorly or because they cannot "locate" it in memory? Likewise, with physiological measurements, we do not always know which psychological response is being reflected: For example, anger and fear produce very similar physiological reactions.

The process of selecting and designing a dependent variable depends upon the aspects of reliability and validity you are willing to sacrifice. When studying physiology, we recognize that we may not positively know the underlying emotion being reflected in a response and thus direct our efforts toward more clearly identifying it. When studying cognitive processes, we recognize the difficulty of drawing valid inferences and therefore attempt to build in controls that increase confidence in these inferences. And when obtaining participants' self-reports, we recognize the potential unreliability and attempt to minimize its impact. As with the independent variable, a design is guided by the questions "What is it you wish to study?" and then "What potential flaws must you deal with?"

REMEMBER   Select a procedure for its strengths and then try to minimize its weaknesses.

Recall that any operational definition of a variable gives a limited and potentially biased perspective. One strategy for bolstering our conclusions is to use *converging operations*—different approaches that "converge" on the same behavior. You can employ this strategy by testing the same participants on multiple dependent variables within a single study. If you reach the same conclusion about a treatment or behavior from each measure, you have greater confidence that you are not being misled by any one of them. For example, let's say we obtain physiological measurements and self-reports of participants' emotional state. If they report greater anxiety when they are physiologically more anxious, we have greater confidence in the validity of inferences drawn from either variable. Measuring participants on more than one dependent variable is also very cost-effective, yielding considerably more information for the effort involved in a study. On the other hand, it's not always necessary or even a good idea to employ multiple measures. A single variable—especially if it is an established, accepted measure—can be satisfactory. Using just one variable is particularly beneficial when we do not want to actually weaken reliability and validity by overloading participants with many confusing tasks or making their participation in a study too tedious.

Designing the Dependent Variable

Assuming you've selected a construct- and content-valid dependent variable, you must determine exactly how you'll use it to produce participants' scores. The primary concern at this point is to develop a reliable procedure, so that any time participants exhibit a particular behavior, they are consistently assigned the same particular score. The way to accomplish this is first through your scoring criteria. **Scoring criteria** define the system for assigning different scores to different responses. These criteria determine if a response is correct or not, what constitutes the beginning and end of a response, how to distinguish one response from another, and all of the other decisions necessary for consistently assigning a particular score to a particular response. Then we'll "know" what participants did or did not do to receive a certain score, and that any other individual who received that same score did the same things.

You need scoring criteria even for apparently straightforward variables. Say you're going to test participants' memory by presenting them a list of words, and then counting the words correctly recalled. Is it a correct response if someone writes "bare" but the list presented "bear"? What if for "mother" people recall "mom"? What if participants recall the correct words but in a different order than in the list?

Scoring criteria will be even more elaborate when a behavior is more difficult to quantify, as when measuring aggressiveness, sexism, or motivation, because here often you must evaluate a participant's behavior subjectively. For example, in the temperature study, we might define an aggression score as the number of aggressive acts exhibited toward the researcher. Then the question is what do we mean by an aggressive act? The strategy is always to minimize inconsistency and bias by minimizing the *interpretation* you must give to a behavior. Instead, look for observable, concrete behaviors that have a distinct beginning and end. Thus, we could define aggressive acts in terms of such observable behaviors as yelling, hitting, slamming things on the desk, and so on.

You must also define how to assign scores when such behaviors occur. Does each word a participant yells count as one aggressive act, or is each uninterrupted string of words one aggressive act? Does a nasty look receive the same aggression score as a punch? And so on. Or, if you are observing whether someone smiles in response to a stimulus, how shortly after the stimulus must a smile occur in order to be considered a response to that stimulus? How long must a smile last for it to be counted?

Participants *never* behave in an ideal way. You must try to anticipate every possible variation on the expected response, so if it happens, you know how to score it. For help, refer to the literature to find acceptable scoring criteria. Beyond this, your decisions are usually arbitrary: Simply define one way to score each behavior so that you eliminate inconsistency, sloppiness, and error.

_____

REMEMBER   Precise scoring criteria that focus on observable behaviors are necessary for measuring a behavior reliably.

One important goal for your scoring criteria is that they result in a sensitive measure.

Creating a Powerful Design through a Sensitive Measure

The goal of an experiment is to observe different behaviors as the conditions of the independent variable change. Therefore, the measurement procedure must *discriminate* or distinguish between behaviors, giving a different score each time a behavior is different. Only when two individuals exhibit the identical behavior should they receive the same score. If a slight difference in behavior produces a different score, then we have a **sensitive dependent measure.** A sensitive measure produces different scores for small differences in behavior. This lets us observe even a small influence on responses that a manipulation may produce.

Sensitivity is increased through observing responses that can differ subtly, and by precisely measuring those differences. For example, a 5-point rating scale is more sensitive than a yes-no question. Here's why. Say we're comparing male and female participants, asking each to indicate yes or no to whether they're in a good mood. The men are in a really good mood, so they say "yes." The women are in an OK mood, so they respond "yes." This is an insensitive measure because it does not distinguish the subtle differences between participants' moods, instead lumping them together and indicating they're all the same. Thus even though there is a difference in mood between the two conditions, we will not see it in the data (and the experiment will be a failure). Say that instead, however, participants indicate their mood using a 5-point Likert scale, where 1 indicates a very bad mood and 5 a very good mood. Here the men might score 5s, but the women might produce 4s. Now we'll detect the differences in mood that are present between the men and women (and the study will be a success). For even greater sensitivity, we might use a 7-point scale (to even distinguish between men in a very good mood from men in an almost very good mood, and so forth), or for even greater sensitivity, we might measure mood using precise physiological equipment. Always try to measure the amount or degree of a behavior precisely, as opposed to measuring a yes-no type of response.

Recall that a powerful design is one that is likely to produce a clear and convincing relationship. A more sensitive measure produces a more powerful design. This is because part of producing a convincing relationship is to produce large differences in scores *between* conditions, and thus large differences between the average or mean scores per condition. With a sensitive measure, we are more likely to see differences in participants' scores, even when the independent variable produces only small differences in behavior. (Above, the rating scale showed the subtle differences between the men's good mood and the women's OK mood.) Conversely, because an insensitive measure produces the same score for different behaviors, it results in an unpowerful design. Here—as when the men and women answered yes-no—we might miss differences in behavior that exist between the conditions. Then, even though nature is related as we predict, we obtain data indicating that, as the conditions change, the dependent scores do not.

REMEMBER For a sensitive dependent variable, *precisely* measure *subtle* differences in behavior.

Part of creating a sensitive measure is to avoid restricting the range.

Avoiding a Restricted Range of Scores

So that we can distinguish subtle differences in participants' behavior, it should be possible for them to obtain any of a wide range of different scores. If the design artificially limits participants to only a few possible scores, then we have the problem of a restricted range. **Restriction of range** occurs when the range of possible scores on a variable is limited. For example, people can exhibit great differences in aggressiveness, so our procedure should allow scores that also reflect these differences. If we restrict the range, however, everyone scores close to or at the same score, *regardless* of the independent variable. Therefore, we are less likely to see a relationship in which there are different scores as the conditions change.

To avoid a restricted range, first consider the scores you will assign. If in the temperature study participants can obtain an aggression score of only 1, 2, or 3, the range is restricted. But if they can score anywhere between 0 and 100, the range is not restricted. Second, look for aspects of the testing situation that, *practically speaking,* limit the behaviors or scores that might occur.

One such aspect is when the task is too easy or otherwise biased so that all scores are likely to be near the highest possible score. In that case, the data will show **ceiling effects:** The lowest potential scores—from the worst-scoring participants—are very high, so scores cannot differ much because would-be higher-scoring individuals cannot get much higher (everyone's scores are "hitting the ceiling"). For example, if in the temperature study we accept almost any action as being aggressive, then not-so-aggressive people will have a high score. Then the range is restricted, because others who get seriously aggressive cannot score substantially higher, and we will fail to discriminate between differences in aggressive behavior.

The range is also restricted if the task is too hard or otherwise biased toward producing low scores. Here the data will show **floor effects:** The highest potential scores—from the best-scoring participants—are very low, so scores cannot differ much because would-be lower-scoring individuals cannot get much lower (everyone's scores are "hitting the floor"). For example, most laboratory subjects will not physically assault a researcher, so it's unreasonable to make high aggression scores depend on such extreme actions: Realistically, no one will obtain high scores, and everyone will have low scores. Then, truly nonaggressive participants cannot score lower than more aggressive ones, and, again, we will fail to discriminate between behaviors. (In fact, most social settings bias participants against acting aggressively, so floor effects are likely. To make participants more inclined to respond aggressively in our study, we might have the experimenter provoke participants in all conditions by being rude and nasty to them [as in Bell, 1980].)

Thus, a sensitive procedure is, in part, one that avoids ceiling and floor effects. To achieve this, the typical participant should start off with scores in the middle between very low and very high scores. But it should also be realistically possible to obtain higher or lower scores as the conditions of the independent variable change.

> **REMEMBER**   Always strive for a sensitive procedure that will reflect slight differences in behavior and that will produce an unrestricted range of scores.

Observing Reliable Behaviors

So far we've discussed the reliability of the dependent variable in terms of flaws that the experimenter might introduce by measuring a behavior and assigning scores to it in an inconsistent and misleading manner. However, unreliability can also come from inconsistency in the *behavior* itself. If a participant's behavior is an atypical, unrepresentative response to a condition, then it and the resulting score will be misleading. Instead, we want each participant's score in a condition to be *typical* of his or her score in this situation, reflecting a reliable, representative example of the participant's *typical* behavior in this situation.

There are two general approaches to increasing the reliability of the behaviors we observe: Practice trials and multiple trials.

Practice Trials   A participant's behavior—and score—may be unrepresentative because he or she has not "warmed up" on the measurement task. When this is a possibility, we provide **practice trials**: We test participants as in the real study, but we ignore their scores from these trials when analyzing the results. (A "trial" is one complete measurement or observation.) Practice trials are especially useful when studying physical reactions, as in a reaction-time task. Or, if the task is complicated or involves elaborate equipment, practice trials ensure that participants understand the task. In addition, practice trials allow people to get used to being observed, so they are behaving more naturally by the time we collect the real data.

Multiple Trials   A major component of reliability is the number of real trials a participant performs in a condition. A score that is based on only one trial may reflect all sorts of extraneous factors: A participant might be momentarily distracted or might guess well; the trial might be especially easy or difficult; or some other aspect of the situation may make the trial peculiar. In such a case, the response and score are not representative of a participant's typical response and score.

To avoid the bias from one unique trial, we observe each participant several times in a condition, observing **multiple trials.** Again we are using the strategy of balancing out extraneous variables. We assume that differences in a participant's motivation or attention on different trials balance out, that easy trials balance with hard ones, and so on. We then compute each participant's total score or we compute an average (mean) score for each participant's scores from all of his or her trials. When interpreting these summary scores, we are more confident that they reliably reflect the typical response, because we have balanced out the random fluctuations found in individual trials.

Thus, in the temperature study, we might be inclined to simply ask participants the one question: "How aggressive do you feel toward the researcher?" But, they may not interpret "aggressive" as we intend, they may not recognize their feelings as aggression, or they may not wish to divulge this negative emotion. To overcome such problems, we should instead ask participants several questions that, from different perspectives and using different wording more completely address participants' positive and negative feelings. Then, by scoring and combining responses to all questions, we can produce one score that should accurately reflect a participant's level of aggressiveness toward the experimenter. Likewise, if we're studying memory by testing recall of a list of words, we present several lists per condition, so that we balance out differences in the familiarity, pronounceability, or memorability of any one list. Or, if measuring reaction time to a stimulus, we present many trials per condition to balance out differences in any single stimulus, and to balance momentary physical differences that result in being very fast on some trials and asleep at the switch on others.

There is no magic number of trials you should observe per condition, although to prevent confounding, all conditions should have the same number of trials. Observe more trials when each trial is more easily influenced by extraneous variables and likely to be unreliable. For example, reaction time is usually measured in milliseconds, so responses—and scores—can be easily influenced by extraneous influences. Therefore, we usually measure many trials per condition (in the range of 40 to 200) to produce a reliable estimate of a participant's typical reaction time. On the other hand, if a behavior is less influenced by momentary, extraneous variables, only one or a few trials are necessary. Also consider the influence that multiple trials will have on participants and their performance. People can perform many reaction-time trials quickly and easily; they cannot, however, perform great elaborate tasks for hours on end without becoming unduly fatigued or stressed. (If many trials are necessary and mental or physical fatigue is a problem, break up the testing over a series of days.) Also, multiple trials may not be possible if we are surprising participants with a particular stimulus or response. (You can only surprise someone once!) As with everything in research, weigh the pros and cons of your choices (and check the literature to see what others have done).

——————
REMEMBER Providing practice trials and testing multiple trials tends to increase the reliability of the data.

Although multiple trials add reliability, they also create the problem of order effects.

The Problem of Order Effects

Multiple trials introduce a new extraneous variable called order effects. **Order effects** are the influence on a particular trial that arises from its position in the sequence of trials. Order effects have two components.

Practice effects are the influence on performance that arises from practicing a task. Even after practice trials, participants may perform initial trials poorly because they are still not warmed up. After more trials, performance may improve because participants become quicker or more accurate. With even more trials, however, performance may decrease again because participants become fatigued or bored.

The other component is **carry-over effects,** the influence that a particular trial has on performance of subsequent trials. Carry-over effects can arise first from simply experiencing a trial. For example, if one trial happens to be very frustrating, this feeling may "carry over," lowering performance on subsequent trials. Trials might also be especially boring, easy, or anxiety-provoking, all of which can influence responses to later trials.

Carry-over effects also arise from a **response set,** which is a bias toward responding in a particular way because of previous responses made. This occurs whenever responding becomes more of a habit than a natural reaction to the stimulus. Thus you have a response set when completing a multiple-choice exam if, after the first few questions, you superstitiously believe the correct answer is always choice 4. You might also develop response sets from strategies that have proven successful. For example, unscramble each of the following words:

ookb

reet

oatc

oabt

You can solve the first three words quickly because of the response set that says to always place the final letter first. If you stumble on the fourth word, however, it's because this strategy no longer works.

The problem with practice and carry-over effects is that a response is some-what unique because of *where* in the sequence it occurs. Above, your solution of each word is faster or slower than it would be if the word was in a different location in the sequence. Therefore, participants' overall performance is tied to the unique order used, and so the summary scores are an unreliable indication of the typical response, especially when compared to other orders.

REMEMBER Order effects result from practice, from carry-over of the experience of a trial, and from response sets.

Counterbalancing Order Effects

To solve the problem of order effects we again use the strategy of balancing. Here we balance the effect of any single order by including different orders. Balancing order effects is called counterbalancing. **Counterbalancing** is systematically changing the order of trials for different participants in a *balanced* way to *counter* the biasing influence of any one order. For example, say that in a temperature study comparing 70 vs. 90 degrees, we measure how aggressive participants feel toward the experimenter by having them answer 10 different questions. If we number the questions 1 through 10, a simple counterbalancing scheme is to present the questions to half of the participants in each condition in the order 1 through 10, and to present the questions to the remaining participants in the order 10 through 1. This design is shown in Table 3.3. Each X repre-

Table 3.3 Diagram of Temperature Experiment with the Order of Trials within Each Condition Counterbalanced

Each X Represents a Participant's Summary Score from 10 Questions

	Independent Variable of Temperature	
	70-Degree Condition	90-Degree Condition
Participant's Scores Obtained with Order 1–10	X X X X	X X X X
Participant's Scores Obtained with Order 10–1	X X X X	X X X X
	$\overline{X}$	$\overline{X}$

sents a participant's summary score for the 10 questions, such as his or her mean aggressiveness score. We then ignore the order in which participants completed the questions and look at *all* aggression scores found in each condition. To summarize these scores, we usually compute the mean of the scores in each condition, computing the mean of all summary scores in each column. (That's right: We compute the average of participants' individual average scores.) Higher scores in the 90-degree condition will support the hypothesis that increasing temperature increases aggressiveness. Further, we are confident that the results are not biased by the particular order in which questions were answered, because there is not one particular order present. If we were to test additional people using other orders, we would have even more confidence that the order of trials was not biasing the results. (There are several variations of this technique discussed in Chapter 5.)

> **REMEMBER** When you measure multiple trials, it is appropriate to counterbalance the order of trials.

Note that some researchers use the term *counterbalancing* when balancing any extraneous variable, in addition to the variable of order. Thus, if a male experimenter tests half the participants in each condition and a female tests the remainder, we have counterbalanced for experimenter gender. If half the participants in each condition are male and half are female, we have counterbalanced participants' gender.

Judging a Behavior and Inter-rater Reliability

So far we've discussed measuring rather concrete, obvious behaviors. Special problems arise, however, when in experimental or descriptive designs a score is based on a researcher's subjective judgment about a participant's behavior. For example, in the temperature study, instead of using a questionnaire to measure participants' aggressiveness, we might secretly observe and rate their aggressive actions toward the experimenter (perhaps watching them through a one-way mirror). Not only will the necessary scoring criteria be rather elaborate, but then we must apply them reliably. The problem is, we—the experimenters—know that participants are "supposed" to be more aggressive with hotter temperatures, and try as we might, we cannot prevent this expectation from biasing how we'll rate their behaviors in the different conditions. Therefore, we cannot be relied on to produce objective, reliable, and valid judgments about participants' behavior.

To solve this problem, we enlist the aid of **raters** to judge participants' behavior. These are people who are usually kept in the dark—"blind"—to our hypothesis and the specific conditions they are viewing, and who are trained to use our scoring criteria. Such raters provide us with much greater confidence in subjective scores. For example, in research into whether chimpanzees can learn American Sign Language, one test is whether a chimp can correctly name objects. The problem is that the researcher might cue the chimp as to the correct sign to use, or erroneously give the chimp credit for a sign because it was "close enough" to the desired sign. To eliminate these biases, one researcher shows the object, and another "rater," who cannot see the object, observes and records the chimp's sign. Raters are also common in studies that involve subjectively scoring such behaviors as creativity or nonverbal communication.

Of course, one rater might not reliably score a given behavior. At times the rater might miss or forget part of a participant's action. Over the course of a study, the rater might become more attuned and sensitive, or become fatigued and less motivated. And finally, one rater might judge a behavior differently than would another. (What you consider a neutral facial expression, I might consider an aggressive glare.) Any rater can introduce such errors, and we usually cannot eliminate them.

As you know, when we cannot eliminate an extraneous influence, we try to balance it out. The approach with raters is to employ **multiple raters,** having more than one rater judge each participant's behavior. Then we combine the ratings from the different judges, usually computing the mean rating given to each participant. This mean should balance out the biases of each individual rater, giving us a more reliable measure of each participant's behavior. Further, multiple raters form a sample of observers from which we can infer that any observer would judge the behavior in roughly the same way, so we can generalize the results with greater confidence.

To be convinced that the raters are consistent, it is important to determine their inter-rater reliability. **Inter-rater reliability** is the extent to which raters agree in the scores they assign to participants' behavior. We can determine inter-rater reliability by computing the percentage of agreements between raters—for example, the percentage of times that raters agreed on the sign a chimp produced. (Better than 90% agreement is usually considered reliable.) Or, as discussed in Chapter 8, we may "correlate" the scores from two raters. In the temperature study, for example, hopefully we'll find that low aggression scores assigned to a participant by one rater are consistently matched by low scores assigned by the other, but when high scores are given by one, they are also given by the other.

REMEMBER   When designing the dependent variable, consider multiple raters and inter-rater reliability.

For help remembering the questions to ask when designing the dependent variable, consult Checklist 3.2.

After designing the independent and dependent variables, the next step is to control any remaining extraneous variables.

CHECKLIST 3.2   Questions to consider when designing a dependent variable

❏ Does the variable provide content and construct validity?

❏ Will the variable be confounded?

❏ Will the variable provide external validity?

❏ Do dependent scores reflect common, real-life behavior?

❏ Are scoring criteria complete and sensitive to differences in behavior?

❏ Is range unrestricted, with no ceiling/floor effects?

❏ Are practice trials needed?

❏ Are multiple trials needed?

❏ Are order effects counterbalanced?

❏ Are raters with high inter-rater reliability needed?

Controlling Extraneous Variables

Get used to the idea that *any* aspect of the research situation—the participants, the researcher, the measurement procedure, and the environment—can influence an individual's behavior and thus mislead us. Therefore, look for extraneous variables to control by considering these four components. For each, try to anticipate and eliminate anything that might threaten the reliability or validity of your study. The goal is to prevent extraneous variables from fluctuating *within a condition* (so that all participants experience the condition in the same way) and *between the conditions* (so that, except for the independent variable, everything is the same in the different conditions). You can view all fluctuating extraneous variables as essentially resulting in inconsistency either within or between conditions. Therefore, the basic strategy is to build in consistency. Thus, everyone in the temperature study should be dressed the same way, seated the same distance from the heater, acclimated to the temperature to the same extent and for the same length of time, treated the same by the experimenter, perform the same task while sitting in the room, and so on. If everything is the same for all participants except for the conditions of the independent variable, then we will have greater confidence that we "know" what the scores and relationship reflect.

Also, consistency is important for another reason. Recall that ultimately you'll look at the relationship between the scores in your data, and you want a powerful design that produces a strong and convincing relationship. *Anything can potentially influence participants' scores.* Inconsistency in a study will lead to a weak, inconsistent relationship. That is, inconsistency between conditions will produce inconsistent differences in scores between conditions, and inconsistency within conditions will produce inconsistent scores within conditions. For example, say that some participants in each condition are dressed warmly while others are not, and that increased temperature does increase aggression as we think. Therefore, within any condition, some participants will be substantially hotter and more aggressive than others, so that we'll see a wide range of different aggression scores for that condition. Recall that a wide range of scores in each group produces a weak relationship. Further, higher room temperature will increase aggression scores by an inconsistent amount depending on how participants are dressed, so we'll see an inconsistent trend toward increasing aggression with higher temperatures. As you know, the problem with a weak, unconvincing relationship is that it can potentially cause us to conclude that there is actually no relationship here, so that we miss the real relationship that exists in nature.

REMEMBER The key to designing a convincing experiment is to build in consistency within and between conditions.

Although every study will necessitate its own controls, there are several general techniques for creating consistency.

Instructions to Participants

Participants themselves can introduce all sorts of extraneous variables during the testing session: Any perspective or attitude that participants take or anything they do can cause them to experience a condition in a way that differs from that of other participants. Then there is inconsistency within and between conditions. We control participants' behavior through the instructions we give them at the beginning of their participation.

Instructions must clearly explain what the task is and how participants should approach it: Describe the sequence of events, identify the stimuli participants should attend to, and explain how they should indicate a response. The goal is to have all participants perform precisely the same intended task, without introducing extraneous stimuli or behaviors that make the task different for different participants.

Creating effective yet consistent instructions requires considerable effort because if you must stop during testing of a participant to further explain the task or correct a behavior, then *your* actions become another inconsistency. Therefore, instructions should be clear for the least sophisticated participants, avoiding psychological jargon and unfamiliar words. They should anticipate participants' questions. (Should people guess when responding? Should they hurry?) Instructions should also prohibit unwanted behaviors. (Participants should not look around, fidget, or talk, so they don't miss crucial aspects of the task.) And the same instructions should be presented to all participants. (When manipulating a variable through instructions, change only the necessary parts and avoid a confounding by keeping constant all other aspects.) Never "ad lib" instructions, because you can't reproduce them reliably. Instead, read them from a prepared script and be sure everyone understands them. (If you tell participants to read and understand written instructions, you can't be sure they'll do so.) To reliably present the instructions, speak in an easily reproduced, neutral voice, or, better yet, play a tape recording of them. To help make this all work, researchers usually dress and behave rather formally, because this elicits greater compliance from participants.

Using Automation

The way we present stimuli, obtain responses, and assign and record scores during the measurement task is another major potential source of inconsistency. The way to control extraneous variables here is through **automation**: Using electronic or mechanical devices to present stimuli and to measure and record responses. Electronic timers, slide projectors, video and audio recorders, and computers ensure controlled and reliable stimulus presentations. Automating the data-collection process ensures that the scoring system is consistently and accurately applied and provides for more reliable and sensitive measurement. Automation also eliminates experimenter errors and inconsistency that may result because (1) the experimenter is so busy directing the study that parts of a behavior are missed and (2) the experimenter has expectations about how the study should turn out and thus inadvertently influences participants or records scores accordingly.

With automation, however, you must guard against the problem of instrumentation effects. **Instrumentation effects** are changes in the measurement materials that occur because of use, making the measurements less reliable. This occurs when, over the course of a study, slides, films, and videotapes become scratched and blurred, paper materials get mutilated, or equipment and timers become less accurate. Part of the "instrumentation" is the experimenter, who may become more experienced, more bored, or more crazed as time passes, and who may inadvertently change the procedure. Because of changes in the material or procedure, the measurements obtained late in a study can be different from those obtained early on, making the experiment unreliable overall.

To minimize instrumentation effects, always keep equipment in order and make copies of materials so that all participants can be presented with pristine stimuli. Also, be vigilant to keep the experimenter's behavior constant. Finally, test some participants from each condition during the early, middle, and late stages of the study, so that potential instrumentation effects are balanced in all conditions and thus cannot confound the study.

> *REMEMBER*   Although automation improves reliability and precision, instrumentation effects reduce reliability because the materials change through use.

Testing Participants in Groups

When building in consistency, an important issue is whether to test participants individually or in groups. Group testing is most common when the task requires written responses, such as on a questionnaire. The advantages of group testing are: (1) collecting data is more efficient and (2) if you can test all participants in a condition at one time, then everyone will experience the same consistent condition. The disadvantage is that participants may make noise, block one another's view, or otherwise distract one another so that many extraneous variables are introduced. Therefore, you need to control such behaviors carefully when testing groups. Usually, you can do this through particularly explicit instructions. How successful you'll be—and the wisdom of group testing in general—depends on the particular experiment and how susceptible participants will be to the presence of others.

Pilot Studies

To be sure that they have developed a reliable and valid procedure, researchers often conduct a pilot study. A **pilot study** is a miniature version of a study that researchers use to test a procedure prior to the actual study. (Note that a pilot study is different from a manipulation check: Pilot studies occur *before* a study; manipulation checks occur *during* the study.) Using participants similar to those in the actual study, pilot studies determine such matters as whether the instructions are clear, whether the task can be done given time constraints or other demands, and whether you have developed a workable, sensitive, and reliable scoring procedure. In addition, a pilot study allows you to train raters and to confirm that they have high inter-rater reliability. It also allows you to work out any bugs in the equipment or procedure so that the study runs smoothly and consistently.

Pilot studies are also used to create and validate stimuli. For example, say that our independent variable involves showing participants films that contain different amounts of violence. Our personal judgment is of little help in determining the amount of violence in a film, because we might be particularly sensitive or insensitive to violence. Therefore, we would show the films to pilot subjects and have them rate the amount of violence each contains.

For any problems identified, we alter the stimuli, task, or instructions and conduct more pilot studies until we have the desired situation in each condition.

> **REMEMBER** To maintain consistency in the testing procedure, create clear instructions, use automation but limit instrumentation effects, consider group testing, and conduct pilot studies.

Eliminating Participants from the Data

Even with all of these precautions, research never runs as smoothly as planned (Murphy's Law always applies). Some participants will behave strangely. (I've had them go to sleep!). Others may be downright uncooperative, some may be too "dim" to grasp the instructions, or others may be biased because they've learned the details of the study from a previous participant. A fire drill may occur while testing someone or your equipment may blow a fuse.

In such situations, participants are not experiencing the study that you designed: They are not being exposed to the independent variable reliably, they are not responding as directed, or they are being influenced by extraneous variables. Therefore, you may exclude their scores from your data. You must be *very* sure that these participants do not belong in the study, and you cannot exclude them just because their scores do not confirm your prediction. (That's rigging the results and committing fraud: You might as well make up the data.) When in doubt, therefore, include a participant's data. But, if scores are obtained in a clearly inappropriate situation, you can exclude them. Then test additional participants to fill in for those you've excluded. (Any study that produces many excluded participants, however, is a problem, because it contains a consistent hidden factor that is selecting a biased sample and thus may reduce external validity.)

 ## Putting It All Together

With this chapter, you know a little more about designing a good study (actually, you know a lot more). We're not finished yet, because as you'll see in the next chapters, we still have to consider a participant's reactions to being tested, whether we have an ethical design, and which characteristics of participants may influence the results. However, you are on your way toward conducting valid and reliable experiments, and because the issues are largely the same, you also understand how to approach descriptive designs. In *any* research, you should carefully examine your operational definitions, create clear instructions, consider automation and multiple trials, watch out for order effects, or use multiple raters with high inter-rater reliability. On the other hand, don't develop a false sense of security about the "proof" that such controls provide. We are still only collecting evidence, and the techniques we've discussed are necessary simply for producing "good" convincing evidence.

You may be thinking that producing good evidence requires remembering an overwhelming number of details. (As a friend once remarked, "First you have to think about *everything*!") However, instead of approaching these issues as a long list to memorize, view them as a way to think about the research setting: You're creating a complete social and physical environment in which to observe participants, and you must take charge of all aspects of this environment. If instead you prefer a list, Checklist 3.3 presents the issues we've discussed. (A few more items will be added to the list in the following chapters.)

| CHECKLIST 3.3 | Questions to consider when designing an experiment |

☐ What is the hypothesis?

☐ Is the hypothesis testable, falsifiable, precise, rational, and parsimonious?

☐ What is the appropriate population?

Designing the independent variable

☐ Will the variable provide content and construct validity?

☐ Will the operational definition prevent confounding?

☐ Will the conditions generalize well?

☐ Will the temporal aspects of the design generalize?

☐ Does the factor reflect common, real-life situations?

☐ Is a control group appropriate?

☐ Is the manipulation strong, without diffusion of treatment?

☐ Is a manipulation check needed?

Designing the dependent variable

☐ Does the variable provide content and construct validity?

☐ Will the variable be confounded?

☐ Will the variable provide external validity?

☐ Do dependent scores reflect common, real-life behavior?

☐ Are scoring criteria complete and sensitive to differences in behavior?

☐ Is range unrestricted, with no ceiling/floor effects?

☐ Are practice trials needed?

☐ Are multiple trials needed?

☐ Are order effects counterbalanced?

☐ Are raters with high inter-rater reliability needed?

Creating consistent procedures

☐ Are instructions clear and complete?

☐ Can automation be used without instrumentation effects?

☐ Is group or individual testing of participants best?

☐ Is a pilot study needed?

CHAPTER SUMMARY

1. *Confederates* are people enlisted by a researcher to create a particular social situation for participants.

2. An *intervening variable* is an internal characteristic that is influenced by the independent variable, which in turn influences the dependent variable.

3. A *state characteristic* is a transient attribute that can be experimentally manipulated. A *trait characteristic* is a more permanent attribute that is not easily manipulated.

4. A *control group* is measured on the dependent variable but receives zero amount of the independent variable, or otherwise does not receive the treatment. An *experimental group* receives a nonzero amount of the independent variable.

5. A *powerful design* is likely to produce a clear and convincing relationship in the sample data. A *strong manipulation* adds power by creating conditions that produce large differences in dependent scores between the conditions.

6. *Diffusion of treatment* occurs when participants in one condition are aware of the treatment given in other conditions.

7. A *manipulation check* is a measurement, in addition to the dependent variable, used to confirm that the independent variable had its intended effect.

8. The dependent variable may involve *forced-choice* procedures (including *yes-no* and *sorting tasks*) and *self-reports* (including *Likert-type* rating questions).

9. *Scoring criteria* define the system for assigning dependent scores to participants' responses. The system should provide for a *sensitive* measure that produces different scores for small differences in behavior.

10. *Restriction of range* occurs when the range of possible scores on a variable is limited. *Ceiling effects* restrict the range because all scores tend to be very high, so scores cannot get much higher. *Floor effects* restrict the range because all scores tend to be very low, so scores cannot get much lower.

11. Reliability is improved with *practice trials* and by observing each participant on *multiple trials* within each condition.

12. *Order effects* are the influence on a particular trial that arises from its position in the sequence of trials. *Practice effects* are the influence that comes from practicing a task. *Carry-over effects* are the influence that experiencing a trial has on subsequent trials. A *response set* is a bias toward responding in a particular way because of previous responses made.

13. *Counterbalancing* controls for order effects by presenting different orders of trials within each condition.

14. When scores are based on subjective evaluation of a participant's behavior, use *multiple raters.* They should have high *inter-rater reliability,* the extent to which raters agree in the scores they assign.

15. The key to designing a convincing experiment is to build in *consistency*, both *within* and *between* conditions.

16. Consider *automation* for presenting stimuli and measuring scores. *Instrumentation effects* produce unreliable measurements because of changes in equipment and materials that occur through use. *Instructions, group testing,* and *pilot studies* also determine the consistency of a procedure.

KEY TERMS

automation *(100)*
carry-over effects
  (94)
ceiling effects *(91)*
confederates *(77)*
control group *(80)*
counterbalancing
  (95)
diffusion of treatment
  (84)
experimental group
  (80)
floor effects *(91)*
forced-choice
  procedure *(86)*
inter-rater reliability
  (97)

intervening variable
  (77)
instructions *(99)*
instrumentation effects
  (100)
Likert-type question
  (87)
manipulation check
  (85)
multiple raters *(97)*
multiple trials *(93)*
order effects *(94)*
pilot study *(101)*
powerful design *(83)*
practice trials *(92)*
practice effects *(94)*
raters *(96)*

reaction time *(86)*
response set *(94)*
restriction of range
  (91)
scoring criteria *(89)*
self-reports *(87)*
sensitive dependent
  measure *(90)*
sorting task *(87)*
state characteristic
  (77)
strong manipulation
  (83)
trait characteristic
  (78)
yes-no task *(86)*

REVIEW QUESTIONS

1. What does it mean to use (a) a "forced-choice" procedure? (b) "Likert-type" questions? (c) a "sorting task"?

2. (a) What does the term *self-reports* mean? (b) What is the major disadvantage of this procedure?

3. (a) What is a powerful design? (b) Why is creating a powerful design important?

4. (a) What is a strong manipulation? (b) Why do we seek strong manipulations?

5. (a) What is a control group? (b) What is an experimental group? (c) Why do we employ control groups?

6. (a) What is meant by reliable manipulation of the independent variable? (b) Why is reliable manipulation important?

7. (a) What is a manipulation check? (b) What is the difference between a pilot study and a manipulation check?

8. (a) Why do we give participants practice trials? (b) Why are multiple trials generally better than a single observation? (c) What problem arises with multiple trials?

9. (a) What are practice effects? (b) What are carry-over effects? (c) What is a response set?

10. What is counterbalancing?

11. What is a sensitive measurement procedure?

12. In terms of fluctuating extraneous variables, what is the key concern when developing a testing procedure?

13. What are the pros and cons of testing participants in groups?

14. (a) What do we mean by automation? (b) Why can automation be good for a study? (c) Why can automation be bad for a study?

15. To study nonverbal communication, your conditions involve presenting a picture of a person making different kinds of faces (smiling, frowning, smirking). You ask participants to indicate the person's emotional state as either happy or sad. (a) What flaws are built into dependent scores? (b) How can you improve this procedure?

16. To study how practice influences physical ability, you manipulate three conditions of the amount of practice that participants have playing basketball and then measure the number of baskets they make out of 50 tries. Your participants are all physical education majors. (a) What flaw is built into these scores? (b) How can you improve this procedure?

17. In question 16, (a) to make the task challenging, you have participants stand at the far end of the basketball court when testing their basket-shooting. What flaw is present in this procedure? (b) Instead, you have participants stand almost directly underneath the basket. What flaw is present now?

18. In a study of memory, you read aloud one list of either similar or dissimilar words and then measure participants' memory for the list. (a) What problems might occur because you read the lists? (b) How can you eliminate them? (c) What problem might now arise over the course of testing many people?

19. In question 18, you ask participants to write down the list of words. (a) To reliably score recall, what decisions should you make? (b) How could you ensure you did not score the responses in a biased fashion? (c) What aspect of reliability must you then check?

20. In question 18, (a) what problem affects the reliability of the memory *behavior* you are observing? (b) What preliminary task can you add to improve reliability? (c) How can you expand your observations of each participant to improve reliability? (d) What problem have you created? (e) Precisely describe how you would deal with the problem.

21. After delivering different speeches to participants to make them more or less sexist, you examine their sexism in each condition by observing whether they help a confederate of the opposite sex. (a) What can you do to check that your speeches actually altered sexism? (b) If the speeches had little or no effect, what design principle would be your goal when rewriting them? (c) What would be your approach for accomplishing this? (d) What would you do to be sure you had created effective speeches before conducting the study again?

DISCUSSION QUESTIONS

1. Your conditions consist of three types of instructions on how to be logical. The dependent variable is participants' ability to solve three logic problems. (a) What threats to reliability and validity are present in this dependent measure? (b) How would you deal with them?

2. You compare the number of typing errors that people produce when copying material onto a computer when using either a black-and-white or color monitor. (a) What potential sources of inconsistency in and between conditions might arise? (b) How would you control such variables?

3. You conduct the temperature study discussed in this chapter, comparing the levels of 70, 80, and 90 degrees Fahrenheit. You'll ask participants 10 questions about their aggressiveness toward the researcher. Diagram how you'll counterbalance order effects, as well as participants' gender in each condition.

4. You create different conditions by playing different types of music to participants. After a while, you suddenly pull out and shoot a (blank) pistol. You then measure participants' anxiety level in order to determine whether different types of music cause people to remain more or less calm in the face of startling stimuli. (a) What threat to internal validity might arise as you test more and more people? (b) How would you counteract it?

5. You wish to study how hard participants will work for food depending on how hungry they are. (a) Create an operational definition for manipulating the independent variable and diagram your design. (b) Evaluate your definition in terms of construct, content, and internal and external validity.

4

Risk, Deception, and the Ethics of Research

GETTING STARTED

To understand this chapter, recall the following:

- From Chapter 2, recall what the components of an experiment are, and the differences between laboratory and field experiments.

- From Chapter 3, recall that for power, we seek a strong manipulation and a sensitive measure that avoids a restricted range and floor/ceiling effects. Also recall what we mean by automation and diffusion of treatment.

Your goals in this chapter are to learn:

- What demand characteristics are and how to prevent them from threatening a study.

- What research ethics are and how to design and conduct an ethical study.

- What animal research involves and the ethical issues in animal research.

As you've seen, researchers often must be rather devious: We *do* things to participants and sometimes they aren't the nicest experiences, we manipulate—or some would say "rig"—the situations under which participants are observed, we control participants' extraneous behavior, and often the behavior we want to observe is a personal affair that people would rather keep to themselves. Yet, researchers are a part of society, subject to the same restrictions and responsibilities as anyone else. Therefore, part of designing a study involves considering whether you've crossed the line. In this chapter we discuss the ethical issues that arise in human—and animal—research and how to handle them.

Before we get to ethics, however, we'll first discuss one more important potential flaw to deal with when designing a study, because how we deal with it has a major impact on the ethics of a study. The flaw is called demand characteristics.

Demand Characteristics

Imagine you are a participant in an "experiment" taking place in an elaborate "laboratory." A "psychologist" with lab coat and clipboard puts a plate of cookies in front of you and says, "Normal people crave cookies at this time of day, so eat if you want." I bet you'll eat one. On the other hand, imagine the psychologist says, "Only people who have no self-control eat at this time, but eat if you want." I'll bet you don't. In any situation, the social and physical surroundings provide cues that essentially "demand" that we behave in a certain way. In research, these cues are called demand characteristics. A **demand characteristic** is an extraneous cue that guides or biases a participant's behavior. Participants rely on demand characteristics to answer such questions as "What's really going on here?" "What am I supposed to do?" and "How will my response be interpreted?" Demand characteristics arise despite the instructions we provide, and participants don't necessarily respond to them intentionally or even consciously.

Demand characteristics can be grouped in terms of the four components of a study. First, participants bring with them certain attitudes that influence their behavior. Research procedures are mysterious, and rumor has it that psychologists do strange things to people and study only intelligence, sexual deviance, and crazy people. Therefore, while participants are trying to determine what is really going on, they are also on guard: They are sensitive to the whole idea of being "studied" and may alter their behavior accordingly. This is the demand characteristic called reactivity. **Reactivity** is the bias in responses that occurs because participants are aware that they are being observed. Participants know they're under the gun, and they "react" to the mere presence of an experimenter who is observing and possibly "analyzing" their behavior. Therefore, some participants may be overly cooperative, doing and saying what they think they are "supposed" to. Others may be overly contrary, providing behaviors that are the opposite of those the researcher seeks. Still others may, simply because we're observing them, behave in very unnatural ways.

As an example, consider the interesting study by Strack, Martin, and Stepper (1988). They hypothesized that the facial muscles used for smiling provide feedback that further improves mood. (In other words, not only does being happy make you smile, but smiling makes you happy.) To test the hypothesis, they measured the dependent variable of mood after participants held a pen in their mouths using their teeth (which mimics smiling) or using their puckered lips (which does not mimic smiling). The problem was to be sure that participants' mood and how they indicated it was not influenced by demand characteristics. But, because of reactivity, some participants might laugh and act happy simply because they think it's expected. Others who feel happy may respond as sad so that they don't divulge their inner feelings. Still others might become very self-conscious, nervous, or giddy so that their response is not what they'd normally do, or they make more errors than they normally would. In fact, such reactivity can even be physiological: For example, when measuring blood pressure, the mere act of attaching the measuring cuff to people raises their blood pressure.

In addition, participants also respond to another important demand characteristic called social desirability. **Social desirability** occurs when people provide what they consider to be the socially acceptable response. Essentially, participants "edit" their responses so that they aren't embarrassed or so they won't appear weird or abnormal. Thus, in the smile study, some participants may act happy, not so much because they *are* happy, but because they think it's the normal response. Others may want to act happy but inhibit this because they're afraid they'll be perceived as weird.

The environment in which a study takes place can also provide cues to participants. The surroundings may distract participants or cause them to react to extraneous factors. Often participants use such things as random noises, changes in lighting, or a broken pencil point as cues for erroneously concluding what is being studied and how they should respond. This is especially true in fancy laboratories with one-way mirrors and complex equipment that can play on someone's fears. (Once, in a study involving a bank of electronic timers, I had to convince participants that they would not be electrocuted by having them look under their chairs to see there were no wires!)

The measurement procedure that participants must perform also communicates demand characteristics that participants use to modify their responses. For example, in studies of mental imagery, participants must envision a previously presented map, and the time they take to mentally travel between different locations on the map is measured. Participants take longer when the locations on the map are more distant. However, this result might occur not because it reflects how participants travel along mental maps, but because participants know that longer distances "should" take longer, so they "oblige." Or, in a different situation, participants might interpret an opinion survey as really being a personality test. Then, instead of honestly answering the questions, they will respond in ways they think projects their ideal personality.

Finally, the experimenter is an important source of demand characteristics. Researchers usually dress and behave rather formally to inspire serious cooperation from participants. But, our formality can inhibit participants' normal reactions. On the other hand, if we act and dress too informally, we may encourage inattentiveness and sloppy performance. Further, people are very sensitive to **experimenter expectancies,** which are cues the experimenter provides about the responses that participants should give in a particular condition. These cues occur because the researcher knows the predictions of the study and may inadvertently communicate them. Then the ultimate self-fulfilling prophecy is produced. In the smile study, for example, we expect people to be happier when mimicking a smile. Subtle actions on our part can register on participants, and, sure enough, they'll respond with the predicted mood.

As these examples illustrate, demand characteristics cause people to play a role, being good (or not so good) participants who perform on cue. The problem is that they are responding to these cues, instead of to our variables. Then, for example, reactivity or social desirability may restrict the range of scores, reducing the sensitivity and power in the study. If we're measuring aggressiveness, for example, all participants might stifle their aggression so they don't look bad. This will produce low scores for all conditions, producing floor effects. If we're measuring "niceness," we're likely to see ceiling effects. In addition, we lose internal validity because it is the cues that cause a particular response, instead of the independent variable. Thus, if people act happy when smiling because they think it's expected, then it will appear that our manipulation influences their behavior when it really has no effect. Or the cues may cause participants to behave contrary to our prediction: If they force themselves to act sad when using their smile muscles, it will appear that our manipulation does not influence their behavior as we predict, when otherwise it would. We also lose reliability, because scores are different from what they would be if such cues were not present. And because not all participants react to the same cues in the same way, scores will be inconsistent. Finally, we lose external validity because the results will not generalize to other situations where such demand characteristics are not present.

REMEMBER   Demand characteristics are cues that bias participants, resulting in responses that are not valid, reliable reactions to our variables.

Fortunately, we have several techniques for controlling demand characteristics.

General Controls for Demand Characteristics

Our first line of defense against demand characteristics is to provide participants with as few cues as possible. If they have no cues, their only recourse is to act naturally. Thus, instructions to participants should not divulge the specific purpose, manipulation, or predictions of a study. Note: Any time we keep participants in the dark regarding the specifics about a condition they receive, we are using a **single-blind procedure.** In addition, instructions should not include extraneous, distracting information (such as placing an unnecessary time limit on a task). Also, hide threatening equipment and avoid threatening actions or extraneous comments by the experimenter.

It is especially important to limit the cues from the experimenter. A prime reason for using automation is that equipment will not communicate experimenter expectations. When a potentially biasing experimenter must be present, however, you should use a double blind. In a **double-blind procedure,** both the participants and the researcher who interacts with them are unaware of the specific condition being presented. The original researcher trains others to actually conduct the study, but they do not know the conditions or predictions—they are "blind" to them. Such procedures are especially common when testing the effect of a drug or other medical treatment. If the researcher knows when a particular drug is being administered, his or her expectations about its effects may be communicated to patients. These expectations *alone* can produce the expected physical reaction or recovery from an illness. If the experimenter is blind to such information, however, no expectations can be communicated.

> **REMEMBER** A double-blind procedure keeps both the researcher and the participants blind to the conditions, so that their expectations do not influence the results.

Our second defense against demand characteristics is to make those cues that must be present as neutral as possible. Thus, the researcher tries to be rather bland, being neither overly friendly nor unfriendly. In the instructions, we try to neutralize participants' fears and suspicions by presenting the task without implying that it is difficult or easy and without indicating what the "normal" or expected response is. Further, we encourage participants to respond naturally and honestly, and tell them that they should not be upset if they make errors, and that we are not using the data for any sinister purpose. Thus, for example, when conducting a memory study we might tell participants that we are simply studying memory processes, that we expect errors to occur, and that regardless of their performance, it will not reflect on their personality or intelligence. Also, we try to provide a response format that participants are comfortable with: We have children act out responses using toys or we give college students a paper-and-pencil test. And we try to select a researcher with whom participants will be comfortable when performing the task (in terms of gender, age, and so on). This is especially important when responses are likely to be influenced by reactivity and social desirability (for example, in a study of sexual fantasies), because participants' willingness to risk making mistakes or to honestly divulge personal information depends on the characteristics of who is observing them. (You behave very differently in a locker room than when meeting a date's parents!)

If a procedure is especially likely to produce reactivity, we attempt to neutralize it by making participants more comfortable by allowing them to "habituate" to it. With **habituation,** we familiarize participants with a procedure before beginning actual data collection. For example, one reason to have participants perform practice trials is so the researcher's presence becomes a "habit" and is no longer disruptive. Or, when testing children—who often respond poorly to strangers—we play with them and get to know them before testing begins. We also allow participants to habituate to any equipment being used: If we are videotaping responses, we allow participants to become comfortable with being recorded before the study begins.

Our final defense is to have participants ignore demand characteristics by creating experimental realism. **Experimental realism** is the extent to which the measurement task engages participants. The goal is to create a measurement task that people find so interesting or engrossing that they "forget" about demand characteristics. Thus, in the smile study, if the task is so engrossing that participants forget about the pen in their mouth, the results will be less influenced by demand characteristics. Experimental realism does not mean, however, that the task is like real life, so experimental realism is different from ecological validity. With experimental realism, the task may be very strange and unreal, but because they're involved in it, participants' responses are actual, honest responses to it.

You should apply the preceding strategies to virtually all designs. Don't forget that experiments are not the only research we conduct. Descriptive studies—in which we may simply observe participants' behavior, provide them with questionnaires, and so on—are subject to the same types of demand characteristics as experiments. Therefore, when conducting descriptive studies, try to minimize and neutralize cues as well. If, however, an experimental or descriptive design will still produce very strong demand characteristics despite using these techniques, then you may need to use unobtrusive measures or deception.

Using Unobtrusive Measures and Deception

When the procedure for measuring the dependent variable will strongly encourage reactivity and social desirability, researchers sometimes employ unobtrusive measures. With an **unobtrusive measure**, we measure participants' behavior without making them aware that the measurement is being made. Thus, an unobtrusive measurement of aggressiveness might involve observing participants through a one-way mirror. Other unobtrusive measures may include the use of hidden cameras and recorders. Or we may observe telltale evidence left by participants (for example, to measure how far people sit from one another, we could measure the distance separating their chairs after they've left the room). In each case, participants cannot be overly influenced by demand characteristics if they are unaware of the measurement being made.

Sometimes an unobtrusive measure is used in conjunction with deception. **Deception** involves the creation of an artificial situation or "cover story" that disguises a study. Participants are then unaware of the manipulation or the behavior actually being studied, so they do not feel pressured to respond in a certain way. For example, in the smile study, imagine what you would do if a researcher simply said, "Here, hold this pen in your lips." You'd probably feel very self-conscious and behave unnaturally. The original researchers eliminated such problems by telling participants that the study investigated how physically impaired people use their mouths to do tasks that others do by hand. Then, while holding the pen in either their lips or teeth, participants used the pen for various tasks, including marking various stimuli. Among the stimuli were several cartoons, and participants' rating of how humorous they found the cartoons was the dependent variable for measuring their mood. Thus, what might have been a bizarre task was transformed into a rational, engaging task in which participants were less self-conscious and responded in a more natural way.

Likewise, Schachter, Goldman, and Gordon (1968) sought to measure how much food people would eat under different conditions. But blatantly watching people as they eat is likely to make them highly reactive. Therefore, the researchers told participants that they were in a taste study in which they were to rate the taste of different crackers, and that they should eat as many crackers as necessary. The real dependent variable was the number of crackers eaten. Note that a task designed to distract participants from demand characteristics (such as rating the taste of crackers) is referred to as a **distractor task.**

Conversely, we can sometimes use demand characteristics to our advantage, disguising a task by incorporating elaborate scientific-looking procedures. For example, Duclos et al. (1989) manipulated the posture that people adopted in order to determine how posture influences mood. So that the participants would maintain a posture without being overly conscious or suspicious of it, fake electrodes for measuring "brain activity" were attached to them, and they were told that their posture was important for accurate measurements.

A special type of deception is often used in conjunction with a control condition (a condition that receives zero amount of the independent variable). Because only the experimental group receives the treatment, it also only experiences the associated demand characteristics. Therefore, we have a confounding: The experimental group behaves differently from the control group either because of the treatment or because of the accompanying demand characteristics. For example, let's say we give an experimental group a drink of alcohol while a control group receives nothing. Any impairment the experimental group exhibits may be due to the alcohol, or it may arise because giving people alcohol implies that we expect them to act drunkenly, so they do.

To keep such demand characteristics constant, control groups are given a placebo. A **placebo** provides the demand characteristics of a treatment. Thus, we would give the above control group something that smells and tastes like alcohol but that is not alcohol. Then we communicate to both groups the same demand characteristics for acting drunkenly, so any differences in their behavior are due to the real alcohol given to the experimental group. Similarly, when testing other drugs, we give placebo "sugar" pills or injections to the control group so that all participants experience the same procedure and form the same expectations. And in studies that require the experimental group to perform an involved task prior to making a response, we have the control group perform a similar, placebo task to eliminate differences between the groups in terms of motivation or fatigue. Note that placebos also help to reduce *diffusion of treatment*. They make it more difficult for participants to identify a control or experimental condition, so they are less likely to be biased by their knowledge about the study. Likewise, other forms of deception can be used to prevent diffusion of treatment, because if participants can't readily identify the treatments, they can't tell others, or be influenced themselves.

REMEMBER A placebo is given to control groups so that they experience the same demand characteristics as experimental groups.

Deception is not always necessary or wise (as with everything in research, you must balance the pros and cons). Research has shown, for example, that if we manipulate the independent variable of room temperature, we should not try to hide this by, say, offhandedly remarking that the room's thermostat is broken. Participants will often guess that the study deals with temperature anyway (Bell & Baron, 1976). Catching the researcher in a lie will worsen the demand characteristics, because then participants *know* they should be on guard.

Concealing the Experiment

When we are especially concerned about reactivity and social desirability, the final approach is to conceal the entire experiment. Many studies, for example, have been performed while participants sit in a waiting room, supposedly waiting to be taken into the experiment. Mathews and Cannon (1975) studied how the noise level in a room influenced a person's willingness to help a confederate who dropped some books. Doing this in a formal laboratory with the experimenter watching might communicate that helping behavior was being studied and that the expected behavior was to help. Instead, a confederate dropped the books while walking past the participant in the "waiting room," and the person's response was unobtrusively observed.

The most extreme way to conceal an experiment is to move out of the laboratory and conduct a *field experiment*. Here we unobtrusively conduct the experiment by observing people in shopping malls, student unions, and so on. One reason that field experiments have greater external validity is that they can disguise the fact that an experiment is being conducted. For example, Isen and Levin (1972) discreetly manipulated participants' mood by allowing some people the pleasant experience of finding money in the change return of a pay phone. Then a passing confederate dropped a manila folder, and the dependent variable was whether participants helped the confederate. Similarly, Mathews and Cannon (1975) conceptually replicated their above study of the influence of background noise on a person's helping behavior. They had a confederate drop books on a sidewalk in front of random passersby, while another confederate operated a noisy lawn mower. Such field studies overcome the reactivity or social desirability that occurs with laboratory experiments because reactivity, experimenter cues, and so on are minimized, and the situation tends to have high experimental realism. Likewise, recall that descriptive studies are typically conducted in the field, resulting in greater external validity. This is primarily because the researcher plays a much less active and obvious role, the environment is more natural, and there is greater realism, so there are usually fewer demand characteristics present that bias participants away from behaving naturally.

REMEMBER   Reduce demand characteristics through minimizing cues, habituation, experimental realism, unobtrusive measures, deception, and field experiments.

For help remembering the questions to ask when dealing with demand characteristics in a study, consult Checklist 4.1.

It is often because of demand characteristics that psychological research becomes most devious and creative. In fact, researchers can probably manipulate virtually any independent variable, get participants to do just about anything,

CHECKLIST 4.1   Questions to consider when identifying and preventing demand characteristics

Will demand characteristics be present?

❏ Will the participants react to being observed?

❏ Will the participants give socially desirable responses?

❏ Will the environment bias the participant's responses?

❏ Will the experimenter's characteristics or expectancies influence scores?

Choices for preventing demand characteristics

❏ Do you keep participants "blind" to the procedure?

❏ Do you keep cues as neutral as possible?

❏ Should you have participants "habituate" to being observed?

❏ Should you use automation?

❏ Should you use single- or double-blind procedures?

❏ Do you use tasks with experimental realism?

❏ Should you hide measurement tasks using unobtrusive techniques?

❏ Do you provide a placebo for control group?

❏ Should you disguise conditions with deception or a field experiment?

and have them divulge their most private and personal feelings. This raises the important question, however, of whether researchers *should* do such things.

Research Ethics

As a researcher in psychology, you face a dilemma: On the one hand, you need a well-controlled, informative study, even if this means being deceptive, eliciting responses that participants want to keep private, or doing things that cause them discomfort. We justify these actions on the grounds that good, sound scientific knowledge is needed to benefit humanity. On the other hand, you should treat participants properly because they have basic rights to privacy, to respect, and to safety. Therefore, the central issue in **research ethics** is the concern for balancing a researcher's right to study a behavior with the right of participants to be protected from abuse.

The Cooperativeness of Participants

Why do people allow themselves to be mistreated by a researcher? First, researchers are often viewed as authority figures and, as with all authority figures, people tend to think that they are benevolent and honest. Second, people assume that research is valuable for society, so they believe their participation is important. The result is that participants respect the goals of research and trust the researcher, so they are open to abuse.

An example of how motivated participants are was demonstrated in a classic study by Orne (1962), who tried to give participants a task they would refuse. He gave each person 2,000 sheets of paper, each of which contained 224 addition problems. No justification for the task was given, and participants were merely told that the researcher would return "sometime." Five and one-half hours later, the participants were still working, but the experimenter gave up! In the next attempt, participants were told that, after completing each sheet, they should tear it up into a minimum of 32 pieces and then continue with the next sheet. Participants performed this task for *several hours* until, again, the experimenter gave up. The subjects later reported that they viewed this meaningless task as some sort of important psychological endurance test.

As the preceding illustrates, an overriding demand characteristic in any study is for participants to be cooperative. In fact, people cooperate even to their own detriment. The classic example of this is Milgram (1963), who convinced participants that they were assisting him to train a "learner" confederate to learn verbal stimuli. Each time the learner made an error, the participants pressed a switch that he or she believed administered an increasingly larger electrical shock to the learner. Despite protests from the learner (who could be heard but not seen, and who eventually emitted deathly silence), and despite the fact that the electrical switches were labeled "DANGER: SEVERE SHOCK," a *majority* of participants delivered what they believed was as much as 450 volts of electricity! (The electrical outlets in your home deliver at least 110 volts.)

Milgram applied no coercion other than to tell participants to continue, using only the authority that they had implicitly given him. Yet they complied, even though they believed they were harming another person, and in many cases became *very* emotionally and physically distressed themselves. Further, these were not young, impressionable freshman college students, but adults of various ages and backgrounds.

Milgram was soundly criticized for his tactics, but there are many studies suggesting that a researcher can probably get participants to put up with almost anything: They are willing to suffer great mental or physical discomfort, and they are reluctant to protest or to protect themselves. However, merely because people volunteer for a study does not mean that we have the right to take advantage of them. In essence, there is an implicit contract between participants and researchers. Their side of the contract is to help in the study and to trust us. Our side of the contract is to not abuse their trust. Being ethical means living up to our part of the bargain.

REMEMBER We must treat participants ethically, because they are helping us and trust us not to harm them.

The APA Principles of Ethical Conduct

To assist researchers when dealing with ethical issues, the American Psychological Association (APA) adopted the Ethical Principles of Psychologists and Code of Conduct (1992). These principles govern the full range of a psychologist's activities. In particular, they deal with the care of human and nonhuman research participants and apply to any type of study (not just experiments). For now, we'll discuss human participants. These principles can be summarized as follows.

Identify Potential Risks The first ethical consideration is for you to determine whether your design presents any risk to participants. Begin by identifying potential **physical risks:** Is there anything in the study that could physically endanger participants? Are you manipulating a potentially dangerous independent variable? Could measuring the dependent variable be harmful? Is all equipment working properly and safely, and will presenting stimuli cause pain or physical damage? Are you adhering to all accepted procedures when injecting drugs, drawing blood, and the like?

Second, identify potential **psychological risks:** Will participants experience undue anxiety, depression, or other unpleasant feelings because you are invading their privacy, producing negative emotions, or lowering their self-esteem? Distress can occur directly as the result of a manipulation, as when we intentionally cause people to become sad or depressed. Distress may also result indirectly. For example, you might think Milgram's study was not so unethical because no one actually got hurt. But if Milgram had not disconnected the electrical wires, the participants would have killed—murdered—the learner! Think about how they felt when *that* dawned on them.

When identifying potential risks, consider not only your procedure but also your participants. Having healthy teenagers perform strenuous exercise may not be risky, but it is risky for the elderly or for people with heart conditions. Likewise, films containing sex, violence, and mayhem are standard fare for some adult moviegoers, but they may be upsetting for others, or for children.

Dealing with deception is a particularly difficult issue. On the one hand, Christensen (1988) found that among people who had participated in deceptive and nondeceptive experiments, those in the deceptive studies enjoyed the experience more, became better educated about psychological research, and did not mind being deceived. On the other hand, this does not mean you can freely deceive participants on a whim. Deception may be harmful because, when participants learn of it, they may feel foolish, depressed, or angry. Therefore, the APA guidelines explicitly require that deception be used *only* when it is a necessary component of a design.

Thus, in evaluating the ethics of deception, first consider whether it is necessary for producing the desired study. (It is doubtful, for example, that Milgram could have elicited such extreme obedience without using deception.) Second, consider the amount of deception involved. The greater the deception—the bigger the lie—the more objectionable it is. Finally, and most important, consider how severe the psychological impact of the deception will be. The extreme emotional reactions resulting from Milgram's deception are a serious ethical concern, whereas the more minor reactions arising from the deception in our smile study are much less objectionable.

Protect Participants from Physical and Psychological Harm   Once the potential risks in a study are identified, you must try to eliminate or at least minimize them. If participants will be stressed or embarrassed, can you alter the design to eliminate these feelings and still get at the intended behaviors? In particular, recall that we seek a *strong manipulation* of the independent variable that may involve exposing participants to a large amount of the variable or exposing them for a long time. Balance this goal with the ethical goal of minimizing the negative impact of the treatments: Can you "tone down" the manipulation so that it affects participants but still is not too extreme? Thus, if we want to make one group more depressed than another, we don't need to make the first group suicidal! In fact, consider whether the study will work if, instead, we make one group happier than another. We can also minimize risks by screening out high-risk individuals. If the study involves exercise, for example, screen out people with a heart condition. If we're manipulating depression, screen out people who are already clinically depressed.

One important rule is to minimize participants' anxiety by keeping all information about them confidential. They are never identified in publications or discussed in casual conversations. (Often we assign participants a number instead of recording their names, so they remain anonymous.)

Justify Remaining Risks   For any risks to participants that remain in a design, you must fairly and honestly decide whether they are justified by the study's scientific worth. That is, the knowledge to be gained from a study must clearly and convincingly justify the risk to participants. Thus, when weighing the risks in a study, ask such things as Will the study demonstrate something *new* and *important* about a behavior? Is determining causality important enough to justify manipulating the variable as an independent variable, or could you forego causality and use a descriptive/correlational study with people who have already experienced the variable in the real world? Will a highly stressful or invasive dependent variable tell you that much more about a behavior than a more mundane, less-objectionable one? Throughout, recognize that as the potential for physical or psychological risk increases, you must have a corresponding increase in the scientific worth of the study. If not, don't conduct the study.

> **REMEMBER**   The primary ethical concern in any study is to minimize potential harm to participants and to ensure that any remaining risk is justified.

Ethical issues are not always clear-cut, so seek the advice of others. In fact, to conform to the APA's Ethical Principles (as well as to federal and state regulations), colleges and research institutions maintain a **Human Subjects Review Committee** (also called an Institutional Review Board, or IRB). This committee consists of individuals from various disciplines, so a broad perspective is represented. The committee's job is to review a study's procedures to ensure the ethical treatment of participants. All researchers must obtain approval from their IRB *before* conducting any type of study.

One thing a review committee always looks at is how you'll deal with the issue of informed consent.

Obtain Informed Consent   Out of respect for the participants' right to control what happens to them, you must inform them about the study *prior* to their participation and then let them decide whether they wish to participate. That is, obtain **informed consent.** The APA's Ethical Principles state that informed consent is required unless there is minimal risk, such as when we merely observe anonymous people in a field setting. But always obtain informed consent when conducting laboratory experiments. The usual procedure is to provide participants with a written description that contains four components.

First, describe the purpose and procedures of the study. Sometimes you must withhold specific details to prevent diffusion of treatment and to reduce demand characteristics, but usually you can provide general information without biasing the participants. Tell them as much as you can. In addition, participants have the right to know what you'll do with their data and you should tell them if their individual performance will be kept confidential (this information will also reduce reactivity). If you have a very good reason for violating confidentiality, explain it and indicate how you'll communicate participants' performance to others.

Second, explicitly warn participants of any physical or psychological risks associated with the procedure, describing any details that could reasonably be expected to influence a person's decision to participate in the study. Even if you cannot divulge all aspects of a procedure, you must warn participants of any negative consequences of it. (For example, Milgram should have at least warned his subjects that they might learn some unpleasant things about themselves.)

Third, inform participants that they are free to discontinue their participation at any time during the study, *without penalty*. Volunteering for a study produces such strong demand characteristics to be cooperative that this option *does not* occur to people. Be sure that withdrawing is a realistic option, without any hidden coercion because participants are enrolled in a class or have a job where the study is being conducted.

Finally, obtain participants' signatures as their explicit consent to participate. In the case of minors and others who are not capable of making this decision, obtain consent from their parents or guardians.

Take Care of Participants after the Study   Finally, after a study, any negative consequences of the procedure must be removed so that participants feel as good about themselves as they did when they entered the study. First, alleviate any concerns they have by providing a **debriefing.** Here we fully inform participants about all aspects of the study, including the manipulation and any deception used and why. Second, remove any adverse physical or emotional reactions in participants that you may have created. Thus, if we tested the effects of alcohol, we care for participants until they are sober. If we created anxiety or depression, we try to reverse these feelings, explaining why we think they are normal reactions to our manipulation. If follow-up counseling or check-ups are needed, we provide qualified, professional help. Finally, give participants a means of contacting you later in case unforeseen problems arise.

REMEMBER   Always obtain informed consent, debrief participants, and care for them after the study.

Regardless of whether you're conducting an experimental or descriptive study, you should approach these ethical issues in the same manner. To help you remember them all, they're listed in Checklist 4.2.

The Ethics of Unobtrusive Measures and Field Research

Ethical issues get particularly complicated with unobtrusive and deceptive procedures, especially in terms of whether we're violating a participant's right to informed consent. In a laboratory setting, however, participants are aware that they will be observed even if they cannot see the observer, so using one-way mirrors and other unobtrusive measures is usually acceptable. Likewise, in a waiting-room situation, participants have given their tacit agreement to be observed by showing up for the study. If such a procedure might embarrass, victimize, or

CHECKLIST 4.2   Ethical questions to consider when designing a study

- ☐ Are there physical risks to participants?
- ☐ Are there psychological risks to participants?
- ☐ Can you eliminate or minimize risks?
- ☐ Can you justify risks in terms of the scientific value of results?
- ☐ Will you obtain informed consent?
- ☐ Will you provide debriefing and care for participants after the study?
- ☐ Will you submit the planned procedure to the IRB for review?

otherwise harm a person, however, then explicit prior informed consent is needed.

When people know they are participating in a descriptive study or experiment in the field, we deal with informed consent and debriefing as described above. However, the most difficult ethical situation arises with unobtrusive or hidden field research. After all, it involves the ultimate deception, because participants are not even aware a study is being conducted! As a result, they have not formally volunteered, nor have they been given a chance to provide informed consent. The problem is that, without informed consent, we are essentially spying on people.

The classic example of this dilemma is a study by Middlemist, Knowles, and Matter (1976). They wanted to study the "personal space" that people use to comfortably separate themselves from others in social settings. Their goal was to eliminate demand characteristics while measuring whether an invasion of one's personal space created physical tension. Their solution was to observe males as they visited the urinal in a public restroom! They invaded personal space by having a confederate use the adjacent urinal, and the measure of participant's resulting tension was the amount of time each took to urinate. To be unobtrusive, a researcher occupied one of the stalls and used a periscope to observe each participant, timing the interval between unzipping and rezipping.

We might justify this study by claiming that it is "scientific research" for the "good of humanity." But, some would argue, this is no different from when a government agency or the police spy on citizens, claiming that it helps catch criminals. After all, spying is spying, and it is wrong to invade people's privacy and violate their rights, regardless of whether it is for scientific advancement and the good of humanity or for national security and rooting out evil.

Others would argue that a public behavior is just that—public—and so it's open to anyone's observation. Thus, a male who uses a public restroom has tacitly agreed to be observed by other males. Conversely, if a male wishes to keep his urinal behavior private, he should not use a public restroom. From this perspective, some researchers claim that it is unethical for scientists *not* to conduct unobtrusive field research, because then they would miss potentially valuable information.

There is no easy resolution to this debate. You might suggest that we obtain informed consent after the study, but by then participants' rights are already violated (and telling people afterwards might be more upsetting than not informing them at all). Instead, it is again the researcher's responsibility to weigh the violation of a person's rights against the potential scientific information to be gained. Therefore, first decide just how "public" participants consider a behavior to be. Are you invading their expected privacy? How strenuously would they object if you asked their permission? How upset would they be if they found out about your spying after the fact? (If you are unsure of the answers, conduct a pilot study in which you ask people these questions.)

Then weigh the invasion of privacy against the potential scientific benefits. For example, Koocher (1977) argued that the above urinal study needlessly invaded participants' privacy because it replicated findings already demonstrated by other, less questionable techniques. (But see the reply of Middlemist, Knowles, & Matter [1977].) Also consider whether the procedure really needs to be conducted as an unobtrusive field study. Do the benefits of a field study outweigh the resulting ethical problems and reduced control that would not be problems in straightforward laboratory research? And finally, remember that the APA's Ethical Principles state that deception must be necessary and that informed consent is required unless the risk to participants is minimal. The more the behavior being studied is an innocuous, mundane public behavior, and the greater the necessity for an unobtrusive field experiment, the more the study can be justified ethically.

In addition to the issues of informed consent, you must also be especially sensitive to the issue of risk in field experiments. Risk is especially important when it comes to the independent variable, because field experiments allow us to manipulate all sorts of real-life situations. However, we are *not* free to abuse the unsuspecting public in the name of "science." (You don't have the right to yell "Fire!" in a crowded theater just to see what happens!) In a laboratory setting, informed consent and the lack of experimental realism are protection for participants: Because they have volunteered to experience our artificial situation, it has less of a real impact on them. In field experiments, however, this is not the case. Our deceptions and pranks can cause people to become really frightened, really angry, or really dangerous. Therefore, researchers have an even greater responsibility to respect and protect participants. In short, there are limits to our right to conduct field studies that impose on others. And, as usual, after resolving these ethical issues for ourselves, we obtain approval from our Human Subjects Review Committee.

REMEMBER You must be particularly sensitive to the ethics of unobtrusive field research.

Role Playing and Simulations

One possible solution when a laboratory or field procedure is just too risky is to have people simulate being in the experiment through **role playing:** Participants pretend they are in a particular situation and we either observe their behavior or have them describe how they would behave. Because the situation is not real, physical or psychological harm is unlikely. Still, caution must be exercised. For example, Haney, Banks, and Zimbardo (1973) created a prison simulation that unexpectedly turned sinister: College men pretending to be guards or prisoners exhibited the worst, most dangerous behaviors associated with a real prison.

In practice, role playing is used infrequently because it has very limited validity and reliability. First, demand characteristics can run rampant: Participants may alter their reactions or descriptions to conform to perceived expectations or to keep their real behaviors private. (Would people simulating the Milgram electric-shock study actually admit that they'd electrocute someone?) Second, people often cannot accurately predict how they would respond. For example, in studies of personal space, participants have given verbal descriptions, manipulated dolls, or drawn lines on paper to indicate how far they would stand from someone else. Yet such predictions seldom match the person's actual behavior when observed under real conditions (Hayduk, 1983).

Research Involving Animals

So far, we've discussed the ethical issues regarding human participants. Psychological research, however, is not limited to the study of humans, and we face similar ethical concerns with animal participants. First, however, let's consider why we even study animals.

In part, psychologists study animals simply because they demonstrate interesting behaviors. For example, researchers conduct laboratory and field research to study the migratory habits of various animals, to study the social-dominance hierarchies in a species, or to simply understand the behaviors an animal exhibits in a normal day's routine. Researchers also study the behavior of a species to compare it with other species, such as when we compare the cognitive capabilities of animals with those of humans. As a result, we have learned that gorillas and chimpanzees can use American Sign Language to communicate, and that a variety of animals understand symbolic relationships.

Researchers also study animals to test an "animal model" regarding some behavior that can then be generalized to all species, including humans. For example, much of what we know about basic brain functioning is based on models that originated from animal research. A common design is to surgically alter an area of the brain and then determine how a behavior is different relative to the behavior in unaltered animals. For example, researchers have learned a great deal about the role the hypothalamus plays in eating behavior by surgically damaging different parts of the hypothalamus in white rats. Researchers also test animal models without using surgical techniques. For example, much of what we know about genetics comes from the breeding of rats and mice. Likewise, animal research has been the basis for many developments in learning and conditioning: Ivan Pavlov's principles of classical conditioning were based on the behavior of dogs, and B. F. Skinner's work on operant conditioning was based on the behavior of rats and pigeons.

Though some people are incensed by the comparisons, animal research often has substantial external validity, generalizing well to many aspects of human behavior, such as education, clinical therapy, and the workplace. Humans are animals, too, and some laws of nature apply to all animals in the same ways. For example, a hypothalamus is a hypothalamus, and the model of how a rat's hypothalamus influences eating behavior has generalized well to humans. Likewise, animal research is often the first step in the development of a new drug or physical treatment. When the treatment works with animals, it often works with humans.

Controls Used with Animal Research

Many animal studies are true experiments conducted in a laboratory: We obtain a random sample of animals (sometimes trapped in the wild but usually purchased from commercial suppliers), randomly assign them to conditions, and apply all of the previous controls we've discussed for reliably and validly manipulating the independent variable. For internal validity, we keep constant the extraneous variables that might produce a confounding, so we maintain their cages and environment consistently for all animals, test them in the same manner, and so on. Similarly, for a valid and reliable dependent variable, we define the scoring criteria, provide practice trials, observe multiple trials, and counterbalance order effects.

Believe it or not, experimenter expectancies and demand characteristics can even be a problem in animal studies. A researcher can inadvertently make errors in measuring or recording scores that are biased toward confirming the research hypothesis. And a researcher's expectations can produce subtle differences in the way that animals are handled and tested, biasing their behavior so that they confirm the hypothesis. These problems even occur when dealing with something as simple as a rat learning a response (Rosenthal, 1976), but they are especially serious when dealing with higher species. In particular, the experimenter must avoid the famous problem of "Clever Hans" (Pfungst, 1911). Hans was a horse that apparently could perform addition! If asked for the sum of 2 plus 2, Hans pawed the ground 4 times; if asked 3 plus 3, he pawed 6 times. It turned out, however, that when Hans was blindfolded, he mysteriously lost his mathematical abilities! Apparently Hans produced correct answers by watching his owner. At the point when the correct sum was reached, the owner showed a relaxed look and Hans stopped pawing the ground.

To minimize such biases, researchers handle all animals in the same way, automate where possible, and use multiple raters and double-blind procedures when subjectively scoring responses. Further, control groups are given appropriate placebos and are handled and tested in the same ways as experimental groups. For example, when testing a drug or surgical procedure, control animals are injected with a placebo or undergo the anesthesia and surgery without receiving the actual treatment. As a result, they experience the same trauma that experimental animals experience.

> **REMEMBER** We control extraneous variables in research involving animals in the same ways as in research involving humans.

The Ethics of Animal Research

There is a continuing debate among scientists and the general public about the ethics of conducting laboratory experiments with animals. It is true that such research often exposes animals to unpleasant and harmful manipulations: In addition to surgical procedures, animals experience independent variables involving electric shocks, food or water deprivation, exposure to toxins, and other aversive conditions. Further, the way to conduct a manipulation check of a surgical procedure is to perform an autopsy. And, even with nonsurgical procedures, animals may be physically or psychologically altered by the treatments, so they usually cannot be studied again and are destroyed.

On the one hand, some animal rights advocates say that animal experiments are unethical because they violate the rights of animals to live free and unharmed. They argue that even though humans have the ability to exploit other animals, we do not have the right to do so. Some even make the more radical argument that laboratory studies of animals do not even provide useful information, so there is no justification for what is seen as animal abuse. From these perspectives, the only ethical way to study animals is through descriptive studies conducted in natural settings.

On the other hand, animal researchers argue that most experiments are justified by the knowledge they produce: The previous criticism is wrong in that animal research has most definitely added substantially to the well-being of humans (and other animals) in important ways. Animal research has been the basis for virtually all modern drugs and surgical techniques, for the identification of numerous toxins and carcinogens, and for many psychological principles. From this perspective, it would be *un*ethical if researchers did *not* conduct animal research to benefit society. Thus, the argument here is that researchers have the right—and the responsibility—to pursue any useful scientific information.

This issue boils down to whether you think the goal of benefitting humans takes precedence over the rights of other animals. If you think it does, then animal research is justified, because there is no other way to obtain the data. It would be more unethical to perform experimental surgical or medical procedures on humans: We cannot undo surgical alterations, and, when first testing a drug, we may have no idea of the harmful side effects that can occur. Likewise, we cannot control the breeding practices of humans in order to study genetics, nor can we administer to humans many of the aversive conditions that have led to important discoveries with animals.

In addition, there are scientific and practical reasons for conducting animal laboratory studies. Descriptive research limits the variables and controls we can employ, so this approach is an inadequate substitute. Also, laboratory research with animals can be conducted quickly and efficiently: Animals are easily obtained and housed, their environment can be controlled and manipulated easily, and, for genetic studies, they have a short gestation period.

Regardless of where your personal feelings fall in this debate, it is wrong to think of animal research as involving the mindless torture of abused animals. As with all people, some researchers may be less than ethical and mistreat their animals. For the vast majority of researchers, however, laboratory animals are valued participants in whom much time, energy, and expense have been invested. It is in the researchers' interest to treat them well, because animals that are abused make poor subjects for a reliable and valid study. Furthermore, the APA's Ethical Principles (1992) provide guidelines for the treatment of research animals, and there are federal, state, and local regulations for the housing and care of animals as well. Because of such rules, animals are well cared for, undergo surgery in sterile settings with anesthesia, and are disposed of in a humane manner.

Finally, the APA's ethical guidelines require that we evaluate animal research in the same way we do human research. First, the harm caused to an animal must be minimized. Thus, we prefer designs that provide positive events as opposed to aversive events, we prefer mildly aversive events to drastic ones, and we prefer temporary external manipulations to permanent surgical ones. Second, we are not frivolous in the treatment of animals, so every aspect of a procedure must be necessary. As usual, the key is whether the procedure is justified by the scientific importance of the information that will be learned. Finally, every research institution must have an institutional review board that ensures the ethical treatment of animal subjects.

REMEMBER Acceptable animal research minimizes the harm done to subjects and must be justified as scientifically important.

Scientific Fraud

There is one more aspect of ethics to consider. Unfortunately, one reason that scientists must always be skeptical about research findings is that other scientists are sometimes guilty of fraud. They may report data from a study inaccurately, they may publish data when no research was conducted, or they may be guilty of *plagiarism,* passing off the ideas and conclusions of others as their own. Often their motivation is to provide further support for their previous conclusions: They needed a replication that failed to materialize, so they "faked" the data. At other times, they are responding to professional pressures to be productive researchers.

An example of the problems caused by fraud is that of Sir Cyril Burt, the first British psychologist to be knighted. Burt studied the inheritability of intelligence, concluding that intelligence is genetically determined. In fact, this view became so pervasive that at one time it influenced the educational system in Great Britain. From the genetic perspective, it made sense to limit education to those who had the innate intelligence to benefit from it. Therefore, based on an intelligence test, children would either go on to high school and college, or end up virtually relegated to the coal mines (Hearnshaw, 1979). However, using Burt's research to justify such a program turned out to be a mistake, because Dorfman (1978) convincingly showed that Burt had faked his results (but there is some doubt about this conclusion too [Joynson, 1989]).

Science tries to prevent fraud in two ways. First, most published research reports undergo **peer review:** Prior to publication, a report's manuscript is sent to several psychologists who are knowledgeable about the research topic. They review the study, checking that conclusions make sense, appropriate procedures are followed, ideas are not plagiarized, and so on. It is hoped, therefore, that fraudulent research will not make it into the research literature. Second, science prevents fraud through replication: Fraudulent conclusions that do make it into the literature will not be supported by subsequent replication efforts. Then, even though not identified as fraudulent, these conclusions will be dropped from the accepted literature.

Regardless though, it is unethical to perpetrate any form of scientific fraud. This includes falsifying results, as well as keeping secret a result that contradicts one's views. In particular, because you are a beginning research report writer, you must be very careful to avoid plagiarism. (As discussed in Appendix A, always reference your source for any idea that you got from reading other research.) Remember that fraud not only violates every rule of science, but it also causes enormous harm: Given the extent to which researches share and integrate research findings, a fraudulent finding can undermine many areas of psychological knowledge. There is no justification for research fraud.

Putting It All Together

Don't underestimate the influence that demand characteristics—especially reactivity and social desirability—can have on the results of a study. Therefore, play psychologist: Use what you know about human nature, defense mechanisms, anxiety, and the like to anticipate demand characteristics. Also, place yourself in the role of a participant and see how you'd feel. Then imagine you're someone just the opposite of you, and see how that person would feel. If people are likely to be biased—or downright dishonest—in their responding, then alter the situation so they'll comfortably and honestly respond to your variables as you intend.

Also, research ethics are not some stuffy topic to merely give lip-service to in a textbook. Unethical practices are unacceptable to the community of scientists, and, practically speaking, you'll never get them past an Institutional Review Board: For a clearly risky procedure, there usually is no convincing scientific justification. As you've seen, one study never definitively "proves" a hypothesis. As a result, conducting an unethical or dangerous study is just not worth it.

To help you remember about demand characteristics and the ethical issues, along with all of the other questions to consider when designing an experiment, consult Checklist 4.3.

CHECKLIST 4.3   Questions to consider when designing an experiment

❏ What is the hypothesis?

❏ Is the hypothesis testable, falsifiable, precise, rational, and parsimonious?

❏ What is the appropriate population?

Designing the independent variable

❏ Will the variable provide content and construct validity?

❏ Will the operational definition prevent confounding?

❏ Will the conditions generalize well?

❏ Will the temporal aspects of the design generalize?

❏ Does the factor reflect common, real-life situations?

❏ Is a control group appropriate?

❏ Is the manipulation strong, without diffusion of treatment?

❏ Is a manipulation check needed?

Designing the dependent variable

❏ Does the variable provide content and construct validity?

❏ Will the variable be confounded?

❏ Will the variable provide external validity?

❏ Do dependent scores reflect common, real-life behavior?

❏ Are scoring criteria complete and sensitive to differences in behavior?

❏ Is range unrestricted, with no ceiling/floor effects?

❏ Are practice trials needed?

❏ Are multiple trials needed?

❏ Are order effects counterbalanced?

❏ Are raters with high inter-rater reliability needed?

Creating consistent procedures

☐ Are instructions clear and complete?

☐ Can automation be used without instrumentation effects?

☐ Is group or individual testing of participants best?

☐ Is a pilot study needed?

Will reactivity, social desirability, or demand characteristics from the environment, task, or experimenter influence scores?

☐ Will the participants react to being observed?

☐ Will the participants give socially desirable responses?

☐ Will the environment bias the participant's responses?

☐ Will the experimenter's characteristics or expectancies influence scores?

☐ Do you keep participants "blind" to the procedure?

☐ Do you keep cues as neutral as possible?

☐ Should you have participants "habituate" to being observed?

☐ Should you use automation?

☐ Should you use single- or double-blind procedures?

☐ Do you use tasks with experimental realism?

☐ Should you hide measurement tasks using unobtrusive techniques?

☐ Do you provide a placebo for control group?

☐ Should you disguise conditions with deception or a field experiment?

Considering ethical issues

☐ Are there physical risks to participants?

☐ Are there psychological risks to participants?

☐ Can you eliminate or minimize risks?

☐ Can you justify risks in terms of the scientific value of results?

☐ Will you obtain informed consent?

☐ Will you provide debriefing and care for participants after the study?

☐ Will you submit the planned procedure to the IRB for review?

CHAPTER SUMMARY

1. *Demand characteristics* are extraneous cues that guide or bias a participant's behavior.

2. *Reactivity* is the demand characteristic occurring because participants are aware that they are being observed.

3. *Social desirability* is the demand characteristic occurring because participants want to behave in a socially acceptable manner.

4. *Experimenter expectancies* is the demand characteristic from cues the researcher provides about the responses participants should give.

5. To reduce demand characteristics, minimize or neutralize cues that may bias participants' responses. This includes using *habituation, unobtrusive measures, deception,* and *unobtrusive field experiments.*

6. *Habituation* familiarizes participants with a procedure before actual data collection begins.

7. An *unobtrusive measurement* is done without making participants aware they are being measured.

8. With *experimental realism,* participants are engaged by the task and thus are less concerned with demand characteristics.

9. A *placebo* provides the demand characteristics of a treatment.

10. In a *single-blind* procedure, participants are unaware of the nature of the treatment. In a *double-blind* procedure, the researcher who tests participants and the participants are unaware of the nature of the treatment.

11. *Research ethics* deal with balancing the right of a researcher to study a behavior with the right of participants to be protected from abuse.

12. The *APA's Ethical Principles of Psychologists and Code of Conduct* require that animal and human participants be protected from physical or psychological harm and that potential harm is scientifically justified.

13. All research is reviewed by the appropriate institutional review committee.

14. Researchers should obtain *informed consent,* should *debrief* participants, and should take care of them after the study.

15. In *role playing,* participants pretend they are in a particular situation.

16. Animal research is conducted to study animals and to test models that can be generalized to humans. This research requires the same controls, including dealing with demand characteristics, as those found in research with humans.

17. Ethical research with animals minimizes the risk to them and is scientifically justified.

18. Science prevents fraud through replication and *peer review.*

KEY TERMS

APA's Ethical Principles *(118)*
debriefing *(121)*
deception *(113)*
demand characteristic *(109)*
distractor task *(114)*
double-blind procedure *(112)*
experimenter expectancies *(111)*
experimental realism *(113)*

habituation *(112)*
Human Subjects Review Committee *(120)*
informed consent *(120)*
peer review *(128)*
placebo *(114)*
physical risk *(118)*
psychological risk *(118)*
reactivity *(109)*
research ethics *(117)*

role playing *(124)*
scientific fraud *(127)*
single-blind procedure *(111)*
social desirability *(110)*
unobtrusive measure *(113)*

REVIEW QUESTIONS

1. (a) What do we mean by demand characteristics? (b) In terms of reliability, internal validity, and external validity, how do demand characteristics harm a study?

2. (a) What is experimental realism, and why do we seek it? (b) How is experimental realism different from ecological validity?

3. (a) What are unobtrusive measures? (b) Why do researchers use unobtrusive measures or deception?

4. What is meant by research ethics?

5. What are the three major issues about risks you must resolve to *design* an ethical study?

6. What are the two major steps you must include to *conduct* an ethical study?

7. (a) Why is informed consent needed? (b) What four things must you provide participants to obtain "informed consent?"

8. (a) What is role playing? (b) What is the advantage of this approach? (c) What is the disadvantage of this approach?

9. In the smile study discussed in this chapter, should participants in a condition be tested individually or in groups? Why?

10. In terms of demand characteristics, (a) why could automation be good for a study? (b) Why could it be bad?

11. (a) In terms of demand characteristics, what potential confounding occurs between a control group and an experimental group? (b) How do you eliminate this confounding?

12. (a) What important ethical issue occurs in unobtrusive field research? (b) According to the APA's Ethical Principles, when don't you need to obtain informed consent?

13. In study 1, the researcher is intentionally either friendly or unfriendly, predicting that being friendly will induce greater levels of cooperation from participants. In study 2, the researcher reads either a list of similar or a list of dissimilar words and then measures participants' memory for the list. (a) How might the researcher bias the outcome of each study? (b) How can this bias be eliminated in each study?

14. You wish to test the proposal that women become more sexually aroused by erotic films depending on whether the plot has a weak or strong theme of love and romance. After showing participants one type of film, you measure the dependent variable using a questionnaire about their arousal. (a) What demand characteristics are a major problem? (b) How would you reduce these demand characteristics? (c) What ethical problems might arise with this study?

15. In question 14, instead of a questionnaire, you decide you must personally interview each participant. (a) What technique for controlling demand characteristics should you use? (b) What aspects of the researcher should you control?

16. (a) What are two major criticisms of laboratory animal research? (b) How would you answer these criticisms?

17. When conducting a study, a researcher wears a white lab coat and carries a clipboard and stopwatch. How might these details influence the internal and external validity of the study?

18. Consider the hypothesis that greater exposure to violence on television results in more aggressive behavior. (a) For ethical reasons, what might be the best design for determining whether this relationship exists? (b) What is the trade-off in being ethical?

19. Your experiment tests whether studying for more time results in higher test grades. You select participants from your research methods class and have them study for either 0, 1, 2, or 4 hours before they take their regular course exam on Chapters 4 and 5 in this book. Ethically speaking, what's wrong with this design?

20. You deliver different speeches to make participants more or less sexist. Then you measure their sexist attitudes using a questionnaire titled "Survey of Sexist Attitudes." (a) What about your independent variable and the measurement task might produce invalid results? (b) Why is it that your manipulation could appear to work even though it does not really alter participants' views? (c) Why could your manipulation appear not to have worked although it really did alter their views? (d) How would you attempt to avoid this problem?

21. In question 20, you instead measure participants' sexism by observing whether they help a confederate of the opposite sex. (a) What demand characteristics might cause helping behavior here? (b) Why might you *fail* to observe differences in attitudes under the different conditions? (c) How would you attempt to avoid this problem?

DISCUSSION QUESTIONS

1. Say that again you conduct a study in which you play one of several types of music to people, and then suddenly pull out and shoot a (blank) pistol. You measure participants' anxiety level in order to determine whether different types of music cause people to remain more or less calm in the face of startling stimuli. (a) How might demand characteristics influence your data? (b) What specific information must you include when obtaining informed consent? (c) What risks are present in this study? (d) To minimize risks, what aspects of the participants you select should be considered? (e) What should your debriefing include? (f) What major flaw will occur in this study as you continue to conduct it? (g) Should you conduct this study? Why?

2. You have discovered a new drug treatment for a serious mental illness that you wish to test. What conflicting ethical and design principles do you face when considering whether to include a control condition?

3. You want to unobtrusively observe children at a day-care center, judging how aggressively they behave when playing with dolls after watching an adult behave aggressively. (a) What problems do you foresee arising from demand characteristics? (b) How would you deal with these biases? (c) Why is this design a problem ethically? (d) Explain how you would meet each of the APA guidelines in this study.

4. For the study in question 14, the film lasts 25 minutes and is in black and white. The questionnaire consists of 20 Likert-type statements in which the scale for each is between 1 (strongly agree) and 5 (strongly disagree.) Write the instructions you would give to participants, create an informed consent form, and determine what you would say during the debriefing.

5

Controlling Participant Variables Using Between-Subjects and Within-Subjects Designs

GETTING STARTED

To understand this chapter, recall the following:

- From Chapter 2, recall what reliability and internal and external validity are.
- From Chapter 3 recall why we use multiple trials and what order effects are.
- Also from Chapter 3, recall what the restriction of range is, what a powerful design is, and why a powerful design is important.

Your goals in this chapter are to learn:

- How participant variables influence external validity.
- How fluctuating variables create error variance that limits how convincing—powerful—a relationship is.
- How participant variables influence reliability and internal validity.
- What constitutes a between-subjects design and how to control participant variables in this design.
- What constitutes a within-subjects design and how to control participant variables in this design.
- The difference between matched groups and repeated measures designs.
- What randomization, partial counterbalancing, and complete counterbalancing are.

135

*S*o far, we've taken the participants in a study pretty much for granted. Yet participants are thinking, feeling, and behaving organisms who can modify any measurement procedure. Therefore, an important aspect of designing a study is to consider the characteristics of the participants. In this chapter you will see how to recognize participant variables that can influence your results, examine techniques for controlling such variables, and consider the impact that such controls have on the interpretation of a study.

How Participant Variables Influence External Validity

Participants respond differently to a manipulation because no two individuals are identical. *Participant variables* are inherent, personal characteristics that distinguish one individual from another. Physically, participants differ in gender, age, metabolism, hormones, the speed their neurons fire, musculature, coordination, height, and weight. Because their physical machinery is not identical, their physical reactions are not identical. Cognitively, they differ in style, strategies, intelligence, and memory, so they do not all process a stimulus identically. They also differ in terms of personal histories and experiences, social and economic standing, and so on. As a result, some are more familiar with a task than others, they are influenced by moods in different ways, and they have different motivations. Socially, their attitudes and personality differ, so some will be more reactive, more competitive, or more attentive.

To communicate all of these differences, we sometimes use the catch-all phrase **individual differences**, referring to the characteristics that make individuals different from one another and thus produce different responses to the same situation. When discussing participant variables, we really mean any variable that makes one individual different from another.

Depending on the situation, a participant variable can be an independent variable, a dependent variable, or an extraneous variable. For now, we'll discuss how extraneous participant variables can influence a study. This begins when defining the relevant population.

Defining the Population

Remember that it is the external validity of a design that allows us to accurately generalize results to the population, describing how all individuals would behave under the conditions of our experiment. Participant variables are extremely important to external validity, because they define the population we can generalize to. We define the population by creating selection criteria. **Selection criteria** define participants in terms of the characteristics we require for allowing them to participate in the study. The criteria that define a sample also define the population it represents. Therefore, we create selection criteria so that, ideally, the sample is *representative* of our target population: It is a good example, accurately reflecting the individuals and thus the behaviors and scores that are found in the population we wish to study.

Defining the sample first depends on the constructs and hypothesis being investigated. When studying the behavior of children, for instance, the sample and population should be composed of children of a specified age. Recognize, however, that a population is not a fixed entity defined by one variable. Members of a population may differ along many variables: The population of children, for example, contains males and females from different cultures and backgrounds, with different abilities, and so on. How well results generalize to the population depends on how much the sample has in common with the population in terms of *all* of the participant variables that can influence responses. If individuals having a particular characteristic are excluded, we may end up with a biased and unrepresentative example of the population, thus creating a biased picture of how all members of the population behave. In short, the selection criteria should produce a sample that is similar to the population along all relevant participant variables so that the sample is essentially a miniature version of the population.

> **REMEMBER** A sample should reflect the important characteristics of the population being studied.

Limitations on the Representativeness of a Sample

Recall that we randomly select participants so that every individual in the population has the same chances of being selected. As discussed in Chapter 2, we may use *simple random sampling* (similar to drawing names from a hat) or *systematic random sampling* (selecting every *n*th name from a list). By selecting participants in an unbiased and unselective manner, we allow the diverse characteristics of the population to occur in the sample as often, and to the same degree, as they occur in the population. As a whole, therefore, the individuals in the study should be representative of the population. However, certain de facto limitations will always be present to prevent some members of the population from being selected. First, the entire population may not be identifiable. For example, if you peruse the research on alcoholism and its treatment, you'll find that it is largely limited to males. Historically, female alcoholics have been unwilling to identify themselves, so they have been unavailable as research subjects.

Second, we are unable to contact all identifiable members of the population. Usually the sample is limited to those people living near us. If we then solicit participants using the telephone directory, the population is further limited, excluding the rich and famous with unlisted numbers, as well as poor people who have no phone. Many experiments are even more limited, because the samples are made up of students at the researcher's university. Further, we are often able to reach only certain students—those enrolled in psychology courses.

Because of such limitations, we usually cannot obtain a truly random sample from the population. In practice, many researchers solicit participants by announcing an experiment in college classes or by posting announcements on bulletin boards or in the college newspaper. Under these circumstances, selection is random only to the extent that we try to give every potential participant in the available portion of the population an equal opportunity to volunteer for the study. Often we then test all volunteers who meet the selection criteria, or we use simple or systematic random sampling to select from those who constitute the volunteer pool.

By excluding some members of the population, we may overrepresent some participant variables and fail to represent others, so that the sample is unrepresentative of the population. For example, because of its admission standards and cost, a particular college will attract a certain type of student. Then, whether such limitations seriously reduce external validity depends upon the behavior under study. If we are studying consumer attitudes toward a product and exclude poor people from the sample, we ignore an important segment of the population and thus reduce external validity. However, if poor people cannot afford the product, then they *should* be excluded from the sample. Likewise, some behaviors of college students, such as memory or other cognitive processes, may not generalize well to the adult population as a whole, because college students are better educated and smarter than adults in general.

Researchers often use college students as subjects because students are conveniently available and findings about many of their basic behaviors do generalize well to the larger population. For some behaviors, however, you may need to broaden the population. Milgram's infamous electric-shock study did not rely on college students, because, given their age and position, they might have been especially responsive to authority figures. Instead, the general adult population was sampled. Always consider the population you wish to generalize to, and determine whether any limitations in the sample will seriously reduce the validity of your conclusions. If so, take the necessary steps to obtain a more representative sample. Chapter 9 examines techniques for contacting a wider range of participants.

Sample Size and Representativeness

Working within the available population, we then seek to adequately represent it. An important aspect of this process is deciding on N: The symbol N stands for the number of participants in a study, and n stands for the number of participants observed in a condition (adding all of the ns equals N). To maximize external validity, the general rule is "the more the merrier": The larger a sample, the more of the population that is observed, so it is more likely that the sample will include all relevant types of participants. Therefore, we are more likely to obtain an accurate, representative sample rather than a biased, misleading one. Conversely, with only a few participants, we are more likely to obtain a sample having rather atypical characteristics, so that it is not representative of the population.

"The more the merrier" does not mean that you need to test hundreds of participants per condition. The range of N in laboratory experiments is often between 50 and 100, with ns in the range of 15 to 30. The results of such studies are replicated with considerable frequency, at least in terms of the general pattern of results. Thus, with Ns in this range, one random sample is roughly comparable to another, and the findings they produce *are* externally valid. Of course, if more participants can easily be tested, they further increase the external validity of a study.

You are not required to have the same number of participants—"equal ns"— in all conditions. However, remember that you want to generalize the results of each condition and seek the same level of confidence in each. Therefore, avoid having only a few participants in a particular condition. Instead, divide them so that there is close to the same number of participants per condition and therefore an adequate, comparable representation of the population in each. (Note, too, that statistical procedures are most accurate with close to equal ns, and they are often much easier to perform with equal ns.)

Limitations on the Representativeness of Volunteers

Even with a large N from a not-too-limited portion of the population, the representativeness of a sample still can be limited because only some individuals will end up participating in the study. Then the external validity of the results suffers because of the peculiar characteristics of these participants.

First, external validity is limited because of the volunteer bias. The **volunteer bias** is the bias that arises because a sample contains only those individuals who are willing to participate in the study. There are considerable differences between people who volunteer for a study and those who do not (Rosenthal & Rosnow, 1975). Among other things, volunteers tend to have a higher social status and intelligence, to exhibit a greater need for approval, and to be less authoritarian and conforming. Also, participants who find the research topic interesting or personally relevant are more likely to volunteer, as are those who expect to be positively evaluated.

Also, those who complete a study may be biased because they are not naive about psychological research. **Subject sophistication** is a bias that occurs when participants are knowledgeable about research. People may have participated in previous experiments, or they may have studied research methods or the psychological topic under investigation. Participants also gain experience and knowledge about our manipulations over the course of their participation. Because of this knowledge, they may be more or less susceptible to reactivity and other demand characteristics, or they may be aware of our deceptions or predictions and more prone to diffusion of treatment. Then their behavior is different from the general, unsophisticated population. (And note that subject sophistication even applies to animal participants that, through experience, become more relaxed or anxious during testing, learn how to perform a task better, and so on.)

REMEMBER   Participants may form a biased sample because of *volunteer bias* and *subject sophistication*.

Although these threats to external validity are not entirely controllable, you can try to limit them. Try to make the mechanics of volunteering and participating in the study easy for all potential participants. And initially solicit a wide range of both sophisticated and unsophisticated subjects. As usual, also consider a study's possible flaws when interpreting it. During debriefing you can question participants about their sophistication or their reasons for volunteering to gauge how biased the sample is.

How Fluctuating Variables Influence a Relationship through Error Variance

Once you have identified the sample's characteristics that you seek for maximizing external validity, then consider any additional participant variables that may influence your results. Remember, we want to control any extraneous variable that can fluctuate *within* a condition or *between* conditions. To understand how such fluctuating variables influence the mathematical relationship you obtain, let's examine a specific example.

Say that we're interested in the hypothesis that people who witness a crime or other event recall the event better when they are hypnotized. We decide to create two samples of participants who will each watch a videotape of a supposed robbery. Later, one group will be hypnotized to the same extent and then answer 30 questions about the details of the robbery. The other group—the control condition—will answer the questions without benefit of hypnosis. Thus, the conditions of the independent variable are the presence or absence of hypnosis, and the dependent variable is the number of questions answered correctly. (For ethical safeguards, we use a trained hypnotist, obtain explicit consent after informing participants about the hypnosis, ensure that there is little risk from the hypnosis, fully debrief participants, and obtain prior approval from our IRB.) You can envision this design as shown in Table 5.1. Each X stands for a participant's recall score—the total number of questions each correctly answers. We hope to

Table 5.1 Diagram of Hypnosis Study

The independent variable is degree of hypnosis and the dependent variable is recall.

	No Hypnosis	Hypnosis
Recall	X	X
Scores	X	X
→	X	X
	X	X
	X	X
	$\overline{X}$	$\overline{X}$

demonstrate a relationship in which, as the amount of hypnosis increases, recall scores also tend to increase. Likewise, we can summarize the scores in each condition by, for example, computing the mean $(\overline{X})$ of the scores in each column. Comparing these should show that, "on average," scores increase with increased hypnosis.

To allow a clear interpretation of the variables and behaviors under study, we apply all of the controls discussed previously. Thus we seek a reliable and strong manipulation of hypnosis so that when under hypnosis, all participants are equally and deeply hypnotized, and when in the control group, all participants are equally alert and awake. It is because we want a reliable presentation of the robbery that we show the same videotape to all participants, and we would want to develop reliable and valid questions that really measure each person's memory of the robbery. For a reliable measure of an individual's memory, we ask 30 questions and then produce a summary score for each person. But remember that a problem with multiple trials is order effects, the influence of practice, fatigue, or experience over a sequence of trials. Any one order in which participants complete the 30 questions—with its peculiar effects—could bias scores so they are especially high or low. Therefore, we might control order effects by testing half of the participants in each condition under one of two orders. For internal validity, we eliminate confoundings so that differences in recall scores between the conditions are really due to differences in hypnosis. And we seek external validity so that the way the samples perform is really the way the general population performs.

At the same time, we cannot claim to have demonstrated anything about a behavior unless we find a mathematical relationship in the sample data, so our conclusions are only as good as the data we collect. (Garbage in, garbage out!) Therefore, we also seek a *powerful* design that produces a clear and convincing relationship. For example, compare the powerful and unpowerful examples in Table 5.2. In the unpowerful data, instead of there being one recall score associ-

Table 5.2 Possible Data from Hypnosis Study Showing Unpowerful and Powerful Relationships

Unpowerful		Powerful	
No Hypnosis	*Hypnosis*	*No Hypnosis*	*Hypnosis*
30	20	10	30
10	8	10	30
23	29	10	30
15	23	10	30
17	20	10	30
$\overline{X} = 19$	$\overline{X} = 20$	$\overline{X} = 10$	$\overline{X} = 30$

ated with one condition and a different recall score consistently associated with the other, we see a weak relationship that barely shows a consistent increase in scores with hypnosis: There is a wide range of *different* scores *within* each condition, increases produced by hypnosis are small when they occur, and the pattern is inconsistent because sometimes there is not an increase—scores remain the same or even decrease between no hypnosis and hypnosis. On the other hand, the powerful data produce a much stronger relationship, providing a much more convincing demonstration that hypnosis improves memory. First, hypnosis makes a relatively big difference in recall scores. Second, there is clearly one recall score associated with the control condition, and a different one under hypnosis, so that the pattern is consistently shown for all participants.

Two important statistical terms are used as shorthand for describing the inconsistency in scores within a condition. First, when there are differences among the scores in a group, the scores are described as **variable,** or as showing **variability.** As you'll see in Chapter 6, one statistical measure of variability is the statistic called the "variance." Therefore, the second name for the inconsistency or differences among scores within the conditions of an experiment is **error variance.** As you've seen, part of producing a powerful study is to minimize the inconsistency or error variance, so that you have a clearer, more convincing relationship.

REMEMBER   To produce a strong and convincing relationship, minimize error variance, the differences among scores found within each condition.

The Connection between a Powerful Relationship and Reliability and Validity

Here is a key part of designing a study: The techniques for producing a reliable and valid study are the *same* as those for producing a convincing—powerful—relationship between the scores. Both goals are achieved by controlling extraneous variables that may fluctuate *between* or *within* a condition. For example, variables that fluctuate within a condition threaten reliability because the situation is different for each individual, causing him or her to respond differently. This also produces differences in scores within each condition, producing a weaker, less convincing relationship. Likewise, extraneous variables that fluctuate between conditions produce confoundings and reduce internal validity, because we cannot know whether differences in the scores between conditions are due to the manipulation or to the extraneous variables. Such fluctuating variables also weaken the relationship because their influence will vary from one minute to the next, producing a less consistent pattern of increasing or decreasing scores.

Ideally, therefore, we seek to control *all* extraneous variables so that everything that might influence the results is the same between and within conditions.

This includes environmental, researcher, and measurement variables, as well as participant variables.

To identify participant variables to control, look for any characteristic of an individual that is substantially correlated with—related to—the independent or dependent variables. First, look for differences among participants that might influence the impact of the independent variable. In the hypnosis study, for example, people differ in how easily they are to hypnotize, how long they will remain "under," and so on. If participants differ along this variable, then everyone in the hypnosis condition will not experience the same hypnosis, producing inconsistent differences in recall between the conditions. Or say we're studying the effects of alcohol. Because of differences in weight, metabolism, or tolerance, people will be more or less affected by a particular amount of alcohol, producing an inconsistent effect of each condition of the independent variable.

Second, look for differences among participants that might influence how a response on the dependent variable is made. For example, a person's inherent memory ability will influence his or her recall of the videotaped robbery. Or if we have participants read a description of the robbery, a person's vocabulary and reading skills are correlated with, and thus might influence, his or her comprehension of the description, in turn influencing retention of it. These variables will produce differences in recall scores between or within conditions, although they will have nothing to do with the effect of our manipulation.

REMEMBER   A participant variable that is correlated with the influence of the independent variable or with performance on the dependent variable is a potential variable to control.

Generally, when the stimulus is rather concrete and elicits a physical response, look for participant variables that influence physical responses. These may be physiological, such as participants' height or degree of coordination, or psychological, such as their cognitive abilities or motivation. For stimuli and responses that involve social behaviors or attitudes, look for variables that influence social processes, such as personality or cultural differences. Of course, the research literature is helpful in identifying important participant variables to control: Research specifically related to your study will indicate variables that others believed needed controlling, and general research investigating individual differences will indicate variables that can influence the behavior you're studying.

For help in remembering the various ways that participant variables influence a study, consult Checklist 5.1.

As you'll see in the remainder of this chapter, you can control participant variables in a number of ways. When considering which to use, you must simultaneously decide how you'll select participants for each condition. That's because there are two general approaches to use when creating conditions, and each determines how to control important participant variables. The first technique is to create a between-subjects design.

CHECKLIST 5.1	Questions to consider when controlling participant variables

❑ Do the characteristics of participants limit generalizability?

❑ Is the sample size (*N*) sufficient to represent the population?

❑ Does the volunteer bias or subject sophistication influence the results?

❑ Are extraneous participant variables strongly correlated with the independent or dependent variable?

❑ Will fluctuating participant variables within conditions reduce reliability and the relationship's strength?

❑ Will fluctuating participant variables between conditions reduce internal validity and the relationship's strength?

Controlling Participant Variables in a Between-Subjects Design

In a **between-subjects design**, a different group of participants is randomly selected for each condition of an independent variable. You can recognize this type of design, because participants are tested under only one level of the independent variable. We simply select one random sample for one condition, and a different, separate sample for the other condition(s).

Whether a between-subjects design is appropriate depends first on whether it's appropriate to compare one group of participants in one condition to an entirely different batch of participants in another condition. For example, in the hypnosis study, we might not want participants to have practice by seeing the videotape and answering the memory questions in more than one condition. If this is an important consideration, we may choose a between-subjects design.

For a between-subjects design to be appropriate, however, it must also provide acceptable control over extraneous participant variables. With a between-subjects design, our first line of defense for controlling participant variables is random assignment.

Random Assignment

In a between-subjects design involving a true independent variable, we randomly assign participants to each condition. This controls participant variables by randomly mixing them, so that differences in a variable are balanced out in each condition. For example, by randomly assigning people to our hypnosis conditions, some who have a good memory and some who do not should end up in each condition. Overall, differences in recall scores between the conditions should not be due to differences in the memory ability of participants, so this potential confounding should be eliminated.

Be careful, however, to assign participants in a truly random way, avoiding any hidden variable that determines their assignment. For example, we wouldn't assign students who sit in the front of a class all to one condition and those sitting in the back to the other. Where a student sits is not random, so we might confound the conditions with various personal characteristics. Similarly, do not assign to the same condition all people who first volunteer for a study. Those who participate early in a study may be more prompt, compulsive, or ambitious than later subjects. Instead, randomly assign participants to different conditions as they arrive, so that such characteristics are spread out between conditions.

Pros and Cons of Random Assignment   Given how frequently research findings can be replicated, random assignment—and random selection—are powerful tools for producing balanced, representative samples in each condition. This is especially heartening because we often cannot identify the important participant variables to be controlled. With random assignment, we don't need to know the variables that are being controlled, because whatever they are in the population, we allow them to occur in a balanced way in each condition.

There are, however, three potential problems with random assignment. First, random assignment does not guarantee a balance of participant variables within each condition. Thus, for example, by chance we might still have people in one hypnosis condition who all have a much better memory than those in another, so that the independent variable is confounded. Second, random assignment works less well with small samples, so if ns are small, we are still likely to have groups that differ along important participant variables. Third, when random assignment does balance out a variable effectively, the variable then fluctuates *within* each condition. Remember that the reason we control a variable is because we think that more or less of it *does in fact* have more or less of an impact on the independent or dependent variable. Therefore, random assignment intentionally changes such variables within each condition, producing potentially large differences—large error variance—among the dependent scores within each condition. This will weaken the relationship and reduce the power of a study. For example, random selection and assignment should produce participants in the *same* hypnosis condition having different memory abilities. This may then cause them to produce different recall scores, so that we end up with a weaker, less consistent relationship.

Because of these potential problems, researchers sometimes instead actively control individual participant variables. One approach is to balance a variable.

Balancing Participant Variables

We do not leave the balancing of a critical participant variable to random chance, because the possibility of a serious confounding is too great. Instead, we control the variable by systematically balancing or "counterbalancing" its influence within each condition.

To balance a participant variable, we first make the variable part of the selection criteria. For obvious physical or personal characteristics (gender and age), we merely solicit participants who meet the criteria. For less obvious characteristics, we **pretest** participants: Prior to conducting the study, we measure potential participants on the variable to be controlled. For example, we may measure a physical attribute (strength), a cognitive skill (reading ability), or a personality trait (anxiety level). Recognize that conducting a pretest is no different from measuring participants on a dependent variable, so you need a valid and reliable measurement technique that takes into account such issues as scoring criteria, sensitivity, demand characteristics, order effects, and so on.

Using the pretest information, we create a separate subject "pool" for each aspect of the participant variable we wish to balance. For example, in the hypnosis study, we could control participants' gender by creating a pool of males and a pool of females. To control for memory ability, we could identify those males and females who have good and poor eyewitness memory using an appropriate pretest. Then we assign participants so that each pool is represented in each condition in a balanced way. For example, we could randomly select and randomly assign participants so that 25% of those assigned to each condition are from the male good-memory pool, 25% are from the female good-memory pool, and so on. This design is shown in Table 5.3. The Xs in each row represent participants'

Table 5.3 Diagram of the Hypnosis Experiment Showing Balancing of Gender and Memory Ability

Each row represents people having the same gender and memory ability.

Participant Pool	No Hypnosis	Hypnosis
Male Good Memory	XXX . . .	XXX . . .
Female Good Memory	XXX . . .	XXX . . .
Male Poor Memory	XXX . . .	XXX . . .
Female Poor Memory	XXX . . .	XXX . . .
	$\overline{X}$	$\overline{X}$

scores from the corresponding pool. To determine the effect of the conditions of hypnosis, we ignore gender and memory ability and average all scores vertically in a condition. Then the scores in each condition should be equally influenced by differences in memory ability and gender, so that any differences between conditions cannot be confounded by these variables. (All other design issues still apply, so again we could also counterbalance the order in which participants complete the 30 questions, and so on.)

This procedure introduces an important new term: Above, when we ignore the gender and memory ability of participants and obtain an overall mean score in each column, we are "collapsing" across the participant variables. **Collapsing** across a variable means that we combine scores from the different amounts or categories of that variable. In the hypnosis study we collapsed across gender and memory ability. If we used a male experimenter with half the participants in each condition and a female experimenter with the other half, we would collapse across experimenter gender by combining the scores of people tested by both experimenters, computing one overall mean for each condition. Likewise, when we test participants on multiple trials in a condition, we average them together, so we collapse across trials.

REMEMBER Collapsing across a variable means that we combine the scores from the different levels of the variable.

Pros and Cons of Balancing If we find a relationship, then, because we've balanced the participant variable, we can be sure that it was not a confounding, so we have greater internal validity. We also have greater external validity, because we demonstrate the relationship even with the different levels of the variable present in each condition. In the hypnosis study, we are sure gender and memory ability do not confound the results, and we demonstrate a more general relationship because different genders and memory abilities are present.

Of course, that's if we find a relationship. As with random assignment, the drawback to counterbalancing is that it involves changing a variable *within* conditions, so there may be greater variability in the scores within each condition. Above, by including in each condition the scores of males and females who have good and poor memories, we are likely to see larger variability in recall scores than if we tested only males or only people with a good memory. Thus, counterbalancing can produce a relatively large error variance, so we obtain a less consistent relationship and have less power.

Also, if you think about it long enough, you can identify any number of variables to counterbalance in any study. The drawback is that extensive balancing schemes greatly complicate the design of a study. Further, because different participants must be tested with each level of a balanced variable, this can dramatically increase the number of individuals required in each condition. And finally, a pretest may alert participants to the variables under study or to the purpose and predictions of the research. This knowledge can lead to diffusion of treatment, or it can communicate demand characteristics that participants respond to during the experiment proper. (To avoid such problems, some form of deception in the pretest may be necessary.)

> **REMEMBER** Balancing a participant variable ensures that it cannot confound the results, but it may result in increased error variance, and pretesting may communicate demand characteristics.

With random assignment and counterbalancing, our *hope* is that, overall, the group tested in one condition is comparable to the group in the other condition. The problem, however, is that the balancing act just described simply may not work, and then the independent variable is confounded by a participant variable. Instead, to gain greater control, we can more directly ensure that the individuals in one condition are comparable to those in the other conditions. One way to do this is to use a matched-groups design.

Matched-Groups Designs

In a **matched-groups design,** each participant in one condition "matches" a participant in the other conditions on one or more extraneous participant variable. For example, to control the participant variable of memory ability, we could create two samples containing participants who are the same—have "matching" memory abilities.

To create matched samples, first identify pairs of participants who have the same matching score on the variable to be controlled (using a pretest if necessary). Then randomly assign each member of the pair to one condition. Thus, we would identify matching pairs of people who have the same memory ability and assign one member of each pair to a condition. If we select two people who have a very good memory, we'll randomly assign one person to the hypnosis condition and the other person to the control condition. Likewise, someone with a terrible memory in one condition is matched with a person having an equally terrible memory in the other condition, and so on.

We can also match participants on more than one variable. For example, we might want to create matching samples in terms of gender as well as memory ability. This would produce the design shown in Table 5.4. Each row contains the scores of a matched pair of participants: The first pair consists of two males, both with a good memory. The second pair is two females, both with a good memory, and so on. Think of a row as representing a very small experiment with one participant per condition. Any difference in the scores between the conditions cannot be due to differences in participants' memory ability or gender, because these variables are constant. Then, because having one participant per condition is not a reliable approach, we replicate this study with other pairs.

You can match participants using any relevant participant variable, such as weight, age, physical ability, or the school they attend. You can also rely on natural pairs to match participants. For example, roommates or husband-and-wife teams are already matched in terms of having the same housing arrangements.

Table 5.4   Diagram of the Hypnosis Experiment

Each row represents two people who are matched on gender and memory. Xs represent each person's recall score.

	No Hypnosis	Hypnosis
Pair 1: Male Good Memory	X	X
Pair 2: Female Good Memory	X	X
Pair 3: Male Poor Memory	X	X
Pair 4: Female Poor Memory	X	X
	$\overline{X}$	$\overline{X}$

Another common approach is to test identical twins, assigning one of each pair to each condition. Because genetic influences are equated, any differences in a behavior between groups must be due to environmental causes. Likewise, in animal research, pairs may be created from litter mates to match them on variables related to their experiences.

If it is difficult to find participants who have the same score on the matching variable, you can rank-order participants and create pairs using adjacent ranked scores. Thus, above, the two males whose memory ability ranks them as first and second in our subject pool would form one pair; the two with the next best memory would form the next pair, and so on.

REMEMBER   In a matched-groups design, each participant in one condition matches a participant in every other condition in terms of one or more extraneous variables.

Pros and Cons of Matched Groups   The advantage to matching is that it ensures that in every condition there is a participant with virtually the same score on the variable(s) we wish to control. This keeps these variables constant across the conditions, eliminating this potential confounding. By controlling memory ability and gender in the preceding experiment, for example, we have greater internal validity for inferring that differences between the conditions are due to our treatment.

There are, however, limitations to a matched-groups design. Again, we have the problem that pretesting may create diffusion of treatment or communicate demand characteristics. Also, we are again intentionally changing the levels of an extraneous variable within each condition, so we might increase the variability of scores within each condition. Again, this produces a less powerful or convincing relationship. (But as you'll see in Chapter 6, the statistical analysis for matched groups makes this less of a problem than with the previous techniques we've discussed.) Finally, there is the practical problem that, to find matching participants, we may have to pretest many individuals or settle for a very small N. This is especially so with a design that involves several conditions of the independent variable, in which matching triplets or larger numbers can be very difficult if not impossible.

> **REMEMBER** A matched-groups design ensures that the conditions are comparable on the matching variable, but matching can increase error variance, and it can be impractical.

Limiting the Population

An alternative to counterbalancing or matching a participant variable is to limit the population based on that variable, so that we keep the variable constant. Then the variable cannot influence the results. For example, if we expect males and females to differ greatly in how hypnosis influences their memory, we might limit the population to males only or to females only.

We limit the population through selection criteria. We pretest participants to identify those who meet the criteria and are approximately the same on the participant variable. For example, we might create a pool of males who all have the same very good eyewitness memory. Then, from this pool, we would randomly select and assign participants to the conditions.

Pros and Cons of Limiting the Population   There are two advantages to selecting participants from a more limited population. First, this increases internal validity by eliminating a potential confounding that might occur with random assignment: By testing only males, for example, we need not be concerned about whether gender is balanced in each condition. Second, this increases power by reducing the error variance: The more similar the participants, the less variable the scores are likely to be within each condition. Above, differences in scores within a condition that might occur between males and females will not occur when all participants are males.

There are also two drawbacks to limiting the population. First, if we become too selective, we may overly restrict the range of scores. For example, by limiting the study to just men with a very good memory, we might see little or no difference in recall scores between the hypnosis conditions. Second, because we are more selective in choosing participants, they represent a more limited population, and so external validity is reduced. Thus, if we test only males, we will have no evidence for generalizing to females.

Researchers usually opt for increased power and internal validity, even at the expense of external validity. Therefore, the advantages of limiting the population usually outweigh the disadvantages.

> **REMEMBER** Limiting the population eliminates potential confounding by a participant variable and reduces error variance, but at the possible cost of restricted range and reduced external validity.

Selecting the Approach for Dealing with Participant Variables

Random assignment, counterbalancing, matching, and limiting the population are not mutually exclusive procedures. We could, for example, limit the population to only one gender and then balance or match memory ability. And regardless of the extent to which we counterbalance and limit the population, we still rely on random selection and random assignment to balance any other participant variables within and between conditions.

In selecting a procedure or combination of procedures, you are faced with two considerations. First, how important is the variable? The more likely it is to influence the results, the more you must actively control it. Never leave the control of a highly influential variable to random assignment: Either counterbalance it, match it, or limit the population to keep it constant.

Second, weigh the goal of having the power to find a convincing relationship with the goal of making externally valid inferences about the relationship. The larger the number of variables that we balance, the more that variables that influence scores are changing, so the greater the error variance may be. Conversely, keeping a variable constant by limiting the population reduces potential error variance, but at the cost of reduced external validity because a more unique type of participant is being tested.

Recognize that the same problems arise when controlling *any* environmental, researcher, or measurement variable as well. For example, we could balance experimenter gender, using a male experimenter with half of the people in each hypnosis condition and a female experimenter with the other half. This would produce greater generalizability, because we demonstrate the relationship with both types of experimenter. But we would balance this variable because we expect that whether a male or female experimenter is present *makes a difference* to participants and to their scores. Therefore, counterbalancing will produce greater variability in scores within the conditions. If only a male or only a female experimenter was present throughout, however, we would see less error variance, but we would also demonstrate the relationship in a more unique situation.

> **REMEMBER** When deciding to control *any* extraneous variable, consider its threat to reliability and internal validity versus whether your control will substantially increase error variance or limit external validity.

There is no easy solution to this predicament. You should strive for a happy medium, but, if pushed, researchers generally risk producing a unique situation. So, counterbalance only those few variables that are *likely* to confound the independent variable or that *seriously* bias dependent scores. Control other, more minor variables by keeping them constant.

You can see all of the questions to consider when designing a between-subjects study in Checklist 5.2. If the answers to these questions are such that you cannot solve the problem of controlling participant variables, you might instead use a within-subjects design.

Controlling Participant Variables in a Within-Subjects Design

On the one hand, a problem with the preceding methods is that we may not even know the important participant variables to control in a particular study. Also, for situations in which we need to control participant variables, often there are *many* to control, and it's almost impossible to counterbalance or match on numerous variables. On the other hand, however, the more variables we can match participants on, the more we eliminate potential confounding. In fact, the ideal would be to have participants in all conditions who are identical in every respect. The way to have identical participants is to test the *same* individual in each condition. Therefore, when matching or counterbalancing is unworkable but the study calls for tightly controlling participant variables, we employ a within-subjects design. In a **within-subjects design**, the same participants are tested under all levels of an independent variable. Another name for a within-subjects design is repeated measures. In a **repeated-measures design**, we repeatedly measure the same participants under all conditions of an independent variable.

For example, in the hypnosis study, consider all of the cognitive, motivational, physiological, and experiential differences between participants that

CHECKLIST 5.2   Questions to consider when selecting a between-subjects design

❏ Will random assignment control important participant variables?

❏ Will balancing control important participant variables?

❏ Will matching control important participant variables?

❏ Will pretesting create major problems?

❏ Will limiting the population restrict generalizability?

❏ Will controls add error variance that weakens the relationship?

might influence their memory. We're not sure which of these variables are the most important to control, and even if we were, counterbalancing them all in a between-subjects design would be unworkable, limiting the population would severely limit generalizability, and finding participants who match on so many variables would be impossible. The solution is a repeated-measures design: We'd show one group of participants two videotapes of two different robberies—once when participants are hypnotized and once when not—and for each condition we'd have them complete a series of 30 questions to measure their recall of the robbery.

Notice that repeated measures is different from multiple trials. With multiple trials, we repeatedly observe a participant *within* a condition to obtain a reliable estimate of the typical response to that condition. (We're asking participants 30 questions—30 trials—to obtain a reliable recall score for them in a condition.) With repeated measures, regardless of the number of trials per condition, we repeatedly observe the same participant under all conditions of a factor to control participant variables. (We're observing participants under both the control and experimental conditions to keep such variables as their memory ability constant.)

The layout for this design is shown in Table 5.5. Each row represents the summary recall score from one participant tested under both conditions, so although we have one sample of participants, we have two samples of scores. Again, think of a row as representing an experiment with one participant in both conditions. Any difference in recall cannot be due to participant variables, because they are all constant. Then, for greater reliability, we replicate this study with other participants.

All of the usual design requirements apply. Repeated measures don't control for differences among participants *within* a particular condition, so we rely on

Table 5.5   Diagram of Repeated-Measures Design of Hypnosis Experiment

Each row represents one person tested under both conditions. Each X represents a person's recall score for the trials in the condition.

	No Hypnosis	Hypnosis
Participant 1 (Male, Order1)	X	X
Participant 2 (Male, Order2)	X	X
Participant 3 (Female, Order1)	X	X
Participant 4 (Female, Order2)	X	X
	$\overline{X}$	$\overline{X}$

random assignment or counterbalancing to control individual differences here. Thus, for example, as in Table 5.5, we control participants' gender within each condition by counterbalancing it, testing an equal number of males and females. Further, we still have the problem of order effects owing to the order in which participants complete the 30 recall questions within a condition. Therefore, we might control order effects by testing each half of the participants under one of two orders (indicated in Table 5.5 as order1 and order2).

Collapsing vertically in each column, the mean score for each condition summarizes the recall scores per condition. These scores in either group should not be particularly influenced by participants' gender or by the order in which they completed the recall questions because no one gender or order is present. And, because the same people are being observed, all participant variables should be constant between the two conditions. Therefore, any differences in scores between the samples cannot be confounded by differences in participants' memory abilities, attentiveness, and so on, because such variables are represented equally in both conditions.

Note that a special type of repeated-measures design is used when participants are measured before and after some event or treatment. In a **pretest-posttest design,** participants are measured on the dependent variable before they experience the condition of the independent variable, and then again after they receive the treatment. Thus, for example, to test whether meditation reduces physical stress, we might measure the same person's blood pressure before and after a period of meditation. Or to determine the effectiveness of a new weight-loss diet, we would measure each person's weight before and after a period of dieting.

> **REMEMBER**   A repeated-measures design matches participants along all participant variables by testing each participant under all conditions of an independent variable.

Pros and Cons of Repeated Measures

The strength of repeated measures is that they should eliminate potential confounding from virtually all participant variables: Differences between the conditions should not be due to differences produced by these variables because each participant, with the same characteristics, is in every condition. Repeated-measures designs can also produce a number of problems, however. Although repeated measures will keep more permanent participant variables constant, not all aspects of participants will remain the same because *individuals change from moment to moment.*

First, participants eventually become aware of all our conditions. Therefore, at some point, participants may identify what they think is the purpose and hypothesis of the study, producing diffusion of treatment or creating demand characteristics that lead to unnatural behavior.

Second, because we must test the various conditions in a sequence that occurs over time, scores will be influenced by several factors that occur due to the passage of time. **Subject history** refers to the fact that participants continue to have a life and experience things that can change them and influence their responses. Similarly, scores are influenced by **subject maturation:** As someone grows older and more mature, he or she changes in ways that influence responses. Thus *subject history* refers to changes due to participants' external experiences, whereas *maturation* refers to changes due to their internal development and growth. Both, however, can *severely* reduce internal validity: A response to one condition measured now and a response to another condition measured later may be confounded by changes in a participant because of history and maturation.

Further, repeated measures can produce substantial "subject mortality." This doesn't mean that participants literally die (usually). Rather, **subject mortality** refers to the loss of subjects because their participation dies out before the study is completed. Also known as "subject attrition," this can occur in a between-subjects design or anytime that participants refuse to continue their testing in a condition. It is most common with repeated testing that requires a considerable amount of time per participant, so that, to reduce fatigue and overload, we spread out testing over several days. Then people show up for initial sessions but do not return for later ones. The problem is, mortality effects are selective: People who continue to participate may find the study more interesting, perform better at the task, be more committed to helping science, or be more desperate for college credit or money. In any case, the results are biased. For example, in testing a new diet, the people who give up on dieting are likely to disappear. Those who stay may be so motivated that *any* diet would work well. Then what is apparently the influence of the test diet is actually due to a characteristic of the participants. Likewise, in any type of design, subject mortality results in only a certain type of participant, and so we lose external validity for generalizing to the broader population.

To counter these influences, try to conduct repeated measures (and multiple trials) within a short time span. Also, attempt to make the mechanics of participating in the study easy, with a task that is interesting, so that its completion does not require extremely dedicated volunteers. And pay attention to the degree of subject mortality that occurs, so that you can gauge how biased the sample is.

REMEMBER The results of a repeated-measures design can be biased by subject history, subject maturation, subject morality, and diffusion of treatment.

Finally, a major problem with repeated measures is that they produce a new kind of order effects. As you've seen, order effects are the influence of performing a series of trials. These effects include (1) practice effects—getting better at responding over trials; (2) fatigue effects—getting worse at responding over trials; (3) carry-over effects—the experience of any one trial that influences scores on subsequent trials; and (4) response sets—from previous trials, developing a habitual response for subsequent trials.

Previously, we discussed order effects as they occur over multiple trials *within* a particular condition. With repeated measures, however, these same effects also occur *between* conditions. After all, from a participant's perspective, changing from one condition to another largely involves an additional sequence of trials—more of the same, as it were. Thus, in the hypnosis study, by the time participants get to the second condition they may be tired and inattentive, or they may be very good at identifying the details of a robbery, or they may be very reactive to having the experimenter around. If the second condition was performed first, however, these influences might not be present.

Further, order effects interact with the previous problems of subject maturation, history, and morality. If a particular condition was performed at a different point in the sequence, perhaps maturation and history would not have changed participants so much. Or perhaps subject mortality would have selected a different type of participant who performs differently if other, less boring conditions were performed first.

Thus, we never know whether performance in one condition is higher or lower than in another condition just because of the order effects operating on that condition. We cannot prevent order effects, but we can attempt to balance their influence.

Methods for Controlling Order Effects

To control for order effects in a repeated-measures design with two conditions, we counterbalance the order in which participants perform the conditions: Half the participants perform condition 1 followed by condition 2, and the remaining participants perform condition 2 followed by condition 1. Thus, in the hypnosis study, half the participants would be tested first with the control condition, and half would start with the experimental condition, as shown in Table 5.6. All other design requirements still apply, so the participants' gender is counterbalanced. Because we're testing multiple trials, we also control for order effects within conditions by testing different participants under different orders (indicated as order1 and order2). When we examine all scores in a condition—collapsing in a column—the mean recall score within the control or experimental groups should not be particularly influenced by participants' gender or by the order in which they completed the recall questions. And, because the same person is being observed, virtually all participant variables should be constant between conditions. Further, any differences between the two conditions are not due to a particular order in which the conditions were performed, because both possible orders of conditions are present.

With only two conditions, the preceding counterbalancing scheme is quite adequate. For more than two conditions, there are several common techniques for controlling order effects. To see them, say that we expand the hypnosis study

Table 5.6 Diagram of Hypnosis Experiment Showing Counterbalancing of Order of Conditions

The top half of the diagram shows participants tested with one order, and the bottom half shows those tested in the reverse order.

Participants Tested in Control Condition First	No Hypnosis	Hypnosis
Participant 1 (Male, Order1)	X	X
Participant 2 (Male, Order2)	X	X
Participant 3 (Female, Order1)	X	X
Participant 4 (Female, Order2)	X	X
Participants Tested in Experimental Condition First		
Participant 5 (Male, Order1)	X	X
Participant 6 (Male, Order2)	X	X
Participant 7 (Female, Order1)	X	X
Participant 8 (Female, Order2)	X	X
	$\overline{X}$	$\overline{X}$

by adding a third condition, comparing the influence on memory from a no hypnosis, a mild hypnosis, and a deep hypnosis condition. For each condition, we'd still present participants a videotape of a robbery and then have them complete 30 recall questions. We're still using repeated measures, but with more than two conditions we may deal with order effects using either complete counterbalancing, partial counterbalancing, or randomization.

Complete Counterbalancing of Conditions

Complete counterbalancing is the process of balancing order effects by testing different participants with different orders, so that *all* possible orders are present.

For example, let's call the three conditions of the new hypnosis study, A, B, and C. Three conditions produce six possible orders:

ABC   ACB   BCA   BAC   CAB   CBA

Notice two things about these orders. First, each condition appears in every position within the sequence: A appears twice as the first condition, twice as the second condition, and twice as the third condition (likewise for B and C). Second, every possible sequence is included: For the sequence beginning with A, the two possible orders ABC and ACB are included, and so on. Thus, complete counterbalancing balances both a condition's position in the sequence and the order of the conditions coming before and after it. Applying this technique to the hypnosis study, we have the diagram shown in Table 5.7. For one-third of the participants, condition A is first, so performance under this condition might be biased because of its location in the sequence. However, condition B also occurs first for one-third of the participants, as does condition C, so these conditions are equally biased. Likewise, each condition occurs second at times, and third at times. Note that, within each order of conditions, we still balance other variables of concern:

Table 5.7   Diagram of Completely Counterbalanced Expanded Hypnosis Experiment

Each row represents participants tested under a particular sequence of the three conditions.

	Conditions		
Orders	*A* *No Hypnosis*	*B* *Mild Hypnosis*	*C* *Deep Hypnosis*
Participants Tested Using ABC	XXX ...	XXX ...	XXX ...
Participants Tested Using ACB	XXX ...	XXX ...	XXX ...
Participants Tested Using BCA	XXX ...	XXX ...	XXX ...
Participants Tested Using BAC	XXX ...	XXX ...	XXX ...
Participants Tested Using CAB	XXX ...	XXX ...	XXX ...
Participants Tested Using CBA	XXX ...	XXX ...	XXX ...
	$\overline{X}$	$\overline{X}$	$\overline{X}$

We balance gender, so that both males and females perform each order, and we counterbalance the order in which the trials in each condition are performed. Therefore, when we examine all scores in a condition—in a column—the recall scores should not be particularly influenced by participants' gender or by the order in which they completed the recall questions. And there should be no confoundings between conditions: (1) by participant variables; (2) by order effects within the 30 trials per condition; or (3) by history, maturation, mortality, or order effects occurring because of when in the sequence each condition was performed.

The term *complete counterbalancing* also applies when counterbalancing the order of multiple trials *within* a condition. If in the study just described, for example, all possible orders of the 30 recall questions within a condition were represented, then we'd have also completely counterbalanced the order of trials.

You may have noticed that the design of this study is very complex! Complete counterbalancing tends to create a design that rapidly becomes unworkable, especially if you are also counterbalancing other variables. Further, you may need many more participants so that you can test some under each order. Such problems suggest that we might be going overboard by completely counterbalancing order effects. After all, the goal is simply to ensure that the results are not confounded or unduly influenced by one particular order. Therefore, instead you may want to only partially counterbalance.

Partial Counterbalancing of Conditions

Partial counterbalancing is the process of balancing order effects by testing different participants using only some of the possible orders. For example, with three conditions, it is common to use the following three orders of conditions:

ABC   BCA   CAB

As here, typically a partial counterbalancing scheme systematically changes the position at which a condition occurs in the sequence but does not change the conditions coming before or after the condition. (The procedure for creating this type of counterbalancing scheme is sometimes called a "Latin square design.") Applying this scheme to the hypnosis study, we have the diagram shown in Table 5.8. Much simpler!

But we have balanced only practice effects or other biases that occur because of where in the sequence a condition occurs (first, second, or third). Partial counterbalancing does not control for carry-over effects (the influence on one condition resulting from having performed a previous condition). The scheme shown in Table 5.8 does not balance potential carry-over effects, because B follows A and C follows B in two-thirds of the sequences, but C never immediately follows A. Therefore, when carry-over effects are likely to occur between conditions, we instead include all orders, and use complete counterbalancing.

Table 5.8   Diagram of Partially Counterbalanced Expanded Hypnosis Experiment

Each row represents those participants tested under a particular sequence of the three conditions.

	Conditions		
Orders	A No Hypnosis	B Mild Hypnosis	C Deep Hypnosis
Participants Tested Using ABC	XXX	XXX	XXX
Participants Tested Using BCA	XXX	XXX	XXX
Participants Tested Using CAB	XXX	XXX	XXX
	$\overline{X}$	$\overline{X}$	$\overline{X}$

REMEMBER   Partial counterbalancing presents some of the possible orders of conditions to control practice effects. Complete counterbalancing includes all possible orders to control practice and carry-over effects.

The term *partial counterbalancing* also applies to multiple trials within each condition. If in the preceding designs half the participants per row also performed the individual trials in order 1 through 30 and the remaining participants per row performed 30 through 1, we'd have also partially counterbalanced the order of trials within conditions.

Counterbalancing is used typically when there are only a few possible orders, so that order effects can be handled efficiently and systematically. When there are many possible orders and the goal is simply to include some different sequences in an unsystematic way, an alternative approach is randomization.

Randomizing the Order of Conditions

Randomization is the process of balancing order effects by randomly creating different orders under which different participants are tested. In the hypnosis study, we could randomize the order of conditions by randomly creating a sequence for each participant. Likewise, we could randomize the order of trials within a condition by essentially shuffling the 30 questions in a condition for each participant.

In fact, with some tasks you can simultaneously randomize both the order of trials and the order of conditions. Say we're conducting a study that measures participants' reaction time to recognize whether individually presented words occurred in a previously read paragraph. We compare conditions involving 20 words of either 1, 2, or 3 syllables. To randomize, in every 15 trials we can randomly select and mix 5 trials from each condition. When we unscramble the responses, each condition will have been performed at the beginning, middle, and end of the sequence, and each particular trial will have been sometimes performed early in the sequence and sometimes performed later in the sequence. On the other hand, we do not usually intermix conditions when each condition requires us to stop and change the instructions or procedure. Instead, to prevent confusion, participants complete all trials in one condition before going on to the next condition. This method is known as "blocking" trials (trials are performed as a group or "block"). Then we control order by having different participants perform the conditions in different orders.

Choosing a Design

From this chapter, you've seen that there is much to consider when deciding whether to use a between-subjects or within-subjects design. A repeated-measures design is preferred when participants' responses are likely to be strongly influenced by individual differences in cognitive strategies, physical abilities, or experiences. Essentially, this design is used when it makes sense to compare a person or animal in one condition to the same person or animal in the other conditions. Thus, studies involving memory and learning are usually conducted in this way, as are studies that examine a sequence—such as when we study the effects of practice or maturation. (As always, reading the relevant research literature will help you to make this decision.) Further, we may select such designs because, as you'll see, repeated-measures (and matched groups) are analyzed in a way that results in reduced error variance, producing a more powerful design than a comparable between-subjects design.

Other design considerations, however, may prevent you from using repeated measures: First, consider whether a particular condition might produce rather permanent changes in behavior so that the condition has unique carry-over effects. **Nonsymmetrical carry-over effects** occur when the carry-over effects from one order of conditions do not balance out those of another order. Such effects occur whenever performing task A and then task B is not the same as performing task B and then task A. For example, we would not want to test the same participants in more than one condition if each entailed some sort of surprise. Likewise, once you have taught participants something in one condition, you cannot "unteach" them in a subsequent condition. Or, as is often the case in animal research, a condition may involve some surgical technique that cannot be undone. In such situations, counterbalancing will not effectively balance out the bias produced by a particular order of conditions. Instead, use a between-subjects design, because no carry-over effects are possible.

Also, do not underestimate the influence of subject history, maturation, and mortality. These can be more detrimental to a study than the lessened control occurring in a between-subjects design. In addition, a repeated-measures design often places greater demands on your ability to create stimuli. Typically you will need many more stimuli when participants are exposed to all conditions than when they are exposed to only one condition. In the between-subjects version of the hypnosis study, for example, you'd need only one videotape of a robbery with 30 recall questions to show to all conditions. In the within-subjects version with three levels of hypnosis, you'd need three different videotaped robberies. Yet the tapes would have to be very comparable in terms of the details and events in the story as well as in the lighting, sound, and mechanics of taping. You'd also need a different set of 30 questions for each robbery, yet with all being comparable in terms of wording, reading level, degree of memory difficulty, and so on. Any differences in the tapes, story details, or questions could be a confounding. Although you may be able to create comparable materials (that's why we have pilot studies), you want to be sure that this is possible and that such effort is really necessary before you select such a design.

Finally, consider the advantages of repeated measures versus the disadvantages of counterbalancing. As you've seen, controlling *any* variable through counterbalancing changes the variable within a condition and thus tends to produce greater variability among scores within the conditions. Repeated measures designs almost always require extensive counterbalancing (or randomization), and so including the influence of many changing variables tends to greatly increase error variance, reducing the power to show a clear and convincing relationship.

The key to selecting your design depends on the number and importance of participant variables that must be controlled. If numerous uncontrolled participant variables could seriously reduce reliability and validity, then a repeated-measures design is preferred despite the difficulties it entails. If there are only a few crucial participant variables, however, a repeated-measures design can create more problems than it solves, and so a better choice may be to identify the most serious variable to control and to match participants on that variable in a matched-groups design. You can also still obtain valid and reliable results from a between-subjects design, especially if you balance important participant variables or limit the population.

REMEMBER Between-subjects designs are preferred if carry-over effects are nonsymmetrical, if the task does not allow repeated testing, or if extensive counterbalancing is unwise.

You can summarize the questions to consider when designing a within-subjects design using Checklist 5.3.

In fact, you've seen a number of issues to consider when dealing with participant variables. Whether to use a between-subjects design, matching, or repeated measures is a *major* aspect of designing any study. To help you remember all of the pros and cons associated with the techniques we've discussed, consult Table 5.9.

| **CHECKLIST 5.3** | Questions to consider when selecting a within-subjects design |

❑ Must many participant variables be controlled?

❑ Are subject history, maturation, and mortality a problem?

❑ Do stimuli and other aspects fit a repeated-measures design?

❑ Will nonsymmetrical carry-over effects occur?

❑ Is randomization or partial or complete counterbalancing of order of conditions needed?

Table 5.9 Pros and Cons Associated with the Different Methods for Controlling Participant Variables

Method	*Pros*	*Cons*
Random Assignment	1. Produces balanced representative samples	1. May not balance important variables 2. Works poorly with small ns 3. May increase error variance
Balancing a Variable	1. Prevents confounding by the variable	1. May increase error variance 2. Complicates design and inflates N 3. Pretest may bias participants
Matching Groups	1. Keeps matched variable constant between conditions	1. Finding matching participants is difficult 2. May increase error variance 3. Pretest may bias participants
Limiting Population	1. Eliminates fluctuating variable 2. Reduces error variance	1. May restrict range of dependent scores 2. Reduces external validity
Repeated Measures	1. Eliminates confounding from all participant variables 2. Requires small N 3. Design is statistically more powerful	1. Allows diffusion of treatment 2. Confounding by subject history and maturation 3. Subject mortality reduces external validity 4. Order effects require balancing that reduces power 5. Increases stimulus requirements 6. Incompatible with nonsymmetrical carry-over effects

Putting It All Together

When you start to counterbalance order and other extraneous variables, the process of designing a study can become very complex. But you don't have to control *everything*. Although you want data from a well-controlled experiment, you must actually get the data! Don't try to control so many variables that you can't conduct the study. Instead, control those variables that seriously confound the results or severely reduce reliability. Keep in mind that when you institute a control to eliminate one problem, you often produce other problems. Therefore, you are never going to produce the perfect study, so produce the best study you can within practical limits.

And finally, one more time, to review all of the questions to consider regarding participant variables, along with all of the previous questions you've considered when designing an experiment refer to the checklist located on the inside front cover of this text.

CHAPTER SUMMARY

1. *Participant variables* are personal characteristics that distinguish one subject from another, resulting in *individual differences* in how each responds to the same situation.

2. *Selection criteria* are the characteristics of participants that we require for allowing them to participate in a study.

3. A *pretest* may be needed to identify participants who meet the selection criteria.

4. External validity depends on the sample size *(N)*, on whether participants are drawn from a limited population, and on whether participants differ from nonparticipants because of participant variables, including the *volunteer bias* and *subject sophistication*.

5. The inconsistency or *variability* in the dependent scores within each condition reduces the strength of the relationship. This inconsistency is referred to as *error variance*.

6. Participant variables correlated with the influence of the independent variable or with performance on the dependent variable should be controlled because they reduce reliability and internal validity. They also increase error variance and reduce our ability to find a strong, convincing relationship.

7. In a *between-subjects design,* a different group of participants is randomly selected for each condition of an independent variable.

8. In a between-subjects design, participant variables are controlled by balancing them through *random assignment,* by *systematically balancing* them, by keeping them constant through *limiting the population,* and by *matching participants.*

9. *Collapsing* across a variable means that we combine the scores from the different levels of the variable.

10. Random assignment can control for many unknown participant variables, but it may not evenly balance them, and if it does, it increases error variance.

11. Balancing a variable prevents it from confounding the results and increases external validity, but at the cost of increased complexity, a larger *N,* and increased error variance.

12. Limiting the population prevents confounding and minimizes error variance, but at the cost of reduced external validity.

13. In a *matched-groups design,* each participant in one condition is matched with a participant in every other condition along an extraneous variable. This controls the variable between conditions, but pretesting creates problems and matching is not always workable.

14. In a *within-subjects* or *repeated-measures* design, each participant is measured under all conditions of an independent variable.

15. A repeated-measures design that entails measuring participants before and after some event is called a *pretest-posttest design.*

16. Repeated measures are especially prone to confounding by subject history and maturation, by subject mortality, and by order effects.

17. *Subject history* refers to the fact that participants continue to have experiences that can change them and influence their responses.

18. *Subject maturation* refers to the fact that, as an individual grows older and more mature, he or she changes in ways that influence responses.

19. *Subject morality* refers to the loss of participants because their participation dies out before the study is completed.

20. With *complete counterbalancing,* different participants are tested with different orders so that all possible orders of conditions or trials are present. With *partial counterbalancing,* participants are tested using only some of the possible orders of conditions or trials. With *randomization,* different participants are tested using different random orders of conditions or trials.

21. *Nonsymmetrical carry-over effects* occur when the carry-over effects from one order of conditions do not balance out those of another order.

KEY TERMS

between-subjects
   design   *(144)*
complete
   counterbalancing
   (157)
collapsing   *(147)*
error variance   *(142)*
individual differences
   (136)
matched-groups
   design   *(148)*
nonsymmetrical carry-
   over effects   *(161)*

partial
   counterbalancing
   (159)
pretest   *(146)*
pretest-posttest design
   (154)
random assignment
   (144)
randomization   *(144)*
repeated-measures
   design   *(152)*
selection criteria
   (136)

subject history   *(155)*
subject maturation
   (155)
subject mortality
   (155)
subject sophistication
   (139)
variability   *(142)*
variable   *(142)*
volunteer bias   *(139)*
within-subjects design
   (152)

REVIEW QUESTIONS

1. What is meant by the term *selection criteria?*

2. (a) How can participant variables influence external validity? (b) How can they influence internal validity? (c) How can they influence reliability?

3. You conduct a study involving the members of your class. (a) What limitation on external validity might arise? (b) Why might this limitation not arise?

4. What is meant by (a) volunteer bias? (b) subject mortality? (c) subject sophistication? (d) How does each bias your results?

5. (a) What do N and n symbolize? (b) Why is a larger N important for external validity? (c) What range of n is usually adequate?

6. You conduct a study measuring a participant's helpfulness in aiding a confederate to study for a psychology exam. In each condition, people must help for five consecutive days. What aspect of your participants might bias the results?

7. How do you identify participant variables that might confound a study?

8. (a) How does random assignment to conditions control participant variables? (b) When is balancing participant variables more appropriate than random assignment? Why?

9. What problems arise with pretesting?

10. (a) What does it mean to collapse across a variable? (b) What is error variance, and how does it affect a study?

11. (a) What positive impact does counterbalancing participant variables have on a study? (b) What negative impact does it have?

12. (a) What positive impact does limiting the population have on a study? (b) What negative impact does it have?

13. (a) How is a between-subjects design created? (b) How do you control participant variables here? (c) Why would you choose this design?

14. (a) How is a matched-groups design created? (b) How does it control participant variables? (c) Why would you choose this design?

15. (a) How is a within-subjects design created? (b) How does it control participant variables? (c) What is the other name for this design? (d) Why would you choose this design?

16. (a) What problems are created by repeated measures in terms of changes in participants? (b) What problems are created by repeated measures in terms of the measurement task?

17. (a) What is the difference between partial counterbalancing and complete counterbalancing? (b) What is the advantage and disadvantage of each?

18. (a) What is the advantage of counterbalancing or matching in terms of internal and external validity? (b) What is the disadvantage of both procedures? (c) How do you resolve this conflict?

19. Identify the type of design being used in the following. (a) When studying the effects of a new memory-enhancing drug on Alzheimer's patients, testing a group of patients before and after administration of the drug. (b) When studying the effects of alcohol on motor coordination, comparing one group of people given a moderate dose of alcohol with another group given no alcohol. (c) When studying whether males and females are persuaded differently by a female speaker. (d) The study in (c), but with the added requirement that for each male of a particular age there is a female of the same age. (e) When studying how the amount of body fat changes in a group of athletes, measuring it weekly over a two-month training program.

20. You conduct a repeated-measures design, comparing a condition in which you train people to improve their memory with a control condition. What problem is produced here that counterbalancing the order of conditions will not solve?

21. A student proposes comparing the conditions of "male" and "female" in a repeated-measures design. (a) Why or why not is this an acceptable approach? (b) What control techniques can be applied instead?

DISCUSSION QUESTIONS

1. You conduct a repeated-measures study of the effects of three different types of motivational messages. Participants listen to one message every day for two weeks, then they complete a 20-question test of well-being, and then they begin listening to the next message, and so on. (a) Specify your scheme for dealing with order effects. (b) What three problems will arise with your

participants during the study that might confound the results? (c) What problem is likely to be created by any one message that makes repeated measures a problem? (d) What ethical problems are present here?

2. You decide to conduct the study in question 1 as a between-subjects design instead. (a) Describe this design. (b) How does it eliminate the problems in 1(b) and 1(c)? (c) What new problems does it create?

3. For the studies in questions 1 and 2, (a) what participant variables are important for you to control? (b) Which of these would you control by limiting the population, and how would you do it? (c) Which of these would you control by balancing, and how would you do it? (d) What positive or negative impact will each approach have?

4. During the preceding studies, one participant was out sick for a week. (a) What should you do about this person's data and why? (b) What new selection criterion should you add? (c) What impact might this criterion have on the strength of the observed relationship? (d) How does this criterion affect external validity?

Part II

The Statistical Analysis of Experiments

Now that you understand how to design experiments, we'll discuss how to analyze them. In the upcoming chapter we'll review the descriptive and inferential statistical procedures used in simple experiments involving one independent variable. Then in Chapter 7 we'll look at how to analyze more complex experiments that involve more than one independent variable.

6

Applying Descriptive and Inferential Statistics to Simple Experiments

GETTING STARTED

To understand this chapter, recall the following:

- From Chapter 2, recall what a relationship is, and how we generalize the sample relationship to the population.

- From Chapter 3, recall what a sensitive measure is.

- From Chapter 5, recall what a powerful design is, what variability or error variance is, what collapsing is, and what a between- and within-subjects design is.

Your goals in this chapter are to learn:

- What the "type" and "strength" of a relationship is.

- What the four scales of measurement are.

- How an experiment is summarized using the means of the conditions.

- How the standard deviation and variance summarize the strength of a relationship.

- How to interpret and graph the results of an experiment.

- The logic of inferential statistics and the errors they produce.

As you know, psychological research measures behaviors and events to demonstrate relationships. Therefore, once you've collected the data, the next step is to examine and interpret the observed relationship. This chapter reviews the common statistical procedures that researchers use when analyzing the results of experiments. First we'll examine the common procedures for summarizing sample data, and then we'll review the common methods for drawing statistical inferences about a relationship in the population.

Selecting the Statistical Procedures

You perform essentially the same statistical analysis of any experiment, regardless of whether it's a laboratory or field experiment, or whether it's a true experiment (with a true independent variable that allows random assignment of participants to groups) or a quasi-experiment (which does not allow random assignment). There are two major types of statistics: First, **descriptive statistics** are for summarizing and describing the important characteristics of data. (Don't confuse descriptive *research* with descriptive *statistics*. Descriptive research refers to designs that describe *behaviors*. Descriptive statistics are used to describe *data* from any type of design, whether it be experimental or descriptive.) These procedures tell us whether a relationship is present and, if so, what the particular characteristics of the relationship in each condition are.

Second, we want to generalize this sample relationship, describing the relationship we'd expect to find if we could observe everyone in the population. **Inferential statistics** are for deciding if a sample relationship represents a relationship found in the population. Then these procedures also help us to describe the characteristics of the relationship in the population.

> *REMEMBER*   You must always apply the appropriate descriptive and inferential procedures to a study.

There are many ways to describe and summarize a relationship, so part of designing a study is to identify the appropriate statistical procedures to use. You should do this when *designing* the study, because otherwise it's possible to complete a study that cannot be analyzed. Further, some statistical procedures are better than others, and whether you can use the best procedure depends on other design decisions.

Which statistical procedures to use depends on two major issues. The first is the design you have: Different kinds of experiments are analyzed using certain statistics, and descriptive studies are analyzed using others. Second, the procedure to use depends on the way that you measure a behavior and obtain the scores. You can measure scores using one of four **scales of measurement:** nominal, ordinal, interval, and ratio.

With a **nominal scale,** each score identifies membership in a particular category—for example, if you assign a "1" to identify people as "Republican" and a "2" to identify them as "Democrat." The numbers on football jerseys, the letters representing blood-type, whether someone passes or fails a test, and a person's gender are examples of nominal scales.

With an **ordinal scale,** the scores indicate rank order relative to other participants: A score of 1 means the most or least of the variable, a 2 means the second most or least, and so on. The letter grade you get in a college course and military rank are other examples of ordinal scales.

With an **interval scale,** the scores reflect an amount of a variable, but zero does not truly mean zero amount, so negative scores are possible. For example, temperature is usually measured on an interval scale. "Zero degrees" does not mean that zero amount of heat is present, only that the temperature is less than 1 degree and more than −1 degree. Likewise, when measuring participants' over- and underestimates of the weight of an object, or the balance in their checking accounts, we are using interval scales.

With a **ratio scale,** the scores reflect an amount, but zero means zero amount, so negative scores are not possible. Measuring participants' errors on a test, the calories they consume in a day, or the amount of money in their pocket involves ratio scales.

For help remembering the different scales of measurement, consult Table 6.1.

Impact of a Particular Scale of Measurement

There are three important reasons to pay attention to the scale of measurement. First, different scales provide different degrees of precision and *sensitivity*. Recall that a sensitive measure is one that distinguishes subtle differences in behavior.

Table 6.1 Summary of Types of Measurement Scales

Each column describes the characteristics of the scale.

	Type of Measurement Scale			
	Nominal	*Ordinal*	*Interval*	*Ratio*
What does the scale indicate?	Quality	Relative quantity	Quantity	Quantity
Is there a true zero?	No	No	No	Yes
How might the scale be used in research?	To identify males and females as 1 and 2	To judge who is 1st, 2d, etc., in aggressiveness	To convey over- and underestimates	To measure the number of correct answers on a test

Nominal scores only grossly discriminate between participants, because they essentially categorize based on a yes/no decision. Ordinal scales are somewhat more sensitive, but they still lack precision. (In a race, for example, we cannot tell whether those in first place are only slightly ahead or miles ahead of those in second.) However, interval or ratio scales—especially when involving fractional scores—are most sensitive because they can reflect very small differences in behaviors.

The second reason to pay attention to your scale of measurement is that only certain descriptive procedures can be used with certain types of scores. It makes no sense, for example, to compute a football team's average jersey number, or the average position of all runners in a race.

Third, the scale of measurement determines which inferential procedure is appropriate. With interval or ratio scores, we are also concerned with whether the scores form at least an approximately **normal distribution.** To answer this question, check the research literature to see how others treat your variable. If the scores are normally distributed, you can usually use a procedure from the category of **parametric inferential statistics.** When interval or ratio scores are not normally distributed, or when you measure nominal or ordinal scores, you should use one of the **nonparametric inferential statistics.**

REMEMBER   The statistical procedures to apply and the sensitivity of scores depend on the scale of measurement used to measure the dependent variable.

Psychological research usually involves interval or ratio scores that meet the requirements of parametric procedures. In the following sections we'll discuss the most common procedures used with such data. First, though, let's review the characteristics of the relationship that we ultimately describe.

Understanding the Characteristics of a Relationship

As a very simple example, let's say we conduct an experiment to investigate that old rumor that the more you study, the better you perform on a test. We'll manipulate the independent variable of amount of time participants study a set of material in a controlled laboratory, using the conditions of studying for either 1, 3, or 5 hours. After studying for the assigned time, we'll measure the dependent variable of participants' performance on a college-like multiple-choice test. We could conduct either a between- or within-subjects design, and regardless, all of the usual issues of producing reliable, valid, and consistent results apply. With the data in hand, we'll look for the relationship in which increased test grades are associated with increased study time.

Any relationship, whether in an experiment or descriptive study, forms the same pattern: As the scores on variable X change, the scores on variable Y change in a consistent fashion. But how do we decide which variable to call X or Y? In any study, the researcher implicitly asks, "For a given score or amount of one variable, what scores occur on the other variable?" The "given" variable is always the X variable, and the "other" variable is always the Y variable. In the preceding we're asking, "For a given amount of study time, what test grades occur?" So study time is X, and test grades is Y. In fact, an experiment always asks, "For a given level of the independent variable, what scores occur on the dependent variable?" Therefore, the independent variable is always the X variable, and the dependent variable is always the Y variable. (A participant's "score" on the independent variable is the condition under which he or she is tested.) Also, note that there is a special language for describing a relationship. We use the general format "Y scores change **as a function of** changes in X." In our experiment, we're examining changes in test grades as a function of changes in hours spent studying. In fact, because the independent variable is always X, experiments always look for a change in scores on the dependent variable as a function of changes in the independent variable.

To summarize any relationship, there are two aspects to examine. First, the **type of relationship** is the overall direction in which the Y scores change as the X scores increase. One type of relationship is a linear relationship. In a **linear relationship,** as the X scores increase, the Y scores change in only one direction, continuously increasing or continuously decreasing in a straight-line pattern. For example, say that we obtain scores like those in Figure 6.1. Both data sets show linear relationships, because in both the scores change in one direction. However, there are two subtypes of a linear relationship. Data Set A shows a **positive linear relationship,** in which as the independent variable *(X)* increases, the dependent *(Y)* scores increase. On the other hand, Data Set B, shows a **negative linear relationship,** in which as the independent variable *(X)* increases, the dependent *(Y)* scores decrease.

The second characteristic of a relationship to examine is its strength. The **strength of the relationship** is how consistently the Y scores change as the X variable increases. Coincidentally, in Figure 6.1, both relationships are perfectly consistent and thus have maximum strength: All participants with the same study-time score have the same test score, and when study time changes, test scores all change in a perfectly consistent way.

REMEMBER   The important characteristics of a relationship to understand are its type (direction) and its strength (consistency).

You can also see these characteristics in the graphs in Figure 6.1. Hours studied (the X variable) is plotted on the X axis, and test scores (the Y variable) are plotted on the Y axis. Each "dot" on the graph is called a "data point," representing a participant's X-Y pair. (Such a graph is called a scatterplot.) Data Set A shows a positive linear relationship, because the pattern indicates that as the level of study time increases, test scores also increase. Data Set B shows a negative linear relationship, indicating that as the study time increases, test scores decrease. Each scatterplot also shows a perfectly consistent relationship, because there is only one data point above each X, indicating that all participants in a particular condition received the same test score. (Their data points are all on top of one

Figure 6.1 Data producing perfect positive and negative linear relationships

Each column shows test scores after studying for either 1, 3, or 5 hours.

	Data Set A: Perfect Positive Relationship			Data Set B: Perfect Negative Relationship		
	Hours Studied (X)			*Hours Studied (X)*		
	1	*3*	*5*	*1*	*3*	*5*
Test	20	50	80	80	50	20
Scores (Y)	20	50	80	80	50	20
⟶	20	50	80	80	50	20

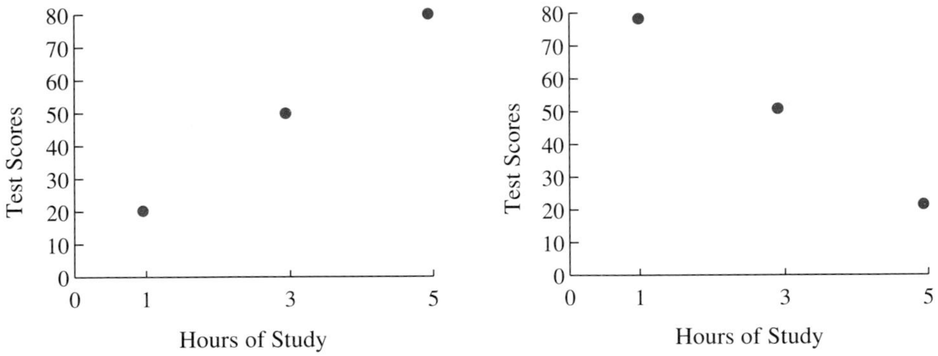

another.) All of the data points fall on a straight line, so these are perfect *linear* relationships.

Perfect relationships, however, do not occur in real research.

Intermediate Relationships   Most relationships have an intermediate strength: A value of Y *tends* to be paired with a value of X, and as X changes, the value of Y *tends* to change in a consistent fashion. Figure 6.2 presents examples of intermediate-strength relationships. (Note that the pattern here is idealized so you can see it, but real data never form such balanced symmetrical patterns!) These data show **variability** in the Y scores, because the test scores at a particular study time differ from one another. Recall that the generic name for the inconsistency or variability among scores in a relationship is **error variance.** It is the variability or error variance in Y scores at each X that works against the strength of a relationship. Instead of consistently seeing one test score at one level of study time, we see (1) different test scores paired with one level of study time, and/or (2) the same test score paired with different amounts of study time.

Figure 6.2   Data producing intermediate-strength relationships

Each column shows test scores after studying for either 1, 3, or 5 hours.

Data Set A: Strong Positive Relationship			Data Set B: Weak Positive Relationship		
Hours Studied			*Hours Studied*		
1	*3*	*5*	*1*	*3*	*5*
10	40	70	10	30	50
20	50	70	30	50	70
20	50	80	50	70	90

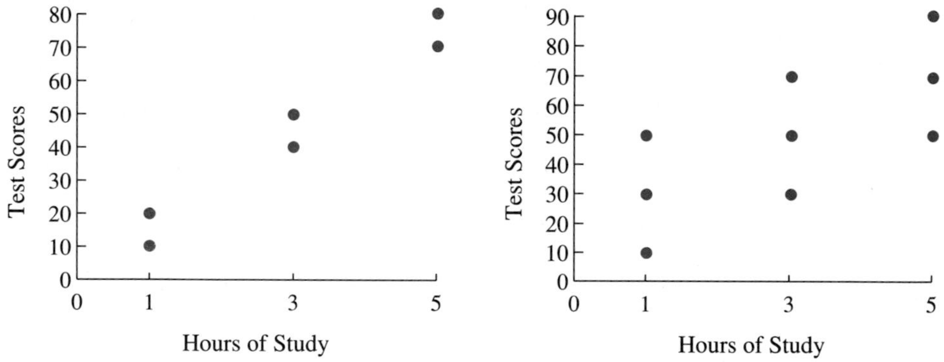

Considering the amount of variability, data Set A shows a relatively stronger relationship because test scores at a study time do not differ from one another by very much, and the same test scores don't occur at different study times. Thus, there is "close" to one value of Y at each X. Data Set B, however, shows a relatively weaker relationship because here more frequent and larger differences occur among test scores at a particular study time, and the Ys at one X often are the same Ys found at other Xs.

These patterns can also be seen in the scatterplots. In Graph A, different test scores are associated with each study time, so several data points appear above each X. However, the data points are not vertically spread out much, indicating relatively small error variance and a strong relationship. Conversely, Graph B shows a weaker relationship, because the greater vertical spread among the data points above each X shows greater variability in Y scores.

Recall that the consistency of the relationship is one aspect of how *powerful* data are. Power is the idea that, if a relationship exists in nature, we want the sample data to reflect it in a clear and convincing manner so that we don't miss it. A stronger relationship is harder to miss and is thus more powerful.

REMEMBER The smaller the variability of the *Y* scores at each *X*, the stronger and more powerful the relationship is.

Zero Relationship At the other extreme, Figure 6.3 shows data that form zero relationship. This pattern is as far from a relationship as you can get. There is not one or even close to one test score associated with one study time, nor is there a trend toward changing Y scores as X changes. Instead, the same batch of Y scores tends to show up at every value of X.

Nonlinear Relationships We do not always have a linear relationship. In a **nonlinear relationship,** as the *X* variable increases, the pattern of changing *Y* scores does not fit one straight line. Figure 6.4 shows two examples of nonlinear relationships. (Again, such symmetrical patterns are the ideal, not the norm.) In Graph A, as the X scores increase, at first the Y scores also increase, but beyond a certain X, the Y scores change direction and tend to decrease. Coincidentally, these data show a relatively strong relationship, because there is relatively little variability in Y scores at each X. In Graph B, as X scores increase, at first Y

Figure 6.3 Data producing no relationship

Hours Studied		
1	*3*	*5*
30 50 70	30 50 70	30 50 70

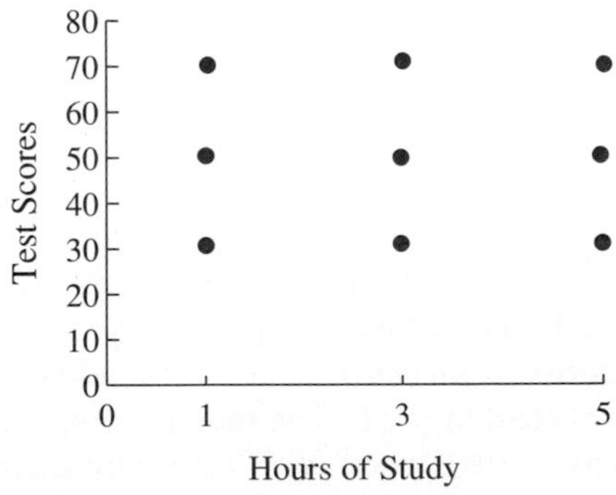

Figure 6.4   Scatterplots showing nonlinear relationships

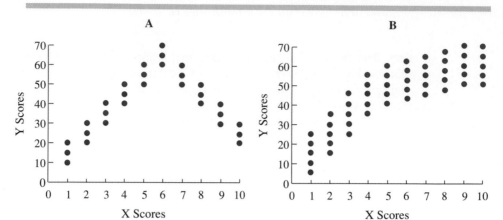

scores tend to increase sharply, but beyond a certain X they change their direction, tending to increase only slightly. Coincidentally, these data show a weaker relationship, because there is larger variability in Y scores at each X.

Other nonlinear relationships might follow any pattern that repeatedly changes direction. Regardless, the strength of the relationship is always how consistently one or close to one value of Y is associated with one particular value of X.

Applying Descriptive Statistics to Experiments

So far, we've simply looked at a table or graph to see how the individual scores change from one condition to the next. However, in real research we test larger Ns, and then we might have a confusing array of many numbers with a relationship hidden in them. Also, we need more quantitative ways of describing a relationship than merely "eyeballing" it. Therefore, the first step is always to compute descriptive statistics. To begin with, we describe central tendency and variability.

Describing Central Tendency

To summarize the pattern of increasing test scores with increased study time, we first need to know whether the scores in a particular condition are generally low, medium, or high. Therefore, we summarize the dependent scores in each condition by computing a **measure of central tendency.** There are three common measures of central tendency. (1) The **mean** score, symbolized by $\overline{X}$, is the average of a group of scores. It is used with normally distributed interval or ratio scores.

(2) The **median** is the 50th percentile, meaning that 50% of the scores are at or below this score. It is computed with non-normal interval or ratio scores, or with ordinal scores. (3) The **mode** is the most frequently occurring score. It is used with nominal scores. Each of these is used to indicate where the *center* of a group of scores *tends* to be located. (Calculations can be found in Appendix C.1.)

REMEMBER The measure of central tendency used in an experiment is determined by the scale of measurement that you applied to the *dependent* scores.

Usually, psychological research involves normally distributed interval or ratio scores. Then the mean is interpreted as the score "around" which the scores in a condition tend to be clustered. For example, say we obtained data such as those in Table 6.2. Looking first at the scores, you see that test scores tend to increase with increased study time. To summarize this we compute the mean test score for each condition: The 1-hour condition produced scores "around" the mean score of 20, the 3-hour condition produced a different distribution of scores around 25, and the 5-hour condition produced still another distribution around 31.67. *A relationship is present whenever there are differences between the means of the conditions.* Further, the way the mean scores change as the conditions change indicates the type of relationship present. Here, because the means tend to increase as study time increases, we know that the individual test scores on which each mean is based also tend to increase as study time increases. Conversely, if the means in all conditions were the same value, this would indicate that essentially the same distribution of test scores is present in each condition and, thus, that no relationship exists. (We look for the same patterns when the median or mode is computed in each condition.)

Recognize that not all of the means must differ for a relationship to be present. For example, we might find that only the means in the 1-hour and 3-hour levels are different. This is still a relationship, because, at least sometimes, as the conditions change, the dependent scores also tend to change.

Table 6.2 Test Scores as a Function of Hours Studied

	Hours Studied		
	1-Hour Condition	*3-Hour Condition*	*5-Hour Condition*
Test Scores	5 25 30	15 25 35	20 25 40
	$\overline{X} = 20.00$	$\overline{X} = 25.00$	$\overline{X} = 31.67$

> **REMEMBER**   When the mean scores for the conditions differ, then individual dependent scores are changing with the conditions, so a relationship is present.

Graphing the Results of an Experiment

Instead of plotting the individual data points, published research usually presents the results of an experiment using a **line graph.** We create a line graph when the levels of the *independent variable* are measured using an ordinal, interval, or ratio scale of measurement. The hours someone studies is a ratio scale, so the previous data are plotted as the line graph in Figure 6.5. The independent variable is always *X*, so the *X* axis is labeled with our conditions. We computed the mean score in each condition, so the *Y* axis is labeled as the mean dependent score. Then each data point is the mean score for a condition, and adjacent data points are connected with straight lines. (If the median or mode is appropriate for your dependent variable, then it is plotted as the *Y* variable.) The data points are connected with straight lines, because we assume that the relationship continues in a straight line between the points shown on the *X* axis. Thus, we would assume that the mean of a 4-hour condition would fall on the line that connects the means for the 3- and 5-hour conditions.

> **REMEMBER**   On a graph of an experiment, the independent variable is always plotted on the *X* axis.

The vertical location of each mean in Figure 6.5 implies a group of test scores around that location. When the vertical location of the mean changes as the conditions change, we know that there is a group of higher or lower test scores for each condition, and therefore a relationship is present. As shown here,

Figure 6.5   Line graph showing mean test scores as a function of study time

Each data point is the mean score for a condition.

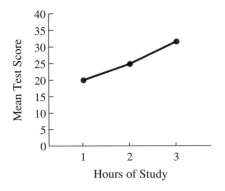

a line graph that generally slopes upward indicates a largely positive linear relationship. If the line slopes downward, it indicates a negative linear relationship, and if the line fluctuates up and down, it indicates a nonlinear relationship. A horizontal line graph indicates no relationship, because it shows no change in means—or scores—as the conditions change.

Experiments are not always summarized using line graphs. If the *independent* variable reflects a *nominal* scale of measurement, we create a **bar graph** in which the height of each bar reflects a data point, and the bars do not touch. For example, say that in a different study, all participants studied for the same amount of time, but we compared the mean test performance of students majoring in either physics, psychology, or English. Such *categories* might produce the data in Figure 6.6. This shows a relationship because the tops of the bars do not form a horizontal line, so there are different means and thus different scores in each condition. However, the bars communicate that we arbitrarily placed psychology to the left of English. Therefore, if we inserted the additional category of sociology between psychology and English, we could not assume that the mean for sociology majors would fall on a line running between the means for psychology and English majors.

REMEMBER The measurement scale of the dependent scores determines which measure of central tendency to calculate, and the scale of the independent variable determines the type of graph to create.

Figure 6.6 Bar graphs showing mean test scores as a function of college major

The height of each bar corresponds to the mean score for the condition.

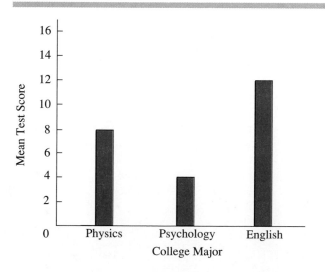

Finally, notice that you must have at least three conditions—and three data points on a graph—to see a nonlinear relationship. With just two conditions, one group's mean can be only higher or lower than the other group's, so the data can depict only a linear relationship, even if the relationship in nature is nonlinear. Therefore, when designing a study and selecting the number of conditions you'll test, an important consideration is the type of relationship that you seek to demonstrate. When practical, research typically involves at least three conditions, in case the relationship is nonlinear. The maximum tends to be six to eight conditions, which is more than adequate for describing most relationships.

Describing Variability

To see the strength of a relationship in an experiment, we often compute the variability of the dependent scores in each condition. **Measures of variability** are numbers that summarize the extent to which scores in a distribution differ. When the mean is the appropriate measure of central tendency, the appropriate measures of variability are the sample variance and the sample standard deviation. The **sample variance** is the average squared difference between each dependent score and the mean. The **sample standard deviation** is the square root of the sample variance. (Calculations can be found in Appendix C.2.) The standard deviation can be most directly interpreted as indicating roughly the "average" amount that the scores in the condition deviate from the mean of the condition.

The larger the standard deviation and variance, the more the scores in a condition differ from the mean, and thus the greater the inconsistency in the scores in that condition. Recall that the inconsistency in a relationship is *error variance,* so by looking at the pattern of variances or standard deviations across all conditions, we see the error variance. The original scores (in Table 6.2) produce the means and standard deviations shown in Table 6.3. The 1-hour condition produced scores around the mean of 20, but individual scores differ above or below this by an "average" of about 10.8. The 3-hour condition produced scores around 25, but individuals here differ by about *plus or minus* 8.16. And in the 5-hour condition, participants differ from the mean of 31.67 by about 8.5. Are

Table 6.3   Mean and Standard Deviation of Test Scores in Each Condition of Study Time

	Independent Variable: Hours Studied		
	1-Hour Condition	*3-Hour Condition*	*5-Hour Condition*
Mean	20.00	25.00	31.67
Standard Deviation	10.80	8.16	8.50

these large amounts? Well, back in Table 6.2 the lowest test score in the experiment was 5 and the highest was 40, so overall the test grades differ by as much as 35 points. Therefore, this relationship is *relatively* consistent, because the scores in each condition differ by about only 8 to 10 points. (If each standard deviation equaled zero, we would find one Y score in each condition and have a perfectly consistent relationship.)

As you'll see in Chapter 7, we compute a statistic (called the "effect size") to obtain a less subjective description of the strength of a relationship.

REMEMBER We usually summarize the relationship in an experiment by computing the mean and standard deviation in each condition and by plotting a line or bar graph.

Interpreting the Overall Relationship

The next step would be to perform the appropriate inferential procedure. If the data pass this test, then the preceding descriptive statistics are the basis for testing the hypothesis of the study and for interpreting the results. Look again at the results in Table 6.3 and note the type of relationship. We originally predicted that test grades would increase as study time increased. Because the means form a largely positive linear relationship, these data confirm our hypothesis. A negative or very nonlinear relationship would contradict our prediction and disconfirm the hypothesis. In a different study, the hypothesis might lead us to predict only some kind of relationship, and then a positive, negative, or nonlinear relationship would confirm the hypothesis.

Also note the *strength* of the relationship, because the inconsistency in a relationship suggests the extent to which *other* variables influence the behavior. Recall that there are two general causes for differences among scores within a condition. First, there may be unsystematic external variables operating on participants. For example, within a study-time condition, perhaps sometimes the laboratory was noisy or the experimenter was distracting, so studying was less effective for some participants than for others. This would produce differences among test scores even though all had studied the same amount. Second, different scores result from individual differences among participants. People in our study will exhibit differences in intelligence, aptitude, and motivation that can cause them to score differently on the test, even when they study the same amount.

Thus, the extent to which test scores are consistently related to study time suggests the extent to which test grades are "caused" by study time alone. A very strong relationship will suggest that amount of study time has a major, controlling effect on test scores: It seems to be *the* variable that determines a score, with other variables having only a minor influence on test grades. Conversely, a weak relationship would suggest that, in addition to study time, there are other factors that substantially influence test grades.

Following this line of reasoning, we begin to interpret our results "psychologically," explaining how we think these variables operate in terms of the theoretical explanations, models, and constructs about learning and memory that initially led us to conduct this study.

> **REMEMBER**   Research is interpreted on the basis of the type and strength of the relationship found in the sample data.

We cannot, however, *confidently* draw any conclusion until we've performed the appropriate inferential procedures.

Applying Inferential Statistical Procedures

Ultimately, we want to generalize the sample relationship to everyone in nature—to everyone in the population. However, we can never be certain how the population would behave, because there is no guarantee that the sample accurately *represents* the population. How representative a sample is depends on the luck of the draw of the participants and their scores that are selected. Just by chance, our data might contain too many high scores or too many low scores relative to the population, so that a sample is *un*representative to some degree. In statistical terms, we say we have sampling error. **Sampling error** results when the characteristics of the sample data are different from the population they represent. Because of the luck of the draw, the *sample* is in *error* in representing the population.

> **REMEMBER**   Sampling error results from the luck of which scores are obtained so that the sample is different from the population it represents.

There is always the possibility of sampling error, and so *sampling error is the reason researchers perform inferential statistics*. We would like to say that if we measured the entire population under each condition, we would find different scores—and means—in each condition like those in our sample data. BUT! Maybe we're being mislead by sampling error so that if we tested everyone in the population under each condition, we would find the *same* batch of scores (and the same mean) each time, in which case this relationship is *not* present in the population.

For example, assume that we could see the scores for everyone in the population under our different levels of study time, producing Figure 6.7. Although there is no relationship here, imagine that the three circles on the graph enclose the scores that, simply by chance, we happened to obtain in each condition of our experiment. Because of chance—sampling error—the scores in the samples tend to increase with amount of study time, even though they do not increase for everyone in the population—*in nature*. Likewise, the sample means tend to

Figure 6.7 Hypothetical population scatterplot

This scatterplot shows a sample relationship even though no such relationship exists in the population.

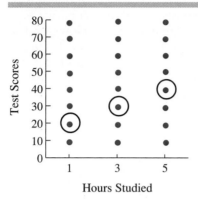

increase, even though the same mean would be found for each condition in the population.

Thus, even though we may find a mathematical relationship in the sample, it may not represent a real relationship that occurs in nature. Instead, the data may *coincidentally* form a relationship by chance. Therefore, before we can generalize any relationship we observe, we must first decide whether the relationship in the sample is "believable," representing a relationship that actually exists in nature. To do so, we apply inferential statistics.

The Logic of Inferential Statistics

In statistical terminology, we can sum up the preceding issue using two hypotheses. On the one hand, the predicted relationship might not exist in the population: The **null hypothesis** implies that, because of sampling error, the sample data poorly represent the *absence* of the predicted relationship in the population. On the other hand, the sample data might represent the real relationship found in the population: The **alternative hypothesis** implies that the sample data reflect the presence of the predicted relationship in the population. (Note that we're not talking about whether the data are reliable or valid. Whatever the scores measure, we're saying that they form a real relationship.)

We can never know whether a real relationship exists. We can, however, determine the probability of obtaining a particular sample relationship by chance when there is no real relationship. The logic of all inferential statistics is this: Say we obtain a very weak, barely consistent sample relationship. The null hypothesis says this pattern is due to chance, and in reality the sample poorly represents no relationship. This hypothesis makes sense, because the odds are high that a few scores might pair up by chance even when no real relationship exists. Therefore, we "retain" the null hypothesis.

However, with a stronger relationship the null hypothesis becomes less convincing. Say we obtain a perfectly consistent relationship. Again, the null hypothesis says that this pattern is due to sampling error. However, the probability is incredibly small that, *by luck,* we would select scores that match up perfectly when there is no relationship in nature. Such a low probability is taken as evidence that disconfirms the null hypothesis. Because such a sample relationship is *too unlikely* to be produced by sampling error, we "reject" the null hypothesis. Then the only explanation left is the alternative hypothesis that the data represent a real "believable" relationship.

REMEMBER   We reject the null hypothesis when it is too unlikely that we'd obtain our data if a real relationship does not exist in nature.

Selecting an Inferential Procedure

How we determine the probability of obtaining a particular relationship by chance depends on the characteristics of the design (the scale of measurement used, the way the relationship is summarized, how many groups are involved, and so on). Therefore, you must select the appropriate inferential procedure to use. So far we've examined the influence of manipulating *one* independent variable, discussing **one-way designs.** Then, if we have normally distributed interval or ratio scores, we select a *parametric* procedure.

Parametric Procedures   The most common parametric procedures for a one-way design are the two-sample *t*-test and the analysis of variance.

The **two-sample *t*-test** is performed when we examine only two conditions of one independent variable. We could use the *t*-test, for example, if we compared only the effects of 1 hour versus 3 hours of study time. However, you calculate *t* in one of two ways, depending on how you select your participants. When you use either a repeated-measures design or a matched-groups design, you should perform the **dependent samples *t*-test.** When you select a random sample for each condition without repeated-measures or matching, you should perform the **independent samples *t*-test.**

When you test three or more conditions of one independent variable, perform the **one-way analysis of variance (ANOVA),** computing an *F*. (When there only two conditions, you can use either the *t*-test or ANOVA.) Thus, the original study-time experiment examined studying for 1, 3, or 5 hours, so here we'd perform ANOVA. However, there are again two sets of formulas, depending on whether you have a between- or within-subjects design. But here's a confusing tidbit: Statistically, *between* and *within* are defined differently than they were before. In the research terminology of Chapter 5, matched-groups produce a between-subjects *design* and repeated measures produce a within-subjects design. However, perform the **within-subjects ANOVA** when you have a repeated-measures *or* matched-groups design. Perform the **between-subjects ANOVA** when you don't use matching or repeated measures.

Table 6.4 shows the designs for the *t*-test and ANOVA. Regardless of whether you've got a between- or within-subjects design, the logic is the same. Essentially, we first collapse across all counterbalanced variables to compute the mean of each condition (each column). As you've seen, different means in different conditions indicate a relationship, and the bigger the differences, the more convincing the relationship. Then we compute a statistic—*t* or *F*—that summarizes the sample relationship by comparing the difference in scores between conditions relative to the error variance within conditions. If *t* or *F* is large enough, then we conclude that the scores (or means) differ so much between conditions that we have a believable relationship.

Nonparametric Procedures Sometimes you'll have scores that are measured using a nominal or ordinal scale of measurement, and then you should use a non-parametric inferential statistic. As with the *t*-test or ANOVA, these procedures also produce a statistic that summarizes the sample relationship.

You'll obtain ordinal scores in a study for one of two reasons. Sometimes participants' scores on the dependent variable are directly measured using ranked scores (such as when you have "raters" rank-order participants on some characteristic). At other times you initially measure the dependent variable using interval or ratio scores, but because they violate the rules of parametric procedures, you transform the scores by assigning them ranks: The highest original score is ranked 1, the next highest is ranked 2, and so on. Then the logic is similar to that of the previous tests. For example, say we ranked the performance of eight students on a test after they studied for 1 or 3 hours, giving the highest test grade in

Table 6.4   Diagram of a *t*-Test and One-Way ANOVA

Each X represents a participant's score on the dependent variable.

	t-Test		One-Way ANOVA		
	Hours Studied			*Hours Studied*	
	1	*3*	*1*	*3*	*5*
	X	X	X	X	X
	X	X	X	X	X
	X	X	X	X	X
	X	X	X	X	X
	$\overline{X}$	$\overline{X}$	$\overline{X}$	$\overline{X}$	$\overline{X}$

the **experiment** a rank of 1, the second highest score in the study a 2, and so on. Now we look for the pattern the ranks form as shown below:

Hours Studied

1	3
3	1
6	2
7	4
8	5

There is apparently a relationship here, because participants tend to consistently score higher—obtaining lower ranks—when they study longer. It looks like a relationship, but maybe the lower ranks occurred in the 3-hour condition simply by luck. To test this, if you test two conditions without matching or repeated measures, compute the **Mann-Whitney test.** If you test more than two conditions in this way, perform the **Kruskal-Wallis test.** If you test two conditions but use matching or repeated measures, compute the **Wilcoxon test.** If you test more than two conditions using this design, compute the **Friedman test.** In each of these, if the obtained statistic is large enough, then we conclude that we have a believable relationship.

Finally, sometimes your dependent variable involves categorizing participants using a nominal scale. There is no common inferential procedure for a matched-groups or repeated-measures design. However, if you don't use matching or repeated measures and you're examining one factor, then compute the **one-way chi square.** For example, say that we wish to categorize all those who failed the exam in terms of whether they studied for 1, 3, or 5 hours. Say that we found the following frequency of failing participants in each category:

Hours Studied

1	3	5
12	5	2

It looks like a relationship exists here, because the frequency of category membership—how often participants fail—changes depending on the number of hours studied. (With no relationship, we'd see about the same number of participants in each condition.) But, maybe we have these frequencies just because of sampling error. Therefore, we compute the chi square—χ^2—and if it is large enough, then we conclude that we have a believable relationship.

The formulas for parametric and nonparametric procedures, and instructions for using them are presented in Appendix C. To help you select a procedure, the previous discussion is summarized in Table 6.5.

Interpreting Significant Results

In each of the previous procedures, the larger the obtained statistic we compute, the stronger the relationship, and so the less likely that it is due to sampling error. To decide whether the obtained statistic is large enough for us to reject the null hypothesis, we compare it to the "critical value." (For details, see the specific procedure in Appendix C.) If the obtained value is *greater* than the critical value, then we reject the null hypothesis and accept the alternative hypothesis. We communicate this decision by stating that the results are significant. A **significant** sample relationship is too unlikely to occur by chance, so we assume that it represents the real, predicted relationship found in the population. You'll also read research that finds "significant differences," meaning that the differences

Table 6.5 Parametric Procedures and Their Nonparametric Counterparts Used in Experiments with One Independent Variable

Between-Subjects Analysis (No Matching or Repeated Measures)

Number of Conditions	Parametric Scores (Interval or Ratio)	Nonparametric Scores	
		Ordinal	Nominal
Two	Independent samples *t*-test	Mann-Whitney test	Chi square
Three or more	Between-subjects ANOVA	Kruskal-Wallis test	Chi square

Within-Subjects Analysis (Matched Groups or Repeated Measures)

Number of Conditions	Parametric Scores (Interval or Ratio)	Nonparametric Scores	
		Ordinal	Nominal
Two	Dependent samples *t*-test	Wilcoxon test	none
Three or more	Within-subjects ANOVA	Friedman test	none

between the means of the conditions are too large to explain as mere sampling error, so they must represent real differences that occur in the population. In such cases, we conclude that we have a believable sample relationship and go on to interpret and generalize it accordingly.

> *REMEMBER* In every study, you must determine whether or not the sample relationship is significant.

Comparing the Conditions in ANOVA

You are not finished with inferential procedures when you obtain a significant F in any ANOVA that involves more than two levels of the factor. A significant F indicates only that two or more conditions differ significantly, but it does not indicate *which* conditions differ significantly. Therefore, the next step is to perform post hoc comparisons. **Post hoc tests** compare all possible pairs of conditions to determine which ones differ significantly from each other. In the literature you'll encounter several post hoc tests (each named after their developers), such as the Scheffé test, the Newman-Keuls test, or the Duncan test. The different procedures differ in how likely they are to produce significant results versus producing errors. An in-between procedure is the Tukey HSD test. (This and analogous procedures for nonparametric procedures are shown in Appendix C.)

Performing these procedures is similar to performing a t-test on each pair of means from the factor. Thus, in the study-time experiment, we'll end up comparing the means of the 1- and 3-hour conditions, the means of the 1- and 5-hour conditions, and the means of the 3- and 5-hour conditions. This will identify where, among the three levels of study time, significant differences in test scores occur. Then we will infer that there is a "real" relationship involving only those conditions that differ significantly, and we will discuss only these differences when generalizing the results.

Instead of computing F and then performing post hoc tests, researchers sometimes take a different approach and perform planned comparisons. **Planned comparisons** compare only some conditions in an experiment. In the study-time experiment, for example, a hypothesis might lead us to compare the 1-hour condition to every other condition, but without comparing the 3-hour to the 5-hour condition. Planned comparisons are also called a priori comparisons. (In these procedures, F need not be computed.)

> *REMEMBER* Perform either post hoc comparisons or planned comparisons to determine which levels in a factor differ significantly.

Estimating the Population Mean

If the results of the study-time experiment are significant, then we'll use the mean in each level to estimate the mean we'd find if we studied the entire population.

(A population mean is called mu, symbolized as μ.) For example, if our sample mean of 20 in the 1-hour condition differs significantly from the other means, we'd estimate that after testing the population under this condition, the population's μ would be "around" 20. However, the sample of students in that condition probably does not *perfectly* represent the population, so we probably have some sampling error in this estimate. To factor in sampling error, we compute a confidence interval. A **confidence interval** describes a range of μs, any one of which the sample mean is likely to represent. You can see this in the following diagram:

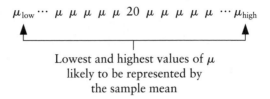

Lowest and highest values of μ
likely to be represented by
the sample mean

Computing the confidence interval involves computing the lowest and highest value of μ that the sample mean is likely to represent. In the example, this gives us a range of values around 20. Then, even if our sample mean contains sampling error, we conclude that μ is probably within this range. (Computations are shown in Appendix C.9.)

Restrictions on Interpreting Significant Results

Based on a significant sample relationship (and post hoc tests and confidence intervals), we can begin to describe the relationship we'd expect to find if we could study everyone in the population. On the one hand, this means we are confident that we know how nature works in this situation. On the other hand, remember that researchers are always cautious in their conclusions. When making inferences about a significant relationship, bear in mind two restrictions.

First, a significant result does not "prove" that the relationship exists in the population. All we have "proved" is that chance—sampling error—would be unlikely to produce our data if a relationship does not exist in the population. But unlikely does not mean impossible. It's still possible that the relationship does not occur in the population and simply by the luck of the draw we obtained data that give the appearance of a relationship. Thus, whenever results are significant, it's possible that we've made a Type I error. A **Type I error** occurs when we reject the null hypothesis, but it is the correct hypothesis. In other words, we say the data reflect a real relationship—and the independent variable works—when in fact they do not.

Thus sometimes (although we never know when) the null hypothesis is really true. In that case, rejecting null is a Type I error (and retaining it is the correct decision). However, in setting up an inferential test, we set **alpha,** symbolized by α, which is the probability that we will make a Type I error. Psychologists have agreed that alpha can be no greater than .05, so that the probability that we'll reject a true null hypothesis is always less than .05. Thus, on the one hand, it is unlikely that we've made a Type I error, but on the other hand, it's still possible.

The second restriction is that the term *significant* indicates only that the *numbers* in the data are unlikely to occur if the sample represents a population of *numbers* in which the relationship does not exist. It does not mean that these numbers accurately reflect our variables, or that the behaviors and constructs are related in the way that we've hypothesized. Therefore, as usual, you must evaluate the study in terms of reliability and the various types of validity we've discussed in previous chapters to be sure that you are not being misled by flaws in the design. Only if you've performed a well-designed study can you be confident that the relationship between the scores reflects the relationship between the *variables* that you think are present. If so, you'll be confident both that you're not being mislead by flaws in the design, and that you're not being mislead by sampling error. Then, you can confidently interpret the relationship "psychologically" in terms of the variables and constructs you set out to study.

> **REMEMBER** Significant results may *not* represent a real relationship in the population or reflect the relationship between the variables that you think they do.

Interpreting Nonsignificant Results

If the inferential statistic we obtain is not greater than the critical value, then the results are not too unlikely to occur through sampling error. Therefore, we do not reject the null hypothesis. We describe such results as **nonsignificant.**

If results are not significant, we have not "proved" that the predicted relationship does not exist in the population (and we have not proved that the independent variable doesn't work as predicted). We have simply found that chance could reasonably produce data such as ours when a real relationship does not exist. But just because chance *could* do so does not mean that it *did* so. For example, let's say we obtain a very weak, nonsignificant relationship when comparing the influence of different study times. There are three possible reasons why this might happen. (1) Maybe we're correct and there is no real relationship here, and to the extent that we see a sample relationship, it's because of sampling error. (2) Maybe there *is* this relationship in the population and the sample perfectly represents it, but being so weak, we—and our statistics—misinterpret it as reflecting sampling error. (3) Maybe there is a very strong relationship in nature, but, because of sampling error, we have an unrepresentative sample that produced this weak example of it.

With nonsignificant results, we have merely failed to reject the null hypothesis, so both it and the alternative hypothesis are still viable proposals: Literally, we cannot decide whether the relationship exists in the population or not. Therefore, we do not say anything about the relationship: We do not perform any additional statistical procedures to describe the relationship, we do not conclude whether it confirms or disconfirms our original hypothesis, and we do not even begin to interpret it psychologically.

> **REMEMBER** Nonsignificant results provide no convincing evidence—one way or the other—as to whether a "real" relationship exists.

Because it's possible that a particular relationship exists in the population even though our results are nonsignificant, it is also possible that we are making an error whenever we retain the null hypothesis. A **Type II error** occurs when we retain the null hypothesis when it is false and the alternative is the correct hypothesis. (The probability of a Type II error is called beta, symbolized as β). Thus, sometimes (we also never know when) the null hypothesis is really false. Retaining null is a Type II error (and rejecting it is the correct decision). Here we conclude that there is no evidence for the relationship in nature (no evidence that our manipulation works) when in fact the relationship exists (and the manipulation may work!).

Statistical Power and Research Design

Type I and Type II errors are mutually exclusive: If it's possible you've made one type of error, then you cannot have made the other. Your potential to make a Type I or a Type II error is determined by the true state of affairs: Is null really true or really false? Whether you've then made that error depends on whether you've rejected or retained null.

Psychology seeks to avoid Type I errors, so that we avoid building a science around chance relationships that do not really exist in nature. (That's why we make α so small.) However, we also want to avoid Type II errors, so that we identify the real relationships and thus learn something about nature. This ability is so important that it has a special name: **Power** is the probability that we will reject the null hypothesis on those occasions when null is actually false, correctly concluding that the sample data reflect a real relationship. In other words, power is the probability that we will not make a Type II error.

Power is important because, after all, why bother to conduct a study if you're unlikely to reject the null hypothesis even when the predicted relationship really *does* exist? Therefore, whether you have sufficient power is crucial whenever you retain the null hypothesis. (Some introductory statistics books discuss directly calculating the power in a study, or see Cohen, 1988). However, you cannot add power after a study is complete. Instead, you must create a powerful design, so that you'll have confidence in your decision if later on, you end up retaining the null hypothesis.

The concept of power has shown up in previous chapters when we discussed producing a powerful design—a design that produces a strong, convincing sample relationship. Now you can understand the logic behind this: We are talking about only those times when the null hypothesis is false and there really *is* a relationship in nature. On those occasions, we "should" reject the null hypothesis, so our results "should" be significant. Therefore, maximizing power essentially means that we maximize the probability that results will be significant. As you've seen, an inferential procedure uses the strength of a relationship to determine how likely it is to occur by chance (sampling error). On those times when the null hypothesis really is false, it is better to have a stronger sample relationship, because then the obtained inferential statistic we compute will be *larger*. The larger the obtained value, the more likely that it will be larger than the critical value. Then, instead of missing a real relationship by concluding that it is due to chance, we make the correct decision, concluding that the results are significant. There are two general approaches for maximizing the power in a study.

First, as we've seen in previous chapters, we create a powerful design that is likely to result in a strong, convincing sample relationship. We seek large differences in scores—and means—between the conditions (because this adds to the strength of a relationship). We do this by using a *strong manipulation* and obtaining *sensitive measurements*. We also minimize error variance within conditions (because such differences in scores work against the strength of the relationship). We do this by building in controls that eliminate the influence of extraneous variables from the participants, experimenter, environment, or measurement task that create inconsistency in scores.

An additional, new component of a powerful design involves N, the number of participants that you test. *The greater the N, the more powerful the design.* The size of N is important, because a relationship of a given strength is more "believable" if it's based on more observations. For example, while two participants might be likely to produce a particular relationship by chance when there is no real relationship present, 200 are not. This logic is built into significance testing because the larger the N, the larger will be the obtained inferential statistic we compute. Also, N determines the *degrees of freedom*, or *df*, in a study. A larger N produces larger *df*, and the larger the *df*, the smaller the critical value to which we compare our obtained statistic. The smaller the critical value, the more likely that the obtained statistics exceeds it, so the more likely that the results are significant. (Note, however, that we are discussing relatively small samples. Generally, an N of 30 is needed for minimal power, and increasing N up to 121 increases power substantially. However, an N of 500 is not much more powerful than an N of, say, 450.)

REMEMBER   The stronger the sample relationship and the larger the N, the more powerful the study.

The second approach is to use powerful statistics. First, because of their theoretical foundations, parametric inferential procedures are more powerful than nonparametric procedures: Data that are analyzed using a parametric test are more likely to be significant than if the same data are analyzed using a nonparametric procedure. Therefore, try to design any study so that you can use parametric procedures.

With designs testing only two conditions, power is also determined by whether you perform a **one-tailed** or **two-tailed test.** With two means, the relationship can only be linear, and if you predict which level's mean will be larger and which will be smaller, you can predict either a positive or a negative relationship. Then perform the one-tailed test. Perform a two-tailed test when you cannot predict whether the relationship will be positive or negative. (Analyses with three or more conditions always use a two-tailed test.) A one-tailed test is more powerful than a two-tailed test. However, if the sample relationship turns out to be the opposite of what you've predicted, then the relationship is not significant. Therefore, if you are not sure of the prediction, use the safer two-tailed test, because you can find a significant relationship regardless of its type and still draw inferences from the study.

REMEMBER The power of a design is increased by using parametric procedures and one-tailed tests.

Putting It All Together

The lesson that should be obvious at this point is that issues of reliability, validity, and control are *the* issues in research design. You've seen how we attempt to design a study so that we accurately and only measure the variables of interest, while controlling all other variables. If we don't, these flaws can mislead us when we interpret the results psychologically. You've also seen how these same flaws influence our statistical interpretations because they lessen our power. Our statistical interpretations are critical to our psychological interpretations, because results must be significant before we can draw any inferences about a relationship. Thus, eliminating flaws in the design is doubly important so that you (1) obtain powerful data and do not miss a relationship when it exists, and then (2) draw the correct psychological interpretations about that relationship.

CHAPTER SUMMARY

1. Experiments investigate changes in the dependent variable *as a function of* changes in the independent variable.

2. *Descriptive statistics* summarize and describe the important characteristics of a sample of data. *Inferential statistics* are procedures for deciding whether a sample relationship represents a relationship that actually exists in the population.

3. A *nominal scale* reflects the category a participant falls in; an *ordinal scale* reflect a participant's rank order; an *interval scale* measures an amount and negative scores are possible; and a *ratio scale* measures an amount, but negative scores are not possible.

4. *Parametric* inferential statistics are usually used with normally distributed interval or ratio scores. *Nonparametric* statistics are used with non-normal interval/ratio scores, or with nominal or ordinal scores.

5. To describe a relationship, determine (a) the *type* of relationship—the direction in which the Y scores change as the X scores change, and (b) the *strength* of the relationship—the extent to which one value of Y is consistently associated with one value of X.

6. In a *positive linear relationship,* as the X scores increase, the Y scores also tend to increase. In a *negative linear relationship,* as the X scores increase, the Y scores tend to decrease. In a *nonlinear relationship,* as the X scores increase, the Y scores change their direction of change. When no relationship is present, the distribution of Y scores at one X is virtually the same as at other Xs.

7. *Measures of central tendency* summarize a distribution of scores, indicating the score around which the distribution tends to be centered. The common measures are the mean, the median, and the mode. Which measure to compute depends on the scale used to measure the dependent variable.

8. In graphing the results of an experiment, the independent variable is plotted on the X axis and the dependent variable is on the Y axis. A *line graph* is created when the independent variable is measured using an ordinal, ratio, or interval scale. A *bar graph* is created when the independent variable is measured using a nominal scale.

9. *Measures of variability* describe how much the scores differ from one another. The common measures of variability are the *variance* and the *standard deviation.*

10. The *strength* of a relationship in an experiment indicates the degree to which changes in dependent scores are caused by changing the levels of the independent variable.

11. The *null hypothesis* implies that the sample poorly represents the absence of the predicted relationship in the population. The *alternative hypothesis* implies that the sample data reflect the presence of the predicted relationship in the population.

12. A *one-way design* has only one independent variable. The *two-sample t-test* is the appropriate parametric inferential procedure when there are only two conditions and the *analysis of variance (ANOVA)* is appropriate when there are two or more levels. Use the *dependent-samples t-test* or the *within-subjects ANOVA* with matching or repeated measures. Otherwise, use the *independent-samples t-test* or the *between-subjects ANOVA.*

13. With ranked data (without matching or repeated measures), compute the *Mann-Whitney test* with two conditions and the *Kruskal-Wallace test* with more than two conditions. With matching or repeated measures, use the *Wilcoxon test* with two conditions and the *Friedman test* with more than

two conditions. Use the *one-way chi square* with nominal data and two or more conditions.

14. *Alpha (α)* is the probability of making a Type I error.

15. In a *one-tailed inferential* test, only a positive linear relationship or only a negative one is predicted. In a *two-tailed test,* either a positive or a negative relationship is predicted.

16. *Significant* indicates that the sample relationship is too unlikely to occur if the predicted relationship does not exist in the population. *Nonsignificant* provides no convincing evidence, one way or the other, about the predicted relationship.

17. In ANOVA, *post hoc tests* compare all possible pairs of conditions to determine which ones differ significantly. *Planned comparisons* are performed to compare only some pairs of conditions.

18. A *confidence interval* describes a range of values of the population mean *(μ),* any one of which the sample mean is likely to represent.

19. A *Type I error* is rejecting the null hypothesis when it is true. A *Type II error* is retaining the null hypothesis when it is false.

20. Power is the probability of rejecting the null hypothesis when it is false. Power is increased by maximizing the differences in scores between conditions, minimizing the error variance, and by increasing N. Also, parametric statistics are more powerful than nonparametric statistics, and one-tailed tests are more powerful than two-tailed tests.

KEY TERMS

alpha *(α) (191)*
alternative hypothesis *(185)*
ANOVA *(186)*
as a function of *(174)*
bar graph *(181)*
between-subjects ANOVA *(187)*
confidence interval *(191)*
dependent samples *t*-test *(186)*
descriptive statistics *(171)*
error variance *(175)*
Friedman test *(188)*

independent samples *t*-test *(186)*
inferential statistics *(171)*
interval scale *(172)*
Kruskal-Wallis test *(188)*
line graph *(180)*
linear relationship *(174)*
Mann-Whitney test *(188)*
mean *(178)*
measure of central tendency *(178)*

measures of variability *(182)*
median *(179)*
mode *(179)*
negative linear relationship *(174)*
nominal scale *(172)*
nonlinear relationship *(177)*
nonparametric inferential statistics *(173)*
nonsignificant *(192)*
normal distribution *(173)*

null hypothesis *(185)*
one-tailed test *(195)*
one-way analysis of
   variance (ANOVA)
   (186)
one-way chi square
   (188)
one-way designs
   (186)
ordinal scale *(172)*
parametric inferential
   statistics *(173)*
planned comparisons
   (190)

positive linear
   relationship *(174)*
post hoc tests *(190)*
power *(193)*
ratio scale *(172)*
sample standard
   deviation *(182)*
sample variance
   (182)
sampling error *(184)*
scales of measurement
   (171)
significant *(189)*

strength of the
   relationship *(174)*
two-sample *t*-test
   (186)
two-tailed test *(195)*
Type I error *(191)*
Type II error *(193)*
type of relationship
   (174)
Wilcoxon test *(188)*
within-subjects
   ANOVA *(187)*

REVIEW QUESTIONS

1. What two major characteristics of a study determine the type of statistical procedures you should use?

2. When do you perform parametric or nonparametric procedures?

3. (a) What is the difference between positive and negative linear relationships? (b) What is the difference between linear and nonlinear relationships?

4. In the following chart, identify the characteristics of each variable.

Variable	Measurement Scale
Gender	_____
Academic Major	_____
Time	_____
Restaurant Ratings	_____
Speed	_____
Position in Line	_____
Change in Weight	_____

5. For each of the following, what is the independent and dependent variable, what scale of measurement is being used with each variable, and how would you graph the results? (a) You examine whether amount of graffiti changes as a function of a males' versus a females' restroom. (b) You study the relationship between students' choice to sit toward the front, middle, or back of a classroom and their grade in the class. (c) You conduct a study of memory for pictures as a function of participants' mood, ranging from very sad to very happy.

6. Summarize the steps involved in describing and interpreting the results of an experiment.

7. (a) What is the mode? (b) What is the median? (c) What is the mean? (d) With what type of data is the mean appropriate?

8. How does the size of a measure of variability communicate (a) the size of the differences between the scores in a distribution and (b) how consistently the participants scored close to the same score?

9. (a) What is sampling error? (b) Why does the possibility of sampling error present a problem to researchers when inferring that a relationship exists in nature?

10. (a) What does the null hypothesis communicate? (b) What does the alternative hypothesis communicate?

11. (a) When do you use a one-tailed or a two-tailed test? (b) What is the advantage and disadvantage of each?

12. What does it mean to have significant results in terms of (a) the obtained and critical values? (b) the likelihood of obtaining our sample relationship if the null hypothesis were true?

13. (a) Why is it important to create a powerful design? (b) What four things can you do when designing a study to increase power? (c) What two statistical aspects should you consider to increase your power?

14. Consider the results of the following experiments.

Experiment 1

Condition 1	Condition 2	Condition 3
12	30	45
11	33	48
14	36	49
10	35	44

Experiment 2

Condition 1	Condition 2	Condition 3
18	8	3
13	11	9
9	6	5

(a) What should you do to summarize these experiments? (b) Which experiment produced the stronger relationship? (c) In each experiment, what does the amount of error variance tell you about the impact of the independent variable?

15. Consider the following graph:

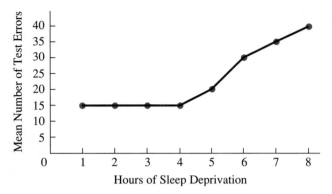

(a) Interpret specifically the relationship. (b) Give a title to the graph, using "as a function of." (c) If you participated in this study and had been deprived of 5 hours of sleep, estimate how many errors you would make. (d) If we tested all the people in the world after 5 hours of sleep deprivation, how many errors would you expect each to make? (e) What symbol stands for your prediction in part d? (f) What statistical issue arises in your conclusion in part d? (g) What issue of validity arises in part d?

16. In an experiment, a researcher observes that participants' interest in a lecture increases as a function of whether they are paid $1, $5, or $25 to listen to it. What statistical procedures must be performed before we can accept that each amount of money causes a difference in interest level?

17. A television commercial claims that "ultra-bleach" toothpaste significantly reduces tooth decay compared with other brands. What does this statement imply about (a) the type of research method used and (b) the statistical procedures performed and their outcome?

18. Say that the researcher in question 17 used an alpha equal to .25. What problems are raised by this alpha level?

19. A researcher hypothesizes that males and females are the same when it comes to intelligence, predicting a nonsignificant difference. Why is this hypothesis impossible to test statistically?

20. Researcher A finds a significant negative relationship between increasing stress level and participants' ability to concentrate. Researcher B replicates this study but finds a nonsignificant relationship. Identify the statistical error that each researcher might have made.

21. Dr. Grumpy administered the Grumpy Emotionality Test to people while varying the amount of sunlight present. The resulting line graph slants downward. What does this tell you about (a) the means for the conditions,

(b) the raw scores for each condition, and (c) the relationship between emotionality and sunlight?

DISCUSSION QUESTIONS

1. A researcher wonders whether attending a private or public high school influences performance on a test of social skills. Say she finds significant results. (a) What is the probability that she made a Type I error, and what would the error be in terms of the independent and dependent variables? (b) What is the probability that she made a Type II error, and what would the error be in terms of the independent and dependent variables? Say she finds nonsignificant results. (c) What is the probability that she made a Type I error, and what would the error be in terms of the independent and dependent variables? (d) What is the symbol for the probability that she made a Type II error, and what would the error be in terms of the independent and dependent variables?

2. If we conduct the study-time experiment discussed in this chapter using a between-subjects design, random selection and random assignment should result in a mix of different participants for each condition. (a) How might this mix adversely affect the power of the study? (b) Should this be a within-subjects design instead? (c) Describe completely how you would study whether increased test grades increase as a function of increased study time.

3. A researcher obtains a large degree of error variance in an experiment on children's ability to remember a passage they read as a function of the number of hours they have previously watched television. (a) What does this statement indicate about the scores in each condition? (b) What might cause such variability? (c) What impact will such variability have on the statistical results? (d) What impact will it have on the conceptual interpretation of the variable of television watching?

4. Immediately prior to an exam, we ask students the number of hours they studied. We then conduct an experiment by randomly selecting a group of 10 participants who had studied for 1 hour and a group of 10 who had studied for 2 hours. The mean exam scores for the two groups were 35 and 50, respectively. An independent samples t-test yielded an obtained $t = +1.70$. (a) For alpha $= .05$, what conclusion do you draw from this study? (b) What statistical flaw should concern you, and how would you fix it? (c) If t had equaled $+2.70$, what conclusion would you draw? (d) In part c, what additional information about the data would you seek? (e) How confident are you in your conclusions in part c and why? (Hint: Remember to consider the type of experiment this is.)

7

Designing and Analyzing Multifactor Experiments

GETTING STARTED

To understand this chapter, recall the following:

- From Chapter 5, recall what a between-subjects, a matched-groups, and a repeated-measures design is.

- From Chapter 6, recall the purpose of a one-way ANOVA, what a significant *F* indicates, and when to perform post hoc tests.

- Also from Chapter 6, recall how the consistency of a sample relationship indicates the impact that the independent variable has.

Your goals in this chapter are to learn:

- What two-way factorial designs are and why researchers conduct them.

- How to collapse across a factor and what a significant main effect indicates.

- How to calculate the cell means and what a significant interaction indicates.

- What measures of effect size indicate.

- How to interpret the results of a two-way experiment.

- The logic of experiments having three or more factors.

Believe it or not, so far we have discussed *simple* experiments. They are simple because they involve manipulating only one independent variable and performing only the most basic statistical analyses. In actual practice, however, psychologists often manipulate more than one independent variable. Using the terminology of ANOVA, an independent variable is a factor, so manipulating more than one independent variable produces a **multifactor experiment.**

To introduce you to multifactor experiments, this chapter first discusses between- and within-subjects experiments containing two factors. As with other designs, the approach here is the same regardless of whether you manipulate true or quasi-independent variables. We'll focus on analyzing such experiments, because once you understand the procedures involved, the interpretation is straightforward. (Don't worry though, this is only a conceptual review and summary, without the calculations. The formulas for these analyses are presented in Appendix C.) We'll also discuss the logic of designs involving more than two factors—and a few other advanced topics—so that if you encounter them in the literature, you'll understand their basics.

The Reason for Multifactor Studies

A multifactor design has two advantages over a single-factor design. First, in most natural settings there are varying amounts of many variables present that combine to influence a behavior. By manipulating more than one independent variable in an experiment, we can examine the influence of these combinations on a behavior. When the combination of different amounts of our independent variables produces an effect on dependent scores, we have an *interaction*. The primary reason for conducting multifactor studies is to observe the interaction between independent variables.

A second advantage of multifactor designs is that once you have created a design for studying one independent variable, often only a minimum of effort is required to study additional factors. Thus, multifactor studies can be an efficient and cost-effective way of determining the effects of—and interactions among—several independent variables.

Finally, multifactor experiments are often produced when you set out to study only one factor but then counterbalance an important extraneous variable. As you'll see, instead of collapsing across and ignoring such a variable as we've done in previous chapters, we can treat it as an additional factor and examine its influence on dependent scores as well.

The Two-Way Between-Subjects ANOVA

Recall that when you manipulate one independent variable, you have a *one-way design*. Not surprisingly, in a **two-way design** the researcher simultaneously manipulates two independent variables within one study. The logic in a two-way study is the same as that for a one way-design: For each variable, we formulate hypotheses and make predictions regarding the effect of the manipulation on the dependent variable. Here's an example from real research. As part of a multifactor design, Berkowitz (1987) examined the hypothesis that the more positive a participant's mood, the more that person will help others. Berkowitz induced either a positive, negative, or neutral mood in participants by having them read 50 mood-influencing statements. The experimenter then asked each person for help in scoring data sheets from a fictitious experiment. The number of columns of data scored within a 5-minute period was the dependent measure of helping. The design of this factor is shown in Table 7.1.

All of the principles we've discussed for designing the independent and dependent variable and controlling extraneous variables also apply to a multifactor design: Berkowitz limited the population and sample to females, devised a plausible request for help that minimized reactivity and other demand characteristics, kept the experimenter's behavior constant, and developed constant scoring criteria. Because the amount of help that a person provides involved a ratio scale, computing the mean helping score in each condition is appropriate. Thus, averaging vertically across the scores in each column in Table 7.1 yields the mean for each mood level, showing how helping scores change as a function of improving mood. To be sure that any relationship we see here is not due to sampling error, we'll perform an ANOVA. But matching participants seems unnecessary, and repeated measures of the same participants under all three moods might produce uncontrollable carry-over effects. Therefore, in statistical terms, this is a between-subjects factor.

Another of Berkowitz's hypotheses about helping behavior was that heightened self-awareness—or self-consciousness—increases helpfulness. To test this hypothesis, the researcher manipulated participants' self-awareness by having some see their reflection in a mirror throughout the experiment while others did not. This portion of the design can be envisioned as shown in Table 7.2.

Table 7.1   Diagram of the Factor of Mood

Each X represents a participant's helping score, and each $\overline{X}$ represents the mean helping score in a condition.

Mood Factor		
Negative	Neutral	Positive
X	X	X
X	X	X
X	X	X
X	X	X
$\overline{X}$	$\overline{X}$	$\overline{X}$

Table 7.2 Diagram of the Factor of Self-Awareness

Each row represents a level of self-awareness, each X represents a participant's helping score, and each $\overline{X}$ represents the mean helping score in a condition.

Self-Awareness Factor

High Self-Awareness (Mirror)	X X X X X X X X X	$\overline{X}$
Low Self-Awareness (No Mirror)	X X X X X X X X X	$\overline{X}$

The only novelty in this diagram is that the two conditions are arranged horizontally, so that each *row* identifies a different level of awareness. Again we apply the necessary controls: Demand characteristics are reduced by explaining that the mirror is part of another study being conducted in this lab, and, in the no-mirror condition, the mirror is present but turned away from participants. Averaging horizontally across the scores in each row yields the mean helping score for each level of self-awareness. This factor also involves no matching or repeated measures, so it, too, is a between-subjects factor.

To create a two-way design, we manipulate *both* mood and self-awareness. The diagram of this design is shown in Table 7.3. Note that the columns still represent the levels of mood, and the rows still represent the levels of self-awareness. Each small square in the diagram is called a cell. A *cell* is produced by the combination of a level of one factor with a level of the other. For example, the upper left cell in Table 7.3 contains the scores of people who received the combination of high self-awareness and negative mood. Their mean helping score, the *cell mean,* is 2.0.

Table 7.3 Two-Way Design for Studying the Factors of Type of Mood and Level of Self-Awareness

The means shown here are similar to those found in Berkowitz (1987), Experiment 2.

		Mood Factor			
		Negative	Neutral	Positive	
	High	$\overline{X} = 2.0$	$\overline{X} = 8.9$	$\overline{X} = 16.8$	$\overline{X} = 13.9$
Awareness Factor					
	Low	$\overline{X} = 2.4$	$\overline{X} = 9.6$	$\overline{X} = 9.5$	$\overline{X} = 7.2$
		$\overline{X} = 2.2$	$\overline{X} = 9.3$	$\overline{X} = 13.2$	

Researchers have a code for communicating the layout of a multifactor design. The design in Table 7.3 has one factor with three levels and one factor with two levels, so it is called a "three by two" design, written as "3 × 2" (or "2 × 3"). The number of digits indicates the number of factors in the study, and each digit indicates the number of levels in that factor. Thus, if we had two factors, each with two levels, we'd have a 2 × 2 design. (You can have any number of levels in either factor.) Also, because we combine all levels of one factor with all levels of the other factor, it is a **complete factorial design** (or simply a factorial design). If for some reason we did not include all cells (for example, omitting testing the positive mood–low self-awareness cell) we would have an *incomplete* factorial design. (Incomplete factorial designs require special statistical procedures.)

> *REMEMBER* In a *complete factorial design,* all levels of one factor are combined with all levels of the other factor.

All of the controls devised for each factor still apply in the two-way design. The major difference in multifactor designs lies in the way we analyze and interpret the results. As always, the goal is to determine whether a significant relationship exists between the independent and dependent variables. Usually, the dependent variable is measured with interval or ratio scores that form normal distributions so the data meet the rules for the two-way analysis of variance. As with the one-way ANOVA, however, there are different formulas depending on how you select and assign participants to the levels of each factor. If, as in the example, you have simply randomly assigned participants to every cell in a two-way design, with no matching or repeated measures, then perform the **two-way between-subjects ANOVA** (calculations are shown in Appendix C.5). As you'll see, the two-way ANOVA essentially creates a series of one-way ANOVAs. First, we examine the relationship produced by each individual independent variable.

Main Effects

When we examine the effect of an individual independent variable, we examine its main effect. The **main effect** of a factor is the influence that changing it has on the dependent scores, ignoring any other factors in the study. In our helping study, for example, we determine the main effects on participants' helping behavior produced by (1) changing the levels of their mood and (2) changing the levels of their self-awareness.

To find the main effect of mood, we examine the scores as if they were from the one-way design shown in Table 7.4. The small box is our original 3 × 2 diagram. Then we *collapse* vertically across the different self-awareness conditions, ignoring the levels of self-awareness just as we've collapsed across counterbalanced variables in prior chapters. To compute the mean score in a column, you

Table 7.4 Diagram of the Main Effect of Mood

In each column are the two cell means from the original diagram in Table 7.3.

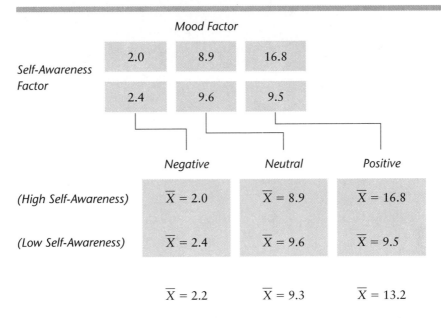

can either average all participants' scores in that column or average together the cell means in that column. The means obtained from columns are the *main effect means* for that factor. Thus, the main effect means are 2.2 for negative mood, 9.3 for neutral mood, and 13.2 for positive mood.

Although these means appear to show a relationship between mood and helping, we have the usual problem: It might be that there is no "real" relationship here, and instead the means for this factor *appear* to show a relationship because of sampling error and the luck of the draw of who was tested. As usual, this is the null hypothesis, and we test it in the two-way ANOVA by computing a "main effect F" based on the means from the column factor. If the F is significant, then changing a person's mood produces significant differences in helping scores. Remember, however, that a significant F indicates only that, somewhere in the factor, at least two of the levels differ significantly. Therefore, as you saw in Chapter 6 with one-way designs, you perform post hoc comparisons (such as the Tukey *HSD* test) to determine which main effect means of 2.2, 9.3, and 13.2 differ significantly from one another. Then, as usual, you examine the means, determine the type and strength of relationship they form, and so on to describe and interpret "psychologically" how changing mood level influences helping behavior.

Once you have analyzed the main effect of one factor, you then analyze the main effect of the next. To find the main effect of self-awareness, we examine the one-way design shown in Table 7.5. Here we collapse horizontally across the mood factor, ignoring whether participants had a negative, neutral, or positive

Table 7.5   Diagram of the Main Effect of Self-Awareness

In each row are the cell means from the original diagram in Table 7.3.

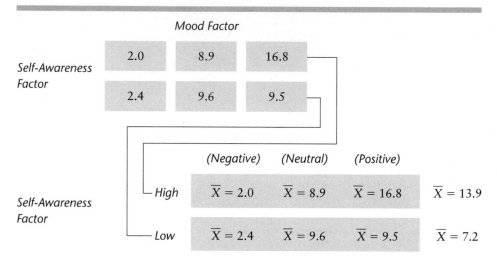

mood, to obtain the overall mean helping score of each row. To compute each mean, you can again either average all scores in the row or, as shown, average the cell means in the row. Then you have the main effect means for high self-awareness (13.9) and low self-awareness (7.2).

Although these means appear to reflect a relationship between awareness level and helping, we again are faced with the null hypothesis that this, too, is not a real relationship. Therefore, you compute a second main effect *F* to test the differences between the means of the rows. If it is significant, then at least two of these main effect means differ significantly. In this design, the factor contains only two levels, so the significant difference must be between low and high self-awareness. If there had been more than two levels, post hoc comparisons would be performed to determine which means differ significantly. Once you know which conditions are part of a "real" relationship, you then examine and interpret the relationship as we've done previously.

After examining the main effects for each variable, the final step is to examine the interaction effect.

Interaction Effects

An **interaction effect** is the influence that combining levels from the factors has on dependent scores. In the helping study, for example, we examine how a particular mood level combined with a particular self-awareness level influences scores, compared with the influence when other levels of mood or awareness are present.

The interaction of two factors is called a **two-way interaction.** It is identified using the number of levels in each factor. Here one factor has three levels and one has two, so we have a "three by two" ("3 × 2") interaction.

To examine a two-way interaction, we do not collapse across or ignore either of the original factors. Instead, we treat each *cell* in the study as a level of the interaction factor. You can think of this factor as the original six cell means arranged in the one-way design shown in Table 7.6.

The relationship in an interaction is complex because it involves three variables that are changing: two independent variables and the dependent variable. *To interpret an interaction, look at the relationship between one factor and the dependent scores, and see how that relationship changes as the levels of the other variable change.* As in the left portion of Table 7.6, under low self-awareness, changing mood from negative to neutral increases helping scores, but changing mood from neutral to positive then slightly decreases them. (This is a nonlinear relationship.) However, this relationship is not found on the right; under high self-awareness, mean helping scores consistently increase as mood improves (forming a linear relationship.)

Thus, you know that an interaction is present when the effect of changing one factor is not consistent for each level of the other factor: The effect of improving mood under high self-awareness is not the same as that under low self-awareness. In other words, any conclusion we make about the effect of changing the levels of one factor *depends on* which level of the other factor we're talking about: Whether we should conclude that improving participants' mood always increases their helping behavior in a linear fashion depends on whether

Table 7.6   Interaction of Type of Mood and Self-Awareness Level

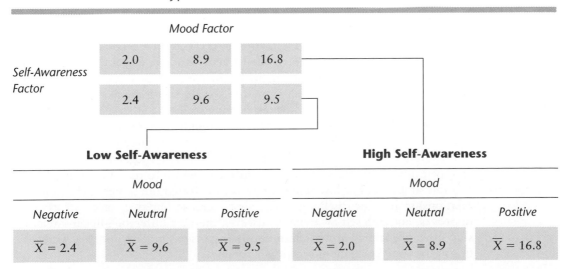

we're talking about participants having high or low self-awareness. Or, from the opposite perspective, whether we should conclude that helping is greater with high or low self-awareness depends on which mood level we're talking about.

> **REMEMBER**   A *two-way interaction* indicates that the relationship between one factor and the dependent scores depends on which level of the other factor is present.

Conversely, an interaction would *not* be present if the pattern of cell means produced by changing mood for high self-awareness is the same as that for low self-awareness. When there is no interaction present (1) the effect of changing one factor is the same for all levels of the other factor, and (2) the influence of changing the levels of one factor does not depend on which level of the other variable is present.

Of course, once again we have a problem. Although these means *appear* to show an interaction, this might be due to sampling error while there is not a "real" interaction in nature. Therefore, we calculate another, separate *F* for the interaction. (You can think of the interaction as a one-way ANOVA for the six levels of the interaction, but technically this tests the difference between the cell means *after* those differences related to each main effect have been removed.) As usual, if the interaction *F* is significant, then somewhere among the cell means there are significant differences. And also as usual, you then perform post hoc tests to determine specifically which cell means differ significantly. Finally, as usual, you examine the means that differ significantly, describing the type and strength of the relationships present and interpreting them "psychologically."

But first, recognize that an interaction can be a beast to interpret. Therefore, always graph the interaction.

Graphing the Interaction   An interaction is graphed on a *single* graph. As usual, label the *Y* axis as the mean of the dependent variable. Label the *X* axis as the levels of one factor (usually placing the factor with the most levels here). Usually you'll create a line graph. Then show the second factor by drawing a separate line for each of its levels. Thus, for our helping study, we label the *X* axis with the three mood levels. Then we connect the data points from the three cell means for high self-awareness with one line and those from the three cell means for low self-awareness with a different line as in Figure 7.1. (A legend or key is always included in such graphs to define the different lines.) To read the graph, look at one line at a time. For low self-awareness (the dotted line), there's the nonlinear relationship in which helping scores first increase but then level off as mood improves. For high self-awareness, however, there's a different—linear—relationship in which helping scores continuously increase as mood improves. Therefore, this graph shows that an interaction is present.

Figure 7.1   Graph of an interaction, showing mean helping scores as a function of mood and self-awareness level

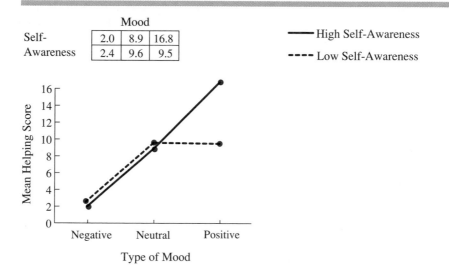

Note that there is one more way to recognize when an interaction is present. An interaction can produce an infinite variety of different graphs, but an interaction will always produce lines that are *not parallel*. Remember that each line summarizes the relationship between X (the factor) and Y (dependent scores). A line that is shaped or oriented differently depicts a different relationship between X and Y. Thus, when the lines from an interaction are not parallel, we have a different relationship between X and Y depending on which level of the other factor we examine.

For example, let's say our data turned out to produce one of the graphs in Figure 7.2. On the left, changing mood level has an opposite effect depending on the self-awareness condition. On the right, the slopes of the lines are different, indicating that improving mood with high self-awareness more dramatically increases helping scores than does improving mood with low self-awareness. On the other hand, when *no* interaction exists, the lines are parallel. Say that our data produced one of the graphs in Figure 7.3. In both, the lines indicate that as mood level changes, the scores change in the same way *regardless of* level of self-awareness. Thus, neither graph shows an interaction. (The difference in the height of the two lines in each graph simply shows the main effect of self-awareness: On the left, the low awareness groups consistently scored higher, while on the right they consistently scored lower.)

Think of a significant interaction F as indicating that somewhere in the graph, the lines significantly differ from parallel. A nonsignificant F indicates

Figure 7.2   Two graphs showing that an interaction is present

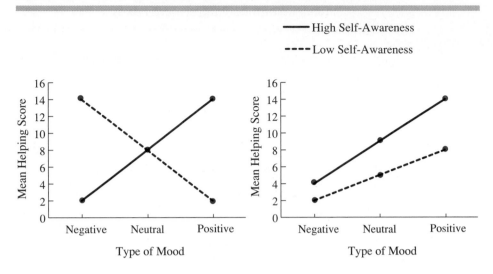

that any deviance from parallel is likely to be due to sampling error in representing parallel lines—no interaction—in the population.

> **REMEMBER**   When an interaction is present, the lines on a graph are not parallel, indicating that the relationship between the X factor and Y variable changes with changing levels of the other factor.

Figure 7.3   Two graphs showing no interaction

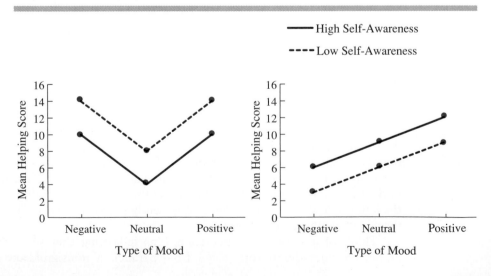

Visualizing the Main Effects from the Interaction Graph You can also graph the means from any main effect using the same procedures for graphing a one-way design discussed in Chapter 6. However, when reading a research article, you are generally expected to visualize the main effects from a graph of the interaction. Because cell means are averaged together to obtain main effect means, you should envision the data points for the main effect of a factor as the average of the appropriate data points in the interaction graph.

To see how this is done, assume that we obtained the data in Figure 7.4. On the graph at the left, the asterisks show where the overall mean for each level of mood is located after mentally collapsing vertically across high and low self-awareness (averaging the two data points in each circle). Plotting the line formed by these points on a separate graph (with the X axis labeled for mood level) would show the main effect of type of mood. On the graph at the right, the asterisks show where the overall mean for each level of self-awareness is located after collapsing across mood (mentally averaging the three data points in each circle). Plotting the line formed by these points on a separate graph (with the X axis labeled for low and high self-awareness) would show the main effect of self-awareness.

Of course, we don't believe the graph of an interaction unless its F is significant. Even then, all of the means might not differ significantly. Therefore, you must investigate a significant interaction further.

Simple Main Effects Here's a new technique for investigating an interaction. A **simple main effect** is the effect of one independent variable at one level of a second independent variable. Essentially we examine the overall relationship within any row or any column in the diagram of the study. For example, we might

Figure 7.4 Main effects seen in the graph of an interaction

The dots are cell means and the asterisks are visualized main effect means.

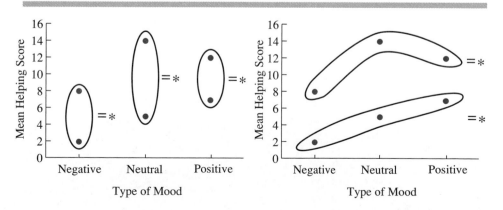

examine the simple main effect of changing mood under the high self-awareness condition, looking only at these cell means from the original interaction:

	Negative	*Neutral*	*Positive*
High self-awareness	$\overline{X} = 2.0$	$\overline{X} = 8.9$	$\overline{X} = 16.8$

The simple main effect is analyzed as a one-way ANOVA on these cell means, but with somewhat different computations. (See, for example, Hinkle, Wiersma & Jurs, 1998). If this *F* is significant, it indicates that in the high self-awareness condition, changing mood produces a significant relationship, and that significant differences occur somewhere among these three means. This information is helpful if, for example, there is not a significant simple main effect for mood in the low self-awareness conditions. Then we'd know that the interaction reflects a relationship for high self-awareness and no relationship for low self-awareness.

Post Hoc Comparisons in the Interaction   A more common approach is to examine all means in the interaction by performing post hoc comparisons. You can again perform the Tukey HSD test discussed previously, but the computations for an interaction are different from those for a main effect (as shown in Appendix C.8).

Note that we do *not* compare every cell mean to every other cell mean. In Table 7.7, we would not compare the cell mean for negative mood–high self-awareness to the mean for neutral mood–low self-awareness, because doing so would create a *confounded comparison:* The cells differ along more than one fac-

Table 7.7   Cell Means as a Function of Type of Mood and Level of Self-Awareness

The connected cells illustrate a confounded comparison.

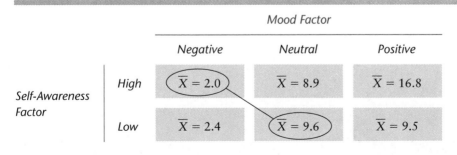

		Negative	Neutral	Positive
		Mood Factor		
Self-Awareness Factor	High	$\overline{X} = 2.0$	$\overline{X} = 8.9$	$\overline{X} = 16.8$
	Low	$\overline{X} = 2.4$	$\overline{X} = 9.6$	$\overline{X} = 9.5$

tor, so we cannot identify which factor produced the difference in scores (the change in mood or the change in awareness?). Thus in the diagram of a study, do not compare cells that are diagonally positioned. Instead, post hoc comparisons in the interaction should involve only **unconfounded comparisons**—comparisons of cell means that differ along only one factor. Therefore compare all possible pairs of cell means that are in the *same row,* and compare all possible pairs of cell means that are in the *same column.*

> **REMEMBER** In the interaction, a *simple main effect* involves a one-way ANOVA performed on a row or column of cell means. Post hoc tests compare all pairs of means within every row and column.

Interpreting the Two-Way Experiment

In a multifactor ANOVA, whether any one *F* is significant is not influenced by whether the other *F*s are significant. Also, after we have performed post hoc comparisons on the main effect means and the cell means, any combination of significant differences between means is possible. So that you can see the results of your various comparisons, Table 7.8 shows a way to identify the significant differences that we might find in the helping study. Outside the diagram, main effect means that differ significantly are connected by a line. Inside the diagram, interaction cell means that differ significantly are connected by a line.

We interpret main effects in a two-way study the same way we would in a one-way design. Thus, from Table 7.8, we would *like* to conclude that, overall, the main effect for awareness indicates that people with high self-awareness help more than those with low awareness (comparing the means of 13.9 and 7.2).

Table 7.8   Summary of Significant Differences in the Helping Study

Each line connects two means that differ significantly.

Likewise we would like to claim that overall, the main effect of each improvement in mood is to produce higher scores (comparing 2.2 to 9.3 to 13.2).

The problem is that main effect means are based on an average across the cell means of the interaction. But when we examine these cell means, the significant interaction *contradicts* the overall influence of the main effects. Literally, the effect of a factor *depends* on the other factor and vice versa. Thus, looking at the cell means, high self-awareness does not always produce significantly higher scores than low self-awareness: Instead, it does so only in the positive mood condition. Likewise, improving mood does not always increase scores: With high self-awareness it does, but there is no significant difference between neutral and positive mood in the low self-awareness condition.

Because an interaction indicates that the effect of one factor depends on the level of the other, you usually *cannot* make an overall, general conclusion about any main effects when the interaction is significant. Instead, the interpretation of the study is based on the significant interaction. In the helping study, therefore, our interpretation would center on explaining why, regardless of self-awareness level, negative mood produced less helping than neutral mood, but positive mood increased helping only when participants also experienced high self-awareness. We might propose, for example, that whether they are self-aware or not, a negative mood is sufficiently aversive to make people unwilling to help. For a positive mood to increase helpfulness, people must also have a high level of self-awareness so that they attend to their mood. We do not, however, pay attention to the main effects of mood or awareness level.

Usually, only when the interaction is not significant can we base the interpretation of a study on the significant main effects.

REMEMBER   The two-way ANOVA produces an *F* for each main effect and for the interaction. When the interaction is significant, we usually cannot draw a general conclusion about each main effect's influence.

Using Counterbalanced Variables to Produce Two-Way Designs

As another example of a two-way design, recall that if you think that an extraneous variable might seriously confound an independent variable or otherwise influence your results, you should actively control it, usually through counterbalancing. In such cases you can *analyze* the study as a two-way design, even though you originally set out to test one independent variable in a one-way design. For example, say that in a different study we wanted to compare the influence of only a person's positive or negative mood on how helpful another person is perceived to be. In each condition we present participants with a set of mood-inducing statements. Then they read descriptions of several fictitious people and rate each one's perceived helpfulness. We might wish to counterbalance for participants' gender, such that half of the people in each condition are male and half are female. Or we might control order effects by changing the order in which the fictitious individuals are described and rated. These designs are shown in Table 7.9.

Analyzing these studies as two-way designs provides much more information than if, as in previous chapters, we ignored—collapsed—gender or order and created a one-way design. In addition to obtaining an *F* for the influence of mood, we will also obtain an *F* for gender, to see whether the overall means for males and females differ. Or we'll obtain an *F* for order of trials, to see whether one order produced a difference in scores relative to the other. We can also examine the interaction between these variables and mood. If the interaction is significant, then we will discover that the effect of manipulating mood depends on a person's gender or on the order in which trials are performed.

A further advantage of treating these designs as two-way designs involves error variance. Recall that a problem with counterbalancing is that it can add error variance: Combining males and females produces greater differences in scores within each column than does testing only one gender. By treating gender as a separate factor, however, the ANOVA removes the differences between males and females that contribute to error variance, instead treating them as differences in scores that are related to gender. This reduces the amount error variance that is present when the mood factor is analyzed, so there should be a stronger relationship between mood and dependent scores that is more likely to be significant.

Thus, always consider whether you should analyze any single-factor study as a multifactor design involving counterbalanced variables. You will obtain considerably more information from a study that, regardless, you are going to conduct in the same way. Likewise, remember that your goal as a researcher is not only to demonstrate a relationship but to understand it. Therefore, after you've performed your primary analyses, explore the data. You might group scores along any potentially relevant variable: Did the time of day during which participants were tested produce differences? Does their age relate to their performance? The more precisely you examine the data, the more precisely you'll be able to describe the variables that influence a behavior and to explain how it operates.

Table 7.9 Two-Way Designs Produced by Counterbalancing Either Gender or Order of Trials

	Mood Factor				Mood Factor		
	Positive	*Negative*			*Positive*	*Negative*	
Males	$\overline{X}$	$\overline{X}$	$\overline{X}$	*Order 1*	$\overline{X}$	$\overline{X}$	$\overline{X}$
Females	$\overline{X}$	$\overline{X}$	$\overline{X}$	*Order 2*	$\overline{X}$	$\overline{X}$	$\overline{X}$
	$\overline{X}$	$\overline{X}$			$\overline{X}$	$\overline{X}$	

The Two-Way Within-Subjects ANOVA

As you know, statistically, a within-subjects factor controls participant variables by measuring the same subjects repeatedly in all levels of the factor, or by matching different participants along an extraneous variable. If you (1) repeatedly measure the same group of participants in all conditions of two independent variables, (2) match participants in all cells, or (3) have matched groups on one variable and repeated measures on the other, and the data are appropriate for a parametric procedure, then you should analyze the results using the **two-way within-subjects ANOVA.** Although the calculations for this procedure (in Appendix C.6) are different from those for a two-way between-subjects ANOVA, its logic and interpretation are identical.

Here's another example from real research. An issue in cognitive psychology is how different aspects of a stimulus can interfere with successful processing of the stimulus. The classic example of this is the "Stroop interference task" (Stroop, 1935), which examined participants' reaction time to report the color of the ink that a word is printed in when the word is the name of some other color. For example, you'd see the word yellow printed in green ink. A variation of this approach involves numbers (as in Flowers, Warner, & Polansky, 1979). To see how this works, quickly indicate the *number* of numbers indicated in each row:

2   2   2

three three

Say that we replicate this study presenting one row of numbers at a time. In one factor, interference is created because the number present is incongruent with the number of numbers present (e.g., 2 2 2), or interference is not created because the number present is congruent with the number of numbers present (e.g., 2 2). In a second factor, we present a row of digits (e.g., 2 2 2) versus a row of words (e.g., two two two). The dependent variable is a person's reaction time to report the number of numbers present in a row. You can envision this 2 × 2 factorial design as shown in Table 7.10.

To control all of the extraneous participant variables that could influence cognitive processing and reaction time, we test the same participants in all conditions, so this is a 2 × 2 repeated-measures design. (Depending on the study, we could instead have any number of levels in either factor.) Then, as usual, we apply the appropriate controls, such as creating comparable stimuli for each condition, testing multiple trials per condition, and counterbalancing order effects that are due to the order of trials per condition and the order of conditions.

We collapse across the different orders, computing each participant's mean reaction time in each of the four cells (as in Table 7.10). Again, view the two-way within-subjects ANOVA as a series of one-way ANOVAs. Collapsing vertically across the conditions of whether words or digits were presented, we can examine the main effect for the factor of type of pairing. Apparently, incongruent pairings produced interference, resulting in a slower mean reaction time (.542 seconds)

Table 7.10   2 × 2 Repeated-Measures Design for the Factors of Digit-Word and Congruent-Incongruent Pairings

Each X represents a participant's mean reaction time. Cell means are taken from Flowers et al. (1979), Table 1.

		Type of Pairing		
		Congruent (2 2)	Incongruent (2 2 2)	
Type of Number	Digit	X X $\overline{X} = .493$ X X	X X $\overline{X} = .543$ X X	$\overline{X} = .518$
	Word	X X $\overline{X} = .505$ X X	X X $\overline{X} = .542$ X X	$\overline{X} = .524$
		$\overline{X} = .499$	$\overline{X} = .542$	

than with congruent pairings (.499 seconds). Next, collapsing horizontally across type of pairing, we examine the main effect for the type of number presented. Apparently, mean reaction time for digits (.518 seconds) was faster than for words (.524 seconds). Finally, we examine the interaction, comparing the four cell means. When congruent numbers producing no interference were presented, participants responded to digits more quickly than to words (.493 seconds vs. .505 seconds, respectively). But when incongruent numbers producing interference were presented, there was virtually no difference in reaction time between digits and words (.543 seconds vs. .542 seconds, respectively).

However, each of these apparent influences on reaction time might really be mere sampling error. Therefore, we compute an *F* for each main effect and an *F* for the interaction. We perform post hoc comparisons for those main effects that are significant and have more than two levels. If the interaction is significant, we perform post hoc comparisons or analyze the simple main effects. Then we explain psychologically why the difference between digits and words disappears when the incongruent, interfering stimuli are present. If the interaction is not significant, we focus on any significant main effects: Why, overall, did participants respond more quickly to digits than to words, and why did any type of incongruent pairing (using words or digits) produce interference?

> **REMEMBER**   A *two-way within-subjects ANOVA* is used when you create matched groups or repeatedly measure the same participants in all conditions of two independent variables.

 ## The Two-Way Mixed ANOVA

Recall that a problem in creating a matched-groups design is that it can be difficult to find sufficient numbers of matching participants. A problem when using repeated measures is that they create order and carry-over effects (including nonsymmetrical ones), so that we may have an unworkable counterbalancing scheme. These problems are multiplied in a two-way design. Therefore, we may prefer to create a within-subjects factor only when it critically requires control of participant variables, and test the other variable as a between-subjects factor. When a design features a "mix" involving one within-subjects factor and one between-subjects factor, it is called a **two-way mixed design.**

One common mixed design arises when you begin with one factor that is set up as a *pretest-posttest design.* Recall that here we measure the same participants both before and after presenting the treatment. Let's take another example from real research, this one involving "subliminal perception." Such research typically entails presenting a stimulus that is visible only very briefly—say, for about 5 milliseconds. (It takes about 150 milliseconds to blink.) The hypothesis is that the stimulus can in some way be processed, even though people do not consciously recognize that it was even present.

Before we proceed, let's look at the findings regarding subliminal perception. There is *no* accepted evidence that brief messages hidden in advertisements make you buy a product, or that hidden messages in music turn you into a devil-worshiping psychopath! These misconceptions can be traced to a *rumor* about a study from the 1950s (relayed in McConnell, Cutler & McNeil, 1958). The subliminal messages "Buy popcorn" and "Drink Coca-Cola" were supposedly inserted in a film being shown at a theater, and the sale of refreshments at the theater's concession stand supposedly increased dramatically. However, the duration of each message was supposedly only 1/3000 of a second (an impossible speed for a 1950s movie projector), no control group was used, and no distinction was made between refreshments bought during the movie and those bought before the movie started. Further, these results were never reported in any journal, and there are no published replications of this or similar claims under controlled conditions. (To understand how such misconceptions become part of the folklore, consider two possible explanations: [1] the public's fear of brainwashing and other such mysteries, and [2] self-proclaimed "experts" who say that subliminal messages are effective, and who will *sell* you information to "prove" it.)

There is, however, well-controlled experimental evidence that a subliminal stimulus can register. In cognitive research, first flashing the word *doctor* allows faster recognition of *nurse* when it is then presented at normal speed than does first flashing the word *bread* (Meyer & Schvanveldt, 1971). In social research, flashing words that describe honesty or meanness produce a corresponding bias in participants' later description of a confederate (Erdley & D'Agostino, 1988). In clinical research, flashing soothing types of subliminal messages appears to have a positive influence (Silverman & Weinberger, 1985).

Let's consider a study conducted by Silverman, Ross, Adler, and Lustig (1978). They tested males' ability at dart-throwing before and after presentation of the subliminal message "Beating Dad is OK." The message was hypothesized to reduce residual guilt developed from childhood feelings of competition with father figures.

A *poor* way to design this study is shown in Table 7.11. If the mean dart scores are significantly higher after the message, we'd *like* to conclude that the message improved performance. But! There is something seriously wrong with this design in terms of potential confoundings. Here's a hint: Remember maturation, history, reactivity, and practice effects? Perhaps the after-message scores improved because of changes in these variables. That is, maybe the men acclimated to being tested, their brains matured and developed better eye-hand coordination, or they got better at dart throwing because of the practice provided by the before-message condition.

To eliminate these competing hypotheses, we need a control group that does everything the experimental group does but, instead of seeing the message "Beating Dad is OK," sees a placebo message that does not alleviate guilt. Adding a control group creates a between-subjects factor, with some individuals tested with the experimental message and others tested with the control message. This gives us the much better two-way mixed design shown in Table 7.12.

If the dependent variable meets the criteria for parametric procedures, we compute *a two-way mixed design ANOVA* (calculations are provided in Appendix C.7), and again, the design need not be a 2 × 2. Again think of this as a series of one-way ANOVAs, using the same logic as in previous examples (*all multifactor ANOVAs are treated as a series of one-way ANOVAs*). Therefore, as usual,

Table 7.11   Diagram of a Poorly-Designed One-Way Dart-Throwing Experiment

Xs represent each subject's dart score.

Before Message	After Message
X	X
X	X
X	X
X	X
$\overline{X}$	$\overline{X}$

Table 7.12   Diagram of the Two-Way, Mixed-Design Dart-Throwing Experiment

		Repeated-Measures Factor		
		Before Message	*After Message*	
	Participants with "Dad" message	X X X	X X X	$\overline{X}$
Between-Subjects Factor				
	Participants with control message	X X X	X X X	$\overline{X}$
		$\overline{X}$	$\overline{X}$	

we'll compute and test an *F* for the column factor (comparing the Before-After means), an *F* for the row means (comparing the influence of the "Dad" vs. the control message), and an *F* for the interaction, indicating whether the cell means differ significantly. (For each, if there were more than two levels, again perform post hoc tests.)

The main effects, however, are not likely to indicate anything interesting. When we collapse vertically and obtain the main effect means of Before-message and After-message, both the experimental and control messages will be included. Therefore, any difference between these two means will show only that scores change between the two testings. But such differences may be due to the experimental message or to maturation and practice effects. We cannot tell. Likewise, collapsing horizontally across Before and After gives the main effect means for the two types of messages. If the "Dad" message produces a higher mean than the control message, we will not know whether this occurred because the Before scores were higher or because the After scores were higher.

The specific test of the hypothesis that the "Dad" message increases performance comes when comparing the four cell means in the interaction. Ideally, we would predict a significant interaction that produces the graph shown in Figure 7.5. This shows an interaction (the lines are not parallel), and ideally the post hoc comparisons will confirm the following: (1) that there is no difference in the Before scores for the two groups, suggesting that the study is not contaminated by initial differences in dart-throwing skills between the two groups of men; (2) that there is no change in scores from Before to After for the control group, sug-

Figure 7.5 Ideal interaction between pretest vs. posttest and control vs. experimental cells

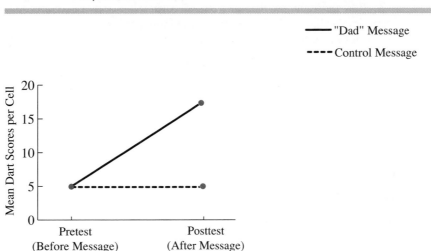

gesting that maturation, acclimation to testing, practice, and so on are not producing a Before-After difference in the experimental group; and (3) the After scores of men receiving the "Dad" message are significantly higher than those receiving the control message. This combination of findings would convincingly support the hypothesis that the "Dad" message does improve dart-throwing. (As this example illustrates, with a little thought you can predict and understand interaction effects, so, regardless of the type of design, don't think solely in terms of main effects.)

You have a mixed design whenever you set out to investigate two independent variables, one of which is best tested as a within-subjects factor while the other is best tested as a between-subjects factor. Thus, you might originally seek to investigate only one within-subjects factor but end up also examining the effects of a counter-balanced between-subjects variable. Or you might start with a between-subjects variable but then also analyze the repeated-measures factor of multiple trials, so that you can examine practice effects.

REMEMBER In a *two-way mixed design,* you have one within-subjects factor and one between-subjects factor.

The Three-Way Design

The beauty of ANOVA is that it can be applied to even more complex experiments with as many factors as you wish, regardless of whether the factors are all between-subjects, all within-subjects, or mixed. You may add more independent variables or analyze more counterbalanced control factors.

For example, say that we add the variable of participants' gender (male vs. female) to the previous two-way dart study. With three factors, we have a **three-way design,** which with two levels of each factor is a 2 × 2 × 2 design. Say that we obtained the data for this *mixed* design shown in Table 7.13. The previous 2 × 2 design for males is on the left. On the right, that design is replicated, but with females. If the data fit the criteria of a parametric procedure, then a three-way mixed-design ANOVA is appropriate.

Main Effects

Because there are three independent variables, the ANOVA produces a separate *F* for three main effects. As usual, to find a main effect, we collapse across the other factors. Thus to find the main effect of gender, we average all of the males' scores together (for the box on the left, $\overline{X} = 12.5$) and all of the females' scores together (in the box on the right, $\overline{X} = 9.5$). Apparently, males were better at throwing darts than females. To find the main effect of Before message vs. After message, we average together the columns containing Before scores, regardless of gender ($\overline{X} = 9.0$), and the columns containing After scores ($\overline{X} = 13.0$). Apparently, participants scored higher on the posttest than on the pretest. Finally, the main effect of type of message is the average of the scores in the rows of the "Dad" message ($\overline{X} = 12.5$) and in the rows of the control message ($\overline{X} = 9.5$). Apparently, people who saw the "Dad" message scored higher than those who saw the control message.

Table 7.13   Diagram of a Three-Way Design for the Factors of Before and After Messages, Type of Messages, and Participant Gender

Each mean is the mean dart score of participants in that cell.

	Males		Females	
	Before Message	*After Message*	*Before Message*	*After Message*
"Dad" Message	$\overline{X} = 10$	$\overline{X} = 20$	$\overline{X} = 8$	$\overline{X} = 12$
Control Message	$\overline{X} = 10$	$\overline{X} = 10$	$\overline{X} = 8$	$\overline{X} = 10$

Two-Way Interactions

Three factors produce three two-way interactions, and each has a separate *F*. Collapsing across gender produces the interaction of Before-After and Dad-Control messages, shown here:

	Before	*After*
"Dad"	$\overline{X} = 9$	$\overline{X} = 14$
Control	$\overline{X} = 9$	$\overline{X} = 10$

The mean in each cell is based on both males' and females' scores. Note that the difference between the Dad and control messages is greater in the After-message condition. (To put it another way, the difference between Before message and After message depends on the type of message.) Apparently, therefore, there is an interaction between these two factors.

To produce the other two-way interactions, we collapse across the third factor as shown here:

	Gender and Type of Message Interaction			*Gender and Before-After Interaction*	
	Male	*Female*		*Male*	*Female*
"Dad"	$\overline{X} = 15$	$\overline{X} = 10$	*Before*	$\overline{X} = 10$	$\overline{X} = 8$
Control	$\overline{X} = 10$	$\overline{X} = 9$	*After*	$\overline{X} = 15$	$\overline{X} = 11$

On the left, collapsing across Before-After produces the interaction between gender and Type of Message. Note that the difference between the "Dad" and control messages is greater for males than it is for females. (To put it another way, the difference between males and females depends on which message they receive.) Thus there is an apparent interaction between gender and type of message.

On the right, collapsing across Type of Message produces the interaction between gender and Before-After. Here males show a greater increase from Before to After than do females. (In other words, the difference between males and females depends on whether we examine the Before scores or the After scores.) Thus, we apparently have a two-way interaction here.

The Three-Way Interaction

Finally, we do not collapse across any factor, computing an *F* for the three-way interaction: This is the effect of simultaneously changing the levels of all three factors. We saw that in a two-way interaction, the effect of one variable changes depending on the level of the second factor we examine. In a **three-way interaction,** the two-way interaction between any two variables changes depending on which level of the third factor we examine. (Conversely, if the three-way interaction is not significant, then we have basically the same two-way interaction regardless of the level of the third factor we examine.) By graphing the original cell means from Table 7.13, we have the three-way interaction in Figure 7.6. As this shows, the interaction between Before-After and Dad-Control depends on whether participants are male or female. For males, there is a dramatic change from pretest to posttest scores with the "Dad" message, but the control males show no change. For females, there is a different two-way interaction: There is slight improvement in dart-throwing following the control message, suggesting that the control females benefited from practice at throwing darts. Following the "Dad" message, experimental females showed a slight, additional improvement beyond the practice effects of the control females. Thus, the "Dad" message had a minimal positive influence on females, so maybe they aren't intensely guilty about competing with their fathers to begin with. There's dramatic improvement after the "Dad" message among males, however, so maybe males do feel guilty

Figure 7.6 Graphs showing how the two-way interaction between pretest and posttest and "Dad"–control message changes as a function of participant gender

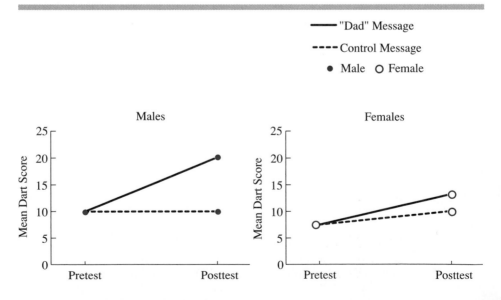

about this competition, and thus the message reduces an otherwise serious restriction on their performance.

REMEMBER   A three-way interaction shows that the interaction between any two factors is not consistent across the levels of the third factor.

In a published report of this research (using the APA format discussed in Appendix A), this interaction would be graphed on *one* set of X-Y axes, using four different styles of lines. As shown in the legend in Figure 7.6, for example, we can use solid lines for experimental groups and dashed lines for controls, combined with solid dots for males and open dots for females. Thus, •———————• connects the means of the Male-Experimental group, ○———————○ connects the means of the Female-Experimental group, •- - - - - - - - -• connects those of the Male-Control group, and ○- - - - - - - - -○ connects those of the Female-Control group.

Of course, we would not believe any of the previous interpretations unless the main effects and interactions were significant, and for each we'd perform post hoc comparisons to determine which specific means differ significantly. Then, as usual, we would interpret the results by first focusing on significant interactions, because they contradict main effects. A significant three-way interaction, however, also contradicts any two-way interactions: We saw that the two-way interaction between Dad-Control and Before-After *depends on* whether it involves males or females. Therefore, the interpretation of a three-way design focuses on the significant three-way interaction. Thus, based on Figure 7.6, we would attempt to explain the psychological reasons behind why the "Dad" message produced a dramatic improvement in scores for males but a small improvement for females. If the three-way interaction is not significant, we focus on significant two-way interactions. If these interactions are not significant, then we focus on significant main effects.

The Two-Way Chi Square

Recall that there are times when we do not measure the *amount* of a variable but, rather, we count whether someone falls in one or another *category* of a variable. In Chapter 6 we used the one-way chi square to determine whether the frequency of category membership differed significantly along one variable. With two such variables, we compute the **two-way chi square,** again calculating χ^2. This procedure requires two variables that are used to categorize participants, with no matching or repeated measures. For example, we might categorize people in terms of their gender and political party, counting the frequency of male Republicans, female Republicans, and so on. Also, the two-way chi square is used if there are two variables on which we are categorizing participants, regardless of whether we call each an independent or dependent variable. Let's say that in our original helping study we conduct a manipulation check and categorize those participants who report having a negative or a positive mood after testing. Then we count the number of people who helped as a function of type of mood. A requirement of chi square, however, is that the responses of *all* participants in the sample be included, so we must count both the frequency of participants who helped *and* of those who did not. Let's say we obtain the data shown in Table 7.14. Here we have a 2 × 2 design in which we categorize participants along two variables: whether they were in a positive or negative mood and whether they were helpful or not. (Other designs might be a 2 × 3, a 4 × 3, etc.)

Although this looks like a two-way ANOVA, the two-way chi square examines only the *interaction* of the two variables. That is, we determine whether the frequencies in the categories of one variable *depend* on which category of the other variable we examine. (The two-way chi-square is also called the "test of independence.") Here we will determine whether the frequency of helping or not helping is independent of participants' mood. Essentially, we ask whether a relationship exists between the two variables. When the variables are independent, there is no relationship between category membership on one variable and category membership on the other variable. In Table 7.14, however, the two variables appear somewhat related or dependent: Saying "No" is more often associated with being in a negative mood, and saying "Yes" is more often associated with being in a positive mood.

The null hypothesis is that the variables are "really" independent in the population, and that any appearance of a relationship is due to sampling error. If the obtained χ^2 is significant (calculations in Appendix C.13), we conclude that the variables are dependent. For the helping study we would conclude that the frequency of helping or not helping depends on a person's mood. As in any other study, we then examine the type and strength of the relationship and, using this information, attempt to explain "psychologically" why those participants in a positive mood were more likely to help.

> **REMEMBER**   A significant *two-way chi square* indicates that category membership along one variable is dependent on or related to category membership along the other variable.

Table 7.14   Frequency of Participants Who Helped or Did Not Help as a Function of Their Reported Mood

		Mood	
		Negative	Positive
Helping	Yes	5	18
	No	20	2

Describing Effect Size

Our discussions have treated all independent variables as being of equal importance. In nature, however, some variables are more important than others. Therefore, a critical question in any experiment is "How important is this independent variable?" In answering this question, do not confuse importance with significance. "Significant" only indicates that the data reflect a "real" relationship and not a chance pattern of scores produced by sampling error. To be important, a variable must first produce a significant relationship. But a significant relationship is not necessarily important.

In experiments, we determine a variable's importance by measuring its effect size. **Effect size** is an indication of how dramatically an independent variable influences a dependent variable. Presumably, manipulating the independent variable "causes" participants' scores—and behavior—to change. The effect size indicates the extent to which the manipulation causes this change.

One crude measure of effect size is the difference between the means of the conditions. Say that after manipulating mood we obtain the helping scores shown here:

Mood Level		
Negative	Neutral	Positive
0	5	12
4	13	19
8	18	29
$\overline{X} = 4$	$\overline{X} = 12$	$\overline{X} = 20$

The difference between these means averages out to 8 points. Because this seems to be a relatively large difference in helping scores, we can argue that mood is important in determining a person's helping behavior.

The problem, however, is that we have no way of knowing whether a difference of 8 points is really a large difference in nature, so we must be very subjective when evaluating it. Further, an important variable need *not* produce large differences in the behavior. Rather, a scientifically important variable will *consistently* influence the behavior in question. Recall that the degree of consistency or inconsistency in a relationship—the amount of error variance—indicates the extent to which variables other than our factor influence dependent scores. Thus, although changing mood above produces relatively big differences in *means,* there is considerable error variance, so mood is not the only, major determinant of individual helping scores.

Therefore, when describing an independent variable's effect size, we usually compute how *consistently* the variable influences the behavior. The generic name for this computation is the proportion of variance accounted for.

Understanding the Proportion of Variance Accounted For

To evaluate the importance of a relationship, we must compare it with something. We determine how informative a relationship is compared with the information we'd have if we were not aware of the relationship. To do this, we examine the data from two perspectives. First, we examine the scores as if there were no independent variable—as if we had simply measured the entire sample of participants on the dependent variable. Then we determine how much information is gained if we do not ignore the independent variable.

In an experiment, the term *proportion of variance accounted for* is a shortened version of *the proportion of total variance in the dependent scores that is accounted for by the relationship with the independent variable.* The total variance in dependent scores is simply a measure of how much all of the scores in the study differ from one another when we ignore the independent variable. For example, let's say we perform a simple version of our mood study, comparing the helping scores of people in the conditions of positive or negative mood. We obtain the scores shown below.

Finding the Total Variance in Dependent Scores	Finding the Systemic Variance in Dependent Scores	
	Negative	*Positive*
4 8	4	8
4 8	4	8
4 8	4	8
Overall $\overline{X} = 6$	$\overline{X} = 4$	$\overline{X} = 8$

On the left, we ignore the levels of the independent variable and simply compute the total variance in the scores—how much the six scores differ from the overall mean of the study. On the right, we do not ignore the independent variable, grouping scores according to the conditions. Look what happens: All of the differences in scores occur *between* the conditions with no differences in scores *within* a condition. In other words, there is no error variance. Rather, all of the differences between scores form systematic variance. **Systematic variance** refers to the differences in scores that occur with changes in an independent variable. It is changes in scores that are associated with—related to—changing the conditions.

Because this is a perfectly consistent relationship, all of the total variance is systematic variance. Thus, the mood factor accounts for 100% of the variance. Or, as a proportion, it accounts for 1.0 of the total variance in helping scores. In an experiment, the **proportion of variance accounted for** is the proportion of total variance in dependent scores that is systematic variance. In other words, it is the proportion of total variance in scores that is associated with or related to changes in the independent variable.

We "account" for the variance in helping scores in that we know when and why different scores occur. Participants will have a score of 4 when their mood is negative. They will have a *different* score of 8 when their mood is positive. Thus the effect size of the mood manipulation is 1.0: It produces or accounts for *all* of the observed differences in helping behavior.

A perfectly consistent relationship does not normally occur, so we usually won't account for 100% of the variance. For example, we might obtain the following helping scores:

Total Variance in Dependent Scores		Systematic Variance Owing to Mood	
		Negative	Positive
2	6	2	6
4	8	4	8
6	10	6	10
Overall $\overline{X} = 6$		$\overline{X} = 4$	$\overline{X} = 8$
Total Variance = 6.67		Error Variance = 2.67	

Again, on the left, we ignore the independent variable and obtain the total variance, the amount that all scores differ from the mean of the experiment. Calculating the variance, we find 6.67. On the right, when we do not ignore the independent variable, we see that although there is a relationship, there is also some error variance. With negative mood, scores are around the mean of 4, but some are above and some are below. With positive mood, scores are around 8. Essentially, we compute the error variance by determining the amount the scores in each condition differ from the mean of the condition and then average across the different conditions. Here the error variance is 2.67.

Of all the differences between the scores in a study, to some extent the differences are associated with changing the independent variable, and to some extent they are not. In other words, the total variance is the sum of the systematic variance plus the error variance. Thus, out of a total variance of 6.67, about 2.67 is error variance and the remainder is systematic variance. Whether 2.67 represents a large amount is difficult to judge, so to make this number easier to interpret, we transform it into a proportion of the total: 2.67 divided by 6.67 equals .40. In this study, 40% of the total variance in scores is error variance. This means that 60% of the total variance is not error variance, so it must be systematic variance. Thus, the effect size of the independent variable is .60: Of all the differences in the study, 60% of them are associated with and presumably caused by changing the independent variable.

One other way to interpret the proportion of variance accounted for is in terms of how well the relationship allows us to predict each participant's score—and behavior. When ignoring the independent variable, we would predict each participant's score as the overall mean score, and be in error—be "off"—by whatever amount the actual scores differ from the mean. The differences between the actual scores and the overall mean is the total variance, so using the overall mean of 6, we are off by an "average" of 6.67. However, when we consider the conditions of the independent variable, our best estimate of participants' scores is the mean of their condition. By predicting that people will score around 4 when in a negative mood and around 8 when in a positive mood, we are closer to their actual scores than if we predicted a score of 6 for them. How much closer? Using the mean of each condition, our predictions are off by an average of 2.67, compared with being off by 6.67 when we ignore the relationship. In other words, our errors when using this relationship are 40% of what they are when we ignore the relationship, so using the relationship improves predictions by 60%: We are, on average, 60% closer—60% more accurate—when we use the means of the conditions to predict scores than when we use the overall mean of scores. Thus, by using the relationship between helping and mood, we are 60% more accurate in predicting, explaining, and understanding the differences in helping scores than if we do not consider this relationship.

> **REMEMBER** The *proportion of variance accounted for* is the proportional improvement in predictions that is achieved when we use a relationship to predict scores, compared with if we did not use the relationship.

In actual research, the effect size of a particular factor is usually in the neighborhood of .15 to .30. In plain English, the proportion of variance accounted for tells us how much better off we are by knowing about and using a relationship than if we had never heard of it. Therefore, we can use the proportion of variance accounted for to evaluate the importance of different independent variables. Say that variable A accounts for .10 of the variance in a particular behavior, while variable B accounts for .20 of the variance. Variable B is twice as important for understanding the behavior as variable A: We are twice as accurate in knowing when and why participants will exhibit a particular score and behavior under the conditions of B than we are by knowing their condition under A. Essentially, by studying variable B we are 20% better at understanding the behavior than if we had not studied this variable. By studying variable A, we are only 10% better off than if we had not bothered. (Recognize, however, that effect size indicates importance in a statistical sense, not in a practical sense: A variable that accounts for only 3% of *deaths* is, practically speaking, very important. Scientifically, though, it does not advance our knowledge greatly.)

Any time you obtain a *significant* effect of an independent variable in an experiment you should determine its effect size. (With a nonsignificant result, you cannot believe that a "real" relationship even exists, so a nonsignificant effect always accounts for zero proportion of the variance.) The proportion of variance accounted for is *the* way to determine whether a relationship is scientifically important or merely much ado about nothing. In fact, the American Psychological Association (1994) now wants all published research to include a measure of effect size. Effect size has not always been reported in the literature, and huge, elaborate experiments often have been performed to study what are actually very minor variables. By computing effect size, you determine the importance of your variables.

> **REMEMBER** The *effect size* of a manipulation indicates how dramatically it influences dependent scores and, thus, how important it is for understanding the dependent behavior.

Computing the Proportion of Variance Accounted For

Mathematically, comparing the total variance to the error variance to compute the proportion of variance accounted for as we did earlier can be accomplished by simply computing an appropriate *correlation coefficient* and then *squaring* it. (Recall that a correlation coefficient is a statistic that summarizes the strength of a relationship, and as you saw above, the weaker a relationship, the smaller the proportion of variance accounted for.) As usual, however, there are different formulas to use, depending on your scale of measurement and the nature of your design.

1. **The Point-Biserial Correlation Coefficient** When you have only two conditions of the independent variable and perform a *t*-test, compute the squared **point-biserial correlation coefficient.** Symbolized as r_{pb}^2, this statistic describes the effect size of two conditions of the independent variable on an interval or ratio dependent variable (calculations in Appendix C.9).

2. **Eta Squared** When you perform either a between- or within-subjects ANOVA, determine the proportion of variance accounted for by computing **eta squared,** symbolized as η^2 (calculations appear in Appendix C.9). There are also nonparametric versions of η^2 for use with ranked scores (also given in Appendix C). In multifactor designs, a separate η^2 is computed for each significant main effect and interaction. Then use the size of each to determine the emphasis you should give to the effect when interpreting the study. The larger the η^2 the more important the main effect or interaction was in influencing scores in your experiment, so the more central it should be in your interpretation. Note that the one exception to the rule of always focusing on the significant interaction is when it has a very small effect size. An interaction

contradicts the general, overall pattern shown in a main effect. However, if the interaction has a very small effect size, then it only slightly and inconsistently contradicts the overall main effect. In this case, you can focus your interpretation on any substantial significant main effects instead.

3. **The Phi and Contingency Coefficients**   There is no measure of effect size for a one-way chi square. But with the two-way chi square, describe effect size by computing either of the following (shown in Appendix C.13). When dealing with a 2 × 2 design, compute the squared **phi coefficient**. When dealing with a two-way design that is *not* a 2 × 2 (e.g., a 3 × 2, a 3 × 3, etc.), compute the squared **contingency coefficient**. Each indicates how much you can account for or predict the frequency of category membership on one variable by considering category membership on the other variable. In the study described back in Table 7.14, for example, we would see the degree to which the frequency of helping behavior is determined by participants' mood.

A Word about Multivariate Statistics and Meta-Analysis

In the literature, you'll encounter two types of research approaches that expand on the type of ANOVA we have discussed; they include more variables or take a broader perspective. The first approach is called "multivariate statistics."

Everything we've discussed so far has involved *one* dependent variable, and the statistics we've performed are called **univariate statistics.** Researchers can, however, measure participants on two or more dependent variables in one experiment. For example, in our mood study, we might have measured helping behavior as well as participants' attitudes toward the experimenter, described the kind of a day they'd been having, and any other reactions that might be influenced by mood or be related to helping behavior. Statistics for multiple dependent variables are called **multivariate statistics.** These include the multivariate *t*-test and the multivariate analysis of variance (MANOVA). Although these are very complex procedures, the basic logic still holds: If the results are significant, the observed relationship between the independent variables and dependent variables is unlikely to be the result of sampling error. Given these significant results, the researcher then examines the influence of the independent variables on each dependent variable at a time, using the *t*-tests or ANOVAs we've discussed.

The other approach involves "meta-analysis." Recall that, ultimately, confidence in the external validity of research is developed through repeated studies that literally and conceptually replicate a finding. Rather than subjectively evaluating the extent to which several studies support a particular hypothesis, however, researchers analyze the studies using meta-analysis. **Meta-analysis** is a statistical procedure for combining, testing, and describing the results from different studies. For example, Carlson, Marcus-Newhall, and Miller (1990) performed a meta-analysis of some 22 published studies that investigated the influence of cues for aggression (e.g., weapons) on participants' aggressive behavior. With meta-analysis, researchers generally take one of two approaches: Either they determine whether the experiments taken together consistently show a significant effect of a particular variable, or they estimate the effect size of a variable based on all of the studies.

On the one hand, a meta-analysis provides objective methods for generalizing a variable's effect, and because the results are based on many participants tested under varying procedures, we have a high degree of confidence in the conclusions. On the other hand, a meta-analysis glosses over many differences in operational definitions, controls, measurement procedures, and other aspects of the studies. Therefore, although a meta-analysis adds to our understanding of a behavior, we must necessarily speak in *very* general terms.

Putting It All Together

There is no limit to the number of factors you can have in a study or test in an ANOVA. You can study four independent variables in the same study and perform a four-way ANOVA, or you can create a five-way design, and so on. There are, however, practical limits to such designs. The number of participants needed becomes quite large, and the counterbalancing scheme or stimulus requirements become extremely complex. Although with effort these problems can be solved, researchers are also limited by their ability to interpret such studies. If you conduct a "simple" four-way study—a ($2 \times 2 \times 2 \times 2$) design—the ANOVA provides separate *F*s for four main effects, six two-way interactions, four three-way interactions, and one monster four-way interaction (there would be eight lines on its graph). If this sounds very complicated, it's because it *is* very complicated. Three-way interactions are difficult to interpret, and interactions that contain more than three factors are practically impossible to interpret.

Remember that a major concern of science is to simplify the complexity found in nature. Duplicating this complexity in a study is counterproductive. Therefore, unless you have a very good reason for including many factors in one experiment, it is best to examine only two or, at most, three factors at a time. Then conduct additional experiments to investigate the influence of other variables. In each, you can perform a literal replication of portions of your previous studies, thus greatly increasing their internal and external validity. And, although you will not learn of the simultaneous interactions of many variables, you will understand what you do learn.

CHAPTER SUMMARY

1. In a *multifactor experiment,* the researcher examines several independent variables and their interactions. In a *complete factorial design,* all levels of one factor are combined with all levels of the other factor.

2. In a *two-way between-subjects ANOVA,* there is no matching or repeated measures of participants in conditions of either of the two independent variables that are manipulated. In a *two-way within-subjects ANOVA,* matched

groups or the same repeatedly measured participants are tested in all conditions of two independent variables. In a *two-way mixed design,* one within-subjects and one between-subjects factor is examined.

3. In any two-way ANOVA, an *F* is computed for the *main effect* of each factor and for the *interaction.*

4. A *main effect* of a factor is the effect that changing the levels of that factor has on dependent scores, while collapsing across—ignoring—all other factors in the study.

5. An *interaction effect* is the influence that the combination of levels from the factors has on the dependent scores. In a *two-way interaction,* the relationship between one factor and the dependent scores is different for and depends on each level of the other factor. When the cell means of a significant interaction are graphed, the lines are not parallel.

6. A *simple main effect* is the effect of one factor at one level of a second factor within the interaction. Post hoc comparisons in an interaction should involve only *unconfounded comparisons*—comparisons of cell means that differ along only one factor.

7. Because an interaction contradicts the overall pattern suggested by the main effects, the interpretation of a study usually focuses on the significant interaction.

8. A *three-way design* produces three main effects, three two-way interactions, and a three-way interaction. In a *three-way interaction,* the two-way interaction between two factors changes as the levels of the third factor change.

9. The *two-way chi square procedure* is used when counting the frequency with which participants fall into the categories of two variables. If χ^2 is significant, the frequency of participants in the different categories of one variable depends on their category membership along the other variable.

10. For any significant main effect or interaction, the *effect size* indicates how dramatically the variable influences the dependent scores.

11. The *total variance* in dependent scores indicates how much all of the scores in the study differ, and it equals the error variance plus the systematic variance. *Systematic variance* refers to the differences in scores that occur with, or are associated with, changes in the conditions.

12. Calculating effect size as the *proportion of variance accounted for* indicates the proportion of total variance in dependent scores that is systematic variance. It reflects the proportional improvement in predictions that is achieved when we use a relationship to predict scores, compared with if we do not use the relationship.

13. The effect size is calculated as (1) the squared value of the *point-biserial correlation coefficient* when performing a *t*-test, or (2) *eta squared* for each significant factor or interaction effect when performing ANOVA.

14. The effect size in a significant 2×2 chi square is the squared *phi coefficient.* With a two-way design that is not a 2×2, effect size is the squared *contingency coefficient.*

15. *Multivariate statistics* are inferential statistical procedures used when a study involves more than one dependent variable.

16. *Meta-analysis* involves statistical procedures for combining, testing, and describing the results from different studies.

KEY TERMS

complete factorial
   design *(206)*
contingency coefficient
   (234)
effect size *(229)*
eta squared *(233)*
interaction effect
   (208)
main effect *(206)*
meta-analysis *(234)*
multifactor experiment
   (203)
multivariate statistics
   (234)
phi coefficient *(234)*

point-biserial
   correlation
   coefficient *(233)*
proportion of variance
   accounted for
   (231)
systematic variance
   (230)
three-way design
   (224)
three-way interaction
   (226)
two-way between-
   subjects ANOVA
   (206)

two-way chi square
   (227)
two-way design
   (203)
two-way interaction
   (209)
two-way mixed design
   (220)
two-way within-
   subjects ANOVA
   (218)

REVIEW QUESTIONS

1. (a) What are the reasons for conducting multifactor designs? (b) What is a complete factorial design?

2. A student hears about a 2×3 design and concludes that six factors were examined. Is this correct? Why or why not?

3. What is the difference between a two-way within-subjects ANOVA and (a) a two-way between-subjects ANOVA? (b) a two-way mixed ANOVA?

4. Identify the Fs that are computed in a two-way ANOVA involving factors A and B.

5. (a) What is the difference between a main effect mean and a cell mean? (b) What does it mean to collapse across a factor?

6. (a) A significant main effect indicates what about an independent variable? (b) A significant interaction indicates what about an independent variable? (c) Why do we usually base the interpretation of a two-way design on the interaction when it is significant?

7. A researcher studies participants' frustration levels when solving problems both as a function of the difficulty of the problem and as a function of whether they are math or logic problems. She finds that logic problems produce more frustration than math problems, that greater difficulty leads to greater frustration, and that more difficult logic problems produce greater frustration than more difficult math problems. In the ANOVA performed for this study, what effects are significant?

8. In question 7, say the researcher instead found that math and logic problems lead to the same frustration levels, that frustration consistently increases with greater difficulty, and that this is true for both math and logic problems. In the ANOVA performed for this study, what effects are significant?

9. You are studying the volunteer bias. You advertise your experiment first as a memory study and again later as an attitude study. For each, you pass around a sign-up sheet in some psychology courses and then count the number of volunteers who actually show up for the experiment. (a) What statistical procedure should you use? (b) What factor (or factors) do you examine?

10. A researcher examines performance on an eye-hand coordination task as a function of three levels of reward and three levels of practice, obtaining the following cell means:

		Reward		
		Low	Medium	High
Practice	Low	4	10	7
	Medium	5	5	14
	High	15	15	15

(a) What are the main effect means for reward, and what do they indicate about this factor? (b) What are the main effect means for practice, and what do they indicate?

11. (a) In question 10, is an interaction likely? (b) How would you perform unconfounded post hoc comparisons of the cell means? (c) What would be confounded comparisons?

12. (a) In question 10, why does the interaction contradict your conclusions about the effect of reward? (b) Why does the interaction contradict your conclusions about practice?

13. (a) What is a simple main effect? (b) In question 10, what will the simple main effects of reward (at each practice level) apparently indicate?

14. (a) What is the difference between systematic variance and error variance? (b) What does the total variance refer to? (c) What does the proportion of variance accounted for refer to?

15. In question 10, the researcher reports that the effect size of reward is .14, that the effect size of practice is .31, and that the interaction accounts for .01 of the variance. What does each value indicate about the influence of these effects?

16. Why does the proportion of variance accounted for indicate how important a variable is?

17. What statistic indicates proportion of variance accounted for in (a) a *t*-test design? (b) an ANOVA? (c) a chi square?

18. In a research report, you read that the researcher used (a) a meta-analysis or (b) a multivariate statistic. Based on this information, what do you know about each study?

19. The following are the cell means of three experiments. For each experiment, compute the main effect means and indicate whether there appears to be an effect of A, B, or A × B.

	Study 1				*Study 2*				*Study 3*	
	A_1	A_2			A_1	A_2			A_1	A_2
B_1	2	4		B_1	10	5		B_1	8	14
B_2	12	14		B_2	5	10		B_2	8	2

20. In question 19, if you graph the cell means (labeling the *X* axis with factor A), what pattern will you see for each interaction?

21. After performing a 3 × 4 ANOVA, you find that all *F*s are significant. What other procedures should you perform?

22. (a) When is it appropriate to compute the effect size in a two-way ANOVA? (b) For each effect, what does the effect size tell you?

23. In an experiment, you measure the popularity of two brands of soft drinks (factor A), and for each brand you test males and females (factor B). The following table shows the main effect and cell means from the study:

Factor A: Brand

		Brand X	Brand Y	
Factor B: Gender	Male	14	23	18.5
	Female	25	12	18.5
		19.5	17.5	

(a) Describe the graph of the interaction means when factor A is on the X axis. (b) Does there appear to be an interaction? Why? (c) Why will a significant interaction prohibit you from making conclusions based on the main effects?

DISCUSSION QUESTIONS

1. Create a graph of the interaction in the reaction-time study shown in Table 7.10, placing "type of number" on the X axis.

2. Design a two-way study, diagram it, and place mean scores in each cell that appear to produce the predicted main effects and interactions.

3. In a between-subjects design, you investigate participants' hypnotic suggestibility as a function of whether they meditate before being tested and whether they were shown a film containing a low, medium, or high amount of fantasy. For the following data, perform all appropriate statistical analyses and determine what you should conclude about this study.

Amount of Fantasy

		Low	Medium	High
	Meditation	5 6 2 2 5	7 5 6 9 5	9 8 10 10 10
Amount of Meditation	No Meditation	10 10 9 10 10	2 5 4 3 2	5 6 5 7 6

4. When designing a two- or three-way repeated-measures study with many trials and conditions, (a) what potential biases and confoundings owing to participants might be especially prominent? (b) What ethical concern arises regarding the demands you place on participants?

Part III

Beyond the Typical Laboratory Experiment

It's time to shift mental gears. Our previous discussions have focused on true laboratory experiments involving groups of human participants. Such studies are common in psychological research, because they usually produce the greatest internal validity for arguing that a particular variable causes people's behavior to change. However, the goal is always to design the best study so that we can most clearly and confidently answer the question at hand. Therefore, psychologists often choose an alternative to the typical laboratory design. In some cases, the reason may be that the laboratory setting creates an artificial setting and the observed behavior is too unnatural. At other times, the variables cannot be manipulated or measured in a way that conforms to an experiment. And sometimes the hypothesis being tested and the goals of the research require a different approach. In these situations, other designs—or a combination of designs—are better suited for answering the research question. In the following chapters, we examine these other designs.

8

Correlational Research and Questionnaire Construction

GETTING STARTED

To understand this chapter, recall the following:

■ From Chapter 2, recall what descriptive research is and what reliability and the different types of validity are.

■ From Chapter 4, recall what the restriction of range is, and understand the concept of inter-rater reliability.

■ From Chapter 6, recall what a positive and negative linear relationship is, what the strength of a relationship is, and how variability weakens the relationship.

Your goals in this chapter are to learn:

■ The difference in how to analyze correlational data and experimental data.

■ How to interpret a correlation coefficient.

■ The logic of significance testing of a correlation coefficient.

■ How the regression equation is used to predict the Y scores for a given X.

■ How correlation is used to demonstrate reliability and validity.

■ How to design questionnaires and interviews.

Recall that researchers do not test only experimental or causal hypotheses but also descriptive hypotheses. The most common descriptive approach in psychological research is the **correlational design.** Here we test the hypothesis that a relationship between the variables is present. The term *correlation* is synonymous with *relationship,* so in using a correlational design we set out to describe the relationship—examine the correlation—between variables.

This chapter will first discuss the logic of correlational designs and contrast them with experimental designs. Then we'll review basic correlational statistics and discuss a number of ways they are used. Finally, we'll cover two major tools that are commonly used for gathering data in correlational designs: interviews and questionnaires.

The Difference between True Experiments and Correlational Studies

Although both experimental and correlational designs are for demonstrating a relationship, they differ in *how* the researcher goes about it. To illustrate, consider a research hypothesis from industrial-organizational psychology: Supposedly "job satisfaction," the degree to which workers find their jobs satisfying, is related to their wages. In a true experiment, we might attempt to demonstrate this by manipulating the independent variable of amount of pay that participants receive while performing a laboratory task. For example, we could randomly assign people to various pay levels and have them perform a "job" of assembling "widgets" out of toy building blocks. Then, after an interval, we'd obtain participants' answers to a series of questions that measure their job satisfaction. Our research hypothesis implies the question, "For a given pay rate, what is a person's job satisfaction?" Recall that the "given" variable is always graphed as the X variable, and that we examine Y scores as a function of X. Therefore, we place the independent variable of pay rate on the X axis and the dependent variable of job satisfaction on the Y axis. For now, we'll create a *scatterplot* of the individual data points that we might obtain, as shown in scatterplot A of Figure 8.1. (As usual, I've created unrealistically symmetrical scatterplots so that you can easily see the pattern.)

The important thing to recognize here is that, by randomly assigning participants to a pay condition, we, the *researchers,* determine each person's X score—that is, we decide whether their "score" will be $3, $6, or $9. Then we show that, for an *assigned X,* people tend to produce a certain Y score. On the other hand, the distinguishing aspect of a correlational design is that we do not manipulate the X variable: We do not determine participants' X scores by randomly assigning them to an amount of the variable to experience. Rather, the scores on both variables reflect an amount or category of a variable that an individual has *already* experienced. Thus, to conduct this study using a correlational design, we might randomly select some people who are already employed at jobs and then

Figure 8.1   Job satisfaction scores as a function of pay rate

The results in scatterplot A were gathered in a true experiment; those in scatterplot B were gathered in a correlational study.

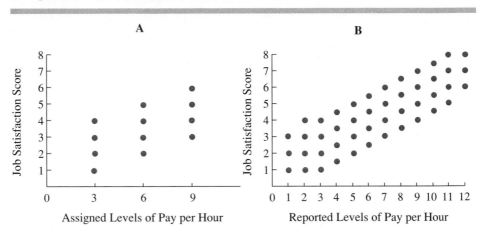

measure their hourly pay and their job satisfaction. As shown in scatterplot B of Figure 8.1, we examine the same relationship as in the experiment: We again ask the question "For a given pay rate, what is a person's job satisfaction?"—so pay rate is still the X variable. But! Here we show that for a *reported* X score of pay rate, people tend to produce a certain Y score of job satisfaction. Thus, the defining feature of a correlational design is that the participants are not randomly assigned to the levels of the X variable as with a true independent variable, although participants' scores on the X variable are analogous to the levels of a factor in an experiment. (If instead we had asked, "What is a person's pay rate for a given satisfaction level?" then satisfaction level would be the X variable and pay rate would be the Y variable.) Regardless, in a correlational design, we then look for the relationship in which as X scores change, Y scores also change in a consistent fashion.

> **REMEMBER**   The distinguishing aspect of a correlational design is that a participant's score on the X variable is an amount or category of the variable that the participant already demonstrates or has experienced.

Any of the approaches to measuring variables in experiments can also be used in correlational designs. A common approach is to measure participants' scores using different tests and then to correlate their scores (e.g., relating participants' intelligence test scores with their creativity test scores). Sometimes questions measuring several variables are included in one test (e.g., the *Minnesota Multiphasic Personality Inventory* or *MMPI* measures numerous variables), and then the researcher correlates scores from each variable. Researchers also examine the relationship between test scores and a physical or physiological attribute (e.g., relating participants' self-esteem scores to their gender). Or we may obtain data from records, such as when examining police shooting incidents or the attendance records of factory workers. We may have participants create the record themselves by having them keep a diary to record certain behaviors. We may also examine environmental events (e.g., correlating daily temperature changes with the frequency of violence or depression). We may also measure one or the other variable in a laboratory procedure, such as correlating reaction times with intelligence or personality scores.

Interpreting Correlational Designs

Our confidence in the conclusions drawn from a correlational design is influenced by the same concerns you saw previously with experiments. Thus, the procedures for measuring each variable should have construct and content validity. They should be reliable and provide sensitive measurements that can detect subtle differences in behavior. Extraneous influences such as demand characteristics, response sets, and the volunteer bias should be eliminated. And, as always, we seek consistency throughout by considering the four components of any study—the participants, environment, researcher, and measurement task.

However, recall that, compared to experiments, correlational designs have two flaws that severely reduce internal validity for concluding that differences in the X variable *cause* differences in Y scores. The first flaw is that we do not randomly assign participants to a score on the X variable. Therefore, we do not control participant variables by randomizing and thus balancing them across the different X scores. Because of this, differences between participants on the X variable are very likely to be confounded by differences in extraneous variables. For example, in our job-satisfaction study, workers who differ in their existing pay rates might also differ in job type, length of employment, or education level. Because the variable of pay rate is confounded with these variables, we cannot say that it is pay that *causes* job satisfaction.

The second flaw in correlational designs is that often we cannot be certain that X occurred before Y. Yet to conclude that X causes Y, we must *know* that X occurred first. For example, we cannot know for sure that a worker's low pay rate occurred first, so that it caused low job satisfaction. Perhaps for some reason participants were first dissatisfied with their job and, because of resulting poor motivation and performance, they then received low pay. Or perhaps a third variable was first operating: Perhaps some workers suffered discrimination, and this caused both low pay and low job satisfaction.

Thus, the relationship found in a correlational design might mean that changes in X cause changes in Y as we think. The problem is that changes in Y might cause changes in X, or some third variable might produce differences in both the X and Y scores. Therefore, a single correlational study is, at best, only interpreted as *suggesting* that changes in X cause changes in Y. Because of our lack of confidence in such a statement, correlational designs are best for testing a descriptive hypothesis that a relationship exists between the variables. (Recall that in a true experiment, we do randomly assign participants to conditions, and they do experience a condition before the dependent variable. Therefore, this design is best for testing a hypothesis about a causal variable.)

> *REMEMBER* Causal relationships are not inferred from a correlational design, because (1) the absence of random assignment allows for potential confoundings and (2) the order of occurrence of the variables is unknown.

Reasons for Using the Correlational Approach

Though we must accept the limited evidence for causality found in a correlational design, it is still a legitimate research method. In fact, a correlational design may be preferable for several reasons.

First, because of ethical and practical considerations, some relationships cannot be studied using a true experimental design. For example, physical and sexual abuse, accidents, crime, and recreational drug use are important psychological variables. Ethically, however, we cannot study such variables by randomly assigning people to experience them in a true experiment. Likewise, there are many variables we simply cannot manipulate, such as a person's career, race, gender, personality traits, or mental and physical illness. On the other hand, such variables and behaviors do occur in the real world, so we *can* study them through correlational methods. Thus, for example, we can measure the amount of abuse people have experienced and relate it to other behaviors or characteristics. Further, through literal and conceptual replication, together with experimental studies of relevant constructs, researchers can eventually develop some degree of confidence in causal relationships involving such variables.

Second, correlational procedures are useful for discovering new relationships. For example, we might measure workers on numerous variables that we suspect are related to job satisfaction (their work history, training level, motivation, pay, and so on) and then discover which variables produce relationships. Such research is useful not only for describing behavior but also for identifying relationships that might be causal that we can then investigate using experimental designs.

In addition, a laboratory experiment creates a rather artificial situation and involves only participants who will come to us. An advantage of the correlational approach is that often it can be conducted *outside* of the laboratory, where, potentially we have greater ecological and external validity. For example, measuring the pay and job satisfaction of employed workers is a more valid way to study this relationship than studying laboratory subjects who make widgets.

Finally, recall that part of understanding a behavior is being able to predict when it will occur. The relationship found in a correlational study may be better for predicting behaviors than that found in an experiment, because part of the greater external validity of a correlational design is that it usually provides a more complete description of the relationship. Typically, an experiment involves a limited set of conditions (X scores) with gaps between them. As shown back in scatterplot A of Figure 8.1, for example, we studied only the three pay rates of $3, $6, and $9 dollars per hour. Therefore, we have no data for predicting satisfaction levels for a $5 or $7 rate. In a correlational study, however, we are likely to obtain a wider variety of X scores to relate to Y, thus possibly improving predications. Look again at scatterplot B of Figure 8.1. Here, actual workers reported pay rates between $3 and $12 per hour, so we have data for predicting job satisfaction scores throughout a much wider range of pay rates.

A correlational design is especially preferred in applied research involving the creation of a "selection test." If, for example, people must take a test when applying for a job, they are taking a selection test. The logic is that previous correlational research might have shown that those employed workers who score higher on the test also tend to be better workers. Therefore, only those job applicants who perform above a certain score on the test will be hired, because we predict that they will also be better workers. Similar selection tests are being used when people take college entrance exams, which allow us to predict their future college performance. Or when clinical patients take diagnostic tests, which allow us to identify those who are at risk of developing emotional problems.

REMEMBER Correlational designs are useful for discovering relationships, they solve ethical and practical problems, and they may provide better validity and accuracy in predictions.

Analyzing Data with Correlational Statistics

Usually data from correlationals research is analyzed by first computing a correlation coefficient. A **correlation coefficient** is a statistic—a number calculated using the pairs of X and Y scores in the sample data—that summarizes the type and strength of the relationship that is present. However, computing a correlation coefficient does *not* create a correlational *design*. A correlational design occurs whenever you do not randomly assign participants to the levels of the variable, *regardless* of how the data are analyzed. You can compute correlations within experimental designs, and you can apply ANOVAs or *t*-tests to correlational designs. Generally the rule is this: On the one hand, ANOVA, *t*-tests, and similar procedures are the primary analysis when the X variable consists of a few different levels or X scores. Then we examine the mean Y score per condition and look at how the means change as a function of changes in X. On the other hand, correlational statistics are the primary method of analysis when the X variable consists of a wide range of scores. Usually we don't compute the mean of Y for each X here, because we'd end up with an unwieldy number of different means that would be difficult to compare. For example, using an ANOVA to compare the mean job-satisfaction score for each of 20 different pay rates would be overwhelming. Instead, we use the correlation coefficient to summarize the *entire* relationship formed by all of the data at once. This is the major advantage of a correlation coefficient: It takes a very complex relationship involving a wide range of scores and simplifies it into one easily interpreted statistic.

As with other statistics, the specific correlation coefficient to compute depends on the nature of the *X* and *Y* scores we measure. Most psychological research typically involves the **Pearson correlation coefficient,** which is the parametric procedure used to describe the *linear* relationship between normally distributed interval or ratio scores (calculations are given in Appendix C.11). Symbolized by *r*, this statistic is technically the "Pearson Product Moment Correlation Coefficient." Also, a common nonparametric procedure is the **Spearman correlation coefficient.** This coefficient is employed when both variables are measured using an ordinal scale, showing participants' rank order (calculations given in Appendix C.12). Other types of coefficients are used with other types of data, but, regardless, we interpret every coefficient in the same way.

To see how the correlation coefficient communicates the type and strength of a relationship between variables, let's say that we correlate workers' overall job satisfaction scores with their corresponding pay rates, as shown in Figure 8.2. These are both normally distributed ratio scales, so we compute the Pearson *r*. Summarizing the data in this way is usually the starting point for most correlational research, because a straight-line relationship is the simplest, most common type. An *r* will have a value between −1.0 and +1.0. A positive coefficient indicates a positive linear relationship (as in scatterplot A of Figure 8.2.) A negative value indicates a negative linear relationship (as in scatterplot B). The absolute value of the coefficient communicates the strength of the relationship. A value of ±1.0 indicates a perfectly consistent relationship which, as in A of Figure 8.2,

Figure 8.2   Data producing perfect positive and negative linear relationships between job satisfaction and hourly pay rate

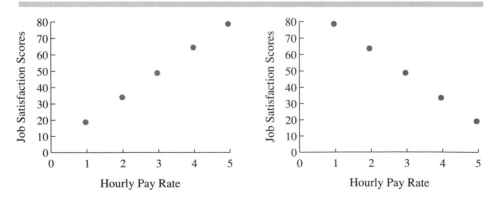

has *one* value of Y associated with only one value of X so that all data points fall on a straight line. A value less than ±1.0 is essentially the degree to which the data *approximate* a perfect linear relationship. The way to interpret an *r* less than ±1 is to compare it to 1: The closer the *r* is to 1, then the closer to one value are the Y scores at an X, and the more the scatterplot forms a straight line. For example, Figure 8.3 shows two intermediate-strength relationships. As the coefficient approaches 0, it indicates a less consistent linear relationship, with greater variability in Y scores at each value of X. Note that the components of a relationship in a correlation are analogous to those in an experiment, so the variability in Y scores at each X is again the *error variance*. In Figure 8.3, scatterplot A shows greater error variance and thus a less consistent relationship, which produces a lower correlation coefficient than that in scatterplot B.

(As a frame of reference, note that a relationship in psychological research is considered reasonably strong when it produces an *r* in the neighborhood of +.40. An *r* of +.60 is downright impressive.)

At the opposite extreme, Figure 8.4 shows data that do not form a relationship, and so *r* will equal zero. This pattern is as far as you can get from that of a perfect straight line, and *r* = 0 is as far as you can get from ±1.

Of course, merely calculating the correlation coefficient is not enough. As you saw with experiments, it might be that the relationship in the sample data is the result of sampling error—a coincidental pairing of X-Y scores so that we happen to see a linear pattern. For example, it's possible that in nature, job satisfaction and pay rate are *not* really related, but by luck, the workers we selected at each pay rate produced satisfaction scores that tend to fall in a line, creating the

Figure 8.3   Two scatterplots showing intermediate-strength relationships between job satisfaction scores and hourly pay rate

Data in A produce a smaller *r* than data in B.

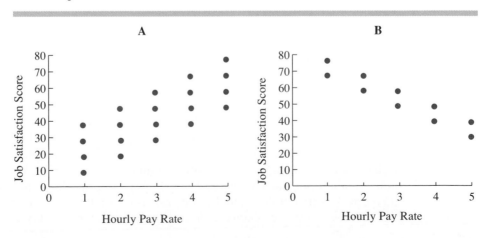

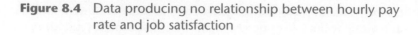

Figure 8.4   Data producing no relationship between hourly pay rate and job satisfaction

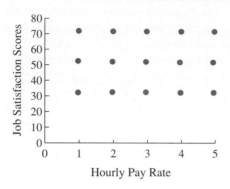

illusion of a relationship between these variables. If so, then the *r* we've calculated reflects nothing more than sampling error, poorly representing a population correlation of 0. Therefore, you must always determine whether any correlation coefficient you've computed is significant (as described in Appendix C.11).

If the correlation coefficient is significant, we're confident that the relationship is not a chance occurrence. Then, we interpret the study by examining the value of the correlation coefficient. Say, for example, the variables of job satisfaction and pay rates produce an *r* of +.50 that turns out to be significant. First, we know that there is a positive linear relationship here. Originally, we predicted a positive relationship, so this *r* confirms the hypothesis. (Recall that in statistics, such a prediction involves a one-tailed test.) A negative *r* would contradict and thus disconfirm the hypothesis. In a different study, we might predict merely some kind of relationship, either positive or negative (and use a two-tailed test). Then either a positive or negative value of *r* would confirm the hypothesis.

Further, an *r* of +.50 indicates a reasonably strong, consistent relationship. As usual, the inconsistency in the relationship suggests the extent to which other variables are operating that we have not taken into account. An *r* of +.90, for example, would indicate extreme consistency, suggesting that only a few, rather unimportant variables are related to job satisfaction in addition to hourly pay. Conversely, an *r* of +.09 would indicate great inconsistency, suggesting the presence of other important variables related to job satisfaction that we have not considered. Following this line of reasoning, we interpret our results "psychologically," considering what the consistency and inconsistency in the relationship indicate about job satisfaction and hourly pay rate, and how they relate to the theoretical explanations, models, and constructs that we began with. However, this is a descriptive, correlational design, so do not infer causality.

For help in understanding the observed relationship, we perform additional statistical procedures, starting with linear regression.

Linear Regression

Perform linear regression only when the Pearson *r* is significant. **Linear regression** is the procedure for predicting participants' scores on one variable based on the linear relationship with their scores on another variable. Thus, once we know there is a significant, believable relationship between pay and job satisfaction, we can then predict a worker's job satisfaction by knowing his or her pay rate. Simultaneously, the linear regression procedure allows us to describe the straight line that summarizes a scatterplot, summarizing the linear relationship in the data.

Perform regression procedures by using the sample data to calculate the **linear regression equation** (shown in Appendix C.11). This equation allows you to graph a straight line that summarizes the scatterplot, called the **linear regression line.** To draw the line, perform the following steps: (1) select some values of *X* and, using the regression equation, calculate the corresponding values of *Y*; (2) plot these *X-Y* data points; and (3) connect the data points with a straight line. For example, an idealized scatterplot and its corresponding regression line are shown in Figure 8.5. The regression line fits the scatterplot so that the distance some *Y* scores are above the line equals the distance other *Y* scores are below the line. Thus, the line summarizes the scatterplot by, on average, passing through the center of the *Y* scores at each *X*. Think of the regression line as reflecting the linear relationship hidden in the data. Because the actual *Y* scores fall above and

Figure 8.5 Idealized scatterplot showing a linear regression line

The arrow indicates *Y'* for *X* = 1.

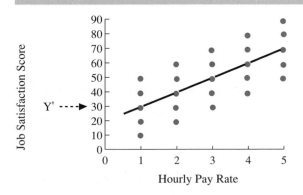

below the line, the data only more or less fit a straight line. But there's no system for drawing a more or less straight line. Instead, the regression line is what a perfect version of the linear relationship in the data would look like.

You read the regression line by traveling vertically from any X until you intercept the regression line and then traveling horizontally until you intercept the Y axis. The value of Y that falls on the regression line above any X is called "Y prime," symbolized as Y'. Each Y' is a summary of the Y scores at an X based on the overall linear relationship in the data. Because there is balance of the Y scores above and below the line at each X, the value of Y' at an X is *more or less* the Y score that everyone at that X obtained. Therefore, Y' is our best prediction of an individual's Y score at a value of X. **Y prime** is the predicted value of Y for those who score at a particular value of X. By entering the value of any X into the regression equation, we can calculate the corresponding Y' score. In Figure 8.5, for example, we predict a Y' of 30 for an X of $1. The Y scores are evenly spread out *around* (more or less than) each value of Y'. So, considering the entire linear relationship, participants with an X of $1 scored *around* a Y of 30, so 30 is our best prediction and summary for any other person scoring an X of $1.

> **REMEMBER** The *linear regression equation* summarizes the linear relationship in a sample of data, producing the *linear regression line*. From this, we use the relationship to predict the Y score—Y'—at any X.

It is by using the regression procedure that we create **selection tests.** First we measure a sample on both the X and Y variables so that we can determine the regression equation. Then we can test new individuals on the X variable. We enter their X scores into the regression equation and calculate the corresponding values of Y'. If a person's predicted Y' score meets our "criterion," he or she is selected for the job, and so on. Thus, for example, students must take the Scholastic Aptitude Test (SAT) to be admitted to some colleges, because researchers have already established that SAT scores are somewhat positively correlated with subsequent college grades. Therefore, by applying regression techniques to the SAT scores of would-be college students (their X scores), we can predict their future college performance (their Y' score). If the predicted grades are too low, the student is not admitted to the college. Because of this procedure, in correlational designs the X variable is also called the *predictor variable* and the Y variable is also called the *criterion variable*.)

Errors in Prediction and the Variance Accounted For

It is not enough to say that a relationship can be used to predict scores. We should know the amount of error to expect in such predictions so that we know how much credence to give them. To estimate the amount of error we'll have when predicting unknown scores, we examine how well we can predict the known scores in a sample. That is, we'll pretend we don't know the Y scores in the sample, predict them using the regression equation, and then compare the predicted Y' scores to the actual Y scores. The predictions for some participants will be close to their actual Y scores, while predictions for others may contain considerably more error. Therefore, to summarize the error across the entire relationship, we compute *something like* the "average error" in the predictions.

To understand this, look again at Figure 8.5. For those people paid $1 an hour, we'll predict a satisfaction score of 30. The **error in prediction** is the difference between the score we predict for someone—Y'—and the score they actually got—their Y score. The workers paid $1 actually scored as high as 40 or 50, so we're off by -10 and -20 points for them, and so "on average" we're off by about -15 points. Likewise, others scored as low as 10 or 20, so we're off by an average of about $+15$ for them. Thus, when we predict a satisfaction score of 30 for each of these workers, when we're wrong we'll be in error by about ± 15 points.

To summarize the relationship, we determine the errors we'd have at the other pay rates, and then average them together to find one number for the whole sample. Although the actual calculations are slightly more involved, we essentially end up with the overall "average" error in predictions we have when we use this relationship—the average difference between the Y' we predict for participants and the actual Y scores they obtained. These calculations produce the statistic called the standard error of the estimate. The **standard error of the estimate** communicates the amount by which the actual Y scores in a sample differ from their corresponding predicted Y' scores. Let's say that when $r = +.50$, the standard error of the estimate equals 2.0 (calculations shown in Appendix C.11). We interpret this number as indicating that "on average" our predicted Y's differ from participants' actual Y scores by about 2 points.

REMEMBER Whenever you compute a correlation coefficient, it is appropriate to compute the standard error of the estimate to describe the "average" prediction error you'd have using the linear regression procedure.

Notice that the size of r gives a hint about your prediction errors. The larger the r, the closer the Y scores are to the regression line, so there is less difference between the Y' we predict for participants and the Y score they actually obtain. When r is ± 1, everyone at an X has the same Y score, they all fall on the regression line, and so there is zero difference—no error—between the predicted and actual Y scores, and the standard error of the estimate equals 0. Conversely, as r approaches 0, there are larger differences among the Y scores at each X, so there will be larger differences between the Y' and the actual Y scores at that X.

It is difficult to determine whether being off by an average of, say, 2 points is a lot, so it's still difficult to evaluate the prediction errors occurring with this relationship. Instead, a less subjective way of evaluating the accuracy of predictions is to determine the **proportion of variance accounted for.** In Chapter 7, you saw that this statistic is the proportion of the total variance in Y scores that we can predict or account for by knowing the condition under which a participant was tested. Because a condition of the independent variable is simply a special type of *X* score, the proportion of variance accounted for is *always* the proportion of the total variance in *Y* scores that is accounted for by knowing participants' *X* scores.

Recall that the proportion of variance accounted for is the proportion of total variance in *Y* that is *systematic variance*—the extent to which differences in *Y* are systematically related to changes in *X*. In making this calculation, we again determine the improvement in predictions we have when we use the relationship to predict scores, as compared to when we do not use the relationship. For example, let's say that we obtained the job satisfaction scores shown in Figure 8.6. On the left are the scores we obtained and all of the differences between them constitute the total variance. Without utilizing the relationship with pay rate, we cannot predict any of these differences. On the right is the regression line for this study. To the extent that the satisfaction scores tend to increase with pay, some differences in satisfaction scores are now predictable. To this extent the scores exhibit systematic variance. At the same time, to some extent the *Y* scores do not follow this trend, so they also exhibit error variance. Therefore, a predicted *Y'* score only gets us in the neighborhood of the actual *Y* scores: For example, in this relationship we know that people tend to score around 20 when paid \$1 and around 30 when paid \$2, but we don't know precisely when they score 10, 20, 30, or 40. Thus, compared to when we don't utilize the relationship, using a person's pay rate improves our accuracy in predicting job satisfaction by some proportion.

The proportion of variance accounted for in a correlational design equals the **squared correlation coefficient.** Thus, after a Pearson *r* has been computed, the

Figure 8.6 Proportion of variance accounted for in a job satisfaction study

Differences between scores on the left constitute the total variance. By correlating the scores with pay rates on the right, we identify both systematic and error variance.

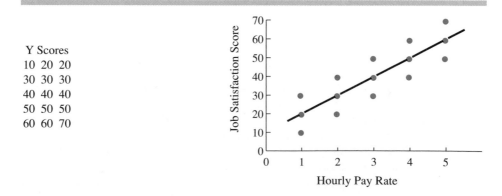

Y Scores
10 20 20
30 30 30
40 40 40
50 50 50
60 60 70

value of r^2 indicates the proportion of total variance in Y scores that is systematically associated with changing X scores. Essentially r^2 communicates the proportional improvement in predicting Y scores that occurs when we calculate the regression equation and use it to predict Y scores, compared with when we do not use this procedure. Thus, say that the r in the job satisfaction study is $+.40$. Then the variable of pay rate accounts for $.4^2$ or $.16$ of the variance in satisfaction scores: We are, on average, 16% more accurate at predicting—and understanding—differences in satisfaction if we consider a person's pay rate than if we don't consider his or her pay rate. (Likewise, squaring other types of correlation coefficients provides the same kind of information about the relationship found in those situations.)

In a correlational design, r^2 is *not* called a measure of effect size: To say that X has an effect would be to imply causality. Instead, r^2 is called the **coefficient of determination.** However, as with effect size, we compare the values of r^2 from different relationships to evaluate which is the most useful, scientifically important relationship. Thus for pay rate and job satisfaction, r is $+.40$, producing an r^2 of $.16$. But say that the correlation between years on the job and satisfaction is $r = +.20$, producing an r^2 of $= .04$. Because $.16$ is four times $.04$, the relationship involving pay rate is four times as systematic as that involving years on the job. In these data, then, pay rate is four times as useful for predicting scores and, thus, four times more important for understanding differences in job satisfaction. (All of the measures of proportion of variance accounted for that we've discussed are for describing sample data. They are *very* rough estimates of how useful the relationship is if applied to the population.)

REMEMBER The squared correlation coefficient indicates the proportion of variance in Y that is accounted for by the relationship with X, so it indicates how useful the relationship is.

Maximizing the Power of the Correlation Coefficient

Remember *power?* It's the probability of not rejecting the null hypothesis when there really is a relationship between the variables. Power is also important with correlation coefficients. If a coefficient is not significant, you don't know whether it describes a "real" relationship, so you cannot perform linear regression or compute r^2, and you cannot draw any conclusion about how the variables or underlying constructs are related. At such times, however, it would be a shame if you were missing a real relationship because you had insufficient power: It's silly to conduct *any* type of study where you're unlikely to reject null when it's really false. Therefore, to ensure that you won't miss a relationship that actually exists in the population, you should create correlational designs that maximize power.

Remember, the discussion of power is confined to those times when the null hypothesis is false, so you should obtain a *significant* coefficient. We maximize power by creating a design that will produce a strong relationship and thus a large coefficient that is likely to be significant. To illustrate, say that the graphs in

Figure 8.7 depict the results of two studies investigating the relationship between hourly pay and job satisfaction. Study A produces a pattern that closely approximates a straight line, forming a relatively narrow ellipse that produces a relatively large correlation coefficient that is likely to be significant. Study B, however, produces a relatively wider, more circular pattern. This will produce a smaller coefficient that is less likely to be significant, so we might miss finding this relationship. Study B has two problems that produced this pattern of scores.

First, study B reflects greater variability in *Y* scores at each *X*. The fact that the *Y* scores do not closely fit the straight (regression) line is precisely what a low correlation coefficient indicates. Thus, to increase power, we seek to control any extraneous variables that might produce error variance. Further, we seek a precise and sensitive measurement of each variable. If, for example, we round off the pay rates to whole-dollar amounts, then we may be forcing different job satisfaction scores to occur at the same pay score, artificially increasing error variance.

Second, study B suffers from **restriction of range.** We obtained a limited range of pay scores, so a scatterplot with so much error variance does not produce much of a linear pattern. These data are misleading, producing a smaller *r* than would be found if the range were not restricted: Had study B included pay scores below $3 and above $5, even with the same variability in *Y* scores, the overall pattern would be relatively more linear, producing a larger coefficient that was more likely to be significant. (We can place either variable on the *X* axis, so restricting the range of either will produce a truncated, circular scatterplot and an artificially low correlation coefficient.)

Often, restriction of range in a correlational study is due to the participants selected. For example, in our study we should avoid selecting only workers who have the same job because they will all receive very close to the same pay. Similarly, if we're correlating students' overall college grade-point average with their

Figure 8.7   Scatterplots from two studies of the relationship between hourly pay rate and job satisfaction

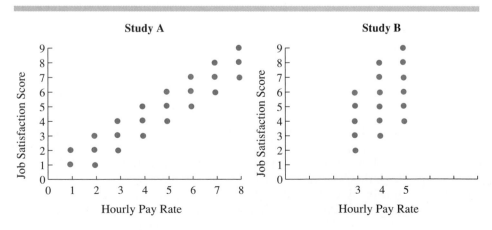

later job success, our selection criteria should not be limited to honor students or to students taking a particular course: Such selectivity could produce *ceiling* or *floor* effects, or otherwise restrict the range of grade-point averages.

In addition, there are three general principles for increasing the power of correlational designs. First, we increase power by increasing N. Correlational designs frequently entail less control of extraneous variables, which can increase error variance and weaken the relationship. Therefore, researchers often compensate by using larger Ns than those found in experiments, often in the range of several hundred participants. Second, recall that parametric statistical procedures are more powerful than nonparametric procedures, so when possible, we prefer to measure scores using an interval or ratio scale that meets the requirements of the parametric Pearson correlation coefficient. And third, remember that the Pearson r describes the extent to which the data form a *linear* relationship. We compute r when we predict a linear relationship, or when we wish to determine the degree to which a linear relationship is present. However, if the data form a distinctly nonlinear pattern, they will not fit a straight line very well, and the coefficient may not be significant. Then we lose power because we conclude that there is no relationship when, in fact, a consistent and significant nonlinear relationship exists. Therefore, to maximize power, compute the coefficient that is appropriate for the type of relationship in the data.

> **REMEMBER** Maximize the size of the correlation coefficient by minimizing error variance, avoiding restricted range, testing a large N, and computing parametric, linear statistics when appropriate.

Additional Uses of Correlation

Recall that any time you develop a new measurement task, you must be concerned with demonstrating its reliability and validity.

In addition to describing the overall results of a study, computing a correlation coefficient is the statistical technique for demonstrating the reliability and validity of a new measurement procedure in any experimental or correlational design.

Ascertaining Reliability

As you know, if a measurement procedure is reliable, then whenever a participant consistently exhibits a particular behavior, he or she should receive the same score. There are three ways a correlation coefficient is used to show reliability.

First, recall that often a measurement involves judging or rating a participant's behavior, and for reliability we use multiple raters. To demonstrate that the behavior is judged reliably, we need to show high *inter-rater reliability,* the consistency of ratings by any two raters. For example, say that we are studying creativity and have two judges rate how creative participants are when "doodling." If the judges are reliable, then we should see a large positive correlation between their ratings: We should find that low creativity scores assigned to a participant by one rater were consistently matched by the other, while high scores given by one were also given by the other.

A similar approach is used to show the reliability of a testing procedure that does not involve raters. **Test-retest reliability** indicates that participants tend to obtain the same score when tested at different times. For example, if a college exam has test-retest reliability, a student who produces a low score now should also produce a low score later, and a student scoring high now should also score high later. In other words, test-retest reliability is evident when there is a high, positive correlation between the scores obtained from the two testings. Likewise, a physiological measurement has test-retest reliability if scores from the same participants tested twice are positively correlated.

Test-retest reliability reflects the reliability of a participant's total score on a test from one testing *session* to another. A different approach is to determine whether the *trials* within *one* testing session are reliable. **Split-half reliability** indicates that participants' scores on some trials consistently match their scores on other trials. Typically we first split a test in half, comparing the odd-numbered trials to the even-numbered trials. (This balances order effects due to fatigue or practice.) Then we compute a summary score—such as a mean of the total number correct—for each participant on each half of the test. Then we correlate the summary scores. For example, if the questions on a college exam have split-half reliability, then students scoring low on the odd questions should also score low on the even questions, and so on. Likewise, we might determine the split-half reliability of a series of reaction-time trials by correlating the times from even- and odd-numbered trials.

> **REMEMBER**   Test-retest reliability is the correlation between repeated testings, and split-half reliability is the correlation between different trials within one test.

For any of the preceding, a coefficient of +.80 or better is usually required for the procedure to be considered reliable.

Ascertaining Validity

Recall that the issue of validity is whether a procedure actually measures what it is intended to measure. Believe it or not, one approach to demonstrating validity is simply a researcher's judgment that the procedure looks valid. **Face validity** is the extent to which a measurement procedure appears to measure what it's intended to measure. Thus, if we judge that on its "face" a procedure looks reasonable, we have one very limited way of arguing that the procedure is valid. For example, a reaction-time task has face validity if it appears to measure the time taken by people to perform a mental operation. An intelligence test has face validity if it appears to measure intelligence.

REMEMBER Face validity means that a procedure is valid because it looks valid.

To produce more objective evidence of validity, however, we use correlational procedures. One approach is to determine the convergent validity of a procedure. **Convergent validity** is the extent to which the scores obtained from one procedure are positively correlated with scores obtained from another procedure that is already accepted as valid. For example, say that we develop a new test for measuring job satisfaction. Then we give the same people both our test and another accepted test. If our test is valid, then when workers are satisfied, they should obtain high scores on both our and the old accepted test. When they are dissatisfied, they should score low on both tests. Therefore, there should be a strong, positive correlation between the scores from the two tests. If so, we can argue that both procedures "converge" on and measure job satisfaction.

On the other hand, **discriminant validity** is the extent to which the scores obtained from one procedure are *not* correlated with the scores from another procedure that measures other variables or constructs. Thus, our job satisfaction test is valid if it does not correlate with accepted measures of personality or motivation. In this case, we would argue that the procedure "discriminates" between what it is and is not intended to measure.

REMEMBER With convergent validity, a procedure correlates with another procedure that is valid. With discriminant validity, a procedure does not correlate with other, unintended measures.

Even though two *procedures* correlate with each other, this does not necessarily mean that they reflect the intended *behaviors*. After all, it might be that neither our new test nor the old accepted test actually measures job satisfaction. Therefore, another approach for demonstrating validity is to correlate the scores from a procedure with an observable behavior. **Criterion validity** is the extent to which a procedure can distinguish between participants on the basis of some behavior. There are two subtypes of criterion validity.

Concurrent validity is the extent to which a procedure correlates with an individual's *present* behavior. For example, say that our definition of job satisfaction is such that it should be negatively related to absenteeism. Concurrent validity would be demonstrated if people who scored high on the satisfaction test were seldom absent, while those scoring low were frequently absent. Then we'd think the test is valid, because test scores correlate with an actual behavior in exactly the way they should if the test does measure what it's supposed to measure.

On the other hand, **predictive validity** is the extent to which a procedure correlates with an individual's *future* behavior. For example, say we used our satisfaction test to predict participants' future absenteeism. The test has predictive validity if, when we later examine their absentee rates, workers' actual rates are positively correlated with their predicted rates.

> *REMEMBER* Criterion validity is the extent to which a procedure relates to a specific behavior, either distinguishing the behavior concurrently or predicting future behavior.

Not surprisingly, predictive validity is of paramount importance when creating selection tests: After all, we use these tests to predict someone's future performance. What is surprising is that a measurement can lack construct, content, and even face validity but still have predictive (and concurrent) validity. Essentially, in such cases the procedure does distinguish an individual's behavior, but we don't understand why. For example, we might find that the number of cups of coffee a worker drinks daily is an accurate predictor of—is positively correlated with—later job satisfaction. Even if we haven't a clue as to why this relationship occurs, coffee consumption still has predictive validity.

To help you remember the names of the various approaches to reliability and validity, consult Table 8.1.

Table 8.1   Summary of Methods for Ascertaining Reliability and Validity

Reliability	
Inter-rater	Ratings from two raters are positively correlated.
Test-retest	Each participant's test and retest scores are correlated positively.
Split-half	Participants' scores from half of the trials positively correlate with their scores from the other half of the trials.
Validity	
Face	Procedure appears valid.
Convergent	Procedure correlates with other accepted measures.
Discriminant	Procedure does not correlate with other unintended measures.
Criterion	
Concurrent	Procedure correlates with a present behavior.
Predictive	Procedure correlates with a future behavior.

Conducting Research Using Interviews and Questionnaires

A common method of gathering data in descriptive research is to ask people questions using interviews and questionnaires. (The preceding procedures for ascertaining validity and reliability are especially common in the development of such questions.) However, don't make the mistake of thinking that questionnaires and interviews are used solely in descriptive designs. Such self-reports are often used in experiments to measure the dependent variable and as a manipulation check.

When you design an interview or questionnaire, your first step should be to search the psychological literature for existing questionnaires and tests. Typically, the term *questionnaire* implies that there are no correct or incorrect answers, while *test* implies that there are correct and incorrect answers or that, based on previous research, there are at least typical and atypical answers. The advantage of using existing procedures is that their reliability and validity have already been established. Detailed descriptions of various psychological tests can be found in research reports, as well as in specific reference books (e.g., Robinson, Shaver, & Wrightsman, 1991). Thus, for example, we would find there is a widely accepted questionnaire for measuring job satisfaction, the "Job Descriptive Index" (Smith, Kendall, & Hulin, 1969). When selecting a questionnaire, remember from Chapter 3 that we distinguish between a state characteristic (a temporary, changeable attribute) and a trait characteristic (a rather stable, unchanging attribute). In the literature, you'll find questionnaires for measuring specific state or trait characteristics.

On the other hand, creating your own questions involves a lot of work, and then you must demonstrate their reliability and validity. If you choose to develop your own questions, you'll have a number of decisions to make. As an example, say that we set out to create a procedure for measuring job satisfaction.

The first step is to consider the type of questions to ask.

Using Closed-Ended versus Open-Ended Questions

In a **closed-ended question**, the researcher provides the alternatives from which the participant selects. Multiple-choice, true-false, yes-no, and rating-scale questions are all closed-ended questions. Some closed-ended questions that might reflect job satisfaction are:

(a) At work, my favorite activity is
   1. Working with my hands.
   2. Solving mental problems.
   3. Supervising others.
   4. Completing paperwork.

(b) At work I become angry
   1. Never.
   2. Once in a while.
   3. Frequently
   4. Most of the time.

(c) Check all the words that describe your co-workers:
    __ Stimulating
    __ Stupid
    __ Helpful
    __ Boring

(d) On most days, do you look forward to going to work?
    1. Yes
    2. No

Closed-ended questions are also called "objective" questions, and that is their overwhelming strength: A response can be assigned a score objectively and reliably, with a minimum of subjective interpretation or error on the researcher's part. For example, in question (a) above, when participants select choice 1, we can assign them a score of 1 on that question, reliably assigning the same score to all people who prefer working with their hands.

The disadvantage of closed-ended questions is that they may yield limited information. First, they measure only the variable(s) we've selected. In question (b), we asked about anger at work, but participants might feel that happiness is the more relevant emotion. Second, participants can select only from the choices provided, even if they would like to give a different response. In question (c), perhaps a worker considered co-workers to be "intelligent," a response that is not available. For these reasons, closed-ended questions are used when reliability is a major concern but we are not interested in discovering new variables that might be relevant.

Conversely, in an **open-ended question,** the participant determines both the alternatives to choose from and the response. Any question equivalent to an essay question, whether written or oral, is open-ended. Thus, we might ask the open-ended questions "Describe your favorite activities at work" and "How often do you become angry at work?" Open-ended questions can also be projective. In a **projective test** the participant describes or interprets an ambiguous stimulus. This approach is used when participants might not be conscious of their feelings, or when social desirability is likely to prevent them from explicitly revealing them. Instead, people will "project" their feelings into the ambiguous situation. Two classic examples of projective tests are the *Rorschach test,* in which participants interpret ambiguous inkblots, and the *Thematic Apperception Test,* in which they interpret ambiguous pictures.

The advantages of open-ended questions are the opposite of those of closed-ended questions. Open-ended questions allow people to provide a wide range of responses, so researchers may discover new relevant variables. Further, participants can respond in their own words, so they are not limited to just the one perspective or phrasing that is present in a closed-ended question. On the other hand, the disadvantage of open-ended questions is that scoring each response requires subjective interpretation by the researcher, so scores may not be reliable. Two people who should be given the same score because their behaviors are the same might obtain different scores because of differences in the wording of their responses. (How would you score the responses "The paperwork is easy" versus

"The paperwork is very easy"?) Also, the scoring of open-ended questions is highly susceptible to experimenter biases and expectations.

As usual, we counteract problems of subjective scoring by using double blinds and multiple scorers who demonstrate high inter-rater reliability. The crucial component, however, is the scoring criteria. One way to score open-ended questions is the technique called content analysis. In **content analysis** we score a participant's written or spoken answer by counting specified types of responses. We can assign a score based on the number of times a certain word, a certain feeling, or a particular perspective occurs. For example, a worker's score might simply reflect the number of positive references made to paperwork, regardless of whether the word *very* occurs. (See Krippendorf, 1980, for further information on content analysis.)

Even with strict scoring criteria, open-ended questions tend to provide less reliable and objective data, so they are used when reliability is not a major concern. In particular, open-ended questions are used with initial research into some unexplored behavior so that we can identify potentially relevant variables, or when each participant's response is likely to be unique.

Of course, you may employ both open-ended and closed-ended questions in the same questionnaire. This mix has the advantage of providing both reliable questions that are narrow in scope and less reliable questions that are wider-ranging.

Using Interviews versus Questionnaires

You must also decide whether to use an interviewer to ask the questions or to provide participants with a written questionnaire to complete. The advantage of interviewers is that they ensure that participants complete the questions as instructed. In addition, an interviewer can react to the information provided by a participant, either requesting clarifying information or exploring additional topics that arise. The drawback to interviewers, however, is that they can heighten the demand characteristics of reactivity and social desirability, or they may inadvertently communicate expectancies about the desired response.

Just the opposite is true of questionnaires: The interaction between the researcher and participant is minimal, so there is less risk of biasing participants with experimenter expectations. Reactivity and social desirability also may be reduced, because completing a questionnaire anonymously can be much less threatening than talking to another person. Questionnaires also provide more efficient data collection, because many people can be tested at one time. The disadvantages of questionnaires, however, are that participants might not complete them as instructed, and the information obtained is limited to the inflexible questions presented.

The role of an interviewer is not all-or-nothing. At one extreme is the structured interview. In a **structured interview,** participants are asked specific, predetermined questions in a controlled manner. The most structured interview is when the interviewer simply reads closed-ended questions to participants and records their responses. The interviewer reads each question in a neutral manner with no additional comments or hints, and responds to a participant's extraneous comments by merely repeating the question. (This approach is common, for example, in telephone surveys or when testing young children.) A less structured interview may involve asking open-ended questions, but the interviewer follows a script to ensure that all participants are treated in a consistent fashion. (This approach is commonly used in intelligence tests.)

At the opposite extreme is an unstructured interview. In an **unstructured interview** the researcher has a general idea of the open-ended questions that will be asked, but there is freedom of discussion and interaction between participant and interviewer. Such interviews are commonly used when a researcher begins studying a behavior or is developing a complete description of an individual, such as during a clinical diagnosis. The lack of structure allows us to explore a wide range of issues, but the trade-off is that we lose reliability, and the interviewer might lead participants into saying things they do not mean.

REMEMBER   Interviews are preferred when the researcher must react to a participant's responses, but questionnaires are more reliable and less susceptible to demand characteristics.

Constructing Questions

The principles for creating questions in interviews and questionnaires are largely the same. Any question constitutes a *trial* in which what we ask is a stimulus and a participant's answer is his or her response. Therefore, we exercise the same concerns when designing a question that we did when presenting an independent variable and measuring a dependent variable.

First, recognize that participants must interpret the meaning of a question and that we must interpret the meaning of their response. For valid inferences, you should minimize the extent to which participants must decide what it is we are asking. For example, the question "Do you experience job satisfaction with your job?" is a problem because most workers will not know what *we* mean by job satisfaction. Instead, we should ask participants to report specific behaviors. If job satisfaction is related to being paid enough, we should ask workers whether they are paid enough. Then *we* translate their responses back into our variables and constructs. Therefore, the elements of a question should have construct validity, reflecting the hypothetical construct as it's defined, as well as content validity, so that the question and the response actually and only reflect the variable or behavior you seek to measure. In addition, each question should have face validity, temporal validity, ecological validity, concurrent validity, and predictive validity.

Second, you should design questions that are sensitive to the subtle differences that exist between people. We create a question to *discriminate* or differentiate between participants on the variable being measured. We assume that there are differences between people on the variable because, otherwise, why bother to measure it? Therefore, you should design sensitive and precise questions that people will answer differently, to reflect such differences. Also, we want to measure the full range of behaviors, so design questions that avoid ceiling effects, floor effects, or any other restriction of range in participants' scores. This includes watching out for questions that create demand characteristics resulting in selected responses because of reactivity, social desirability, or perceived experimenter expectancies. Realize that this goal may contradict the goal of having face validity. The problem is that the more obvious it is to a researcher that a question measures a particular variable, the more obvious it is to participants, too. Because this can then increase demand characteristics, researchers sometimes sacrifice face validity by disguising questions or by measuring a behavior less directly.

Finally, recall that a score should reflect a participant's "typical" behavior. However, any response might be atypical because of a question's unique wording or perspective, or because the participant experiences a momentary distraction or misinterprets the question. As usual, we counter such problems by increasing reliability through multiple trials: We create a number of different questions designed to measure the same variable or behavior. By varying the wording and perspective across different questions, we should balance out the unique aspects of any one question. Then we produce a summary score for each participant, such as the total number correct or mean score. This provides a more reliable estimate of a person's typical response to such items. Also, computing a summary score from many questions increases sensitivity, because participants' scores will tend to span a wider range, so that we are more likely to distinguish between one individual and another.

REMEMBER The goal of question construction is to reliably and validly discriminate between participants on the variable being studied.

When generating questions, try to create many examples that reflect a variable. Then select those questions that are best suited to your purposes. Select questions using the following criteria.

Wording the Questions Phrase questions so that you are confident you know what participants are communicating by their response and so that you can discriminate between different people. To meet these goals, avoid the following types of questions.

First, avoid **double-barreled questions**. These are questions that have more than one component. Consider the question "Should you be given more flexibility and less supervision on your job?" What if a person agrees to one part but not the other? The meaning of any response here will not be clear to you, so instead, ask two separate questions. Always phrase a question so that it states just one idea.

Second, avoid **leading questions.** These are questions that are so loaded with social desirability or experiment expectancies that there is one obvious response. Consider the question "Should very bad workers who are always late receive low pay?" This question won't discriminate between participants, because everyone knows what the correct answer "should be." Always phrase questions in a neutral manner, avoiding biased or inflammatory statements.

Third, avoid **Barnum statements.** These are questions that are so global and vague that everyone would agree with them or select the same response for them. (They are named after P. T. Barnum, who was famous for such statements.) For example, asking "Do you sometimes worry?" or "Have you had difficulty in some college courses?" will elicit the same answer from virtually everyone. This is the problem with horoscopes and palm readings: They are so general that people can always think of personal experiences that seem to fit. Always phrase a question so that it targets a specific behavior.

Finally, avoid questions that contain *undefined terms.* For example, asking "Should workers who are always late receive low pay?" will leave you wondering how participants interpret "always" and "low pay." Instead, either define such terms in the question or have participants provide the definition in their response. Thus, you might ask "What pay should a worker receive who is late for work an average of twice a week?" In this version you define "always late" and you allow participants to define "low pay" in their response.

REMEMBER   A question should be a clear, precise, and unbiased statement of a single idea, to which different participants are likely to respond differently.

Creating the Responses for Closed-Ended Questions   The preceding guidelines also apply to the wording of the response alternatives in closed-ended questions. Each alternative should be constructed to maximize your confidence that you know what participants wish to communicate when they select it. Therefore, the choices should be worded in a precise and unbiased manner, should convey one idea each, and should be mutually exclusive.

You must also determine the **response scale,** which is the number and type of choices to provide for each question. For example, we might ask yes-no (or true-false) questions, such as "Do you deserve a raise in pay?" Then we can assign a score of 1 for "yes" and a score of 2 for "no" (or arbitrarily pick any other two numbers). With only two scores, however, we have the problem of a restricted range, so we cannot finely discriminate between participants: We'll gloss over differences between those who firmly believe a statement is true and those who think it is only somewhat or sometimes true. Also, if we are scoring a test for correct answers, someone's *apparent* correct response might actually be a lucky guess.

To alleviate problems of restricted range, sensitivity, and guessing, increase the number of response choices. Multiple-choice questions are most appropriate for measuring factual information or discrete responses. For example, we might ask:

Do you deserve a raise in pay?
1. No
2. Yes, a $1 raise
3. Yes, a $2 raise
4. Yes, more than a $2 raise

Four choices allow us to discriminate more precisely. However, the fourth choice does not distinguish between those who seek a $3 raise and those who seek a $4 or $5 raise. To obtain finer discriminations, we'd provide additional choices.

When measuring responses that fall along a continuum, we often employ *Likert-type* questions. These consist of a declarative statement accompanied by a rating scale. Most often, the scale is "anchored" at each end by the words *agree* and *disagree*. Thus, we might ask:

My hourly salary is sufficient for me.

   1   2   3   4   5

Strongly   Strongly
Agree   Disagree

We can also change the wording of the question to measure other experiences and attitudes, using such anchors as *seldom/frequently* or *like/dislike*.

Notice that creating a Likert-type question involves three decisions. First, consider the wording of the anchors. Including the word "strongly" implies extreme feelings. Because of social desirability, participants may be less likely to select the extreme positions of 1 or 5. Labeling the anchors with only *agree/disagree* would imply less extreme feelings, and thus would be more likely to get a wider range of responses. However, we'd also have a less clear definition of what participants were communicating. The way to resolve this issue depends on how threatening a particular question is. Usually, we define the anchors clearly and then attempt to minimize demand characteristics by our wording of the statement being rated.

Second, you must select the number of response alternatives. A five-point rating scale discriminates among only five levels of agreement. When greater sensitivity is needed, include more alternatives. (Do not allow participants to place responses between the points on the scale, because such responses cannot be scored reliably.) How large a scale you should select depends on participants' ability to differentiate their feelings. On a scale of 1 to 20, for instance, people probably cannot distinguish between a 16 and a 17. Instead, they are likely to guess between the two, and then your interpretation of what a 16 or 17 indicates is in error. Resolving this issue depends on the particular question, but we usually use scales with between 5 and 7 choices.

Finally, note that with 5, 7, or any odd number of choices, there is one neutral "middle of the road" choice. The more threatening an issue, the more likely it is that everyone will play it safe and choose the midpoint. This defeats our primary purpose of discriminating among participants. The solution is to use an even number of choices. With six options, for example, there is no middle point, so participants must commit one way or the other. In general, use an odd-numbered scale when you assume that people can be legitimately neutral on an issue, and use an even-numbered scale to counter strong demand characteristics or to force participants to take a stand.

Once you have created the basic questions to ask, you can often generate additional, comparable questions for multiple trials merely by changing the wording and perspective. For example, to measure how interesting workers find their job, we can ask them to answer these two questions:

My job is interesting.

1   2   3   4   5

STRONGLY   STRONGLY
AGREE   DISAGREE

My job is boring.

1   2   3   4   5

STRONGLY   STRONGLY
AGREE   DISAGREE

Then we "code" similar responses across related questions with the same score. That is, strongly agreeing with "My job is interesting" is equivalent to strongly disagreeing with "My job is boring." Therefore, we can record a response of 5 on the "boring" question as a score of 1, a 4 as a 2, and so on. Then for both questions, the lower the score, the more interesting the job. Likewise, with multiple-choice questions we score the choices so that each score reflects the same response (e.g., a 1 is assigned to any choice implying minimum job satisfaction).

Dealing with Order Effects

Because multiple questions are essentially multiple trials, we again face the problem of order effects. Practice effects, for example, occur if participants first find the questions to be novel or they feel great reactivity; but with more questions, they become comfortable, or later, they become fatigued or bored. Likewise, carry-over effects occur if participants respond in a biased fashion to later questions because of earlier questions. (Have you ever found that the way one question is worded on an exam provides the answer to a later question?) Participants can also develop response sets, especially over repeated closed-ended questions. If, for example, initial multiple-choice questions consistently call for choice 1, participants may superstitiously select choice 1 for subsequent questions. Or if people select the strongly agree option on initial Likert-type questions, they may continue to make this response automatically.

There are several techniques for dealing with order effects:

1. **Provide practice questions**   By providing practice questions prior to presenting the questions of interest, we allow participants to warm up to the question format and to habituate to their content, without contaminating the data.

2. **Use funnel questions**   These are general questions that lead to more specific questions. Just as a funnel opens large and then narrows, we order questions from the general to the specific. Often an initial open-ended funnel question is followed by more specific, closed-ended questions, creating a block of questions that all pertain to the same issue. This order gets participants thinking about a topic before they can be biased by the specific choices provided in subsequent closed-ended questions. Thus, for example, we might first ask workers to describe their general satisfaction with their pay, and then follow up with specific multiple-choice or Likert-type questions.

3. **Use filter questions**   These are general questions that determine whether participants should answer additional, detailed questions. For example, an interviewer might ask a worker whether he or she has experienced sexual harassment on the job, and if the answer is "no," the interviewer would not ask any additional follow-up questions about harassment. (On a questionnaire, participants would be instructed to skip the follow-up questions.) Thus, we "filter out" those participants who would be needlessly fatigued, annoyed, or biased by answering irrelevant questions. In addition, the follow-up questions can be more clearly phrased, because they're directed at a subset of participants (here, at only those who have experienced harassment).

4. **Counterbalance order effects**   We can balance out the effects of one particular order by creating different orders of questions for different participants so that questions that appear early in some questionnaires appear later in others, and vice versa. Across all participants completing the different versions, the total sample will not be biased by one unique order of questions.

5. **Prevent response sets**   To prevent rote responding, we vary the question format to try to force participants to read and think about each question. Thus, in multiple-choice questions, we randomly vary which choice is correct. In Likert-type questions, we present both positive and negative statements to be rated, and we vary the scale by mixing agree/disagree with frequently/infrequently, and so on. We may also intermix multiple-choice with Likert-type questions. Note, however, that we do not drastically change the format from question to question. Rather, we generally present a block of one type of question (containing, say, 10 questions) before changing to a different format for the next block of questions. In this way, we avoid confusing participants and increasing their errors, while still minimizing response sets.

6. **Use alternate forms**   **Alternate forms** are different versions of the same questionnaire given to different participants. Here we change the order, wording, and perspective of questions so that the questionnaires appear to be different

yet still measure the same variables. Alternate forms are especially useful when we must measure the same participants repeatedly as in a pretest-posttest design. For example, say we wanted to measure workers' job satisfaction immediately before and after giving them a raise. We would not use the identical questionnaire both times, because people might duplicate their previous responses on the second testing in order to appear consistent, or they might intentionally change their responses because they think we expect them to. Ideally, the alternate forms will hide the similarity of participants' past and present responses so that they answer the second version honestly. (Alternate forms involve different questionnaires, so we must ensure that they are comparable in terms of validity and reliability.)

Creating Catch Trials

Sometimes participants do not follow instructions when completing questionnaires and interviews. Some people give no thought to the questions and select answers randomly, just so they can be finished. Others are untruthful, responding solely to demand characteristics. And still others make errors when responding. We can incorporate specific questions to "catch" such participants.

To identify people who may be answering questions randomly, we can include a specific question several times throughout the questionnaire, but reorder the choices. Consider these examples:

When working I prefer to be
1. Left alone.
2. Supervised occasionally.
3. Supervised frequently.

When working I prefer to be
1. Supervised occasionally.
2. Supervised frequently.
3. Left alone.

A person's preference should be the same on both questions. Anyone who fails to be consistent is either completing questions randomly or recording responses erroneously.

To identify participants who are responding to demand characteristics, we can create questions for which we know the truthful response. Say that when questioning teenagers about their use of drugs, we are concerned that peer pressure may cause some to overstate their drug involvement. To identify these people, we might ask the following:

I have taken the pill known as a "watermelon"
1. Never.
2. Between 1 and 5 times.
3. Between 5 and 10 times.
4. More than 10 times.

There is no pill known as a watermelon. All participants should select response 1, unless they are untruthful (or made an error).

With such questions, we can estimate the frequency with which participants were untruthful or made errors when responding to all questions. Also, we can use such questions to eliminate untrustworthy individuals from the data.

Conducting Pilot Studies

Pilot studies are extremely valuable when developing questionnaires and interviews. Instead of having pilot subjects complete the questions, however, you can ask them questions about the questions to confirm any assumptions you might have. Thus, you can check that the questions convey the intended meaning, that the rating scale is appropriate for differentiating their feelings, that the response scale fits the nature and wording of the question, or that there are minimal demand characteristics present. You can also check that, as when we equated the interesting and boring questions, the responses you see as equivalent are actually equivalent for participants. (One indication of this would be a strong correlation between responses to any two questions you think are equivalent.) Based on participants' responses, alter any problem questions and conduct additional pilot studies until you have constructed the desired questions.

A pilot study can also be used to determine whether a questionnaire has convergent or discriminant validity compared with other questionnaires, or to determine criterion validity by correlating scores with a present or future behavior. Likewise, you can determine whether alternate forms of a questionnaire have comparable reliability and validity. For example, we can have the same participants complete each separate alternate version in a test-retest procedure, or complete a combined version that we then separate in a split-half procedure. Either way, participants' scores from the two forms should produce a high, positive correlation. In addition, both forms should show high convergent and criterion validity with other measures.

Administering the Questionnaire or Interview

Administering a questionnaire or interview requires the same controls that are found in experiments. You should limit or balance participant variables so that the sample is representative. You should control the environment so that there are no extraneous distractions. You should avoid complicated and tiring questions so that participants do not make errors in responding. You should provide unbiased instructions for completing the questions (even if they seem self-explanatory). And you should keep the behaviors of the researcher neutral and consistent.

To minimize demand characteristics, first be careful when creating a title for your questionnaire. Ask yourself if a title is really necessary. Does it bias participants? (Think how you would respond to a questionnaire titled "Survey of Deviant Sexual Fantasies." What if it were titled "Survey of Common Sexual

Fantasies"?) Second, consider whether deception is needed, in the form of "filler" or "distracter" questions. These are not included in the data but they alter the overall appearance of the questionnaire and disguise its actual purpose. (For example, you might include filler questions about nonsexual fantasies to reduce reactivity to sexually oriented questions, and title the questionnaire "Survey of Common Fantasies.")

Ethical considerations are always important. A questionnaire or interview should not be unduly stressful for participants, and, as with all research, your procedure should be approved by your institution's Human Subjects Review Committee. Participants' responses are always kept confidential, and care should be taken to alleviate their fears about what the questions will divulge about them or what the data will be used for. As always, you must obtain explicit informed consent: The fact that people complete a questionnaire or interview is *not* informed consent, because they might feel coerced in the same way they might during an experiment. On completion of testing, be sure to provide a debriefing.

After collecting the data, apply the appropriate statistical techniques to summarize the results and make the proper inferences. You must again consider the scale of measurement you've used, but otherwise statistics don't care whether your scores are measured by a questionnaire, by an interview, or by any other approach. Thus, for Likert-type questions, you can summarize each participant's responses by computing a mean rating per participant. For a test, you can determine the total number of correct or incorrect responses. For multiple-choice or open-ended questions, you can count the frequency of certain responses. You can then combine individual scores to compute the overall mean or total score to summarize a sample. If you're comparing different samples or changing the conditions of an experiment, you can perform *t*-tests, ANOVA, chi square, and the like using the summary scores to identify significant differences between the groups in terms of how each responds to your questions. Or you can compute the appropriate correlation coefficient to relate a participant's summary score on your questions with a score measured by another questionnaire or by some other procedure. If your questions measure several variables, you can correlate participants' scores on these "subtests." And when testing different samples or conditions of an experiment, you can compute the correlation for each group and then determine whether the coefficients for the groups differ significantly.

If the data produce a significant result, then you have demonstrated a "believable" relationship involving participants' responses to your questions. Then, as usual, you interpret the results "psychologically," relating your results back to the constructs and models you began with. However, remember that you are obtaining participant's *self-reports* about their behaviors or feelings, instead of directly observing them. Even with all of the preceding controls, there is always room for skepticism about whether participants' responses actually reflect the variables you're attempting to measure.

To help you remember the various issues when constructing a questionnaire or interview, Checklist 8.1 summarizes the previous sections.

CHECKLIST 8.1	Question construction

Should closed- or open-ended questions be used?

❏ Is reliability or breadth of information most needed?

Should an interview or a questionnaire format be used?

❏ How strong are demand characteristics?

❏ Must responding be structured for the participants?

❏ What breadth of information is needed?

Are questions worded correctly?

❏ Are double-barreled questions avoided?

❏ Are leading questions avoided?

❏ Are Barnum statements avoided?

❏ Are undefined terms avoided?

What is the response scale?

❏ Are measurements sensitive to subtle differences?

❏ Are multiple-choice or Likert-type questions appropriate?

❏ What description should anchor Likert-type questions?

❏ How many choices should each scale contain?

❏ Is an odd or even number of choices needed?

How will questions be administered?

❏ Are practice questions needed?

❏ Are funnel or filter questions needed?

❏ Are demand characteristics a problem?

❏ Are ethical obligations being met?

❏ Have order effects, especially response sets, been avoided?

❏ Are alternate forms needed?

❏ Are catch trials needed?

❏ Are clear instructions provided?

❏ Is a pilot study needed?

A Word about Advanced Correlational Procedures

Often researchers examine relationships involving more than two variables, and then there are a number of advanced correlation and regression procedures to use. Although these procedures are appropriate regardless of how the variables are measured, they are frequently found in questionnaire and interview research. Four methods that you will find in the literature are multiple correlation and regression, discriminant analysis, partial correlation, and factor analysis.

Multiple Correlation and Regression

Often, researchers discover more than one variable that predicts a behavior. For example, let's say that we can predict job satisfaction based on workers' pay rate, and that we can also predict job satisfaction based on workers' feelings toward their supervisor. If we want the most accurate prediction of job satisfaction, we should simultaneously consider *both* a worker's pay and his or her feelings toward a supervisor. **Multiple correlation** and **multiple regression** are employed when *multiple* predictor *(X)* variables are used to predict one criterion *(Y)* variable. These procedures are similar to those discussed earlier. The multiple correlation coefficient, called the multiple R, indicates the strength of the relationship between the multiple predictors and the criterion variable. The multiple regression equation allows us to predict an individual's Y score by simultaneously considering his or her scores on the different variables. And the squared multiple R is the proportion of variance in the Y variable accounted for by using the X variables to predict Y scores.

Discriminant Analysis

A variation of multiple correlation is used when the Y variable reflects *qualitative* differences between participants. This procedure is common in clinical research, for example, when using test scores to categorize people who are schizophrenic versus borderline personality versus paranoid, and so on. **Discriminant analysis** is for categorizing participants along a qualitative Y variable using several quantitative predictor *(X)* variables. The procedure calculates what are essentially selection criteria or "cutoff" scores. Individuals whose combined scores fall below a cutoff score are categorized in group A of the Y variable (e.g., as borderline personality). Those whose score are above the cutoff score are classified in group B (e.g., as paranoid). And those with scores beyond a higher cutoff score are categorized in group C (e.g., schizophrenic). By using this technique, researchers determine the best X variables and the best cutoff scores for maximally separating or "discriminating" between individuals so that there is a minimum of overlap or similarity between the groups.

Partial Correlation

Sometimes instead of using multiple predictors, we take the opposite approach: We wish to examine the relationship between one X and Y variable, without including the influence of other X variables. For example, say we wish to examine the relationship between job satisfaction and pay rate. However, this relationship might be tinged by workers' feelings toward their supervisor. Essentially, there might be an *interaction,* such that the relationship between workers' pay and job satisfaction *depends* on their feelings toward their supervisor. The ideal would be to find workers who all feel the same way toward their supervisor, so that, with this variable constant, we can examine just the relationship between job satisfaction and pay rate. Unfortunately, it may be impossible to keep such an extraneous variable constant in the real world. It *is* possible mathematically, however, to keep its influence constant. A **partial correlation** indicates the correlation between two variables while keeping the influence of other variables constant. Essentially, this procedure would remove the influence that workers' feelings toward their supervisor has on their job satisfaction. What would remain are only the differences in job satisfaction that are correlated with pay rate.

Factor Analysis

So far, our approach has been to begin with a specific hypothesized relationship and then to create questions to test whether two or more variables are related. A more exploratory approach, however, is to create a variety of questions that address many aspects of a general behavior and then to determine which are correlated. From such relationships, we attempt to identify the common, underlying component that they measure. The statistical procedure used in this process is called factor analysis. **Factor analysis** uses the correlations between responses to discover the underlying components they reflect.

For example, in a general questionnaire about the workplace, say we find that a question about being absent from work is positively correlated with a question about taking long lunches: People who are frequently absent tend to frequently take long lunches. Both questions appear to tap the same underlying attitude about work—call it the "lack-of-dedication" factor. At the same time, say that these two questions are not correlated with questions about the importance of friendly co-workers or the time spent in casual conversation, but that these latter questions are highly correlated with each other. These questions appear to tap another aspect of the workplace—call this one the "sociability" factor. Likewise, we might find an "ambition" factor, because questions about how hard people work, how much they desire promotion, and how much they seek added responsibility are found to be correlated. From such results, the factors of dedication, sociability, and ambition become the constructs of interest when we describe workers. Further, these factors might then be related to other behaviors, such as workers' overall job satisfaction.

REMEMBER *Multiple correlation, discriminant analysis, partial correlation,* and *factor analysis* are used when we examine relationships involving several variables.

Putting It All Together

This chapter discussed a number of complex issues that arise when creating questionnaires, as well as several fancy statistical procedures that are used in correlational research. Regardless of how elaborate it is, however, remember that a correlational study cannot be used to infer the causal variable in a relationship. Recall that even with all of the controls used in an experiment, you must be cautious when inferring causality because there may be a hidden confounding. In a correlational design with no random assignment, there is almost certain to be a confounding. Therefore, always be on guard for identifying this approach. In the newspaper, for example, you might read about teenagers who committed suicide after listening to a particular rock and roll album, or about serial killers who were abused as children. If you think about it, these statements involve a correlational approach, because the "participants" here were not randomly assigned to the levels of either variable. Therefore, the apparent causal variable is confounded with other potential causes. The apparent cause might be the actual cause (we're open-minded, remember), but such reports do not indicate this.

CHAPTER SUMMARY

1. In a *correlational design,* the researcher measures participants' scores on two or more variables to observe a relationship. Causality cannot be inferred because participants are not randomly assigned to the levels of a variable, and which variable occurred first is unknown.

2. The *Pearson correlation coefficient* is computed when the *X* and *Y* scores are normally distributed and measured using an interval or ratio scale. The *Spearman correlation coefficient* is computed when both variables are measured using an ordinal scale.

3. A *linear correlation coefficient* will range between $+1$ and -1. The sign indicates the type of relationship. The smaller the absolute value of the coefficient, the greater the variability in the *Y*s at each *X*, the greater the vertical width of the scatterplot, and the less accurately *Y* scores can be predicted from *X* scores.

4. *Linear regression* is used for predicting scores on one variable based on the linear relationship with another variable. The *linear regression equation* is used to predict a *Y* score, called *Y prime (Y'),* for a particular *X*. The *linear regression line* summarizes a linear relationship, with the values of *Y'* falling on the line.

5. The *standard error of the estimate* communicates the amount by which the *Y* scores in a sample differ from the corresponding predicted *Y* scores. The *squared correlation coefficient,* called the *coefficient of determination,* is the

proportion of total variance in *Y* scores that is accounted for by the relationship with *X*.

6. The size and power of a correlation coefficient is increased by minimizing error variance, avoiding restricted range, testing a large *N*, and using parametric, linear procedures when appropriate.

7. *Test-retest reliability* indicates that participants tend to obtain the same overall score when repeatedly tested at different times. *Split-half reliability* indicates that their scores on some trials consistently match their scores on other trials.

8. With *face validity* a procedure appears to be valid. With *convergent validity* a procedure is correlated with other procedures that are accepted as valid. With *discriminant validity* a procedure is not correlated with procedures that measure other things.

9. With *criterion validity* the scores from a procedure correlate with an observable behavior. With *concurrent validity* a procedure correlates with a present behavior. With *predictive validity* a procedure accurately predicts a behavior.

10. The goal of psychological questions is to reliably and validly discriminate between individuals on the variable of interest.

11. With *closed-ended questions* participants select from alternatives provided by the researcher. With *open-ended questions* participants determine the alternatives to choose from.

12. With *projective tests* participants create a description or interpretation of an ambiguous stimulus, thus projecting their hidden feelings or attributes.

13. *Content analysis* is the procedure used to score open-ended questions by looking for specific words or themes.

14. In a *structured interview,* participants are asked specific, predetermined questions. In an *unstructured interview,* the questions are less rigidly predetermined.

15. Questions should avoid (a) *double-barreled questions,* which have more than one component; (b) *leading questions,* which are biased so that there is only one obvious response; (c) *Barnum statements,* which are global truisms to which everyone responds in the same way; and (d) questions containing *undefined terms.*

16. A *response scale* is the number and type of choices provided for each question.

17. When using Likert-type questions, consider whether the rating scale (a) has anchors that overly bias participants, (b) contains choices that participants can discriminate between, and (c) forces them to indicate a preference.

18. When asking a series of questions, take care to eliminate order effects, especially those due to response sets.

19. *Funnel questions* are general questions that lead to more specific follow-up questions. *Filter questions* are general questions for determining whether more detailed follow-up questions should be asked.

20. *Alternate forms* of a questionnaire contain differently worded questions that measure the same variables. They are especially important when testing in a repeated-measures design.

21. *Multiple regression* and *multiple correlation* predict scores on one Y variable using multiple X variables. *Discriminant analysis* categorizes subjects along a qualitative criterion variable using several predictor variables. *Partial correlation* determines the correlation between two variables while keeping the influence of other variables constant. *Factor analysis* identifies a common underlying factor by determining which questions are correlated.

KEY TERMS

alternate forms   *(271)*
Barnum statement
   (268)
closed-ended question
   (263)
coefficient of
   determination
   (257)
concurrent validity
   (261)
content analysis
   (265)
convergent validity
   (261)
correlation coefficient
   (249)
correlational design
   (245)
criterion validity
   (261)
discriminant analysis
   (276)
discriminant validity
   (261)
double-barreled
   question   *(267)*

error in prediction
   (255)
face validity   *(260)*
factor analysis   *(277)*
filter question   *(271)*
funnel question   *(271)*
leading question
   (268)
linear regression
   (253)
linear regression
   equation   *(253)*
linear regression line
   (253)
multiple correlation
   and regression
   (276)
open-ended question
   (264)
partial correlation
   (277)
Pearson correlation
   coefficient   *(250)*
power of the
   correlation
   coefficient   *(257)*

predictive validity
   (261)
projective test   *(264)*
proportion of variance
   accounted for
   (255)
response scale   *(268)*
restriction of range
   (258)
selection test   *(254)*
Spearman correlation
   coefficient   *(250)*
split-half reliability
   (260)
squared correlation
   coefficient   *(258)*
standard error of the
   estimate   *(255)*
structured interview
   (265)
test-retest reliability
   (260)
unstructured interview
   (266)
Y prime   *(254)*

REVIEW QUESTIONS

1. What is the difference between an experiment and a correlational study in terms of (a) the hypothesis being tested? (b) how the researcher collects the data? (c) how the researcher examines the relationship?

2. What are the two reasons you can't conclude that you have demonstrated a causal relationship based on correlational research?

3. (a) How do you decide which variable to call X in a correlation? (b) What other names are given to the X and Y variables?

4. (a) What is the advantage of computing a correlation coefficient? (b) What two characteristics of a linear relationship are described by a correlation coefficient? (c) When do you compute a Pearson correlation coefficient? (d) When do you compute a Spearman coefficient?

5. (a) Why do you perform linear regression? (b) What is Y'? (c) What does the standard error of the estimate indicate?

6. As the value of r approaches ± 1, what does it indicate about (a) the shape of the scatterplot? (b) the variability of the Y scores at each X? (c) the closeness of Y scores to the regression line? (d) the accuracy with which you can predict Y if X is known?

7. (a) Why is the proportion of variance accounted for equal to 1 with a perfect correlation? (b) Why is it zero when there is no relationship? (c) Why don't you compute r^2 when the correlation is not significant?

8. (a) How do you maximize the power of a correlational design? (b) What produces a restricted range? (c) Why should it be avoided? (d) How is it avoided?

9. Say that you find a large correlation between the amount of orange juice people consume and the number of their yearly visits to a doctor. Is this evidence that drinking more orange juice causes people to be healthier so that they don't have to go to the doctor?

10. A researcher uses an unstructured interview to measure how aggressive a sample of children are. (a) What approach should she use to score their responses? (b) How should she ensure that a participant's score is reliable? (c) How should she ensure that those doing the scoring are reliable?

11. A researcher correlates participants' ability to concentrate and their ability to remember, finding $r = +.30$. He also correlates ability to visualize information and memory ability, finding an $r = +.60$. (a) He concludes that the relationship between visualization and memory is twice as consistent, and therefore twice as informative as that between concentration and memory. Why do you agree or disagree? (b) What advanced statistical procedures can

the researcher use to improve his predictions about memory ability even more?

12. A researcher finds that variable A accounts for 25% of the variance in variable B. Another researcher finds that variable C accounts for 50% of the variance in variable B. Why, by accounting for greater variance, does variable C produce a relationship that is scientifically more important?

13. A student complains that it is unfair to use scores from the Scholastic Aptitude Test (SAT) to determine college admittance because she might do much better in college than predicted. (a) What statistic(s) will indicate whether her complaint is correct? (b) What concern about the test's validity is she actually addressing?

14. A researcher measures both how loudly students play music when studying and their exam grades. She tests a very large N, obtaining a significant r of $+.10$. She concludes that playing loud music has a dramatic impact on exam grades. What two errors has she made?

15. A researcher uses mathematical ability to predict sense of humor. He measures creativity in terms of how funny a participant finds three puns to be. He tests 10 math majors and finds a nonsignificant r. (a) What characteristic of his participants might account for this result? (b) What problem with his criterion variable might account for this result? (c) What other obvious improvement in power can he achieve?

16. In question 15, say that previous research has shown that people with very high or very low math skills tend to find puns humorous, but those with intermediate skills do not. How can this finding account for the nonsignificant r?

17. (a) What is the difference between test-retest reliability and split-half reliability? (b) Why would we prefer to show the split-half reliability of a college exam instead of its test-retest reliability?

18. (a) What is the difference between convergent and divergent validity? (b) How does criterion validity differ from the types of validity in part (a)? (c) What are the two types of criterion validity, and how is each determined?

19. (a) What are the advantages and disadvantages of open-ended questions? (b) of closed-ended questions?

20. For each of the following, indicate whether you should use a written questionnaire, a structured interview, or an unstructured interview: (a) when measuring the attitudes of first-graders, (b) when measuring the contents of people's daydreams, (c) when measuring people's attitudes toward researchers.

21. I ask my students to rate their agreement with the following statements. What is wrong with the wording of each statement? (a) The material in this book is sometimes difficult. (b) I like reading this book, but I dislike the sta-

tistics. (c) A good student will like this book. (d) With this book I can get an acceptable grade.

22. A friend says that his reactions to inkblots couldn't possibly indicate anything about him. (a) What aspect of the test's validity is he reacting to? (b) Why is the test doing what it is intended to do?

23. On a personality test, the question "Do you prefer cooked carrots or raw carrots?" is asked several times. (a) Why might a researcher include the responses to this question when predicting someone's personality? (b) For what other reason(s) might the researcher ask this question?

24. (a) What are alternate forms? (b) What concerns are important when creating them? (c) When are they necessary?

25. As you read a research article, what can you determine about the research when you see that (a) multiple correlation and regression procedures were performed? (b) a discriminant analysis was performed? (c) a partial correlation was performed?

26. From a factor analysis of a personality questionnaire, a researcher identifies the factors of sociability, extroversion, and depression as constituting personality. How were these factors identified?

DISCUSSION QUESTIONS

1. You wish to examine how well people do on a test of problem-solving ability as a function of how anxious they are. (a) Why and how would you conduct this as an experiment? (b) Why and how would you conduct this as a correlational design? (c) How would you analyze the relationship in each case?

2. The original research into smoking and lung cancer showed that people who smoked more often also developed lung cancer more often. (a) Tobacco companies deny that this finding is evidence that smoking causes cancer. Are they correct? (b) This finding has been replicated numerous times in human studies, and experiments show that white rats exposed to cigarette smoke develop lung cancer. Are tobacco companies still correct in disputing the above claim?

3. A student complains that a college exam was unfair because it contained some questions that only a few students answered correctly. How would a researcher justify the inclusion of such questions?

4. Research has found that people from certain races score an average of as much as 15 points lower on standard intelligence tests than do people from other races. This finding has been used as evidence that some races are inherently less intelligent than others. (a) What considerations would cause you to qualify such a conclusion? (b) What would you say to those people who dismiss this conclusion as blatant racism? (c) What are the ethical issues involved in disseminating these findings to the public?

5. In a study, you measure how much participants are initially attracted to a person of the opposite sex *(X)* and how anxious they become during their first meeting with him or her *(Y)*. For the following ratio data:

Participant	X	Y
1	2	8
2	6	14
3	1	5
4	3	8
5	6	10
6	9	15
7	6	8
8	6	8
9	4	7
10	2	6

(a) Appropriately summarize this relationship. (b) Is it significant? (c) Compute the linear regression equation. (d) What anxiety score do you predict for any person who produces an attraction score of 9? (e) When using this data, what is the "average" amount of error you should expect in your predictions? (f) What is the proportion of variance in *Y* that is accounted for by *X*? (g) Why or why not is this a valuable relationship? (h) Is how much people are attracted to others a major cause of how nervous they become during their initial meeting?

9

Field Experiments and Single-Subject Designs

GETTING STARTED

To understand this chapter, recall the following:

- From Chapter 2, recall how random selection and random assignment produce a representative sample and eliminate confounding by participant variables.

- From Chapter 3, recall what diffusion of treatment and manipulation checks are.

- From Chapter 4, recall what demand characteristics are, including reactivity, social desirability, and experimenter expectancies.

- From Chapter 5, recall what the volunteer bias, maturation, history, and carry-over effects are.

Your goals in this chapter are to learn:

- The pros and cons of field experiments.

- The different probability and nonprobability sampling techniques.

- The flaws in field experiments with the public and with specific groups, and how to counter the flaws in each.

- The pros and cons of conducting small *N* research.

- The different types of single-subject designs.

*I*n addition to correlational studies, psychological research involves other designs that are different from the standard laboratory study. Sometimes an experiment is conducted outside of a laboratory, and sometimes we study only one participant. In this chapter we examine these common alternatives: field experiments and single-subject designs.

Field Experiments

Throughout this book, you've seen that controlled laboratory experiments provide the greatest *internal validity:* At the conclusion of such experiments we are confident that we know what occurred within them, so we can confidently conclude that changes in the independent variable caused changes in the dependent variable. Yet, recall that although laboratory experiments increase internal validity, they simultaneously limit *external validity,* the extent to which findings generalize to other individuals or settings.

The problem is that a laboratory setting is artificial because participants know they are being studied and a researcher is present who does not behave the way people in real life behave. Therefore, the study can suffer from reduced *experimental realism,* because participants cannot forget they are involved in a study and thus cannot be totally engaged by the task. Their behavior can be biased by *demand characteristics* such as *experimenter* expectancies and *reactivity.* The results can lack *ecological validity* because we observe what individuals can do and not necessarily what they typically do. And our participants can be unrepresentative because of *volunteer bias, mortality effects,* and a *limited population.* The bottom line is that the results of a laboratory experiment can be peculiar because of our procedure, so that the observed relationship is found only in a literal replication of our design with very similar subjects.

Sometimes this is an acceptable state of affairs. When the hypothesis involves basic research into hypothetical constructs and basic behaviors, researchers are usually most concerned with internal validity, and so they conduct a laboratory experiment. When studying mental tasks, for example, we conduct reaction-time experiments under laboratory conditions, because we're concerned with a basic component of cognitive processing rather than with the way in which the mental tasks translate into everyday behaviors. When we seek greater external validity, however, we leave the laboratory and perform the study in the real world, conducting field research. When we seek to demonstrate a causal relationship, we perform a **field experiment.** There are four advantages to conducting field experiments.

1. We can make observations in natural settings, so such studies generally have a high degree of external and ecological validity. Our findings should generalize to the real world because they are obtained in the real world.

2. We can take the experiment to the participants, so the sample can be taken from either a select target population or from the general population.
3. We can observe behavior when individuals are psychologically engaged by a real situation, so we have greater experimental realism. This advantage is especially important because, instead of relying on potentially unreliable self-reports of what people say they do, we can observe what they actually do.
4. We can go out into the real world and replicate laboratory studies to ensure the generality of their findings. After learning about a behavior in the lab, we go out and see whether it operates the way we think it does.

Remember that a field experiment still incorporates the procedures of an experiment. As much as possible, we randomly assign participants to conditions, reliably manipulate the conditions of an independent variable, control extraneous variables, and measure the dependent variable in a reliable, sensitive, and powerful manner. We analyze the results using *t*-tests, ANOVAs, or nonparametric procedures. If the results are significant, we examine the scores from each condition as well as the differences between them, and we consider the type and strength of the relationship observed. We then attempt to explain the psychological processes reflected by the results. Because we've conducted an experiment, we have internal validity for arguing that manipulating the independent variable caused the dependent scores to change. Because we've conducted a field experiment, however, we also have external validity for concluding that the findings apply to common, realistic situations and actually reflect natural behaviors.

REMEMBER *Field experiments* are conducted to show a causal relationship in a natural setting.

Sampling Techniques

In previous examples of experiments, we relied on the random selection of participants from the available pool, often consisting of college students. Given our emphasis on internal validity, however, we accept that such samples are not truly "random" because they are restricted to only those people we can solicit and bring to the laboratory. This "pseudo-randomness" can then weaken external validity, because we might be observing an unrepresentative sample. An unrepresentative sample is different from the population, leading to inaccurate descriptions of the typical behavior that occurs in the population.

You can use additional sampling techniques, however, when selecting a sample for *any* type of experimental, correlational, or descriptive design. These techniques are especially common in field research, because, by taking the study to participants, we can be more selective in defining the target population and the techniques used to select participants.

Researchers often identify potential participants from governmental or commercial mailing lists, or from membership lists of social or civic groups. On the one hand, such lists should not include people from outside the target population. In a survey of voter attitudes, for example, we should survey only those people who vote, so we might use a list of people who voted in the last election (although this does not mean they will vote in the next election). On the other hand, we should not exclude any important segments of the population—a list of voters from the last election does not include people who are going to vote for the first time. Likewise, a survey about gun control should not include only registered gun owners, but it should not totally exclude them either. Thus, to obtain a representative sample, the goal is to include all of the important subgroups in the target population.

How we go about obtaining a sample is, in research language, our "sampling technique." There are two general types of sampling technique: probability and nonprobability sampling.

Probability Sampling Techniques   In **probability sampling,** every potential subject has an equal likelihood of being asked to participate. By giving everyone an equal chance, we allow each participant characteristic that occurs with a certain frequency in the population to occur with that same frequency in the sample. As you saw in Chapter 2, one form of probability sampling is **simple random sampling,** in which we randomly select participants from a list of the population. Another form is **systematic random sampling,** in which we select every *n*th person from the population list.

Both simple and systematic random sampling rely on chance, so we might *not* contact all of the types of individuals in the population, especially those who constitute a small proportion of it. To ensure that the various subgroups of the population are represented in a study, we may instead use stratified sampling. In **stratified random sampling** we identify the important subgroups in the population and then randomly select individuals from each group so that their representation in the sample is proportional to their representation in the population. That is, we select a proportion of the total *N* from each group so that we proportionally represent the important "strata" in the population. For example, if government records reveal that 70% of the target population is male, then 70% of the sample should be male. If the sample *N* is to be 100, then from the identified males, we randomly select 70 males (and thus 30 females). If a person declines to participate, we select another male to replace him. We can also combine selection criteria: For example, if 5% of the population are females who own guns, we randomly select 5 participants from the pool of female gun owners. Other "strata" that are typically included in field research are socioeconomic level, race, and geographic location. Notice, however, that we still rely on random sampling and random assignment within a strata, because this balances out any other participant variables that might otherwise bias the results.

Sometimes it is too expensive or too difficult to contact the individuals in a population. In such cases we might use an alternative sampling technique called cluster sampling. In **cluster sampling** certain groups, or "clusters," are randomly selected and then all members of each group are tested. To study homeless people, for example, we might randomly select a few areas in a city where homeless people are found and then study all the individuals we can locate in each area. Similarly, to study workers at a large factory, we might select departments randomly and study the workers in each. Because the clusters are randomly selected, there should be no bias in participant selection, so the sample should be reasonably representative.

> **REMEMBER** Simple random sampling, systematic sampling, *stratified sampling,* and *cluster sampling* are *probability sampling* techniques that provide all individuals in the population an equal chance of being selected.

Nonprobability Sampling Techniques   In **nonprobability sampling,** every member of the population does *not* have an equal opportunity to be selected. Therefore, we are likely to miss certain types of individuals, resulting in a less representative sample.

Nonetheless, a common form of this approach is **convenience sampling,** in which we study participants who are conveniently available. Studying the students sitting in the student union or the people riding a bus involves convenience samples. However, these are not random samples, because only those people who are present at the one place and time of the study have any chance of being selected, and the reason they are present is usually not a random event. Therefore, a convenience sample is representative of a very limited population composed of only the same types of people found in the same situation as in the study.

To at least some extent, most "random" samples are also convenience samples: Given a researcher's limitations in terms of travel, time, and cost, there will always be some members of the population who have no chance of being selected. For example, if we have permission to conduct a study only in one portion of a factory, the resulting sample is not representative of all factory workers. Similarly, we are relying on convenience sampling when selecting college-level, introductory psychology students, because they represent the population of students who happen to be taking introductory psychology.

Another type of nonprobability sampling that can produce a more representative sample is **quota sampling.** As in stratified sampling, we ensure that the sample has the same percentage—the same "quota"—of each subgroup as in the population. Unlike stratified sampling, however, in quota sampling we do not randomly sample from each subgroup. Instead, we rely on convenience samples to fill each quota. For example, say that we want 20 six-year-olds and 20 seven-year-olds in a sample. If we obtain these participants by testing a convenient class of first-graders and a convenient class of second-graders, we are using quota sampling.

Finally, sometimes we want to study a "hidden" population, such as when we study drug addicts or prostitutes. Then we use **snowball sampling.** Here we identify one participant, and from him or her we obtain the names and locations of other participants, and from them we identify others, so that the sample tends to build or "snowball." However, such a sample is probably not very representative, because only those people within our network of acquaintances have any chance of being selected, and they may be different from others in the population.

For a summary of the preceding sampling techniques, see Table 9.1. Both probability and nonprobability sampling techniques play a role in the two general types of field experiments: those involving the general public and those involving selected groups.

Field Experiments with the General Public

One approach to field experiments is to conduct the study in an unrestricted public area in order to generalize to the "typical citizen." This kind of study is usually conducted in one of two ways: Either the researcher targets certain people and observes their response to a condition of an environmental independent variable, or the researcher (or a confederate) creates a condition by approaching par-

Table 9.1 Summary of Sampling Techniques

Probability Sampling	
Simple	Randomly select participants from the population.
Systematic	Select every nth individual from a population list.
Stratified	Randomly select from subgroups, proportionate to each group's representation in the population.
Cluster	Randomly select clusters and test all members per cluster.
Nonprobability Sampling	
Convenience	Select participants who are conveniently available.
Quota	Obtain convenience samples to represent subgroups, proportionate to each group's representation in the population.
Snowball	Locate participants through other participants.

ticipants and exhibiting a behavior to elicit a response. Essentially, we conduct the study we'd like to conduct in the laboratory, except that the demand characteristics associated with a formal laboratory and experimenter would seriously reduce the validity and reliability of the results. In the field, therefore, we disguise the fact that an experiment is being conducted, using deception and unobtrusive measures.

Such field experiments are especially common when studying social behaviors. For example, Isen and Levin (1972) studied helping behavior—"bystander intervention"—as a function of a participant's mood. They manipulated mood by allowing some people to find money in the change return of a pay phone. Then a passing confederate dropped a manila folder, and the dependent variable was whether participants helped the confederate. Similarly, Shaffer, Rogel, and Hendrick (1975) staged a theft at a college library. A confederate (the "victim") sat with a participant and then left, either asking or not asking the participant to watch his belongings. Another confederate then approached, searched the belongings, and stole the victim's wallet. The dependent variable was whether the participant tried to stop the thief. Researchers have also examined such things as whether or not a confederate waitress touched restaurant patrons influenced the size of the tip they then left (Crusco & Wetzel, 1984). Or, in studying "personal space," Albas and Albas (1989) conducted a fictitious poll while measuring how far the participant came to stop from a pollster. The study manipulated the factors of the meeting occurring in the safety of a shopping mall versus a less-safe city park, and whether the pollster made eye contact or did not because of wearing dark glasses.

Limitations of Studies with the Public   As with any study, field experiments are not perfect. We still lack construct and content validity if the operational definition of a variable does not measure what we intend. We still may lack ecological validity, because the situation is somewhat contrived. (Would a real thief riffle through someone's belongings when another person is sitting at the same table watching?) External validity is still limited to situations similar to the ones we study. (Helping was studied when a *nonviolent* theft occurred in a *library*.) And, finally, demand characteristics may still be present, because participants are suspicious and uncooperative (thinking "What kind of weirdo is this?"), or because they give socially desirable responses.

Field experiments are also limited in terms of controlling participant variables. Random selection of participants is limited, because we use some degree of convenience sampling, selecting from among those people who are present at the time and location of the experiment. (People in a park or mall might not represent people who are seldom found there.) Also, we may have to impose selection criteria that further limit random selection: In the library study, participants must be sitting alone, and people sitting alone might act differently from those who are not. Convenience sampling can also be imposed by experimenter bias: Perhaps the pollsters in the park conveniently avoided a potential participant who seemed threatening to them! And we continue to rely on volunteers who may be unrepresentative of nonvolunteers: People who stop for the pollster might be different from those who do not, including exhibiting a different sense of personal space.

In addition, field experiments allow less control of potentially confounding variables that reduce internal validity. We cannot always balance participant variables because random assignment of subjects to conditions is limited. (For example, personal-space differences supposedly due to the safety of a park or mall might actually be due to differences between the types of people found in the park and mall.) Or whether people stop and help a pollster might actually be due to the time of day and where they are going. Or the size of the tip left might depend on how much money a participant has or the perceived quality of the waitress's service. Further, often there can be no control group: We cannot measure the personal space of those people who do not stop and talk to the pollster.

Field experiments also allow a less consistent testing situation, because in the real world, it is difficult to consistently manipulate an independent variable. In particular, a confederate's behavior may be inconsistent because he or she must react to a participant's more natural, uncontrolled behavior. (Some people may be gabby, some not.) Also, we have less control over environmental variables, such as the number of other people present, wind and temperature conditions, or horns blowing and other distractions.

This loss of control also reduces the reliability of scores and statistical power. We cannot provide instructions to guide participants, so we may encounter a wide variety of responses. (For example, some people might pace while talking with a pollster, so that we cannot reliably measure their personal space.) Obtaining multiple trials per person to increase reliability is usually not possible, because a deception works only once, or a passerby will volunteer only if a task is brief. Likewise, repeated-measures designs are usually not possible. Further, we are often able to obtain only gross measurements of a behavior. (We can indicate only whether a person did or did not attempt to stop the thief, not how much he or she wanted to help.) Not only do such measurements reduce precision and sensitivity, but the data must often be in terms of categorizing or rank-ordering participants, so we are limited to using less powerful, nonparametric statistics.

Controls Used with the Public To defeat the above flaws we use the usual methods. To improve random selection and generality, for example, researchers use the equivalent of cluster sampling, testing at several locations (e.g., several randomly selected shopping malls) in a counterbalanced way. We also usually use systematic random sampling, selecting every nth person who appears and meets our selection criteria. We can also stratify the sample—for example, by observing every nth female until we have the desired proportion of females in the sample. Systematic and stratified sampling make selection more random and eliminate experimenter biases in selecting participants. And we balance participant variables, time of day, and other potential confoundings by randomly alternating the treatment condition assigned as each participant is selected.

For consistency, we set criteria for selecting each participant (doing so only when a certain number of people are present, when no major momentary distractions are occurring, etc.). We control for effects due to one confederate by using several confederates, having each test a portion of the participants in each condition, and we attempt to keep the appearance and behavior of all confederates consistent. Finally, we strive for sensitive scoring criteria using quantitative measurements and parametric procedures where possible. For even greater reliability and validity, we can ask participants questions directly as a manipulation check following our unobtrusive observation of them, we can use multiple raters, and we can test a relatively large *N*.

Even with such controls, however, you must be especially careful to critically evaluate all field experiments and to temper your conclusions that changing the independent variable caused the dependent variable to change. The trade-off of internal validity for external validity means that we do obtain a general idea about the influence of a variable on a behavior in a natural setting, but we lose precision and confidence in the description of exactly how the variable caused the behavior, and how the behavior was exhibited.

Field Experiments with Selected Groups

The other approach to field experiments involves entering the field to study a specific group of participants that already exists. Sometimes we are unable to disguise the study, especially when we have to provide instructions and incorporate the same trappings as those in a laboratory experiment. At other times we operate more unobtrusively. Either way, however, there is some existing factor that creates the group we wish to study, and this factor provides greater external validity. Usually this is the case because we are studying a behavior that occurs only in certain situations or with certain individuals. This type of field experiment is common in the workplace, with researchers studying such diverse groups as airplane pilots, police officers, factory workers, professional sports teams, or nurses. In each case, the participants are of interest because they exhibit specific types of behavior, they operate in a role of authority or have a certain status, or for such mundane reasons as that they normally wear uniforms.

Selected groups are also found outside of the work setting. In one of the first studies of personal space, Felipe and Sommer (1966) felt that the effects of invading an individual's personal space could not be examined unless it occurred in an environment where such "crazy behavior" would not be viewed as bizarre. Therefore, their manipulation involved whether a confederate sat very close to patients in a mental institution! Similarly, educational research often involves existing groups of students. Or researchers may gain access to a select group by studying young children at a day-care center or elderly people at a senior citizen's home. In an interesting twist on this selected group approach, Gladue and Delaney (1990) investigated whether men and women become more attractive to one another as the closing time of a bar approaches by studying an existing group of patrons at a bar. Using a repeated-measures design, the researchers asked participants to rate the attractiveness of the other patrons on several occasions during the evening. They confirmed that attractiveness increased as time wore on. (Interestingly, the ratings were *not* positively correlated with alcohol consumption, so alcohol could not have caused increased attractiveness!)

Limitations of Studies with Selected Groups   In addition to the usual loss of control that frequently occurs with field experiments, there are several special problems in testing selected groups. One problem is that researchers are often limited to convenience sampling of those groups that they can obtain permission to test. Another major problem occurs if we use cluster sampling but assign one intact group to each condition. Then we are not randomly assigning participants to conditions, so our manipulation is probably confounded: If, for example, a condition contains all workers from the same department, the reason they are in that department—rather than our manipulation—might cause them to behave differently from workers in another condition. Also, the public may not be as obedient or adventurous as the typical college student. Some workers might refuse to try a particular working condition, or parents might object to their children being in a control or mildly aversive condition. The resistance of such participants is not random, so participant selection and assignment to conditions is likewise not random. Also, in a repeated-measures design, we may see substantial subject mortality, further reducing the randomness of our selection.

Another limitation of studies involving selected groups is that merely by entering an established field setting the researcher can alter the situation and make it artificial and contrived. Therefore, to preserve the natural environment, we prefer to use an unobtrusive measure, although this may not be possible. Most nursery schools, for example, do not have a one-way mirror, and the management or union at most companies will not allow us to videotape workers. As an alternative, we can ask participants' regular supervisor or teacher to act as the experimenter. But such people are not trained researchers, so they may greatly bias the results. For example, the data may not be valid or reliable for our purposes if a substitute experimenter assigns dependent scores, because the purpose and criteria of a supervisor's rating may be very different from those of a researcher. Also, supervisors' or teachers' expectations, as well as subtle variations in their treatment of participants, can produce a self-fulfilling prophecy. In a classic study, Rosenthal and Jacobson (1966) found that when students were identified as about to "bloom" intellectually, their teacher assigned them higher intellectual development scores, despite the fact that in reality the identified students had originally been randomly selected and were not about to bloom at anything.

Existing-group designs are especially prone to *diffusion of treatment*. Recall from Chapter 3 that this problem occurs when people in one condition are aware of the treatment received by people in other conditions. With field experiments, group membership may overlap or change during the course of a study: Shift workers might change to a different shift and thus be exposed to another condition. Or people in existing groups might gossip about the experiment: Senior citizens might talk to others who have not been tested, or children in one class might learn of a desirable treatment given to another class. Such information can then lead participants to react to their conditions in a biased, unnatural manner.

Finally, note that a special kind of demand characteristic sometimes operates among participants who form a cohesive group, called the **Hawthorne effect.** It is named for a group of workers at Western Electric Company's Hawthorne factory who participated in a study of worker productivity (Roethlisberger & Dickson, 1939). The researchers manipulated numerous variables that should have decreased productivity, but, regardless, participants continuously *increased* their productivity! Afterwards, participants indicated that because their employer and the researchers had given them special attention, a team spirit had developed, and they felt compelled to be cooperative and to continuously increase their productivity. (There is, however, some controversy over this account: see Bramel & Friend, 1981.) Nonetheless, the term Hawthorne effect has come to refer to a change in participants' performance—usually an improvement—that occurs from the novelty of being in a study and having a researcher pay attention to participants. Although this effect can be found in any type of study, it is prevalent when participants already form a cohesive group.

Note that the Hawthorne effect is different from reactivity, which is a participant's reaction to being observed or "analyzed." If participants are unnaturally motivated to stick at a boring task because of their enthusiasm for a study, we have the Hawthorne effect. If their performance is then unnatural because of their nervousness about being videotaped, we have reactivity.

REMEMBER The *Hawthorne effect* is a bias in participants' performance resulting from the apparently special treatment and interest shown by a researcher.

Controls Used with Selected Groups   By now, you're familiar with the methods used to overcome the above limitations. We seek random assignment of participants to conditions, so in a factory study, for example, we would try to ensure that some workers from each department are assigned to each condition. To minimize diffusion of treatment, we explain to participants why they should not talk to one another, and we test all conditions close together in time. We also give all conditions the same appearance, by disguising the control condition with a placebo or by using deception. Then, if participants learn about another condition, it will sound the same as their own. We also test participants from different locations in a counterbalanced way, because this not only improves generalizability but also helps to prevent diffusion of treatment (people from different localities are unlikely to have contact with one another). Further, if supervisors or teachers must serve as the researchers, we give them explicit training and use a double-blind procedure. And, finally, to counter demand characteristics such as the Hawthorne effect, we present neutral cues and instruct participants to behave naturally, and not in the way they think the experimenter wants them to.

Ethics and Field Experiments

Don't forget, ethical concerns are always important, and as usual, you must evaluate a field experiment to ensure that participants experience a minimum of psychological and physical stress, and to protect their rights. When conducting a field experiment in which participants are aware of the study, deal with issues of risky variables, deception, unobtrusive measures, debriefing, and informed consent in the usual ways. Of particular concern is avoiding any implicit coercion of participants; we do not want them to participate because they think they must in order to keep their job or to be viewed favorably by their boss, teacher, or peers.

Remember that unobtrusive field experiments involving the public present the additional question of whether it's ethical to even conduct the study, because participants are not even aware a study is being conducted. Therefore, recognize that conducting the experiment automatically places you in the position of violating participants' right to informed consent, so you must tread lightly. The APA's Ethical Standards requires that you obtain informed consent unless there is *minimum* physical or psychological risk to the participants. However, you are manipulating real-life variables and measuring real-life reactions. On the one hand, people will react to the situation or to a confederate in a real way (that's why you perform such studies). On the other hand, this real situation may be very frightening or disturbing to participants. Thus, always evaluate the reactions that participants might have. How frightened will participants be by thinking they are alone in a library with a possibly dangerous thief? How will participants react to being approached in a city park by someone wearing dark glasses? What will people make of a waitress in a restaurant who constantly touches them? In such scenarios, *you* are responsible for protecting participants from physical or mental distress. And, as usual, after you think you've resolved the ethical issues, you must submit the study for review by your Institutional Review Board.

> *REMEMBER* You must be particularly sensitive to the ethics of field experiments.

 ## Small N Research and the Single-Subject Design

So far, we have focused on experiments involving *groups* of people or animals. However, there is an entirely different kind of experiment in which only one participant is studied. A **single-subject design** is a repeated-measures experiment conducted on one participant. Typically, the experiment (with an N of 1) is then replicated on a few more participants, so this research is also known as **small N research.** Before considering the particulars of such designs, let's discuss why we would want to use them.

The Argument for Small *N* Designs

Some researchers argue that there are three unacceptable flaws in experiments involving groups of participants (Sidman, 1960). The first pertains to error variance, the random differences between scores found within the conditions. Typically with group designs, we use random assignment of participants and counterbalancing of extraneous variables. Because we therefore include the influence of fluctuating variables within each condition, the design itself produces much of the error variance. The inconsistency in scores then makes it difficult to see a relationship hidden in the data (so that we must rely on obtuse, inferential statistics). This is especially a problem given how seldom researchers usually report a variable's effect size (the proportion of variance accounted for). Further, researchers then ignore the differences in behavior reflected by error variance and the variables that cause them. We ignore differences in behavior between participants (*intersubject* differences) and different behaviors in the same participant from moment to moment (*intrasubject* differences). Yet these variables are potentially important aspects of the behavior under study.

The second flaw in group designs is that, because of the variability in individual scores, we must compute the mean (or similar measures) in each condition. Yet a mean score may misrepresent the behavior of any and all individuals (how often does the mean score accurately describe your performance on an exam?) A classic example of this problem occurred when Eysenck (1952) examined group means and found that neurotic patients undergoing psychotherapy showed no improvement compared with those who had never entered therapy. He then concluded that therapy is basically useless! Later, however, Bergin (1966) demonstrated that, individually, some people do improve while others worsen, and that this is why Eysenck's means showed no change. A further problem is then that—incredibly—after using group means to describe a relationship, we turn around and generalize the findings to individuals! Psychology studies the laws of behavior as they apply to the individual, but in group designs we never examine a relationship in terms of the individual.

The third flaw in group designs involves the problem of demonstrating a consistent, reliable effect of the independent variable. Usually we demonstrate a relationship only once in a particular study, typically testing participants only briefly under the various conditions. Then we rely on inferential statistics to conclude that the study is reliable. That is, if the results are significant, the relationship is unlikely to be due to random chance. Instead, it is likely to be caused by something that makes it reproducible, so a significant relationship is also described as a reliable relationship. We do not, however, have any *empirical* evidence that the relationship is reproducible. Other researchers might replicate the study, but their situation and participants inevitably will differ from ours. And in their replication, researchers also seldom demonstrate empirically that their relationship is reliable.

REMEMBER Group designs ignore the causes of error variance, they rely on mean scores to describe individuals, and they do not empirically show that an effect is reliable.

Small *N* designs address these problems in the following ways:

1. They control participant variables and individual differences not by balancing them but by keeping them constant. With only one participant, there can be no intersubject differences in scores. At any point, if we see an inconsistency in the participant's response, we know that some extraneous variable is responsible, so we can attempt to identify and understand it.

2. Our "analysis" of the data is usually accomplished by visual inspection. (That's right, we don't perform statistics when *N* = 1!) Instead, we look at a graph of the data to see whether there is a relationship between the independent and dependent variables. Because we rely on visual inspection, we accept that there is an effect only when it is obvious. The size of the effect, then, is the obvious amount that the participant's response changes between conditions.

3. To be sure that the effect of the independent variable is reliable, we perform the manipulation repeatedly on the same participant, or we perform a replication of the experiment on a few additional participants. Each replication is treated as a separate study, however, so we don't gloss over individual differences by combining their results. Ultimately, then, because the relationship is based on individuals, we are studying reliable relationships in the psychology of individuals.

The Logic of Baseline Designs

If an experiment contains only one participant, then of course it must be a repeated-measures design. Typically, the study involves only two levels of the independent variable: a *control condition* with zero amount of the variable present and a *treatment condition* with some nonzero amount of the variable present. Under each condition, we measure the participant's behavior with a dependent variable that usually reflects the quantity of responding, such as the rate of responding over time or the magnitude of responses. For example, the old standby of counting the number of times a rat presses a lever under different conditions of reward fits this design.

Observing the participant under a control condition establishes a baseline. A **baseline** is the level of performance on the dependent variable when the independent variable is not present. It is used for comparison to the level of performance when the variable is present. To establish the baseline, the participant is observed for a substantial period of time, observing numerous responses. Once the participant has habituated to the procedure so that the baseline is stable, we have the typical response rate when the treatment is not present. Then we introduce the experimental or treatment condition and establish the participant's response rate in this situation. If the response rate with the treatment is different from that without the treatment, we have demonstrated an effect of the independent variable.

Baseline designs are most often associated with animal research. Because of the flaws in group studies, baseline designs became the mainstay of B. F. Skinner and others who study instrumental conditioning. This approach is often referred to as the "experimental analysis of behavior" (and the *Journal of the Experimental Analysis of Behavior* is devoted to it). In a typical baseline experiment, a researcher might place a rat in a cage containing a lever and then establish the baseline rate of lever-pressing. Or a pigeon's baseline rate of pecking at a target might be established. A particular reward, punishment, or environmental stimulus is then introduced, and once responding is again stable, the response rate with the treatment is compared to the baseline rate. The procedure is then replicated on several other animals, with the results from all published as one research report.

Baseline designs are also performed with humans. For example, in applied studies of "behavior modification," researchers establish baselines for anxiety attacks, phobias, psychotic episodes, eating disorders, and other problem behaviors. Then they introduce rewards, punishments, or other forms of treatment and observe the change in the frequency or magnitude of the behavior. Similar designs are also used in industrial settings to demonstrate the effects of various treatments on a worker's productivity, or in educational settings to study factors that improve a child's learning.

The fundamental logic of baseline designs is to compare the baseline response rate with the treatment response rate, but as the following sections show, there are two general design approaches we can take.

Reversal Designs

The simplest approach would be to test a participant first when the independent variable is not present, in order to obtain the baseline (call this condition A). Then we could observe the participant after the variable is present (call this condition B). This simple "AB" design could be used to show that rats, for example, will press a lever more often when food is dispensed as a reward than in a baseline condition when food is not dispensed.

By showing that responding is different with the treatment, we might be tempted to conclude that the treatment has an effect. If this is all we do, however, we are open to the rival hypothesis that it was some confounding factor that produced the change in responding. Maybe some confounding environmental stimulus led to the increased lever-pressing. Or, perhaps changes in the rat's ongoing history or maturation coincidentally caused the increased lever-pressing (or maybe the rat got bored and started pressing to entertain itself).

To demonstrate that it is the presence of the treatment and not some other variable that is controlling the participant's behavior, the strategy is to return the participant to the control condition after the treatment condition is over. If responding "reverses" to the baseline rate, we have evidence that the behavior is controlled by the treatment. This approach is called a reversal design. In a **reversal design**, the researcher repeatedly alternates between the baseline condition and the treatment condition. When we present the baseline phase, the treatment phase, and then the baseline phase again, the design is described as an **ABA reversal design.** For even more convincing evidence, we can reintroduce the treatment condition again, employing an ABAB design (or any extended sequence, such as an ABABAB design).

To see the effects of the manipulation, we graph the results, as shown in Figure 9.1. Going from testing under condition A to testing under condition B, we see that the introduction of food leads to increased responding. Then, after removing the reward and returning to condition A, the response "extinguishes," eventually returning to its original baseline rate. Reintroducing the reward reinstates the response rate, and so on. Because it is unlikely that a confounding variable would repeatedly and *simultaneously* change with each of the conditions, we are confident that our treatment caused the behavioral change. Then replicating this study on a few other participants further reduces the possibility that the behavioral change was due to a confounding variable that coincidentally changed with the treatment.

REMEMBER A reversal design demonstrates the effect of a variable by repeatedly alternating between testing with and without the treatment condition.

Multiple-Baseline Designs

Recall that any repeated-measures design can introduce the problem of carry-over effects from one condition to the other. If the previous reversal designs are

Figure 9.1 Ideal results from an ABAB reversal design

Lever-pressing rate is shown to be a function of the presence or absence of a food reinforcer.

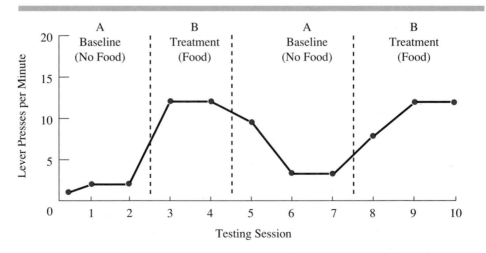

to work, the carry-over effect of the treatment must be reversible. Many treatments, however, involve a permanent, irrevocable change. For example, once a rat has learned to respond to a stimulus, some learning may always remain, so that the animal's responding never returns to the original baseline rate. Further, some clinical treatments are not reversible for ethical reasons. For example, it might be unethical for a researcher to discontinue a treatment that reduces a person's phobic reactions, just for the sake of the research.

If we do not reverse the treatment in such situations, we do not eliminate the possibility that the change in behavior was due to maturation, to history, or to environmental effects that occurred coincidentally with the treatment. The solution is to employ a multiple-baseline design. A **multiple-baseline design** reduces the possibility of confounding factors by examining more than one baseline. The logic is that we eliminate potential confoundings by demonstrating that the behavior changes only when the treatment is introduced, regardless of when it is introduced. There are three general variations of the multiple-baseline design.

One approach is to establish **multiple baselines across participants.** Here we measure a baseline for several individuals on the same behavior, but we introduce the treatment for each at a different time. For example, the argument that maturation, history, or some other variable might cause a rat to increase lever-pressing relies on the idea that the variable changed at the precise moment that we introduced the treatment. To counter this argument, we might obtain the baselines for several rats, but for each we introduce the food reward at a different point in time. Let's say we obtain the data shown in Figure 9.2. We eliminate the argument that some other variable produced the results, because even though we start the treatment at a different time for each rat, the treatment still alters the behavior. An incredible coincidence would be required for a confounding variable to change simultaneously with the different onset of treatment for each rat. (This approach is also used when replicating the previous reversal design with different participants, by varying the time at which the ABA conditions are instituted for each participant.)

A second approach is to collect **multiple baselines across behaviors.** Here we measure a baseline for several behaviors from one participant and apply the treatment to each behavior at a different time. For example, say we are concerned with a child who is disruptive in school and we establish baselines for aggressive acts, for temper tantrums, and for attention-seeking behavior. We develop a treatment involving verbal feedback that should reduce all of these behaviors. The treatment is applied first to one behavior, later to the second behavior, and still later to the third. If the incidence of each type of behavior drops only when the treatment is introduced, it is implausible that an extraneous confounding variable coincidentally caused the change in each behavior.

Alternately, we might hypothesize that the treatment will affect only one of the above behaviors. After introducing the treatment, we should find that the target behavior changes but that the other behaviors remain at their baseline rate. If so, we can be confident that it was not changes in some extraneous variable that produced the change, because it should have changed all of the behaviors.

The third approach is to establish **multiple baselines across situations.** Here we establish baselines for one behavior on the same participant, but in different situations. For example, we might establish a baseline for a child's temper

Figure 9.2   Idealized data from a multiple-baseline design across participants

Note the different points in time at which a food reward was introduced.

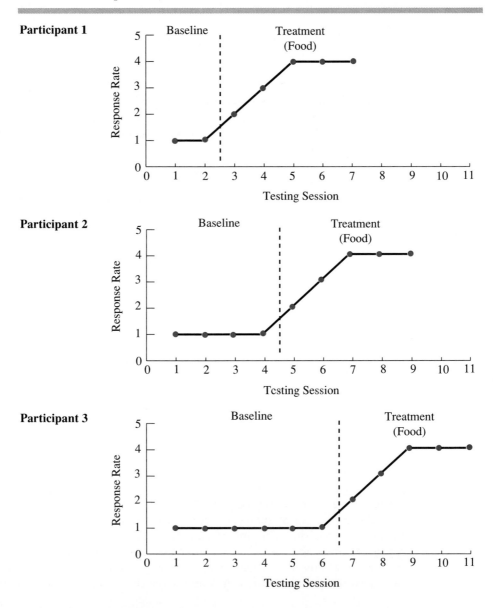

tantrums when at school and also when at home. Then at different points in time we apply a treatment phase to eliminate the tantrums. It is unlikely that an extraneous variable that decreases tantrums would coincidentally occur with the treatment at different times, *and* at school and at home.

REMEMBER A multiple-baseline design shows the effect of a variable by demonstrating a change in the target behavior only when the treatment is introduced.

For a summary of the layout of the different baseline designs, consult Table 9.2.

Design Concerns with Baseline Research

In any baseline design, the behavior and procedure we use to observe it must first produce a stable or consistent baseline. Therefore, we try to operationally define the dependent variable in a way that minimizes variability, and we observe the baseline condition for a sufficient period of time so that there are no clear increasing or decreasing trends in responding. Likewise, each treatment condition should be observed until the behavior is stable, so that we can clearly compare the effects of the presence and absence of the variable.

Table 9.2 Summary of the Different Types of Baseline Designs Commonly Used in Single-Subject Research

Design	Layout
Reversal Design (ABA)	Alternates between control and treatment conditions
Multiple Baseline	Compares influence of treatment with baseline under different situations
Across Participants	Examines treatment effect after different-length baseline for one behavior from different participants
Across Behaviors	Examines treatment effect on different behaviors from one participant
Across Situations	Examines treatment effect on one behavior from one participant in different situations

As usual, we must be careful to avoid any confounding. In particular, to balance changes due to participants' ongoing history and maturation, we ensure that each baseline phase has the same duration as each treatment phase. Also, given that some behaviors are influenced by physiological or seasonal cycles, we prevent confounding by balancing the testing over the entire cycle. We do so either by extending the baseline and treatment phases so that each encompasses the complete cycle or, when replicating with other participants, by testing each at a different point in the cycle.

In multiple-baseline studies involving different behaviors from the same individuals, it is important that the behaviors be independent of one another. If they are not, then an extraneous variable (rather than the treatment) might actually cause one behavior to change, leading to changes in the other related behaviors. Therefore, this design is best for behaviors that are not highly correlated with each other, so that once the treatment is applied to one behavior, the baseline rate of the other behaviors does not change until we introduce the treatment.

Other Approaches to Single-Subject Designs

There are many variations to the single-subject approach (see, for example, Barlow & Hernsen, 1984). Although baseline studies usually compare the control condition to one treatment condition, we can also use this design to study the effects of several levels of a variable. For example, we can first observe the control, baseline condition (A), then observe one treatment level (B), then observe a different treatment level (C), and so on. To reverse the effects of each treatment, we insert the control condition between each treatment, producing an ABA-CADA design.

It's also possible to investigate an interaction effect—the combined effect of two independent variables. However, in a baseline design, we investigate the effect of combining *one* specific level from one variable with *one* specific level of another. For example, we can determine whether there is a particular combined effect of presenting one amount of food with one amount of water as a reinforcer. In addition to control conditions, we test one animal with only food as a reward, then with both food and water, and then with only food again. In testing another animal, we present only water first, then food and water, and then only water. By comparing performance in the food-only and water-only conditions to the control conditions, we see their respective effects. And by comparing performance in the food-plus-water conditions to performance with water-only and food-only, we see whether there is a combined effect that is different from either individual effect. If there is, we have an interaction, a particular influence on responding that occurs with the combination of food and water.

In addition to the baseline designs we have discussed, the term *single-subject design* can also refer to the kinds of repeated-measures experiments described in previous chapters. We test only one participant, but we measure the dependent variable in terms of discrete trials, compute a mean or other summary score per condition, and so on. This approach is common when we study a person with an extraordinary attribute, such as when someone has an extraordinary memory, an unusual physiological characteristic, or, in clinical research, a unique set of symptoms.

Choosing between Single-Subject and Group Designs

The major advantage of single-subject designs is that they allow us to examine a relationship between variables in a single individual. Further, sometimes they are necessary because the behavior of interest is found in an extremely small percentage of the population, and a researcher can find only a few individuals to study. Sometimes, too, a design entails so much time and effort per participant that a single or small N is required. And single-subject designs are useful for initially exploring a behavior, or for studying variables that cause error variance in group studies.

The disadvantages of these designs stem first from the fact that they involve repeated measures. They become less feasible the more that carry-over effects occur. In addition, they are not commonly used for studying an interaction involving several levels of each factor, because they create impossibly complex schemes. Finally, any single-subject design is wiped out by mortality effects: Rats may die during a study, and humans require extreme patience and motivation for long-term participation. The solution to such problems is often a between-subjects group design. Such designs also can be conducted more quickly, and they allow for the use of deception and other procedures that often are not feasible with repeated measures.

As usual, selecting a design depends on the hypothesis and variables being studied, as well as on all of the concerns for flaws that we've discussed. Of particular importance is finding a balance between internal and external validity. On the one hand, the potentially great control of variables in a single-subject design achieves a high degree of internal validity. So we would select a single-subject design especially when the possible influence of fluctuating participant variables is of primary concern. On the other hand, a major drawback of single-subject research is its limited external validity. Because results are tied to one or a few unique participants, individual differences can make our results very different from those we would find with other participants. (Remember, random sampling does not work so well at balancing participant variables with very small samples.) At the same time, the results are tied to a highly controlled and individualized setting, so generalizability is limited to only similar settings. A group design, however, provides greater confidence that the conclusions generalize to other individuals and settings.

REMEMBER Single-subject designs provide substantial internal validity but have limited external validity.

The pros and cons of a single-subject design are listed in Table 9.3.

Table 9.3   Pros and Cons of a Single-Subjects Design

Pros	Cons
High internal validity	Limited external validity
Eliminates intersubject variance and examines intrasubject variance	Repeated measures influenced by mortality and carry-over effects
Describes relationship for an individual	Biased by characteristics of individual studied
Empirically demonstrates reliability of effect	Not practical for studying interactions

Putting It All Together

The typical laboratory study of groups of humans is the most common in psychology, because it is practical and efficient, it provides a relatively high degree of internal validity, and it provides some external validity for generalizing to other situations and to humans in general. The question of whether to take this approach, however, depends on your reasons for conducting the study. You should conduct field research when you seek increased generalizability to real-world behaviors and other individuals—something the generic laboratory study does not provide. You should conduct a single-subject design when you seek to eliminate error variance, especially variability due to differences in participants, which group designs incorporate. And don't forget research with animals, that you can conduct either when you want to study animal behavior or when it's the only way to even remotely study a human behavior.

The variations on the typical experiment that you've seen in this chapter are a strength of psychological methods, because they provide a form of *converging operations* that allow us to study a behavior using different perspectives and procedures. Ideally, to form a complete body of knowledge, psychology needs both laboratory experiments and field experiments, because the reduced internal or external validity of one is made up for by the other. Likewise, researchers need group studies and single-subject designs to confidently build our understanding of a behavior. Single-subject designs give a specific description of a relationship as it applies to one case. Group designs give a general description of how a relationship tends to operate over numerous cases.

CHAPTER SUMMARY

1. A *field experiment* is an experiment conducted in a real-life setting in order to increase external validity.

2. With *probability sampling techniques* every potential participant has an equal likelihood of being selected. With *simple random sampling* participants are selected in a random fashion. With *systematic random sampling* every *n*th individual is selected from a list of the members of the population. With *stratified random sampling* participants are proportionately randomly selected from within each important subgroup in the population. With *cluster sampling* certain groups are randomly selected and then the members of each group are observed.

3. With *nonprobability sampling,* every member of the population does not have an equal opportunity to be selected. With *convenience sampling,* participants are those who are conveniently available. With *quota sampling,* the population is proportionately sampled, but convenience samples fill each quota. With *snowball sampling,* potential participants are identified by other participants.

4. Field experiments may lose internal validity because extraneous variables are difficult to control. They may lose reliability because participants' behaviors are unreliable and measurements are imprecise and lack sensitivity.

5. A special demand characteristic common to field experiments is the *Hawthorne effect,* a bias in a person's behavior resulting from the special treatment and interest shown by a researcher.

6. When conducting field experiments, consider the ethics of invading a person's privacy, manipulating variables that can have a real impact, and not obtaining informed consent.

7. Group designs have been criticized on the grounds that (a) they ignore the variables that cause inter- and intrasubject differences reflected by error variance, (b) they rely on mean scores that may barely show an effect and are inaccurate for describing any individual, and (c) they do not empirically show that an effect is reliable.

8. A *single-subject* or small *N* design involves a complete repeated-measures experiment conducted on each of a few participants. The advantages of this design are that it (a) keeps participant variables constant, (b) provides a clear indication of the effect size of a variable, and (c) empirically demonstrates the reliability of the effect.

9. A *baseline* is the level of performance on the dependent variable when the independent variable is not present. It is then compared to performance when the *treatment* is present.

10. A *reversal design* (such as an ABA design) repeatedly alternates between the baseline condition and the treatment condition.

11. When the influence of a manipulation cannot be reversed, a *multiple-baseline design* is used. Here, a baseline is established for one behavior from several participants, for several behaviors from one participant, or for one behavior from one participant in several situations.

12. Single-subject designs are appropriate when studying a detailed description of one individual, when the treatment does not produce large carry-over effects, and when many observations per subject are necessary. Otherwise, a group design is preferable.

KEY TERMS

ABA reversal design
    (300)
baseline   *(298)*
baseline design   *(299)*
cluster sampling
    (288)
convenience sampling
    (289)
field experiment
    (286)
Hawthorne effect
    (295)
multiple-baseline
    design   *(301)*
multiple baselines
    across behaviors
    (301)

multiple baselines
    across participants
    (301)
multiple baselines
    across situations
    (302)
nonprobability
    sampling   *(289)*
probability sampling
    (288)
quota sampling
    (289)
reversal design   *(299)*
simple random
    sampling   *(288)*
single-subject design
    (296)

small *N* research
    (296)
snowball sampling
    (289)
stratified random
    sampling   *(288)*
systematic random
    sampling   *(288)*

REVIEW QUESTIONS

1. (a) What is the difference between a laboratory experiment and a field experiment? (b) What is the difference between correlational field research and a field experiment?

2. In terms of validity, (a) what is the major advantage of field experiments over laboratory experiments? (b) What is the major disadvantage?

3. What are the disadvantages of field experiments in terms of (a) the consistency of your procedures? (b) the reliability of your scoring? (c) power?

4. (a) What is the advantage of probability sampling over nonprobability sampling? (b) Why is the "randomness" and thus the representativeness of any random sample limited?

5. (a) What is the difference between simple and systematic random sampling? (b) What is stratified random sampling? (c) What is cluster sampling?

6. (a) What advantage and disadvantage are associated with convenience sampling? (b) What is quota sampling? (c) What is snowball sampling?

7. You test the effectiveness of motivational training by providing it to half of your college's football team during training camp. The remaining members form the control group, and the dependent variable is the coach's evaluation of each player. (a) Why might diffusion of treatment influence your results? (b) How could the Hawthorne effect influence your results? (c) How could the coach bias your results?

8. In question 7, why would you test the football team instead of conducting a laboratory study of random psychology students?

9. To determine whether attractiveness influences a pledge's acceptability to a sorority, you present participants from one sorority with descriptions of potential pledges accompanied by photos of unattractive females. Those from another sorority are given the same descriptions along with photos of pledges of medium attractiveness, and so on. (a) What confounding is present in this study? (b) How would you eliminate it?

10. In question 9, (a) why would you choose this design over randomly selecting females from a psychology course? (b) Compared to a laboratory study, what flaws are *not* eliminated by this design?

11. (a) What is a reversal design? (b) What is the logic for eliminating confoundings in this design? (c) What is the major factor that prohibits its use?

12. (a) What is a multiple-baseline design involving one behavior from several participants? (b) What is the logic for eliminating confoundings in this design?

13. (a) What is a multiple-baseline design involving several behaviors from one participant? (b) involving one behavior for one participant in several situations?

14. Let's say you conduct a single-subject study of the influence of relaxation training on "state" anxiety (measured on the basis of heart rate). (a) Should this study involve an ABA reversal design or a multiple-baseline design? (b) Describe the specific design to use.

15. (a) In question 14, what are three advantages to using a single-subject design? (b) What are two disadvantages?

DISCUSSION QUESTIONS

1. You wish to examine the influence of wall color on people's mood. (a) How would you conduct this as a laboratory study? (b) as a field experiment on the public? (c) as a field experiment on existing groups? (d) What are the pros and cons of each design?

2. Using the food-plus-water example of a reversal design discussed in this chapter, sketch graphs that would show an interaction.

3. How would you answer people who criticize field experiments as an invasion of people's privacy?

4. You have developed a new therapy that helps people to quit smoking. (a) What are the advantages and disadvantages of testing the therapy using a group design (such as in a pretest-posttest design)? (b) What are the advantages and disadvantages of testing the therapy using a small N design? (c) Describe the specific baseline design you could use to demonstrate that the therapy helps people to quit smoking. (d) What would you look for in your data to support this hypothesis?

10

Quasi-Experiments and Descriptive Designs

GETTING STARTED

To understand this chapter, recall the following:

- From Chapter 2, recall why participants are randomly assigned to conditions and the difference between a true and quasi-independent variable.

- Also from Chapter 2, recall the nature and goals of descriptive research.

- From Chapter 3, recall what trait and state characteristics are.

- From Chapter 5, recall what the effects of subject mortality and subject history are.

- From Chapter 7, recall what an interaction is.

- From Chapter 9, recall the definition of a correlational design and its issues of internal and external validity.

- From Chapter 9, recall the different types of sampling techniques.

Your goals in this chapter are to learn:

- The common types of quasi-experimental designs and their pitfalls.

- The different approaches to observational research.

- How field surveys are conducted.

- The ethical issues in descriptive research.

*S*o far we've examined correlational designs and true experiments. But psychological research also uses two other general techniques—quasi-experiments and descriptive designs—and this chapter discusses each in detail. We'll also introduce research conducted on a grand scale, called program evaluation. All of these are legitimate research methods, although, as you'll see, they have both strengths and weaknesses. None of these designs is especially complex, but be forewarned: There are a number of variations—each with its own name—so pay attention to the terminology.

Understanding Quasi-Experiments

Recall that in a true experiment, the researcher randomly assigns participants to the conditions of the independent variable, so it is the researcher who determines each individual's "score" on the *X* variable. Sometimes, however, the nature of the variable is such that participants cannot be randomly assigned to conditions. For example, let's say we think that personality type influences creative ability. We cannot randomly assign people to a certain personality, so, instead, we compare the creative abilities of a group of people already having one type of personality to a group having another type, and so on. The layout of this design is shown in Table 10.1. Such a design is a quasi-experiment. As discussed in Chapter 2, the participants in a **quasi-experiment** are assigned to a particular condition because they have already experienced or currently exhibit that condition of the variable. The term *quasi* means "seemingly," so this design has the appearance of a true experiment. Because we do not truly manipulate the independent variable, a quasi-experiment involves a **quasi-independent variable:** We lay out

Table 10.1 Diagram of One-Way Quasi-Experiment

	Personality Types		
	Condition 1	Condition 2	Condition 3
Creativity Scores ⟶	X X X X X X	X X X X X X	X X X X X X
	$\overline{X}$	$\overline{X}$	$\overline{X}$

the design and compare the scores between conditions as in a true experiment, but we only appear to administer the independent variable.

It is important to recognize that, although the preceding design looks like an experiment, any quasi-experiment actually bears a remarkable resemblance to a correlational design. In both, participants have a score on the X variable because they have already experienced or currently exhibit that level of the variable. Thus, whether we call it an experiment or not, the above design is equivalent to a study in which we merely approach a number of people, measure their personality and their creativity, and then look at the relationship between their scores. Therefore, technically, a quasi-experiment is a correlational design that tests the hypothesis that a relationship exists.

The name "quasi-experiment," however, communicates two important differences from a correlational design. First, in a correlational design, participants determine the range of X scores obtained, and then the researcher examines the relationship across the full range. In a quasi-experiment, the researcher chooses a few, specific values of the X variable to examine. Thus, we might identify only three personality types as the conditions of our quasi-independent variable, while in a true correlational design, participants might demonstrate many different personality types.

The second distinction is that a correlational design usually implies that there is little control of extraneous variables, whereas a quasi-experiment usually implies more control. Thus, our quasi-experiment would presumably maintain better control of researcher, environmental, and task variables than the correlational version. Ideally, such controls will yield a more reliable and internally valid study for describing the relationship.

A quasi-experiment, then, is a more controlled version of a correlational design. Because it is essentially a correlational design, however, a quasi-experiment still has two major limitations. First, its greater internal validity does not extend to extraneous participant variables. By not randomly assigning participants to conditions, we do not balance participant variables between and within conditions, so the conditions may be confounded by such variables. For example, people differing in personality type might also differ in intelligence, physiology, genetics, or history, any one of which can actually be the cause of differences in their creativity.

Second, we often cannot identify the true temporal order in which the variables occur. For example, someone's personality might cause a certain creativity level to develop, but it's also possible that one's creativity level causes a certain personality to develop. Because of these restrictions, a quasi-experiment—even when conducted under highly controlled laboratory conditions—provides little confidence that differences in the independent variable cause differences in the dependent variable.

REMEMBER A quasi-independent variable is confounded by participant variables, so it severely restricts internal validity for inferring the cause of a behavior.

Still, a quasi-experiment is a common research approach. In fact, a large portion of psychological research involves this method, because many of the most interesting and informative relationships in psychology include quasi-independent variables. At the same time, however, we simply accept that the results of a single study only *suggest* a causal variable and that, as usual, we build confidence in a conclusion only through replication and converging operations. That is, say that through many literal and conceptual replications—using correlational designs and quasi-experiments—we consistently find a particular type of relationship between personality and creativity. With such results, we will eventually develop a fair degree of confidence that personality type causes differences in creativity.

Quasi-experiments generally occur in one of three situations: When the independent variable involves a participant variable (e.g., personality type), when it involves an environmental event (e.g., hurricanes or having a particular classroom teacher), and when it involves the passage of time (e.g., such as the factor of age). We'll discuss each type separately in the next three sections.

Quasi-Independent Variables Involving Participant Variables

Researchers are studying a quasi-independent variable whenever they study a participant variable. Such variables include differences in individuals in terms of their anxiety, depression, self-esteem, attitudes, cognitive or physical characteristics, history and experiences, or socioeconomic classifications. We "manipulate" such variables to the extent that we select the different types of participants that are present in the experiment. Thus, for example, researchers have compared the conditions of male versus female using a host of dependent variables (usually finding gender differences). Likewise, research has examined differences in how left- and right-handers perform various cognitive and artistic tasks. In field research, researchers use quasi-independent variables when they examine factory workers whose jobs differ in level of responsibility, pay rate, and so on. Likewise, the study in Chapter 9 comparing participants found in a shopping mall to those in a city park was a quasi-experiment. Quasi-independent variables also occur in animal research that compares the behaviors of different species or compares animals who differ in innate aggressiveness or dominance. In addition, a quasi-independent variable is involved any time the conditions compare "normal" with "abnormal" participants, as is often the case in clinical research.

Creating the Conditions Using a Participant Variable

Identifying the participants for each condition requires first measuring individuals on the quasi-independent variable. Often it is necessary to pretest—either observing potential participants' overt behavior or administering a questionnaire that measures their characteristics. (Often the quasi-independent variable is the level of a rather permanent "trait" characteristic that participants exhibit.) Using the scores from the pretest, we then operationally define each condition.

For example, let's say we hypothesize a relationship between a person's having low, medium, or high self-esteem and his or her willingness to take risks. From the research literature we can obtain any number of existing self-esteem tests, and one classic measure of risk-taking is the distance at which people stand from the target in a ring-toss game. After administering the self-esteem test to a large pool of people, we'll use their scores to select participants for each condition. Because few people are likely to exhibit an identical level of self-esteem, however, we can define low self-esteem as a test score of between 0 and 10, medium self-esteem as a score between 45 and 55, and high self-esteem as a score between 90 and 100. The design for this study is shown in Table 10.2. Except for the absence of random assignment to conditions, this design is the same as in a true experiment. We face all of the usual concerns, such as ethics, standardized procedures, demand characteristics, reliable scoring, pilot studies, and so on. Also, we can combine the factor of self-esteem with other variables in a factorial design: We might also manipulate the number of confederates present when a person tosses rings. We can include any combination of true and quasi-independent variables.

How effectively the conditions of a quasi-independent variable are manipulated hinges on the selection pretest. (Because this test is itself a measurement procedure, we have the usual design concerns to consider with it, such as scoring criteria, sensitivity, reliability, and demand characteristics.) Then, as always, we seek a valid manipulation of the independent variable, so for example, the above pretest must validly identify differences in self-esteem. Also, we seek a reliable, consistent manipulation, so the self-esteem scores should reliably reflect differences in self-esteem. Finally, we seek to maximize statistical power by creating a

Table 10.2 Diagram of a One-Way Experiment with the Quasi-Independent Variable of Self-Esteem Level

	Self-Esteem Level		
	Low (0–10)	*Medium* (45–55)	*High* (90–100)
Risk-Taking Scores ⟶	X X X X X	X X X X X	X X X X X
	$\overline{X}$	$\overline{X}$	$\overline{X}$

strong manipulation. Therefore, participants should have *very* distinctly low, medium, and high self-esteem scores so that the conditions are very different from one another, producing large differences in risk-taking.

The Problem of Regression Toward the Mean

There is a potential flaw in reliability that can occur whenever we seek to identify participants who are relatively extreme on a variable. Recall that any measurement technique can be unreliable to some extent, containing measurement error because of random distractions and flukes. Simply by chance, these influences can conspire in such a way that some participants obtain extreme scores: Some people will be particularly lucky or unlucky at guessing answers, some might feel particularly good while others might be having a bad day, or there might be quirks in the measurement procedure that cause some to score especially well or especially poorly. Such random, momentary influences will not always be present, however, and they do have a way of averaging out. Therefore, if we measure the same individuals again, their scores will tend to be less extreme, simply by chance. This time, the high scores won't be so high and the lows won't be so low. Instead, all scores will tend to be more toward the middle. Because the mean falls in the middle of the scores, another way to say this is that a participant's typical score will tend to be closer to the mean. This outcome is known as regression toward the mean. **Regression toward the mean** occurs when, because of inconsistent random factors, extreme scores tend to change in the direction of moving closer to the mean.

The problem with regression toward the mean is that with it we do not have a strong manipulation. For example, people identified by the pretest as having very high or very low self-esteem scores are likely to actually exhibit a more average level of self-esteem. Therefore, our three conditions may not actually differ in self-esteem as much as we think. Even if self-esteem does cause risk-taking, with smaller differences between the levels of self-esteem, we may find small, possibly nonsignificant differences in risk-taking.

An additional problem is that regression toward the mean also threatens internal validity, because what appears to be a change in scores due to the treatment may actually be nothing more than a change in random measurement error. For example, say that in a different study we test a counseling technique for raising a person's low self-esteem, using a pretest-posttest design. We identify people having very low self-esteem, then apply the treatment, and then measure their self-esteem again. To some extent the peculiarities that produced very low self-esteem when we tested participants the first time will not be present the second time. Therefore, their second score will tend to be higher (closer to the mean), *regardless* of whether the treatment works or not!

We try to counteract regression toward the mean by using multiple trials from the most reliable selection tests possible. Also, we can include a control group—another group that is measured at the same times as the experimental group but does not experience the treatment. The extent to which the control group's scores change will show the extent of extraneous influences, including that of regression toward the mean.

> **REMEMBER** Regression toward the mean is a change in extreme scores toward less extreme scores that occur because random influences are not consistently present.

Interpreting the Quasi-Experiment

Even in a quasi-experiment, you should attempt to control extraneous participant variables. You can select participants from a limited population or match them on relevant variables (e.g., we might select only children and match them across the conditions on their ring-tossing ability). You might control other participant variables by balancing them (e.g., by selecting an equal number of males and females for each level of self-esteem). And of course we use random sampling: We randomly select participants to pretest, and if enough people meet the criteria for a condition, we randomly select from among them those people we'll actually study. Recognize, however, that such controls do not eliminate the problem that a quasi-independent variable is still likely to be confounded by other extraneous participant variables.

Also recall that to minimize error variance, you want to eliminate differences *within* each group. In particular, the more that participants differ on the independent variable within a condition, the more that dependent scores will also differ. Therefore, the range of selection scores that create each condition should be narrowly defined. Thus, in our self-esteem study, the goal is to select very similar people *within* each condition in terms of self-esteem, because then they should score consistently in terms of risk-taking. And, whenever there is lessened control and potentially large error variance, you can compensate by testing a relatively large N.

Finally, recall that any pretest can add to demand characteristics because it alerts participants to the variables under study and thus causes them to behave differently than they otherwise would. To counter this, we might use deception to disguise both the pretest and the purpose of the study. Also, recognize that in any correlational study we can test the variables in the order that is least biasing to participants, capitalizing on the fact that one variable does not truly precede the other anyway. Therefore, we might first measure many people on the dependent variable of risk taking so that they are not biased, and then give them the selection test to determine who will be placed in each condition when we analyze the data.

Thus, from the preceding discussion, you can see the four major threats to internal validity that arise in a quasi-experiment involving participant variables:

1. Lack of random assignment may lead to confounding by other participant variables.
2. Regression toward the mean may yield misleading results.
3. The selection device may produce demand characteristics.

4. Differences between participants on the independent variable *within* conditions may produce error variance in dependent scores, reducing the effect of the independent variable.

You analyze the results of quasi-experiments using the same procedures as in previous experiments. Compute the mean (or other summary measure) for each condition and then perform the *t*-test, ANOVA, or other inferential procedure that is appropriate for the study's design. However, unless you have created a matched-groups or a pretest-posttest design, a quasi-independent variable virtually always requires a between-subjects analysis. Also, despite the problems of causality, it is again appropriate to compute the effect size of any significant quasi-independent variable.

As usual, the final step is to attempt to explain psychologically how and why the independent and dependent variables are related in nature. But tread softly around the issue of causality. In our example, people who differ in self-esteem probably also differ on many other hidden variables. Therefore, we have little confidence that it is self-esteem that causes differences in risk-taking.

Quasi-Independent Variables Involving Environmental Events: The Time-Series Design

A second type of quasi-experiment arises when investigating the effect that an uncontrollable, environmental event has on behavior. Natural disasters (such as floods, hurricanes, and earthquakes) can dramatically affect an individual's mental health. Governments, schools, and industries institute programs that can influence a person's productivity and satisfaction. And societal events, such as wars, riots, and economic recessions, can alter individuals' expectations and attitudes.

Usually such variables cannot be studied in the laboratory (how do you create a war?). Instead, researchers study such events using the general quasi-experimental approach known as a time-series design. A **time-series design** is a repeated-measures design in which participants' behavior is measured prior to the occurrence of an event and again after it has occurred. Although this sounds like the typical pretest-posttest design, it is a quasi-experiment because participants cannot be randomly assigned to receive the treatment: We cannot randomly select those people who will experience an earthquake or who will have their school adopt a new program. We also have difficulty in creating control groups, and we cannot control the occurrence of the independent variable (in a city hit by a hurricane, not everybody experiences the same ferocity). We therefore have considerably less internal validity for concluding that the independent variable causes the dependent behavior, as well as less external validity for concluding that the same relationship is found with other individuals and settings.

While there are numerous approaches to time-series designs, the four major types are discussed below. (See Campbell & Stanley, 1963, for the definitive brief text on such designs.)

One-Group Pretest-Posttest Designs

In the **one-group pretest-posttest design,** we obtain a single pretest measure on a group and then, after the event, obtain a single posttest measure of the group. For example, Nolen-Hoeksema and Morrow (1991) examined the mental stress of people before and after an earthquake. Or, Frank and Gilovich (1988) hypothesized that wearing black uniforms leads to more aggressive behavior, so they examined the number of penalty minutes incurred by a professional hockey team before and after it changed to black uniforms.

Note that such designs provide extremely weak internal validity for inferring the causes of a behavioral change. The overwhelming problem is that they lack a control group. For example, without knowing the penalty scores of a control hockey team that is repeatedly measured, we have no idea whether the penalty scores might have changed in the experimental group, even if the uniforms had *not* been changed. To see this, look at the two graphs in Figure 10.1.

On the left, the one-group design appears to show that changing uniforms produced an increase in penalties. However, with a control group, we might have obtained the data on the right, which shows that with or without the uniform change, penalty minutes increased. This outcome would suggest that some other, confounding factor simultaneously changed and that this actually produced the increase in penalties: Maybe all teams became more aggressive, or the referees began calling more penalties than they had previously. Or, because the pre- and posttests are separated by a period of time, there is always the possibility that the scores changed because of participants' ongoing history and maturation: Maybe aggressiveness naturally increases as players become older and more experienced. Maybe the results reflect mortality effects, with less aggressive players leaving the team between measurements. Or, if researchers interviewed participants, maybe they introduced a confounding through experimenter expectations or created a

Figure 10.1 Graphs showing the potentially missing information when a control group is not present in a pretest-posttest design

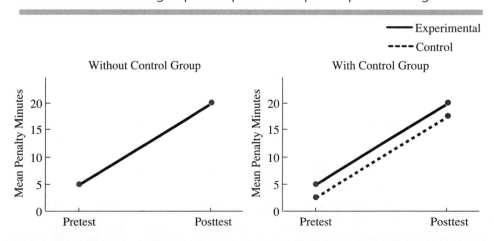

Hawthorne effect that altered later scores. And maybe the results reflect regression toward the mean: Perhaps at the pretest, players were coincidentally experiencing very low penalty rates, and the increase at the posttest merely reflects natural fluctuations in scores.

Similar problems arise if we study the job satisfaction of workers before and after a major change in a factory's production schedule or if we examine the mental stress of people before and after an earthquake. When a study involves a simple one-group pretest-posttest design, there is no way to eliminate such flaws. Therefore, because the conclusions from such a study are so weak, this design is typically used only when no alternative design is possible.

> **REMEMBER**   In the one-group pretest-posttest design, the absence of a control group means that we cannot eliminate the possibility that extraneous variables caused the dependent scores to change.

Nonequivalent Control Group Designs

You might think that the solution to the problems with the one-group design is simply to add a control group. Implicitly, however, we always seek an *equivalent* control group. By *equivalent* we mean a control group that is similar to the experimental group in terms of participant variables and in terms of experiences between the pretest and the posttest. In true experiments, we attempt to obtain an equivalent control group by (1) randomly assigning participants to conditions so that we balance participant variables, and (2) keeping all experiences the same for both groups. Thus, the ideal would be to randomly select half of a team to change uniforms and the other half not to. Or to select half of a city to experience an earthquake. Then the experimental and control groups would have similar characteristics and similar experiences between the pretest and posttest. Ideally, the only difference between the groups would be that one group experiences the treatment, so then any differences in their posttest scores could be attributed to it.

The problem, of course, is that we cannot create such an equivalent control group. In most cases, all members of the relevant participant pool automatically experience the treatment. The best we can do is to obtain a **nonequivalent control group**—a group that has different characteristics and different experiences during the study. For example, we might observe another hockey team that did not change to black uniforms during the same season we observe our experimental team. This would be a nonequivalent control group because different teams have players with different styles of play, different coaches, different game strategies, and different experiences during the season. Likewise, if we selected people who live in a different city as the control group for people who experience an earthquake, this, too, would be a nonequivalent group, because people living in another city might be intrinsically different and have different daily experiences. Nonetheless, a nonequivalent control group is better than nothing.

To analyze such results, however, we should not simply compare the posttest scores of the experimental and control groups. Any difference here is confounded by initial differences between the groups and by differences in experiences during the study. Instead, we can examine the *difference* between the pretest and posttest scores in each group. To illustrate, let's say the hockey teams produced the penalty data shown in Figure 10.2. Computing the difference for each group indicates the *relative* change that occurs from pretest to posttest. The experimental team showed an increase in penalty minutes from a mean of 4 to a mean of 10 minutes—a difference of 6. The control team showed an increase from 10 to 12—a difference of only 2. Regardless of the actual number of penalties in each group, the important finding is that, over the same time period, there was a larger increase for the team that changed uniforms.

To determine whether this difference is significant, we could first compute a pretest-posttest difference score for each player in the control group and in the experimental group. Then, because this is a between-subjects design involving two independent samples of difference scores, we could perform the independent samples *t*-test, comparing the mean difference score for the control group with that of the experimental group. Alternatively, we could perform a two-way ANOVA on the raw penalty scores and examine the interaction. As Figure 10.2 shows, the relationship between pre- and posttest and penalty minutes *depends* on whether we are talking about the control group or the experimental group, so there is apparently a significant interaction here. If the interaction is not significant, then the data may form essentially the pattern shown in the right-hand graph back in Figure 10.1. This would show that the relationship between pre- and posttest and penalty scores does not depend on whether a team changed uniforms.

Figure 10.2   Possible data for a nonequivalent control group design

These data show penalties for both experimental and control teams over the same pretest and posttest period.

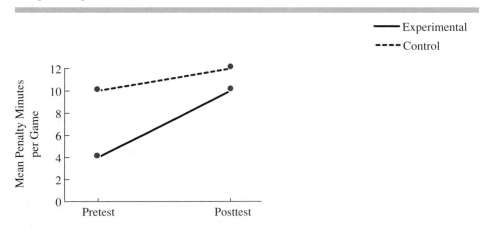

A nonequivalent control group design provides some degree of improvement in internal validity compared to the previous one-group design. The nonequivalent control group helps to eliminate potential confounding, but *only* from factors that are *common* to both groups. In the hockey study, for example, Figure 10.2 suggests that there was no confounding factor common to both teams that produced the increase in penalties. If any maturation, history, or environmental effects common to all hockey players had been responsible for the results, then the difference between pretest and posttest would be the same for both teams. Because the experimental group exhibited a larger change, something else was present for only that team which produced the change. However, it's still possible that this "something else" was *not* the change in uniforms. A nonequivalent groups design does not eliminate the possibility of a unique confounding or a random fluctuation that occurred only in the experimental group. Thus, it might have been some event specific to only the experimental team that actually brought about the increase in penalties (maybe a new coach was hired who actively promoted more aggressive play).

> **REMEMBER**   A nonequivalent control group design eliminates only potential confounding by variables that are common to both the experimental and control groups.

Interrupted Time-Series Designs

Sometimes we do not have access to a control group that is even approximately equivalent. For example, it is difficult to imagine the control group for survivors of an airplane crash or for those who have served as president of the United States. In such cases, we can test whether the pretest-to-posttest change in scores would have occurred without the treatment by examining the scores of the experimental group at other times before and after the treatment. In an **interrupted time-series design,** we make observations at several spaced times prior to the occurrence of the independent variable and at several times after it. In fact, this was the approach taken by Frank and Gilovich (1988), who examined the penalty records for 10 years before and 6 years after the hockey team changed to black uniforms. Their results were similar to those shown in Figure 10.3. The researchers also incorporated the idea of a nonequivalent control group by comparing the team to the entire league. To do this, they transformed the team's yearly total penalty minutes to a *z*-score (each *z*-score describes the team's score relative to the average penalty time for the entire league, so that an average score produces a *z* of zero, a below-average score produces a negative *z,* and an above-average score produces a positive *z*). As you can see in Figure 10.3, before the uniform change the team was consistently below the league average in penalties, but after the change it was consistently above average.

From such a pattern we see two things. First, the many pretest and posttest observations demonstrate the normal random fluctuations in scores from year to year. These are not as large as the change from before to after the uniform

Figure 10.3   Data for interrupted time-series design

Shown here are the yearly penalty records (in *z*-scores) of the hockey team before and after changing to black uniforms.

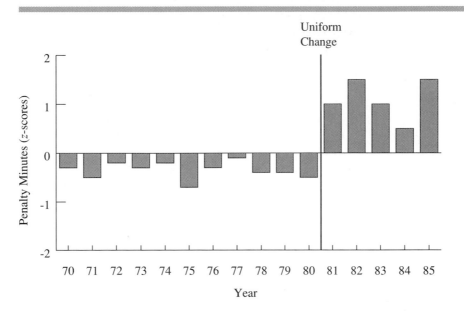

change, so the apparent effect of changing uniforms cannot be dismissed as a random fluctuation. Second, because we see a long-term, stable level of responding before the treatment and a long-term, stable level after the treatment, it is unlikely that history, maturation, or environmental variables produced the observed change. These variables would be expected to operate over the entire 16-year period, producing similar changes at other points in time. Yet the change occurred only when the treatment was introduced. (Advanced statistical procedures are available for determining whether this is a significant change; see Cook and Campbell [1979]).

Thus, the interrupted time-series design allows us to confidently conclude that the pretest-to-posttest change in dependent scores did not result from a random fluctuation in scores or from a repeatedly occurring confounding variable. The one weakness in the design is that some variable might have coincidentally changed *once* at the same time that the treatment was introduced. For example, hockey teams change players yearly, and perhaps by chance more penalty-prone players were acquired during the same year as the uniform change. However, such an explanation would require a rather exceptional coincidence, considering all of the changes in the makeup and experiences of the team over this 16-year period. Therefore, we have substantial confidence that the change in behavior isdue to the treatment. (Frank and Gilovich [1988] provided additional confidence by also reporting a true experiment held in a laboratory that also demonstrated that wearing black does increase aggressiveness.)

REMEMBER The numerous pretest and posttest observations of an inter-rupted time-series design reduce, but do not eliminate, the possibility that the treatment is confounded with some other event.

Multiple Time-Series Designs

To further increase confidence in the conclusions from a quasi-experiment, we can combine the interrupted time-series design and the nonequivalent control group design, creating a **multiple time-series design.** Here, we observe an experi-mental group and a nonequivalent control group, obtaining several spaced pretest scores and several spaced posttest scores for each. Thus, for example, we might examine several years of penalty records both for the team that changes uniforms and for another team that does not, as shown in Figure 10.4. This fig-ure shows the effect of the treatment in two ways. First, with the experimental group, the change in behavior occurs only after the treatment has been intro-duced, and otherwise there is one stable behavior before and a different stable behavior after the treatment. Second, the change from pretest to posttest scores in the experimental group is larger than that in the control group.

Although there might still be some confounding factor that occurred simulta-neously with the treatment, the fact that it does not produce the same results in the control group means that it is specific to the experimental group. Further, the

Figure 10.4   Data for a multiple time-series design

The yearly penalty record of a hockey team before and after changing to black uniforms, and of a nonequivalent control team.

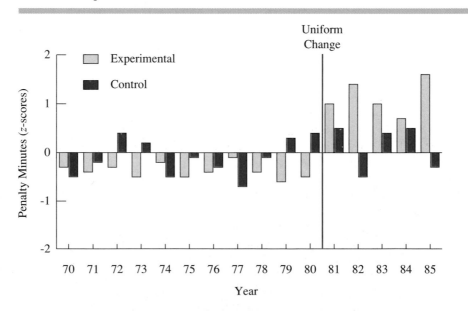

fact that throughout all these years it occurs only once and simultaneously with the treatment indicates that it would have to be an extreme coincidence. Together, therefore, these findings make it very unlikely that a confounding variable produced the change in the experimental group.

> *REMEMBER* A multiple time-series design examines numerous pretest and posttest observations for both an experimental and nonequivalent control group.

 ## The Quasi-Independent Variable of the Passage of Time

One more important quasi-independent variable in psychology is the passage of time. The entire field of developmental psychology is built around the variable of age, focusing on how it relates to changes in social, emotional, and cognitive behavior. Researchers also study the passage of time in other settings, as when comparing experienced workers with inexperienced workers or following an individual's change in memory ability over the course of a day. These are quasi-independent variables, because we cannot randomly assign people to be a certain age or to experience only a certain amount of work. Therefore, such studies are like the previous time-series designs, in that we sample participants' behavior at different points, before and after the passage of a certain amount of time. However, they differ from time-series designs in one important way. In time-series designs, an environmental event was the variable of interest, while the accompanying passage of time between measurements allowed for potential confoundings from maturation and history. In the present designs, the passage of time—with the accompanying maturation and history—is the variable of interest, while environmental events are potential confoundings.

There are three general approaches to studying the passage of time: longitudinal designs, cross-sectional designs, and cohort designs.

Longitudinal Designs

In a **longitudinal design,** we observe the effect of the passage of time by repeatedly measuring a group of participants. For example, let's say we want to study vocabulary development in a group of children. To do so, we'll test them yearly from ages 4 to 8 (as in Gathercole, Willis, Emslie, & Baddeley, 1992). As shown in Table 10.3, such a design is set up and analyzed in the same way as any other repeated-measures experiment. Collapsing vertically, any differences between the mean scores for the conditions will reflect changes in vocabulary skills as a function of age. As usual, this factor can be part of a multifactor design, in which other true or quasi-independent variables are examined.

Table 10.3 Diagram of a One-Way Longitudinal Study Showing Repeated Observations of Each Child at Different Ages

Xs *represent vocabulary scores.*

	Age (in Years)				
	4	5	6	7	8
Participant 1	X	X	X	X	X
Participant 2	X	X	X	X	X
Participant 3	X	X	X	X	X
Participant 4	X	X	X	X	X
Participant 5	X	X	X	X	X
	$\overline{X}$	$\overline{X}$	$\overline{X}$	$\overline{X}$	$\overline{X}$

We might also study briefer periods of time. For example, Nelson and Sutton (1990) examined white-collar workers over a nine-month period to determine how they coped with work-related stress. And, as mentioned in Chapter 9, Gladue and Delaney (1990) technically used a longitudinal design when they questioned patrons in a bar repeatedly to see whether they rated others as more attractive as closing time approached.

The overriding advantage of a longitudinal study is that, as a repeated-measures design, it keeps participant variables reasonably constant between the conditions. Thus, observing the same children as they age keeps constant such variables as participants' genetic makeup, their parents, the environments they're raised in, and so on.

There are, however, several disadvantages to longitudinal designs. First, just keeping in touch with participants over a lengthy period can be difficult, so these studies often involve a small N, and the results may be biased by subject mortality. Second, the design is repeated measures, and so successive conditions may be confounded by order effects (which cannot be counterbalanced). Third, and most important, a longitudinal study is inherently confounded by any extraneous variable that participants experience during the study. For example, an increase in a boy's vocabulary between age 4 and 5 might appear to reflect normal development but might actually be due to his learning to read or watching certain television shows. Finally, a longitudinal study may lack *temporal validity,* poorly generalizing to future generations, because the society and culture are constantly changing. A study of language development in the 1950s, for example, might not generalize to children in the 1990s, because of such recent innovations as educational television and preschool education.

REMEMBER Longitudinal designs are confounded by extraneous events that occur during the course of the study, and they may not generalize over time.

Cross-Sectional Designs

We can also study the passage of time using a **cross-sectional design.** This is a between-subjects quasi-experiment in which different participants are observed at different ages or at different points in a temporal sequence. Thus, for example, we might select a cross-section of ages, testing the vocabulary of a group of 4-year-olds, a different group of 5-year-olds, and so on, as shown in Table 10.4. Basically, this is an example of the design we discussed earlier in which the researcher selects participants for each condition using a participant variable—except that the variable here is based on time. (Again, this factor may be part of a multifactor design, which also examines other true or quasi-independent variables.)

The major advantage of a cross-sectional design is that the study can be conducted rather quickly and easily. The major disadvantage is that the conditions might differ in terms of many confounding variables. For example, the 5-year-old participants will differ from the 4-year-olds in genetic makeup, family environment, and other variables that might cause differences in their vocabulary scores.

> **REMEMBER** Cross-sectional designs involve a between-subjects comparison of different age groups. They might be confounded by any other variable that also distinguishes the groups.

In fact, a special confounding can occur in cross-sectional studies because of differences in subject history. It is called a cohort effect. **Cohort effects** occur when age differences are confounded by differences in subject history. The larger the differences in age, the greater the potential for cohort effects. For example, let's say we study memory ability as a function of age by testing people born in the United States in 1930, 1950, and 1970. These groups differ not only in age but also in that each group grew up during a different era. Therefore their backgrounds differ in terms of health and nutritional care, educational programs, and

Table 10.4   Diagram of a One-Way Cross-Sectional Study Showing Observations of a Different Group of Children at Each Age

	Age (in Years)				
	4	*5*	*6*	*7*	*8*
Vocabulary Scores →	X X X X X	X X X X X	X X X X X	X X X X X	X X X X X
	$\overline{X}$	$\overline{X}$	$\overline{X}$	$\overline{X}$	$\overline{X}$

cultural experiences: One group reached adolescence during World War II, another during the birth of television, and the third when drugs and "disco" were common. Thus, any observed differences in memory ability might actually be due to these differences in history. Further, if each group's unique background influences performance, then the results will generalize poorly to other generations having different backgrounds.

> **REMEMBER**   Cohort effects are the confounding of age differences with generational history differences.

A more subtle but equally detrimental problem is that a particular testing procedure may not be appropriate for widely divergent age groups. If you test participants' knowledge of common popular culture, for example, older people may be unable to identify the names of current rock and roll bands or to understand computer games. But if you test knowledge of political or historical events, older people may perform better, because they lived through the events.[1] Likewise, different age groups will not be equally motivated or equally engaged by a particular procedure. The elderly simply might not want to play at tasks like memorizing word lists or holding a pen in their mouths to make them smile. Take care, therefore, to ensure that differences in the mental and physical abilities, experiences, and motivations of different age groups do not confound the variable of age.

Because of the greater likelihood of potential confoundings, cross-sectional designs are generally considered to be less effective than longitudinal designs. However, especially if you match participants across conditions on relevant variables, such designs do provide an immediate comparison of individuals who differ in age or time-related experiences.

Cohort Designs

You cannot completely prevent cohort effects, but you can identify when they are present by using a cohort design. A **cohort design** is a longitudinal study of several groups, each from a different generation. For example, let's say we repeatedly study the vocabulary development in one generation of children beginning when they were 4 years old in 1990 and in another generation of children beginning when they were 4 in 1994. As shown in Table 10.5, this design is set up and analyzed in the same way as any other two-way experiment. Collapsing over scores vertically produces the mean score for each age, and differences between the means show the main effect of age. This factor provides the longitudinal, developmental information. Collapsing scores horizontally produces the main-effect mean for each generation. If there is no significant difference between these

---

[1]To demonstrate how people remember an unusual event, I used to ask students to recall what they were doing when President John F. Kennedy was assassinated. Now they answer, "I wasn't born yet!"

Table 10.5 Diagram of a Two-Way Cohort Study

Xs represent vocabulary scores.

		Repeated Measures over Age						
		4	5	6	7	8		
1990	*1*	X	X	X	X	X		
Participants	*2*	X	X	X	X	X	$\overline{X}$ ←	
	3	X	X	X	X	X		
	4	X	X	X	X	X		*Generation*
								Main
1994	*1*	X	X	X	X	X		*Effect*
Participants	*2*	X	X	X	X	X	$\overline{X}$ ←	
	3	X	X	X	X	X		
	4	X	X	X	X	X		
Age Main								
Effect ⟶		$\overline{X}$	$\overline{X}$	$\overline{X}$	$\overline{X}$	$\overline{X}$		

means, then there is no evidence that the scores differ on the basis of a child's generation. If there is a difference between the two groups, however, then cohort effects are present, and the developmental results are less likely to generalize to other generations. Likewise, the absence of a significant interaction between generation and age would suggest that changes in scores as a function of age are basically similar—parallel—regardless of each generation's history. A significant interaction, however, would indicate that the type of changes with age that we see *depends* on which generation is examined—in which case we have a cohort effect.

> **REMEMBER** A cohort design is the longitudinal study of several groups, each from a different generation.

To help you remember the names and procedures of all the preceding quasi-experimental designs, they are summarized in Table 10.6.

Descriptive Research

The final general research approach for us to discuss is **descriptive research:** studies designed to describe a behavior, the situation it occurs in, or the individuals exhibiting it. You already know that, while demonstrating causality, true experiments involve some description of the behavior under study. Likewise, correlational designs—including quasi-experiments—are descriptive procedures used to

Table 10.6 Summary of Quasi-Experimental Designs

Types of Design	Procedure
Designs involving participant variables	Create conditions on the basis of a participant's characteristic
Time-series designs	
One-group pretest-posttest design	Measure one group once before and once after the event
Nonequivalent control group design	Perform pretest and posttest on both an experimental and nonequivalent control group
Interrupted time-series design	Obtain repeated measures from one group, both before and after the event
Multiple time-series design	Conduct interrupted time-series design on both an experimental and control group
Designs involving temporal variables	
Longitudinal design	Obtain repeated measures as a function of age or experience
Cross-sectional design	Use a between-subjects design based on age or experience
Cohort design	Examine repeated-measures factor based on age and between-subjects factor based on generation

test a hypothesis that a relationship exists between two (or more) variables. Outside of these contexts, however, the term descriptive research usually conveys the intention only to observe and describe participants or their behavior, so we do not manipulate or control any variables. Further, sometimes such studies do not look for a specific hypothesized relationship, so we do not necessarily correlate changing variables, and instead we describe only one individual or measure with only one variable. The goal here is simply to describe a certain behavior or type of individual. Therefore, descriptive research is usually conducted as field research in order to minimize demand characteristics and increase external validity.

REMEMBER The focus of descriptive research is to describe a behavior, the situation in which it occurs, or the individuals who exhibit it.

On the one hand, the disadvantage of such descriptions is that we examine a behavior without much control, so there is great potential for confoundings, and we might miss hidden influence or misinterpret what we see. Therefore, with descriptive research we can only speculate on the causes of a behavior. On the other hand, there are three advantages of descriptive research:

1. Descriptions are informative. For example, we might describe the mating rituals of frogs in the wild or the actions of drivers in a large city, because these are interesting behaviors. For applied research, we might describe consumer attitudes or the behaviors of drug addicts.
2. Descriptions are the starting point for identifying variables and building hypothetical constructs that can be tested later using other methods. For example, much research in clinical psychology developed from the constructs of Sigmund Freud, even though he only observed and described behaviors. Likewise, descriptions can provide an indirect test of a theory or model. (A researcher might ask, for example, "Are the predictions from a Freudian model confirmed by a description of a schizophrenic?")
3. Description is sometimes the only way to study a behavior or situation, because it is either practically or ethically impossible to produce it in an experiment. For example, the only way to learn about the migratory behaviors of whales or the childhood experiences of a serial killer is by observing and describing them.

Thus, descriptive research is a legitimate approach, even though we cannot use it to confidently infer the causes of behavior. In addition to correlational designs, descriptive research falls into two general categories: field surveys and observational studies.

Field Surveys

In a **field survey** people complete a questionnaire or interview in a natural setting so that we can infer the responses we would see if we could poll the population. Field surveys may apply to a narrowly defined population, as when, for example, surveying nurses treating AIDS patients to gauge their burn-out rates (George, Reed, Ballard, Colin, & Fielding, 1993). They are also used to describe the attitudes of the general population, as when, for example, surveying the public's reactions to crime (Harrison & Gfroerer, 1992) or describing consumer attitudes (Fornell, 1992). Field surveys are also used to describe common experiences: The Roper Organization (1992) asked a sample of Americans how often they had experienced ghosts and UFOs (more than 30% reported they had!).

All of the considerations about questionnaires discussed in previous chapters should be applied to a field survey: construct and content validity; reliable scoring; clear questions with precise, mutually exclusive choices; and controlled consistent behavior on the part of the interviewer. In particular, because we often deal with unsophisticated participants, we want to focus on having them describe concrete behaviors. Also, because in the real world people might be frazzled and busy, we counterbalance the order of questions across different participants and include "catch questions." In this way we control for and identify response biases that occur when people half-heartedly respond in order to finish the task quickly.

In addition to a good questionnaire, the key to field surveys is the sample. Because we are especially concerned about the external validity provided by survey research, we want to obtain a representative sample, a sample that truly reflects the characteristics and responses found in the population. To improve our chances of doing so, we typically survey a rather large N, often involving hundreds of participants. The survey may be conducted at a particular location, such as a shopping mall or other public place, because we believe members of the target population frequent that place. Or, if we are unable to reach a representative sample at any one location, we reach a broader segment of the population either by mailing the survey or by conducting it over the telephone.

Mailed versus Telephone Surveys   Mailing a survey is most useful when a large sample is needed and/or a lengthy questionnaire is being used—and when the researcher is not in a hurry to get the data. A major problem with mailed surveys, however, is that some people will not bother to complete and mail them back to us (even though we always include a stamped, addressed return envelope). The "return rate" can be very low, with only 10% or 20% of the surveys being returned. In such a case, we may have a sample that is very unrepresentative of the population. Therefore, some researchers use the rule of thumb that to have confidence in a mailed survey, the return rate should be at least 50%.

There are many techniques for improving return rates (see Kanuk & Berenson [1975] for a review). First, include a cover letter that explains the survey's purpose, tells why it is important for participants to complete it, and provides complete information about the researchers and how they can be contacted. Second, make sure that the survey presents the appropriate *face validity:* It should be well organized, neat, and professional, and it should look like a serious, precision psychological instrument. Third, both for reliability and to increase return rates, use closed-ended or brief open-ended questions so that it is easy for participants to follow the instructions and to accurately and rapidly complete the survey. Sometimes researchers include a small reward for participation, or they mail a follow-up letter to remind people to complete the survey. The goal is to convince participants that you are conducting legitimate research and to engage their interest and cooperation.

Surveys can also be conducted over the telephone (see Lavrakas, 1993). These usually consist of structured interviews, in which the interviewer reads the participant a series of closed-ended questions. With only one interviewer, a telephone survey can be a *very* lengthy enterprise. If there are sufficient funds to hire many interviewers, however, data collection can be accomplished quickly. For this reason, telephone surveys are used, for example, during election campaigns to get the momentary "pulse" of the voters. Also, telephone surveys may achieve a higher response rate than mailed surveys because people are less likely to refuse when a person directly requests their help. Conversely, some people may *not* participate because they consider such surveys to be demanding interruptions in their lives. And many people are wary because "psychological surveys" have frequently been used as a cover for obscene phone calls and for telemarketing scams.

Again, the key to enlisting participants is an effective initial introduction. A professional, straightforward, yet friendly manner will add to your credibility and engage people. Clearly identify yourself and allow participants to verify who you are (e.g., give them your phone number). Describe the survey, the time needed to complete it, its purpose, and the way in which responses will be handled. Keep the length of the questioning brief.

To improve the reliability of a telephone survey, keep each question and the response choices simple: Participants do not have the questions in front of them, so they must rely on their memory, and thus errors are likely. Further, remember that the interviewer's behavior is important. Therefore, interviewers should be trained to stick to the script, reading the questions in an unbiased manner and providing no additional information or hints. To the degree possible, the interviewer should respond to a participant's comments by politely repeating the survey question.

Once you have identified the method for conducting a survey, you must decide how to assemble a representative sample.

Selecting the Sample   As with *any* type of research, surveys can be biased first by the manner in which you identify the population of potential participants. On the one hand, we want to avoid including people from outside of the target population. Thus, to contact senior citizens, we might obtain addresses from senior citizen groups. On the other hand, we do not want to exclude any important segments of the population: Some senior citizens do not belong to any group. Thus, the first step is to identify all of the important subgroups in the target population that should be represented in the sample.

A survey can still be biased by the manner in which we select the sample from the target population. From a mailing list, we might simply contact every person. If this is not feasible, we can use any of the sampling techniques discussed in Chapter 9.

When we have a large list of potential participants, *probability sampling*—simple and systematic random sampling—can be very effective. To ensure that the various subgroups of the population are accurately represented, however, surveys often employ *stratified random sampling*. Recall that this is when we identify the important subgroups in the population and then randomly select people from each of them. This technique is used in professional telephone surveys at election time, and though each survey typically involves only about 1,000 participants, the pollsters are extremely accurate in predicting the outcome of an election involving some 50 million voters!

If we cannot obtain a list of individuals in the population from which to randomly select, we may use *cluster sampling* and randomly select certain locations or groups to survey. Or we may use *nonprobability sampling* techniques, such as *convenience sampling*, *quota sampling*, or *snowball sampling*.

With any of the preceding approaches, a survey can still be biased if it involves hidden criteria that eliminate certain participants. For example, the time of day we telephone is important, because at noon on weekdays we may find only a certain type of person at home, or calling at dinnertime may be biased against parents who are busy with small children to feed. Likewise, when distributing surveys at a public place, remember that the time and place we select, our manner of dress, and our approach to potential participants can all produce a biased sample.

In addition, participants have their own reasons for participating, so our results are prone to the volunteer bias. Those who do not participate might be a certain type (e.g., very busy or very lazy) and those who do participate might be a different type (e.g., very inactive or bored). An especially important bias is how strongly participants feel about the issues being raised in the survey. For example, a mailed survey about abortion in the United States is most likely to be completed by those who very strongly favor abortion or very strongly oppose it. This is the danger with radio and television call-in surveys: The callers are probably a biased sample, consisting of those people who, for some reason, are especially motivated to make the call. In field surveys, always consider whether you have missed the "silent majority."

> **REMEMBER**   In survey research, take care to identify the appropriate population and to obtain a representative sample.

Analyzing Survey Results   To summarize the results of a survey, use the standard statistical techniques already discussed. Rely on descriptive statistics, computing summary statistics such as the mean rating for questions, counting the frequency of certain responses, and describing the variability in scores. You might also correlate scores from different questions that measure different variables. As usual, determine whether correlations are significant and use *t*-tests, ANOVA, and the chi square procedure to identify significant differences between different groups that you've surveyed.

Because we conduct field surveys to describe the population, we frequently compute a confidence interval. Recall that a confidence interval is a range of values, one of which we would expect to find if we could test the entire population. Thus, for example, if a sample of nurses produces a certain mean rating about dealing with AIDS patients, a confidence interval would provide a range of values within which we expect the average rating of the population of nurses to fall. Likewise, confidence intervals are involved when we report the frequency of a certain response. In this context, however, they are usually called the **margin of error.** If, for example, pollsters report that 45% of a sample support the president's policies, they may also report a margin of error of ±3%. This communicates that if we could poll the entire population, the actual percentage of people who support the president is expected to be within 3 percentage points of 45%, or between 42% and 48%.

Recognize, however, that even if we use sophisticated sampling techniques and have a large *N*, the results of a survey will lack external validity to some degree. Any sample we select is likely to be different from any other sample we might have selected Also, the more we use convenience and other nonprobability sampling techniques, the less representative a sample will be. Finally, because surveys reflect how people feel at the time of the survey, they may have little *predictive validity* for describing how people will feel later.

Observational Studies

In a field survey, participants know they are being surveyed, and there is some interaction between them and the researcher, even if only through the mail. A different approach to descriptive research is to use observational techniques. In **observational research,** we observe participants in a less obtrusive manner. There are three general observational methods.

In **naturalistic observation,** the researcher observes a wide variety of behaviors in an unobtrusive manner. Naturalistic observation usually implies a rather unstructured and unsystematic approach in which we have not identified a specific, limited behavior or situation to study. To be unobtrusive, we may use hidden cameras, observe from camouflaged hiding places, or simply blend in with the crowd in a public place. If unobtrusive techniques are not possible, then at a minimum we *habituate* participants to our presence before beginning the study. For example, the famous studies performed by Jane Goodall (1986, 1990) involved naturalistic observation of chimpanzees. After they had habituated to her presence, she was able to observe their general lifestyles in the wild. Likewise, Mastrofski and Parks (1990) performed an observational study of police officers in action by riding with the officers on patrol.

More commonly, researchers perform **systematic naturalistic observation.** We are again unobtrusive, but here we identify a particular behavior to observe so that we are more "systematic" in our observations. For example, Heslin and Boss (1980) observed the nonverbal interactions of people being met at an airport. This approach is also common in studies of animals in the wild; Boesch-Acherman and Boesch (1993), for example, observed the use of natural tools by wild chimpanzees.

Sometimes the behavior of interest involves private interactions between members of a group that cannot be seen from afar. Then we may perform **participant observation,** in which the researcher is an active member of the group being observed. Usually, the researcher's activities are "disguised" or hidden from participants. In a classic example, Rosenhan (1973) arranged for "normal" people to be admitted to a psychiatric hospital to observe how patients were treated. Less frequently, the participant observer is "undisguised."

REMEMBER The basic approaches in observational studies are *naturalistic observation, systematic observation,* and *participant observation.*

The Pros and Cons of Observational Designs

The overriding advantage of an observational design is that, through unobtrusive observation, we are describing behaviors in a natural setting that are not influenced by reactivity or other demand characteristics. Therefore, such procedures can be very useful as a starting point for identifying potentially important variables, and they provide the ultimate natural setting for testing models or predictions about a behavior that are derived from more controlled research settings. There are, however, several disadvantages.

1. We do not obtain informed consent. Especially with participant observation, there is the ethical question of violating a person's expectation of privacy.
2. Descriptions are highly susceptible to experimenter expectations, so that we may see only what we expect to see. This is especially a problem with participant observation, because the researcher can inadvertently cause participants to behave in the expected way.
3. Usually we cannot randomly sample from the population, so we must rely largely on convenience samples of those individuals we can find to observe.
4. Instead of measuring or quantifying responses, we often have only a verbal description of a behavior we've observed. Such *qualitative data* may lack precision and accuracy, and they are not very sensitive to subtle differences in behavior.
5. The preceding problems along with the fact that we have no control of any variables, mean that observational designs have little validity for even identifying the presence of a relationship between variables, let alone for identifying causal relationships.

To minimize these problems, we can use an assortment of systematic techniques. For example, we may develop scoring criteria using *content analysis* as discussed in Chapter 9, looking for certain movements, speech patterns, facial expressions, and so on. Then we might count the frequency of each specific behavior or measure its duration. Or we might use *time sampling,* in which we break the observation period into intervals and then determine whether the behavior occurs during each interval. And, when dealing with groups, we might observe the entire group all at once, or we might observe only one individual for a certain time, then observe another, and so on.

To facilitate accurate data recording and to minimize the time spent *not* observing, we produce structured scoring sheets so that we can simply check off categories of behaviors. Or we automate by tape-recording participants or our verbal descriptions of them for later scoring. To reduce experimenter biases, we use multiple observers and double-blind procedures. And, finally, to improve external validity, we attempt to obtain more "random" samples, either through systematic random sampling of every *n*th individual or through random selection of clusters.

Additional Sources of Data in Descriptive Approaches

The term *observational research* usually implies that a researcher was physically present to observe participants. In the research literature, however, you'll encounter other procedures that are used to collect data. Whether the researcher's goal is simply to describe individuals or to test a hypothesis about a specific relationship, the three common terms that further identify a design are archival research, ex post facto research, and case studies.

Archival Research   The term **archival research** communicates that written records constitute the source of our data on one or more variables. Typically, these records come from schools, hospitals, government agencies, or police. For example, Faustman and White (1989) examined medical and psychiatric records to describe stress disorders found in some war veterans. In applied archival research, Kiesler (1993) described the extent to which nonpsychiatric hospitals are actually involved in the treatment of psychiatric cases. Archival research is also used to describe social trends and events, as in Connors and Alpher's (1989) analysis of the alcohol-related themes in country-western songs. (They concluded that in such songs alcohol is usually used for drowning one's sorrows.)

The advantage of archival research is that it allows access to behaviors that would otherwise be unobservable. It also allows us to verify participants' self-reports (e.g., we can compare actual college-grade records to participants' reported grades). However, archival research also presents some disadvantages. First, obtaining access to all pertinent records can be difficult or impossible. Second, we are obliged, whenever possible, to obtain informed consent from the people described in the records, because we are invading their privacy.

A third disadvantage of archival research is that the accuracy and appropriateness of our data depend entirely on the people who created the records. Usually the records are not made with a researcher's question in mind, so they may not address our variables. Further, they may contain verbose, open-ended descriptions, requiring much subjective interpretation on our part. We can attempt to quantify such descriptions using content analysis, but different record-keepers may give such different descriptions that a consistent, reliable approach is not possible. Often, too, there are few controls in place to prevent errors, or to prevent the inclusion of the record-keeper's personal biases. Thus, we often have considerably less confidence in archival data than in data derived from our own direct observations.

Ex Post Facto Research   In **ex post facto research,** the study is conducted after the events of interest have occurred. (*ex post facto* means "after the fact"). Usually, this approach involves examining archival records. Thus, for example, the study of hockey team penalties was ex post facto because it involved past penalty records. Likewise, Anderson and Anderson (1984) conducted an ex post facto correlational study by examining crime statistics and daily temperature records to determine whether the number of criminal assaults increased with higher temperatures. Less commonly, ex post facto research may involve having participants report a past event, such as completing a questionnaire regarding their stress levels before and after an earthquake.

The problem with ex post facto designs is again that we obtain potentially unreliable data. Often, we cannot precisely quantify the variables and events that occurred nor ensure that they reliably occurred for all participants. Likewise, written records are only as accurate as the people keeping them, and participants' self-reports may be biased and error-prone. Also, we usually cannot randomly assign participants to conditions after the fact, so at best we have a quasi-experiment and thus cannot infer the cause of any behavior.

Case Studies   A **case study** is an in-depth study of one situation or "case." Usually the case involves a single participant. However, a case study is different from a single-subject experiment, because here we are not manipulating any independent variables. Some researchers distinguish between a case study, implying a prospective, longitudinal approach, and a case history, implying a retrospective, archival approach. Either way, such studies are frequently found in clinical research, providing an in-depth description of a particular patient's clinical symptoms and reactions to therapy (e.g., Stagray & Truitt, 1992). Case studies may also involve normal behavior, as when Neisser (1981) studied the memory distortions of a government witness by comparing records of the events to the witness's testimony. On the other hand, a case can also involve a specific event or organization, as in Anderson's (1983) study of the government's decision-making procedures during the "case" of the Cuban missile crisis. The advantage of case studies is that they provide an in-depth description of an individual or event. The disadvantage is that, because they are essentially longitudinal studies, they are confounded by the occurrence of any extraneous factor during the period being studied, and because they are also archival studies, they may yield data with poor reliability and validity. Further, the selection of the participant or case is often a convenience and not random, and with an *N* of only 1, the external validity of a case study may be poor, probably *not* typifying other cases.

> **REMEMBER**   Although case studies provide in-depth descriptions of one individual or event, they might lead to inaccurate and unrepresentative findings.

A summary of the various terms used in descriptive research is presented in Table 10.7.

Ethical Issues in Descriptive Research

The ethical issues in descriptive research are the same as in experiments: To minimize the risks to participants and to justify any risk in terms of the knowledge we will gain. Here the risks arise because being observed by a researcher or completing a survey might be embarrassing, stressful, or unpleasant for participants.

Table 10.7 Summary of Terminology Used in Descriptive Research

Field survey	Polling people in the field
Observational research	Observation of participants by
Naturalistic observation	unobtrusive, rather unstructured observation
Systematic observation	unobtrusive but rather structured observations
Participant observation	unobtrusive, systematic observations, with researcher a member of the group being observed
Archival research	Any type of design in which data are collected from formal records
Ex post facto research	Any type of design in which data are collected after events have occurred
Case study	In-depth description of one individual, group, or event

If the participants are aware that a study is being conducted, follow the usual rules: all responses are kept confidential, and participants' fears about what the data will divulge about them or what it will be used for are alleviated. Always obtain explicit informed consent, even with field surveys. And always provide a debriefing.

The principal ethical dilemma arises with unobtrusive research. From one perspective, observational techniques are another name for spying on people. With disguised participant observation, we are present under false pretenses and violate a person's expectation of privacy. With archival studies, we might end up examining private records without obtaining the person's consent. Therefore, as with any form of unobtrusive field research, we may be violating participants' rights.

As usual, it's your responsibility to weigh the violation of a person's rights—and how private they'll consider a behavior to be—against the potential scientific information that you'll gain. Also, remember that prior informed consent is required unless the physical and mental risk to participants is minimal. And, as usual, descriptive procedures must also be approved by your institution's Human Subjects Review Committee.

A Word about Program Evaluation

There is one other type of design that you should be familiar with. This one incorporates a combination of the various procedures already discussed. It is most common when researchers conduct studies on community human services programs, such as programs for preventing or treating drug and alcohol abuse (e.g., Werch, Meers, & Hallan, 1992) or educational programs such as Project Head Start (e.g., McKey et al., 1985). **Program evaluation** refers to a variety of procedures for developing and evaluating social programs. This is the ultimate applied research because such programs are essentially grand experiments in social change (Campbell, 1969). They are based on the experimental principle that by providing some form of treatment to participants—to society—we'll see a corresponding change in behavior. Program evaluation provides feedback to administrators and service providers as well as providing scientific information about the effect of a program as a quasi-independent variable.

Although this research encompasses many procedures (see Posavac & Carey, 1989), it usually consists of four basic phases:

1. *Needs assessment.* Before designing a particular program, researchers identify the services that are needed and determine whether potential users of the program will use it.
2. *Program planning.* When designing the program, researchers apply findings from the literature that suggest the best methods to implement for the behavior and situation being addressed.
3. *Program monitoring.* Once the program is implemented, researchers monitor the program to ensure that it provides the intended services and that clients are using them.
4. *Outcome evaluation.* Eventually, researchers determine whether the program is having its intended effect, by using a time-series study that compares behaviors before and after the program's implementation.

The data in each of these phases come from such sources as field surveys of the community; archival studies of hospital, school, and police records; and interviews, unobtrusive observations, and case studies of service providers and clients. On the one hand, such procedures suffer from all of the flaws we've discussed, especially because they are quasi-experiments. On the other hand, program evaluation serves a very real applied need, and flawed data are better than no data (as long as the flaws are recognized and considered).

> **REMEMBER** Program evaluation involves procedures for creating and evaluating social programs.

Putting It All Together

The names of the designs discussed in this chapter communicate different procedures, but they are not always rigidly defined either-or terms. Think of them as approaches that can be mixed and matched to suit your particular research question or to identify a characteristic of your study. For example, the hockey penalty study discussed earlier was simultaneously an archival, ex post facto, quasi-experimental, interrupted time-series study of one case. Each of these terms communicates different strengths and weaknesses of the study, so they should cause you to think about the reliability of scores, potential confoundings, and the generality of the conclusions that are drawn.

Perhaps the most important thing to remember about quasi-experiments is that they often look like true experiments, especially when a quasi-independent participant variable is being studied in a laboratory setting. When evaluating your own research or that designed by others, remember that you won't find a red flag signaling the nature of the design. Therefore, you must always carefully examine whether the participants are randomly assigned to the conditions of a variable. If not, then the results only *suggest* the causes of the behavior being studied.

CHAPTER SUMMARY

1. In a *quasi-experiment* involving a *quasi-independent variable,* participants cannot be randomly assigned to conditions. Instead, they are assigned to a condition based on some inherent characteristic. Because the independent variable is probably confounded by other participant variables, quasi-experiments have much less internal validity than true experiments.

2. Effective manipulation of a quasi-independent variable involving a participant variable hinges on the selection of participants for each condition who are similar to each other but very different from those in other conditions.

3. *Regression toward the mean* occurs when, because of inconsistent random factors, extreme scores tend to change in the direction of coming closer to the mean.

4. A *time-series design* is a quasi-experimental repeated-measures design in which a behavior is sampled at different times.

5. A *one-group pretest-posttest* design has no control group.

6. In a *nonequivalent control group design,* the control group and the experimental group have different characteristics and different experiences during the study.

7. In an *interrupted time-series design* observations are made at several spaced times prior to the treatment and at several times after it.

8. In a *multiple time-series design* both an experimental group and a nonequivalent control group are observed at several times before the treatment and several times after it.

9. In a *longitudinal design* participants are repeatedly measured to observe the effect of the passage of time.

10. A *cross-sectional design* is a between-subjects experiment in which partici-
    pants are observed at different ages or at different points in a temporal
    sequence.

11. *Cohort effects* occur when differences in age are confounded by differences
    in subject history.

12. A *cohort design* is a factorial design consisting of a longitudinal study of sev-
    eral groups, each from a different generation.

13. In some *descriptive research* the goal is to describe a behavior, the situation
    in which it occurs, or the individual exhibiting it. The three major types of
    descriptive research are *correlational studies, field surveys,* and *observa-
    tional studies.*

14. A *field survey* involves having people complete a questionnaire or interview
    in the field, either in person, by mail, or over the telephone.

15. A confidence interval or the *margin of error* is computed when estimating
    the population's responses to a field survey.

16. In *naturalistic observation* the researcher observes participants' behaviors in
    an unobtrusive and unsystematic manner. In *systematic naturalistic observa-
    tion* the researcher unobtrusively observes a behavior in a systematic man-
    ner. And in *participant observation* the researcher is a member of the group
    being observed.

17. *Ex post facto research* is conducted after a phenomenon has occurred.
    Archival research is conducted using participants' records. And a *case study*
    involves an in-depth description of one individual, organization, or event.

18. *Program evaluation* involves procedures for developing and evaluating so-
    cial programs.

KEY TERMS

archival research
  (337)
case study (338)
cohort design (328)
cohort effects (327)
cross-sectional design
  (327)
descriptive research
  (329)
ex post facto research
  (337)
field survey (331)
interrupted time-series
  design (322)
longitudinal design
  (325)

margin of error
  (334)
multiple time-series
  design (324)
naturalistic
  observation (335)
nonequivalent control
  group (320)
observational research
  (335)
one-group pretest-
  posttest design
  (319)
participant
  observation (335)

program evaluation
  (340)
quasi-experiment
  (312)
quasi-independent
  variable (312)
regression toward the
  mean (316)
systematic naturalistic
  observation (335)
time-series design
  (318)

REVIEW QUESTIONS

1. (a) What is the difference between a true experiment and a quasi-experiment? (b) In what way are quasi-experiments and correlational designs similar? (c) In what way are they different?

2. (a) What three types of variables are studied as quasi-independent variables? (b) Why can't we confidently infer causality from a quasi-experiment?

3. (a) How do you design a quasi-independent variable in order to study a participant variable? (b) What is the goal when using the scores from a selection pretest to create conditions? (c) What bias might be produced by a pretest?

4. At the beginning of a gym class, you obtain the highest score on a physical-fitness test. During the semester, however, your scores get worse, while the initially unfit students tend to score higher. You conclude that the gym class helps unfit people but harms the most fit. (a) What rival hypothesis involving random factors might explain these results? (b) How would it cause the changes in scores? (c) How would you test your hypothesis?

5. (a) What is a one-group pretest-posttest design? (b) What is missing from this design? (c) What extraneous variables might confound this design?

6. (a) What is a nonequivalent control group design? (b) What potential confounding variables does it eliminate? (c) What potential confounding variables are not eliminated?

7. (a) What is an interrupted time-series design? (b) What potential confounding variables does it eliminate? (c) What potential confoundings does it not eliminate?

8. (a) What is a multiple time-series design? (b) What potential confounding variables does it eliminate? (c) What potential confoundings does it not eliminate?

9. (a) What is a longitudinal design? (b) What is its major advantage? (c) What is its major flaw?

10. (a) What is a cross-sectional design? (b) What is its major strength? (c) What is its major weakness?

11. (a) What are cohort effects? (b) What is a cohort design? (c) What is the advantage of this design? (d) How do you determine whether cohort effects are present?

12. What does the term *descriptive research* convey?

13. (a) When do researchers mail surveys? (b) When do they use telephone surveys? (c) Why is it important to ensure high participation rates in both types of surveys?

14. (a) What is the difference between naturalistic observation, systematic observation, and participant observation? (b) What are the strengths of observational designs? (c) What are their weaknesses?

15. (a) What is archival research? (b) What is ex post facto research? (c) What are the major weaknesses of these designs? (d) Why do researchers use them?

16. (a) What is a case study? (b) What is the strength of this approach? (c) What is its weakness?

17. What is program evaluation?

18. The results of a survey indicate that 33% of all college students are extremely concerned about their future job prospects. The reported margin of error is ±5%. What does this number indicate?

19. A student wants to perform a longitudinal study by measuring yearly the self-esteem scores of a group of students as they pass through their freshman, sophomore, junior, and senior years in college. To control order effects, he wants to counterbalance the order in which participants are tested in these four repeated-measures conditions. What would you tell him?

20. A student measures the happiness of a group of sorority pledges at the beginning of the semester and again at the end of the semester in which they've been admitted to the sorority. She finds that the latter scores are higher and concludes that joining a sorority increases a woman's happiness. (a) What is the name of this design? (b) What major flaw is present? (c) What rival hypotheses might explain her results? (d) What would you do to improve the study?

DISCUSSION QUESTIONS

1. You wish to conduct a field survey to describe the nation's attitudes toward gun control. With a closed-ended questionnaire in hand (a) How would you identify the population? (b) How would you contact participants and have them complete the questionnaire? (c) How would you select your sample? (d) How would you summarize the data? (e) Evaluate your design.

2. Using the questionnaire in question 1, how would you conduct a quasi-experiment to determine whether people who differ in their attitudes toward gun control also differ in how frightened they become when confronted by a thief? (You might adapt the study from Chapter 9, in which participants are confronted by a supposed thief in a college library. Or you might create a study in which participants are in a waiting room, thinking that they are waiting for an experiment to begin.)

3. You measure the maturity levels of students at four times during the college year (factor A). You compare freshman from 10 years ago with present-day freshman (factor B). (a) What type of variable is factor A? (b) What type of variable is factor B? (c) What type of design have you created?

4. In question 3 you obtain the following cell means. What should you conclude about (a) the presence of cohort effects? (b) how maturity changes during a college student's year?

	Time 1	Time 2	Time 3	Time 4
10 Years Ago	10	20	30	40
Present Day	25	25	25	25

5. In two nonequivalent control group designs you obtain the following mean stress scores for people before and after an earthquake. (a) What should you conclude about whether the treatment caused the change in scores in the experimental group in Study A? (b) What other hypotheses are plausible? (c) What should you conclude in Study B? (d) What hypotheses are eliminated in Study B? (e) What possible confounding is still possible in Study B?

	Study A				Study B	
	Before	After			Before	After
Control	20	50		Control	60	70
Experimental	30	60		Experimental	50	85

Part IV

Putting It All Together

Believe it or not, you now understand the vast majority of the designs and statistical analyses used in psychological research. Because we always want valid and reliable data, there are actually few differences in the mechanics of designing and conducting most research, and you are familiar with all of the important issues. The trick now is to be able to apply your knowledge. The following chapter provides you with practice at applying design principles by working through several structured scenarios, so that you really can put it all together.

11

Examples of Designing and Evaluating Research

Topic 1: Attribution of Arousal

Topic 2: Time Perception

Topic 3: Fear of Success in Females

Topic 4: Creativity

Additional Research Topics

Belief in Astrology
Serial-Position Effects
Attractiveness and Height
The Influence of Color
Self-Consciousness and "Choking under Pressure"

*T*his chapter presents a number of research scenarios within which you can practice making design decisions in a structured way. (It may also provide some ideas for studies that you might want to pursue on your own.) For each topic, you'll encounter questions that put you in the role of the researcher who designs, evaluates, and replicates a specific study. To get the most out of these exercises, don't just read along passively. Instead, actively and thoughtfully participate as if you really were the researcher conducting the study.

We'll examine the first four topics in depth, focusing on a specific study and the additional studies that developed from it. Then we'll briefly review five other research topics that suggest various designs. (For each design discussed, remember that there are flaws in any research study, so there are other approaches you might take.)

Finally, recall that the details in designing and evaluating any study boil down to the following key questions:

1. *Purpose of study?* Is it to test a causal hypothesis, to demonstrate a correlation, or to describe a behavior?
2. *Type of behavior studied?* Does it involve a participant characteristic, a response to concrete stimuli, or a response to a social interaction?
3. *Type of design?* Is the study a true experiment or a quasi-experiment? Does it involve a single-subject, correlational, or observational design? Should it be conducted in the field or laboratory?
4. *Type of participant and sampling?* Will you generalize to a specific population? What selection criteria are needed? How will you sample the population? Will participants be representative?
5. *Control of participant variables?* What confounding participant variables are present? Should you counterbalance in a between-subjects design or use a repeated-measures design?
6. *How to manipulate variables?* Should you vary instructions or stimuli? Should you use confederates? Do you have a strong, consistent, and valid manipulation? Do you need a manipulation check? Are there confounding variables present?
7. *How to measure variables?* Will you examine overt behaviors or self-reports? Will participants be tested individually? Are the scoring criteria sensitive? Are you reliably and validly scoring the behavior?
8. *Procedural problems?* Is there experimental realism? Are there order effects, demand characteristics, or other biases present? Should you conduct a pilot study?
9. *Materials needed?* What materials and apparatus do you need for consistent and comparable stimuli and for reliable measurements?
10. *Ethical problems?* Are you harming participants or violating their rights? Is deception justified? Have you obtained informed consent and provided a debriefing?

11. *Statistical analysis?* What is your *N*? Have you maximized power and minimized error variance? Do your scores fit a parametric or nonparametric procedure? Should you perform a between-subjects or a within-subjects analysis?

12. *Validity of conclusions?* Do the results clearly confirm your hypothesis? Are there rival hypotheses that reduce your internal validity? Do you have external, construct, ecological, and temporal validity?

Refer to this list as you consider each of the following studies.

Topic 1: Attribution of Arousal

When people become physiologically aroused by one stimulus, their emotional response to other stimuli is heightened. In particular, researchers have proposed that the heightened physiological arousal to a fearful stimulus is "misattributed" (misdiagnosed) as romantic attraction toward a member of the opposite sex. Dutton and Aron (1974) tested this proposal in several studies.

> What are the hypothesis and purpose of this study?
>
> What are the variables to be studied, and which design is appropriate?
>
> How would you elicit the dependent behavior?
>
> What sampling would you use, and should you control subject variables?

The hypothesis is that greater attraction to a member of the opposite sex occurs when participants experience fear from some other source. Because causation is the issue here, a true experiment is appropriate. The independent variable is amount of fear, a temporary "state" characteristic. The dependent variable is the amount of attraction a participant experiences. Although you might perform a field experiment, let's first discuss a laboratory setting, as in Experiment 3 in Dutton and Aron (1974).

The study calls for a confederate who will be the object of attraction. Thus, the manipulation is to create conditions of different levels of fear in participants while a confederate is present. The dependent measure is the participants' attraction to the confederate. Because we'd be unlikely to change a person's attraction to the confederate in a repeated-measures design, a between-subjects design with a single trial per participant is appropriate.

Participants are tested individually, because in a group they might be inhibited and not divulge any attraction. To keep the attractiveness of the confederate constant, one confederate serves for all conditions. Regarding participant variables, Dutton and Aron used a female confederate, thus requiring male participants. They should not know the confederate and ideally should have a minimum of other romantic entanglements (engaged or married people might resist feeling, or at least reporting, any attraction). Participants should be the same age as the confederate, and you might limit or balance race and nationality. Otherwise, there is no unique population here, so a random sample from available college students is sufficient.

Now, how should you manipulate participants' fear? You could arrange for an "accident" that raises anxiety or concoct an "experiment" that directly harms participants to make them fearful. But ethically these tactics are inappropriate, and all you really need to do is threaten them with something that will make them fearful. At the same time, the threat should be realistic within the context of an experiment, and also allow you to manipulate the amount of fear. You might threaten to hit participants or to embarrass them, for example, but this might cause unintended responses, such as anger or refusal to participate. Instead, Dutton and Aron capitalized on the reputation of psychology experiments by telling participants that they would be electrically shocked as part of the study.

How would you create the conditions to manipulate fear?

How would you confirm that the intended effect occurred?

Dutton and Aron manipulated fear by threatening participants with different levels of shock. The shock was described as either small (low fear condition) or large (high fear condition). To produce a strong manipulation, they described the small shock as "a minor tingle which some people actually find pleasant" and the large shock as "quite painful." (You might add a control group threatened with no shock.)

A manipulation check ensures that the procedure actually influences participants' fear, so at some point we'd actually measure their anxiety level as a function of their assigned shock level.

How would you measure the dependent variable?

Instead of observing participants' behavior and then trying to infer how attracted they were, Dutton and Aron asked participants how sexually attracted they were to the confederate. But rather than asking "Is she attractive?" they achieved greater sensitivity by presenting a 5-point Likert scale with the questions "How much would you like to ask her out?" and "How much would you like to kiss her?" Included in the questionnaire was a manipulation check in the form of the question: "How do you feel about being shocked?" Participants' ratings were on a scale of like/dislike, and the researchers interpreted "greater dislike" as indicating "greater fear." They also included an additional, less threatening measure of arousal by having participants describe an ambiguous picture in a projective test. Each description was examined for sexual content using content analysis and, for reliability, was scored by two scorers.

If you consider the reputation of psychology experiments, you'll see that participants might be very suspicious and show a high degree of reactivity and social desirability.

How would you ensure experimental realism?

A deceptive cover story is needed so that participants encounter the confederate and are assigned a shock level in a convincing and realistic way. Dutton and Aron introduced the confederate to the participant as a second "participant." Both were ostensibly there for an experiment in which two people would be tested simultaneously, to study the effects of punishment (shock) on learning. The researcher then tossed a coin supposedly to determine which of the two would receive the high or low shock condition (but actually to randomly assign the real participants to their conditions). Then, because it was not necessary to actually administer the shock, participants completed the questionnaire.

How would you address demand characteristics?

To reduce reactivity and social desirability, Dutton and Aron presented the questionnaire under the guise that personality characteristics and feelings between participants can influence this type of learning study. The confederate and participant were taken to separate cubicles while the experimenter "set up the shock equipment." For face validity, the questionnaire contained several "filler" questions about the participants, along with the attraction and fear questions and the projective test.

What procedural or ethical problems must be addressed?

Because any subtle differences in the behaviors or demeanor of the confederate might alter her attractiveness, her behavior must be "scripted" so that she acts the same way with all subjects. Keeping where she sits constant is also important because participants need to see her and yet not be too near or far away. Keeping her "blind" to the hypothesis is advisable, because she might otherwise emit subtle cues that could confound conditions. The experimenter must behave consistently as well. A pilot study to practice and de-bug the procedure is definitely needed.

Ethically there is a problem if participants feel coerced into receiving shock and experiencing fear. Dutton and Aron solved this problem by telling participants they would be shocked and then obtaining informed consent, thus giving them the opportunity to leave before the study continued. Although the researcher lied to participants because they were not actually shocked, the lie would cause them to expect more harm than they experienced—ethically a much better situation than causing them to expect less harm than they actually experienced.

Select *N,* and diagram the study.

What statistical procedures will you perform?

Because of the very controlled setting and the small variability of rating scores, Dutton and Aron had sufficient power to obtain significant results with 20 participants per condition. The study is diagrammed in Table 11.1. Ratings from the "date" and "kiss" questions were averaged together, producing each participant's score. These are ratio scores that fit the requirements of a parametric procedure. Therefore, a between-subjects (independent samples) *t*-test is appropriate. (If you included a control group or other levels, or if you included additional factors, you would perform a between-subjects ANOVA.) With higher ratings indicating greater attraction, Dutton and Aron obtained an overall mean attraction rating of 2.8 in the low-fear condition, which differed significantly from the mean rating of 3.5 in the high-fear condition.

Another analysis is also required: The manipulation check must confirm that the shock conditions produced high and low anxiety levels. The rating scores from the question about "disliking the shock" can also be analyzed using the independent-samples *t*-test. Dutton and Aron found that the mean dislike rating for the high-shock group was significantly larger than for the low-shock group, suggesting that their manipulation altered participants' fear levels as intended.

What conclusions can you draw from this study?

What issues of validity need to be addressed?

Significantly higher attraction scores in the high-fear group confirm the hypothesis that attraction is heightened by fear from an extraneous source, so there is support for the idea that participants misattribute their greater fear of the shock as being greater attraction to the confederate.

Table 11.1   Diagram of the Misattribution Study

	Conditions		
	Low Shock *(Low Fear)*	*High Shock* *(High Fear)*	
Each X *Represents* *Participant's Mean* *Attraction Score*	X X X X X	X X X X X	*N* = 40
Overall Mean *Attraction*	$\overline{X} = 2.8$	$\overline{X} = 3.5$	

One important concern, however, is whether demand characteristics have limited internal validity for concluding that greater fear causes greater attraction. Maybe the participants were dishonest because of reactivity, social desirability, and experimenter expectations. (After all, it doesn't take a genius to realize that if a "psychologist" tells you that a shock is very unpleasant, you should then indicate that you dislike the idea of being shocked!) It's possible, therefore, that participants were *not really* more or less fearful in their respective conditions. If so, then we don't know why they were more or less attracted to the confederate. Also, is there external validity for concluding that this relationship occurs in other settings? Participating in an experiment is not the usual context in which you think about your sexual attraction to another person. This setting is very contrived, and everything depends on how convincing the confederate and experimenter were.

How would you replicate this study under more natural conditions?

We need a field experiment to test this hypothesis in a more naturalistic setting, using a natural fear-arousing stimulus. The idea is to catch participants after experiencing some positive yet fear-arousing event, so any thrill-seeking activity would suffice. For example, you could test at a "bungee cord–jumping" event or at a roller-coaster ride. Dutton and Aron selected a narrow, wobbly, foot-bridge suspended high above a scenic canyon to create the experimental condition of high fear. Nearby, was a wide, solid, and sturdy bridge over the canyon, which served as the "control bridge" for the low (no) fear condition.

How would you conduct this experiment?

You might strategically place the confederate so that participants walk by her, and then question them to determine their attraction to her. However, participants might not even notice her. Dutton and Aron solved this problem with the following procedure: After a male had crossed the bridge, a female interviewer approached him to answer a questionnaire for a "study" about the effects of scenic attractions on creativity. Among the filler items was a brief projective test, which was later scored for sexual imagery by two trained raters. In addition, participants were offered the interviewer's phone number, so they could later call to "discuss the study." Whether participants took the phone number and whether they called were taken as indications of greater attraction to the interviewer. As a control, a male interviewer also tested some males and offered his phone number.

How would you analyze these results?

Dutton and Aron measured three dependent variables here. First, the sexual imagery scores from the projective test produced an inter-rater correlation coefficient of $+.87$. Then each participant's imagery score was a ratio score, so the data were entered into two between-subjects *t*-tests using the conditions of high and low fear. When the interviewer was female, participants who crossed the scary bridge provided significantly greater sexual imagery than did those who crossed the control bridge. When the interviewer was male, no significant difference was found.

Second, the scores for accepting the interviewer's telephone number and for actually calling consist of two yes-no, categorical or nominal variables. Dutton and Aron found that 9 out of the 18 high-fear males who took the female interviewer's phone number actually called her. Only 2 out of the 16 low-fear men called. The male interviewer received 2 calls out of the 7 high-fear participants who took his number, and 1 call out of 6 from the low-fear group. To determine whether calling rates for the control and experimental groups differed significantly, Dutton and Aron performed one chi square procedure for the female interviewer and one for the male interviewer. They reported significant differences only for the female interviewer.

What procedural and control problems exist in this design?

First, you must confirm that the two bridges actually produce high and low fear, respectively. Because directly asking participants about their fear might have caused suspicion, Dutton and Aron relied on a pilot study in which other, similar males who crossed each bridge answered a questionnaire and confirmed the effect of the bridges.

A second problem is that random sampling was not possible here, because only those males who actually crossed a bridge and who volunteered to complete the questionnaire were tested. (Also, only those of a certain age who were unaccompanied by a female were approached.) Most critical is the fact that the participants themselves decided which bridge to cross. Given that participants were not randomly assigned to the conditions, this is a quasi-experimental design. Therefore, in addition to the bridge they crossed, participants might have differed along many other variables. In particular, those who crossed the scary bridge were probably more adventurous and perhaps this made them more likely to call the interviewer and to project more sexual imagery in their stories. In a replication, Dutton and Aron created a more comparable control group by selecting men who had also crossed the scary bridge but who then loitered about until (presumably) the fear had dissipated. They found results similar to those reported above. Nonetheless, it is not appropriate to say that greater fear *caused* the higher attraction scores in this study.

What additional research on this topic would you suggest?

A general question concerns the construct validity of arguing that people actually misattribute or misinterpret extraneous arousal as heightened sexual attraction. Do participants really not know that they were scared by the bridge or electric shock? If they identify the actual source of their physiological arousal, then they are not misattributing it, and some other factor is responsible for heightened sexual attraction. Because of this question, several alternative explanations for these results have been proposed (see Allen, Kendrick, Linder, & McCall, 1989).

Conceptual replications of misattribution effects are also appropriate. For example, Cohen, Waugh, and Place (1989) observed couples entering and leaving a movie theater and noted that more touching occurred after a scary movie than after a dull one. White and Knight (1984) demonstrated heightened attraction due to misattribution of arousal from physical exercise (running in place). However, misattribution has not always been successfully replicated (e.g., Kendrick, Cialdini, & Linder, 1979). To extend this research, consider that most studies involve male participants. But would the same results occur with female participants and a male confederate? Would they occur with homosexual males or females and a same-sex confederate? Also, studies have been conducted regarding the effects of alcohol consumption on sexual arousal (e.g., McCarty, Diamond, & Kaye, 1982) and on the dynamics of people meeting in bars, reacting to "opening lines," and so on (e.g., Cunnigham, 1989). Both topics would seem relevant to the situation where fear and sexual attraction converge. Further, little evidence is available regarding misattribution of other emotions, such as anger. And, finally, it is unclear whether this process works in reverse, such that increased sexual attraction might be misattributed and result in increased fear in a fearful situation.

Topic 2: Time Perception

Have you ever taken a long car trip and noticed that the drive home seemed to take less time than the drive to your destination, even though on the clock both trips took the same amount of time? This experience is an example of the observation that the more a time interval is "filled" with stimuli, the longer it seems to have lasted. As you go toward your destination, the scenery and sights are novel, so that the travel time is mentally "filled" with many interesting stimuli. Then, although only 30 minutes have elapsed, they are overestimated as "feeling like 40." On the return trip, however, you've seen all the sights, so the interval is mentally unfilled. Then the elapsed 30 minutes feel like 30 or perhaps even 20 minutes.

Based on such observations, Ornstein (1969) hypothesized that people judge the duration of an interval using their memory for the stimuli that occurred during the interval. When the memory is in some sense "larger," the interval is perceived as longer. He therefore set out to show that the more stimuli a person encounters during an interval, the longer the interval is judged to have been.

What are the hypothesis and purpose of this study?

What are the variables to be studied, and which design is appropriate?

How would you elicit the dependent behavior?

What sampling would you use, and should you control
participant variables?

This study tests the hypothesis that filling an interval with more stimuli causes it
to be perceived as longer. Because any extraneous event during an interval helps
to "fill" it and thus confounds the study, you should conduct a controlled laboratory experiment. You can create a true experiment by randomly assigning participants to conditions of the independent variable, which is the number of stimuli
filling an interval. The dependent behavior is participants' estimate of the duration of the interval. Presumably, time perception is similar in all normal humans,
so you can randomly sample from available college students.

When studying any cognitive process, you are likely to find large individual
differences, but you can control them by performing a repeated-measures design.
In our case, however, once participants know that they will be estimating an
interval, they might count or otherwise mentally time it. One solution to this
problem is to use repeated measures but also to disguise and deemphasize the
time-estimate response. Ornstein, for example, buried the request for a time estimate in a questionnaire that participants completed after each interval. Alternatively, you might use a between-subjects design so that in each condition you
truly surprise people with a request to estimate the interval. Although this
approach is better because it guarantees that participants are not prepared for the
time estimate, let's adopt Ornstein's repeated-measures design.

How would you define your conditions and institute needed
controls?

The obvious approach is to directly vary the number of stimuli presented to participants during an interval. Ornstein varied the number of tones that they heard.
Or you might vary the number of visual stimuli presented, or change the nature
of the task performed during the interval. Let's assume that you use the tones
Ornstein used.

You must also define the duration of the interval. Although there is research
literature on the perception of very brief, millisecond intervals, Ornstein defined
an ecologically realistic interval of 9 minutes and 20 seconds. (You wouldn't
want an interval as obvious as 60 seconds or 5 minutes, because people would be
likely to guess these.) The key, then, is to create a strong manipulation by filling
the interval with a substantially different number of tones in each condition.
Ornstein created three conditions, with the tones occurring at the rate of 40, 80,
or 120 tones per minute. The duration of the tones was constant regardless of the
condition, but the pauses between them was varied so that the tones occurred
regularly throughout the interval.

How would you measure the dependent variable?

Here a person's direct estimate of the interval's duration is needed. Thus, Ornstein asked participants to estimate the duration in minutes and seconds. This score is objective and participants can easily record their own responses. Alternatively, if you believed that people are unable to translate their subjective impressions of time into these terms reliably, you could ask them to estimate the interval nonverbally by drawing a line to represent its length (Mulligan & Schiffman, 1979).

What testing procedure and what materials are needed?

As long as the experimenter does not communicate expectations or create undue pressure and thus reactivity, the researcher can be present during testing. For reliability, produce an audio tape recording of the three intervals, using electronic clocks and tone generators to create the stimuli. To eliminate distractions, play the recording over headphones, at a constant volume for all participants. (Be sure to select only people with normal hearing.)

To create a realistic situation and prevent participants from forming hypotheses that might bias their estimates, you need a cover story to "explain" why they are listening to recorded tones. For example, your instructions might say that you're studying the relaxing effect of these stimuli, and that participants are to merely relax and sit quietly during the interval. In this way you also minimize any extraneous stimulation that might further fill the interval and influence time estimates. Also, this "relaxation therapy" could require the removal of any jewelry, to ensure that participants do not look at their watches during the interval.

For consistency, participants should estimate an interval immediately after being exposed to it, without any distractions between the interval and the participants' response. Thus, participants could be told that, immediately after the interval, they should turn over the paper in front of them and answer the questions provided there. They would find a questionnaire that includes a question asking them to estimate the interval's length in minutes and seconds, along with other distracting questions regarding their thoughts and relaxation responses. These "other" questions not only add credence to your cover story but also allow you to determine what participants were actually doing during the interval and to obtain a manipulation check of whether they attended to the tones. Afterwards, in your debriefing, stress that participants should not tell other potential subjects about the time-estimation task.

A major procedural problem concerns the order effects produced by repeated exposure to all three conditions: Whether an interval is *relatively* filled might depend on which intervals were previously heard. Likewise, listening to over 9 minutes of tones is a long, boring task, so fatigue effects are likely. However, by testing each third of your participants under the order of conditions ABC, BCA, or CAB, you can adequately counterbalance for order.

What is the prediction of the study and the N to be tested?

Diagram the study and determine the statistical procedures
to be performed.

The prediction is that intervals containing more tones will be estimated as lasting
longer. Because of possibly large error variance due to obtaining estimates in
minutes and seconds, a relatively large N is needed. Based on similar time perception research, you can assume that approximately 50 people per condition will
provide substantial power.

Time-estimate scores are ratio scores that meet the requirements of a parametric procedure. This study has three levels of one within-subjects factor, so perform a one-way within-subjects ANOVA of the design shown in Table 11.2. If
you compute a significant F, perform post hoc comparisons to determine which
means differ significantly. Ornstein found that the interval with 120 tones per
minute was significantly longer than that with 80, and that both of these were
longer than that with 40 tones per minute. Unfortunately, he did not report eta
squared to indicate the effect size of his manipulation, so we do not know how
consistently his varying the number of tones determined time estimates.

The preceding analysis merely indicates whether the subjective impression of
an interval increases as it becomes more filled. However, the estimates may
increase as predicted, but none might have any resemblance to the actual duration of the interval. To see a participant's time estimate in relation to the interval's actual duration, you can subtract the actual duration of the interval from
each estimate. A positive difference indicates that a person overestimated the
duration, saying that it seems longer than it actually was. A negative difference
indicates a person underestimated the duration, saying that it seems shorter than
it actually was. An analysis of the mean differences indicates the effect that filling
an interval has on *errors* when estimating time.

Table 11.2 Diagram of the Time Perception Experiment

The means are from Ornstein (1969), Table 3, p. 56. Each row of Xs
represents the time estimates from the same participant.

Conditions of Number of Tones in the Interval		
40	80	120
X	X	X
X	X	X
X	X	X
X	X	X
X	X	X
$\overline{X} = 6.42$	$\overline{X} = 7.99$	$\overline{X} = 9.00$

What conclusions can you draw from this study?

What are the limitations on your conclusions?

Unless unknown confoundings are present, the above finding confirms the hypothesis that a greater number of stimuli in an interval causes the interval to be perceived as longer.

A limitation is that such tone-filled intervals are never encountered in the real world, so you have limited external validity. You also have reduced generalizability, because your ultimate purpose is to understand the general perception of the passage of *any* time interval.

What factor could be added to this study to increase its generalizability?

The effect of varying the stimuli in an interval should be tested with intervals of different lengths, so that the results are not tied to just one interval. Thus, you could create a second factor by presenting both the condition containing the preceding interval (to replicate Ornstein's study) and another condition containing a different size interval. You might include the interval of 4 minutes 40 seconds, which is one-half the size of Ornstein's (but you could add intervals of any size that make sense).

How would you analyze this design, and what will it indicate?

Because you now have the two factors of number of tones per minute and the length of the interval, a two-way ANOVA is appropriate. However, you should not analyze participants' actual estimates of the duration of the interval. If their estimates bear any resemblance to reality, then the two interval sizes would automatically produce differences in estimates (you'd expect about a 4-minute difference). To equate the different length of the intervals, again subtract the actual duration from participants' estimates and look at their estimation errors. Say you obtain the mean difference scores shown in Table 11.3. Here the average error in estimates in each cell is positive, so participants consistently overestimated all intervals. The main effect of increasing the number of tones (comparing the column means) still tests the original hypothesis that filling the interval with more stimuli increases its perceived duration: With more tones, overestimates increase, indicating that the interval is perceived as increasingly longer than it actually was. The main effect of duration (comparing the row means) indicates that, overall, the two intervals produced differences in estimation error. Of most interest will be whether there is a significant interaction.

Graph this interaction, labeling the X axis as the conditions of number of tones per minute.

How will a significant or nonsignificant interaction be interpreted?

Table 11.3 Example of Mean Differences between the Actual Interval and Participants' Estimates in a 3 × 2 Design for the Factors of Number of Tones and Interval Duration

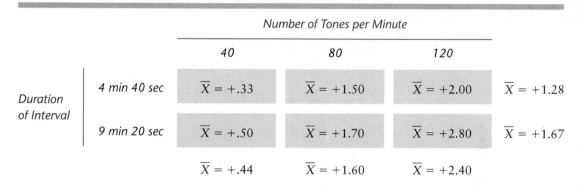

		Number of Tones per Minute			
		40	80	120	
Duration of Interval	4 min 40 sec	$\overline{X} = +.33$	$\overline{X} = +1.50$	$\overline{X} = +2.00$	$\overline{X} = +1.28$
	9 min 20 sec	$\overline{X} = +.50$	$\overline{X} = +1.70$	$\overline{X} = +2.80$	$\overline{X} = +1.67$
		$\overline{X} = +.44$	$\overline{X} = +1.60$	$\overline{X} = +2.40$	

The interaction is graphed in Figure 11.1. If the interaction is significant, you can conclude that the way in which estimates change with more filled intervals *depends* on the duration of the interval. Note that this conclusion would limit your generalizability of the filled-interval hypothesis, because you would find that it applies differently depending on the interval's length. A nonsignificant

Figure 11.1 Interaction between number of tones per minute and interval duration

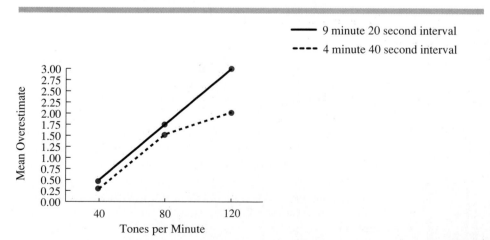

interaction, however, would suggest that the influence of increasing the number of tones is similar—that is, parallel—for both short and long intervals.

So far the results seem to support the hypothesis that people judge an interval as longer when they have a "larger" memory for the contents of the interval. However, there are at least two additional explanations to consider. First, the greater number of tones per minute also creates an interval containing more *complex* stimulation. Perhaps a person's time perception is actually determined by the degree of complexity characterizing the overall event that fills an interval, not merely by the amount of stimulation.

> How might you manipulate the complexity of the stimuli during
> an interval, and what variable must you keep constant?

For a given interval size, the variable to keep constant is the *number* of stimuli presented during the interval. Then vary the complexity of the stimuli presented. In fact, Ornstein (1969) conducted a second study in which participants viewed drawings of geometric shapes that varied in their complexity. You might also vary the complexity of the participant's response to a stimulus, as in Brown (1985), who had people physically trace patterns that varied in complexity. These studies showed that increased complexity did increase the perceived duration of the interval.

The second explanation to consider is that either a larger number of stimuli or a more complex stimulation might produce a less organized memory for the contents of the interval. Stimuli that are simple to us—that we understand—are organized in our memory; stimuli that are complex are not. Thus, any time we organize the stimuli in memory, the interval may seem shorter, while with less organization it may seem longer. Mulligan and Schiffman (1979) tested this hypothesis by manipulating whether participants could make the stimuli more meaningful and organized.

> How would you manipulate the meaningfulness of stimuli
> occurring in an interval?

There are a number of ways you might give more or less meaning to a stimulus. Mulligan and Schiffman (1979) presented participants cartoons either with or without a disambiguating caption that made the cartoon more meaningful. (These cartoons—called "droodles"—are discussed in a very different type of study in Appendix B.) Participants viewed a droodle for a fixed period, either with or without a caption, and then estimated the viewing interval. Estimates were shorter when a caption was provided, presumably because it allowed better organization and simplification of the components of the cartoon in memory.

To further study this phenomenon, cognitive psychologists have many ways of producing differences in retention, complexity, and organization. Using them, you can determine how altering the stimuli or mental task influences time perception.

Also, the preceding research involves retrospective judgments, in which people estimate the interval after it has ended. However, a paradox occurs when people are aware that they will estimate the interval at its start (making a "prospective" estimate). Here the amount of stimulation in the interval has the opposite effect: the more an interval is filled, the *shorter* the interval is judged to be (Hicks, Miller, & Kinsbourne, 1976; but see Brown, 1985). In this context, "time flies when you're having fun" because the fun mentally fills the interval, so time passes quickly. Conversely, "a watched pot never boils" because little is happening, so the interval is mentally unfilled and time drags by. In fact, Cahoon and Edmonds (1980) had participants watch a pot of water come to a boil. They found that the more that participants concentrated on waiting for the water to boil, the longer the interval was judged to be. One possible explanation for this paradox is that when making a prospective time estimate, people do not rely on the amount of stimulation experienced during the interval. Instead, they rely directly on their experience of time. Time estimates become shorter when more stimuli are encountered because greater stimulation directs their attention away from their experience of time. To test whether less attention to time makes it pass rapidly, you can take any established procedure for consuming more or less of a person's attention and incorporate it into a study in which participants estimate an interval's duration.

Topic 3: Fear of Success in Females

Some people argue that the most insidious effect of racism and sexism is that the victims of such biases are conditioned by society to behave in certain ways that match the stereotype. For example, Horner (1972) proposed that women who avoid striving for success in school or occupations may be motivated by "fear of success," or FOS. Given the society of the 1970s, it was reasonable to suggest that women were conditioned to avoid seeking success because they had learned to fear the negative consequences associated with it. In particular, they anticipated being perceived as "unfeminine" and socially undesirable if they were successful. On the other hand, men, Horner proposed, generally exhibit less FOS because, for them, there are fewer negative consequences associated with success. Horner conducted a study to demonstrate that men and women exhibit different levels of FOS.

What are the hypothesis and purpose of this study?

What are the variables to be studied, and which design is appropriate?

What sampling would you use, and should you control participant variables?

This study is for demonstrating the existence of FOS. Because it would be premature to test variables that cause FOS, you should turn to a correlational, descriptive study. The basic proposal is that men and women exhibit different levels of FOS, so at most the design is a quasi-experiment, with the quasi-independent variable of males versus females. The dependent behavior is FOS, presumably a relatively stable "trait" characteristic. The study does not require a specific field setting, so conducting it in a laboratory provides the best control. Presumably, FOS is found throughout the general population, so you can select participants randomly from available college students. Note that the quasi-independent variable of gender is a between-subjects factor, which may be confounded by many other participant variables, including race, age, college experience, and so on. To control these variables, you might either limit the population to a more homogeneous group or produce matched pairs of males and females.

How would you measure the dependent variable?

The key is to operationally define and then measure behaviors that are construct-valid and actually reflect FOS. You might design a situation to cause participants to strive for success, but if they don't, you cannot be sure that this result reflects FOS. But you can measure participants' motives more directly using their self-reports from interviews or questionnaires. Closed-ended questions, however, would be unworkable here, because (1) this is exploratory research, so you don't necessarily know the appropriate questions to ask; (2) people might be unaware of their FOS; and (3) demand characteristics may prevent them from giving honest responses. To avoid such problems, Horner (1972) employed a projective test from which she could infer high or low FOS. Females completed a story that began "After first-term finals, Anne finds herself at the head of her medical school class." Males completed a corresponding story about "John."

What procedure, instructions, and materials are needed?

To ensure reliability, participants completed the story in writing. To focus them on the success of the characters, Horner asked participants to comment on Anne's or John's reactions to their grades, other people's reactions, and their past and future lives. Because only one story was completed per participant, order effects were not a problem.

By counterbalancing the gender of the researcher within each group, you could control for experimenter-produced demand characteristics. (A double-blind procedure would probably not be necessary if you can minimize the interaction between participants and researcher.) Also note that participants can be tested in groups. To minimize reactivity to divulging personal information, you might frame the experiment as a creativity test, English composition test, or as a test of knowledge about social interactions. The materials you would use consist of a sheet of paper with the appropriate description of John or Anne typed across the top. (By providing more sheets you imply that participants can or should write more.)

The design is ethically acceptable because you're testing knowing volunteers, and informed consent can provide straightforward information about the task and situation. However, the hypothesis should not be conveyed until debriefing.

How would you determine each participant's score and ensure a powerful design?

The major problem with a projective, open-ended question concerns reliable scoring. Horner performed a content analysis, operationally defining FOS to be present when a person described Anne or John as having negative feelings or negative experiences as a result of achieving high grades. Horner found, for example, that Anne was described as the stereotypical lonely, unattractive "egghead" who was disliked (and even beat up by classmates when the grades were published!). Multiple scorers (raters) would be appropriate here, and you should check for high inter-rater reliability. A relatively large N is warranted because of potentially high variability in responses and scoring. With so simple a task, you could easily test upwards of 50 people per condition.

You might think that, after scoring the stories, you could assign each participant a score reflecting the number of FOS images in his or her story. However, you do not know that a greater number of FOS images in a story indicates a greater degree of FOS. (Some participants might simply write a more detailed story.) Horner solved this problem by viewing FOS as an all-or-none characteristic. She categorized each participant's story as either exhibiting or not exhibiting FOS and then determined whether more females exhibited FOS than males.

What statistical analysis should you perform?

This is a between-subjects design with nonparametric, nominal, or categorical data, so performing a chi square procedure is appropriate. Technically you should compute the two-way chi square to determine whether the frequency of FOS and non-FOS is independent of participants' gender. This design and the results of Horner's study are shown in Table 11.4. Here a significant result indicates whether the frequency that people produced an FOS story *depends* on

Table 11.4 Diagram of Two-Way Design and Results of Horner (1972)

	Conditions	
	Males (John Story)	*Females* (Anne Story)
FOS Stories	10%	65%
Non-FOS Stories	90%	35%

whether they are male or female. Horner reported that females produced a significantly greater number of FOS stories, although, unfortunately, she did not indicate the strength or consistency of this relationship.

What conclusions can you draw, and are they valid?

Because this is a quasi-experiment, you cannot confidently conclude that gender *causes* the differences in FOS stories. Rather, you can only speculate on how FOS develops in males and females and how it operates to influence behavior. It is reasonable to expect that other people in similar settings would produce similar results, so there is some external validity for this relationship. But you won't know whether FOS actually operates in the real world, whether it actually motivates people, or what all its components are, so ecological, construct, and broad external validity are limited. (Then again, this is just the first study.)

However, even your tentative conclusions hinge on whether there are any confoundings between the two gender conditions. Again, look carefully at Table 11.4.

What is the major confounding between the Male-Female conditions?

The difference in FOS scores between the conditions might be due to the gender of the participants or it might be due to the gender of the *character* in each story: That is, the gender of John and Anne is confounded with the quasi-independent variable of participant gender. To test this hypothesis, Monahan, Kuhn, and Shaver (1974) had both males and females complete stories about both John and Anne. They found that women *and* men showed greater FOS when describing Anne! Thus, there is something about completing the Anne story that produces greater FOS imagery. What is it about Anne's success in medical school that causes both males and females to imagine her as having negative feelings and experiences because of that success?

What bias is built into the stimuli?

The bias is that Anne is in *medical* school, stereotypically a "male" situation. Thus, Horner's study was also confounded because the two conditions differ in terms of whether the gender of the character fits the stereotype of the school. This conclusion was confirmed by Cherry and Deaux (1978), who had males and females describe John and Anne as being either at the head of their *medical-*school class or at the head of their *nursing-*school class. In the medical-school setting, 60% of the Anne stories indicated FOS, compared with only 30% of the John stories. But in the nursing-school setting the shoe was on the other foot: 64% of the John stories but only 30% of the Anne stories indicated FOS. Further, both men and women provided more negative descriptions of John in nursing school and of Anne in medical school.

What do these results indicate about the construct of FOS?

If FOS exists, Horner did not measure it. Essentially her study lacked construct validity: Participants never actually stated that they feared success, and, instead of reflecting some intrinsic motivation, their negative descriptions depended entirely on the context of the story. Apparently, we are all aware of stereotypes and tend to predict unpleasant consequences for someone who violates a stereotype. In particular, when describing someone who is successful at something that is uncommon for their gender, we expect the social consequences of that success to be negative.

Recall that research explanations are supposed to be *parsimonious;* that is, they should not be complicated by unnecessary constructs. Because the preceding study (and similar research) has not demonstrated that FOS is necessary for explaining behavior, the construct has largely been discarded.

What suggestions do you have for further research?

To retain the construct of FOS, you would have to measure it in an objective, valid, and unconfounded manner. For example, you might develop a closed-ended questionnaire to measure FOS and also seek to identify a concrete behavior that reflects avoiding success in real life. Then you could show both *concurrent* and *predictive* validity by determining the correlation between questionnaire scores and actual avoidance of success. Also, because very young children would not be expected to have learned the negative consequences of violating sex-role stereotypes, you might eliminate the bias in Horner's study by testing young children for FOS (assuming young children will have developed FOS). And finally, because society and sex stereotypes presumably have changed since the early 1970s, a replication of the above FOS studies could determine whether there is a generational or "cohort" effect between Horner's participants and those of today.

Topic 4: Creativity

Creativity is often examined in terms of problem solving. In this context, being creative is defined as making new, uncommon associations between ideas to solve a problem. Isen, Daubman, and Nowicki (1987) suggested that one variable that influences creative problem solving is mood or "affect." When experiencing positive affect, people may organize information into broader, more all-inclusive categories, so that they combine highly divergent information. Because of this new organization, they can see unusual connections or novel associations, thus facilitating problem solving.

What are the hypothesis and purpose of this study?

What are the variables to be studied, and which design is appropriate?

What procedure and subjects would you use?

The study is to show that more positive affect causes greater creativity, so a laboratory experiment involving college students is appropriate. Any manipulation that influences a person's "state" characteristic of mood is appropriate. For example, you could present different mood-inducing words or vary the amount of reward that participants receive. In a series of studies, Isen et al. (1987) employed several such procedures, including showing either a five-minute comedy film (consisting of television "bloopers"), a neutral control film (about the normal curve!), or a negative film (a documentary on World War II Nazi concentration camps). Let's use this procedure. Accordingly, your independent variable is the type of film being shown. (Technically, a participant's mood is an intervening variable, which, presumably, is influenced by the type of film viewed.) Because of potential carry-over effects, the films should be presented as a between-subjects factor.

The dependent variable is a participant's score on creative problem solving. Isen et al. presented a number of "brain-teaser" problems to measure creative problem solving, including the Remote Associates Test (Mednick, Mednick, & Mednick, 1964). Here each test question contains three words for which there is one "remote" association. The questions are presented in a questionnaire, and participants fill in the word that provides the association. For example, given the stimuli *mower, atomic,* and *foreign,* the correct answer is *power.*

How would you ensure that the manipulation worked?

How would you ensure reliable measurement of creativity?

A manipulation check is necessary to be sure that the films had the desired effect. Isen et al. accomplished this check by telling participants that the film they were about to see was being pretested for another experiment. Then, after the film was over, they were asked to rate the pleasantness of several unfamiliar, neutral words or to rate statements describing how the film made them feel. Participants confirmed that the films had produced the intended differences in mood. Following these tasks, the Remote Associates Test was performed under the cover story that norms were being established for another study.

To reliably measure creativity, participants completed 21 Remote Associates questions. To control the difficulty of the questions, the researchers used pilot data to select 7 easy, 7 medium, and 7 difficult items. A participant's score was the total number of questions correctly answered. Further, to reliably demonstrate the relationship, the researchers tested between 50 and 100 people in each of their studies, roughly counterbalancing for participant gender.

Diagram this study, and select the statistical procedures you should use.

The study is diagrammed as shown in Table 11.5, and the one-way, between-subjects ANOVA is appropriate. If the *F* is significant, post hoc comparisons and eta squared are computed. Based on Isen et al. (1987), the number of items correctly solved should be significantly higher when participants experience the positive-mood condition than when they experience the neutral condition. Negative mood should not, however, produce a significant difference in creative problem solving compared to the neutral condition.

To obtain greater information from this design, you could analyze an additional, hidden factor.

What additional factor can be analyzed?

What statistical procedure should be used, and what will it show?

The additional factor to be analyzed is the difficulty of the Remote Associates items. Instead of computing an overall total-correct score per subject, you can examine the number correct for each participant when answering the easy, medium, or difficult questions, respectively. In doing so, you create a two-way mixed design. You still have the between-subjects factor containing the three levels of mood, but you also have the repeated-measures factor consisting of easy, medium, or difficult questions. This results in a (3 × 3) mixed ANOVA. From this, you will see the main effect of the mood conditions as well as the main effect of the difficulty of problems. Most interestingly, you will see the interaction between difficulty and mood. This interaction will indicate whether the relationship between a person's mood and his or her creative problem solving *depends* on how difficult the problems are. Notably, when Isen et al. (1987) performed a similar analysis, they found that, regardless of mood level, the difficult questions

Table 11.5 Diagram of Affect and Creativity Experiment

	Conditions of Mood		
	Negative	*Neutral*	*Positive*
Each X Is a	X	X	X
Participant's	X	X	X
Creativity	X	X	X
Score	X	X	X
	X	X	X
	$\overline{X}$	$\overline{X}$	$\overline{X}$

were so difficult they tended to produce a *floor effect,* while the easy items were so easy they tended to produce a *ceiling effect.* Therefore, the interaction of mood and difficulty was not significant.

Although Isen et al. found that positive mood conditions produced higher creativity scores, there is reason to question whether participants truly experienced the different moods. Consider the order in which they performed the various tasks described previously.

What demand characteristics might have biased this study?

After presenting a film, Isen et al. conducted a manipulation check to determine participants' moods. But imagine you are a subject who watches a brief film that is obviously lighthearted or obviously depressing. Then you are asked to rate the pleasantness of words or, worse, to describe how the film made you feel. Wouldn't you suspect that the film was *supposed* to produce a positive or negative mood? Thus, this procedure may have communicated experimenter expectations about the mood that participants were supposed to indicate, and they simply complied. If this were the case, the researchers did not accurately identify the cause of the differences in creativity, because they could not be sure that the intended differences in mood even existed.

To solve this problem, we might present the manipulation check after the creativity test, but having a difficult or easy time in performing the creativity test might change participants' mood from what it was at the beginning of the test. Likewise, we might use different stimuli, but any manipulation that is strong enough to influence mood may also communicate experimenter expectations. Thus, a better design might be to describe the relationship between mood and creativity, but without actively manipulating mood, so that demand characteristics are avoided.

A further problem is that the preceding manipulation check showed that the *average* mood score differed between the conditions, but there was undoubtedly variability in the moods of individuals within each condition. Therefore, this procedure is not a very precise or sensitive way of examining how an individual's mood relates to his or her creativity.

Given these criticisms, when designing an extension of this research you might seek a description of the relationship between participants' specific mood level and their creativity, but without actively manipulating mood.

What design might you use to study this relationship?

What are the hypothesis and purpose of this study?

How would you define and measure the variables?

Given the goals just described, the obvious choice is a correlational study: After measuring participant's existing mood when they enter the study, you can correlate these scores with their scores on a subsequent creativity test. The hypothesis is that mood and creativity are related. The purpose is to show that the relationship exists, but you are no longer trying to show that a positive mood *causes* greater creativity.

To perform a more literal replication of the Isen et al. procedure, you might again operationally define creativity as performance on the Remote Associates Test. To measure the state characteristic of mood, you could again have participants rate the pleasantness of uncommon, emotionally neutral words. (By checking the literature, you can obtain previously used lists of such words.) Your operational definition here is that the higher the pleasantness ratings of the words, the better a person's overall mood.

How would you create the rating scale for items measuring mood?

Because rating a neutral word as *very* pleasant or unpleasant might seem an unnatural task for people, the rating scale can be anchored with only the words *pleasant* and *unpleasant*. Likewise, because people might have a hard time making fine discriminations in the pleasantness of a word, it is appropriate to provide only a 5-point scale. With an odd number of points, you allow participants a middle or neutral rating, which in this context is also appropriate. In your instructions, however, stress that participants should consider all points on the scale.

A pilot study is called for here to determine whether the words are neutral, whether their pleasantness can be rated, and whether the scale is appropriate. You would ask pilot subjects to rate each word on these dimensions and then include only those words in the mood test that are consistently judged to meet these criteria.

How would you construct the mood questionnaire?

To reflect a person's mood reliably, you would want to get a sufficient number of words rated—say, 24 words total. To cancel out any potential response biases, you can counterbalance the placement of *pleasant* and *unpleasant* at the left end of the scale for half of the words and at the right end for the other half.

You might intermix the mood questions with the Remote Associates Test and present them as one questionnaire, but this arrangement could be very confusing for participants. A better approach is to keep the two procedures separate, with individual printed instructions for each.

How would you administer the mood and creativity tests?

There are two reasons that you might have all participants complete the mood questionnaire before completing the Remote Associates Test. First, you would avoid any possible influence that the Remote Associates Test might have on a mood. (Remember, your goal in this design is to *not* manipulate or influence participants' mood.) Second, although your emphasis is definitely *not* on causality, you can strengthen such an inference by having what you believe is the causal variable occur first.

What participants will you select, and how will you sample?

It is most important to test people who differ greatly in their moods and in their abilities to solve the Remote Associates Test. That is, you want to avoid a restricted range on either variable—observing a wide range of different scores on each. This will provide more information and increase statistical power. A target N of around 100 subjects would provide sufficient power.

The hypothesized relationship applies to the general population, so you can randomly select college students. Doing so also gives you the advantage of collecting data in a quiet, controlled laboratory setting. If you had reason to believe that college students would produce a restricted range of scores, however, you might instead conduct a field study in several randomly selected public locations or a mailed survey, using systematic or stratified random sampling techniques.

How would you analyze the data?

First, you must determine each participant's score on each test. For the Remote Associates Test, total the number of correct answers. For the mood test, code all questions so that a higher rating always indicates that the word is rated as more pleasant, implying a more positive affect. Then, each participant's mood score can be either the total or the mean of the ratings that he or she selected.

Both of these variables reflect ratio scales, and implicitly you have assumed a linear relationship here, so compute the Pearson correlation coefficient using each participant's pair of scores. Next, determine whether the coefficient is significant. Your prediction is that there will be a positive correlation between mood and creativity, with higher pleasantness ratings associated with higher creativity scores. Because you predict a specific relationship, perform a one-tailed test of significance.

If r is significant, you can compute the linear regression equation, and then graph the regression line to summarize this relationship. You essentially hypothesized that participants' mood predicts their creativity, so word ratings would be the predictor *(X)* variable and Remote Associates scores the criterion *(Y)* variable. Also compute the standard error of the estimate to determine the "average" amount that participants' actual creativity scores differ from their predicted creativity scores when based on their mood score and the regression equation. You would also compute r^2 to describe the proportion of variance in creativity scores that is accounted for by the relationship with mood. The larger this statistic, the more important mood is for understanding differences in creativity.

What are the important issues of validity in this study?

The first issue is content validity. You want to be sure that pleasantness ratings actually and only reflect the pleasantness that participants attribute to the words. Any flaws in the rating task, or any words that participants have experienced in a way that biases them, will mean that you are not measuring pleasantness as intended. Likewise, the Remote Associates Test must measure a person's ability to make remote associations. If, for example, participants don't know a word's definition, then they will give an incorrect answer for that question because of a variable having nothing to do with making associations.

Your other major concern is construct validity. You have defined creativity as the ability to associate diverse elements in an uncommon way. But creativity may be more than that. Also, your operational definition of being creative is "producing the correct remote associate." But, people who are creative and ingenious might see a unique association that the test does not anticipate, so they would be scored as incorrect. Likewise, the word-pleasantness ratings might reflect a person's mood, but then again they might not. It's possible to be in a very poor mood and still think a word has a pleasant ring to it (*aardvark* springs to mind). Also, there are many aspects to a person's mood (anger, elation, sadness), and you cannot know which, if any, are reflected by these ratings.

For these reasons, you might select any number of published, objective (closed-ended) mood tests from the literature (e.g., Schackman, 1983). An established mood test is usually supported by considerable research showing its validity. Further, such tests often contain subscales, each of which measures a certain component of mood: The items in one scale would measure the factor of "depression," those in another "anxiety," and so on. In fact, if you had used such a test in the preceding study, you could use a participant's score from each subscale as one measure of mood, which you could then correlate with creativity. (In this case, using "multiple correlation and multiple regression" as well as "partial correlation" would be appropriate.)

Of course, these concerns about validity also apply to the Isen et al. (1987) experiments discussed initially. The advantages of your correlational study are that it conceptually replicates their laboratory study while reducing their demand characteristics. And, especially if yours was conducted as a field study, it would add to the external validity and generalizability of the relationship between mood and creativity.

In designing this correlational study, you assumed that performing the Remote Associates Test first might influence participants' subsequent mood scores. As an additional research question, you could actually test whether word pleasantness ratings are changed by the Remote Associates Test.

How would you design this study and create the stimuli?

You could create a pretest-posttest design, with participants performing a word-pleasantness rating test once before the Remote Associates Test and then once after. To prevent participants from merely reproducing earlier ratings, you would create alternate forms, providing two different sets of words to be rated. You would need to demonstrate high test-retest reliability between the two sets and also to counterbalance their use, using each set as the pretest or posttest for one-half of the participants. Then you would examine the difference between the overall (mean) pleasantness ratings before and after the Remote Associates Test.

However, if you merely test a group of people before and after the Remote Associates Test, you will encounter the problems of a one-group pretest-posttest design, having no idea why pleasantness ratings might change between the two testings. After all, you are measuring mood as a state characteristic that, by definition, changes from moment to moment. Therefore, you should also test a control group, measuring their mood twice, with the interval between testing the same as for the experimental group, but without the Remote Associates Test. (This design would be essentially the same as that of the mixed design involving dart throwing that's discussed in Chapter 7.) You would analyze the pleasantness ratings using a 2 × 2 mixed-design ANOVA for the between-subjects factor of experimental-control group and the repeated-measures factor of pre- and posttest. If the interaction is significant, then differences in the pre- and posttest mood scores depend on, and are thus influenced by, whether or not participants perform the intervening Remote Associates Test.

Additional Research Topics

In the research literature, you will find studies that deal with almost every behavior imaginable. What follows are some common and not so common research topics that you can rather easily study.

Belief in Astrology

Astrological horoscopes and personality descriptions contain *Barnum statements* such as "You are generally a happy person, although you sometimes become angry." A person's reactions to such descriptions tells us not only about the popularity of astrology but also about general belief systems. For example, Glick, Gottesman, and Jolton (1989) studied "believers" and "skeptics" to determine how they deal with positive and negative descriptions in horoscopes. They proposed that both types of people would be impressed with the accuracy of positive descriptions (e.g., "You are intelligent"), presumably because such descriptions affirm positive self-perceptions. But they also suggested that only believers in astrology would accept negative descriptions (e.g., "You are indecisive"), because their faith in astrology overrides their self-perceptions. In addition, the researchers tested whether a description not attributed to astrology would be accepted as more accurate, and whether experiencing positive or negative descriptions would alter a person's belief in astrology.

What type of design would you use to study these factors?

Testing any of these factors involves first the quasi-independent variable of conditions of participants who are astrology believers or skeptics. Additional factors then include favorable versus unfavorable personality descriptions, and/or whether or not descriptions are attributed to astrology. The dependent variable would be participants' rating of the accuracy of the descriptions. In their study, Glick et al. (1989) manipulated these factors as between-subjects factors, so that they could also examine the influence of a particular type of experience on a person's attitude toward astrology. They tested this influence with a pretest-posttest design, measuring participants' attitudes toward astrology before and after they participated in the above conditions.

The researchers found that (1) skeptics accept positive personality descriptions as more accurate than negative ones, but believers accept a negative description as being equal in accuracy to a positive one; (2) believers and skeptics alike rated astrological descriptions as more accurate than nonastrological descriptions; and (3) skeptics, more so than believers, became more positive in their feelings toward astrology after receiving favorable horoscopes. Glick et al. proposed that skeptics are more open-minded, so they are more likely to change their opinion about astrology after receiving a positive description. Believers, however, seem to ignore the contradictions from a negative description. This suggests that believers and skeptics differ in terms of how they test these descriptions and evaluate the evidence that supports them.

What suggestions for additional research can you make?

First, it would be interesting to examine how believers and skeptics test astrological predictions. For example, you might present them with a horoscope that is ultimately confirmed or disconfirmed by what "coincidentally" happens later in an experimental setting. Then you could measure how the outcome of a prediction is evaluated by skeptics and believers, and how this evaluation influences their attitudes toward astrology.

Second, when believers are confronted with a negative statement that *disconfirms* their self-perceptions, they continue to maintain their original opinion. The implication is that believers in astrology do not apply the correct logic for testing hypotheses. Recall from Chapter 1 that we discussed using a deck of cards for testing a hypothesis about letters and numbers printed on the cards. Such procedures could be adapted to test for differences in logic and hypothesis testing between skeptics and believers.

Serial-Position Effects

A highly reliable finding in the study of memory is that when people recall a list of words they tend to recall the first few and the last few items in the list best. Because recall changes as a function of an item's serial position in the list, this effect is called the *serial position effect*. Often in these studies, a list consisting of a random string of single digits is spoken, and, for reliability, each participant is tested with a number of lists. To see this effect, we graph the recall scores for the words in a list as a function of where in the list the words occurred. The graph produces a *serial-position curve,* as shown in Figure 11.2. Note that the higher recall of the first items in the list is called the "primacy effect" and the higher recall of the final items is called the "recency effect."

One explanation for the recency effect is that the final few items in a list have most recently entered into memory, so they are in some sense "fresher." Some researchers (e.g., Crowder, 1982) have proposed that these items are better recalled because there is an "echo" in memory of the most recent spoken words. The final word in the list is recalled best because no words come after it that might otherwise interfere with its echo.

How would you test this explanation?

Researchers have tested this proposal by speaking an additional word at the end of the list, called a "stimulus suffix." When the lists consist of digits, the suffix for every list is usually the digit *zero.* Participants are told not to remember the zero; it is merely the signal to recall the list, and they are to otherwise "ignore" it. In control conditions, a tone is the recall signal. Because the tone is so different from the list of words, it should not interfere with the echo of previous words, so the control group should exhibit the typical high recency. Conversely, the zero should reduce the freshness of the final list items and fill the echo, so the experimental group should exhibit reduced recency. In fact, the zero does this, and the lowered recency is called the "suffix effect." (See Turner et al. [1987] for an overview.)

The reason that the suffix disrupts recency is not known. Originally, its effect was thought to be limited to spoken words only. Yet suffix effects have also been

Figure 11.2   Idealized serial position curve

Shown here is participants' recall of 8-item lists as a function of each item's position in the presented list.

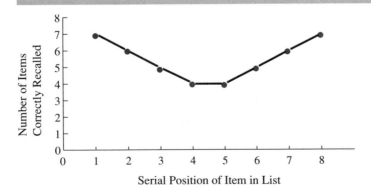

found when the zero is silently mouthed by the experimenter or participants, and among hearing impaired participants when the list and suffix is presented using sign language. In addition, suffix effects have been shown to occur when spoken words in the list have different vowels *(gap, got, gut)* but not when they have different consonants *(gap, tap, map)*. Thus, the suffix effect is not restricted to auditory stimuli, yet it does not always work with auditory stimuli. This inconsistency makes the notion of an "echo" very suspect.

Although there have been many explanations for this effect, one that has received virtually no attention concerns the assumption that participants can in fact "ignore" the zero at the end of the list. But how do they know that the word *zero* is the one to ignore unless they first pay attention to it? You would think that they must first identify this word in order to recognize that it is *not* part of the list to be remembered. A tone, by contrast, may be ignored instantly, because it is so obviously different from the preceding list of words. Thus, we might investigate whether participants can (or do) ignore the zero. If not, is the zero at first treated as part of the list, thereby confusing participants? Or, does a list followed by a zero require greater attention than a list followed by a tone, and does this greater attention cause decreased recall of the list?

How would you study whether participants do ignore the suffix?

You might measure the reaction time of participants to determine whether there are differences in their ability to recognize the end of a list when it is signaled by a tone or zero. If the zero takes longer to recognize, then there is something about it, in terms of the attention it requires, that is different from the control condition. If so, then a confounding has occurred in previous research, because the tone and the zero are not equivalent signals for the end of the list.

Alternatively, you might first identify some words that are easy to recognize and some that are difficult to recognize. Then, using these words in place of the zero, you can see whether they alter the recency effect. Or you might give participants a cue to forewarn them that the zero or tone is about to occur. For example, you might ring a bell just prior to the zero. If reading the list aloud, you could change your tone of voice and inflection, or make a movement, to signal that the zero is about to occur. If such cues eliminate the suffix effect, then you have evidence that the zero normally reduces the recency effect because of the attention it demands or the confusion that it produces.

Attractiveness and Height

Evidence suggests that taller men are typically perceived as more honest, competent, and attractive. Accordingly, Shepard and Strathman (1989) investigated whether women prefer to date taller men and whether they consider taller men more attractive. They also investigated whether men prefer to date shorter women and whether they consider shorter women more attractive.

How would you study the relationship between height
and attraction?

Shepard and Strathman conducted a correlational study, presenting males and
females with a questionnaire that asked for the number and height of their recent
dates as well as for a rating of each date's attractiveness. Participants were also
asked whether they preferred to date a person who was shorter than, taller than,
or the same height as themselves. The researcher's found that females reported
that they dated tall males more frequently than short or medium males. They
also reported a preference for taller men, but they did not rate their taller dates
as more attractive. Interestingly, short and medium-height males reported that
they went out on dates just as often as did tall males. Overall, the males preferred shorter female dates, rated them as more attractive, and dated them more
frequently.

What problem do these self-reports present?

These self-reports may be unreliable for several reasons: (1) Participants might
have inaccurately estimated a date's height, especially after the fact; (2) A date's
personality and compatibility might have influenced participants' perception of
the date's attractiveness; and (3) a "bad" date might have biased participants so
that they remembered their dates as shorter or taller than they actually were. Further, as Shepard and Strathman noted, the females reported fewer dates with
short or medium-height men, but the males, regardless of their height, reported
the same frequency of dates. But, the shorter males were dating *somebody!*
Therefore, the self-reports of either the males or the females must have been in
error.

What suggestions for additional research can you make?

Rather than relying on self-reports about participants' past dating experiences,
Shepard and Strathman (1989) conducted an additional experiment in which
they manipulated height and measured attractiveness. They presented a photograph of the upper bodies of a male and female facing each other. In the photograph, the male was either 5 inches taller, the same height, or 5 inches shorter
than the female. Females rated the man as more attractive when he was taller.
Males, however, did not rate females differently depending on her relative height.
    You might also determine why the females' reports of seldom dating short
men do not correspond to the high frequency of dating reported by short men.
Perhaps the males or females are erroneous in their reports because of pressure to
give the socially desirable response. If so, the number of erroneous reports should
increase when the researcher strongly implies such demand characteristics
through instructions or the task. Also, you might investigate whether the contradictory results occur because of a definitional problem having to do with the
term *taller.* Stereotypically, most people would agree that a man whose height is 7

feet is "tall," and that one who is 5 feet is "short." However, *taller* can be a relative personal term: For a woman whose height is 4 feet 6 inches, a man whose height is 5 feet is "taller." To what extent do males and females use the stereotypic or the personal definition when selecting or describing dates?

There is an ecological issue here as well: Women *are*, on average, shorter than men. The opportunities for dates are greater, then, if women accept taller men and men accept shorter women, so their "preferences" may simply reflect the facts of life. Does the fact that most men are taller than most women lead to a stereotype of the ideal date? As we saw when discussing Horner (1972), people tend to anticipate negative consequences when violating sex-role stereotypes. To what extent do the preceding studies measure stereotyped responses instead of actual attraction? And, finally, is it appropriate to conclude that being taller always makes a male more attractive to a woman? Is there a point at which taller is not better because it becomes "too tall"?

The Influence of Color

Research from environmental psychology suggests that the color of walls, furniture, or floors has an influence on various aspects of behavior. For example, "warm" colors (those close to red) are often believed to be arousing, to increase physical performance, and to improve mood. "Cool" colors (those close to blue) are believed to be soothing, to lower performance, and to have a dulling effect on mood.

How would you design a study to test these beliefs?

One obvious way to manipulate the color in the environment is to test people in different rooms that are painted a different color. In each room, you can have participants perform a physical task or provide responses that indicate their mood. For example, Kwallek, Lewis, and Robbins (1988) asked people to type business forms for 20 minutes after placing them in either a red or blue "office," and then had them complete a questionnaire describing their anxiety, mood, and general arousal. After resting in another room, participants either returned to the same colored office or were switched to the different colored office and then, regardless, performed additional typing and completed another questionnaire. Those who were moved to a different colored office made significantly more typing errors. And the interaction showed that more errors occurred when participants moved from the blue to the red office than when they moved from the red to the blue. The mood data indicated that people remaining in the red office showed greater anxiety and stress, those remaining in the blue office showed greater depression, and those who were moved to different colored offices showed the greatest level of general arousal.

Because moving participants into a different colored room influences their behavior, a problem with this study is that initially placing them in the first office after they've entered the study from someplace else constitutes changing rooms in an uncontrolled manner. As an alternative approach, you might include a control condition that allows you to "reverse" the influence of any previous colored room.

How would you design this study?

Hamid and Newport (1989) studied how the color of a room influences behavior using an ABACAB reversal design. The control or baseline—condition A—was a gray room that presumably neutralized the influence of other colors. A pink room was condition B, and a blue room was condition C. The researchers measured hand-strength and mood in six young children after they had experienced each colored room. Greater physical strength and more positive mood was found in the pink conditions.

What suggestions for additional research can you make?

If there is an influence of color on arousal and performance, then it might extend to colored objects and situations. Would similar effects on typing errors occur depending on the color of the paper in a typewriter or the color of a computer display screen? In the previous chapter we saw the influence of black uniforms on aggression, but the present research suggests that other colors of clothing might also affect behavior. Certainly the idea behind "dressing for success" is that a person's clothing style influences how that person is perceived and judged by supervisors and co-workers (e.g., Forsythe, 1990). Does wearing reddish or bluish clothes also influence perceptions? Also, in this chapter we discussed how participants misattribute their arousal from fear as being due to sexual attraction. Is it possible that arousal from wall color or the color of clothing could be misattributed as sexual attraction? As an applied topic, the colors in business environments might be important for maximizing worker productivity and maximum arousal is sought in athletic events. Does wall color influence a salespersons' or a weight-trainer's success? And, finally, do certain colors play a role when we become overaroused, as discussed below?

Self-Consciousness and "Choking under Pressure"

An unusual behavior to study is the phenomenon of "choking under pressure." Baumeister (1984) proposed that inferior performance ("choking") occurs when we feel so pressured to perform well that we focus too much attention on the process of performing a task and not enough attention on the outcome of the task. Thus, in a self-fulfilling prophecy, the more we worry that things are going badly, the worse they go. Baumeister also proposed that personality characteristics play a role, such that, for example, a person who is more self-conscious should exhibit greater "choking."

How would you design a study to test these proposals?

In an experimental setting, you could create a task for participants in which you manipulate the amount of pressure they feel. The task should be a simple one in which errors are easily measured. For example, you can have people quickly trace a pencil maze, solve simple math problems, or perform a reaction-time task in which they press one of several buttons to make a correct response. Consider Heaton and Sigall (1991), who first classified participants along the quasi-independent variable of high or low self-consciousness. For experimental realism, they had participants in each condition form a "team." Then they manipulated the pressure situation through the additional factors of (1) indicating that the participant's team was behind or ahead, and (2) having participants perform when alone, when watched by their team, or when watched by the opposing team. Choking was measured by the time it took each person to place variously shaped pegs in their corresponding holes. Participants who were low in self-consciousness choked depending on the audience characteristics, while those high in self-consciousness choked when their team was behind.

What suggestions for additional research can you make?

Apparently, people differing in self-consciousness perceive the source of pressure differently. The results for those with high self-consciousness suggest that they choked because of competitive pressure, so you might manipulate the situation for them in terms of the amount of competition involved. The results for those with low self-consciousness suggest that they choked because of their need for social approval, so for them you might manipulate the social setting. Also consider the possibility of replicating this relationship between choking and pressure in a field setting: Perhaps a "stranger" could watch someone playing a game in a video arcade. You might also extend this research to other personality traits, such as looking at whether being task or socially oriented, plays a role in choking. Thus, for example, you might correlate participants' scores on these traits with how much they choke or, as above, examine how these traits interact with different conditions that promote choking. Alternatively, given that high pressure is a form of arousal, you might ask whether the color of the room in which someone is tested influences choking. Finally, you might ask whether a "lucky charm," such as a lucky shirt, is considered lucky because a person did *not* choke when wearing it. (And what color is it?)

Putting It All Together

At this point, you *have* put it all together. By now you understand the basic logic of the studies we've discussed, so you understand psychological research. Congratulations on mastering a complicated topic. If you still feel that you cannot evaluate and conduct the sophisticated research found in the psychological literature, remember that you are at a temporary disadvantage. The major difference between beginning student researchers and professional-level researchers is their knowledge of the psychological issues involved in any topic. You're probably not all that familiar with the existing theory and research on a particular behavior. If you read the literature, however, you'll learn the details of how a construct is conceptualized, along with the commonly used, successful methods of studying it. By filling in these gaps in your knowledge, you'll discover not only that you *can* evaluate and conduct real research but also that it's really a lot of fun.

Reporting Research Using APA Format

GETTING STARTED

To understand this appendix, recall the following:

■ From Chapter 1, recall that a research hypothesis must be testable, falsifiable, rational, and parsimonious.

■ From Chapter 2, recall that research begins with broad constructs, is "whittled down" to precise operational definitions, and then is generalized back to the broad constructs.

■ From Chapter 3, recall the requirements for designing the independent and dependent variable in an experiment.

■ From Chapter 6, recall the uses and interpretation of the mean score in each condition, how to graph an experiment's results, and recall the independent samples *t*-test.

Your goals in this appendix are to learn:

■ The basic components of the psychological literature and how to search it.

■ How to organize the needed information when reporting a study.

■ The parts of an APA-style report and the purpose of each.

■ What information should and should not be reported in a research report.

■ The style and tone that a research report should have.

Recall that science is a community activity in which we try to correct one another's errors by skeptically evaluating each study. Also recall that scientific facts are ultimately built through replication of findings. To allow critical evaluation and to build evidence for a hypothesis through replication, researchers share the results of their studies by publishing them and thus contributing to the *research literature*. This appendix discusses the literature and describes how a research article is created. By knowing the process an author uses in writing an article, you can read the literature more effectively. Also, as a psychology student, you'll probably be reporting your own study sooner or later.

In the following sections, we'll first design an experiment and then see what goes into a manuscript for reporting it in the literature. The final section shows how to create an APA-style research report of the study. Be forewarned that the study here is very simple and does not incorporate all of the design or statistical issues discussed in this book. The idea is to show you the basics. Even though your particular study might be more elaborate, you create a report following the same logic and format.

An Example Study

Let's say that in a cognitive psychology course, you read the study by Bower, Karlin, and Dueck (1975). They studied short-term memory by presenting participants with 28 simple cartoons called "droodles." Each droodle is a meaningless geometric shape, but a particular droodle will instantly become meaningful when an accompanying verbal interpretation is provided. Two examples of droodles are provided in Figure A.1. Some participants were told that droodle A shows a

Figure A.1   Examples of "droodles"

These droodles were accompanied by the following interpretations: (a) "A midget playing a trombone in a telephone booth" and (b) "An early bird that caught a very strong worm."

From G.H. Bower, M.B. Karlin, and A. Dueck (1975), Comprehension and memory for pictures, *Memory and Cognition*, 3(2), 216–222. Reprinted by permission of the Psychonomic Society, Inc. and the author.

"midget playing a trombone in a telephone booth" and that droodle B shows "an early bird that caught a very strong worm." Other participants were not given any interpretation. Bower et al. found that those participants who had been given an interpretation for all droodles could recall (sketch) more of the droodles than those who had not. The authors concluded that the interpretations made the droodles more meaningful, allowing participants to integrate the droodles with their knowledge in memory. Then when participants tried to recall the droodles, this knowledge provided useful "retrieval cues."

However, notice that the accompanying interpretations not only make the droodles meaningful but do so in a humorous way. By using interpretations that are both humorous and meaningful, the droodle study may have been confounded: On the one hand, the interpretations might make the droodles meaningful and thus more memorable, as the authors suggested. On the other hand, the interpretations might make the droodles humorous, and their humor made the droodles more memorable. This second idea leads to a rival hypothesis: When the contexts in which stimuli occur differ in humor, differences in memory for the stimuli are produced. Say that we decide to test this hypothesis.

The hypothesis suggests that greater humor *causes* improved memory, so a well-controlled, internally valid laboratory experiment is in order. In fact, the design of Bower et al. seems appropriate. They compared the effects of an interpretation versus the absence of an interpretation on memory for the droodles. We can investigate our hypothesis by presenting participants with humorous and nonhumorous interpretations. The prediction is that droodles with humorous interpretations will be better recalled.

Before proceeding, we need to be sure the study is rational, ethical, and practical. Rationally speaking, the idea that humor acts as a cue for recalling information seems to fit known memory processes (but we'll check), and understanding memory is a worthwhile psychological study. Ethically, asking participants to remember droodles doesn't appear to cause any harm (but we'll check). And practically speaking, such a study seems doable and does not require inordinate time, expense, or hard-to-find participants or equipment.

As we begin creating the design for the study, we realize that we don't know very much about this topic, so—to the literature!

The Research Literature

Previous research is the ultimate source for learning about a particular psychological topic. Published research provides background in the issues that pertain to your research question so that your hypothesis fits with existing constructs and with the results of previous studies. The literature also suggests numerous ideas for interesting studies and describes established procedures that you can incorporate into your design.

Recall that defining the target population early in the design process helps to develop a more precise hypothesis as well as directing your attention to the most relevant portions of the literature. The Bower et al. experiment studied memory in normal adults. Therefore, we need to find past research on adults regarding (1) how the constructs of "humor" and "meaningfulness" are defined and how they are thought to influence "memory," (2) whether humorous stimuli are better retained than nonhumorous stimuli, and (3) whether other studies using the Bower et al. design have identified flaws in it, have replicated it, or (heaven forbid) have already tested the effects of humorous and nonhumorous interpretations as we will do.

What Constitutes the Research Literature?

The term **research literature** does not mean books or newspapers found in the supermarket or popular magazines such as *Time* or *Psychology Today*. At best, these contain synopses of research articles that most likely omit necessary details. Therefore, go to professional books and psychological journals. Books provide useful background, but because of the time required to create them, even new books can be a few years behind the latest developments. Therefore, focus on journals for the most current developments in a research topic, because they are published once or more a year.

Not all professional journals, however, are of the same quality. In some, the primary requirement for publishing an article is that the author(s) pay the publication costs. These journals have less stringent requirements for quality research. Other journals are "refereed," meaning that each article undergoes "peer review" by several psychologists who are knowledgeable about the topic being studied (as described in the section on scientific fraud in Chapter 4.) To gauge the quality of a journal, check the section that describes its editorial policies. Also, look for journals published by professional organizations of psychologists such as the American Psychological Association, the American Psychological Society, or the Psychonomic Society. One function of these organizations is to disseminate quality research. However, although such journals tend to report convincing research, you still should approach each study with a critical eye.

Searching the Literature

To search the literature, begin with some topic in mind. Most journals are organized around a subarea of psychology (e.g., social, cognitive, abnormal) identified by the journal's title (e.g., *Cognitive Psychology* or the *Journal of Personality and Social Psychology*). By perusing such journals, you may come across articles that you wish to read. If you have a specific research idea, however, you can consult reference sources that search the literature in an organized manner. Remember that, eventually, the goal of any study is to explain "psychologically" the results and behaviors observed in the study. Therefore, this should be your focus when searching the literature. You start by trying to find *all* published research that *might* relate to your topic (and then whittle it down to those that actually do).

Psychological Abstracts   *Psychological Abstracts* is a monthly publication that describes studies recently published in other psychology journals. Its index is organized using the variables and hypothetical constructs commonly studied by psychologists. When using this index, try to be specific, selecting terms you think would be used in the titles of relevant articles. For the droodle study, we would look in recent issues under such terms as humor, meaningfulness, and short-term memory. *Psychological Abstracts* provides a separate author index, so we would also look up the authors of the original droodle study to see if they have reported other similar research. For each article listed, an "abstract"—a brief synopsis—of the study is presented. By reading the abstract, you can determine whether to read the entire article.

Computerized Literature Searches   Many college libraries provide a user-friendly computer program that searches the literature for you. These programs contain a large database covering years of research literature. You simply enter the names of your constructs and variables, and then the computer provides abstracts and the references for studies filed under those terms. The computer will call up many unrelated references for a general term, so cross-reference your terms to ensure a more selective search. For example, merely entering "memory" as a search term will produce hundreds of irrelevant studies. But entering "memory and humor" will call up references more directly related to our study.

Bibliographies of Research Articles   When you find an article on a topic of interest, notice that its bibliography contains references to related studies. By reading the published articles that it cites, and then reading the references in those articles, you can work backward in time and learn about research that came *before* the original study. Sometimes you will also see references to psychological conventions and meetings at which researchers orally presented their research. For a copy of a particular presentation, contact the first author cited in the reference. (For assistance, the American Psychological Association provides a directory of its members' addresses.)

Social Science Citation Index   When you are interested in an article that is several years old, you can search for more recent articles that came *after* the orginal study by using the *Social Science Citation Index*. This publication identifies a research article by authors and date, and then lists other articles published in a given year that have cited it. Thus, for example, we could look up the original 1975 droodle study in the index for 1996, 1997, and so on, to perhaps find more recent related articles.

Review Articles   A review article surveys and summarizes a large body of theoretical and empirical literature dealing with a particular topic. Such articles provide a useful overview as well as references to many specific studies. The title of a review article usually contains the word *review* and some books and journals, such as *Psychological Bulletin* and *Annual Review of Psychology,* specialize in review articles.

References on Testing Materials   Often your design will use a paper-and-pencil test to measure intelligence, personality, creativity, attitudes, emotions, motivations, and so on. Instead of creating your own test and being uncertain of its reliability or its content and construct validity, look for acceptable tests that already exist. To find them, consult reference books that describe common psychological tests. Such books usually have titles indicating that they describe tests (such as *The Mental Measurements Yearbook* or *Measures of Personality and Social Psychological Attitudes*).

You can also use a computerized literature search to find research articles that have employed such tests. To be efficient, cross-reference the name of the attribute to be measured with the term *assessment*. For example, if in a different study you wish to measure depression, using the terms *depression* and *assessment* will limit your search to studies that involve the measurement of depression.

Completing the Droodle Study

The literature provides no studies that cause us to question the original Bower et al. (1975) procedure of presenting droodles as to-be-remembered stimuli. There are no ethical or practical concerns, and because this procedure produced informative and powerful results (they were significant), we can adopt it for our study. In fact, it's desirable to reuse the procedure from previous studies, because then you replicate their findings and you can more directly integrate your results with the literature.

The literature contains many studies that replicate the finding that, for a variety of stimuli, the more meaningful a stimulus is, the better it is retained. For example, when learning a list of words, participants who use each word in a sentence will recall the words better than if they merely think of a rhyme for each word (see Lockhart & Craik, 1990).

Surprisingly, my literature search turned up little research that directly studied how and why humor improves memory (but see MacAninch, Austin & Derks, 1992, and Dixon, Willingham, Strano & Chandler, 1989). Numerous studies, however, show that more *distinctive* stimuli are better retained than less distinctive stimuli (e.g., Schmidt, 1985). For example, in a list of words, a word printed in a different style of print is retained better than other words that are visually similar (Hunt & Elliott, 1980).

The literature will not always address an issue from exactly your perspective, so often you must generalize from previous findings and constructs to fit them to your hypothesis. Thus, in suggesting that humor influences memory, we can propose that a humorous interpretation makes a droodle more distinctive in memory, thereby making it more memorable. Essentially, then, we propose that humor is one component of the construct of distinctiveness—one way to make a stimulus distinctive.

Although the meaningfulness of a stimulus might seem to be the same thing as its distinctiveness, researchers do distinguish between the two concepts. Desrochers and Begg (1987), for example, suggest that distinctiveness is the extent to which unique cues are associated with the particular context in which the stimulus was encountered. Essentially, a distinctive event is notable and thus stands out in memory. Therefore, greater distinctiveness enhances access to the stimulus, allowing us to "find" it in memory. Meaningfulness, on the other hand, is the extent to which the components of the stimulus are organized and integrated. A meaningful event is tied together such that we know all of its "parts." Therefore, once we access a memory of a stimulus, greater meaningfulness enhances recall of the components of the stimulus (see also Einstein, McDaniel & Lackey, 1989).

Although the preceding discussion greatly simplifies the debate about the constructs of distinctiveness and meaningfulness, for our study it boils down to this: On the one hand, the importance of the interpretations in the original droodle study may be that they were humorous, and thus made the droodles more distinctive and in turn more memorable. On the other hand, the importance of the interpretations may have nothing to do with the humor involved. Perhaps they simply made the droodles more meaningful and thus more memorable. Our task is to design a study that clearly shows the influence of humor, separate from the influence of meaningfulness.

By discussing the constructs of memory, humor, and meaningfulness in terms of droodles and their interpretations, we have begun to create operational definitions of them. Now we "whittle down" these constructs, completing the design by defining the specific variables and procedures.

Defining the Variables   Our independent variable involves changing the amount of humor attributed to the droodles by the interpretations. The challenge, however, is to manipulate the amount of humor while producing equally meaningful interpretations. If the droodles are not always made equally meaningful, humor and meaningfulness will be confounded. Then we will be unable to tell whether more humor or more meaningfulness improves retention of a droodle.

What seems to make an interpretation in Bower et al. humorous is that it provides an unusual explanation involving unexpected objects, people, or animals. So if we revise the original interpretations to provide common explanations involving *predictable* objects, people, and animals, they should be less humorous (and less distinctive) but just as meaningful as the originals. For example, from the humorous interpretation "This is a midget playing a trombone in a telephone booth" we can derive the less humorous interpretation "This is a telephone booth with a technician inside, repairing the broken door handle." In both cases the droodle features a telephone booth, so if a telephone booth is particularly meaningful and memorable, it is equally so in both the humorous and nonhumorous conditions. Also, both interpretations involve the meaningful integration of a person, a telephone booth, and an object (either a trombone or a door handle).

Thus, we will have two conditions of the independent variable: In one we provide participants with nonhumorous interpretations, and in the other we provide the corresponding humorous interpretations. If humor is an attribute that aids memory, then the humorous interpretations should produce better recall of the droodles. If humor is not psychologically important in this way, then there should be no difference in retention between the two conditions.

Now, consider all of the details involved in devising a reliable and valid study. First, if there is only one droodle per condition, participants might forget or remember it because of some hidden peculiarity in it. Instead, the original Bower et al. study presented 28 droodles per condition, and we'll use the same number of droodles. The easiest way to obtain the droodles is to use the ones from Bower et al. (To borrow stimuli not fully presented in an article, you can write to the first author of the article.) If instead we decided to create stimuli, then we must control extraneous variables so that all stimuli are comparable. Thus, we would specify rules for creating stimuli so that they all have equal complexity and memorability: All are of equal size, all are drawn in black ink, all contain only two basic geometric shapes, and so on. Although Bower et al. handed each drawing of a droodle to participants, for better control we can present the droodles using a slide projector with an electronic timer or have participants sit at a computer-controlled video monitor.

Also for consistency, all interpretations will contain roughly the same number and type of words, and all will begin with the phrase "This is a . . . " As in the original study, we will test participants one at a time, reading them the interpretation as they first view a droodle. We'll read all interpretations at the same speed and volume, with the same tone of voice and expressiveness. (To further ensure consistency, we might record the interpretations and time the playback to occur when participants view each droodle.) Likewise, the humorous interpretations should all be consistently humorous for a wide range of participants; the nonhumorous interpretations should be consistently nonhumorous; and, as a group, the humorous interpretations should be consistently more humorous than the nonhumorous interpretations.

The dependent variable is recall of the droodles, but we must also decide how to define and measure it. As in Bower et al. (1975), the participants will study each droodle for 10 seconds, so that everyone has the same amount of study time and the same retention period. Immediately after all droodles have been presented, participants will sketch all droodles on sheets of paper containing several, approximately 3-by-3-inch, squares. They will place each droodle in a square, so that we can tell what shapes a participant believes go together to form one droodle.

Completing the Design   We—the researchers—could score the sketches as correct or incorrect ourselves, but our judgment might not be reliable. Instead, therefore, we'll enlist two other people as scorers who are "blind" to the purposes of the study. A response is correct if both scorers agree that it matches an original droodle.

We must also create clear and precise instructions for participants so that they know exactly what to do at each step, and so that we can control their extraneous behaviors. The instructions should be, to the extent possible, worded identically for all conditions, consistently read or recorded, of the same duration, and so on. Further, the researcher must attempt to behave identically when testing all participants, and the environment must be constant for them all.

We must also decide on the specific participants to be examined. Variables such as age, gender, and cultural background might influence what people consider humorous, and we want them all to see the droodles clearly and to understand the interpretations that accompany them. To keep such variables constant, we will randomly select as participants Introductory Psychology students who are similar in age and background, with good eyesight, hearing, and English abilities. To avoid practice effects from showing the same people the same droodles in both conditions, we'll test a separate, independent sample of participants in each condition, and we'll balance gender. To have a powerful *N,* we'll test 40 people per condition, selecting 20 males and 20 females for each.

Finally, we must plan out the statistical analysis. Each person's score will be the number of correctly recalled droodles. These are ratio scores that meet the requirements of parametric statistics, so the inferential statistical procedure we'll use is the independent samples *t*-test. Because we predict that humor will improve recall scores, we have a one-tailed test. (Instead, we could perform the one-way between-subjects ANOVA on the factor of humorous/nonhumorous interpretations.)

Although there are other designs we might create, let's assume we conducted the above study and found that the average number of droodles recalled was 15.2 with nonhumorous interpretations and 20.5 with humorous interpretations. The *t*-test indicated a significant difference, so this is a "believable" relationship. Now we'll interpret the results psychologically, first inferring that humor does influence recall and then working back to the broader hypothetical constructs of how humor and distinctiveness operate on memory.

To share the results with other researchers, we'll prepare a written report of the study following APA format.

Organization of a Research Article

Most psychological research articles follow the rules set down in the **Publication Manual of the American Psychological Association** (1994). Now in its fourth edition, this is the reference source for answering *any* question regarding the organization, content, and style of a research report. Although APA format may at first appear to be a very rigid, arbitrary set of rules, it is necessary. This format minimizes publishing costs by defining precisely the space and effort that a publication requires. It also specifies the information that any report should contain, how the information should be organized, and how it should be reported. Note that the rules here are based on you preparing a manuscript that is ready for delivery to a typesetter, who then prepares it for print. Your job is to follow the prescribed format, *not* to produce the final report or to have it look pretty.

However, especially for beginning researchers, APA format is also a very useful organizational scheme. As a reader, you'll learn where to look in an article to find certain information and how to understand the shorthand codes used to present it. As an author, you'll see how to organize your paper, what to say, and how to say it. And as a researcher, you'll develop a framework for remembering the many design aspects of a study that must be considered. Asking yourself the question "What will I say in each section of a report of this study?" is a cue for remembering the issues that you must deal with.

The sections of an article describe the various aspects of a study in the order in which they logically occur. In Chapter 2 you saw that the flow of a study can be depicted using the diagram in Figure A.2. It shows how, in conducting a study, you work from the general to the specific and then back to the general. Likewise, an APA-style report is organized following these same steps, with four major sections:

- The *Introduction* presents the hypothetical constructs as they are used in past research, develops the hypothesized relationship between the variables for the target population, and provides the specific predictions of the study.
- The *Method* section describes the specifics of the design and how the data were collected.

Figure A.2   The parallels between research activity and APA format

The flow of a research study is from a general hypothesis to the specifics of the study, and then back to the general hypothesis. The APA format also follows this pattern.

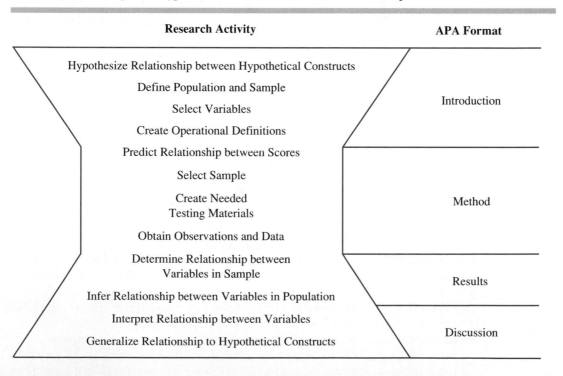

- The *Results* section reports the descriptive and inferential statistics performed and describes the statistical relationship found.
- The *Discussion* section interprets the results first in terms of the variables and then generalizes to the broader relationship between the hypothetical constructs with which we began.

REMEMBER The organization of a research report follows the logical order of the steps performed in conducting the research.

The ultimate goal of APA format is precision in communication. At the same time, you need to conserve space and avoid overstatements or redundancy. Thus, strive to state each idea clearly, to say it once, and to report only the necessary information. To meet the goal of precise yet concise communication, both the author and the reader make certain implicit assumptions.

The Assumptions of the Author and Reader

The reader assumes that the author understands statistics and research methods, that the author has described any unusual or unexpected events, and that he or she is a reasonable, ethical, and competent researcher. Many things are left unsaid in a research article, because the reader can assume that commonly accepted procedures were used and that the details of the procedures are unimportant. Thus, for example, you need not state "I compared the obtained statistic to the critical value" because all researchers know this must be done. Stating it would be redundant.

Likewise, an author assumes that the reader is a competent psychologist. Therefore, a report does not give readers a detailed background of the topic under study, because the assumption is that they already know something about it, or that they will read the references provided. The author also assumes that the reader understands statistics and research methods. *Do not teach statistics and design principles to the reader.* Do not say "Reliable data were important because . . ." or "A *t*-test was performed because . . . " The reader should already know why reliability is important and why a *t*-test is performed. Finally, always use common terminology (such as reliable, valid, confounding) but without providing definitions. The author assumes that the reader either understands such terms or will find out what they mean.

As the author, you should focus on providing readers with the information they cannot get elsewhere: *your thoughts and actions as a researcher.* What conclusions did *you* draw from a previous article? What do *you* mean when using a particular hypothetical construct? What logic did *you* use in deriving a hypothesis or prediction? And what do *you* think a result indicates about the behavior under study? As the author, you are the expert, so give the reader the benefit of your wisdom. Your job is to describe clearly and concisely all of the important mental and physical activities you performed in creating, conducting, and interpreting the study. The goal is to provide readers the information necessary to (1) understand the study, (2) evaluate the study, and (3) perform a literal replication of the study.

REMEMBER   A good report allows the study to be fully understood, scientifically evaluated, and literally replicated.

Some Rules of Style

There are many specific rules for preparing a research article, so refer to the *Publication Manual* for complete instructions. What follows are some general rules for preparing a research article that conforms to APA style:

1. A report describes a completed study, so it is written in the past tense ("I predicted that . . ."). The exception is to state in the present tense any conclusions that apply to present or future situations ("Humor influences recall by . . .").
2. Cite all sources from which you obtained information, using only the last names of the author(s) and the date. You may use the reference as the subject of a sentence: "Smith and Jones (1992) defined distinctiveness as . . ." Or you may state an idea and provide the reference in parentheses: "Distinctiveness is defined as . . . (Smith & Jones, 1992)." (In a parenthetical citation, "&" is used instead of "and.") When citing an article with three to six authors, include all names the first time you cite it. Thereafter, refer to it using only the first author and the Latin phrase *et al.* Thus, first we say "Bower, Karlin, and Dueck (1975)," but subsequently we say "Bower et al. (1975)." When citing an article with more than six authors, even the first time you cite it use only the first author and *et al.*
3. Refrain from directly quoting an article. Instead, paraphrase and summarize the idea, so that *you* tell the readers what they should understand about the idea. Also, address a study itself, not its authors. For example, the phrase "Bower et al." refers primarily to a reported experiment, not to the people who conducted it. Thus, we write "The results are reported *in* Bower et al. (1975)" instead of "The results are reported *by* Bower et al. (1975)."
4. To distinguish your study from other studies, refer to it as "this study" or "the present study." However, do not use these phrases in a way that attributes human actions to nonhuman sources, as in "This study attempted to demonstrate that . . ." Instead use "I" as the subject of these verbs. (Use "we" *only* if you have a co-author.)
5. Use accepted psychological terminology as much as possible. When you use a nonstandard term or you name a variable, define the word the first time you use it and then use that word consistently. In the droodle study, we'll define *humorous* and use only this term, rather than mixing in terms such as *funny* or *entertaining*. This prevents confusion about whether we mean something slightly different by *funny* or *entertaining*. In addition, avoid using contractions or slang terms. A reader from a different part of the country or another country may not understand such terms.

6. Avoid abbreviations. They are justified only if (a) a term consists of several words, (b) it appears *very* frequently throughout the report, and (c) you are not using many different abbreviations. If you must abbreviate, do so by creating an acronym, using the first letter of each word of the term. Define the complete term the first time it is used, with its acronym in parentheses. Thus, you might say "Short-term Memory (STM) is . . . ." Then use *only* the acronym, *except* as the first word of a sentence: There, always use the complete term.

7. Use words when describing numbers between zero and nine, and digits for numbers that are 10 and larger. However, use digits for any size number if (a) you are writing a series of numbers in which at least one is 10 or larger, or (b) the number contains a decimal or refers to a statistical result or to a precise measurement (such as a specific score or the number of participants). Thus, you would say "The three conditions, with 5 individuals per condition . . . ." Also, never begin a sentence with a number expressed in digits.

8. In research published before 1994, you'll see the generic term *subjects* refers to the individuals that researchers study. A post-1994 change in APA style now requires the use of less impersonal and more precise terms. The generic term to use is *participants,* but where appropriate use more descriptive terms such as students, children, men, women, rats, and so on. In addition, APA rules stress that you avoid gender-biased language. Thus, refer to the gender of participants using the equivalent terms *male* and *female* and to individuals as *he* or *she*. When possible, use neutral terms such as *chairperson*.

9. Finally, use precise wording. In the droodle study, we won't say that participants "saw" or "looked at" a droodle, or that they "forgot" a droodle, because we don't *know* that these events occurred. We know only that participants were presented a droodle or failed to recall it.

The Components of an APA-Style Research Article

These are the components of an APA-style manuscript in the order in which they occur:

> Title page
> Abstract page
> Introduction
> Methods
>> Participants
>> Materials or Apparatus
>> Procedure
> Results
> Discussion
> References
> Tables and Figures

All parts are typed double-spaced, and without "justifying" the righthand margin. The following sections examine each component in detail, using examples from a manuscript of the droodle study. (The complete manuscript is presented in Appendix B.) Throughout this discussion, compare the previous steps we went through when designing the study—and all that was said—to what is actually reported. Translating and summarizing your thoughts and activities are the keys to creating a research report.

The Title

A **title** allows readers to determine whether they want to read the article. It should clearly communicate the variables and relationship being studied, but it should consist of no more than 12 words. Titles often contain the phrase "as a function of." For example, "Helping Behavior as a Function of Self-Esteem" indicates that the researcher examined the relationship between participants' helping behavior and different amounts of their self-esteem. A title such as "Decreased Errors in Depth Perception as a Function of Increased Illumination Levels" provides the added information that the observed relationship is negative, such that greater illumination is associated with fewer errors. Because illumination level can be manipulated easily, this title probably describes an experiment in which "illumination level" was the independent variable and "errors" was the dependent variable.

Titles also often begin with the phrase "Effect of," as in "Effect of Alcohol Consumption on Use of Sexist Language." The word *effect* means "influence." Such a title is a causal statement, implying that an experiment was conducted and that changes in the independent variable (amount of alcohol consumed) caused a change in the dependent variable (amount of sexist language used by participants). Note the difference between effect (usually a noun) and affect (usually a verb). If *X affects Y,* then there is an *effect* of X on Y. (Here's a trick for remembering this distinction: *Effect* means *end result,* and both begin with *e.* *Affect* means *alter,* and both begin with *a.*)

The title you create should provide sufficient information for readers to determine whether the article is relevant to their literature search. Choose terms that are specific, and never use abbreviations or terms that need to be defined. Thus, for our study, we won't include "droodles" because most people won't know what they are. Instead, we might use the title "Effect of Humorous Interpretations on Immediate Recall of Nonsense Figures." This wording identifies the variables, specifying that we are studying short-term memory of drawings. Contrast this with such terrible titles as: "A Study of Humor and Memory" (of course it's a study!), or "When Does Memory Work Better?" (what does "work" mean?). Either of these would be useless for determining whether the article is relevant to a specific research topic.

In an APA-style manuscript, the title page is a separate page containing the title, your name, and the formal title of your college or university. A sample title page appears in Figure A.3 on the next page. The title page is page number 1, with the number placed in the upper right corner of the page, as it is on *all* other pages. (The minimum margin all around is 1 inch).

Figure A.3   Sample title page of a research manuscript

Notice the location and spacing of the various components.

```
                                                Effect of Humorous     1
            Running head: EFFECT OF HUMOROUS INTERPRETATIONS ON RECALL




                              Effect of Humorous Interpretations on
                              Immediate Recall of Nonsense Figures
                                       Gary W. Heiman
                                      Podunk University
```

The title page also contains two other components. First, left of the page number is typed the **manuscript page header,** consisting of the first two or three words from *your* title. The header appears on all subsequent pages, so if any pages become separated, the publisher can identify them as belonging to your manuscript. (This is another reason for all researchers not to use titles beginning "A Study of.") Second, on the first line below the header is typed the words **Running head:** followed by an abbreviated title. This running head will be printed at the top of each page in the published article. (On this page of your textbook, the running head is "Reporting Research Using APA Format.")

The Abstract

The title page is followed by the **abstract,** which is a brief summary of the study. The abstract describes the specific variables used, important participant characteristics, a brief description of the overall design, and the key relationship obtained. It also indicates the theoretical approach taken in interpreting the results, though often without giving the actual interpretation.

Although the abstract accompanies the article, it is also reproduced in *Psychological Abstracts,* so it must be able to stand alone, containing no abbreviations or uncommon terms (no "droodles"). It should include only details that answer the reader's question: "Is this article relevant to my literature search?" Most authors write the abstract after they have written the report, so they can summarize the key points more easily. If you find it difficult to compress a lengthy paper into 100 to 120 words, think of the abstract as an elaboration of the title. Given the title, what else would you say to communicate the gist of the article? The abstract for the droodle study appears in Figure A.4.

REMEMBER The *title* describes the relationship under investigation. The *abstract* summarizes the report. Together, they allow readers to determine whether the article is relevant to their literature search.

The Introduction

The **Introduction** should reproduce the logic you used to derive your hypothesis and to design the study to test it. It is the Introduction that shows the "whittling down" process, beginning with broad descriptions of behaviors and hypothetical constructs and translating them into the specific variables of a study. It then describes the predicted relationship between scores that will be measured using the operational definitions.

Researchers read an introduction with two goals in mind. First, a reader wants to understand the logic of the study. Thus, the author should introduce the hypothesis and the psychological explanations being tested, the general design (e.g., whether correlational or experimental), the reasons that certain operational definitions are used, and why a particular result will support the predictions and

Figure A.4 Sample abstract page

The abstract page is page number 2, with a centered heading reading "Abstract." The abstract itself is one paragraph long. Note that the first line is not indented.

```
                                              Effect of Humorous     2


                               Abstract
          The effect of humor on the immediate recall of simple visual
          stimuli was investigated. Eighty college students (20 men and 20
          women per condition) viewed 28 nonsensical line drawings that
          were each accompanied by either a humorous or nonhumorous verbal
          interpretation. Although the interpretations were comparable in
          the meaningfulness they conveyed, those participants presented
          with humorous interpretations correctly recalled significantly
          more drawings than those presented nonhumorous interpretations.
          The results suggest that a meaningful and humorous context
          provides additional retrieval cues beyond those cues provided by
          a meaningful yet nonhumorous context. The effect of the cues
          produced by humor is interpreted as creating a more distinctive
          and thus more accessible memory trace.
```

hypothesis of the study. Both the purpose of the study and the population under study should be clear. (Unless specified, we assume that the relationship being studied applies to the broadest population.) Readers also evaluate the hypothesis of the study and its logic. Are the explanations circular pseudo-explanations? Are there rival hypotheses and extraneous variables to be considered?

Second, a reader looks for empirical evidence that supports the hypothesis. The Introduction is where virtually all references to past research occur, including those studies that do and do not support the hypothesis. Further, if the study is successful, the author will attempt to interpret and explain the findings "psychologically," so the Introduction also contains the conceptual and theoretical issues to be discussed later in the paper.

The reader assumes that, unless otherwise noted, a study cited in support of a hypothesis is reasonably convincing. Previous studies are reported very briefly, usually with the author merely citing them by name (rather than explaining them in detail) to indicate that they provide support. If discussed at all, previous studies are described in terms of the specific information the author judged to be important when deriving his or her hypotheses. The details of a study are provided only when (1) they are necessary for the reader to understand the author's comments about that study, or (2) they are necessary for showing support for the author's position. Therefore, the Introduction does not usually contain such details as the number of participants, the statistics used, or the specifics of the design used in the studies cited. (If readers want that kind of detail, they should go read the studies themselves.)

A portion of the Introduction for the droodle study appears in Figure A.5. Although you know how the study turns out, the Introduction is written as if you do not, describing the process you went through *before* collecting the data.

In the droodle study, the Introduction begins within the larger context of the hypothetical constructs of meaningfulness and its influence on memory. Then we work logically from the broad ideas to the specific example of the droodle study. We immediately focus, however, on the perspective taken to study the hypothetical constructs. We orient the reader, providing the major relevant conclusions from past research and their references. We also identify when we are merely speculating. The purpose of the study is stated *early* in the Introduction—in this case, at the end of the first paragraph. In subsequent paragraphs, we further retrace our logic, defining what we mean by the constructs of meaningfulness and distinctiveness and explaining how humor might influence memory. Then we describe how we define and manipulate humor while keeping meaningfulness constant.

Notice that you must make a connection between past research and the present study. Usually, after presenting previous findings, you can point out a question or flaw that has not been addressed. Once the background and important issues are discussed, you might say something like "However, this interpretation does not consider . . ." or "This variable, however, was not studied . . ." Then, address the problem you have raised.

A good strategy is to logically lead up to a final paragraph that says something like "Therefore, in the present study . . ." Then state the specific hypothesis and relationship to be studied, describe your general approach for defining and

Figure A.5 Sample portion of the introduction

Note that the title is repeated and that we do not label this section as the Introduction.

Effect of Humorous   3

Effect of Humorous Interpretations

on Immediate Recall of Nonsense Figures

Researchers have consistently demonstrated that retention of to-be-learned material improves when the material is presented in a context that leads to meaningful processing (Lockhart & Craik, 1990). In particular, Bower, Karlin, and Dueck (1975) presented college students with a series of "droodles," which are each a meaningless line drawing that can be made meaningful by presentation of an accompanying verbal interpretation. Those individuals who were provided the interpretations correctly recalled (sketched) significantly more of the droodles immediately following their presentation than did those individuals given no interpretations. However, each interpretation in Bower et al. (1975) defined a droodle in a humorous fashion, using unexpected and incongruent actors and actions. Thus, differences in the meaningfulness attributed to

manipulating the variables, and specify your prediction. The details of how the data were collected are provided in the next section.

> *REMEMBER* The Introduction presents all information that will be used to interpret the results: The conceptual and theoretical logic of the study, relevant past research, and the predictions of the study.

The Method

Next comes the **Method** section, which contains the information needed to understand, critique, and exactly replicate the data-collection procedures. To collect data we need participants, testing materials and equipment, and a specific testing procedure and design. APA format requires that these categories be presented in three separate subsections, in this order: (1) Participants, (2) Materials or Apparatus, and (3) Procedure. The beginning of our Method section is shown in Figure A.6.

Participants   Here, you describe the participants you've enlisted so that other researchers can obtain comparable participants and look for uncontrolled participant variables. Thus, identify important characteristics (e.g., gender, age, school affiliation) and specify any criteria used when selecting them. If animals are tested, identify their species, genus, and strain and your supplier. Always report the number of individuals tested. Because their motivation is important, describe any form of reimbursement that was used. Also, in this section or in a letter sent to the journal editor, an author must certify that the participants were treated in accordance with the ethical principles of the APA.

Materials or Apparatus   This section immediately follows the Participants section (see Figure A.6). Usually it is called Materials because most studies involve mainly testing materials such as stimulus objects, tests and printed material, slides, drawings, and so on. You may call this section Apparatus if testing mainly involves equipment such as computers, recording devices, and the like. (If extensive discussion is required, you can divide this section into two sections.) Regardless of its title, describe the relevant materials and apparatus you prepared, but

Figure A.6   Sample portion of the method section

Notice the placement of the headings, as well as the use of capital letters and underlining.

```
              humorous interpretations should be more frequently recalled
          than those accompanied by nonhumorous interpretations.
                                 Method
          Participants
                  Forty female and 40 male undergraduate students from an
          introductory psychology course at Podunk University each
          received $3.00 for their voluntary participation. All were
          between 20 and 22 years of age (mean age = 20.7 years), were
          born in the United States, were raised in English speaking
          families, and had normal or corrected eyesight and hearing.
          Participants were randomly assigned to either the humorous or
          nonhumorous condition, with 20 males and 20 females in each
          condition.
          Materials
                  The 28 droodles from Bower et al. (1975) were reproduced,
          each consisting of a black-ink line drawing involving two
```

without explaining how they are used. Again, organize the information according to the logical order in which the components occur: We'll present a droodle, give an interpretation, and then measure retention.

Supplies must be described clearly so that the reader can understand, evaluate, and reproduce them. Therefore, if supplies are purchased, indicate the manufacturer and model, or the edition or version. If materials are borrowed from previous research, briefly describe them and provide the citation. If you build equipment, describe it so other researchers can reproduce it. If you create visual stimuli, describe the rules used to create them in terms of their dimensions, their color, and so on. If you create verbal stimuli, describe the rules used to select them, such as the length of words or sentences, their meaning and content, their difficulty level, and so on. For any paper-and-pencil tests, describe the number of questions, the format of each question, and the way in which participants indicate their responses. Also report information about the reliability and validity of a procedure. For example, the speed and error rates of equipment should be indicated because such rates affect reliability. With paper-and-pencil tests, either note their previously demonstrated validity and reliability or briefly report any procedures you performed to determine this.

Note that all physical dimensions are reported using the metric system, and that common units of measurement are abbreviated. Table A.1 provides the most common abbreviations used in psychological research. If you measure in nonmetric units, report the measurement both in nonmetric and in converted metric units.

Keep in mind that only *important* elements are reported. Readers know the necessary steps in designing a study, and generally understand why and how each component is chosen. (They've *taken* this course!) Therefore, do not specify such things as how participants were randomly selected or how you determined their age. Likewise, do not describe obvious equipment (e.g., whether participants used a pencil or a pen to complete a questionnaire, or what furniture was present in the room where testing took place). Note a detail only if it (1) would not be

Table A.1   Common Abbreviations Used in the APA Format

Notice that these abbreviations do not take periods.

Unit	Symbol	Unit	Symbol
centimeters	cm	meters	m
grams	g	milliliters	mL
hours	hr	millimeters	mm
kilograms	kg	minutes	min
liters	L	seconds	s

expected by a reasonable researcher or (2) would seriously influence the reliability or validity of the results.

Procedure   The **Procedure** section describes how you brought the participants, materials, and apparatus together to actually perform the study. A portion of this section from the droodle study is presented in Figure A.7.

The best way to organize this section is to follow the temporal sequence that occurred in your study. The first thing we do is give participants their instructions, so first summarize these instructions. Then describe the tasks performed by the participants in the order they were performed, as well as any controls you included, such as counterbalancing groups or randomizing trials. A useful strategy is to initially describe those aspects of the procedure that are common to all participants and then to distinguish one condition from another: always work from the general to the specific. (Briefly report here the outcome of any pilot study you conduct, or in the above Materials section, wherever the pilot study most directly applies.)

Along the way, the various parts of the Method section should communicate the complete design of the study. If not, an optional *Design* section may be added. Here you describe the layout of the study in terms of the conditions, par-

Figure A.7   Sample portion of the procedure section

with a loop attached to the lower right side. The humorous interpretation was "This shows a midget playing a trombone in a telephone booth." The nonhumorous interpretation was "This shows a telephone booth with a technician inside fixing the broken door handle."

    Response forms for recalling the droodles consisted of a grid of 3 by 3 in. (7.62 cm by 7.62 cm) squares printed on standard sheets of paper.

Procedure

    Participants were tested individually and viewed all 28 droodles accompanied by either the humorous or nonhumorous interpretations. Participants were instructed to study each droodle during its presentation for later recall and were told that the accompanying interpretation would be helpful in remembering it. A timer in the slide projector presented each ticipants, and variables used (so that essentially a reader can diagram the study as we have in previous chapters). But note that this section should be necessary only if you're describing a very complicated design, involving numerous groups or variables, or elaborate steps in testing.

In some instances, still other sections may be created—but, again, only if they're truly necessary. For example, if we took extensive steps to determine the reliability of a procedure and this element was central to the study, we might describe these steps in a *Reliability of Measures* section.

> **REMEMBER** The Participants section describes the important characteristics of subjects, the Materials or Apparatus section describes the characteristics of the testing materials and equipment, and the Procedure section describes the testing situation and design.

The Results

The next section is the **Results,** which reports the statistical procedures you performed and the statistical outcomes you obtained. However, *don't* interpret the results here, only report them. A portion of the Results section for the droodle study appears in Figure A.8. Describe the results in the same order in which you

Figure A.8   Sample portion of the results section
Notice that the heading is centered.

```
          instructed to recall the droodles in any order, sketching each
          droodle within one grid on the response sheet.
                                    Results
               Two assistants who were unaware of the purposes of the
          study scored the participants' sketches. A sketch was considered
          to indicate correct recall if both scorers agreed that it
          depicted a droodle. (On only 2% of the responses did the scorers
          disagree.) Each participant's score was then the total number of
          correctly recalled droodles.
               The mean number of droodles correctly recalled was 20.50 in
          the humorous interpretation condition (SD = 3.25) and 15.20 in
          the nonhumorous interpretation condition (SD = 4.19). With an
          alpha level of .05, a one-tailed independent samples t-test
          indicated a significant difference between the conditions,
          t(78) = 6.32, p <.05. The relationship between amount of humor
```

perform the steps of the analysis. First, you must have some scores to analyze, so begin by describing how you operationally defined and tabulated each participant's score. (We described how each droodle was scored as correct or incorrect.) Also describe any transformations performed on the raw scores, such as if you converted each participant's number correct to a percentage. It is at this point that any information regarding the reliability of the data is noted (such as the inter-rater reliability of the scorers).

Any analysis then involves first computing the descriptive statistics that summarize the scores and relationship. We usually report the mean and standard deviation for each condition. Note that the symbol for a mean is "M" and for a standard deviation is "SD." Write "The mean number of droodles," however, not "the M number of droodles."

You would next perform the appropriate inferential procedure, so next report the formal name for the procedure and describe how it was applied to the data. Then report the results of the analysis. You must indicate the alpha level you used and report all significant *and* nonsignificant outcomes, and for each, the terms *significant* or *nonsignificant* must appear. (In a two-way ANOVA, report all main-effect *F*s, even if your interpretation will focus on the interaction.) For any statistic, report the symbol for the obtained value (e.g., *t* or *F*), the degrees of freedom in parentheses, the obtained value, and the probability of a Type I error. In the droodle study, for example, we reported:

$$\underline{t}(78) = 6.32, \underline{p} < .05$$

This indicates that we performed the *t*-test with 78 degrees of freedom, we computed an obtained value of 6.32, and that the probability is less than .05 that such data would occur by chance if there is not really a relationship in the population. (Slightly different formatting rules are used when reporting a statistic whose symbol is from the Greek alphabet. See the *Publication Manual*.) Statistical symbols are to be italicized when published, so they are underlined in your manuscript.

If the results of the inferential procedure are significant, you have convincing evidence of a relationship. At this point, you conduct any secondary analyses that describe the relationship. For example, with a correlation, you also compute the regression line. Or, with a significant *F*, you perform post hoc comparisons. Also, you should indicate the *effect size* of each independent variable, reporting the proportion of variance accounted for by the relationship. (For the droodle study we could include that the squared Point-Biserial correlation coefficient, r_{pb}^2, is .34, indicating that the humor factor accounts for 34% of the differences in recall scores.) For each of these secondary analyses, again identify the procedure and then report the results. (The results from a manipulation check are usually reported here also.)

Remember that any result is significant if the obtained value of *t*, *F*, and so on is larger than the corresponding critical value. You decide either "Yes, it is," or "No, it's not." Therefore, one result cannot be "more significant" than another, nor can you have a "highly significant" result. (That's like saying "more yes," or "highly yes!") Also, do not attribute human actions to statistical procedures, saying such things as "according to the ANOVA . . ." or "the *t* gave significance." Instead, say that "there were significant differences between the means" or that "there was a significant effect of the independent variable."

Figures Because of cost and space considerations, include graphs, tables, or other artwork only when the information is complicated enough that the reader will benefit from a visual presentation. Usually, graphs—called **"Figures"**—provide the clearest way to summarize the pattern in a relationship. However, the author should also have something to say about each figure, telling readers what they should see in it. (For illustrative purposes, a figure is included in the droodle study manuscript, although, technically, the relationship is so simple that the figure is unnecessary.)

Every figure needs to be numbered (even if there's only one). At the point in the narrative where readers should look at the figure, you should direct their attention to it, saying something like "As can be seen in Figure 1 . . . ." Refer to Figure A.9 for the wording as it appears in the manuscript of the droodle study. *Do not,* however, physically place the figure here (the journal publisher would do that). The graph is drawn on a separate page and placed after the references at the *end* of the manuscript. The graph from the sample manuscript appears in Figure A.10. There are many rules for preparing a figure, so check the *Publication Manual.* In general, the height of the *Y* axis should be about 60 to 75 percent of the length of the *X* axis. Fully label each axis, using the names of the variables and their amounts. Use black ink, because color is expensive to publish (and a reader might be color blind!). If the figure contains more than one line in the

Figure A.9 Sample portion of the results section showing reference to a figure

> $\underline{t}(78) = 6.32$, $\underline{p} < .05$. The relationship between amount of humor and recall scores can be seen in Figure 1. Although a positive relationship was obtained, the slope of this curve indicates that the rate of change in recall scores as a function of increased humor was not large.
>
> **Discussion**
>
> The results of the present study indicate that humorous interpretations lead to greater retention of droodles than do

Figure A.10   Sample figure

The caption for the graph reads: "Mean number of droodles correctly recalled as a function of nonhumorous and humorous interpretations."

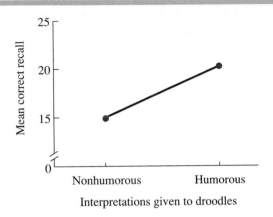

body of the graph, use different symbols for each (e.g., one solid line and one dashed). Then provide a "legend" or "key" to the symbols at the side of the figure. (For an example, see Figure 7.1 or 7.2 in Chapter 7.)

Every figure has an explanatory title, called the **figure caption,** which briefly identifies the variables and relationship depicted. (In the droodle study, the caption is "Mean number of droodles correctly recalled as a function of nonhumorous and humorous interpretations.") Instead of positioning each caption on the corresponding figure (the publisher also does that), place all captions on one **Figure Caption page,** another separate page at the end of the manuscript.

Tables   Create a table of results rather than a figure when it is important for the reader to see the precise numerical values of means, percentages, and so on. A **table** is called for only when there are too many numbers to efficiently include in the narrative. All tables are numbered consecutively, and, as with figures, the reader is directed to them by you at appropriate points in the Results section. The actual tables are placed at the end of the manuscript. Note that you *do* place the title for each table on the table itself. For example, say that we had reason to compare male versus female participants, and we examined their recall of the individual droodles depending on whether the interpretation referred to humans, animals, plants, or objects. If we present this information in the narrative, it will be very dense and difficult to follow. Instead, a table is the way to go, as shown in Table A.2. (The *Publication Manual* provides detailed instructions for laying out different tables.)

The title should clearly yet concisely summarize the table, and the layout should be such that the table can be easily understood. Type the table so it's against your left-hand margin, and limit using horizontal lines to only when they're really needed (vertical lines are almost never needed). All headings should be brief yet clear. Then, only digits are used to express quantities, and each is centered under its heading.

> *REMEMBER* The Results section summarizes the data and the relationship obtained, and reports the outcomes of the inferential procedures performed.

The Discussion

Next, in the **Discussion** section you interpret the results and draw your conclusions. Here the questions originally posed in the Introduction are answered. The Discussion section begins at the point where you have *already* reported a significant relationship (do not report any statistics here), so your first question is "Do the results confirm (1) the predictions and thus (2) the hypothesis?" You can almost always answer this question by beginning the discussion with the phrase "The results of the present study . . ." See Figure A.9 again.

As the term *Discussion* implies, however, do not merely state your conclusions—discuss them. That is, after answering the original research question, your task is to use the answer to explain what you have learned about behavior. Recall

Table A.2:   Example APA-Style Table

Notice the table's title is underlined, and the table is double-spaced.

Table 1

Recall of Droodle Types for Males and Females

| | Gender | | | |
| | Males | | Females | |
Type	M	SD	M	SD
Human	2.33	0.68	3.55	1.01
Animal	2.14	0.46	4.21	0.98
Plant	5.70	1.86	3.23	2.79
Object	4.99	2.30	1.45	0.99

from the diagram back in Figure A.2 that, in the Discussion section, you work backward, from the specific to the general. So, beginning with the narrowly defined relationship in the study, generalize to the relationship between the variables that might be found with other individuals or situations. Then generalize the findings based on the variables to the constructs you originally set out to study.

Begin by focusing on the descriptive statistics you've reported (inferential statistics are no help here). Your job is to become a psychologist again, translating the numbers into descriptions of behaviors and explanations of the variables that influence them. For example, the droodle study produced higher recall scores with humorous interpretations. This indicates better retention, a mental *behavior* that is different from what occurred when nonhumorous interpretations were given. Thus, based on the scores in each condition, as in Figure A.11, the discussion proposes how manipulating humor influences the memory system. Of course, we cannot discount those droodles given nonhumorous interpretations, because they were frequently recalled, and the addition of humor had no great effect. Thus, as here, researchers factor into their conclusions what the direction and rate of change in scores indicate, what the consistency or inconsistency in the relationship indicates, and what the proportion of variance accounted for indicates. Recall that, in studies with more than two conditions, only some conditions might represent an actual relationship. In such cases also consider why and how these results occur.

Figure A.11   Sample portion of the discussion section

```
                                    Effect of Humorous     8

nonhumorous interpretations. Because the meaningfulness of the

droodles provided by the interpretations was presumably constant

in both conditions, it appears that humor provides an additional

source of retrieval cues. This conclusion is consistent with the

proposal that humor increases the distinctiveness of a stimulus,

thereby facilitating recall by increasing the accessibility of

the stimulus in memory.

    The improvement in recall produced by humor, however, was

relatively small. This result may be due to the fact that all

droodles were made meaningful, although sometimes by a

nonhumorous interpretation. As in other research (Lockhart &
```

All explanations must rationally fit with previous findings and theoretical explanations. Thus, the goal is to provide an integrated and consistent explanation, answering the question "Given your findings and past findings, what is the present state of knowledge about the behavior or construct?" In the droodle study, for example, we relate our findings to current explanations of the role of distinctiveness and meaningfulness in memory. Notice, however, the use of such words as *presumably, probably,* and *apparently.* Do not say "prove" or provide explanations as if they are fact. And although you may say *causes* or *influences,* the difficulty in identifying causal variables should lead you to use these words cautiously.

You must also consider any major flaws in the design that limit confidence in your conclusions. When looking for flaws, however, do not use the tired old argument that the data may not be representative or that a larger sample is needed. Your significant inferential statistics have eliminated these arguments. Instead, any questions you raise should be based on these important design issues:

1. *Reliability.* Did changing the interpretations given to the droodles consistently manipulate the variable of humor? Did we consistently and only measure a person's recall of the droodles?
2. *Internal validity.* Were the humorous and nonhumorous interpretations truly equal in meaningfulness? Perhaps the unusual elements in a humorous interpretation yield a broader, more wide-ranging meaning. If so, then by manipulating humor we also manipulated meaningfulness, and greater meaningfulness might have increased recall scores. If it is likely that this (or another) confounding occurred, then we have reduced internal validity for saying that amount of humor influenced recall.
3. *External validity.* Is it appropriate to generalize this relationship to other people and situations? Did participants have an unusual sense of humor, so that the results are unique? Droodles are simple visual stimuli, so can we generalize the effect of humor to verbal material or to complex visual material?
4. *Content and Construct validity.* Do the recall scores actually reflect "memory" for the droodles? Have we correctly defined "meaningfulness" and "humor"? In particular, we only speculated that humor produces "distinctiveness," but we have no empirical evidence of this.

Although you should attempt to prevent potential flaws when designing a study, they are sometimes unavoidable. Do not try to hide a major flaw. Instead, evaluate the study and either provide counterarguments to explain why a potential flaw does not seriously reduce your confidence in a conclusion, or qualify and limit your conclusions in light of the flaw.

Researchers often conclude the Discussion section by pointing out the next steps to be taken in the research area. Remember, as the author you are the expert, so indicate what hypotheses should be tested next. (For example, we would note the lack of evidence that humor makes a stimulus more distinctive, and suggest that researchers attempt to confirm this hypothesis.)

REMEMBER   The Discussion section answers the questions posed by the study, interpreting the results in terms of what is now known about the underlying behavior.

The Reference Page

The final section following the Discussion is the **Reference** page(s). This lists alphabetically the complete references for all sources cited in the article. *Each source should be one that you have read.* If, for example, you learn about Jones's article from reading Smith's report, you should read Jones, too (because Smith might be misleading). If you do not, then your reference to Jones should indicate that it is "as cited in" Smith.

As shown in Figure A.12, each reference is typed as a paragraph. (The published version will be converted to the normal hanging-indent format, as in the References in this book.) For a journal article, provide the last name and first initials of all authors, listed in the same order as they appear in the article. Next, give the year of publication, the article's title, and the title of the journal, its vol-

Figure A.12   Sample portion of reference page

Notice the punctuation and underlining.

                                                    Effect of Humorous   10
                              References
        Bower, G. H., Karlin, M. B., & Dueck, A. (1975).
Comprehension and memory for pictures. <u>Memory and Cognition, 3,</u>
216–220.
        Desrochers, A., & Begg, I. (1987). A theoretical account of
encoding and retrieval processes in the use of imagery-based
mnemonic techniques: The special case of the keyword method. In
M. A. McDaniel & M. Pressley (Eds.), <u>Imagery and related</u>
<u>mnemonic processes: Theories, individual differences, and</u>
<u>applications</u> (pp. 56–77). New York: Springer-Verlag.
        Einstein, G. O., McDaniel, M. A., & Lackey, S. (1989).
Bizarre imagery, interference, and distinctiveness. <u>Journal of</u>
<u>Experimental Psychology: Learning, Memory, and Cognition, 15,</u>
137–146.
        Hunt, R. R., & Elliott, J. M. (1980). The role of

ume number, and the page numbers of the article. The *Publication Manual* provides slightly different rules for referencing books, book chapters, monthly magazines, and so on.

Putting It All Together

Most research ideas come from the literature. Authors may suggest rival explanations for their results, or point out untested hypotheses. Also, no study is perfect, so you may find flaws that suggest a research hypothesis. Or you may discover two published studies that contradict each other, so you can design a study to resolve the debate. You can also literally replicate a study, but it is more interesting and informative to add a new twist or perspective to the design that simultaneously expands our knowledge. For example, in replicating the droodle study, you might add a third, no-interpretation, control condition.

Developing your research ideas will be easier if you recognize that any published article makes the study *sound like* it was a smooth-running, perfectly planned, well-organized process. In reality, it wasn't. An article will not report all the people who volunteered for the study but never showed up. It will gloss over the difficulty the researcher had in finding an artist who could draw droodles or the hours it took to invent their interpretations. And it will not mention the several prior attempts, using different stimuli or procedures, that failed to produce interpretable results. Thus, although an article might give you the impression that the researcher was omniscient and that the study ran like clockwork, don't be fooled. Research is much more challenging—and more fun—than that.

CHAPTER SUMMARY

1. A research report is organized based on the sequence in which the various aspects of the study occur.

2. Most psychological articles follow the rules in the *Publication Manual* of the *American Psychological Association,* so that they conform to "APA format."

3. *Psychological Abstracts* contains the abstracts of articles published in other psychological journals.

4. The *Social Science Citation Index* is used to identify recent articles that cite a previous article.

5. A report should not present information that is redundant with a reader's knowledge or other reference sources. Rather, it should provide the necessary information for (a) understanding the study, (b) evaluating it, and (c) literally replicating it.

6. The *Title* should clearly communicate the variables and relationship being studied. The *Abstract* should summarize the report. Together, these elements allow readers to determine whether they want to read the article.

7. The *Introduction* presents all information that will be used to interpret the results. It reconstructs the logic and cites the literature the researcher used in working from the hypothetical constructs to the specific predicted relationship of the study.

8. The *Method* section provides the information needed to understand, critique, and literally replicate the data-collection procedures. It consists of three subsections: *Participants, Materials* or *Apparatus,* and *Procedure.*

9. The *Participants* section describes the subjects of a study in terms of their characteristics, their total number, and the reimbursement given.

10. The *Materials* or *Apparatus* section describes the characteristics of the stimuli, the response materials, and the equipment used to test participants. Information about the reliability and validity of the material and apparatus is also included here.

11. The *Procedure* section describes the situation(s) in which participants were tested. It should summarize the instructions given to participants and the task(s) performed by them, and complete the description of the design.

12. The *Results* section describes the statistical procedures performed and the outcomes obtained. In this order, it (a) describes the scores, (b) reports the descriptive statistics, (c) identifies each inferential procedure performed, and (d) reports the results of the procedure. Report primary analyses first, followed by secondary analyses.

13. In the *Discussion* section, the results are interpreted and the conclusions are drawn. The initial questions posed by the study are answered and the findings are related to past findings, providing an integrated description of a behavior or construct. It is here that major potential flaws in the study are discussed.

14. In an APA-style manuscript, after the Discussion section comes the *References,* the *Tables,* the *Figure Caption page,* and the *Figures.*

KEY TERMS

abstract *(398)*
apparatus section *(402)*
discussion section *(409)*
figures *(407)*
figure caption *(408)*
figure caption page *(408)*
introduction *(398)*
manuscript page header *(398)*

materials section *(402)*
method section *(401)*
participants section *(402)*
procedure section *(404)*
Publication Manual of the American Psychological Association (391)

Psychological Abstracts (387)
reference page *(412)*
research literature *(386)*
results section *(405)*
running head *(398)*
Social Science Citation Index (387)
table *(408)*
title *(396)*

REVIEW QUESTIONS

1. Why is it necessary to conduct a literature search?

2. How would you go about finding literature that investigates the possible connection between violence on television and heightened aggressiveness in adolescents?

3. You find an article related to the topic of television and aggressiveness in adolescents. How can you use this article to find relevant research that occurred prior to it?

4. The article you find was published in 1988. How would you use this article to find more recent related research?

5. You wish to measure the aggressiveness of a sample of adolescents. Other than creating your own test, what two approaches can you take to find a valid and reliable test of aggressiveness?

6. What information should you include in the title of a research article?

7. What information should you include in the abstract of a research article?

8. From another researcher's perspective, what is the purpose of reading your title and abstract?

9. (a) How do you create the page header that appears at the top of each page of a manuscript? (b) What is the running head, and how is it used?

10. (a) Summarize the information that is presented in the Introduction. (b) In general terms, what information about a study is not yet included here?

11. (a) What are the three standard components of the Method section? (b) What information is contained in each subsection? (c) In general terms, what information about a study is not yet reported in the Methods section?

12. (a) How is the Results section organized? (b) In general terms, what information about a study is not yet reported here?

13. (a) When should you include a figure in a research report? (b) When should you include a table?

14. (a) How is the Discussion section related to the Introduction? (b) In addition to drawing a conclusion about your specific prediction, what other issues are addressed in the Discussion section?

15. For each of the following statements, indicate two reasons that its format is incorrect: (a) "40 students will hear the music and be tested." (b) "Because the critical value is 2.45 and the obtained value is 24.7, the results are very significant." (c) "The mean scores in the respective conditions for men were 1.4, 3.0, 2.7, 6.9, 11.8, 14.77, 22.31, 25.6, 33.7, and 41.2. For girls, the mean scores were . . ." (d) "To create the groups, the participants were split in half, with five individuals in each." (e) "The results were significant, indicating the null hypothesis should be rejected. Therefore, I conclude that the

relationship demonstrates . . ." (f) Title: "Type of Interpretation as a Function of Remembering Funny Droodles."

DISCUSSION QUESTIONS

1. In question 15, revise each statement so that it uses correct APA style.

2. Examine a published research article and discuss how it follows the diagram presented in Figure A.2.

3. (a) What practical application might the droodle study have, for example, in the preparation of lectures or textbooks? (b) Why might your confidence in such a generalization be limited? (c) How would you use the literature to increase your confidence?

4. A researcher obtains a correlation coefficient of $r = .434$, which is not quite significant (the critical value is .44). Several participants, however, behaved contrary to the researcher's predicitons. The study has potential life-saving applications, so to produce a significant r the researcher eliminates the data from these "bad" participants and publishes the study. What is your reaction to this decision?

5. Perform an updated literature search about (a) distinctiveness versus meaningfulness and memory; (b) the original 1975 droodle study; (c) the influence of humor on memory.

Sample APA-Style Research Report

Effect of Humorous   1

Running head: EFFECT OF HUMOROUS INTERPRETATIONS ON RECALL

Effect of Humorous Interpretations on

Immediate Recall of Nonsense Figures

Gary W. Heiman

Podunk University

Abstract

The effect of humor on the immediate recall of simple visual
stimuli was investigated. Eighty college students (20 men and 20
women per condition) viewed 28 nonsensical line drawings that
were each accompanied by either a humorous or nonhumorous verbal
interpretation. Although the interpretations were comparable in
the meaningfulness they conveyed, those participants presented
with humorous interpretations correctly recalled significantly
more drawings than those presented nonhumorous interpretations.
The results suggest that a meaningful and humorous context
provides additional retrieval cues beyond those cues provided by
a meaningful yet nonhumorous context. The effect of the cues
produced by humor is interpreted as creating a more distinctive
and thus more accessible memory trace.

Effect of Humorous Interpretations

on Immediate Recall of Nonsense Figures

Researchers have consistently demonstrated that retention of to-be-learned material improves when the material is presented in a context that leads to meaningful processing (Lockhart & Craik, 1990). In particular, Bower, Karlin, and Dueck (1975) presented college students with a series of "droodles," which are each a meaningless line drawing that can be made meaningful by presentation of an accompanying verbal interpretation. Those individuals who were provided the interpretations correctly recalled (sketched) significantly more of the droodles immediately following their presentation than did those individuals given no interpretations. However, each interpretation in Bower et al. (1975) defined a droodle in a humorous fashion, using unexpected and incongruent actors and actions. Thus, differences in the meaningfulness attributed to the droodles may have been confounded by differences in the humor associated with the droodles. The purpose of the present study was to investigate the effect of humorous interpretations when the meaningfulness of the droodles is kept constant.

Few studies can be found that directly examine how the humor associated with a stimulus influences recall of the stimulus. However, it is reasonable to speculate that the relevant dimension of humor may be that it is simply one type of context that makes a stimulus meaningful. Desrochers and Begg (1987) defined the meaningfulness of a stimulus as the extent to

which the components of the stimulus are organized and
integrated. Therefore, meaningfulness provides retrieval cues
that enhance recall of the components of the stimulus, once the
stimulus has been accessed in memory. From this perspective,
either a humorous or a nonhumorous context should produce
equivalent recall of stimuli, as long as both contexts provide
an equivalent level of meaningful organization.

On the other hand, humor may play a different role than
that of only providing a meaningful context. Because it provides
an unusual and unexpected interpretation, humor may make a
stimulus more distinctive in memory. The distinctiveness of a
stimulus is defined as the number of novel attributes that it
can be assigned (Schmidt, 1985). Research has shown that greater
distinctiveness does improve retrieval (Hunt & Elliott, 1980).
Desrochers and Begg (1987) and Einstein, McDaniel, and Lackey
(1989) suggest that distinctiveness is created by unique cues
that are associated with the particular context in which the
stimulus was encountered. Therefore, distinctiveness enhances
access to the overall memory trace for a stimulus. From this
perspective, a humorous context should facilitate recall of a
stimulus to a greater extent than a nonhumorous context,
because, in addition to organizing the components of a stimulus
through its meaning, humor provides additional retrieval cues
that make the memory trace for the stimulus more distinctive and
thus more accessible.

In this study, I tested the above proposals by determining

Effect of Humorous   5

whether droodles accompanied by humorous interpretations are better retained than when they are accompanied by nonhumorous interpretations. For each of the humorous interpretations of Bower et al. (1975), I produced a non-humorous version that would provide an equally meaningful interpretation of the droodle. If humor adds retrieval cues over and above those produced by meaningful processing, then droodles accompanied by humorous interpretations should be more frequently recalled than those accompanied by nonhumorous interpretations.

Method

<u>Participants</u>

Forty female and 40 male undergraduate students from an introductory psychology course at Podunk University each received $3.00 for their voluntary participation. All were between 20 and 22 years of age (mean age = 20.7 years), were born in the United States, were raised in English speaking families, and had normal or corrected eyesight and hearing. Participants were randomly assigned to either the humorous or nonhumorous condition, with 20 males and 20 females in each condition.

<u>Materials</u>

The 28 droodles from Bower et al. (1975) were reproduced, each consisting of a black-ink line drawing involving two interconnected geometric shapes. Droodles were copied to film slides for presentation by a standard Kodak carousel projector (model 28-b).

For each humorous interpretation in Bower et al. (1975), a non-humorous version was created. Each interpretation consisted of a 10 to 14 word sentence, beginning with the phrase "This shows a. . . ." A humorous interpretation referred to an unusual action by unexpected people or animals using incongruent objects. A nonhumorous interpretation was derived by changing the humorous interpretation so that it described common actions by predictable actors using congruent objects. The meaning of each droodle was altered as little as possible, with only the humorous components being replaced with comparable, nonhumorous components. For example, one droodle consisted of a rectangle with a loop attached to the lower right side. The humorous interpretation was "This shows a midget playing a trombone in a telephone booth." The nonhumorous interpretation was "This shows a telephone booth with a technician inside fixing the broken door handle."

Response forms for recalling the droodles consisted of a grid of 3 by 3 in. (7.62 cm by 7.62 cm) squares printed on standard sheets of paper.

<u>Procedure</u>

Participants were tested individually and viewed all 28 droodles accompanied by either the humorous or nonhumorous interpretations. Participants were instructed to study each droodle during its presentation for later recall and were told that the accompanying interpretation would be helpful in remembering it. A timer in the slide projector presented each

Effect of Humorous   7

slide containing a droodle for 10 s, with approximately 2 s between slides. As each slide was presented, I recited the appropriate interpretation. The recall task began immediately after the final droodle was presented. Participants were instructed to recall the droodles in any order, sketching each droodle within one grid on the response sheet.

Results

Two assistants who were unaware of the purposes of the study scored the participants' sketches. A sketch was considered to indicate correct recall if both scorers agreed that it depicted a droodle. (On only 2% of the responses did the scorers disagree.) Each participant's score was then the total number of correctly recalled droodles.

The mean number of droodles correctly recalled was 20.50 in the humorous interpretation condition ($\underline{SD}$ = 3.25) and 15.20 in the nonhumorous interpretation condition ($\underline{SD}$ = 4.19). With an alpha level of .05, a one-tailed independent samples $\underline{t}$-test indicated a significant difference between the conditions, $\underline{t}$(78) = 6.32, $\underline{p}$ <.05. The relationship between amount of humor and recall scores can be seen in Figure 1. Although a positive relationship was obtained, the slope of this curve indicates that the rate of change in recall scores as a function of increased humor was not large.

Discussion

The results of the present study indicate that humorous interpretations lead to greater retention of droodles than do nonhumorous interpretations. Because the meaningfulness of the droodles provided by the interpretations was presumably constant in both conditions, it appears that humor provides an additional source of retrieval cues. This conclusion is consistent with the proposal that humor increases the distinctiveness of a stimulus, thereby facilitating recall by increasing the accessibility of the stimulus in memory.

The improvement in recall produced by humor, however, was relatively small. This result may be due to the fact that all droodles were made meaningful, although sometimes by a nonhumorous interpretation. As in other research (Lockhart & Craik, 1990), the meaningful processing produced by a nonhumorous interpretation may have provided relatively effective retrieval cues. Then the additional retrieval cues produced by the distinctiveness of a humorous interpretation would only moderately improve the retrievability of the droodles. In addition, these results may have occurred because a nonhumorous interpretation given to such a simple visual stimulus produced a reasonably distinctive trace. Additional unique cues provided by a humorous interpretation would then only moderately increase a droodle's distinctiveness, resulting in only a moderate improvement in recall.

It is possible, of course, that humor added to the meaningfulness of a droodle, instead of to its distinctiveness. Desrochers and Begg (1987) suggested that increased meaningfulness results in increased organization of a stimulus

in memory. Humor may have added to the meaningfulness of a
droodle by providing additional ways to organize it, so that its
components were better retrieved. Further research is needed to
determine whether humor produces a more distinctive or a more
meaningful stimulus, especially when the stimulus is more
complex than a simple droodle.

Effect of Humorous   10

References

Bower, G. H., Karlin, M. B., & Dueck, A. (1975). Comprehension and memory for pictures. <u>Memory and Cognition, 3,</u> 216-220.

Desrochers, A., & Begg, I. (1987). A theoretical account of encoding and retrieval processes in the use of imagery-based mnemonic techniques: The special case of the keyword method. In M. A. McDaniel & M. Pressley (Eds.), <u>Imagery and related mnemonic processes: Theories, individual differences, and applications</u> (pp. 56-77). New York: Springer-Verlag.

Einstein, G. O., McDaniel, M. A., & Lackey, S. (1989). Bizarre imagery, interference, and distinctiveness. <u>Journal of Experimental Psychology: Learning, Memory, and Cognition, 15,</u> 137-146.

Hunt, R. R., & Elliott, J. M. (1980). The role of nonsemantic information in memory: Orthographic distinctiveness effects on retention. <u>Journal of Experimental Psychology: General, 109,</u> 49-74.

Lockhart, R. S., & Craik, F. I. M. (1990). Levels of processing: A retrospective commentary on framework for memory research. <u>Canadian Journal of Psychology, 44,</u> 87-112.

Schmidt, S. R. (1985). Encoding and retrieval processes in the memory for conceptually distinctive events. <u>Journal of Experimental Psychology: Learning, Memory, and Cognition, 11,</u> 565-578.

Effect of Humorous   11

Figure Caption

<u>Figure 1</u>. Mean number of droodles correctly recalled as a function of nonhumorous and humorous interpretations.

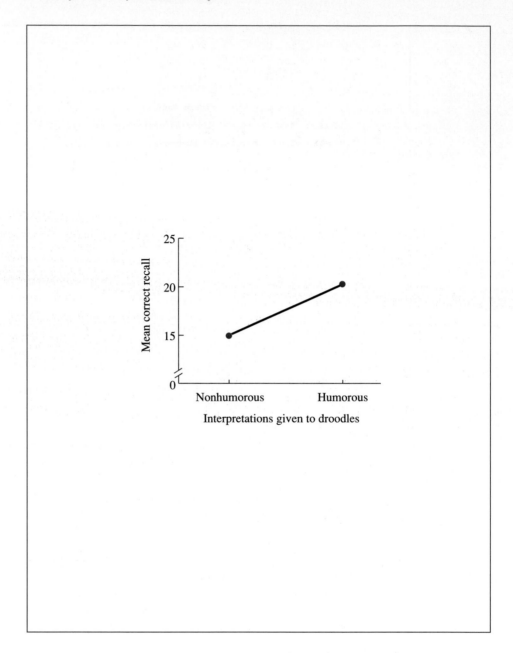

Statistical Procedures

C.1. Measures of Central Tendency
The Mean
The Median
The Mode

C.2. Measures of Variability
The Variance
The Standard Deviation
The Range

C.3. The Two-Sample t-Test
The Independent Samples *t*-Test
The Dependent Samples *t*-Test

C.4. The One-Way Analysis of Variance
The One-Way Between-Subjects ANOVA
The One-Way Within-Subjects ANOVA

C.5. The Two-Way Between-Subjects Analysis of Variance

C.6. The Two-Way Within-Subjects Analysis of Variance

C.7. The Two-Way Mixed-Design Analysis of Variance

C.8. Tukey HSD Post Hoc Comparisons
The Post Hoc Comparison for Main Effect
The Post Hoc Comparison for Interaction Effects

C.9. Measures of Effect Size in t-Tests and ANOVA
Effect Size in *t*-Tests
Effect Size in ANOVA

C.10. Confidence Intervals
Confidence Intervals in *t*-Tests
Confidence Intervals in ANOVA

C.11. Pearson Correlation Coefficient, Linear Regression, and Standard Error of the Estimate
The Pearson Correlation Coefficient
The Linear Regression Equation
The Standard Error of the Estimate

C.12. Spearman Correlation Coefficient

C.13. Chi Square Procedures
The One-Way Chi Square
The Two-Way Chi Square

(continued on next page)

STATISTICAL PROCEDURES

C.14. Mann-Whitney U and Wilcoxon T Tests

The Mann-Whitney U Test for Independent Samples

The Wilcoxon T Test for Dependent Samples

C.15. Kruskal-Wallis H and Friedman χ^2 Tests

The Kruskal-Wallis H Test

The Friedman χ^2 Test

C.1. Measures of Central Tendency

These procedures are discussed in Chapter 6.

The Mean

The mean, X, is found using the formula

$$X = \frac{\Sigma X}{N}$$

where ΣX is the sum of the scores and N is the number of scores in the sample. For the scores 2, 1, 3, 7, 4, 5,

$$X = \frac{\Sigma X}{N} = \frac{22}{6} = 3.667$$

The Median

The median, Mdn, is calculated by arranging all scores in the sample from lowest to highest. If N is an odd number, the median is the score that divides the distribution in two, with an equal number of scores below and above it. If N is an even number, the median is the average of the two middle scores. For the scores 7, 7, 9, 10, 12, 13, 13, 14, 18, the median score is 12.

The Mode

The mode is the most frequently occurring score or scores in the sample. For the scores 1, 2, 2, 2, 3, 3, 4, 4, 4, 4, 4, 5, 5, 6, the mode is 4. For the scores 1, 2, 2, 2, 2, 3, 3, 4, 4, 4, 4, 5, 5, 6, the modes are 2 and 4.

C.2. *Measures of Variability*

Below are formulas for the sample and estimated population variance, the sample and estimated population standard deviation, and the range. Measures of variability are discussed in Chapter 6.

The Variance

There are two ways to calculate variance.

The Sample Variance The sample variance S_x^2, describes how far the sample scores are spread out around the sample mean. The formula is

$$S_x^2 = \frac{\Sigma X^2 - \frac{(\Sigma X)^2}{N}}{N}$$

where ΣX is the sum of the scores and $(\Sigma X)^2$ is the squared sum of the scores, ΣX^2 is the sum of squared scores, and N is the number of scores in the sample. For the scores 2, 3, 4, 5, 6, 7, 8,

$$S_x^2 = \frac{\Sigma X^2 - \frac{(\Sigma X)^2}{N}}{N} = \frac{203 - \frac{(35)^2}{7}}{7} = 4.0$$

The Estimated Population Variance The estimated population variance, s_x^2, is computed using sample data, but it is an estimate of how far the scores in the population would be spread out around the population mean. The formula is

$$s_x^2 = \frac{\Sigma X^2 - \frac{(\Sigma X)^2}{N}}{N - 1}$$

where ΣX is the sum of the scores and $(\Sigma X)^2$ is the squared sum of the scores, ΣX^2 is the sum of the squared scores, and $N - 1$ is the number of scores in the sample minus 1. For the scores of 2, 3, 4, 5, 6, 7, 8,

$$s_x^2 = \frac{\Sigma X^2 - \frac{(\Sigma X)^2}{N}}{N - 1} = \frac{203 - \frac{(35)^2}{7}}{6} = 4.67$$

The Standard Deviation

There are two ways to calculate the standard deviation.

The Sample Standard Deviation   The sample standard deviation, S_x, describes how far the sample scores are spread out around the sample mean. It is calculated as the square root of the sample variance. For the scores of 2, 3, 4, 5, 6, 7, 8,

$$S_x = \sqrt{\frac{\Sigma X^2 - \frac{(\Sigma X)^2}{N}}{N}} = \sqrt{\frac{203 - \frac{(35)^2}{7}}{7}} = 2.0$$

The Estimated Population Standard Deviation   The estimated population standard deviation, s_x, is computed using sample data, but it is an estimate of how far the scores in the population would be spread out around the population mean. It is calculated as the square root of the estimated population variance. For the scores of 2, 3, 4, 5, 6, 7, 8,

$$s_x = \sqrt{\frac{\Sigma X^2 - \frac{(\Sigma X)^2}{N}}{N - 1}} = \sqrt{\frac{203 - \frac{(35)^2}{7}}{6}} = 2.16$$

The Range

The range is the distance between the two most extreme scores in a sample. The formula is:

$$\text{range} = \text{highest score} - \text{lowest score}$$

For the scores 2, 3, 4, 5, 6, 7, 8, the range equals $8 - 2$, which is 6.

 ## C.3. The Two-Sample t-Test

Below are the procedures for performing the independent samples (between-subjects) *t*-test and the dependent samples (within-subjects) *t*-test.

The Independent Samples *t*-Test

This procedure is discussed in Chapter 6. Example data are shown in Table C.1.

Step 1   Determine the sum of scores (ΣX), the sum of squared scores (ΣX^2), the *n*, and the X in each condition.

Step 2   Calculate s_1^2, the estimated population variance based on the scores in the first condition, and s_2^2, the estimated population variance based on the scores of the second condition. Use the formula for the estimated population variance given in section C.2.

Table C.1 Data from Two-Sample Between-Subjects Design

Condition 1	Condition 2
11	13
14	16
10	14
12	17
8	11
15	14
12	15
13	18
9	12
11	11

$\Sigma X = 115$	$\Sigma X = 141$
$\Sigma X^2 = 1365$	$\Sigma X^2 = 2041$
$X_1 = 11.5$	$X_2 = 14.1$
$n_1 = 10$	$n_1 = 10$
$s_1^2 = 4.72$	$s_2^2 = 5.88$

Step 3   Calculate t:

$$t = \frac{(X_1 - X_2) - (\mu_1 - \mu_2)}{\sqrt{\left(\frac{(n_1-1)s_1^2+(n_2-1)s_2^2}{(n_1-1)+(n_2-1)}\right)\left(\frac{1}{n_1} + \frac{1}{n_2}\right)}}$$

where X_1 and X_2 are the means of the two conditions, $(\mu_1 - \mu_2)$ is the difference between the means predicted by the null hypothesis (usually this difference is zero), n_1 is the number of scores in the first condition, n_2 is the number of scores in the second condition, and s_1^2 and s_2^2 are from Step 2.

$$t = \frac{(11.5 - 14.1) - 0}{\sqrt{\left(\frac{(10-1)4.72+(10-1)5.88}{(10-1)+(10-1)}\right)\left(\frac{1}{10} + \frac{1}{10}\right)}}$$

$$t = \frac{-2.6}{\sqrt{(5.30)(.20)}} = \frac{-2.6}{1.030} = -2.524$$

Step 4   Find the critical value of t in Table D.1 of Appendix D. Degrees of freedom, df, equal $(n_1 - 1) + (n_2 - 1)$. For $df = 18$ and $\alpha = .05$, the two-tailed critical value is ± 2.101. Here the obtained t is beyond the critical value, so it is significant. If t is *not* significant, do not perform Step 5.

Step 5 See section C.9 for computing effect size and section C.10 for computing confidence intervals.

The Dependent Samples *t*-Test

This procedure is discussed in Chapter 6. Example data are shown in Table C.2.

Step 1 Calculate the difference, *D*, between the two scores in each pair of scores formed by matching two participants or repeatedly measuring the same participant in both conditions.

Step 2 Calculate *D*, the mean of the difference scores. Here, $D = 18/5 = 3.6$.

Step 3 Calculate s_D^2, the estimated variance of the population of difference scores, found by entering the differences scores into the formula for s_x^2 in section C.2. Here, $s_D^2 = 7.80$.

Step 4 Calculate *t*:

$$t_{\text{obt}} = \frac{\overline{D} - \mu_D}{\sqrt{(s_D^2)\frac{1}{N}}}$$

where μ_D is the average difference score between the conditions described by the null hypothesis (usually this is zero), *N* is the number of pairs of scores, and s_D^2 is from Step 3.

$$t = \frac{\overline{D} - \mu_D}{\sqrt{(s_D^2)\frac{1}{N}}} = \frac{+3.6 - 0}{\sqrt{(7.80)\left(\frac{1}{5}\right)}} = \frac{+3.6}{1.249} = 2.88$$

Step 5 Find the critical value of *t* in Table D.1 of Appendix D. Degrees of freedom, *df*, equal $N - 1$, where *N* is the number of difference scores. Above, for

Table C.2 Data from Two-Sample Within-Subjects Design

Subject	Condition 1	−	Condition 2	=	Difference D	D²
1	11		8		+3	9
2	16		11		+5	25
3	20		15		+5	25
4	17		11		+6	36
5	10		11		−1	1
	X = 14.80		X = 11.20		ΣD = +18	ΣD² = 96

$df = 4$ and $\alpha = .05$, the two-tailed critical value is ± 2.776. If the obtained t is significant, the mean scores in each condition (above, $X_1 = 14.80$ and $X_2 = 11.20$) also differ significantly. If t is *not* significant, do not perform Step 6.

Step 6   See section C.9 for computing effect size and section C.10 for computing confidence intervals.

C.4. The One-Way Analysis of Variance

Below are the procedures for performing a one-way between-subjects ANOVA and a one-way within-subjects ANOVA.

The One-Way Between-Subjects ANOVA

This procedure is discussed in Chapter 6. Example data for a one-way design having three levels (with five participants per level) are shown in Table C.3.

Step 1   Determine k, the number of levels in the factor; then determine the sum of scores (ΣX), the sum of squared scores (ΣX^2), the n, and the X in each level.

Step 2   Also calculate the totals:

$$\Sigma X_{tot} = 40 + 30 + 15 = 85$$

$$\Sigma X_{tot}^2 = 354 + 220 + 55 = 629$$

$$N = 5 + 5 + 5 = 15$$

Table C.3   Data from One-Way Between-Subjects Design

Factor A			
Level A_1	Level A_2	Level A_3	
9	4	1	
12	6	3	
4	8	4	
8	2	5	
7	10	2	*Totals*
$\Sigma X = 40$	$\Sigma X = 30$	$\Sigma X = 15$	$\Sigma X_{tot} = 85$
$\Sigma X^2 = 354$	$\Sigma X^2 = 220$	$\Sigma X^2 = 55$	$\Sigma X_{tot}^2 = 629$
$n_1 = 5$	$n_2 = 5$	$n_3 = 5$	$N = 15$
$\overline{X}_1 = 8$	$\overline{X}_2 = 6$	$\overline{X}_3 = 3$	$k = 3$

Step 3 Compute the correction term (this is the name for a value used in subsequent calculations):

$$\text{Correction term} = \left(\frac{(\Sigma X_{tot})^2}{N} \right) = \frac{85^2}{15} = 481.67$$

Step 4 As you perform the following calculations, create the Analysis of Variance Summary Table shown in Table C.4.

Step 5 Compute the total sum of squares:

$$SS_{tot} = \Sigma X_{tot}^2 - \text{Step 3}$$
$$SS_{tot} = 629 - 481.67 = 147.33$$

Step 6 Compute the sum of squares between groups for factor A:

$$SS_A = \Sigma \left(\frac{(\text{sum of scores in each column})^2}{n \text{ of scores in the column}} \right) - \text{Step 3}$$

$$SS_A = \left(\frac{(40)^2}{5} + \frac{(30)^2}{5} + \frac{(15)^2}{5} \right) - 481.67 = 63.33$$

Step 7 Compute the sum of squares within groups:

$$SS_{wn} = SS_{tot} - SS_A = \text{Step 4} - \text{Step 5}$$
$$SS_{wn} = 147.33 - 63.33 = 84$$

Table C.4 Summary Table of One-Way Between-Subjects ANOVA

Source	Sum of Squares	df	Mean Square	F
Factor A (Between Groups)	63.33	2	31.67	4.52
Within Groups	84.00	12	7.0	
Total	147.33	14		

Step 8 Compute the degrees of freedom:

a) For factor A: $df_A = k - 1$

$$df_A = 3 - 1 = 2$$

b) Within groups: $df_{wn} = N - k$

$$df_{wn} = 15 - 3 = 12$$

c) Total: $df_{tot} = N - 1$

$$df_{tot} = 15 - 1 = 14$$

Step 9 Compute the mean square for factor A:

$$MS_A = \frac{SS_A}{df_A} = \frac{\text{Step 6}}{\text{Step 8.a}}$$

$$MS_A = \frac{63.33}{2} = 31.67$$

Step 10 Compute the mean square within groups:

$$MS_{wn} = \frac{SS_{wn}}{df_{wn}} = \frac{\text{Step 7}}{\text{Step 8.b}}$$

$$MS_{wn} = \frac{84}{12} = 7.0$$

Step 11 Compute *F*:

$$F = \frac{MS_A}{MS_{wn}} = \frac{\text{Step 9}}{\text{Step 10}}$$

$$F = \frac{31.67}{7.0} = 4.52$$

Step 12 Find the critical value of *F* in Table D.2 of Appendix D, using df_A and df_{wn}. Above, for $df_A = 2$, $df_{wn} = 12$, and $\alpha = .05$, the critical value is 3.88. Here the obtained *F* is beyond the critical value, so it is significant. When *F* is significant, perform Step 13.

Step 13 See section C.8 for post hoc procedures, section C.9 for computing effect size, and section C.10 for computing confidence intervals.

The One-Way Within-Subjects ANOVA

This procedure is discussed in Chapter 6. Example data from a one-way repeated-measures design (with five participants) are shown in Table C.5.

Step 1   Determine k, the number of levels of the factor; then determine the sum of scores (ΣX), the sum of squared scores (ΣX^2), the n, and the X in each level. Also calculate the sum of the scores obtained by each subject, ΣX_{sub} (the sum of each row).

Step 2   Also determine the totals:

$$\Sigma X_{tot} = 17 + 34 + 48 = 99$$

$$\Sigma X^2_{tot} = 69 + 236 + 466 = 771$$

$$N = 5 + 5 + 5 = 15$$

Step 3   Compute the correction term:

$$\text{Correction term} = \frac{(\Sigma X_{tot})^2}{N} = \frac{99^2}{15} = 653.4$$

Step 4   As you perform the following calculations, create the Analysis of Variance Summary Table shown in Table C.6.

Step 5   Compute the total sum of squares:

$$SS_{tot} = \Sigma X^2_{tot} - \text{Step 3}$$

$$SS_{tot} = 771 - 653.4 = 117.6$$

Table C.5 Data from One-Way Repeated Measures Design

	Factor A			
	Level A$_1$	*Level A$_2$*	*Level A$_3$*	*ΣX_{sub}*
Subject 1	2	7	9	18
Subject 2	6	8	11	25
Subject 3	3	5	8	16
Subject 4	2	7	10	19
Subject 5	4	7	10	21
				Totals
	$\Sigma X = 17$	$\Sigma X = 34$	$\Sigma X = 48$	$\Sigma X_{tot} = 99$
	$\Sigma X^2 = 69$	$\Sigma X^2 = 236$	$\Sigma X^2 = 466$	$\Sigma X^2_{tot} = 771$
	$n_1 = 5$	$n_2 = 5$	$n_3 = 5$	$N = 15$
	$\overline{X}_1 = 3.4$	$\overline{X}_2 = 6.8$	$\overline{X}_3 = 9.6$	$k = 3$

Table C.6 Summary Table of One-Way Within-Subjects ANOVA

Source	Sum of Squares	df	Mean Square	F
Factor A				
(Between Groups)	96.40	2	48.20	68.86
Subjects	15.60			
A × Subjects	5.60	8	.70	
Total	117.60	14		

Step 6 Compute the sum of squares for factor A:

$$SS_A = \sum \left(\frac{(\text{sum of scores in each column})^2}{n \text{ of scores in the column}} \right) - \text{Step 3}$$

$$SS_A = \left(\frac{(17)^2}{5} + \frac{(34)^2}{5} + \frac{(48)^2}{5} \right) - 653.4 = 96.4$$

Step 7 Compute the sum of squares for subjects:

$$SS_{subs} = \frac{(\Sigma X_{sub1})^2 + (\Sigma X_{sub2})^2 + \cdots (\Sigma X_{subn})^2}{} - \text{Step 3}$$

$$SS_{subs} = \frac{(18)^2 + (25)^2 + (16)^2 + (19)^2 + (21)^2}{3} - 653.4$$

$$SS_{subs} = 15.6$$

Step 8 Compute the sum of squares for the interaction of A by subjects:

$$SS_{A \times subs} = SS_{tot} - SS_A - SS_{subs} = \text{Step 5} - \text{Step 6} - \text{Step 7}$$

$$SS_{A \times subs} = 117.6 - 96.4 - 15.6 = 5.6$$

Step 9 Compute the degrees of freedom:

(a) Factor A: $df_A = k - 1$

$$df_A = 3 - 1 = 2$$

(b) For A by subjects: $df_{A \times subs} = (k - 1)(\text{number of subjects} - 1)$

$$df_{A \times subs} = (3 - 1)(5 - 1) = 8$$

(c) Total: $df_{tot} = N - 1$

$$df_{tot} = 15 - 1 = 14$$

Step 10 Compute the mean square for factor A:

$$MS_A = \frac{SS_A}{df_A} = \frac{\text{Step 6}}{\text{Step 9.a}}$$

$$MS_A = \frac{96.4}{2} = 48.2$$

Step 11 Compute the mean square for A by subjects:

$$MS_{A \times subs} = \frac{SS_{A \times subs}}{df_{A \times subs}} = \frac{\text{Step 8}}{\text{Step 9.b}}$$

$$MS_{A \times subs} = \frac{5.6}{8} = .70$$

Step 12 Compute F

$$F = \frac{MS_A}{MS_{A \times subs}} = \frac{\text{Step 10}}{\text{Step 11}}$$

$$F = \frac{48.2}{.70} = 68.86$$

Step 13 Find the critical value of F in Table D.2 of Appendix D, with df_A as the degrees of freedom between groups and $df_{A \times subs}$ as the degrees of freedom within groups. Above, for $\alpha = .05$, $df_A = 2$, and $df_{A \times subs} = 8$, the critical value is 4.46, so the obtained F is significant. When F is significant, perform Step 14.

Step 14 See section C.8 for post hoc procedures, section C.9 for computing effect size, and section C.10 for computing confidence intervals.

C.5. The Two-Way Between-Subjects Analysis of Variance

This procedure is discussed in Chapter 7. Table C.7 shows example data from a 3×2 between-subjects design, with three scores per cell.

Step 1 In each cell, compute the sum of the scores (ΣX), the sum of the squared scores (ΣX^2), n, and the mean (the interaction means). Determine k_A, the number of levels of factor A. For each column, compute ΣX, n, and the mean (the main effect means of factor A). Then determine k_B, the number of levels of factor B. For each row, compute ΣX, n, and the mean (the main effect means of factor B).

Step 2 Also determine the totals:

$$\Sigma X_{\text{tot}} = 36 + 69 + 68 = 173$$

$$\Sigma X^2_{\text{tot}} = 218 + 377 + 838 + 56 + 470 + 116 = 2075$$

$$N = 3 + 3 + 3 + 3 + 3 + 3 = 18$$

Step 3 Compute the correction term:

$$\text{Correction term} = \left(\frac{(\Sigma X_{\text{tot}})^2}{N}\right) = \frac{173^2}{18} = 1662.72$$

Table C.7 Data from Two-Way Between-Subjects Design

	Factor A $k_A = 3$			
	A_1	A_2	A_3	
B_1	4	8	18	
	9	12	17	
	11	13	15	
	$\overline{X} = 8$	$\overline{X} = 11$	$\overline{X} = 16.7$	$\overline{X} = 11.89$
	$\Sigma X = 24$	$\Sigma X = 33$	$\Sigma X = 50$	$\Sigma X = 107$
	$\Sigma X^2 = 218$	$\Sigma X^2 = 377$	$\Sigma X^2 = 838$	$n = 9$
	$n = 3$	$n = 3$	$n = 3$	
B_2	2	9	6	
	6	10	8	
	4	17	4	
	$\overline{X} = 4$	$\overline{X} = 12$	$\overline{X} = 6$	$\overline{X} = 7.33$
	$\Sigma X = 12$	$\Sigma X = 36$	$\Sigma X = 18$	$\Sigma X = 66$
	$\Sigma X^2 = 56$	$\Sigma X^2 = 470$	$\Sigma X^2 = 116$	$n = 9$
	$n = 3$	$n = 3$	$n = 3$	
	$\Sigma X = 36$	$\Sigma X = 69$	$\Sigma X = 68$	$\Sigma X_{\text{tot}} = 173$
	$n = 6$	$n = 6$	$n = 6$	$\Sigma X^2_{\text{tot}} = 2075$
	$\overline{X} = 6$	$\overline{X} = 11.5$	$\overline{X} = 11.33$	$N = 18$

Factor B $k_B = 2$

STATISTICAL PROCEDURES

Step 4 As you perform the following calculations, create the analysis of variance summary table shown in Table C.8.

Step 5 Compute the total sum of squares:

$$SS_{tot} = \Sigma X_{tot}^2 - \text{Step 3}$$

$$SS_{tot} = 2075 - 1662.72 = 412.28$$

Step 6 Compute the sum of squares for the column factor A:

$$SS_A = \Sigma \left(\frac{(\text{sum of scores in each column})^2}{n \text{ of scores in the column}} \right) - \text{Step 3}$$

$$SS_A = \left(\frac{(36)^2}{6} + \frac{(69)^2}{6} + \frac{(68)^2}{6} \right) - 1662.72 = 117.45$$

Step 7 Compute the sum of squares for the row factor B:

$$SS_B = \Sigma \left(\frac{(\text{sum of scores in each row})^2}{n \text{ of scores in the row}} \right) - \text{Step 3}$$

$$SS_B = \left(\frac{(107)^2}{9} + \frac{(66)^2}{9} \right) - 1662.72 = 93.39$$

Step 8 Compute the total sum of squares between groups (not reported in the Summary Table):

$$SS_{bn} = \Sigma \left(\frac{(\text{sum of scores in each cell})^2}{n \text{ of scores in the cell}} \right) - \text{Step 3}$$

$$SS_{bn} = \left(\frac{(24)^2}{3} + \frac{(33)^2}{3} + \frac{(50)^2}{3} + \frac{(12)^2}{3} + \frac{(36)^2}{3} + \frac{(18)^2}{3} \right) - 1662.72$$

$$SS_{bn} = 313.61$$

Table C.8 Summary Table of Two-Way, Between-Subjects ANOVA

Source	Sum of Squares	df	Mean Square	F
Factor A	117.45	2	58.73	7.14
Factor B	93.39	1	93.39	11.36
A × B Interaction	102.77	2	51.39	6.25
Within Groups	98.67	12	8.22	
Total	412.28	17		

Step 9 Compute the sum of squares for the A × B interaction:

$$SS_{A \times B} = SS_{bn} - SS_A - SS_B = \text{Step 8} - \text{Step 6} - \text{Step 7}$$

$$SS_{A \times B} = 313.61 - 117.45 - 93.39 = 102.77$$

Step 10 Compute the sum of squares within groups:

$$SS_{wn} = SS_{tot} - SS_{bn} = \text{Step 5} - \text{Step 8}$$

$$SS_{wn} = 412.28 - 313.61 = 98.67$$

Step 11 Compute the degrees of freedom:

(a) Factor A: $df_A = k_A - 1$

$$df_A = 3 - 1 = 2$$

(b) Factor B: $df_B = k_B - 1$

$$df_B = 2 - 1 = 1$$

(c) A × B interaction: $df_{A \times B} = (df_A)(df_B) = (\text{Step 9.a})(\text{Step 9.b})$

$$df_{A \times B} = (2)(1) = 2$$

(d) Within groups: $df_{wn} = N - \text{number of cells}$

$$df_{wn} = 18 - 6 = 12$$

(e) Total: $df_{tot} = N - 1$

$$df_{tot} = 18 - 1 = 17$$

Step 12 Compute the mean square for factor A:

$$MS_A = \frac{SS_A}{df_A} = \frac{\text{Step 6}}{\text{Step 11.a}}$$

$$MS_A = \frac{117.45}{2} = 58.73$$

Step 13 Compute the mean square for factor B:

$$MS_B = \frac{SS_B}{df_B} = \frac{\text{Step 7}}{\text{Step 11.b}}$$

$$MS_B = \frac{93.39}{1} = 93.39$$

Step 14 Compute the mean square for A × B interaction:

$$MS_{A \times B} = \frac{SS_{A \times B}}{df_{A \times B}} = \frac{\text{Step 9}}{\text{Step 10.c}}$$

$$MS_{A \times B} = \frac{102.77}{2} = 51.39$$

Step 15   Compute the mean square within groups:

$$MS_{wn} = \frac{SS_{wn}}{df_{wn}} = \frac{\text{Step 10}}{\text{Step 10.d}}$$

$$MS_{wn} = \frac{98.67}{12} = 8.22$$

Step 16   Compute the F for the main effect of factor A:

$$F_A = \frac{MS_A}{MS_{wn}} = \frac{\text{Step 12}}{\text{Step 15}}$$

$$F_A = \frac{58.73}{8.22} = 7.14$$

Step 17   Find the critical value of F for factor A in Table D.2 of Appendix D, for df_A as the degrees of freedom between groups and df_{wn}. Above, for $\alpha = .05$, $df_A = 2$, and $df_{wn} = 12$, the critical value is 3.89 and the obtained F of 7.14 is significant.

Step 18   Compute the F for the main effect of factor B:

$$F_B = \frac{MS_B}{MS_{wn}} = \frac{\text{Step 13}}{\text{Step 15}}$$

$$F_B = \frac{93.39}{8.22} = 11.36$$

Step 19   Find the critical values of F for factor B in Table D.2 of Appendix D, for df_B as the degrees of freedom between groups and df_{wn}. For $\alpha = .05$, $df_B = 1$, and $df_{wn} = 12$, the critical value is 4.75 and so the obtained F of 11.36 is significant.

Step 20   Compute the F for the A × B interaction:

$$F_{A \times B} = \frac{MS_{A \times B}}{MS_{wn}} = \frac{\text{Step 14}}{\text{Step 15}}$$

$$F_{A \times B} = \frac{51.39}{8.22} = 6.25$$

Step 21   Find the critical value of F for the interaction in Table D.2 of Appendix D, for $df_{A \times B}$ as the degrees of freedom between groups and df_{wn}. Above, for

$\alpha = .05$, $df_{A \times B} = 2$, and $df_{wn} = 12$, the critical value is 3.89, and the obtained F of 6.25 is significant.

Step 22   For each significant F, see section C.8 for post hoc procedures, section C.9 for computing effect size, and section C.10 for computing confidence intervals.

C.6. The Two-Way Within-Subjects Analysis of Variance

This procedure is discussed in Chapter 7. Table C.9 shows example data from a 2×2 within-subjects design, with three scores per cell.

Table C.9   Data from 2×2 Within-Subjects Design

		Factor A		
		A_1	A_2	$k_A = 2$
B_1	Subject 1	8	18	
	Subject 2	12	17	
	Subject 3	13	15	
		$\overline{X} = 11$	$\overline{X} = 16.7$	$\overline{X} = 13.85$
		$\Sigma X = 33$	$\Sigma X = 50$	$\Sigma X = 83$
		$\Sigma X^2 = 377$	$\Sigma X^2 = 838$	$n = 6$
		$n = 3$	$n = 3$	
B_2	Subject 1	9	6	
	Subject 2	10	8	
	Subject 3	17	4	
		$\overline{X} = 12$	$\overline{X} = 6$	$\overline{X} = 9$
		$\Sigma X = 36$	$\Sigma X = 18$	$\Sigma X = 54$
		$\Sigma X^2 = 470$	$\Sigma X^2 = 116$	$n = 6$
		$n = 3$	$n = 3$	
		$\Sigma X = 69$	$\Sigma X = 68$	$\Sigma X_{total} = 137$
		$n = 6$	$n = 6$	$\Sigma X_{total}^2 = 1801$
		$\overline{X} = 11.5$	$\overline{X} = 11.33$	$N = 12$
				$k_A = 2$

Factor B
$k_B = 2$

Step 1   In each cell, compute the sum of scores, ΣX, the sum of the squared scores, ΣX^2, n, and the mean (the interaction means). Determine k_A, the number of levels of factor A, and for each column, compute ΣX, n, and the mean (the main effect means of factor A). Determine k_B, the number of levels of factor B, and for each row, compute ΣX, n, and the mean (the main effect means of factor B).

Step 2   Also determine:

$$\Sigma X_{total} = 69 + 68 = 137$$

$$\Sigma X^2_{total} = 377 + 838 + 470 + 116 = 1801$$

$$N = 3 + 3 + 3 + 3 = 12$$

Then create a table in which you collapse across factor B (as in Table C.10), and create another table in which you collapse across factor A (as in Table C.11). Note: the ΣX_{sub} for each subject must be the same in each table.

Step 3   Compute the correction term:

$$\text{Correction term} = \left(\frac{(\Sigma X_{total})^2}{N}\right) = \frac{137^2}{12} = 1564.08$$

Table C.10   A × Subject Table after Collapsing across Factor B

	Factor A		
	A_1	A_2	ΣX_{sub}
Subject 1	17	24	41
Subject 2	22	25	47
Subject 3	30	19	49

Table C.11   B × Subject Table after Collapsing across Factor A

	Factor B		
	B_1	B_2	ΣX_{sub}
Subject 1	26	15	41
Subject 2	29	18	47
Subject 3	28	21	49

Step 4 As you perform the following calculations, create the Analysis of Variance Summary Table shown in Table C.12. (Note that the table has components due to each factor and due to the interaction of factors and subjects.)

Step 5 Compute the total sum of squares:

$$SS_{tot} = \Sigma X^2_{total} - \text{Step 3}$$

$$SS_{tot} = 1801 - 1564.08 = 236.92$$

Step 6 Compute the sum of squares for the column factor A:

$$SS_A = \Sigma \left(\frac{(\text{sum of scores in each column})^2}{n \text{ of scores in the column}} \right) - \text{Step 3}$$

$$SS_A = \left(\frac{(69)^2}{6} + \frac{(68)^2}{6} \right) - 1564.08 = .09$$

Step 7 Compute the sum of squares for the row factor B:

$$SS_B = \Sigma \left(\frac{(\text{sum of scores in each row})^2}{n \text{ of scores in the row}} \right) - \text{Step 3}$$

$$SS_B = \left(\frac{(83)^2}{6} + \frac{(54)^2}{6} \right) - 1564.08 = 70.09$$

Step 8 Compute the total sum of squares between groups (not reported in the Summary Table):

$$SS_{bn} = \Sigma \left(\frac{(\text{Sum of scores in each cell})^2}{n \text{ of scores in the cell}} \right) - \text{Step 3}$$

Table C.12 Summary Table of Two-Way, Within-Subjects ANOVA

Source	Sum of Squares	df	Mean Square	F
Factor				
A	.09	1	.09	.004
B	70.09	1	70.09	52.70
A × B	102.07	1	102.07	23.52
Subjects				
A × S	44.66	2	22.33	
B × S	2.66	2	1.33	
A × B × S	8.68	2	4.34	
Total	236.92	11		

$$SS_{bn} = \left(\frac{(33)^2}{3} + \frac{(50)^2}{3} + \frac{(36)^2}{3} + \frac{(18)^2}{3}\right) - 1564.08$$

$$SS_{bn} = 172.25$$

Step 9 Compute the sum of squares for the A × B interaction:

$$SS_{A \times B} = SS_{bn} - SS_A - SS_B = \text{Step 8} - \text{Step 6} - \text{Step 7}$$

$$SS_{A \times B} = 172.25 - .09 - 70.09 = 102.07$$

Step 10 Compute the sum of squares for Subjects (not reported in Summary Table):

$$SS_{subs} = \frac{(\Sigma X_{sub1})^2 + (\Sigma X_{sub2})^2 \cdots + (\Sigma X_n)^2}{} - \text{Step 3}$$

$$SS_{subs} = \frac{(41)^2 + (47)^2 + (49)^2}{(2)(2)} - 1564.08$$

$$SS_{subs} = 8.67$$

Step 11 Compute the sum of squares for the A × S interaction (Table C.10):

$$SS_{A \times S} = \Sigma \frac{(\text{sum of each A} \times \text{Subject score})^2}{k_B} - \text{Step 3} - SS_A - SS_{subs}$$

$$SS_{A \times S} = \Sigma \frac{(\text{sum of each A} \times \text{Subject score})^2}{k_B} - \text{Step 3} - \text{Step 6} - \text{Step 10}$$

$$SS_{A \times S} = \frac{(17)^2 + (24)^2 + (22)^2 + (25)^2 + (30)^2 + (19)^2}{2}$$
$$- 1564.08 - .09 - 8.67$$

$$SS_{A \times S} = 44.66$$

Step 12 Compute the sum of squares for the B × S interaction (Table C.11):

$$SS_{B \times S} = \Sigma \frac{(\text{sum of each B} \times \text{Subject score})^2}{k_A} - \text{Step 3} - SS_B - SS_{subs}$$

$$SS_{B \times S} = \Sigma \frac{(\text{sum of each B} \times \text{Subject score})^2}{k_A} - \text{Step 3} - \text{Step 7} - \text{Step 10}$$

$$SS_{B \times S} = \frac{(26)^2 + (15)^2 + (29)^2 + (18)^2 + (28)^2 + (21)^2}{2}$$
$$- 1564.08 - 70.09 - 8.67$$

$$SS_{B \times S} = 2.66$$

Step 13   Compute the sum of squares for the A × B × S interaction:

$$SS_{A \times B \times S} = SS_{tot} - SS_A - SS_B - SS_{A \times B} - SS_{subs} - SS_{A \times S} - SS_{B \times S}$$

$$SS_{A \times B \times S} = \text{Step 5} - \text{Step 6} - \text{Step 7} - \text{Step 9} - \text{Step 10} - \text{Step 11} \\ - \text{Step 12}$$

$$SS_{A \times B \times S} = 236.92 - .09 - 70.09 - 102.07 - 8.67 - 44.66 \\ - 2.66$$

$$SS_{A \times B \times S} = 8.68$$

Step 14   Compute the degrees of freedom:

(a) Factor A:

$$df_A = k_A - 1$$
$$df_A = 2 - 1 = 2$$

(b) Factor B:

$$df_B = k_B - 1$$
$$df_B = 2 - 1 = 1$$

(c) A × B interaction:

$$df_{A \times B} = (df_A)(df_B)$$
$$df_{A \times B} = (1)(1) = 1$$

(d) Subjects:

$$df_S = \text{Number of subjects} - 1$$
$$df_S = 3 - 1 = 2$$

(e) A × Subjects interaction:

$$df_{A \times S} = (df_A)(df_S)$$
$$df_{A \times S} = (1)(2) = 2$$

(f) B × Subjects interaction:

$$df_{B \times S} = (df_B)(df_S)$$
$$df_{B \times S} = (1)(2) = 2$$

(g) A × B × Subjects interaction:

$$df_{A \times B \times S} = (df_A)(df_B)(df_S)$$
$$df_{A \times B \times S} = (1)(1)(2) = 2$$

(h) Total:

$$df_{tot} = N - 1$$
$$df_{tot} = 12 - 1 = 11$$

Step 15 Compute the mean square for factor A:

$$MS_A = \frac{SS_A}{df_A} = \frac{\text{Step 6}}{\text{Step 14.a}}$$

$$MS_A = \frac{.09}{1} = .09$$

Step 16 Compute the mean square for factor B:

$$MS_B = \frac{SS_B}{df_B} = \frac{\text{Step 7}}{\text{Step 14.b}}$$

$$MS_B = \frac{70.09}{1} = 70.09$$

Step 17 Compute the mean square for the A × B interaction:

$$MS_{A \times B} = \frac{SS_{A \times B}}{df_{A \times B}} = \frac{\text{Step 9}}{\text{Step 14.c}}$$

$$MS_{A \times B} = \frac{102.07}{1} = 102.07$$

Step 18 Compute the mean square for the A × S interaction:

$$MS_{A \times S} = \frac{SS_{A \times S}}{df_{A \times S}} = \frac{\text{Step 11}}{\text{Step 14.e}}$$

$$MS_{A \times S} = \frac{44.66}{2} = 22.33$$

Step 19 Compute the mean square for the B × S interaction:

$$MS_{B \times S} = \frac{SS_{B \times S}}{df_{B \times S}} = \frac{\text{Step 12}}{\text{Step 14.f}}$$

$$MS_{B \times S} = \frac{2.66}{2} = 1.33$$

Step 20 Compute the mean square for the A × B × S interaction:

$$MS_{A \times B \times S} = \frac{SS_{A \times B \times S}}{df_{A \times B \times S}} = \frac{\text{Step 13}}{\text{Step 14.g}}$$

$$MS_{A \times B \times S} = \frac{8.68}{2} = 4.34$$

Step 21 Compute the F for the main effect of factor A:

$$F_A = \frac{MS_A}{MS_{A \times S}} = \frac{\text{Step 15}}{\text{Step 18}}$$

$$F_A = \frac{.09}{22.33} = .004$$

Step 22 Compute the F for the main effect of factor B:

$$F_B = \frac{MS_B}{MS_{B \times S}} = \frac{\text{Step 16}}{\text{Step 19}}$$

$$F_B = \frac{70.09}{1.33} = 52.70$$

Step 23 Compute the F for the A $\times$ B interaction:

$$F_{A \times B} = \frac{MS_{A \times B}}{MS_{A \times B \times S}} = \frac{\text{Step 17}}{\text{Step 20}}$$

$$F_{A \times B} = \frac{102.07}{4.34} = 23.52$$

Step 24 For each obtained F, find the appropriate critical value in Table D.2 in Appendix D, using as degrees of freedom:

(a) For Factor A: df_A is the df between and $df_{A \times S}$ is the df within. Above, for $\alpha = .05$ and $df_A = 1$, and $df_{A \times S} = 2$, F_{crit} is 18.51, so F_{obt} of .004 is not significant.

(b) For Factor B: df_B is the df between and $df_{B \times S}$ is the df within. Above, for $\alpha = .05$ and $df_B = 1$, and $df_{B \times S} = 2$, the F_{crit} is 18.51, so F_{obt} of 52.70 is significant.

(c) For A $\times$ B: $df_{A \times B}$ is the df between and $df_{A \times B \times S}$ is the df within. Above, for $\alpha = .05$ and $df_{A \times B} = 1$ and $df_{A \times B \times S} = 2$, the F_{crit} is 18.51, so F_{obt} of 23.52 is significant.

Step 25 For each significant F see section C.8 for post hoc procedures, section C.9 for computing effect size, and section C.10 for computing confidence intervals.

C.7. *The Two-Way Mixed-Design Analysis of Variance*

This procedure is discussed in Chapter 7. Table C.13 shown example data from a 2×3 mixed design. Factor A—the Row Factor—is a between-subjects factor (with 3 subjects per level), and factor B—the Column Factor—is a within-subjects factor.

Step 1   In each cell, compute the sum of scores (ΣX), the sum of the squared scores (ΣX^2), n, and the mean (the interaction means). Determine k_A, the number of levels of factor A. For each row, compute ΣX, n, and the mean (the main effect means of factor A). Then determine k_B, the number of levels of factor B. For each column, compute ΣX, n, and the mean (the main effect means of factor B).

Also calculate the sum of the scores obtained by each subject, ΣX_{sub} (the sum of each row).

Table C.13   Data from Two-Way Mixed Design

Factor A is a between-subjects factor, and factor B is a within-subjects factor

		Factor B $k_B = 3$			
		B_1	B_2	B_3	ΣX_{sub}
A_1	Subject 1	4	8	18	30
	Subject 2	9	12	17	38
	Subject 3	11	13	15	39
		$\overline{X} = 8$	$\overline{X} = 11$	$\overline{X} = 16.7$	$\overline{X} = 11.89$
		$\Sigma X = 24$	$\Sigma X = 33$	$\Sigma X = 50$	$\Sigma X = 107$
		$\Sigma X^2 = 218$	$\Sigma X^2 = 377$	$\Sigma X^2 = 838$	$n = 9$
		$n = 3$	$n = 3$	$n = 3$	
A_2	Subject 4	2	9	6	17
	Subject 5	6	10	8	24
	Subject 6	4	17	4	25
		$\overline{X} = 4$	$\overline{X} = 12$	$\overline{X} = 6$	$\overline{X} = 7.33$
		$\Sigma X = 12$	$\Sigma X = 36$	$\Sigma X = 18$	$\Sigma X = 66$
		$\Sigma X^2 = 56$	$\Sigma X^2 = 470$	$\Sigma X^2 = 116$	$n = 9$
		$n = 3$	$n = 3$	$n = 3$	
		$\Sigma X = 36$	$\Sigma X = 69$	$\Sigma X = 68$	$\Sigma X_{tot} = 173$
		$n = 6$	$n = 6$	$n = 6$	$\Sigma X_{tot}^2 = 2075$
		$\overline{X} = 6$	$\overline{X} = 11.5$	$\overline{X} = 11.33$	$N = 18$

Factor A $k_A = 2$

Step 2 Determine the totals:

$$\Sigma X_{tot} = 36 + 69 + 68 = 173$$

$$\Sigma X^2_{tot} = 218 + 377 + 838 + 56 + 470 + 116 = 2075$$

$$N = 3 + 3 + 3 + 3 + 3 + 3 = 18$$

Step 3 Compute the correction term:

$$\text{Correction term} = \left(\frac{(\Sigma X_{tot})^2}{N}\right) = \frac{173^2}{18} = 1662.72$$

Step 4 As you perform the following calculations, create the Analysis of Variance Summary Table shown in Table C.14.

Step 5 Compute the total sum of squares:

$$SS_{tot} = \Sigma X^2_{tot} - \text{Step 3}$$

$$SS_{tot} = 2075 - 1662.72 = 412.28$$

Step 6 Compute the sum of squares for subjects (not reported in the Summary Table):

$$SS_{subs} = \frac{(\Sigma X_{sub1})^2 + (\Sigma X_{sub2})^2 \cdots + (\Sigma X_n)^2}{} - \text{Step 3}$$

$$SS_{subs} = \frac{(30)^2 + (38)^2 + (39)^2 + (17)^2 + (24)^2 + (25)^2}{3} - 1662.72$$

$$SS_{subs} = 122.28$$

Table C.14 Summary Table of Two-Way Mixed Design ANOVA

Source	Sum of Squares	df	Mean Square	F
Between Groups				
Factor A	93.39	1	93.39	12.93
Error Between	28.89	4	7.22	
Within Groups				
Factor B	117.45	2	58.73	6.74
A × B interaction	102.77	2	51.39	5.89
Error Within	69.78	8	8.72	
Total	412.28	17		

Step 7 Compute the sum of squares for the between-subjects, row factor A:

$$SS_A = \sum \left(\frac{(\text{sum of scores in each row})^2}{n \text{ of scores in the row}} \right) - \text{Step 3}$$

$$SS_A = \left(\frac{(107)^2}{9} + \frac{(66)^2}{9} \right) - 1662.72 = 93.39$$

Step 8 Compute the sum of squares for the within-subjects, column factor B:

$$SS_B = \sum \left(\frac{(\text{sum of scores in each column})^2}{n \text{ of scores in the column}} \right) - \text{Step 3}$$

$$SS_B = \left(\frac{(36)^2}{6} + \frac{(69)^2}{6} + \frac{(68)^2}{6} \right) - 1662.72 = 117.45$$

Step 9 Compute the sum of squares for error between subjects:

$$SS_{e:bn} = SS_{subs} - SS_A = \text{Step 6} - \text{Step 7}$$

$$SS_{e:bn} = 122.28 - 93.39 = 28.89$$

Step 10 Compute the total sum of squares between groups (not reported in the Summary Table):

$$SS_{bn} = \sum \left(\frac{(\text{sum of scores in each cell})^2}{n \text{ of scores in the cell}} \right) - \text{Step 3}$$

$$SS_{bn} = \left(\frac{(24)^2}{3} + \frac{(33)^2}{3} + \frac{(50)^2}{3} + \frac{(12)^2}{3} + \frac{(36)^2}{3} + \frac{(18)^2}{3} \right) - 1662.72$$

$$SS_{bn} = 313.61$$

Step 11 Compute the sum of squares for the A × B interaction:

$$SS_{A \times B} = SS_{bn} - SS_A - SS_B = \text{Step 10} - \text{Step 7} - \text{Step 8}$$

$$SS_{A \times B} = 313.61 - 93.39 - 117.45 = 102.77$$

Step 12 Compute the sum of squares for error within subjects:

$$SS_{e:wn} = SS_{tot} - SS_{subs} - SS_B - SS_{A \times B}$$

$$SS_{e:wn} = \text{Step 5} - \text{Step 6} - \text{Step 8} - \text{Step 11}$$

$$= 412.28 - 122.28 - 117.45 - 102.77 = 69.78$$

Step 13 Compute the degrees of freedom:

(a) Factor A: $df_A = k_A - 1$
$$df_A = 2 - 1 = 1$$

(b) Factor B: $df_B = k_B - 1$
$$df_B = 3 - 1 = 2$$

(c) A × B interaction: $df_{A \times B} = (df_A)(df_B) = (\text{Step 13.a})(\text{Step 13.b})$
$$df_{A \times B} = (1)(2) = 2$$

(d) Error between groups: $df_{e:bn} = (k_A)(n - 1)$
$$df_{e:bn} = (2)(3 - 1) = 4$$

(e) Error within subjects: $df_{e:wn} = (k_B - 1)(k_A)(n - 1)$
$$df_{e:wn} = (3 - 1)(2)(3 - 1) = 8$$

(f) Total: $df_{tot} = N - 1$
$$df_{tot} = 18 - 1 = 17$$

Step 14 Compute the mean square for factor A:

$$MS_A = \frac{SS_A}{df_A} = \frac{\text{Step 7}}{\text{Step 13.a}}$$

$$MS_A = \frac{93.39}{1} = 93.39$$

Step 15 Compute the mean square for factor B:

$$MS_B = \frac{SS_B}{df_B} = \frac{\text{Step 8}}{\text{Step 13.b}}$$

$$MS_B = \frac{117.45}{2} = 58.73$$

Step 16 Compute the mean square for the A × B interaction:

$$MS_{A \times B} = \frac{SS_{A \times B}}{df_{A \times B}} = \frac{\text{Step 11}}{\text{Step 13.c}}$$

$$MS_{A \times B} = \frac{102.77}{2} = 51.39$$

Step 17   Compute the mean square for error between groups:

$$MS_{e:bn} = \frac{SS_{e:bn}}{df_{e:bn}} = \frac{\text{Step 9}}{\text{Step 13.d}}$$

$$MS_{e:bn} = \frac{28.89}{4} = 7.22$$

Step 18   Compute the mean square for error within subjects:

$$MS_{e:wn} = \frac{SS_{e:wn}}{df_{e:wn}} = \frac{\text{Step 12}}{\text{Step 13.e}}$$

$$MS_{e:wn} = \frac{69.78}{8} = 8.72$$

Step 19   Compute F for the main effect of A:

$$F_A = \frac{MS_A}{MS_{e:bn}} = \frac{\text{Step 14}}{\text{Step 17}}$$

$$F_A = \frac{93.39}{7.22} = 12.93$$

Step 20   Find the critical value of F for factor A in Table D.2 of Appendix D, using df_A as the degrees of freedom between groups and $df_{e:bn}$ as the degrees of freedom within groups. Above, for $\alpha = .05$, $df_A = 1$, and $df_{e:bn} = 4$, the critical value is 7.71.

Step 21   Compute F for the main effect of B:

$$F_B = \frac{MS_B}{MS_{e:wn}} = \frac{\text{Step 15}}{\text{Step 18}}$$

$$F_B = \frac{58.73}{8.72} = 6.74$$

Step 22   Find the critical value of F for factor B in Table D.2 of Appendix D, using df_B as the degrees of freedom between groups and $df_{e:wn}$ as the degrees of freedom within groups. Above, for $\alpha = .05$, $df_B = 2$, and $df_{e:wn} = 8$, the critical value is 4.46.

Step 23   Compute the F for the A $\times$ B interaction:

$$F_{A \times B} = \frac{MS_{A \times B}}{MS_{e:wn}} = \frac{\text{Step 16}}{\text{Step 18}}$$

$$F_{A \times B} = \frac{51.39}{8.72} = 5.89$$

Step 24 Find the critical value of F for the interaction in Table D.2 of Appendix D, using $df_{A \times B}$ as the degrees of freedom between groups and $df_{e:wn}$ as the degrees of freedom within groups. Above, for $\alpha = .05$, $df_{A \times B} = 2$, and $df_{e:wn} = 8$, the critical value is 4.46.

Step 25 For each F that is significant, see section C.8 for post hoc procedures, section C.9 for computing effect size, and section C.10 for computing confidence intervals.

C.8. Tukey HSD Post Hoc Comparisons

Below are two procedures for using the Tukey HSD Multiple Comparisons test, one for post hoc comparisons within significant main effects and the other for post hoc comparisons within significant interactions.

Post Hoc Comparison for Main Effects

This procedure, discussed in Chapters 6 and 7, may be used with either a between-subjects or a within-subjects design in a one-way ANOVA, or to examine main-effect means in a multifactor ANOVA. It is appropriate *only* if the ns in all levels of the factor are equal.

Table C.15 presents a summary of the one-way between-subjects ANOVA from section C.4.

Table C.15 Data from One-Way Between-Subjects Design

	Factor A	
Level A₁	*Level A₂*	*Level A₃*
9	4	1
12	6	3
4	8	4
8	2	5
7	10	2
$n_1 = 5$	$n_2 = 5$	$n_3 = 5$
$\overline{X}_1 = 8$	$\overline{X}_2 = 6$	$\overline{X}_3 = 3$

$k = 3$

$$MS_A = \frac{SS_A}{df_A} = \frac{63.33}{2} = 31.67$$

$$MS_{wn} = \frac{SS_{wn}}{df_{wn}} = \frac{84}{12} = 7.0$$

$$F = \frac{MS_A}{MS_{wn}} = \frac{31.67}{7.0} = 4.52$$

Step 1   Find "q_k" in Table D.3 of Appendix D, using k (the number of levels in the factor) and df_{wn} (the df used when calculating the denominator of the obtained F). Below, for $k = 3$, $df_{wn} = 12$; and $\alpha = .05$, $q_k = 3.77$.

Step 2   Compute HSD:

$$\text{HSD} = (q_k)\left(\sqrt{\frac{\text{denominator in } F \text{ ratio}}{n}}\right)$$

where "denominator in F ratio" is the MS used as the denominator when calculating the F, and n is the number of scores that each mean being compared is based upon. In the example above, $MS_{wn} = 7.0$ and $n = 5$.

$$\text{HSD} = (3.77)\left(\sqrt{\frac{7.0}{5}}\right) = 4.46$$

Step 3   Determine the differences between all means, by subtracting each mean from every other mean.

Step 4   Compare the absolute difference between any two means to the HSD value. If the difference is *greater* than the HSD, then these two means differ significantly. Above, the difference between $X_1 = 8$ and $X_3 = 3$ is 5, which is greater than 4.46, so these means differ significantly. However, $X_2 = 6$ differs from these means by 2 and 3, respectively. Because 2 and 3 are less than 4.46, X_2 does not differ significantly from the other means.

Post Hoc Comparison for Interaction Effects

This procedure, discussed in Chapter 7, is used to compare the cell means of an interaction in either a between-subjects or a within-subjects design. It involves a correction developed by Cicchetti (1972) that reduces the probability of making Type II errors, based on adjusting k so that it reflects the actual number of unconfounded comparisons being performed.

   Table C.16 presents a summary of the two-way between-subjects ANOVA from section C.5.

Step 1   Determine the "adjusted k" from Table C.17. In the left-hand column, locate the type of interaction being examined, regardless of the order of the numbers describing the factors (e.g., a 3 × 2 design is the same as a 2 × 3 design). In the right-hand column is the adjusted value of k. In the example, the design is a 2 × 3, so the adjusted $k = 5$.

Table C.16 Data from Two-Way Between-Subjects Design

Factor A

		A_1	A_2	A_3
	B_1	4 9 11 $\overline{X} = 8$ $n = 3$	8 12 13 $\overline{X} = 11$ $n = 3$	18 17 15 $\overline{X} = 16.7$ $n = 3$
Factor B	B_2	2 6 4 $\overline{X} = 4$ $n = 3$	9 10 17 $\overline{X} = 12$ $n = 3$	6 8 4 $\overline{X} = 6$ $n = 3$

$$MS_{A \times B} = \frac{SS_{A \times B}}{df_{A \times B}} = \frac{102.77}{2} = 51.39$$

$$MS_{wn} = \frac{SS_{wn}}{df_{wn}} = \frac{98.67}{12} = 8.22$$

$$F_{A \times B} = \frac{MS_{A \times B}}{MS_{wn}} = \frac{51.39}{8.22} = 6.25$$

Table C.17 Values of Adjusted k

Design of Study	Adjusted Value of k
2×2	3
2×3	5
2×4	6
3×3	7
3×4	8
4×4	10
4×5	12

STATISTICAL PROCEDURES

Step 2 Find "q_k" in Table D.3 of Appendix D, using the adjusted value of k and df_{wn} (the df used when calculating the denominator of the F). Above, for $k = 5$, $df_{wn} = 12$, and for $\alpha = .05$, $q_k = 4.51$.

Step 3 Compute HSD:

$$\text{HSD} = (q_k)\left(\sqrt{\frac{\text{denominator in } F \text{ ratio}}{n}}\right)$$

where "denominator in F ratio" is the MS used as the denominator when calculating the F, and n is the number of scores that each mean being compared is based upon. Above, $MS_{wn} = 8.22$ and $n = 3$.

$$\text{HSD} = (4.51)\left(\sqrt{\frac{8.22}{3}}\right) = 7.47$$

Step 4 Determine the differences between all *unconfounded* means, by subtracting each mean from every other mean in the same row or in the same column.

Step 5 Compare the absolute differences between any two means to the HSD value. If the difference is greater than the HSD, then these two means differ significantly.

C.9. Measures of Effect Size in t-Tests and ANOVA

This procedure are discussed in Chapter 7. Compute effect size in t-tests by computing r^2_{pb}, and compute effect size in ANOVA by computing η^2.

Effect Size in t-Tests

This procedure can be used to compute r^2_{pb} in an independent samples (between-subjects) t-test and in a dependent samples (within-subjects) t-test. Calculate r^2_{pb} using the formula:

$$r^2_{pb} = \frac{(t)^2}{(t)^2 + df}$$

where $(t)^2$ is the squared value of the obtained t and df are the degrees of freedom, calculated in the t-test.

For example, in the independent samples t-test in section C.3, $t = -2.524$ and $df = 18$. Thus:

$$r^2_{pb} = \frac{(t)^2}{(t)^2 + df} = \frac{2.524^2}{2.524^2 + 8} = .44$$

Note: The square root of r_{pb} equals the correlation coefficient, r_{pb}, between the indenpendent and dependent variables.

Effect Size in ANOVA

Eta squared (η^2) may be calculated for each between-subjects or within-subjects main effect or interaction in an ANOVA, using the formula

$$\eta^2 = \frac{\text{sum of squares for the effect}}{SS_{tot}}$$

where "sum of squares for the effect" is the sum of squares used in calculating the numerator of the F, whether it is SS_A, SS_B, or $SS_{A \times B}$. The SS_{tot} is the total sum of squares in the ANOVA. For example, the one-way between-subjects ANOVA from section C.4 produced Table C.18.

The effect size for factor A is:

$$\eta^2 = \frac{SS_A}{SS_{tot}} = \frac{63.33}{147.33} = .43$$

(The square root of η^2 equals η, the correlation coefficient between the independent and dependent variables.)

C.10. Confidence Intervals

This procedure is discussed in Chapter 6. Below are the formulas for computing a confidence interval from the results of a t-test and from an ANOVA.

Confidence Intervals in *t*-Tests

The formula for a confidence interval for a population mean, μ, represented by a sample mean is

$$\left(\frac{s_x}{\sqrt{n}}\right)(-t_{crit}) + X \le \mu \le \left(\frac{s_x}{\sqrt{n}}\right)(+t_{crit}) + X$$

Table C.18 Summary Table of One-Way Between-Subjects ANOVA

Source	Sum of Squares	df	Mean Square	F
Factor A	63.33	2	31.67	4.52
Within Groups	84.00	12	7.0	
Total	147.33	14		

Step 1   Compute s_x from the scores in the group, using the formula for the estimated population standard deviation in section C.2.

Step 2   Determine n, the number of scores in the group.

Step 3   Find t_{crit}, the two-tailed value in Table D.1 of Appendix D, for $df = n - 1$, where n is the number of scores in the group. Using $\alpha = .05$ creates a 95% confidence interval and using $\alpha = .01$ creates a 99% confidence interval.

Step 4   Compute X, the mean of the scores in the group.
    As an example, say that a condition in a between-subjects t-test produces the following data: $n = 9$, $s_x = 2.25$, and $X = 11.5$. The two-tailed t_{crit} for $df = 8$ and $\alpha = .05$ is ± 2.306. Thus:

$$\left(\frac{s_x}{\sqrt{n}}\right)(-t_{crit}) + X \leq \mu \leq \left(\frac{s_x}{\sqrt{n}}\right)(+t_{crit}) + X$$

$$\left(\frac{2.25}{\sqrt{9}}\right)(-2.306) + 11.5 \leq \mu \leq \left(\frac{2.25}{\sqrt{9}}\right)(+2.306) + 11.5$$

$$-1.73 + 11.5 \leq \mu \leq +1.73 + 11.5$$

$$9.77 \leq \mu \leq 13.23$$

The 95% confidence interval for the population mean, μ, represented by this sample mean is 9.77 to 13.23.

Confidence Intervals in ANOVA

To compute the confidence interval for the population mean, μ, represented by the mean of any level or cell in an ANOVA, use this formula:

$$\left(\sqrt{\frac{MS_{wn}}{n}}\right)(-t_{crit}) + X \leq \mu \leq \left(\sqrt{\frac{MS_{wn}}{n}}\right)(+t_{crit}) + X$$

Step 1   Determine MS_{wn}, the denominator used in computing F.

Step 2   Determine n, the number of scores that the mean is based on.

Step 3   Find t_{crit}, the two-tailed value in Table D.1 of Appendix D, for the df used in computing the denominator of the obtained F. Using $\alpha = .05$ creates a 95% confidence interval and using $\alpha = .01$ creates a 99% confidence interval.

Step 4   Compute X, the mean of the level or cell being described.
    For example, say that a condition in a between-subjects ANOVA produced a $X = 8.0$ with $n = 5$, and in computing the main effect F involving that condition,

$MS_{wn} = 7.0$, and $df_{wn} = 12$. The two-tailed t_{crit} for $df = 12$ and $\alpha = .05$ is ± 2.179. Thus:

$$\left(\sqrt{\frac{7.0}{5}}\right)(-2.179) + 8.0 \leq \mu \leq \left(\sqrt{\frac{7.0}{5}}\right)(+2.179) + 8.0$$

$$-2.578 + 8.0 \leq \mu \leq +2.578 + 8.0$$

$$5.42 \leq \mu \leq 10.58$$

The 95% confidence interval for the population mean, μ, represented by this sample mean is 5.42 to 10.58.

C.11. Pearson Correlation Coefficient, Linear Regression, and Standard Error of the Estimate

Below are procedures for computing the Pearson r, the linear regression equation, and the standard error of the estimate. These procedures are discussed in Chapter 8.

The Pearson Correlation Coefficient

Example data are shown in Table C.19.

Table C.19   Data for Pearson Correlation Coefficient

Subject	X Score	Y Score	XY
1	1	2	2
2	1	4	4
3	2	4	8
4	2	6	12
5	2	2	4
6	3	4	12
7	3	7	21
8	3	8	24
9	4	6	24
10	4	8	32
11	4	7	28
$N = 11$	$\Sigma X = 29$	$\Sigma Y = 58$	$\Sigma XY = 171$
	$\Sigma X^2 = 89$	$\Sigma Y^2 = 354$	
	$(\Sigma X)^2 = 841$	$(\Sigma Y)^2 = 3364$	

Step 1   Calculate ΣX, the sum of the X scores, and $(\Sigma X)^2$, the squared sum of the X scores.

Step 2   Calculate ΣY, the sum of the Y scores, and $(\Sigma Y)^2$, the squared sum of the Y scores.

Step 3   Calculate ΣX^2, the sum of the squared X scores, and ΣY^2, the sum of the squared Y scores.

Step 4   Calculate ΣXY, the sum after multiplying each X score in a pair times its corresponding Y score.

Step 5   Determine N, the number of pairs of scores in the sample.

Step 6   Calculate r:

$$r = \frac{N(\Sigma XY) - (\Sigma X)(\Sigma Y)}{\sqrt{[N(\Sigma X^2) - (\Sigma X)^2][N(\Sigma Y^2) - (\Sigma Y)^2]}}$$

$$r = \frac{11(171) - (29)(58)}{\sqrt{[11(89) - 841][11(354) - 3364]}}$$

$$r = \frac{199}{\sqrt{[138][530]}} = +.736$$

Step 7   Find the critical value of r in Table D.4 of Appendix D, using degrees of freedom *(df)* equal to $N - 2$, where N is the number of pairs of scores. Above, for $df = 9$ and $\alpha = .05$, the two-tailed critical value is $\pm.602$ (so the obtained r is significant).

The Linear Regression Equation

Step 1   Compute b, the slope of the regression line:

$$b = \frac{N(\Sigma XY) - (\Sigma X)(\Sigma Y)}{}$$

In the Pearson correlation coefficient example (Table C.19), $\Sigma X = 29$, $\Sigma Y = 58$, $\Sigma XY = 171$, $\Sigma X^2 = 89$, $(\Sigma X)^2 = 841$, and $N = 11$:

$$b = \frac{N(\Sigma XY) - (\Sigma X)(\Sigma Y)}{} = \frac{11(171) - (29)(58)}{11(89) - 841} = +1.44$$

Step 2   Compute *a*, the Y-intercept:

$$a = \overline{Y} - (b)(X)$$

Using the preceding data, $\overline{Y} = \frac{58}{11} = 5.27$, $b = 1.44$, and $X = \frac{29}{11} = 2.64$:

$$a = \overline{Y} - (b)(X) = 5.27 - (+1.44)(2.64) = +1.47$$

Step 3   Complete the linear regression equation:

$$Y' = b(X) + a$$

From above, $b = +1.44$ and $a = +1.47$, so:

$$Y' = +1.44(X) + 1.47$$

Step 4   To compute a participant's predicted score, Y', multiply the participant's X score times the slope and add the Y-intercept. For example, using the preceding regression equation, the predicted score for someone scoring an $X = 2$ is

$$Y' = +1.44(2) + 1.47 = 4.35$$

The Standard Error of the Estimate

The standard error of the estimate, $S_{y'}$, is calculated as:

$$S_{y'} = (S_y)(\sqrt{1 - r^2})$$

Step 1   Use the formula for the sample standard deviation in section C.2 to find S_y, the sample standard deviation of the Y scores.

Step 2   Compute r^2, the squared value of the Pearson correlation coefficient.
For the preceding linear regression example, $N = 11$, $\Sigma Y = 58$, and $\Sigma Y^2 = 354$, so $S_y = 2.093$ and $r = +.736$:

$$S_{y'} = (S_y)(\sqrt{1 - r^2}) = (2.093)(\sqrt{1 - .736^2}) = 1.42$$

C.12. Spearman Correlation Coefficient

Below is the procedure for computing the Spearman correlation coefficient, as discussed in Chapter 8.

This procedure is used when participants are rank-ordered on each variable and no two participants receive the same rank within a variable. (Special procedures are needed with "tied ranks"—e.g., if two subjects are ranked first on variable X. Consult a statistics text.)

Example data are shown in Table C.20.

Table C.20   Data for Spearman Correlation Coefficient

Subject	Rank on X Variable		Rank on Y Variable		D	D²
1	4	−	3	=	1	1
2	1	−	1	=	0	0
3	9	−	8	=	1	1
4	8	−	6	=	2	4
5	3	−	5	=	−2	4
6	5	−	4	=	1	1
7	6	−	7	=	−1	1
8	2	−	2	=	0	0
9	7	−	9	=	−2	4

$N = 9$ $\Sigma D^2 = 16$

Step 1   Compute each D, the difference between a subject's X and Y scores.

Step 2   Compute ΣD^2, the sum of the squared Ds.

Step 3   Determine N, the number of pairs of scores in the sample.

Step 4   Compute r_s.

$$r_s = 1 - \frac{6(\Sigma D^2)}{N(N^2 - 1)}$$

$$r_s = 1 - \frac{6(16)}{9(81 - 1)} = 1 - .133 = +.867$$

Step 5   Find the critical value of r_s in Table D.5 of Appendix D, with degrees of freedom *(df)* equal to N, the number of pairs of scores. Above, for $df = 9$ and $\alpha = .05$, the two-tailed critical value is $\pm.683$ (so the obtained r_s is significant).

C.13. Chi Square Procedures

Below are the one-way chi square, the two-way chi square, and the procedures for computing effect size (the phi coefficient and C coefficient).

The One-Way Chi Square

This procedure is discussed in Chapter 6. Example data from a one-way design with two categories are shown in Table C.21.

Step 1 Determine the observed frequency, f_o, in each category (i.e., count the number of subjects falling in each category).

Step 2 Determine the expected frequency, f_e, in each category. This is equal to the probability that a subject will fall in that category if the null hypothesis is true, multiplied by the total N in the study. When we are testing for no difference, the expected frequency in each group equals $f_e = \frac{N}{k}$, where k is the number of categories. Thus, above, for each category, $f_e = \frac{60}{2} = 30$.

Step 3 Compute χ^2:

$$\chi^2 = \Sigma\left(\frac{(f_o - f_e)^2}{f_e}\right)$$

$$\chi^2 = \frac{(20 - 30)^2}{30} + \frac{(40 - 30)^2}{30} = 3.33 + 3.33 = 6.66$$

Step 4 Find the critical value of χ^2 in Table D.6 of Appendix D, for $df = k - 1$, where k is the number of categories. For $\alpha = .05$ and $df = 1$, the critical value is 3.84 (so the obtained χ^2 is significant).

Two-Way Chi Square

This procedure is discussed in Chapter 7. Example data from a two-way design with two categories per variable are shown in Table C.22.

Step 1 Determine the observed frequency, f_o, in each category (i.e., count the number of participants falling in each category).

Table C.21 Data from One-Way Chi Square Design

	Variable A	
Category 1	Category 2	
$f_o = 20$ $f_e = 30$	$f_o = 40$ $f_e = 30$	$k = 2$ $N = 60$

Table C.22   Data from Two-Way Chi Square Design

		Variable A		
		Category 1	*Category 2*	
Variable B	*Category 1*	$f_o = 25$ $f_e = 13.125$ (35)(30)/80	$f_o = 10$ $f_e = 21.875$ (35)(50)/80	Row total = 35
	Category 2	$f_o = 5$ $f_e = 16.875$ (45)(30)/80	$f_o = 40$ $f_e = 28.125$ (45)(50)/80	Row total = 45
		Column total = 30	Column total = 50	N = 80

Step 2   Compute the total of the observed frequencies in each row and in each column. Also determine N, the total number of participants.

Step 3   Compute the expected frequency, f_e, for each cell:

$$\text{cell } f_e = \frac{(\text{cell's row total})(\text{cell's column total})}{N}$$

Thus, for cell A_1B_1 above, $f_e = \frac{(35)(30)}{80} = 13.125$.

Step 4   Compute χ^2:

$$\chi^2 = \Sigma\left(\frac{(f_o - f_e)^2}{f_e}\right)$$

$$\chi^2 = \left(\frac{(25 - 13.125)^2}{13.125}\right) + \left(\frac{(10 - 21.875)^2}{21.875)}\right) +$$

$$\left(\frac{(5 - 16.875)^2}{16.875}\right) + \left(\frac{(40 - 28.125)^2}{28.125}\right)$$

$$\chi^2 = 10.74 + 6.45 + 8.36 + 5.01 = 30.56$$

Step 5   Find the critical value of χ^2 in Table D.6 of Appendix D, for $df =$ (number of rows − 1)(number of columns − 1). For $\alpha = .05$ and $df = (2 - 1)(2 - 1) = 1$, the critical value = 3.84. Only if the obtained χ^2 is significant (as above), go to Step 6.

Step 6   Compute the effect size.

In a 2 × 2 chi square, compute the phi coefficient squared, ϕ^2:

$$\phi^2 = \frac{\chi^2}{N}$$

where χ^2 is the obtained value of chi square and N is the total number of participants in the study. Above, $\chi^2 = 30.56$ and $N = 80$, so $\phi^2 = \frac{30.56}{80} = .38$. (The
square root of ϕ^2 equals ϕ, the correlation coefficient between the two variables.)

In a two-way chi square that is not a 2 × 2 design, compute C^2, the contingency coefficient squared:

$$C^2 = \frac{\chi^2}{\chi^2 + N}$$

where χ^2 is the obtained value of chi square and N is the total number of subjects
in the study. (The square root of C^2 equals C, the correlation coefficient between
the two variables.)

C.14. *Mann-Whitney* U *and Wilcoxon* T *Tests*

Below are the procedures for performing the nonparametric versions of *t*-tests.

The Mann-Whitney *U* Test for Independent Samples

The Mann-Whitney test, discussed in Chapter 6, is analogous to the independent
samples *t*-test for ranked data. It is appropriate when the *n* in each condition is
less than 20. Table C.23 shows such data.

Step 1 Compute the sum of the ranks, ΣR, and the *n* for each group.

Table C.23 Ranked Data from Two-Sample Between-Subjects Design

	Condition 1	Condition 2
Rank-Order Scores	2	7
	1	8
	5	10
	3	4
	6	9
	$\Sigma R = 17$	$\Sigma R = 38$
	$n = 5$	$n = 5$

STATISTICAL PROCEDURES

Step 2 Compute U_1 for group 1, using the fomula

$$U_1 = (n_1)(n_2) + \frac{n_1(n_1 + 1)}{2} - \Sigma R_1$$

where n_1 is the n of group 1, n_2 is the n of group 2, and ΣR_1 is the sum of ranks from group 1. From above,

$$U_1 = (5)(5) + \frac{5(5 + 1)}{2} - 17 = 40 - 17 = 23.0$$

Step 3 Compute U_2 for group 2, using the fomula

$$U_2 = (n_1)(n_2) + \frac{n_2(n_2 + 1)}{2} - \Sigma R_2$$

where n_1 is the n of group 1, n_2 is the n of group 2, and ΣR_2 is the sum of ranks from group 2. From above:

$$U_2 = (5)(5) + \frac{5(5 + 1)}{2} - 38 = 40 - 38 = 2.0$$

Step 4 Determine the obtained value of U. In a two-tailed test, the *smaller* value of U_1 or U_2 is the obtained value of U. Above, the obtained U is $U_2 = 2.0$. In a one-tailed test, one group will be predicted to have the higher ranks and thus the larger sum of ranks. The corresponding value of U from that group is the obtained value of U.

Step 5 Find the critical value of U in Table D.7 of Appendix D, using n_1 and n_2. Above, for a two-tailed test with $n_1 = 5$ and $n_2 = 5$, the critical value is 2.0. The obtained value of U is significant (and the two groups differ significantly) if U is *equal to or less than* the critical value, so the above obtained value is significant. (No procedure is available for directly calculating effect size.)

The Wilcoxon *T* Test for Dependent Samples

The Wilcoxon test, discussed in Chapter 7, is analogous to the dependent samples *t*-test for ranked data. It is used to transform interval or ratio scores to ranked scores. Table C.24 shows such data.

Step 1 Determine the difference score, D, in each pair of the raw interval or ratio scores. It makes no difference which score is subtracted from which, but subtract the scores the same way in all pairs.

Step 2 Determine N, the number of *nonzero* difference scores. Above, disregard subject 10 because there is zero difference, so $N = 9$.

Table C.24   Data from a Two-Sample Within-Subjects Design

Subject	Condition 1	Condition 2	Difference (D)	Ranked Scores	R−	R+
1	54	76	−22	6	6	
2	58	71	−13	4	4	
3	60	110	−50	9	9	
4	68	88	−20	5	5	
5	43	50	−7	3	3	
6	74	99	−25	7	7	
7	60	105	−45	8	8	
8	69	64	+5	2		2
9	60	59	+1	1		1
10	52	52	0	. . .		. . .

$$N = 9 \qquad \Sigma R = 42 \qquad \Sigma R = 3$$

Step 3   Assign ranks to the nonzero difference scores. Ignoring the sign of each difference, assign the rank of "1" to the smallest difference, the rank of "2" to the second smallest difference, and so on.

Step 4   Separate the ranks so that the $R-$ column contains the ranks assigned to negative differences in Step 3. The $R+$ column contains the ranks assigned to positive differences.

Step 5   Compute the sum of ranks, ΣR, for the column labeled $R+$, and compute ΣR for the column labeled $R-$.

Step 6   Determine the obtained value of *T*. In a two-tailed test, *T* equals the *smaller* ΣR found in Step 5. Here, the smaller $\Sigma R = 3$, so the obtained $T = 3$. In a one-tailed test, whether most differences are positive or negative will be predicted, and the ΣR that is predicted to be smaller is the obtained value of *T*.

Step 7   Find the critical value of *T* in Table D.8 of Appendix D, using *N*, the number of nonzero difference scores. Above, for $N = 9$ and $\alpha = .05$, the critical value is 5.0. The obtained *T* is significant (and the two groups differ significantly) when *T* is *equal to or less than* the critical value, so the above *T* is significant. (No procedure for computing effect size is available.)

C.15. *Kruskal-Wallis* **H** *and Friedman* χ^2 *Tests*

Below are the procedures for performing the nonparametric versions of the one-way ANOVA and the corresponding post hoc tests.

The Kruskal-Wallis *H* Test

The Kruskal-Wallis *H* test, discussed in Chapter 6, is analogous to a between-subjects one-way ANOVA for ranks. It requires three or more levels of the factor, with at least five participants per level. Table C.25 shows such data.

Step 1   Compute the sum of the ranks, ΣR, in each condition (i.e., each column). Also note the n in each condition, as well as k, the number of levels.

Step 2   Compute the sum of squares between groups:

$$SS_{bn} = \Sigma\left(\frac{(\Sigma R)^2}{n}\right)$$

where $(\Sigma R)^2$ is the squared sum of ranks for each level and n is the n of the level:

$$SS_{bn} = \left(\frac{(21)^2}{5} + \frac{(35)^2}{5} + \frac{(64)^2}{5}\right) = 88.2 + 245 + 819.2 + 1152.4$$

Step 3   Compute *H*:

$$H = \left(\frac{12}{N(N+1)}\right)(SS_{bn}) - 3(N+1)$$

where N is the total N of the study, and SS_{bn} is from Step 2:

$$H = \left(\frac{12}{15(15+1)}\right)(1152.4) - 3(15+1) = (.05)(1152.4) - 48 = 9.62$$

Step 4   The critical values of *H* are χ^2 values; find these in Table D.6 of Appendix D, using $df = k - 1$, where k is the number of levels in the factor. Above, for

Table C.25   Ranked Data from One-Way Between-Subjects Design

	Factor A	
Level 1	Level 2	Level 3
2	3	14
6	5	15
4	7	10
8	9	12
1	11	13
$\Sigma R_1 = 21$	$\Sigma R_2 = 35$	$\Sigma R_3 = 64$ $k = 3$
$n_1 = 5$	$n_2 = 5$	$n_3 = 5$ $N = 15$

$df = 2$ and $\alpha = .05$, the critical value is 5.99. If the obtained value of H is *larger* than the critical value of χ^2, then the H is significant (and there is at least one significant difference between the groups). When H is significant, go to Step 5.

Step 5 Perform post hoc comparisons by comparing each pair of conditions using the Mann-Whitney procedure in section C.14. Treat each pair of conditions as if they constituted the entire study and rerank the scores. Then compute the obtained U and determine whether it is significant.

Step 6 Compute η^2, the effect size:

$$\eta^2 = \frac{H}{N-1}$$

where H is the value computed in the Kruskal-Wallis test (Step 3), and N is the total number of subjects.

The Friedman χ^2 Test

The Friedman χ^2 test, discussed in Chapter 6, is analogous to a repeated-measures one-way ANOVA for ranks. It requires three or more levels of the factor. If there are only three levels of the factor, there must be at least 10 subjects in the study. If there are only four levels of the factor, there must be at least five subjects. Table C.26 shows such data.

Table C.26 Ranked Scores from One-Way Repeated Measures Design

	Factor A		
	Condition 1	Condition 2	Condition 3
Subject 1	1	2	3
Subject 2	1	3	2
Subject 3	1	2	3
Subject 4	1	3	2
Subject 5	2	1	3
Subject 6	1	3	2
Subject 7	1	2	3
Subject 8	1	3	2
Subject 9	1	3	2
Subject 10	2	1	3
	$\Sigma R_1 = 12$	$\Sigma R_2 = 23$	$\Sigma R_3 = 25$	$N = 10$
	$X = 1.2$	$X = 2.3$	$X = 2.5$	

Step 1   If not already ranked, then rank-order the scores within each participant. That is, assign "1" to the lowest score received by subject 1, "2" to the second lowest score received by subject 1, and so on. Repeat the process for each subject.

Step 2   Compute the sum of the ranks, ΣR, in each condition (i.e., each column).

Step 3   Compute the mean rank in each condition, by dividing the sum of ranks (ΣR) by the number of subjects.

Step 4   Compute the sum of squares between groups:

$$SS_{bn} = (\Sigma R_1)^2 + (\Sigma R_2)^2 + \cdots (\Sigma R_k)^2$$
$$SS_{bn} = (12)^2 + (23)^2 + (25)^2 = 1298$$

Step 5   Compute the Friedman x^2:

$$x^2 = \left(\frac{12}{(k)(N)(k+1)}\right)(SS_{bn}) - 3(N)(k+1)$$

where N is the total number of subjects and k is the number of levels of the factor, and SS_{bn} is from Step 4:

$$x^2 = \left(\frac{12}{(3)(10)(3+1)}\right)(1298) - 3(10)(3+1) = (.10)(1298) - 120 = 9.80.$$

Step 6   Find the critical value of x^2 in Table D.6 of Appendix D, for $df = k - 1$, where k is the number of levels in the factor. Above, for $df = 2$ and $\alpha = .05$, the critical value is 5.99. The obtained x^2 is larger than the critical value, so the results are significant (and there is at least one significant difference between the levels). When x^2 is significant, perform Steps 7 and 8.

Step 7   Perform post hoc comparisons using Nemenyi's procedure.[2]

(a) Compute the critical difference:

$$\text{Critical difference} = \sqrt{\left(\frac{k(k+1)}{6(N)}\right)(\text{critical value of } x^2)}$$

where k is the number of levels of the factor, N is the total number of subjects, and the critical value of x^2 is the critical value used to test the Friedman x^2 (Step 6).

---

[2]As reported in Linton & Gallo, 1975.

$$\text{Critical difference} = \sqrt{\left(\frac{3(3+1)}{6(10)}\right)(5.99)} = \sqrt{(.2)(5.99)} = \sqrt{1.198} = 1.09$$

b. Subtract each mean rank from the other mean ranks. Any absolute difference between two means that is greater than the critical difference is a significant difference. In Table C.26 the differences between the mean rank of 1.2 in condition 1 and the other mean ranks are 1.10 and 1.30, respectively, so they are significant differences. The difference between the means of conditions 2 and 3 is .20, which is not a significant difference.

Step 8   Compute η^2, the effect size:

$$\eta^2 = \frac{\chi^2}{(N)(k) - 1}$$

where χ^2 was computed in the Friedman χ^2 test (Step 6), N is the number of subjects, and k is the number of levels of the factor. Thus:

$$\eta^2 = \frac{\chi^2}{(N)(k) - 1} = \frac{9.80}{(10)(3) - 1} = \frac{9.80}{30 - 1} = .34$$

STATISTICAL PROCEDURES

Statistical Tables

Table D.1 Critical Values of t

Table D.2 Critical Values of F

Table D.3 Values of the Studentized Range Statistic, q_k

Table D.4 Critical Values of the Pearson Correlation Coefficient, r

Table D.5 Critical Values of the Spearman Correlation Coefficient, r_s

Table D.6 Critical Values of Chi Square, χ^2

Table D.7 Critical Values of the Mann-Whitney U

Table D.8 Critical Values of the Wilcoxon T

STATISTICAL TABLES

Table D.1   Critical Values of *t*

	Two-tailed test			One-tailed test	
	Level of significance			Level of significance	
df	$\alpha = .05$	$\alpha = .01$	df	$\alpha = .05$	$\alpha = .01$
1	12.706	63.657	1	6.314	31.821
2	4.303	9.925	2	2.920	6.965
3	3.182	5.841	3	2.353	4.541
4	2.776	4.604	4	2.132	3.747
5	2.571	4.032	5	2.015	3.365
6	2.447	3.707	6	1.943	3.143
7	2.365	3.499	7	1.895	2.998
8	2.306	3.355	8	1.860	2.896
9	2.262	3.250	9	1.833	2.821
10	2.228	3.169	10	1.812	2.764
11	2.201	3.106	11	1.796	2.718
12	2.179	3.055	12	1.782	2.681
13	2.160	3.012	13	1.771	2.650
14	2.145	2.977	14	1.761	2.624
15	2.131	2.947	15	1.753	2.602
16	2.120	2.921	16	1.746	2.583
17	2.110	2.898	17	1.740	2.567
18	2.101	2.878	18	1.734	2.552
19	2.093	2.861	19	1.729	2.539
20	2.086	2.845	20	1.725	2.528
21	2.080	2.831	21	1.721	2.518
22	2.074	2.819	22	1.717	2.508
23	2.069	2.807	23	1.714	2.500
24	2.064	2.797	24	1.711	2.492
25	2.060	2.787	25	1.708	2.485
26	2.056	2.779	26	1.706	2.479
27	2.052	2.771	27	1.703	2.473
28	2.048	2.763	28	1.701	2.467
29	2.045	2.756	29	1.699	2.462
30	2.042	2.750	30	1.697	2.457
40	2.021	2.704	40	1.684	2.423
60	2.000	2.660	60	1.671	2.390
120	1.980	2.617	120	1.658	2.358
∞	1.960	2.576	∞	1.645	2.326

Table D.2 Critical Values of *F*

Critical values for α = .05 are in **dark numbers.**
Critical values for α = .01 are in light numbers.

Degrees of freedom within groups (degrees of freedom in denominator of F ratio)	α	1	2	3	4	5	6	7	8	9	10
1	.05	161	200	216	225	230	234	237	239	241	242
	.01	4,052	4,999	5,403	5,625	5,764	5,859	5,928	5,981	6,022	6,056
2	.05	18.51	19.00	19.16	19.25	19.30	19.33	19.36	19.37	19.38	19.39
	.01	98.49	99.00	99.17	99.25	99.30	99.33	99.34	99.36	99.38	99.40
3	.05	10.13	9.55	9.28	9.12	9.01	8.94	8.88	8.84	8.81	8.78
	.01	34.12	30.82	29.46	28.71	28.24	27.91	27.67	27.49	27.34	27.23
4	.05	7.71	6.94	6.59	6.39	6.26	6.16	6.09	6.04	6.00	5.96
	.01	21.20	18.00	16.69	15.98	15.52	15.21	14.98	14.80	14.66	14.54
5	.05	6.61	5.79	5.41	5.19	5.05	4.95	4.88	4.82	4.78	4.74
	.01	16.26	13.27	12.06	11.39	10.97	10.67	10.45	10.27	10.15	10.05
6	.05	5.99	5.14	4.76	4.53	4.39	4.28	4.21	4.15	4.10	4.06
	.01	13.74	10.92	9.78	9.15	8.75	8.47	8.26	8.10	7.98	7.87
7	.05	5.59	4.47	4.35	4.12	3.97	3.87	3.79	3.73	3.68	3.63
	.01	12.25	9.55	8.45	7.85	7.46	7.19	7.00	6.84	6.71	6.62
8	.05	5.32	4.46	4.07	3.84	3.69	3.58	3.50	3.44	3.39	3.34
	.01	11.26	8.65	7.59	7.01	6.63	6.37	6.19	6.03	5.91	5.82
9	.05	5.12	4.26	3.86	3.63	3.48	3.37	3.29	3.23	3.18	3.13
	.01	10.56	8.02	6.99	6.42	6.06	5.80	5.62	5.47	5.35	5.26
10	.05	4.96	4.10	3.71	3.48	3.33	3.22	3.14	3.07	3.02	2.97
	.01	10.04	7.56	6.55	5.99	5.64	5.39	5.21	5.06	4.95	4.85
11	.05	4.84	3.98	3.59	3.36	3.20	3.09	3.01	2.95	2.90	2.86
	.01	9.65	7.20	6.22	5.67	5.32	5.07	4.88	4.74	4.63	4.54
12	.05	4.75	3.88	3.49	3.26	3.11	3.00	2.92	2.85	2.80	2.76
	.01	9.33	6.93	5.95	5.41	5.06	4.82	4.65	4.50	4.39	4.30
13	.05	4.67	3.80	3.41	3.18	3.02	2.92	2.84	2.77	2.72	2.67
	.01	9.07	6.70	5.74	5.20	4.86	4.62	4.44	4.30	4.19	4.10
14	.05	4.60	3.74	3.34	3.11	2.96	2.85	2.77	2.70	2.65	2.60
	.01	8.86	6.51	5.56	5.03	4.69	4.46	4.28	4.14	4.03	3.94
15	.05	4.54	3.68	3.29	3.06	2.90	2.79	2.70	2.64	2.59	2.55
	.01	8.68	6.36	5.42	4.89	4.56	4.32	4.14	4.00	3.89	3.80

Table D.2 (cont.) Critical Values of *F*

Degrees of freedom within groups (degrees of freedom in denominator of F ratio)	α	\multicolumn{10}{c}{Degrees of freedom between groups (degrees of freedom in numerator of F ratio)}
		1	2	3	4	5	6	7	8	9	10
16	.05	4.49	3.63	3.24	3.01	2.85	2.74	2.66	2.59	2.54	2.49
	.01	8.53	6.23	5.29	4.77	4.44	4.20	4.03	3.89	3.78	3.69
17	.05	4.45	3.59	3.20	2.96	2.81	2.70	2.62	2.55	2.50	2.45
	.01	8.40	6.11	5.18	4.67	4.34	4.10	3.93	3.79	3.68	3.59
18	.05	4.41	3.55	3.16	2.93	2.77	2.66	2.58	2.51	2.46	2.41
	.01	8.28	6.01	5.09	4.58	4.25	4.01	3.85	3.71	3.60	3.51
19	.05	4.38	3.52	3.13	2.90	2.74	2.63	2.55	2.48	2.43	2.38
	.01	8.18	5.93	5.01	4.50	4.17	3.94	3.77	3.63	3.52	3.43
20	.05	4.35	3.49	3.10	2.87	2.71	2.60	2.52	2.45	2.40	2.35
	.01	8.10	5.85	4.94	4.43	4.10	3.87	3.71	3.56	3.45	3.37
21	.05	4.32	3.47	3.07	2.84	2.68	2.57	2.49	2.42	2.37	2.32
	.01	8.02	5.78	4.87	4.37	4.04	3.81	3.65	3.51	3.40	3.31
22	.05	4.30	3.44	3.05	2.82	2.66	2.55	2.47	2.40	2.35	2.30
	.01	7.94	5.72	4.82	4.31	3.99	3.76	3.59	3.45	3.35	3.26
23	.05	4.28	3.42	3.03	2.80	2.64	2.53	2.45	2.38	2.32	2.28
	.01	7.88	5.66	4.76	4.26	3.94	3.71	3.54	3.41	3.30	3.21
24	.05	4.26	3.40	3.01	2.78	2.62	2.51	2.43	2.36	2.30	2.26
	.01	7.82	5.61	4.72	4.22	3.90	3.67	3.50	3.36	3.25	3.17
25	.05	4.24	3.38	2.99	2.76	2.60	2.49	2.41	2.34	2.28	2.24
	.01	7.77	5.57	4.68	4.18	3.86	3.63	3.46	3.32	3.21	3.13
26	.05	4.22	3.37	2.98	2.74	2.59	2.47	2.39	2.32	2.27	2.22
	.01	7.72	5.53	4.64	4.14	3.82	3.59	3.42	3.29	3.17	3.09
27	.05	4.21	3.35	2.96	2.73	2.57	2.46	2.37	2.30	2.25	2.20
	.01	7.68	5.49	4.60	4.11	3.79	3.56	3.39	3.26	3.14	3.06
28	.05	4.20	3.34	2.95	2.71	2.56	2.44	2.36	2.29	2.24	2.19
	.01	7.64	5.45	4.57	4.07	3.76	3.53	3.36	3.23	3.11	3.03
29	.05	4.18	3.33	2.93	2.70	2.54	2.43	2.35	2.28	2.22	2.18
	.01	7.60	5.42	4.54	4.04	3.73	3.50	3.33	3.20	3.08	3.00
30	.05	4.18	3.33	2.93	2.70	2.54	2.43	2.35	2.28	2.22	2.18
	.01	7.60	5.42	4.54	4.04	3.73	3.50	3.33	3.20	3.08	3.00
31	.05	4.17	3.32	2.92	2.69	2.53	2.42	2.34	2.27	2.21	2.16
	.01	7.56	5.39	4.51	4.02	3.70	3.47	3.30	3.17	3.06	2.98

Table D.2 (cont.) Critical Values of *F*

Degrees of freedom within groups (degrees of freedom in denominator of F ratio)	α	Degrees of freedom between groups (degrees of freedom in numerator of F ratio)									
		1	2	3	4	5	6	7	8	9	10
32	.05	4.15	3.30	2.90	2.67	2.51	2.40	2.32	2.25	2.19	2.14
	.01	7.50	5.34	4.46	3.97	3.66	3.42	3.25	3.12	3.01	2.94
34	.05	4.13	3.28	2.88	2.65	2.49	2.38	2.30	2.23	2.17	2.12
	.01	7.44	5.29	4.42	3.93	3.61	3.38	3.21	3.08	2.97	2.89
36	.05	4.11	3.26	2.86	2.63	2.48	2.36	2.28	2.21	2.15	2.10
	.01	7.39	5.25	4.38	3.89	3.58	3.35	3.18	3.04	2.94	2.86
38	.05	4.10	3.25	2.85	2.62	2.46	2.35	2.26	2.19	2.14	2.09
	.01	7.35	5.21	4.34	3.86	3.54	3.32	3.15	3.02	2.91	2.82
40	.05	4.08	3.23	2.84	2.61	2.45	2.34	2.25	2.18	2.12	2.07
	.01	7.31	5.18	4.31	3.83	3.51	3.29	3.12	2.99	2.88	2.80
42	.05	4.07	3.22	2.83	2.59	2.44	2.32	2.24	2.17	2.11	2.06
	.01	7.27	5.15	4.29	3.80	3.49	3.26	3.10	2.96	2.86	2.77
44	.05	4.06	3.21	2.82	2.58	2.43	2.31	2.23	2.16	2.10	2.05
	.01	7.24	5.12	4.26	3.78	3.46	3.24	3.07	2.94	2.84	2.75
46	.05	4.05	3.20	2.81	2.57	2.42	2.30	2.22	2.14	2.09	2.04
	.01	7.21	5.10	4.24	3.76	3.44	3.22	3.05	2.92	2.82	2.73
48	.05	4.04	3.19	2.80	2.56	2.41	2.30	2.21	2.14	2.08	2.03
	.01	7.19	5.08	4.22	3.74	3.42	3.20	3.04	2.90	2.80	2.71
50	.05	4.03	3.18	2.79	2.56	2.40	2.29	2.20	2.13	2.07	2.02
	.01	7.17	5.06	4.20	3.72	3.41	3.18	3.02	2.88	2.78	2.70
55	.05	4.02	3.17	2.78	2.54	2.38	2.27	2.18	2.11	2.05	2.00
	.01	7.12	5.01	4.16	3.68	3.37	3.15	2.98	2.85	2.75	2.66
60	.05	4.00	3.15	2.76	2.52	2.37	2.25	2.17	2.10	2.04	1.99
	.01	7.08	4.98	4.13	3.65	3.34	3.12	2.95	2.82	2.72	2.63
65	.05	3.99	3.14	2.75	2.51	2.36	2.24	2.15	2.08	2.02	1.98
	.01	7.04	4.95	4.10	3.62	3.31	3.09	2.93	2.79	2.70	2.61
70	.05	3.98	3.13	2.74	2.50	2.35	2.23	2.14	2.07	2.01	1.97
	.01	7.01	4.92	4.08	3.60	3.29	3.07	2.91	2.77	2.67	2.59
80	.05	3.96	3.11	2.72	2.48	2.33	2.21	2.12	2.05	1.99	1.95
	.01	6.96	4.88	4.04	3.56	3.25	3.04	2.87	2.74	2.64	2.55
100	.05	3.94	3.09	2.70	2.46	2.30	2.19	2.10	2.03	1.97	1.92
	.01	6.90	4.82	3.98	3.51	3.20	2.99	2.82	2.69	2.59	2.51

Table D.2   (cont.) Critical Values of *F*

Degrees of freedom within groups (degrees of freedom in denominator of F ratio)	α	1	2	3	4	5	6	7	8	9	10
125	.05	3.92	3.07	2.68	2.44	2.29	2.17	2.08	2.01	1.95	1.90
	.01	6.84	4.78	3.94	3.47	3.17	2.95	2.79	2.65	2.56	2.47
150	.05	3.91	3.06	2.67	2.43	2.27	2.16	2.07	2.00	1.94	1.89
	.01	6.81	4.75	3.91	3.44	3.14	2.92	2.76	2.62	2.53	2.44
200	.05	3.89	3.04	2.65	2.41	2.26	2.14	2.05	1.98	1.92	1.87
	.01	6.76	4.71	3.88	3.41	3.11	2.90	2.73	2.60	2.50	2.41
400	.05	3.86	3.02	2.62	2.39	2.23	2.12	2.03	1.96	1.90	1.85
	.01	6.70	4.66	3.83	3.36	3.06	2.85	2.69	2.55	2.46	2.37
1000	.05	3.85	3.00	2.61	2.38	2.22	2.10	2.02	1.95	1.89	1.84
	.01	6.66	4.62	3.80	3.34	3.04	2.82	2.66	2.53	2.43	2.34
∞	.05	3.84	2.99	2.60	2.37	2.21	2.09	2.01	1.94	1.88	1.83
	.01	6.64	4.60	3.78	3.32	3.02	2.80	2.64	2.51	2.41	2.32

Degrees of freedom between groups (degrees of freedom in numerator of F ratio)

Reprinted by permission from *Statistical Methods,* 8th edition, by G. Snedecor and W. Cochran. Copyright © 1989 by the Iowa State University Press, Ames.

Table D.3   Values of the Studentized Range Statistic, q_k

Values of q_k for $\alpha = .05$ are **dark numbers** *and for $\alpha = .01$ are* light numbers.

Degrees of freedom within groups (degrees of freedom in denominator of F ratio)	α	2	3	4	5	6	7	8	9	10
					k = number of means being compared					
1	.05	18.0	27.0	32.8	37.1	40.4	43.1	45.4	47.4	49.1
	.01	90.0	135	164	186	202	216	227	237	246
2	.05	6.09	8.3	9.8	10.9	11.7	12.4	13.0	13.5	14.0
	.01	14.0	19.0	22.3	24.7	26.6	28.2	29.5	30.7	31.7
3	.05	4.50	5.91	6.82	7.50	8.04	8.48	8.85	9.18	9.46
	.01	8.26	10.6	12.2	13.3	14.2	15.0	15.6	16.2	16.7
4	.05	3.93	5.04	5.76	6.29	6.71	7.05	7.35	7.60	7.83
	.01	6.51	8.12	9.17	9.96	10.6	11.1	11.5	11.9	12.3
5	.05	3.64	4.60	5.22	5.67	6.03	6.33	6.58	6.80	6.99
	.01	5.70	6.97	7.80	8.42	8.91	9.32	9.67	9.97	10.2
6	.05	3.46	4.34	4.90	5.31	5.63	5.89	6.12	6.32	6.49
	.01	5.24	6.33	7.03	7.56	7.97	8.32	8.61	8.87	9.10
7	.05	3.34	4.16	4.69	5.06	5.36	5.61	5.82	6.00	6.16
	.01	4.95	5.92	6.54	7.01	7.37	7.68	7.94	8.17	8.37
8	.05	3.26	4.04	4.53	4.89	5.17	5.40	5.60	5.77	5.92
	.01	4.74	5.63	6.20	6.63	6.96	7.24	7.47	7.68	7.87
9	.05	3.20	3.95	4.42	4.76	5.02	5.24	5.43	5.60	5.74
	.01	4.60	5.43	5.96	6.35	6.66	6.91	7.13	7.32	7.49
10	.05	3.15	3.88	4.33	4.65	4.91	5.12	5.30	5.46	5.60
	.01	4.48	5.27	5.77	6.14	6.43	6.67	6.87	7.05	7.21
11	.05	3.11	3.82	4.26	4.57	4.82	5.03	5.20	5.35	5.49
	.01	4.39	5.14	5.62	5.97	6.25	6.48	6.67	6.84	6.99
12	.05	3.08	3.77	4.20	4.51	4.75	4.95	5.12	5.27	5.40
	.01	4.32	5.04	5.50	5.84	6.10	6.32	6.51	6.67	6.81
13	.05	3.06	3.73	4.15	4.45	4.69	4.88	5.05	5.19	5.32
	.01	4.26	4.96	5.40	5.73	5.98	6.19	6.37	6.53	6.67
14	.05	3.03	3.70	4.11	4.41	4.64	4.83	4.99	5.13	5.25
	.01	4.21	4.89	5.32	5.63	5.88	6.08	6.26	6.41	6.54
16	.05	3.00	3.65	4.05	4.33	4.56	4.74	4.90	5.03	5.15
	.01	4.13	4.78	5.19	5.49	5.72	5.92	6.08	6.22	6.35

Table D.3 (cont.) Values of the Studentized Range Statistic, q_k

Values of q_k *for* $\alpha = .05$ *are* **dark numbers** *and for* $\alpha = .01$ *are* light numbers.

Degrees of freedom within groups (degrees of freedom in denominator of F ratio)	α	2	3	4	5	6	7	8	9	10
					k = number of means being compared					
18	.05	2.97	3.61	4.00	4.28	4.49	4.67	4.82	4.96	5.07
	.01	4.07	4.70	5.09	5.38	5.60	5.79	5.94	6.08	6.20
20	.05	2.95	3.58	3.96	4.23	4.45	4.62	4.77	4.90	5.01
	.01	4.02	4.64	5.02	5.29	5.51	5.69	5.84	5.97	6.09
24	.05	2.92	3.53	3.90	4.17	4.37	4.54	4.68	4.81	4.92
	.01	3.96	4.54	4.91	5.17	5.37	5.54	5.69	5.81	5.92
30	.05	2.89	3.49	3.84	4.10	4.30	4.46	4.60	4.72	4.83
	.01	3.89	4.45	4.80	5.05	5.24	5.40	5.54	5.56	5.76
40	.05	2.86	3.44	3.79	4.04	4.23	4.39	4.52	4.63	4.74
	.01	3.82	4.37	4.70	4.93	5.11	5.27	5.39	5.50	5.60
60	.05	2.83	3.40	3.74	3.98	4.16	4.31	4.44	4.55	4.65
	.01	3.76	4.28	4.60	4.82	4.99	5.13	5.25	5.36	5.45
120	.05	2.80	3.36	3.69	3.92	4.10	4.24	4.36	4.48	4.56
	.01	3.70	4.20	4.50	4.71	4.87	5.01	5.12	5.21	5.30
∞	.05	2.77	3.31	3.63	3.86	4.03	4.17	4.29	4.39	4.47
	.01	3.64	4.12	4.40	4.60	4.76	4.88	4.99	5.08	5.16

From B. J. Winer, *Statistical Principles in Experimental Design*, McGraw-Hill, 1962; abridged from H. L. Harter, D. S. Clemm, and E. H. Guthrie, The Probability Integrals of the Range and of the Studentized Range, WADC Tech. Rep. 58–484, Vol. 2, 1959, Wright Air Development Center, Table II.2, pp. 243–281. Reproduced with permission of McGraw-Hill, Inc.

Table D.4 Critical Values of the Pearson Correlation Coefficient, *r*

| | Two-tailed test | | | One-tailed test | |
| | *Level of significance* | | | *Level of significance* | |
df (no. of pairs − 2)	α = .05	α = .01	df (no. of pairs − 2)	α = .05	α = .01
1	.997	.9999	1	.988	.9995
2	.950	.990	2	.900	.980
3	.878	.959	3	.805	.934
4	.811	.917	4	.729	.882
5	.754	.874	5	.669	.833
6	.707	.834	6	.622	.789
7	.666	.798	7	.582	.750
8	.632	.765	8	.549	.716
9	.602	.735	9	.521	.685
10	.576	.708	10	.497	.658
11	.553	.684	11	.476	.634
12	.532	.661	12	.458	.612
13	.514	.641	13	.441	.592
14	.497	.623	14	.426	.574
15	.482	.606	15	.412	.558
16	.468	.590	16	.400	.542
17	.456	.575	17	.389	.528
18	.444	.561	18	.378	.516
19	.433	.549	19	.369	.503
20	.423	.537	20	.360	.492
21	.413	.526	21	.352	.482
22	.404	.515	22	.344	.472
23	.396	.505	23	.337	.462
24	.388	.496	24	.330	.453
25	.381	.487	25	.323	.445
26	.374	.479	26	.317	.437
27	.367	.471	27	.311	.430
28	.361	.463	28	.306	.423
29	.355	.456	29	.301	.416
30	.349	.449	30	.296	.409
35	.325	.418	35	.275	.381
40	.304	.393	40	.257	.358
45	.288	.372	45	.243	.338
50	.273	.354	50	.231	.322
60	.250	.325	60	.211	.295
70	.232	.302	70	.195	.274
80	.217	.283	80	.183	.256
90	.205	.267	90	.173	.242
100	.195	.254	100	.164	.230

From Table VI of R. A. Fisher and F. Yates, *Statistical for Biological, Agricultural and Medical Research*, 6th ed. London: Longman Group Ltd., 1974. Reprinted by permission of Addison Wesley Longman, Ltd.

Table D.5 Critical Values of the Spearman Correlation Coefficient, r_s

Note: *To find the critical value for an* N *not given, find the critical values for the* N *above and below your* N, *add them together, and then divide the sum by 2.*

	Two-tailed test			One-tailed test	
	Level of significance			Level of significance	
N (no. of pairs)	$\alpha = .05$	$\alpha = .01$	N (no. of pairs)	$\alpha = .05$	$\alpha = .01$
5	1.000	—	5	.900	1.000
6	.886	1.000	6	.829	.943
7	.786	.929	7	.714	.893
8	.738	.881	8	.643	.833
9	.683	.833	9	.600	.783
10	.648	.794	10	.564	.746
12	.591	.777	12	.506	.712
14	.544	.715	14	.456	.645
16	.506	.665	16	.425	.601
18	.475	.625	18	.399	.564
20	.450	.591	20	.377	.534
22	.428	.562	22	.359	.508
24	.409	.537	24	.343	.485
26	.392	.515	26	.329	.465
28	.377	.496	28	.317	.448
30	.364	.478	30	.306	.432

Table, "Critical Values of the Spearman Correlation Coefficient, r_s." From E. G. Olds (1949), The 5 Percent Significance Levels of Sums of Squares of Rank Differences and a Correction, *Ann. Math. Statist.*, **20**, 117–118, and E. G. Olds (1938), Distribution of Sums of Squares of Rank Differences for Small Numbers of Individuals, *Ann. Math. Statist.*, **9**, 133–148. Reprinted with permission of the Institute of Mathematical Statistics.

Table D.6 Critical Values of Chi Square, χ^2

df	Level of significance	
	$\alpha = .05$	$\alpha = .01$
1	3.84	6.64
2	5.99	9.21
3	7.81	11.34
4	9.49	13.28
5	11.07	15.09
6	12.59	16.81
7	14.07	18.48
8	15.51	20.09
9	16.92	21.67
10	18.31	23.21
11	19.68	24.72
12	21.03	26.22
13	22.36	27.69
14	23.68	29.14
15	25.00	30.58
16	26.30	32.00
17	27.59	33.41
18	28.87	34.80
19	30.14	36.19
20	31.41	37.47
21	32.67	38.93
22	33.92	40.29
23	35.17	41.64
24	36.42	42.98
25	37.65	44.31
26	38.88	45.64
27	40.11	46.96
28	41.34	48.28
29	42.56	49.59
30	43.77	50.89
40	55.76	63.69
50	67.50	76.15
60	79.08	88.38
70	90.53	100.42

From Table IV of R. A. Fisher and F. Yates, *Statistical Tables for Biological, Agricultural and Medical Research,* 6th ed. London: Longman Group Ltd., 1974. Reprinted by permission of Addison Wesley Longman Ltd.

Table D.7   Critical Values of the Mann-Whitney *U*

To be significant, the U *must be equal to or be less than the critical value. (Dashes in the table indicate that no decision is possible.) Critical values for α = .05 are* **dark numbers** *and for α = .01 are* light numbers.

Two-tailed test

n_2 (no. of scores in Group 2)	α	n_1 (no. of scores in Group 1)								
		1	2	3	4	5	6	7	8	9
1	.05	—	—	—	—	—	—	—	—	—
	.01	—	—	—	—	—	—	—	—	—
2	.05	—	—	—	—	—	—	—	0	0
	.01	—	—	—	—	—	—	—	—	—
3	.05	—	—	—	—	0	1	1	2	2
	.01	—	—	—	—	—	—	—	—	0
4	.05	—	—	—	0	1	2	3	4	4
	.01	—	—	—	—	—	0	0	1	1
5	.05	—	—	0	1	2	3	5	6	7
	.01	—	—	—	—	0	1	1	2	3
6	.05	—	—	1	2	3	5	6	8	10
	.01	—	—	—	0	1	2	3	4	5
7	.05	—	—	1	3	5	6	8	10	12
	.01	—	—	—	0	1	3	4	6	7
8	.05	—	0	2	4	6	8	10	13	15
	.01	—	—	—	1	2	4	6	7	9
9	.05	—	0	2	4	7	10	12	15	17
	.01	—	—	0	1	3	5	7	9	11
10	.05	—	0	3	5	8	11	14	17	20
	.01	—	—	0	2	4	6	9	11	13
11	.05	—	0	3	6	9	13	16	19	23
	.01	—	—	0	2	5	7	10	13	16
12	.05	—	1	4	7	11	14	18	22	26
	.01	—	—	1	3	6	9	12	15	18
13	.05	—	1	4	8	12	16	20	24	28
	.01	—	—	1	3	7	10	13	17	20
14	.05	—	1	5	9	13	17	22	26	31
	.01	—	—	1	4	7	11	15	18	22
15	.05	—	1	5	10	14	19	24	29	34
	.01	—	—	2	5	8	12	16	20	24
16	.05	—	1	6	11	15	21	26	31	37
	.01	—	—	2	5	9	13	18	22	27
17	.05	—	2	6	11	17	22	28	34	39
	.01	—	—	2	6	10	15	19	24	29
18	.05	—	2	7	12	18	24	30	36	42
	.01	—	—	2	6	11	16	21	26	31
19	.05	—	2	7	13	19	25	32	38	45
	.01	—	0	3	7	12	17	22	28	33
20	.05	—	2	8	13	20	27	34	41	48
	.01	—	0	3	8	13	18	24	30	36

Table D.7 (cont.) Critical Values of the Mann-Whitney U

Two-tailed test

	n_1 (no. of scores in Group 1)									
10	*11*	*12*	*13*	*14*	*15*	*16*	*17*	*18*	*19*	*20*
—	—	—	—	—	—	—	—	—	—	—
—	—	—	—	—	—	—	—	—	—	—
0	0	1	1	1	1	1	2	2	2	2
—	—	—	—	—	—	—	—	—	0	0
3	3	4	4	5	5	6	6	7	7	8
0	0	1	1	1	2	2	2	2	3	3
5	6	7	8	9	10	11	11	12	13	13
2	2	3	3	4	5	5	6	6	7	8
8	9	11	12	13	14	15	17	18	19	20
4	5	6	7	7	8	9	10	11	12	13
11	13	14	16	17	19	21	22	24	25	27
6	7	9	10	11	12	13	15	16	17	18
14	16	18	20	22	24	26	28	30	32	34
9	10	12	13	15	16	18	19	21	22	24
17	19	22	24	26	29	31	34	36	38	41
11	13	15	17	18	20	22	24	26	28	30
20	23	26	28	31	34	37	39	42	45	48
13	16	18	20	22	24	27	29	31	33	36
23	26	29	33	36	39	42	45	48	52	55
16	18	21	24	26	29	31	34	37	39	42
26	30	33	37	40	44	47	51	55	58	62
18	21	24	27	30	33	36	39	42	45	48
29	33	37	41	45	49	53	57	61	65	69
21	24	27	31	34	37	41	44	47	51	54
33	37	41	45	50	54	59	63	67	72	76
24	27	31	34	38	42	45	49	53	56	60
36	40	45	50	55	59	64	67	74	78	83
26	30	34	38	42	46	50	54	58	63	67
39	44	49	54	59	64	70	75	80	85	90
29	33	37	42	46	51	55	60	64	69	73
42	47	53	59	64	70	75	81	86	92	98
31	36	41	45	50	55	60	65	70	74	79
45	51	57	63	67	75	81	87	93	99	105
34	39	44	49	54	60	65	70	75	81	86
48	55	61	67	74	80	86	93	99	106	112
37	42	47	53	58	64	70	75	81	87	92
52	58	65	72	78	85	92	99	106	113	119
39	45	51	56	63	69	74	81	87	93	99
55	62	69	76	83	90	98	105	112	119	127
42	48	54	60	67	73	79	86	92	99	105

Table D.7 (cont.) Critical Values of the Mann-Whitney *U*

One-tailed test

n_2 (no. of scores in Group 2)	α	1	2	3	4	5	6	7	8	9
					n_1 (no. of scores in Group 1)					
1	.05	—	—	—	—	—	—	—	—	—
	.01	—	—	—	—	—	—	—	—	—
2	.05	—	—	—	—	0	0	0	1	1
	.01	—	—	—	—	—	—	—	—	—
3	.05	—	—	0	0	1	2	2	3	3
	.01	—	—	—	—	—	—	0	0	1
4	.05	—	—	0	1	2	3	4	5	6
	.01	—	—	—	—	0	1	1	2	3
5	.05	—	0	1	2	4	5	6	8	9
	.01	—	—	—	0	1	2	3	4	5
6	.05	—	0	2	3	5	7	8	10	12
	.01	—	—	—	1	2	3	4	6	7
7	.05	—	0	2	4	6	8	11	13	15
	.01	—	—	0	1	3	4	6	7	9
8	.05	—	1	3	5	8	10	13	15	18
	.01	—	—	0	2	4	6	7	9	11
9	.05	—	1	3	6	9	12	15	18	21
	.01	—	—	1	3	5	7	9	11	14
10	.05	—	1	4	7	11	14	17	20	24
	.01	—	—	1	3	6	8	11	13	16
11	.05	—	1	5	8	12	16	19	23	27
	.01	—	—	1	4	7	9	12	15	18
12	.05	—	2	5	9	13	17	21	26	30
	.01	—	—	2	5	8	11	14	17	21
13	.05	—	2	6	10	15	19	24	28	33
	.01	—	0	2	5	9	12	16	20	23
14	.05	—	2	7	11	16	21	26	31	36
	.01	—	0	2	6	10	13	17	22	26
15	.05	—	3	7	12	18	23	28	33	39
	.01	—	0	3	7	11	15	19	24	28
16	.05	—	3	8	14	19	25	30	36	42
	.01	—	0	3	7	12	16	21	26	31
17	.05	—	3	9	15	20	26	33	39	45
	.01	—	0	4	8	13	18	23	28	33
18	.05	—	4	9	16	22	28	35	41	48
	.01	—	0	4	9	14	19	24	30	36
19	.05	0	4	10	17	23	30	37	44	51
	.01	—	1	4	9	15	20	26	32	38
20	.05	0	4	11	18	25	32	39	47	54
	.01	—	1	5	10	16	22	28	34	40

Table D.7   (cont.) Critical Values of the Mann-Whitney U

One-tailed test

				n_1 (no. of scores in Group 1)						
10	11	12	13	14	15	16	17	18	19	20
—	—	—	—	—	—	—	—	—	0	0
—	—	—	—	—	—	—	—	—	—	—
1	1	2	2	2	3	3	3	4	4	4
—	—	—	0	0	0	0	0	0	1	1
4	5	5	6	7	7	8	9	9	10	11
1	1	2	2	2	3	3	4	4	4	5
7	8	9	10	11	12	14	15	16	17	18
3	4	5	5	6	7	7	8	9	9	10
11	12	13	15	16	18	19	20	22	23	25
6	7	8	9	10	11	12	13	14	15	16
14	16	17	19	21	23	25	26	28	30	32
8	9	11	12	13	15	16	18	19	20	22
17	19	21	24	26	28	30	33	35	37	39
11	12	14	16	17	19	21	23	24	26	28
20	23	26	28	31	33	36	39	41	44	47
13	15	17	20	22	24	26	28	30	32	34
24	27	30	33	36	39	42	45	48	51	54
16	18	21	23	26	28	31	33	36	38	40
27	31	34	37	41	44	48	51	55	58	62
19	22	24	27	30	33	36	38	41	44	47
31	34	38	42	46	50	54	57	61	65	69
22	25	28	31	34	37	41	44	47	50	53
34	38	42	47	51	55	60	64	68	72	77
24	28	31	35	38	42	46	49	53	56	60
37	42	47	51	56	61	65	70	75	80	84
27	31	35	39	43	47	51	55	59	63	67
41	46	51	56	61	66	71	77	82	87	92
30	34	38	43	47	51	56	60	65	69	73
44	50	55	61	66	72	77	83	88	94	100
33	37	42	47	51	56	61	66	70	75	80
48	54	60	65	71	77	83	89	95	101	107
36	41	46	51	56	61	66	71	76	82	87
51	57	64	70	77	83	89	96	102	109	115
38	44	49	55	60	66	71	77	82	88	93
55	61	68	75	82	88	95	102	109	116	123
41	47	53	59	65	70	76	82	88	94	100
58	65	72	80	87	94	101	109	116	123	130
44	50	56	63	69	75	82	88	94	101	107
62	69	77	84	92	100	107	115	123	130	138
47	53	60	67	73	80	87	93	100	107	114

From the *Bulletin of the Institute of Educational Research*, 1, No. 2, Indiana University, with permission of the publishers.

Table D.8 Critical Values of the Wilcoxon *T*

Two-tailed test

N	α = .05	α = .01	N	α = .05	α = .01
5	—	—	28	116	91
6	0	—	29	126	100
7	2	—	30	137	109
8	3	0	31	147	118
9	5	1	32	159	128
10	8	3	33	170	138
11	10	5	34	182	148
12	13	7	35	195	159
13	17	9	36	208	171
14	21	12	37	221	182
15	25	15	38	235	194
16	29	19	39	249	207
17	34	23	40	264	220
18	40	27	41	279	233
19	46	32	42	294	247
20	52	37	43	310	261
21	58	42	44	327	276
22	65	48	45	343	291
23	73	54	46	361	307
24	81	61	47	378	322
25	89	68	48	396	339
26	98	75	49	415	355
27	107	83	50	434	373

Table D.8 (cont.) Critical Values of the Wilcoxon *T*

One-tailed test

N	$\alpha = .05$	$\alpha = .01$	N	$\alpha = .05$	$\alpha = .01$
5	0	—	28	130	101
6	2	—	29	140	110
7	3	0	30	151	120
8	5	1	31	163	130
9	8	3	32	175	140
10	10	5	33	187	151
11	13	7	34	200	162
12	17	9	35	213	173
13	21	12	36	227	185
14	25	15	37	241	198
15	30	19	38	256	211
16	35	23	39	271	224
17	41	27	40	286	238
18	47	32	41	302	252
19	53	37	42	319	266
20	60	43	43	336	281
21	67	49	44	353	296
22	75	55	45	371	312
23	83	62	46	389	328
24	91	69	47	407	345
25	100	76	48	426	362
26	110	84	49	446	379
27	119	92	50	466	397

From F. Wilcoxon and R. A Wilcox, *Some Rapid Approximate Statistical Procedures.* New York: Lederle Laboratories, 1964. Reproduced with the permission of the American Cyanamid Company.

Glossary

AB design A design in which the participant is tested first when the independent variable is not present, then when it is present

Abstract In an APA-style research report, the brief summary of the study (up to 120 words) that immediately follows the title page

Alpha The Greek letter α, which symbolizes the criterion for rejecting the null hypothesis

Alternate forms Different versions of the same questionnaire

Alternative hypothesis The statistical hypothesis describing the population parameters that the sample data represent if the predicted relationship does exist. See also *Null Hypothesis*

Analysis of variance The parametric procedure for determining whether significant differences exist in an experiment involving two or more sample means

ANOVA See *Analysis of variance*

APA's Ethical Principles The code of conduct adopted by the American Psychological Association in 1992 to govern the care of human and nonhuman research participants

Apparatus section The section in an APA-style research report in which materials and apparatus used in the study are described; the section is called Apparatus if testing mainly involves equipment such as computers, recording devices, etc. See also *Materials*

Applied research Research conducted for the purpose of solving an existing, real-life problem

As a function of The way to describe a relationship in a scientific study

Archival research Research for which written records constitute the source of data on one or more variables

Automation The practice of using electronic or mechanical devices to present stimuli and to measure and record responses

Bar graph A graph in which a free-standing vertical bar is centered over each score on the X axis; used when the independent variable implies discrete categories that follow no set order

Barnum statements Questions or statements that are so global and vague that everyone would agree with them or select the same response for them

Baseline The level of performance on the dependent variable when the independent variable is not present, used as a comparison to the level of performance when the independent variable is present

Basic research Research conducted simply to produce knowledge about nature

Between-subjects ANOVA The type of ANOVA that is performed when a study involves no matching or repeated measures

Between-subjects design An experimental design in which subjects are randomly assigned to each condition or are matched across conditions

Carry-over effects The influence that a subject's experience of a trial has on his or her performance of subsequent trials

Case study An in-depth description of one subject, organization, or event

Causal hypothesis A hypothesis that tentatively explains a particular influence on, or cause of, a behavior

Ceiling effects A restriction of range problem that occurs when a task is too easy, causing most or all scores to approximate the highest possible score

Closed-ended question In a questionnaire or interview, a question accompanied by several alternative answers from which the subject must select

Cluster sampling A sampling technique in which certain groups are randomly selected and all subjects in each group are observed

Coefficient of determination The proportion of variance accounted for by a relationship; computed by squaring the correlation coefficient

Cohort design A factorial design consisting of a longitudinal study of several groups, each from a different generation

Cohort effects A situation that occurs when age differences are confounded by differences in subject history

Collapsing across a variable To combine scores from the different amounts or categories of that variable

Complete counterbalancing Testing different participants with different orders so that all possible orders of conditions or trials occur in a study

Complete factorial design A research design in which all levels of each factor are combined with all levels of the other factor(s)

Conceptual replication The repeated test or confirmation of a hypothesis using a design different from that of the original study

Concurrent validity The extent to which a procedure correlates with the present behavior of subjects

Condition An amount or category of the independent variable that creates the specific situation under which participants' scores on the dependent variable are measured

Confederates People enlisted by a researcher to act as other subjects or "accidental" passers-by, thus creating a social situation to which "real" subjects can then respond

Confidence interval A statistically defined range of values of the population parameter, any one of which the sample statistic is likely to represent

Confounded variables See *Confounding*

Confounding A situation that occurs when an extraneous variable systematically changes along with the variable we hypothesize is a causal variable

Construct validity The extent to which a measurement reflects the hypothetical construct of interest

Content analysis A scoring procedure for open-end questions in which the researcher counts specific words or themes in a subject's responses

Content validity The extent to which a measurement reflects the variable or behavior of interest

Contingency coefficient The statistic that describes the strength of the relationship in a two-way chi square when there are more than two categories for either variable; symbolized as C

Control The elimination of unintended, extraneous factors that might influence the behavior being studied

Control group A group of subjects who are measured on the dependent variable but receive zero amount of the independent variable (i.e., do not experience the treatment), thus providing a baseline for determining the effect of the latter on the experimental group

Convenience sampling A sampling approach in which the researcher studies the subjects who are conveniently available

Convergent validity The extent to which the scores obtained from one procedure are positively correlated with the scores obtained from another procedure that is already accepted as valid

Converging operations Two or more procedures that together eliminate rival hypotheses and bolster our conclusions about a particular behavior

Correlational design A research design in which we measure subjects' scores on two or more variables to determine whether the scores form the predicted relationship

Correlation coefficient See *Pearson correlation coefficient; Point-biserial correlation coefficient; Spearman correlation coefficient*

Counterbalancing The process of systematically changing the order of trials for different subjects in a balanced way, so as to counter the biasing influence of any one order

Criterion validity The extent to which the scores obtained from a procedure correlate with an observable behavior, such that the procedure is capable of distinguishing between subjects on the basis of that behavior

Cross-sectional design A quasi-experimental between-subjects design in which subjects are observed at different ages or at different points in a temporal sequence

Debriefing The procedure by which researchers inform subjects about all aspects of a study after they have participated in it, in order to remove any negative consequences of the procedure

Deception   The creation of an artificial situation or a "cover story" that disguises a study

Demand characteristics   Cues within the research context that guide or bias a subject's behavior

Dependent samples *t*-test   The statistical procedure that is appropriate when the scores meet the requirements of a parametric test, the research design involves matched groups or repeated measures, and there are only two conditions of the independent variable

Dependent variable   In an experiment, the variable that is measured under each condition of the independent variable

Descriptive hypothesis   A hypothesis that tentatively describes a behavior in terms of its characteristics or the situation in which it occurs

Descriptive methods   The research methods used to test descriptive hypotheses

Descriptive research   The observation and description of a behavior, the situation it occurs in, or the individuals exhibiting it

Descriptive statistics   Mathematical procedures for summarizing and describing the important characteristics of a sample of data

Descriptive study   A study in which the researcher only observes and measures a behavior or situation, usually in a natural or field setting

Design   The specific manner in which a research study will be conducted

Determinism   The idea that behavior is solely influenced by natural causes and does not depend on choice or "free will"

Diffusion of treatment   A threat to internal validity that arises when subjects in one condition are aware of the treatment given in other conditions

Discriminant analysis   A procedure by which subjects are categorized along a qualitative *Y* variable using several quantitative predictor (*X*) variables

Discriminant validity   The extent to which the scores obtained from one procedure are not correlated with the scores obtained from another procedure that measures other variables or constructs

Discussion section   The section in an APA-style research report in which results are interpreted and conclusions drawn

Distractor task   A task designed to distract participants away from demand characteristics

Double-barreled questions   Questions that have more than one component

Double-blind procedure   A research procedure in which both the researcher who interacts with the subjects and the subjects themselves are unaware of the treatment being presented

Ecological validity   The extent to which an experimental situation can be generalized to natural settings and behaviors

Effect size   An indication of how dramatically an independent variable influences a dependent variable

Empirical knowledge   Knowledge obtained through observation of events

Error in prediction   The amount of error that occurs in predicting unknown scores

Error variance   The variability in *Y* scores at each *X* score

Eta squared   The proportion of variance in the dependent variable that is accounted for by changing the levels of a factor, thus describing the measurement of effect size in a sample; symbolized as η^2

Experiment   A design in which one variable is actively changed or manipulated and scores on another variable are measured to determine whether there is a relationship

Experimental group(s)   Those subjects who receive a nonzero amount of the independent variable (i.e., who experience the treatment) and are then measured on the dependent variable

Experimental methods   The research methods used to test causal hypotheses

Experimental realism   The extent to which the experimental task engages subjects psychologically, such that they become less concerned with demand characteristics

Experimenter expectancies   Subtle cues provided by the experimenter about the responses that subjects should give in a particular condition

Ex post facto research   Research conducted after a phenomenon has occurred

External validity The extent to which our results generalize to other subjects and other situations

Extraneous variables Variables that may potentially influence the results of a study but are not the variables of interest (e.g., subject, researcher, environmental, or measurement variables)

Face validity The extent to which a measurement procedure appears to measure what it is intended to measure

Factor See *Independent variable*

Factor analysis A procedure in which intercorrelations between responses to questionnaire or interview questions are used to discover some common underlying factor

Factorial design. See *Complete factorial design*

Falsifiable The requirement that the test of a scientific hypothesis can possibly show that the hypothesis is incorrect

Field experiment An experiment conducted in a natural setting

Field survey A procedure in which subjects complete a questionnaire or interview in a natural setting

Figures In an APA-style research report, graphs that summarize the pattern in a relationship in a visual presentation

Figure caption An explanatory title provided with a figure in an APA-style research report

Figure caption page A separate page at the end of an APA-style research report that contains all captions for figures in the paper

Filter question General question asked in an interview or questionnaire that determines whether participants should answer additional, detailed questions

Floor effects A restriction of range problem that occurs when a task is too difficult, causing most or all scores to approximate the lowest possible score

Forced-choice procedure A measure in which participants must select from a limited set of choices, such as a multiple-choice test

Friedman test The one-way within-subjects ANOVA for ordinal scores, performed when there are more than two levels of one factor

Funnel question General question asked in an interview or questionnaire that leads to more specific questions

Generalize To apply the conclusions of a study to other individuals or situations

Habituation The process by which subjects are familiarized with a procedure before actual data collection is commenced, in order to reduce reactivity

Hawthorne effect A bias in subjects' behavior—usually an improvement in performance—that results from the special treatment and interest shown by a researcher

Human Subjects Review Committee A committee at colleges and research institutions charged with the responsibility of reviewing all prospective research procedures to ensure the ethical and safe treatment of subjects

Hypothesis A formally stated expectation about a behavior that defines the purpose and goals of a research study

Hypothetical construct An abstract concept used in a particular theoretical manner to relate different behaviors according to their underlying features or causes

Independent samples *t*-test The statistical procedure that is appropriate when the scores meet the requirements of a parametric test, the research design involves a between-subjects design, and there are only two conditions of the independent variable

Independent variable In an experiment, the variable that is systematically changed or manipulated by the researcher; also called a factor

Individual differences The characteristics that make individuals different from one another and that produce different responses to the same situation

Inferential statistics Mathematical procedures for deciding whether a sample relationship represents a relationship that actually exists in the population

Informed consent The procedure by which researchers inform subjects about a laboratory experiment prior to their participation in it, out of respect for subjects' rights to control what happens to them

Instructions   What the researcher tells the participants at the beginning of a study. Instructions describe the sequence of events, identify the stimuli participants should attend to, and explain how participants should indicate responses

Instrumentation effects   Changes in measurement procedures that occur through use of equipment over time, making the measurements less reliable

Interaction effect   The influence that the combination of levels from the factors has on dependent scores

Internal validity   The extent to which the observed relationship reflects the relationship between the variables in a study

Inter-rater reliability   The extent to which raters agree on the scores they assign to a subject's behavior

Interrupted time-series design   A quasi-experimental repeated-measures design in which observations are made at several spaced times before and then after a treatment

Interval scale   A measurement scale in which each score indicates an actual amount, an equal unit of measurement separates consecutive scores, zero is not a true zero value, and negative scores are possible

Intervening variable   An internal subject characteristic that is influenced by the independent variable and, in turn, influences the dependent variable

Introduction   The section of an APA-style research report that presents the hypothetical constructs as they are used in past research, develops the hypothesized relationship between the variables for the target population, and provides the specific predictions of the study

Kruskal-Wallis test   The nonparametric version of the one-way between-subjects ANOVA for ranked scores

Lawfulness   The assumption that events can be understood as a sequence of natural causes and effects

Leading questions   Questions that are so loaded with social desirability or experimenter expectancies that there is one obvious response

Likert-type questions   A measure in which participants rate statements, such as when using a scale of 1 to 5 where 1 indicates "strongly agree" and 5 indicates "strongly disagree"

Linear regression   The procedure for predicting subjects' scores on one variable based on the linear relationship with subjects' scores on another variable

Linear regression equation   The equation that defines the straight line summarizing a linear relationship by describing the value of Y' at each X

Linear regression line   The straight line that summarizes the scatterplot of a linear relationship by, on average, passing through the center of all Y scores

Linear relationship   A relationship between the X and Y scores in a set of data in which the Y scores tend to change in only one direction as the X scores increase, forming a slanted straight regression line on a scatterplot

Line graph   A graph on which adjacent data points are connected with straight lines; used when the independent variable implies a continuous, ordered amount

Literal replication   The precise duplication of the specific design and results of a previous study

Longitudinal design   A quasi-experimental design in which a researcher repeatedly measures a group of subjects in order to observe the effect of the passage of time

Main effect   In a multifactor ANOVA, the influence on the dependent scores of changing the levels of one factor, ignoring all other factors in the study

Manipulation check   A measurement, in addition to the dependent variable, that determines whether each condition of the independent variable had its intended effect

Mann-Whitney test   The nonparametric version of the independent samples t-test for ranked scores

Manuscript page header   In an APA-style research manuscript, the first two or three words of the title typed to the left of the page number on all pages

Margin of error   The confidence interval that is computed when estimating the population's responses to a field survey

Matched-groups design   A research design in which each subject in one condition is matched with a subject in every other condition along an extraneous subject variable

Materials section   The section in an APA-style research report in which materials and apparatus in the study are described; the section is called Materials if testing mainly involves stimulus objects, tests and printed material, slides, drawings, etc. See also *Apparatus section*

Mean   The average of a group of scores, interpreted as the score around which the scores in a distribution tend to be clustered

Measure of central tendency   A score that summarizes the location of a distribution on a variable by indicating where the center of the distribution tends to be located

Measures of variability   Numbers that summarize the extent to which the scores in a distribution differ from one another

Median   The score located at the 50th percentile

Meta-analysis   Statistical procedures for combining, testing, and describing the results from different studies

Method section   The section in an APA-style research report that describes the specifics of the design and how the data were collected; it includes the Participants, Apparatus/Materials, and Procedure subsections

Mode   The most frequently occurring score in a set of data

Model   A generalized, hypothetical description that, by analogy, explains the process underlying a set of common behaviors

Multifactor experiment   An experiment in which the researcher examines several independent variables and their interactions

Multiple baselines across behaviors   The practice of measuring a baseline for several behaviors from one participant and applying the treatment to each behavior at a different time

Multiple baselines across participants   The practice of measuring a baseline for several individuals on the same behavior, but introducing the treatment for each at a different time

Multiple baselines across situations   The practice of establishing a baseline for one behavior on the same participant in different situations

Multiple-baseline design   A research design in which a baseline is established for one behavior from several subjects, for several behaviors from one subject, or for one behavior from one subject in several situations

Multiple correlation and regression   Statistical procedures performed when multiple predictor (X) variables are being used to predict one criterion (Y) variable

Multiple raters   The practice of having more than one rater judge each participant's behavior in a study

Multiple time-series design   A quasi-experimental repeated-measures design in which an experimental group and a nonequivalent control group are observed at several spaced times before and then after a treatment

Multiple trials   The procedure of observing each participant several times in a condition to avoid bias from one unique trial

Multivariate statistics   The inferential statistical procedures used when a study involves multiple dependent variables

Naturalistic observation   The unobtrusive observation of a wide variety of subjects' behaviors in an unstructured fashion

Negative linear relationship   A linear relationship in which the Y scores tend to decrease as the X scores increase

Nominal scale   A measurement scale in which each score identifies a quality or category and does not indicate an amount

Nonequivalent control group   In a quasi-experiment, a control group whose subject characteristics and experiences are different from those of the experimental group

Nonexperimental methods   See *Descriptive methods*

Nonlinear relationship   A relationship between the X and Y scores in a set of data in which the Y scores change their direction of change as the X scores change

Nonparametric inferential statistics Inferential procedures employed to analyze interval or ratio scores that are not normally distributed, or to analyze nominal or ordinal scores

Nonprobability sampling Collectively, the sampling techniques in which every potential subject in the population does not have an equal likelihood of being selected for participation in a study

Nonsignificant Describes results that are considered likely to result from sampling error when the predicted relationship does not exist; it indicates failure to reject the null hypothesis

Nonsymmetrical carry-over effects The result when the carry-over effects from one order of conditions do not balance out those of another order

Normal distribution A frequency distribution for a set of data, usually represented by a bell-shaped curve that is symmetrical about the mean

Null hypothesis The statistical hypothesis describing the population parameters that the sample data represent if the predicted relationship does not exist. See also *Alternative hypothesis*

Objectivity The requirement that a researcher's personal biases, attitudes, or subjective impressions do not influence the study's observations or conclusions

Observational research Research where participants are observed in an unobtrusive manner

One-group pretest-posttest design A quasi-experimental pretest-posttest design for which there is no control group

One-tailed test The test used to evaluate a statistical hypothesis that predicts that scores will only increase or only decrease

One-way ANOVA The analysis of variance performed when an experiment has only one independent variable

One-way chi square The chi square procedure performed when a study examines category membership along one variable

One-way design A research design involving the manipulation of just one independent variable

Open-ended question In a questionnaire or interview, a question for which the subject determines both the alternatives to choose from and the response

Operational definition The definition of a construct or variable in terms of the operations used to measure it

Order effects The influence on a particular trial that arises from its position in a sequence of trials

Ordinal scale A measurement scale in which scores indicate rank order or a relative amount

Parametric inferential statistics Inferential procedures employed to analyze normally distributed interval or ratio scores

Parsimonious The requirement that a scientific hypothesis must be as simple as possible

Partial correlation A procedure in which the correlation between two variables is determined while keeping the influence of other variables constant

Partial counterbalancing Balancing order effects by testing different participants using only some of the possible orders

Participants The individuals in a sample

Participant observation The observation of a group in which the researcher is an active member

Participants section The section in an APA-style research report that describes important characteristics of subjects

Pearson correlation coefficient The correlation coefficient that describes the strength and type of a linear relationship; symbolized as r

Peer review The practice of having a research report manuscript reviewed by several psychologists knowledgeable about the research topic to prevent scientific fraud and to ensure quality research

Phi coefficient The statistic that describes the strength of the relationship in a two-way chi square when there are only two categories for each variable; symbolized as ϕ

Physical risk The potential for something in a study (equipment, presenting stimuli, etc.) to physically endanger participants

Pilot study A miniature version of a study that researchers use to test a procedure prior to the actual study

Placebo An inactive substance that provides the demand characteristics of a manipulation while presenting zero amount of the independent variable, thus serving as a control in an experiment

Planned comparisons In ANOVA, statistical procedures for comparing only some conditions in an experiment

Point-biserial correlation coefficient A statistic that describes the strength of the relationship between two conditions of the independent variable and an interval or ratio dependent variable; symbolized as r_{pb}

Population The infinitely large group of all possible individuals of interest in a specific, defined situation

Positive linear relationship A linear relationship in which the Y scores tend to increase as the X scores increase

Post hoc comparisons In ANOVA, statistical procedures for comparing all possible pairs of conditions, to determine which ones differ significantly from each other

Power The probability that a statistical test will detect a true relationship and allow the rejection of a false null hypothesis

Powerful design An experimental design that is more likely to produce a clear, convincing, and strong sample relationship

Practice effects The influence on performance that arises from practicing a task

Precise The requirement that a scientific hypothesis should contain terms that are clearly defined

Prediction A specific statement as to how we will see a behavior manifested in a research situation, describing the specific results that we expect will be found

Predictive validity The extent to which a procedure allows for accurate predictions about a subject's future behavior

Pretest A measure used to identify and select potential participants, prior to conducting a study

Pretest-posttest design A research design in which subjects are measured before and after a treatment

Probability sampling Collectively, the sampling techniques in which every potential subject in the population has an equal likelihood of being selected for participation in a study

Procedure section The section in an APA-style research report that describes how the participants, materials, and apparatus are brought together to perform the study

Program evaluation The procedures undertaken to evaluate the goals, activities, and outcomes of social programs

Projective test A psychological test in which subjects are asked to create a description or interpretation of an ambiguous stimulus, onto which they project their hidden feelings or attributes

Proportion of variance accounted for The proportion of the error in predicting scores that is eliminated when, instead of using the mean of Y, we use the relationship with the X variable to predict Y scores; the proportional improvement in predicting Y scores thus achieved

Pseudo-explanation A circular statement that explains an event simply by renaming it

Psychological Abstracts A monthly publication that describes studies recently published in psychology journals

Psychological risk The potential for something in a study (manipulation, deception, etc.) to cause participants psychological distress

Publication Manual of the American Psychological Association The definitive reference source for answering any question regarding the organization, content, and style of a research manuscript

Quasi-experiment A study in which subjects cannot be randomly assigned to any condition but, instead, are assigned to a particular condition on the basis of some inherent characteristic

Quasi-independent variable The independent variable in a quasi-experiment

Quota sampling A sampling technique in which, using convenience sampling, the sample has the same percentage of each subgroup as that found in the population

Random assignment A method of selecting a sample for an experiment such that the condition each subject experiences is determined in a random and unbiased manner

Randomization The creation of different random orders of trials or conditions under which different subjects are tested

Raters People enlisted by the researcher to judge participants' behavior. Raters are usually kept blind to the hypothesis and specific conditions and are trained to use the researcher's scoring criteria

Ratio scale A measurement scale in which each score indicates an actual amount, an equal unit of measurement separates consecutive scores, zero means zero amount, and negative scores are not possible

Rational The requirement that a scientific hypothesis should logically fit what is already known about the laws of behavior

Reaction time The amount of time a participant takes to respond to a stimulus

Reactivity The bias in responses that occurs when subjects know they are being observed

Reference page The final section in an APA-style research report in which complete references for all sources cited in the article are listed alphabetically

Regression toward the mean A change in extreme scores toward less extreme scores that occurs because random influences are not consistently present

Relationship A pattern in which a change in one variable is accompanied by a consistent change in the other

Reliability The extent to which a measurement is consistent, can be reproduced, and avoids error

Repeated-measures design A research design in which each subject is measured under all conditions of an independent variable

Replication The process of repeatedly conducting studies that test and confirm a hypothesis so that confidence in its truth can be developed

Representative sample A sample whose characteristics and behaviors accurately reflect those of the population from which it is drawn

Research ethics The concern for balancing a researcher's right to study a behavior with the right of participants to be protected from abuse

Research literature Research studies published in professional books and psychological journals

Response scale The number and type of choices provided for each question in a questionnaire or interview

Response set A bias toward responding in a particular way because of previous responses made

Restriction of range Improper limitation of the range of scores obtained on one or both variables, leading to an underestimation of the strength of the relationship between the variables

Results section The section in an APA-style research report that describes the statistical procedures performed and statistical outcomes obtained

Reversal design A research design in which the researcher alternates between the baseline condition and the treatment condition

Role playing The practice of having participants pretend they are in a particular situation and observing their behavior or having them describe how they would behave; used to reduce physical or psychological risk

Running head The abbreviated title printed at the top of each page in a published research article

Sample A relatively small subset of a population that is selected to represent or stand in for the population

Sample standard deviation The square root of the sample variance

Sample variance The average of the squared deviations of the scores around the mean

Sampling error The difference, due to random chance, between a sample statistic and the population parameter it represents

Scales of measurement Ways to measure scores in a scientific study; the scales are nominal, ordinal, interval, and ratio

Scientific fraud The practice of faking results by reporting data from a study inaccurately, publishing data when no research was conducted, or plagiarizing the work of others

Scientific method The totality of assumptions, attitudes, goals, and procedures for creating

GLOSSARY

and answering questions about nature in a scientific manner

Scoring criteria The system for assigning different scores to different participant responses in a study

Simple main effect The effect of one factor at one level of a second factor

Selection criteria The definition of participants in terms of the characteristics required for allowing them to participate in the study

Selection test A test, such as a college entrance exam, that selects people based on scores and can predict future performance

Self-report A measure in which participants describe their feelings or thoughts

Significant Describes results that are considered too unlikely to result from chance sampling error if the predicted relationship does not exist; it indicates rejection of the null hypothesis

Sensitive dependent measure A precise measurement of subtle differences in behavior

Simple random sampling A sampling technique in which subjects are randomly selected from a list of the members of the population

Single-blind procedure A research procedure in which subjects are unaware of the treatment they are receiving

Single-subject design A repeated-measures experiment conducted on one subject

Small N research A single-subject design (with an N of 1) replicated on a small number of other participants

Snowball sampling A sampling technique in which the researcher contacts potential subjects who have been identified by previously tested subjects

Social desirability The demand characteristic that causes subjects to provide what they consider to be the socially acceptable response

Social Science Citation Index A reference source that identifies a given research article by authors and date, and then lists subsequent articles that have cited it

Sorting task A measure in which participants sort stimuli into different groups

Spearman correlation coefficient The correlation coefficient that describes the linear relationship between pairs of ranked scores; symbolized as r_s

Split-half reliability The consistency with which subjects' scores on some trials match their scores on other trials

Squared correlation coefficient The proportion of total variance in Y scores that is systematically associated with changing X scores

Standard deviation See *Sample standard deviation*

Standard error of the estimate A standard deviation indicating the amount that the actual Y scores in a sample differ from, or are spread out around, their corresponding Y' scores; symbolized as $S_{Y'}$

State characteristic A temporary, changeable attribute that is influenced by situational factors

Stratified random sampling A sampling technique involving the identification of important subgroups in the population, followed by the proportionate random selection of subjects from each subgroup

Strength of the relationship The extent to which one value of Y within a relationship is consistently associated with one and only one value of X; also called the degree of association

Strong manipulation Manipulation of the independent variable in such a way that subjects' behavior is greatly differentiated, thus producing large differences in dependent scores between the conditions

Structured interview An interview in which subjects are asked a specific set of predetermined questions in a controlled manner

Subject history The bias that arises due to participants' experiences that influence repeated measures

Subject maturation The bias that arises due to the changes that occur as an individual grows older and more mature that influence repeated measures

Subject mortality The loss of subjects because their participation dies out before the study is completed

Subjects See *Participants*

Subject sophistication The bias in our results that arises when subjects are knowledgeable about research, such that their responses are not generalizable to the population

Systematic The idea that research observations are obtained in a methodical, step-by-step fashion

Systematic naturalistic observation The unobtrusive observation of a particular behavior or situation in a structured fashion

Systematic random sampling A sampling technique in which every nth subject is selected from a list of the members of the population

Systematic variance The differences in Y scores that occur with, or are associated with, changes in the X variable

Table A display of results in an APA-style research report that lists precise numerical values of means, percentages, etc.

Temporal validity The extent to which our experimental results can be generalized to other time frames

Testable The requirement that it must be possible to devise a test of a scientific hypothesis

Test-retest reliability The consistency with which subjects obtain the same overall score when tested at different times

Theory A logically organized set of proposals that defines, explains, organizes, and interrelates our knowledge about many behaviors

Three-way design A research design involving the manipulation of three independent variables

Three-way interaction The interaction of three factors such that the two-way interaction between two factors changes as the levels of the third factor change

Time-series design A quasi-experimental repeated-measures design in which subjects' behavior is sampled before and then after the occurrence of an event

Title The name given to a research article; no more than 12 words that clearly communicate the variables and relationships being studied

Trait characteristic An attribute that is stable over time and not easily influenced by situational factors

True experiment A study in which the researcher actively changes or manipulates a variable that subjects are exposed to by the researcher

t-test See *Dependent samples t-test; Independent samples t-test*

Two-tailed test The test used to evaluate a statistical hypothesis that predicts a relationship, but not whether scores will increase or decrease

Two-way between-subjects design A research design in which a different group of subjects is tested under each condition of two independent variables

Two-way chi square procedure The chi square procedure performed in testing whether, in the population, frequency of category membership on one variable is independent of frequency of category membership on the other variable

Two-way design A research design involving the manipulation of two independent variables

Two-way interaction The interaction of two factors such that the relationship between one factor and the dependent scores is different for and depends on each level of the other factor

Two-way mixed design A research design involving one within-subjects factor and one between-subjects factor

Two-way within-subjects ANOVA The analysis performed when matched groups or the same repeatedly measured subjects are tested in all conditions of two independent variables

Type I error A statistical decision-making error in which the null hypothesis is rejected even though it is true

Type II error A statistical decision-making error in which the null hypothesis is retained even though it is false

Type of relationship The form of the pattern between the X scores and the Y scores in a set of data, determined by the overall direction in which the Y scores change as the X scores change

Unconfounded comparisons Comparisons of cell means that differ along only one factor

Univariate statistics Statistics that involve one dependent variable

Unobtrusive measures Procedures by which subjects' behavior is measured without their being aware that measurements are being made

Unstructured interview An interview in which the questions are not rigidly predetermined, thus allowing for substantial discussion and interaction between subject and interviewer

Validity The extent to which a procedure measures what it is intended to measure

Variability Showing inconsistency in scores within a condition

Variable Any measurable aspect of a behavior or influence on behavior that may change

Variance See *Sample variance; Error variance; Systematic variance*

Volunteer bias The bias that arises from the fact that a given sample contains only those subjects who are willing to participate in the study

Wilcoxon test The nonparametric version of the dependent samples *t*-test for ranked scores

Within-subjects ANOVA The ANOVA performed when all factors involve matching or repeated measures

Within-subjects design An experimental design in which the same subjects are repeatedly measured in all conditions of the factors

Yes-no task The simplest forced-choice procedure, in which participants are asked questions with "yes" or "no" answers

Y prime The value of Y that falls on the regression line above any X; symbolized as Y'

References

Albas, D. C., & Albas, C. A. (1989). Meaning in context: The impact of eye contact and perception of threat on proximity. *The Journal of Social Psychology, 129,* 525–531.

Allen, J. B., Kendrick, D. T., Linder, D. E., & McCall, M. A. (1989). Arousal and attraction: A response-facilitation alternative to misattribution and negative-reinforcement models. *Journal of Personality and Social Psychology, 57,* 261–270.

American Psychological Association. (1992). Ethical principles of psychologists and code of conduct. *American Psychologist, 47,* 1597–1611.

American Psychological Association. (1994). *Publication manual of the American Psychological Association* (4th ed.). Washington, DC: Author.

Anderson, C. A., & Anderson, D. C. (1984). Ambient temperature and violent crime: Tests of the linear and curvilinear hypotheses. *Journal of Personality and Social Psychology, 46,* 91–97.

Anderson, P. (1983). Decision making by objection and the Cuban missile crisis. *Administrative Science Quarterly, 28,* 201–222.

Barlow, D. H., & Hernsen, M. (1984). *Single case experimental designs: Strategies for studying behavior change* (2nd ed.). New York: Pergamon Press.

Baumeister, R. F. (1984). Choking under pressure: Self-consciousness and paradoxical effects of incentives on skillful performance. *Journal of Personality and Social Psychology, 46,* 610–620.

Bell, P. A. (1980). Effects of heat, noise, and provocation on retaliatory evaluative behavior. *Journal of Social Psychology, 110,* 97–100.

Bell, P. A., & Baron, R. A. (1976). Aggression and heat: The mediating role of negative affect. *Journal of Applied Social Psychology, 6,* 18–30.

Bergin, A. (1966). Some implications of psychotherapy research for therapeutic practice. *Journal of Abnormal Psychology, 71,* 235–246.

Berkowitz, L. (1987). Mood, self-awareness, and willingness to help. *Journal of Personality and Social Psychology, 52,* 721–729.

Boesch-Acherman, H., & Boesch, C. (1993). Tool use in wild chimpanzees: New light from dark forests. *Current Directions in Psychological Science, 2,* 18–21.

Bower, G. H., Karlin, M. B., & Dueck, A. (1975). Comprehension and memory for pictures. *Memory and Cognition, 3*(2), 216–220.

Bramel, D., & Friend, R. (1981). Hawthorne, the myth of the docile worker, and class bias in psychology. *American Psychologist, 36,* 867–878.

Brown, S. W. (1985). Time perception and attention: The effect of prospective versus retrospective paradigms and task demands on perceived duration. *Perception and Psychophysics, 38,* 115–124.

Cahoon, D., & Edmonds, E. M. (1980). The watched pot still won't boil: Expectancy as a variable in estimating the passage of time. *Bulletin of the Psychonomic Society, 16,* 115–116.

Campbell, D. T. (1969). Reforms as experiments. *American Psychologist, 24,* 409–429.

Campbell, D. T., & Stanley, J. C. (1963). *Experimental and quasi-experimental designs for research.* Boston: Houghton Mifflin.

Carlson, M., Marcus-Newhall, A., & Miller, N. (1990). Effects of situational aggression cues: A quantitative review. *Journal of Personality and Social Psychology, 58,* 622–633.

Cherry, F., & Deaux, K. (1978). Fear of success versus fear of gender-inappropriate behavior. *Sex Roles, 4,* 97–100.

Christensen, L. (1988). Deception in psychological research: When is it justified? *Personality and Social Psychology Bulletin, 14,* 664–675.

Cohen, B., Waugh, G., & Place, K. (1989). At the movies: An unobtrusive study of arousal-attraction. *The Journal of Social Psychology, 129,* 691–693.

Cohen, J. (1988). *Statistical power analysis for the behavioral sciences.* Hillsdale, NJ: Lawrence Erlbaum Associates.

Connors, J. G., & Alpher, V. S. (1989). Alcohol themes within country-western songs. *International Journal of the Addictions, 24*, 445–451.

Cook, T. D., & Campbell, D. T. (1979). *Quasi-experimentation: Design and analysis issues for field settings.* Chicago: Rand McNally.

Crowder, R. G. (1982). A common basis for auditory sensory storage in perception and immediate memory. *Perception & Psychophysics, 31*, 477–483.

Crusco, A. H., & Wetzel, C. G. (1984). The Midas touch: The effect of interpersonal touch on restaurant tipping. *Personality and Social Psychology Bulletin, 10*, 512–517.

Cunningham, M. R. (1989). Reactions to heterosexual opening gambits: Female selectivity and male responsiveness. *Personality and Social Psychology Bulletin, 15*, 27–41.

Desrochers, A., & Begg, I. (1987). A theoretical account of encoding and retrieval processes in the use of imagery-based mnemonic techniques: The special case of the keyword method. In M. A. McDaniel & M. Pressley (Eds.), *Imagery and related mnemonic processes: Theories, individual differences, and applications* (pp. 56–77). New York: Springer Verlag.

Dixon, P. N., Willingham, W., Strano, D. A., & Chandler, C. K. (1989). Sense of humor as a mediator during incidental learning of humor-related material. *Psychological Reports, 64*, 851–855.

Dorfman, D. D. (1978). The Cyril Burt question: New findings. *Science, 201*, 1177–1186.

Duclos, S. E., Laird, J. D., Schneider, E., Sexter, M., Stern, L., & Van Lighten, O. (1989). Emotion-specific effects of facial expressions and postures on emotional experience. *Journal of Personality and Social Psychology, 57*, 100–108.

Dutton, D. G., & Aron, A. P. (1974). Some evidence for heightened sexual attraction under conditions of high anxiety. *Journal of Personality and Social Psychology, 30*, 510–517

Eagly, A. H., Ashmore, R. D., MaKijani, M. G., & Longo, L. C. (1991). What is beautiful is good but . . . : A meta-analytic review of research on the physical attractiveness stereotype. *Psychological Bulletin, 110*, 109–128.

Einstein, G. O., McDaniel, M. A., & Lackey, S. (1989). Bizarre imagery, interference, and distinctiveness. *Journal of Experimental Psychology: Learning, Memory, and Cognition, 15*, 137–146.

Erdley, C. A., & D'Agostino, P. R. (1988). Cognitive and affective components of automatic priming effects. *Journal of Personality and Social Psychology, 54*, 741–747.

Eysenck, H. J. (1952). The effects of psychotherapy: An evaluation. *Journal of Consulting Psychology, 16*, 319–324.

Faustman, W., & White, P. (1989). Diagnostic and psychopharmacological treatment characteristics of 536 inpatients with posttraumatic stress disorder. *The Journal of Nervous and Mental Disease, 177*, 154–159.

Felipe, N. J., & Sommer, R. (1966). Invasions of personal space. *Social Problems, 14*, 206–214.

Flowers, J. H., Warner, J. L., & Polansky, M. L. (1979). Response and encoding factors in "ignoring" irrelevant information. *Memory and Cognition, 7*, 86–94.

Fornell, C. (1992). A national customer satisfaction barometer: The Swedish experience. *Journal of Marketing, 56*, 6–21.

Forsythe, S. M. (1990). Effect of applicant's clothing on interviewer's decision to hire. *Journal of Applied Social Psychology, 20*, 1579–1595.

Frank, M. G., & Gilovich, T. (1988). The dark side of self- and social perception: Black uniforms and aggression in professional sports. *Journal of Personality and Social Psychology, 54*, 74–85.

Gathercole, S. E., Willis, C. S., Emslie, H., & Baddeley, A. D. (1992). Phonological memory and vocabulary development during the early school years: A longitudinal study. *Developmental Psychology, 28*, 887–898.

George, J. M., Reed, T. F., Ballard, K. A., Colin, J., & Fielding, J. (1993). Contact with AIDS patients as a source of work-related distress: Effects of organizational and social support. *Academy of Management Journal, 36*, 157–171.

Gladue, B. A., & Delaney, H. J. (1990). Gender differences in perception of attractiveness of men and women in bars. *Personality and Social Psychology Bulletin, 16*, 378–391.

Glick, P., Gottesman, D., & Jolton, J. (1989). The fault is not in the stars: Susceptibility of skeptics and believers in astrology to the Barnum effect. *Personality and Social Psychology Bulletin, 15,* 572–583.

Goodall, J. (1986). *The chimpanzees of Gombe: Patterns of behavior.* Cambridge, MA: Belknap Press.

Goodall, J. (1990). *Through a window: My thirty years with the chimpanzees of Gombe.* Boston: Houghton Mifflin.

Hamid, P. N., & Newport, A. G. (1989). Effect of colour on physical strength and mood in children. *Perceptual and Motor Skills, 69,* 179–185.

Haney, C., Banks, W. C., & Zimbardo, P. G. (1973). Interpersonal dynamics in a simulated prison. *International Journal of Criminology and Penology, 1,* 69–97.

Hanssel, C. E. M. (1980). *ESP and parapsychology: A critical reevaluation.* Buffalo, NY: Prometheus Books.

Harrison, L., & Gfroerer, J. (1992). The intersection of drug use and criminal behavior: Results from the national household survey on drug abuse. *Crime and Delinquency, 38,* 422–443.

Hayduk, L. A. (1983). Personal space: Where we now stand. *Psychological Bulletin, 94,* 293–335.

Hearnshaw, L. S. (1979). *Cyril Burt: Psychologist.* London: Hodder & Stoughton.

Heaton, A. W., & Sigall, H. (1991). Self-consciousness, self-presentation, and performance under pressure: Who chokes and when. *Journal of Applied Social Psychology, 21,* 175–188.

Heslin, R., & Boss, D. (1980). Nonverbal intimacy in airport arrival and departure. *Personality and Social Psychology Bulletin, 6,* 248–252.

Hicks, R. E., Miller, G. W., & Kinsbourne, M. (1976). Prospective and retrospective judgments of time as a function of amount of information processed. *American Journal of Psychology, 89,* 719–730.

Hinkle, P. E., Wiersma, W., & Jurs, S. G. (1998). *Applied statistics for the behavioral sciences* (4th ed.). Boston: Houghton Mifflin.

Horner, M. S. (1972). Toward an understanding of achievement-related conflicts in women. *Journal of Social Issues, 28,* 157–175.

Hunt, R. R., & Elliott, J. M. (1980). The role of nonsemantic information in memory: Orthographic distinctiveness effects on retention. *Journal of Experimental Psychology: General, 109,* 49–74.

Isen, A. M., Daubman, K. A., & Nowicki, G. P. (1987). Positive affect facilitates creative problem solving. *Journal of Personality and Social Psychology, 52,* 1122–1131.

Isen, A. M., & Levin, P. F. (1972). Effect of feeling good on helping: Cookies and kindness. *Journal of Personality and Social Psychology, 21,* 384–388.

Joynson, R. B. (1989). *The Burt Affair.* London: Routledge.

Kanuk, L., & Berenson, C. (1975). Mail surveys and response rates: A literature review. *Journal of Marketing Research, 12,* 440–453.

Kendrick, D. T., Cialdini, R., & Linder, D. (1979). Misattribution under fear-producing circumstances: Four failures to replicate. *Personality and Social Psychology Bulletin, 5,* 329–334.

Kiesler, C. A. (1993). Mental health policy and mental hospitalization. *Current Directions in Psychological Science, 2,* 93–95.

Koocher, G. P. (1977). Bathroom behavior and human dignity. *Journal of Personality and Social Psychology, 35,* 120–121.

Krippendorf, K. (1980). *Content analysis: An introduction to its methodology.* Beverly Hills, CA: Sage.

Kwallek, N., Lewis, C. M., & Robbins, A. S. (1988). Effects of office interior color on workers' mood and productivity. *Perceptual and Motor Skills, 66,* 123–128.

Lavrakas, P. J. (1993). *Telephone survey methods* (2nd ed.). Thousand Oaks, CA: Sage.

Linton, M., & Gallo, P. S. (1975). *The practical statistician: Simplified handbook of statistics.* Monterey, CA: Brooks/Cole.

Lockhart, R. S., & Craik, F. I. M. (1990). Levels of processing: A retrospective commentary on the framework for memory research. *Canadian Journal of Psychology, 44,* 87–112.

Mastrofski, S., & Parks, R. B. (1990). Improving observational studies of police. *Criminology, 28,* 475–496.

Mathews, K. E., Jr., & Cannon, L. K. (1975). Environmental noise level as a determinant of helping behavior. *Journal of Personality and Social Psychology, 32,* 571–577.

May, J. L., & Hamilton, P. A. (1980). Effects of musically evoked affect on women's interpersonal attraction toward and perceptual judgments of physical attractiveness in men. *Motivation and Emotion, 4*(3), 217–228.

McAninch, C. B., Austin, J. L., & Derks, P. L. (1992). Effect of caption meaning on memory for nonsense figures. *Current Psychology: Research and Reviews, 11,* 315–323.

McCarty, D., Diamond, W., & Kaye, M. (1982). Alcohol, sexual arousal, and the transfer of excitation. *Journal of Personality and Social Psychology, 42,* 977–988.

McConnell, J. V., Cutler, R. L., & McNeil, E. B. (1958). Subliminal stimulation: An overview. *American Psychologist, 13,* 229–242.

McKey, R., Cordelli, L., Ganson, H., Barrett, B., McCorkey, C., & Plantz, M. (1985). *The impact of Head Start on children, families, and communities: Final report of the Head Start evaluation, synthesis, and utilization project* (No. OHDS 85-31193). Washington, DC: U.S. Government Printing Office.

Mednick, M. T., Mednick, S. A., & Mednick, E. V. (1964). Incubation of creative performance and specific associative priming. *Journal of Abnormal and Social Psychology, 69,* 84–88.

Meyer, D. E., & Schvanveldt, R. W. (1971). Facilitation in recognizing pairs of words: Evidence of a dependence between retrieval operations. *Journal of Experimental Psychology, 90,* 227–234.

Middlemist, R. D., Knowles, E. S., & Matter, C. F. (1976). Personal space invasions in the lavatory: Suggestive evidence for arousal. *Journal of Personality and Social Psychology, 33,* 541–546.

Middlemist, R. D., Knowles, E. S., & Matter, C. F. (1977). What to do and what to report: A reply to Koocher. *Journal of Personality and Social Psychology, 35,* 122–124.

Milgram, S. (1963). Behavioral study of obedience. *Journal of Abnormal and Social Psychology, 67,* 371–378.

Monahan, L., Kuhn, D., & Shaver, P. (1974). Intrapsychic versus cultural explanations of the "fear of success" motive. *Journal of Personality and Social Psychology, 29,* 60–64.

Mulligan, R. M., & Schiffman, H. R. (1979). Temporal experience as a function of organization in memory. *Bulletin of the Psychonomic Society, 14,* 417–420.

Neisser, U. (1981). John Dean's memory: A case study. *Cognition, 9,* 1–22.

Nelson, D. L., & Sutton, C. (1990). Chronic work stress and coping: A longitudinal study and suggested new directions. *Academy of Management Journal, 33,* 859–869.

Nolen-Hoeksema, S., & Morrow, J. (1991). A prospective study of depression and posttraumatic stress symptoms after a natural disaster: The 1989 Loma Prieta earthquake. *Journal of Personality and Social Psychology, 61,* 115–121.

Orne, M. T. (1962). On the social psychology of the psychological experiment: With particular reference to demand characteristics and their implications. *American Psychologist, 17,* 776–783.

Ornstein, R. E. (1969). *On the experience of time.* Baltimore: Penguin Books.

Pfungst, O. (1911). *Clever Hans (the horse of Mr. von Osten): A contribution to experimental animal and human psychology.* New York: Holt, Rinehart & Winston.

Posavac, E. J., & Carey, R. G. (1989). *Program evaluation* (3rd ed.). Englewood Cliffs, NJ: Prentice Hall.

Robinson, J. P., Shaver, P. R., & Wrightsman, L. S. (1991). *Measures of personality and social psychological attitudes* (Vol. 1). San Diego, CA: Academic Press.

Roethlisberger, F. J., & Dickson, W. J. (1939). *Management and the worker.* Cambridge, MA: Harvard University Press.

Roper Organization. (1992). *Unusual personal experiences: An analysis of the data from three national surveys.* Las Vegas, NV: Bigelow Holding.

Rosenhan, D. L. (1973). On being sane in insane places. *Science, 179,* 250–258.

Rosenthal, R. (1976). *Experimenter effects in behavioral research.* New York: Ervington.

Rosenthal, R., & Jacobson, L. (1966). Teachers' expectancies: Determinates of pupils' I.Q. gains. *Psychological Reports, 19,* 115–118.

Rosenthal, R., & Rosnow, R. L. (1975). *The volunteer subject.* New York: Wiley.

Schackman, S. (1983). A shortened version of the profile of mood states. *Journal of Personality Assessment, 47,* 305–306.

Schacter, S., Goldman, R., & Gordon, A. (1968). Effects of fear, food deprivation and obesity on eating. *Journal of Personality and Social Psychology, 10,* 91–97.

Schmidt, S. R. (1985). Encoding and retrieval processes in the memory for conceptually distinctive events. *Journal of Experimental Psychology: Learning, Memory, and Cognition, 11,* 565–578.

Shaffer, R. M., Rogel, M., & Hendrick, C. (1975). Intervention in the library: The effect of increased responsibility on bystander willingness to prevent theft. *Journal of Personality and Social Psychology, 5,* 303–319.

Shah, I. (1970). *Tales of the Dervishes.* New York: Dutton.

Shepard, J. A., & Strathman, A. J. (1989). Attractiveness and height: The role of stature in dating preference, frequency of dating, and perceptions of attractiveness. *Personality and Social Psychology Bulletin, 15,* 617–627.

Sidman, M. (1960). *Tactics of scientific research.* New York: Basic Books.

Silverman, L. H., Ross, D. L., Adler, J. M., & Lustig, D. A. (1978). Simple research paradigm for demonstrating subliminal psychodynamic activation: Effects of Oedipal stimuli on dart-throwing accuracy in college males. *Journal of Abnormal Psychology, 87,* 341–357.

Silverman, L. H., & Weinberger, J. (1985). Mommy and I are one: Implications for psychotherapy. *American Psychologist, 40,* 1296–1308.

Smith, P. C., Kendall, L. M., & Hulin, C. L. (1969). *The measurement of satisfaction in work and retirement.* Chicago: Rand McNally.

Stagray, J. R., & Truitt, L. (1992). Monaural listening therapy for auditory disorders: Opinions and a case study. *Canadian Journal of Rehabilitation, 6,* 45–49.

Strack, F., Martin, L. L., & Stepper, S. (1988). Inhibiting and facilitating conditions of the human smile: A nonobtrusive test of the facial feedback hypothesis. *Journal of Personality and Social Psychology, 5,* 768–777.

Stroop, J. R. (1935). Studies of interference in serial verbal reactions. *Journal of Experimental Psychology, 18,* 643–662.

Turner, M. L., LaPointe, L. B., Cantor, J., Reeves, C. H., Griffeth, R. H., & Engle, R. W. (1987). Recency and suffix effects found with auditory presentation and with mouthed visual presentation: They're not the same thing. *Journal of Memory and Language, 26,* 138–164.

Wason, P. C. (1968). Reasoning about a rule. *Quarterly Journal of Experimental Psychology, 20,* 273–281.

Werch, C. E., Meers, B. W., & Hallan, J. B. (1992). An analytic review of 73 college-based drug abuse prevention programs. *Health Values, 16*(5), 38–45.

White, G. L., & Knight, T. D. (1984). Misattribution of arousal and attraction: Effects of salience of explanations for arousal. *Journal of Experimental Social Psychology, 20,* 55–64.

Name Index

Adler, J. M., 221
Albas, C. A., 291
Albas, D. C., 291
Allen, J. B., 356
Alpher, V. S., 337
American Psychological Association (APA), 118, 127, 233
Anderson, C. A., 337
Anderson, D., 337
Anderson, P., 338
Aron, A. P., 350–356
Ashmore, R. D., 33
Austin, J. L., 388

Baddeley, A. D., 325
Ballard, K. A., 331
Banks, W. C., 124
Barlow, D. H., 304
Baron, R. A., 115
Baumeister, R. F., 380–381
Begg, I., 388
Bell, P. A., 115
Berenson, C., 332
Bergin, A., 297
Berkowitz, L., 204–205
Boesch, C., 335
Boesch-Acherman, H., 335
Boss, D., 335
Bower, G. H., 384–385, 388
Bramel, D., 295
Brown, S. W., 362, 363

Cahoon, D., 363
Campbell, D. T., 318, 340
Cannon, L. K., 115
Cantor, J., 376
Carey, R. G., 340
Carlson, M., 234
Chandler, C. K., 388
Cherry, F., 366
Christensen, L., 119
Cialdini, R., 356
Cohen, B., 356
Cohen, J., 193
Colin, J., 331
Connors, J. G., 337
Craik, F. I. M., 388
Crowder, R. G., 376
Crusco, A. H., 291

Cunningham, M. R., 356
Cutler, R. L., 220

Daubman, K. A., 367–374
Deaux, K., 366
Delaney, H. J., 293, 326
Derks, P. L., 388
Desrochers, A., 388
Diamond, W., 356
Dickson, W. J., 295
Dixon, P. N., 388
Dorfman, D. D., 128
Duclos, S. E., 114
Dueck, A., 384–385, 388
Dutton, D. G., 350–356

Eagley, A. H., 33
Edmunds, E. M., 363
Einstein, G. O., 389
Elliott, J. M., 388
Emslie, H., 325
Engle, R. W., 376
Eysenck, H. J., 297

Faustman, W., 337
Felipe, N. J., 293
Fielding, J., 331
Flowers, J. H., 218
Fornell, C., 331
Forsythe, S. M., 380
Frank, M. G., 319, 322, 323
Friend, R., 295

Gathercole, S. E., 325
George, J. M., 331
Gfroerer, J., 331
Gilovich, T., 319, 322, 323
Gladue, B. A., 293, 326
Glick, P., 374, 375
Goldman, R., 114
Goodall, J., 335
Gordon, A., 114
Gottesman, D., 374, 375
Griffeth, R. H., 376

Hallan, J. B., 340
Hamid, P. N., 380
Hamilton, P. A., 46, 64
Haney, C., 124

Hanssel, C. E. M., 81
Harrison, L., 331
Hayduk, L. A., 124
Hearnshaw, L. S., 128
Heaton, A. W., 381
Hendrick, C., 291
Hernsen, M., 304
Heslin, R., 335
Hicks, R. E., 363
Hinkle, P. E., 214
Horner, M. S., 363–367, 379
Hulin, C. L., 263
Hunt, R. R., 388

Isen, A. M., 115, 291, 367–374

Jacobson, L., 294
Jolton, J., 374, 375
Joynson, R. B., 128
Jurs, S. G., 214

Kanuk, L., 332
Karlin, M. B., 384–385, 388
Kaye, M., 356
Kendall, L. M., 263
Kendrick, D. T., 356
Kiesler, C. A., 337
Kinsbourne, M., 363
Knight, T. D., 356
Knowles, E. S., 122, 123
Koocher, G. P., 123
Krippendorf, K., 265
Kuhn, D., 366
Kwallek, N., 379–380

Lackey, S., 389
Laird, J. D., 114
LaPointe, L. B., 376
Lavrakas, P. J., 332
Levin, P. F., 115, 291
Lewis, C. M., 379–380
Linder, D., 356
Lockhart, R. S., 388
Longo, L. C., 33
Lustig, D. A., 221

MacAninch, C. B., 388
MaKijani, M. G., 33
Marcus-Newhall, A., 234

Martin, L. L., 110
Mastrofski, S., 335
Mathews, K. E., Jr., 115
Matter, C. F., 122, 123
May, J. L., 46, 64
McCall, M. A., 356
McCarty, D., 356
McConnell, J. V., 220
McKey, R., 340
McDaniel, M. A., 389
McNeil, E. B., 220
Mednick, E. V., 368
Mednick, M. T., 368
Mednick, S. A., 368
Meers, B. W., 340
Meyer, D. E., 221
Middlemist, R. D., 122, 123
Milgram, S., 117–118
Miller, G. W., 363
Miller, N., 234
Monahan, D., 366
Morrow, J., 319
Mulligan, R. M., 362

Neisser, U., 338
Nelson, D. L., 326
Newport, A. G., 380
Nolen-Hoeksema, S., 319
Nowicki, G. P., 367–374

Orne, M. T., 117
Ornstein, R. E., 356–363

Parks, R. B., 335
Pfungst, O., 125
Place, K., 356
Polansky, M. L., 218
Posavac, E. J., 340

Reed, T. F., 331
Reeves, C. H., 376
Robbins, A. S., 379–380
Robinson, J. P., 263
Roethlisberger, F. J., 295
Rogel, M., 291
Rosenhan, D. L., 335
Rosenthal, R., 125, 139, 294
Rosnow, R. L., 139
Ross, D. L., 221

Schachter, S., 114
Schiffman, H. R., 362
Schmidt, S. R., 388
Schneider, E., 114
Schvanveldt, R. W., 221
Sexter, M., 114
Shaffer, R. M., 291
Shah, I., 23
Shaver, P., 263, 366
Shepard, J. A., 377–379
Sidman, M., 297
Sigall, H., 381
Silverman, L. H., 221

Smith, P. C., 263
Sommer, R., 293
Stagray, J. R., 338
Stanley, J. C., 318
Stepper, S., 110
Stern, L., 114
Strack, F., 110
Strano, D. A., 388
Strathman, A. J., 377–379
Stroop, J. R., 218
Sutton, C., 326

Truitt, L., 338
Turner, M. L., 376

Van Lighten, O., 114

Warner, J. L., 218
Waugh, G., 356
Weinberger, J., 221
Werch, C. E., 340
Wetzel, C. G., 291
White, G. L., 356
White, P., 337
Wiersma, W., 214
Willingham, W., 388
Willis, C. S., 325
Wrightsman, L. S., 263

Zimbardo, P. G., 124

Subject Index

ABA designs, 299–300
Abbreviations, in research articles, 395, 403
Abstract section, of article, 398, 399, 418
Affect *vs.* effect, 396
Alpha (α), 191–192
Alternate forms, 271–272
American Psychological Association (APA), 44
  Ethical Principles of Psychologists and Code of Conduct, 118–121, 127
  research article format, 391–413
  sample article, 417–428
Analysis of variance (ANOVA), 186–187
  between-subjects, 187
  comparing conditions in, 190
  confidence intervals in, 462–463
  effect size in, 461
  one-way, 186–187, 435–440
  one-way between-subjects, 435–437
  one-way within-subjects, 187, 438–440
  two-way between-subjects, 203–217, 440–445
  two-way mixed-design, 452–457
  two-way within-subjects, 445–451
Animal research, 124–127
  quasi-independent variables in, 314
Annual Review of Psychology, 387
ANOVA. *See* Analysis of variance (ANOVA)
APA style. *See* American Psychological Association (APA), research article format
Apparatus, in research articles, 402–404
Applied research, 13
Archival research, 337
Arousal, attribution study, 350–356

Assumptions
  reader and author, 393–394
  of science, 46
Astrology study, 374–375
Attractiveness and height study, 377–379
Automation, 100

Bar graphs, 181
Barnum statements, 268, 374
Baseline designs, 298–304
  design concerns with, 303–304
  multiple-, 300–303
Baselines, defined, 80, 298
Basic research, 13
  when to use, 68
Behavior
  context of, 34–35
  observing reliable, 92–94
  problems in inferring causes of, 58–59
  scientific study of, 10–14
Behavior modification, 299
Beta (β) level, 193
Between-subjects ANOVA, 187
Between-subjects design, 144–152
  counterbalancing in, 146–148
  dealing with participant variables in, 151–152
  limiting population in, 150–151
  matched-groups designs, 148–150
  random assignment in, 144–145
Bias
  Hawthorne effect, 295
  reactivity, 109–110
  scientific method and, 4
  subject sophistication, 139
  in surveys, 333–334
  volunteer, 139–140
Bibliographies, research article, 387
Blocking trials, 161

Carry-over effects, 94–95, 155–156
  nonsymmetrical, 161
Case studies, 338
Catch trials, 272–273

Causal hypotheses, 15, 67
Causal relationships, 247–248
Caution, in research, 7
Ceiling effects, 91
Cells, 205
Central tendency measures, 178–180, 430
Chi square
  critical values, 487
  one-way, 188, 467
  two-way, 467–469
Choking under pressure study, 380–381
Closed-ended questions, 263–264
  creating responses for, 268–270
Cluster sampling, 288–289, 333
Coefficient of determination, 257
Cohort designs, 328–329
Cohort effects, 327–328
Collapsing across variables, 147
Color, study on influence of, 379–380
Complete factorial design, 206
Computerized searches, 387
Conceptual replication, 26–27
Concurrent validity, 261
Conditions, 60–61
  complete counterbalancing of, 157–159
  normal/neutral, 81
  partial counterbalancing of, 159–160
  random assignment and, 62–63
  randomizing order of, 160–161
  selecting, 79–85
Confederates, 77
Confidence intervals, 191, 334
  in ANOVA, 462–463
  in *t*-tests, 461–462
Confidentiality, 119
Confounded comparisons, 214–215
Confounding variables, 50–51, 114, 304
  in descriptive research, 58
  in quasi-experiments, 64–65
Construct validity, 48–49, 78
  reporting in articles, 411

Content analysis, 265
Content validity, 48, 78
  reporting in articles, 411
Contingency correlation coeffi-
  cients, 234
Control, of behavior, 11
Control conditions, 298
Control groups, 80–81
Controlled conditions, 9
Controls
  with animal research, 125–126
  choosing, 56
  for demand characteristics,
    111–113
  with selected group studies,
    295–296
  with studies of general public,
    292–293
Convenience sampling, 289, 333
Convergent validity, 261
Converging operations, 27, 39,
    88–89, 306
Correlational research, 56–57,
    244–262
  and correlational statistics,
    249–259
  increasing power of, 259
  interpreting, 247–248
  reasons to use, 248–249
  vs. true experiments, 245–249
Correlational statistics, 249–259
Correlation coefficients,
    249–259
  accounting for prediction/vari-
    ance errors with, 254–257
  contingency, 234
  defined, 249
  of determination, 257
  eta-squared, 233–234
  and linear regression, 253–254
  Pearson, 250, 474–476
  phi, 234
  point-biserial, 233
  power of, 257–259
  for proportion of variance
    accounted for, 233–234
  for reliability, 259–260
  Spearman, 250
  squared, 256–257
  squared contingency, 234
Correlations. *See* Relationships
Counterbalancing, 95–96
  in between-subjects design,
    146–148

complete, 157–159
  in interviews/questionnaires,
    271
  for order effects, 156–160
  partial, 159–160
  to produce two-way designs,
    216–217
Creativity study, 367–374
Criterion validity, 261
Criterion variables, 254
Critical values
  of chi square, 487
  defined, 189
  of *F*, 479–482
  of Mann-Whitney *U*, 488–493
  of Pearson correlation coeffi-
    cient, 485–486
  of Spearman correlation coeffi-
    cient, 486
  of studentized range statistic,
    483–484
  of *t*, 478
  of Wilcoxon test *T*, 494–495
Cross-sectional designs, 327–328

Data points, 174
Debriefing, 121
Deception, 113–115, 119
Degrees of freedom (df), 194
  critical values of, 479–482
Demand characteristics, 109–116,
    117–118
  in animal research, 125
  controls for, 111–113
  defined, 109
  in interviews/questionnaires,
    273–274
  in role playing, 124
  unobtrusive measures and
    deception and, 113–115
Dependent samples *t*-tests, 186,
    434–435, 470–471
Dependent variables, 61–62, 174
  designing, 89–98
  measuring, 86–87, 90–91
  selecting, 86–89
  validity/reliability of, 87–89
Descriptive hypotheses, 15, 67
Descriptive research, 21, 56–59,
    329–339
  advantages of, 331
  and archival research, 337
  and case studies, 338
  defined, 329

and demand characteristics, 113
  ethics in, 338–339
  and *ex post facto* research,
    337–338
  field surveys, 331–335
  inference problems in, 58–59
  observational studies, 335–336
  validity/reliability in, 57–58
  when to use, 67–68
Descriptive statistics, 82, 171,
    178–184
  central tendency, 178–180
  and graphs, 180–182
  interpretation of, 183–184
  and variability, 182–183
Design, research, 8
  choosing, 161–163
  components of, 34–35
  correlational, 56–57
  descriptive, 56–59
  and flawed evidence, 22–23
  selecting, 67–68
  statistical power and, 193–195
  strong manipulation in, 81–85
  two-way, 203–220
Determinism, 5
Diffusion of treatment, 84,
    114–115, 147, 294–295
Direct replication, 26
Discriminant validity, 261
Discussion section, in articles,
    393, 409–412, 423–425
Distractor tasks, 114
Double-barreled questions,
    267–268
Double-blind procedures, 112
Droodle study, 384–385,
    388–391
Duncan test, 190

Ecological validity, 52, 79
Effects, main, 206–208
  graphing, 213–215
  post hoc comparisons for,
    457–458
  simple, 213–214
  in three-way designs, 224
Effects, serial-position, 375–377
Effect size, 183, 229–234
  in ANOVA, 461
  computing, 468–469
  defined, 229
  and proportion of variance
    accounted for, 230–234

reporting in articles, 406–407
in *t*-tests, 460–461
Effect *vs.* affect, 396
Empirical evidence, 8
Environment, 34
and demand characteristics, 110
Environmental events, quasi-
experiments and, 318–325
Environmental variables, 46
Errors
Type I, 191–192, 193
Type II, 193
Error variance, 140–144
defined, 142, 175
Estimated population standard
deviation, 432
Estimated population variance,
431
Eta-squared correlation coefficients, 233–234
Ethical Principles of Psychologists
and Code of Conduct,
118–121, 127
Ethics, 7, 68, 117–124
of animal research, 124–127
APA principles of, 118–121,
127
and descriptive research,
338–339
of field research, 121–123
in interviews/questionnaires,
274
of unobtrusive measures,
121–123
Evaluation of studies, 44–47
Evidence
flaws in, 22–23
scientific, 8–10
Exact replication, 26
Experimental groups, 80
Experimental methods, 20–21,
59–67
independent variables in, 59–60
Experimental realism, 113
Experimenters
expectancies of, 111, 125
as source of demand characteristics, 110–111
Experiments
concealing, 115–116
laboratory *vs.* field, 66–67
true *vs.* quasi, 62–63, 64–66
validity/reliability in, 63–67
Ex post facto designs, 337–338

External validity, 51–53, 64, 79
and participant variables,
136–140
reporting in articles, 411
Extraneous variables, 46–47
controlling, 54–55, 98–102

Face validity, 260–261, 332
Factorial design, 206
Factors. *See* Independent variables
Falsifiability, 15–16
Fatigue effects, 155
Fear of success study, 363–367
Field experiments, 115–116,
286–296
advantages of, 286–287
defined, 67
ethics of, 121–123, 296
with general public, 290–293
sampling techniques, 287–290
with selected groups, 293–296
vs. laboratory, 66–67
Field surveys, 331–335
analyzing results in, 334–335
mailed *vs.* telephone, 332–333
sample selection, 332, 333–334
Figure caption page, 408
Figure captions, 408
Figures, in articles, 407–408
Filter questions, 271
Floor effects, 91–92
Forced-choice procedures, 86–87
Fraud, scientific, 127–128
Friedman χ^2 test, 188, 473–475
Funnel questions, 271

Generalization, 42–43
Graphs, 180–182
Group designs, flaws in, 297–298
Groups, experimental, 80

Habituation, 112–113, 335
Hawthorne effect, 295
Height and attractiveness study,
377–379
Human Subjects Review Commit-
tees, 120
Hypotheses, 14–27
alternative, 185–186
causal, 15
confirmed, 24
creating, 14–15
criteria for, 15–17
definition of, 14
descriptive, 15

descriptive methods and, 21
developing, 33
disconfirmed, 23
experimental methods and,
20–21
flaws in evidence and, 22–23
flaws in research and, 21–22
and hypothetical constructs,
36–38
null, 185–186, 189, 192–193
parsimonious, 16
precise, 16
rational, 16
rival, 24
sources of, 17–19
testing, 19–20, 23–26, 40–44
vs. prediction, 19
Hypothetical constructs, 36–38
defined, 36–37
identifying variables of, 37–38
translating into operational definitions, 38–40
validity of, 48–49

Incomplete factorial design, 206
Independent samples *t*-tests, 186,
432–434, 469–470
Independent variables, 59–60, 174
approaches to manipulating,
76–79
conditions of, 60–61
selecting, 76–79
selecting conditions of, 79–85
true, 62–63
Independent verification, 11
Indirect replication, 26–27
Individual differences, 5, 136, 305
Inferences, 42
problems in behavioral, 58–59
Inferential statistics, 171, 184–189
logic of, 185–186
nonparametric, 187–189
parametric, 186–187
selecting, 186–189
Inferential tests, 191–192
Informed consent, 120–121, 123,
296, 336
Institutional Review Boards (IRB),
120
Instrumentation effects, 100
Interaction effects, 209–215
graphing, 210–214
post hoc comparisons for,
458–460

Interaction effects *(continued)*
post hoc comparisons in, 214–215
and single-subject designs, 304
two-way, 209–210
Internal validity, 49–51, 64, 78–79
defined, 49
reporting in articles, 411
Inter-rater reliability, 96–97, 259–260
Interrupted time-series designs, 322–324
Interval scales, 172, 173
Intervening variables, 77
Interviews
administering, 273–274
and catch trials, 272–273
and order effects, 270–272
questions for, 263–265, 266–270, 275
vs. questionnaires, 265–266
Introduction, in article, 392, 398–401
Invasion of privacy, 123

Kruskal-Wallis *H* test, 188, 472–473

Latin square design, 159–160
Lawfulness, of nature, 5
Leading questions, 268
Likert-type questions, 87, 269
Linear regression, 253–254
Linear regression equation, 253, 464–465
Linear regression line, 253–254
Linear relationships, 174
Line graphs, 180–181
Literal replication, 26
Literature searches, 33, 386–391
bibliographies, 387
computerized, 387
on testing materials, 388
Longitudinal designs, 325–326

Mailed surveys, 332
Main effects, 206–208
graphing, 213–215
post hoc comparisons for, 457–458
simple, 213–214
in three-way designs, 224
Manipulation checks, 85
Mann-Whitney test, 188, 469–470
critical values of *U*, 488–493

MANOVA. *See* Multivariate analysis of variance (MANOVA)
Manuscript page headers, 398
Margin of error, 334
Matched-group design, 148–150
Materials, in research articles, 402–404
Means, 82, 178, 430
and effect size, 229
estimating population, 190–191
regression toward, 316–317
Measurement
scales of, 171–173
and validity, 48–53
variables, 46
Measures, unobtrusive, 113, 121–123
Measures of Personality and Social Psychological Attitudes, 388
Median, 179, 430
Mental Measurements Yearbook, 388
Meta-analysis, 234–235
Method section, in articles, 392, 401–405
materials/apparatus in, 402–404
participants in, 402
procedure in, 404–405
sample of, 421–423
Minnesota Multiphasic Personality Inventory (MMPI), 246
Models, 18–19
Modes, 179, 430
Mood and creativity study, 367–374
Mu (μ), 191
Multifactor experiments, 202–241
defined, 203
effect size description in, 229–234
meta-analysis and, 234–235
multivariate statistics and, 234
reason for, 203
three-way, 223–227
two-way between-subjects ANOVA, 203–217
two-way chi square, 227–228
two-way mixed ANOVA, 220–223
two-way within-subjects ANOVA, 218–220

Multiple-baseline designs, 300–303
across behaviors, 301
across participants, 301
across situations, 302–303
Multiple time-series designs, 324–325
Multiple trials, 92–94
Multivariate analysis of variance (MANOVA), 234
Multivariate statistics, 234

Naturalistic observation, 335
Nature, scientific assumptions about, 4–6
Needs assessment, 340
Negative linear relationships, 174
Newman-Keuls test, 190
N (number of participants), 138–139, 194
Nominal scales, 172, 173
Nonequivalent control group designs, 320–322
Nonlinear relationships, 177–178
Nonparametric inferential statistics, 173
Nonparametric procedures, 187–189, 469–470
Nonsignificant results, 192–193
Nonsymmetrical carry-over effects, 161
Normal distributions, 173
Null hypothesis, 185–186, 189, 192–193

Objectivity, 9
Observational studies, 335–336
One-group pretest-posttest designs, 319–320
One-tailed tests, 195
One-way between-subjects ANOVA, 435–437
One-way chi square, 188
One-way designs, 186–187
One-way within-subjects ANOVA, 187, 438–440
Open-ended questions, 264–265
Open-mindedness, 6–7
Operational definitions, 38–40, 88–89
defined, 38
evaluating, 46
Opinions, 3–4. *See also* Assumptions

Order effects, 94–95, 155–156
  counterbalancing, 95–96
  methods for controlling,
    156–161
  in questionnaires/interviews,
    270–272
  randomizing, 160–161
Ordinal scales, 172, 173
Outcome evaluation, 340

Parametric inferential statistics,
    173
Parametric procedures, 186–187
Parsimonious hypotheses, 16
Participant observation, 335
Participants, 8
  and confidentiality, 119
  cooperativeness of, 117–118
  debriefing, 121
  eliminating from data, 101–102
  identifying potential risks to,
    118–119
  informed consent of, 120–121
  instructions to, 99–100
  number of, 138–139, 194
  protecting from harm, 119
  in research articles, 402
  testing in groups, 100–101
Participant variables, 46,
    135–163
  balancing, 146–148
  in between-subjects design,
    144–152
  and error variance, 140–144
  and external validity, 136–140
  and order effects, 156–161
  pros/cons of control methods
    for, 161–163
  quasi-experiments and,
    314–318
  selecting approach toward,
    151–152
  in within-subjects design,
    152–156
Pearson correlation coefficient,
    250, 263–264, 474–476
  critical values, 485–486
Peer review, 128
Phi correlation coefficients, 234,
    469
Pilot studies, 101, 273
Placebos, 114–115
Plagiarism, 127
Planned comparisons, 190

Point-biserial correlation coeffi-
    cients, 233
Populations
  defining, 136–137
  estimating mean of, 190–191
  identifying, 35–36
  limiting, 150–151
Population variance, 431
Positive linear relationships, 174
Post hoc comparisons, 208,
    214–215
  for interaction effects, 458–460
  for main effects, 457–458
Post hoc tests, 190
Practice effects, 94–95, 155
Practice trials, 92
Precise hypotheses, 16
Predestination, 5
Predicting behavior, 11
Prediction
  errors in, 254–257
  vs. hypotheses, 19
Predictive validity, 261–262
Predictor variables, 254
Pretest-posttest designs, 154,
    220–223
  one-group, 319–320
Pretests, 147–148, 317
Probability sampling, 288–289,
    333
Procedure section, in article,
    404–405
Program evaluation, 339–340
Program monitoring, 340
Program planning, 340
Projective tests, 264
Proportion of variance accounted
    for, 230–234, 255–256
Pseudo-explanations, 10–11
Pseudo-randomness, 287–288
Psychological Abstracts, 387, 398
Psychological Bulletin, 387
*Publication Manual of the Ameri-
    can Psychological Associa-
    tion,* 391, 394

Quasi-experiments, 62–63, 64–66,
    312–329
  defined, 312–314
  interpreting, 317–318
  participant variables and,
    314–318
  passage of time and, 325–329
  time-series design, 318–325

Quasi-independent variables,
    212–213. *See also* Quasi-
    experiments
Questionnaires, 263–275
  administering, 273–274
  and catch trials, 272–273
  and order effects, 270–272
  questions for, 263–265,
    266–270, 275
  vs. interviews, 265–266
Questions
  closed-ended, 263–264
  constructing, 266–270
  double-barreled, 267–268
  leading, 268
  open-ended, 264–265
Quota sampling, 289, 333
Quotations, in research articles,
    394

Random assignment, 62–63,
    64–66, 144–145
Randomization, 160–161
Range, 432
Raters, 96–97
  inter-rater reliability of, 96–97,
    259–260
Rational hypotheses, 16
Ratio scales, 172, 173
Reaction time, 86
Reactivity, 109–110, 115
Reference page, in articles,
    412–413, 426–427
Regression toward the mean,
    316–317
Relationships. *See also* Statistics
  correlation coefficients and,
    250–252
  error variance and, 140–144
  external validity of, 51–53
  and hypothesis testing,
    40–44
  internal validity of, 49–51
  interpreting, 42–43
  linear, 174–175
  nonlinear, 177–178
  strength of, 81–85, 174–177
  strength of and reliability/valid-
    ity, 142–143
  types of, 174
  understanding characteristics of,
    173–178
  zero, 177

Reliability, 47–48
  correlation coefficients for, 259–260
  defined, 47
  in descriptive research, 57–58
  inter-rater, 96–97, 260
  issues of, 63–66
  minimizing threats to, 53–56
  and relationship strength, 142–143
  reporting in articles, 411
  split-half, 260
  test-retest, 260
Remotes Associates Test, 368–374
Repeated-measures designs, 304–305. *See also* Within-subjects design
Replication, 26–27, 53
  conceptual, 26–27
  literal, 26
  to prevent fraud, 128
Representativeness of participants, 136–140
Representative samples, 36
Research. *See also* Scientific method
  animal, 124–127
  applied, 13
  basic, 13, 68
  descriptive methods, 21
  designing, 33–44
  ethics of, 7
  evaluating, 44–47
  experimental methods, 20–21
  flaws in, 21–22
  flow of, 43–44
  goals of, 10–14
  with interviews/questionnaires, 263–275
  searching previous, 385–391
  single studies, 13–14
Research article format, 383–416
  abstract, 398, 399
  assumptions of author and reader, 393–394
  components of, 395–413
  discussion section, 393, 409–412
  introduction, 392, 398–401
  method section, 392, 401–405
  reference pages, 412–413
  results section, 393, 405–409
  sample of, 417–428
  sections in, 391–393
  style rules, 394–395

  title, 396–398
  typing, 396
Researcher variables, 46
Research literature
  defined, 386
  searching, 386–391
Response scales, 268–270
Response sets, 94, 156, 271
Restriction of range, 91–92, 258–259
Results section, in articles, 393, 405–409, 423
  figures in, 407–408
  tables in, 408–409
Reversal designs, 299–300
Review articles, 387
Risk
  in field experiments, 123
  identifying potential, 118–119
Role playing, 124
Running heads, 398

Sample, defined, 35
Samples of participants
  for field surveys, 331–332, 333–334
  limitations on representativeness of, 136–139
  size of, 138–139, 194
Sample standard deviation, 182, 432
Sample variance, 182, 431
Sampling, 35–36
  cluster, 288–289, 333
  convenience, 289, 333
  nonprobability, 289–290
  probability, 288–289, 333
  quota, 289, 333
  representative, 36
  simple random, 35, 288
  snowball, 289–290, 333
  stratefied random, 288, 333
  systematic random, 35, 288
  techniques for field experiments, 287–290
Sampling error, 184
Scales of measurement, 171–173
Scatterplots, 174
Scheffé test, 190
Scientific fraud, 127–128
Scientific method, 2–31
  assumptions in, 4–6
  criteria for evidence in, 8–10
  defined, 3

  hypotheses in, 14–27
  and scientist attitudes, 6–8
Scientists, attitudes of, 6–8
Scores
  content analysis, 265
  variable, 142
Scoring criteria, 89–90
Selection criteria, 136–137
Selection tests, 248–249
Self-consciousness study, 380–381
Self-reports, 88, 274
Sensitivity
  of measurement scales, 172–173
  of measures, 90–91
Serendipitous findings, 12–13
Serial-position curve, 376
Serial-position effects, 375–377
Signal detection analysis, 86
Simple random sampling, 35, 288
Simulations, 124
Single-blind procedures, 111–112
Single studies, 13–14
Single-subject designs, 296–306
  baseline, 298–299, 303–304
  defined, 296
  multiple-baseline, 300–303
  reversal, 299–300
  vs. group, 305
Skepticism, 7
Small *N* research
  arguments for, 297–298
  defined, 296
Snowball sampling, 289–290, 333
Social desirability, 110, 115
Social Science Citation Index, 387
Sorting tasks, 87
Sources, in articles, 394, 412–413
Spearman correlation coefficient, 250
  critical values, 486
Split-half reliability, 260
Squared contingency correlation coefficients, 234
Squared correlation coefficient, 256–257
Standard deviation, 431–432
Standard error of estimate, 255, 465
State characteristics, 77–78
Statistical power, 193–194
Statistics
  descriptive, 171, 178–184
  inferential, 171, 184–189
  interpreting nonsignificant results, 192–193

interpreting significant results, 189–192
for interviews/questionnaires, 274
power of and research design, 193–195
and relationship characteristics, 173–178
scales of measurement in, 171–173
selecting procedures, 171–178
Stimulus suffix, 376
Stratified random sampling, 288, 333
Strength of relationships, 81–85, 142–143, 174–177
Strong manipulations, 81–85
defined, 83
Stroop interference task, 218
Structured interviews, 265–266
Style, research article, 394–395
Subject attrition, 155
Subject history, 155
Subject maturation, 155
Subject mortality, 155, 305
Subjects. *See* Participants
Subject sophistication, 139
Surveys, field, 331–335
Systematic naturalistic observation, 335
Systematic random sampling, 35
Systematic research, 9
Systematic variance, 230–231, 256

Tables, in articles, 408–409
Telephone surveys, 332–333
Temporal validity, 52–53, 79, 326
Testability, 15–16
Testing materials, references on, 388
Test of independence, 228
Test-retest reliability, 260
Theories, 17–18
Three-way designs, 223–227
main effects in, 224
three-way interactions in, 226–227
two-way interactions in, 225
Time, study of passage of, 325–329
Time perception, study on, 356–363
Time-series designs, 318–325
interrupted, 322–324
multiple, 324–325

nonequivalent control group, 320–322
one-group pretest-posttest, 319–321
Title section, of article, 396–398, 417
Trait characteristics, 78
Treatment conditions, 298
True experiments, 62–63, 64–66
T-tests
confidence intervals in, 461–462
dependent samples, 186, 434–435
effect size in, 460–461
independent samples, 186, 432–434
multivariate, 234
nonparametric, 469–470
two-sample, 186, 432–435
Tukey HSD test, 190, 214
post hoc comparisons for interaction effects, 458–460
post hoc comparisons for main effects, 457–458
Two-sample *t*-tests, 186, 432–435
Two-tailed tests, 195
Two-way between-subjects ANOVA, 203–217, 203–220, 440–445
interaction effects, 208–215
main effects and, 206–208
Two-way chi square, 227–228
Two-way interaction, 208–209
Two-way mixed-design ANOVA, 220–223, 452–457
Two-way within-subjects ANOVA, 218–220, 445–451
Type I errors, 191–192, 193
Type II errors, 193

Uncertainty, 6
Undefined terms, 268
Understandability, of nature, 6
Univariate statistics, 234
Unobtrusive measures, 113
ethics of, 121–123
Unstructured interviews, 266

Validity, 48–54
ascertaining, 260–262
concurrent, 261
construct, 48–49
content, 48
convergent, 261
criterion, 261

defined, 48
in descriptive research, 57–58
discriminant, 261
ecological, 52
external, 51–53
face, 260–261
internal, 49–51
issues of, 63–66
minimizing threats to, 53–56
predictive, 261–262
and relationship strength, 142–143
temporal, 52–53
Variability, 142, 175. *See also* Error variance
measures of, 182–183, 431–432
Variables
collapsing across, 147
confounding, 50–51, 58, 114, 304
counterbalancing, 146–148
defined, 37
dependent, 61–62, 86–98
discovering relationships among, 40–44
effect size of, 229–234
environmental, 46
extraneous, 46–47, 54–55
of hypothetical constructs, 37–38
independent, 59–61, 76–85
intervening, 77
measurement, 46
participant, 46
quasi-independent, 212–213
researcher, 46
selecting, 37–38
Variance
accounting for errors in, 254–257
calculating, 431–432
proportion accounted for, 230–234
systematic, 230–231
Volunteer bias, 139–140

Wilcoxon test, 188, 470–471
critical values of *T*, 494–495
Within-subjects designs, 152–156
pretest-posttest, 154
pros and cons of, 154–156

Y prime (*Y*′), 254

Zero relationships, 177

Table 6.5 Parametric Procedures and Their Nonparametric Counterparts Used in Experiments with One Independent Variable

Between-Subjects Analysis (No Matching or Repeated Measures)

Number of Conditions	Parametric Scores (Interval or Ratio)	Nonparametric Scores	
		Ordinal	Nominal
Two	Independent samples *t*-test	Mann-Whitney test	Chi square
Three or more	Between-subjects ANOVA	Kruskal-Wallis test	Chi square

Within-Subjects Analysis (Matched Groups or Repeated Measures)

Number of Conditions	Parametric Scores (Interval or Ratio)	Nonparametric Scores	
		Ordinal	Nominal
Two	Dependent samples *t*-test	Wilcoxon test	none
Three or more	Within-subjects ANOVA	Friedman test	none